The Sale and Management of Flats
Practice and Precedents

The Sale and Management of Flats Practice and Precedents

John Cawthorn
Solicitor

London
Butterworths
1985

United Kingdom	Butterworth & Co (Publishers) Ltd, 88 Kingsway, LONDON WC2B 6AB and 61A North Castle Street, EDINBURGH EH2 3LJ
Australia	Butterworths Pty Ltd, SYDNEY, MELBOURNE, BRISBANE, ADELAIDE, PERTH, CANBERRA and HOBART
Canada	Butterworth & Co (Canada) Ltd, TORONTO and VANCOUVER
New Zealand	Butterworths of New Zealand Ltd, WELLINGTON and AUCKLAND
Singapore	Butterworth & Co (Asia) Pte Ltd, SINGAPORE
South Africa	Butterworth Publishers (Pty) Ltd, DURBAN and PRETORIA
USA	Butterworth Legal Publishers, ST PAUL, Minnesota, SEATTLE, Washington, BOSTON, Massachusetts, AUSTIN, Texas, and D & S Publishers, CLEARWATER, Florida

British Library Cataloguing in Publication Data

Cawthorn, John
Sale and management of flats: practice and procedure.
1. Apartments—Law and Legislation—England
I. Title
344.2064'3 KD829

ISBN 0 406 52670 2

Printed in Great Britain by
Butler & Tanner Ltd, Frome and London

To Jamie, Alex and Gregory

Preface

I wrote my first book, *Residential Estate Conveyancing—Practice and Precedents*, on the prompting of my publishers. I had complained to them that the subject which occupied such a large part of my working life was poorly served, if at all, by the published textbooks. In response, their suggestion was, of course, that I might be prepared to fill the gap myself.

This present book, on the sale and management of flats, differs in its inception only in that the initiative came from me. Its aim has been precisely identical to that which produced the previous one—that is to write a text which may be used, and understood, by the average, busy practitioner and all those involved in management programmes. This book too will, I fear, disappoint the academics and theoreticians for once again theory, case law and erudite discussion have little place here. I have borne in mind my own need, as an average practitioner, in seeking to identify and acknowledge my problem, for a book to tell me how to deal with it and, if necessary, to show me what document to use. I sincerely hope that this approach will be welcomed and found to be useful.

In view of the considerable number of flats and maisonettes in this country it is indeed surprising that textbooks on the subject of their sale and management are so few. The ever-increasing pressures on use of land create the need for further development both now and in the future. Most flats and maisonettes are sold on a leasehold basis and are certainly likely to remain within this category for at least some years. All will depend on how quickly the government reacts to the Law Commission's proposals on land obligations and the obvious unpopularity of leasehold, generally. Virtually all flats, and a fair number of freehold houses now require maintenance; and management programmes are of increasing importance and interest. This book is, therefore, an attempt to provide the busy legal and non-legal practitioner with a sound and practical text on the sale and management of flats whether leasehold or freehold, which involve common areas in need of maintenance.

The book sets out in reasonable detail the basic elements of a lease, and builds around that the descriptions of the various principles of conveyancing. It then moves on to the options and suitability or otherwise of the various management schemes. Next, and this is where the really new ground is broken, the various practical elements of a management programme are discussed describing the various treatments and materials which can be used in the properties which are the subject of management programmes. Finally, the text deals with various peripheral subjects which might well be of interest and use to the readership, including a detailed look into the future development of the law on flats. To conclude, there follows a comprehensive selection of precedents all of which are tried and tested in practice, and which are complementary to the text.

Every author has a long list of people to thank and I am no exception. First on the list must be my wife, Jane, and our three sons, for putting up with, and giving encouragement to, my involvement in this project; and Frances Creeth, who overcame the comedians' description of the traditional mother-in-law to perform sterling duties as project typist. From that point on, there are so many kind people who have helped me that it would be impossible to list all their names here. They are all acknowledged throughout the text, and I feel sure they will forgive me offering corporate thanks here in the preface. There are, however, two areas where I do want to be specific. First, I offer special thanks to the staff of Butterworths, who are unfailingly friendly, helpful and supportive; and second to Tony Wood of Birmingham, who gave me much appreciated moral support, particularly when I decided half-way through the writing of the book to leave Barratts and start my own practice.

The book has been written by one who has for some years been involved not only in the legal side of selling flats, etc but in the management programmes set up for those flats. Therefore the earnest hope of both the author and his publishers is that the book will not only be of use to conveyancers, but to all those involved in management programmes.

The law is stated as at 3 January 1985.

Letchworth, Herts
January 1985

J.W.C.

Contents

CHAPTER 1

Definition of 'flat' and 'maisonette'

This book is about flats and maisonettes, how one deals with the sale of them from a conveyancer's point of view, and how management schemes are formulated for them and implemented throughout the useful lives of the blocks in which they are situated.

That statement is all very well but, before we proceed to our consideration of the various aspects of the subject, we should first of all ask ourselves, 'what is a flat, or a maisonette?' In order to understand the treatment of the subject, we must understand what it is we are referring to when we talk about a 'flat' or a 'maisonette'.

Accordingly, we have to define the two words. The first step must be to look at the everyday meaning of the words to see if these give us any help.

According to the *Shorter Oxford English Dictionary* (3rd edn) the meanings are as follows:

'Flat: 1. A floor or storey in a house
2. A suite of rooms on one floor, forming a complete residence'

'Maisonette: A small house; in recent use, a portion of a house used as a self-contained dwelling'

These definitions are interesting, in that they represent the layman's interpretation of the words, and having seen what these are it becomes fairly clear that the conveyancer's interpretation must of necessity differ somewhat. For instance, a flat is not necessarily, indeed it is very seldom, 'a floor or storey in a house'. This suggests that the whole of the floor is one complete flat which, of course, is not usually the case. The second definition is better, in that 'a suite of rooms on one floor' which 'forms a complete residence' is correct *so far as it goes*, and contemplates that there might be more than one flat on the same floor, but it makes no mention of the presence or otherwise of common parts[1] nor does it contemplate that a flat can be on more than one storey.

As for the definition of a maisonette, the description 'a small house' is, it is suggested, most archaic. On the other hand, the secondary definition of 'a portion of a house used as a self-contained dwelling' is much nearer the mark, the important words being 'self-contained'. However, it still falls some way short of a satisfactory description for the conveyancer so that we must next turn to the legal definitions of the words.

Originally 'flat' was defined in Mozley and Whiteley's *Law Dictionary*[2] as:

1 See later as to the role of common parts in determining the basic difference between a flat and a maisonette.

2 10th edn, 1978, Butterworths. This no longer appears to be up to date.

'a separate and self-contained set of premises, whether or not on the same floor, constructed for use for the purposes of the dwelling and forming part of a building from some other part of which it is divided horizontally. See s 21 of the Housing Subsidies Act 1967. A similar definition is to be found in s 44 of the Housing Act 1964.'

The definition in the Housing Act 1964, s 44 is:

' "flat" means a separate set of premises, whether or not on the same floor, constructed for use for the purposes of a dwelling and forming part of a building from some other part of which it is divided horizontally.'

The definition of flat in the Housing Subsidies Act 1967, s 21, is very similar, but is reproduced in full below so that the reader may note the slight difference in emphasis which this subsequent legislation brought to the definition.

' "flat" means a separate and self-contained set of premises, whether or not on the same floor, constructed for use for the purposes of a dwelling and forming part of a building from some other part of which it is divided horizontally'

It will be noted that in the 1967 definition, the extra words 'and self-contained' have been added to the 1964 definition. One of the latest statutory definition appears to be found in the Housing Act 1980, Sch 19, para 16, where 'flat' is defined as:

'a separate set of premises, whether or not on the same floor, which—
(a) forms part of a building; and
(b) is divided horizontally from some other part of that building; and
(c) is constructed or adapted for use for the purposes of a dwelling and is occupied wholly or mainly as a private dwelling.'

This time the words 'and self-contained' have disappeared. Apart from this omission, there seems to be little difference in the actual meaning of the three definitions. What does seem certain, if nothing else, is that the legislature cannot seem to make up its mind as to how to define the word 'flat'!

While considering the statutory definitions in, inter alia, the 1967 Act we might usefully have a look at the definition therein of 'block of flats'. This is as follows:

' "block of flats", of a given number of storeys means a building containing flats which consists of that number of storeys exclusive of any storey constructed for use for purposes other than those of a dwelling; and for the purposes of this definition a building which consists of a different number of storeys in different parts thereof shall be treated as if each of those parts were a separate building, any question as to the division of any building into such parts, or as to the number of storeys of which any such part consists, or as to the number of flats contained in any such part, being determined by the Minister.'

When we move on to consider a suggested new definition of the word 'flat' that definition will also describe a 'block of flats', and accordingly the preceding wording should be kept in mind.

For a legal or statutory definition of 'maisonette', we can look in vain in Mozley and Whiteley; neither does there appear to be any statutory definition. This is probably because the two words of description, 'flat' and 'maisonette' have been largely thought of as interchangeable, and thus the description of 'flat' is considered to cover that of 'maisonette' as well. Indeed, the additional wording of the description of 'flat' as set out in the 1967 Act[3] is, as we have seen, 'and self-contained', and—as will shortly be demonstrated—whilst a maisonette is self-contained, a flat is not, where the matter of common parts is concerned.

Mention of common parts brings us to the crucial difference between the definitions we have just studied, and the definitions which the reader should bear in mind when reading the rest of this book. However, before we attempt to arrive at a definitive interpretation of the two words, we should summarise the main physical features of flats and maisonettes. This is done below, in table form, so that the relationship of the various aspects of the two different forms of dwelling-units we have just been considering may be contrasted.

FLAT	MAISONETTE
1 Usually on one storey only, but not necessarily so, eg may be on two floors or even more.[4]	1 Similar to flat, in fact it is probably more usual to find a maisonette with more than one storey.
2 If there is more than one storey within the same flat, the means of getting from one storey to the other (or others, if there are more than two storeys) will be self-contained within the flat itself, ie one does not have to go outside the flat itself to get to the other storeys. Thus there may well be internal staircases within the flats themselves, duplicating staircases in the internal common areas.	2 Similar to flats.
3 To qualify for the description, it must form *part only* of the vertical aspect of the building of which it forms part, ie there must be another unit in the same building from which it is divided horizontally.	3 Similar to flats.
4 There may or may not be external common areas, eg garden ground, lawns, paved areas, pathways, roadways etc, which are shared by the flats in any particular building. It is fairly unusual to have separate and exclusive areas for flats, although it is not impossible.	4 Maisonettes are much more likely to have separate gardens, the use of which will be exclusive.
5 A block of flats will have internal common parts, ie there will be a main and/or subsidiary entrance/s, a lobby on the ground floor, staircases and/or lifts, corridors on each floor, which will be used	5 This is where we arrive at the crucial difference between the flat and the maisonette. A building comprising maisonettes will *not* have any internal common parts the maintenance of which is

3 Housing Subsidies Act 1967, s 21.
4 For example, a flat on two floors is sometimes referred to as a 'duplex'—which, although owing a lot to our transatlantic brethren, is at least descriptive.

FLAT	MAISONETTE
by each flat in the building. Admittedly the lower flats are unlikely to use the upper common areas, but in some cases (eg for lift shafts and service) this will be necessary, so that each flat has rights over *all* the internal common parts. Unless the studio flat system of demise is used[5] these common areas will be retained by whoever is managing the building, and no part of them will be actually demised to the individual flats.	shared. Instead, each maisonette will have completely self-contained entrances. A first-floor maisonette will have an entrance staircase which will be completely enclosed from the ground floor unit. Neither owner will have to pass through any part of the building which is not *exclusively* demised to him in order to reach his own unit. We could have said instead of 'his own unit', 'his own front door' but this produces a nice problem in description: is the front door of the first floor maisonette the one at the foot of the staircase opening onto the outside world, or that at the top of the stairs, giving access to the living accommodation unit itself?
6 It follows that there will be some sort of service charge for the internal common areas which will be shared by the flat owners.	6 If entrance ways are self-contained, then there should be no service charge of internal common areas because quite simply there are none.
7 The flat will have the appropriate rights and reservations of support and protection from other units in the same building. If the unit is a flat, by definition there will be another unit either below or above it.[6]	7 Similarly a maisonette will have similar rights and reservations of support and protection, because again by definition, it is a unit which is horizontally divided from another unit in the same building.
8 But unless the flat is demised on the 'studio scheme'[7] the external shell, ie the outside walls, and any internal load-bearing walls, etc and particularly the foundations and the roof will form part of the common parts in respect of which a service charge will be payable.	8 Whilst it is not impossible to set up a scheme of selling maisonettes with the external structure, including foundations and roof, forming common parts, this is fairly unusual, and indeed one of the features which ought to separate a maisonette from a flat is that the roof will belong to the top floor maisonette, and the foundations to the unit on the ground floor. Naturally, the appropriate rights, including maintenance, will be incorporated in the documentation.[8]
9 Because of the above rules, it follows that a block of flats may comprise any number of floors, indeed the only restriction on the number of floors is imposed	9 Equally because of the above rules, it follows that the number of storeys in a block of maisonettes is extremely limited, because over about three storeys one runs

5 See Ch 9, pp. 110–127, below.
6 And see the suggested definition of 'flat' below.
7 As described in ch 9, pp 110–127, below.
8 And refer to Precedent No 1, p 336, below, a typical lease of a maisonette, with appropriate provisions dealing with maintenance of the main fabric and providing for contributions from other owners in the same block.

by the technical problems involved in building to great heights.

out of available space for separate entrances. These will almost always be staircases, and it does not take much imagination to visualise that the space required for separate entrances in a multi-storey block of maisonettes would mean that almost the whole of the lower floor areas would be taken up by self-contained staircases—and thus the whole thing would be self-defeating. Usually three storeys are the maximum whether comprising three single floor units one on top of each other, or two units of two floors and one floor respectively, and in whatever sequence.[9]

By now the reader should have become familiar with the respective concepts of 'flat' and 'maisonette', in so far as they relate to this book and its treatment of the two different units. It is not for one moment suggested that the interpretations which follow are definitive as far as the whole of the conveyancing fraternity are concerned, and there will doubtless be those who will quibble with them.

Nevertheless, it is important that when throughout this book we refer to 'flats' and 'maisonettes', the reader knows precisely what is meant. The following definitions are accordingly offered for reference purposes.

'"Flat" is a separate set of premises which forms part of a building, comprises only part of the vertical aspect of that building, and which shares internal common areas with other sets of premises in the same building. The separate sets of premises may be made up of one or more storeys, but if there is more than one storey, access from one storey to another must be effected without either passing through any of the internal common areas of, or via the outside of, the building.'

'"Maisonette" is a separate set of premises, which forms part of a building, comprises only part of the vertical aspect of that building, but which has a completely separate access to the exterior of the building and does not share any internal common areas with other sets of premises in the same building. Each separate set of premises may be made up of one or more storeys.'

9 This prompts consideration of blocks of unit with front doors leading off 'decks', which may be open or partially closed and which, together with the staircases leading to the decks, are the only common areas. Probably these are, at least technically, flats although in practice they will be treated as, and very often called, maisonettes. However, as this type of development is only usually found in local authority developments, it is not too much of a difficulty in the context of this book's subject.

CHAPTER 2

The history and status of the flat

The flat, and with it the maisonette, as a unit of housing has been around for a great number of years, so that it is by no means a creation of the modern age we live in. Nevertheless, there is no doubt that the flat, as a concept of a particular type of housing, has enjoyed increasing popularity in post-war years.

The concept of a horizontally divided unit of housing can be traced right back to the middle ages, although the more common manifestation of what we would nowadays refer to as a flat, or an apartment, was the 'rooms' that nineteenth-century gentlemen would keep in the main centres of population—usually London. These may or may not have been completely self-contained; certainly some of them would be more in the nature of a service flat.

From the turn of this century onwards, the attraction of the horizontally divided unit of housing enjoying joint use of common areas within the same block became more and more obvious, first in the heavily built up areas, but increasingly in more suburban, and then even rural locations.

When the author migrated from the ranks of private practice to the housebuilding industry in the very late 1960s, there would have been no question at all of any sort of flat or maisonette being built on the sort of developments he was then dealing with—which were a fairly wide range of sites, both in size and type of unit on offer, built by a perfectly ordinary building firm in a perfectly ordinary part of the country, an area encompassing a medium-sized cathedral city, country market towns, and genuinely rural parts.

Now, within the space of no more than 15 years, our expectations have changed completely. We could normally anticipate finding a development of flats or maisonettes in any of these sorts of location, without being in the least surprised.

However, getting back to the development of the horizontally divided unit as a specific type of housing unit, the earlier years of this century found flats being built with more and more frequency, although, of course, not to the same extent as nowadays. Interestingly enough, these flat developments were in the main either for the wealthy—for instance apartments in the heart of fashionable areas of London—or for the poor; witness the developments undertaken by the various trusts such as the Peabody Trust. The middle classes were not catered for, because they had no need or desire to live on top of the attractions of the big cities, and they were well enough off to be able to go into the suburbs and buy their own houses, where there was no need to devise a unit of living accommodation which took up as little ground space as possible.

INCREASE IN POPULARITY

Various constraints have, over the years, combined to make the flat, or the maisonette to a lesser extent, much more suitable as a place to lay one's head. Since the late sixties the real development of the flat as an important feature of the housing scene has occurred, and it seems that every passing year sees development proceeding at an increasing pace. What has given rise to this trend? There are probably two major identifiable reasons:

1 Ease of maintenance

The first, and probably much the less important reason, is that fewer people are prepared to take on the responsibility of running a house, with maintenance of both inside and out, including the looking after of a garden. Of course, there are always going to be those for whom these very things are an attraction in themselves, but in these days of working wives being the rule rather than the exception, young couples especially do not have the time to spare for looking after everything which is associated with a house, and the minimal or non-existent external maintenance associated with a flat is a great attraction. Our young couple will know that whilst they look after the inside of their flat, someone else is going to look after, or 'manage' the common area of the block in which they live—both inside and outside, although they will have to accept the disadvantage of having to pay for this management.[1] But it is precisely because of this little family unit's desire to have as little work as possible to carry out on the unit—ie usually because the wife is working—that they can afford to pay for this management. They will know that when the time comes for them to move on to a larger unit of housing—which this time probably *will* be a house, they will have a ready market for their flat. And they are also probably not going to be in the least worried about having other units on either side of or above and below them—after all, if they bought a terraced or even a semi-detached house they would have lateral neighbours, so the extra neighbours up and down will not bother them.

2 Inflation

The second reason, and much the more powerful influence on the housing market, is inflation. This can be studied in various sectors:

(a) *Land prices*

The cost today of a small site for a modest number of flats is the equivalent of the annual net profit a very successful medium-sized builder would have been expecting to make 15 years ago. The price of land in the London area, and some of the other very large cities, has been a growing problem for a number of years, but that very problem is now manifesting itself in the

1 Although the management scheme may be along the lines of the 'self-help' schemes described in ch 9, pp 110–127, below.

smaller cities, the towns, and even the rural areas. The pressure on land prices may be ascribed to:

(i) *Lack of enough land.* Developers have recognised for some time that there is a shortage of the common basic raw material—land. In some areas there are so many builders chasing so little land that when a parcel does come on to the market, there is a mad scramble for it. Naturally, this only succeeds in pushing up the asking price of the next piece. Then there will be the builder who will pay a stupid price merely to make sure that one of his rivals does not get the land! All the owners of prospective building land will then get wind of this on the jungle drums, and so the mad price spiral goes ever upward.

(ii) *Less 'clean' land.* As well as there being less available land in overall terms, what there is on the market seems to have more and more problems, whether the problems are connected with defective title, stupid restrictive covenants, bad ground, or whatever. As it costs money to put these defects right, this again will add to the inflationary trends.

(iii) *Taxation.* Whatever our politics, the basic concept of a system where all identifiable building land is passed into the hands of some governmental authority for competitive distribution to the (still private!) building industry is probably going to have a great deal in its favour. The problem comes when tax comes into the equation, because there is absolutely no doubt that the taxation of land has been a contributory factor in the spiralling price of land. Just as this book was going to press, however, the Spring 1985 budget abolished Development Land Tax.

(b) *Basic costs*

The price of land is an important element in the build-up of the price of any unit, whether it be a house or a flat. The percentages vary wildly, of course, but as a rule of thumb, 20% is not a bad percentage to be thinking of when one is considering what proportion of the all-up selling price is represented by the land element. But what about the other 80%? Some of it will admittedly be profit—but not too much nowadays!—and some of it will be overheads and other similar administration expenses, but this item will only contribute a significant proportion in the case of the builder of some significant size. The rest will represent the actual cost of building the unit; that is, the bricks and mortar, including the cost of labour as well as of materials.

Inflationary trends continue, and the cost of buiding a normal, everyday unit of housing has probably increased at least tenfold over the last 20 years. Whilst salaries and wages have also tended to keep up with inflation for the most part, the relative positions of the average salary and the average house price now, in the mid-eighties, and 15–20 years ago, means that there is now more financial pressure on the average house-buyer, who is accordingly looking for something which is going to be more in line with his status. Because of this trend, and the pressure on house prices through inflationary movements in the basic building costs, smaller units have to be offered to the public. Viewed in the long term, flats make most use of available land, and, for that matter, building materials and labour (eg flats share common roofs and foundations).

(c) *Movement in borrowers' status*

As far as the mass housing market is concerned, one might as well say that virtually everybody who is buying a house is doing so with a mortgage. Mortgages are only available to those whose status satisfies the requirements of the lender. Given that there is (as we have seen above) a movement towards increasing disparity between the costs of housing and the ability of the house-buying public's income to keep up, there is going to be a negative movement in status, which means that the average house-buyer is tending to look more for a housing unit which is on balance going to have a relatively lower price tag, than if he were going through the same exercise a few years ago.

For this proposition to become clearer, one needs only to recall that 15 or 20 years ago the smallest housing unit that might be anticipated on an average building estate (leaving aside special cases like London and the other very large metropolitan areas) would have been a semi-detached house. Row upon row of this sort of unit was put up, and the first-time buyer would normally expect to be able to buy one. Anything smaller than a semi was unusual. Terraced housing was only to be seen to any great extent in pre-1914 urban areas, flats were units which were much more specialised than they are now and the 'back-to-back'[2] house was a dark legacy of Victorian working class development. As the intervening 15 to 20 years have passed, however, the semi has changed its status. It is no longer the bottom end of the housing market. Rather it is somewhere around the middle of the average housing site, and indeed as a species, it is becoming fairly rare. Certainly the major housebuilders have over the past few years, produced fewer semi-detached houses than almost any other unit.

The first type of property to breach the semi's supremacy was the terraced house, or as the marketing people now refer to them, the 'town house'. Then came the 'back-to-back' unit—ie rather like a pair of semi-detached houses with the semis each split into two units, so that there is basically a unit at each corner. Finally, and in the last few years, the flat has made its presence felt much more as a unit which may be expected to be seen on an average building estate. The underlying reason for this trend is that as one comes down the scale the unit is first, cheaper to build, and second, takes up less land. Better use of space within the units has kept them selling well, and the average prospective purchaser now is just as prepared to look at the town house, back-to-back house, or the flat as was his predecessor 20 years ago to look at the semi.

The above reasons have all been constraints on the average new residential estate, combining to produce the trend to smaller, cheaper, more land effec-

2 'Back-to-back' developments were put up in great numbers. The houses in them afforded no amenity areas, no separate access to the rear, were generally overcrowded, and in some cases represented developers, employers and others taking scandalous advantage of the working classes. When the modern 'back-to-back', described in this chapter, came to be built, the inbuilt prejudice of years had to be overcome.

tive units, but there have been other reasons for the emergence of the flat. These, together with the constraints already discussed, have changed the nature of the flat as a unit of housing from a specialist application to just another variant of the basic unit which may be found on virtually any housing site. The positive reasons for the emergence of the flat are that the leading housebuilders, followed by most of their smaller contemporaries, realised that there was an untapped market for the very small flat, probably a studio unit, or at most a one-bedded unit. Those forming the market had previously lived in 'digs' or bed-sitters, or with their parents, or anywhere they could find to lay their head. By dint of some market research, some very few years ago, the leading housebuilder of the time discovered that there was an apparently untapped, potential market of 120,000 persons who could be interested in, as opposed to the very *temporary* arrangements described above, the purchase of a long leasehold interest in a studio/one-bedroom unit, built in very small blocks placed within the normal housing development, having external elevations of such a nature that it would be difficult for anyone passing to note that what they were looking at was a block of flats, and not some sort of house.

It is now history that the experiment of building these blocks and launching them on the market was successful. This success has itself increased the awareness of the house-buying public of the flat as an acceptable unit of housing on the basis that it is just one of the several *types* of units available to the market, and is not a specialised unit intended for specialised situations.

The trends described above are likely to continue rather than halt or go into reverse. Inflation of some sort is going to be with us for a very long time to come, despite recent encouraging signs. Land will continue to be scarce, and there will be less land available in 'green fields' sites, with more reclaimed land needing to be utilised.[3] The market will continue to be opened out to more and more potential purchasers. This means that the flat in its modern guise is here to stay, whether in blocks included in the normal residential development, or in separate blocks having no relationship to any other concurrent development.

The proof of the preceding narrative is, of course, going to be seen only in statistics.

The first set of figures which are of interest are the percentages of dwelling type in total 'starts'.[4] The last complete year for which figures are available is 1983, and the overall figures are as follows:

Detached houses	28%
Detached bungalows	8%
Semi-detached houses	21%
Terraced houses	21%
Attached bungalows	4%
Flats/maisonettes	18%
	100%

3 Reclaimed land as a description can encompass several different areas, but one important example is land reclaimed by the demolition of old buildings.

4 Source: *National Housebuilding Council: Private Housebuilding Statistics 1983.*

These figures are for England only. The trend of housing types in Scotland is substantially different—eg there are very nearly always many more bungalows built proportionately in Scotland than in England—and inclusion of Scottish figures would distort the true position.[5]

If we then look at the Housing and Construction figures[6] the picture is very much more interesting. These statistics do not refer to *units* of housing, but to number of bedrooms, which is one of the alternative methods of measurement when considering housing statistics. For our purposes, the method of measurement is irrelevant, because what we are looking at here is a like-by-like comparison. Neither are we looking at *percentages*, but numbers of actual properties built, which is much more illustrative.

The figures (which again are for England only) go up to 1984, although the last quarter of 1984 had not been declared at the time of going to press, and so the 1984 figures are extrapolated from those for the first three-quarters of that year.

The first table is for two- and three-bedroom flats completed over the period 1971–1984.

	2 bed	*3 bed*
1971	8,963	1,111
1972	9,140	1,240
1973	9,777	1,545
1974	8,886	1,376
1975	11,183	1,520
1976	9,577	1,349
1977	8,393	968
1978	4,478	920
1979	5,538	792
1980	5,911	612
1981	5,820	664
1982	5,495	499
1983	6,754	593
1984	6,733	688

In all the tables reproduced (which are for the private sector only), account must be taken of the trend in housing starts and completions over the period in question. That trend, overall, was downwards, (although the figures started improving by the end of the period) but both of these tables show that the drop in numbers which occurred in the middle of the period had been reversed by the end, although the starting figures were never regained. However, the very much more interesting table (reproduced overleaf) is that for flats of one bedroom or below (ie studio units) over the same period:

5 In any event, this book is about England and Wales, not Scotland!

6 Source: *Housing and Construction Statistics 1971–1984* (HMSO).

1971	2,867
1972	3,747
1973	3,614
1974	3,452
1975	4,265
1976	3,894
1977	3,607
1978	3,469
1979	2,931
1980	3,616
1981	4,224
1982	6,369
1983	8,658
1984	9,961

This table shows a massive trend upwards. The numbers of one-bedroom flats produced remained fairly constant from the beginning of the period until 1980. From then on, the growth in numbers is impressive. 1981 was the year in which the major housebuilders launched their studio and one-bedroom flats schemes, and the figures reflect these launches, more than doubling in the period 1981–1984. Not only are these 1981 launches reflected in the figures, but also what has obviously been sustained growth in the market.

We can see from these figures, and the underlying trends which we have discussed in the preceding pages, that flats and maisonettes not only have been and continue to be an important sector in the private housing market, but that we are passing through a period—which shows every sign of lasting a long time—when the relevance of the flat, especially the smaller one, has become very much more significant. It follows that everyone concerned with that type of housing—the developer, the manager, the marketing man, as well as the conveyancer, must understand how to deal with it, particularly with regard to the highly specialised aspects.

CHAPTER 3

Flat conveyancing: the choices open to the developer

Moving on from consideration of the definition, history and status of a flat, we should next look at the manner, *from a legal point of view*, in which the flat is going to be sold.

Put simply, there are the alternatives of using either leasehold or freehold conveyancing, just as there are in the sale of ordinary units of housing which are divided only in a vertical plane. But in practice there is really no alternative, given the present state of the law. The only practical course open to the developer of a block of flats is to sell them on a leasehold basis.

Why should freehold be such an unsuitable vehicle for the development of flats?

The answer lies in the established principle of English real property law that the *burden* of a positive covenant will not run with freehold estates. This rule was laid down by the courts as long ago as the last century: a leading case being *Haywood v The Brunswick Permanent Benefit Building Society*[1].This rule is to be contrasted with that in another leading case of the nineteenth century, *Tulk v Moxhay*[2] which some 40 years prior to the *Haywood* case had decided that the burden of a restrictive covenant *would* run with the land so long as certain conditions were satisfied.

For a more detailed discussion on the different effects of the burden (and the benefit) of both positive and restrictive covenants as related to freehold and leasehold estates, the reader is directed to the discussion on pp 309–324 of the Law Commission's proposals on the introduction of a 'Land Obligations Bill', which are designed to clear up the various anomalies inherent in the present system of transfer of land in this country with particular reference to the law of positive and restrictive covenants. There has, in fact, been some considerable disquiet in several quarters, most notably the building societies,[3] about the need to bring in some new system for the conveyancing of land, particularly flats, and the various suggestions made for improvement in the law, including the Law Commissions own proposals, are by no means along the same lines. Nevertheless, the basic problem remains the same until there is some adjustment to this branch of real property law. In relation to flat conveyancing that basic problem can be simply expressed as follows:

(a) The burden of a positive covenant will not run with freehold land.
(b) Covenants between lessors and lessees are treated differently. For a detailed appraisal, the reader should turn to pp 309–324, below dealing with the Law Commission's proposals for reform. Covenants in a lease

1 [1881] 8 QBD 403.
2 [1848] 2 Ph 774.
3 And see ch 29, p 325 on the Building Societies Association's own proposals for reform of the present law.

are entered into either expressly or (under the Law of Property Act 1925, s 79) impliedly on behalf of the covenantor's successors as well as on his own behalf. Under general contract law, the liability will in any event continue despite subsequent changes of ownership on the part of both the lessor and lessee so that there will be cross liabilities by the original lessor to the current lessee, and by the original lessee to the current lessor. Normally, of course, one might expect to find these 'continuing' burdens dealt with by means of indemnity covenants in the conveyancing documentation on the transmission of interests.

Added to this basic principle is the doctrine of 'privity of estate', which preserves enforceability of covenants between the current lessor and the current lessee. Thus in the relationship between lessor and lessee, there is a full range of remedies available to apply to the *current* relationship; in other words, the burden of any positive covenants in a lease *will* run with the leasehold land.

(c) This difference between freehold and leasehold land law so far as enforceability of covenants is concerned is crucial in the development of flats, because in a block of flats there will *always* be common areas, whether internal, external, or both; and each individual flat owner will have to contribute towards the maintenance of the building as a whole. Try as developers might, there is no true flats scheme where this does not apply, even if the burden of contribution whether by means of actual performance or by monetary payment, is contingent. If there is no prospective liability on a flat owner, then he is not living in a flat but a maisonette, which is a quite different animal.[4]

Even the small studio flat schemes described in ch 9, below,[5] have some actual positive contributions, so that the whole question remains one of vital importance.

(d) Thus, prima facie, flats cannot be sold on a freehold basis. However, this statement is not quite true, because flats *can* be sold on a freehold basis, and indeed they have been, but under the umbrella of certain devices which are at best artificial.

A. CHOICES OPEN TO THE DEVELOPER

Having reviewed briefly the state of the law on both freehold and leasehold schemes, we now move on to look at the practical choices open to the developer and those who advise him.

1 Leasehold schemes

The great drawback of leasehold schemes is that they are said to be much less preferable to the general public than freehold ones. This is undoubtedly true, but here I would digress with a personal point of view which to many may seem heretical. I live in Letchworth Garden City, which is one of only two garden cities in the country, and where the great majority of title is

4 See ch 1, p 1, above.
5 See pp 110–127, below.

leasehold. Houses are sold on 999-year leases with a nominal ground rent of £5 per annum. This is collected by the Garden City Corporation, which then distributes the resulting substantial amount to various organisations, schools, charities, etc in the town. Thus the quality of life in the town is arguably better than in surrounding towns, all for the equivalent of 10p per week per householder. Admittedly the Garden City Corporation is more paternalistic than the average commercial lessor, but there is a justifiable comparison.

Most of these housing units are houses, as opposed to flats, but a leasehold term of 999 years never seems to put anyone off, indeed house prices in Letchworth are at a premium since it is acknowledged to be a pleasant town in which to live—and the reason it is more pleasant is a by-product of the rental income! So here we have a conundrum. The arguments against leasehold are, nevertheless, powerful because with a leasehold property the owner only ever has a derivative interest as opposed to freehold, and a derivative interest is felt to be contrary to the dignity of home owners. Yet the overwhelming majority of flats in this country are leasehold, quite simply because there is nothing better available. We can say this before we even look at the specific alternatives available, because of the massive drawbacks of those alternatives. What is more, the general public have become conditioned over the years to accept that a flat is going to be sold leasehold, and there is nothing detrimental in actual practice so far as a potential purchaser of a leasehold flat is concerned. It is, in fact, the only sensible choice to the developer until and unless the law is reformed.

2. Alternative schemes

There is an interesting discussion on the various alternatives open, and consideration of the general state of the present law and the various proposals for reform which have been made, in an article on positive covenants relating to flat blocks by Cedric D. Bell of Huddersfield Polytechnic.[6] The one drawback which many practitioners see as being an encouragement for the passing into history of leasehold flat conveyancing is the right of re-entry which is present in virtually all leases. This is essentially a practical book, and there is not space to launch into an erudite discussion on the 'pros' and 'cons' of there being a right of re-entry, but it is worth noting that the right will only arise and become exercisable if the tenant either does something wrong or fails to pay monies. When anyone buys a flat they should appreciate their responsibilities, and it seems something of a weak argument that those who do not should be protected.

However, we should still look at the other choices open to a developer when setting up his flat scheme. These are as follows.

(a) *Restrictive covenants in freehold sales*

There have been suggestions in some quarters that if all covenants were to be phrased in a negative way, eg those relating to user, excessive noise and the like, then flats would be able to be sold on a freehold basis. But we would still have to cope with the basic problem of the covenant to repair. To phrase

6 Cedric D. Bell 'Law Reform' (1984) 128 SJ 323.

this in a negative manner, eg 'the tenant will not allow the premises to fall into disrepair' is no use, because the covenant is a positive one, whatever the wording used.

If a quasi-building scheme, laying down a set of restrictions to be imposed equally on all flats, were to be set up by the initial documentation, then whoever was a flat-owner at any given time would be able to enforce the restrictions against the other flat-owners for the time being.[7] This would apply whether the units were houses or, as in this case, flats. But a scheme of this sort would still not be able to cope with re-charging of maintenance costs to the individual flats. Perhaps if it were to be stitched into an estate rent charge (see next section) the whole thing *might* work, at least in theory, but the first practical objection would be that it would be difficult enough for some practitioners to understand, let alone the poor prospective purchasers, so on that count alone it would seem to be a non-starter.

(b) *Estate rentcharges*

The Rentcharges Act 1977 introduced a rentcharge of two types (s 2):

(a) a charge, of no more than a nominal amount, to make covenants enforceable against any owner of land for the time being; and
(b) a charge—of an amount that is 'no more than is reasonable for that purpose' to cover the cost of services—including such items as insurance as well as maintenance.

By the 1977 Act, ss 3 (3) (b) and 8 (4) such a rentcharge is exempted from the statutory provisions which govern the redemption/extinguishment of rentcharges, so that in fact it would be able to be created on a perpetual basis, which of course it would have to be if it were to attach to a freehold flat.

If we cast our minds back to the previous section, a building scheme of restrictive covenants could be combined with a services rentcharge, to create freehold flats. However, this would be very cumbersome, because whereas all flat-owners in the same block, under the same building scheme, could enforce those covenants, the right of enforcement of a rentcharge is restricted, as we shall shortly see. So that in effect, a building scheme is virtually a non-starter on a flats scheme.

On the other hand, using rentcharges ought to be an option which could be considered. But it is not, and the reason why flats schemes based on rentcharges are so very rare is that individual flat-owners cannot enforce the covenants against each other. The only person with a right of enforcement is the rentcharge owner (presumably the lessor or the manager). The lessor would probably not want anything to do with owning the rentcharges, as he would equally presumably be selling the flats freehold so that once he had sold the last one he could walk away from the situation. So the manager would have to own the rent charge. But he would only be interested in the service/financial side of the block. Would he be interested in the enforcement of other covenants which related only to the general side of the flats, and not to the management side? Perhaps if there were to be a tenants' management

7 See *Elliston v Reacher* [1908] 2 Ch 665, CA.

company ('tenants' is a misnomer, given a freehold situation, but it is still descriptive and thus reasonably apt) in which the rentcharges were vested this would be the best vehicle, in that there would not be any conflict of interest—or there should not be. However, this book is not exactly a promoter of tenants' management companies as will be seen later.[8] Again we get back to the basic premise that as a vehicle for conveying freehold flats, estate rentcharges are not really a practical consideration.

(c) *Mutual deeds of covenant*

Of all the options open to someone wanting to sell flats on a freehold basis, this is probably the most used, and in some parts of the country, notably a selection of seaside resorts, it is a not uncommon method.

This system relies on the basic principle that although the burden of positive covenants on a freehold flat will not run to subsequent owners, the covenants are perfectly enforceable for ever and a day between the original covenantor and the original covenantee. Thus, why not create *new* covenants every time a flat is sold? Then there would be no difficulties on enforcement.

Like the other freehold options, this sounds reasonable in theory, and it is only when we look at how it works in practice that the drawbacks are apparent:

(a) every time a flat in the block is sold, a deed of covenant must be entered into by the incoming purchaser, the other purchasers remaining in the block and the flat-owner who is selling. This means that someone has got to make sure that on every sale, a deed of covenant is executed. If there is a management scheme, then presumably the manager would have to join in the deeds as well, and he might be willing to take on the administration. Perhaps if the block of flats is registered, a restriction could be entered in the property register to the effect that no transfer would be registered without satisfactory evidence from the manager that the deed of covenant had been entered into. All very well, but yet more work—and if it were the manager's duty to see to this, there would be another item of charge on the service computation;

(b) the sheer scale of the task is horrendous. Imagine that every time a flat in the block is sold, *every* other flat owner has to join in the resulting deed of covenant. The sheer logistics are beyond that which can be coped with easily. The more flats there are in the block, the worse the problem gets. And even if there are only, say, four flats involved, what happens if one of the owners has gone off somewhere, perhaps abroad, and cannot be contacted?;

(c) it is just possible that instead of having the need for individual deeds of covenant, there could be a single 'master' deed which new purchasers could execute. But there are still problems this way, because every time a new purchaser executes the master deed, a copy of the amended deed has to be circulated to all the other flat-owners as proof that the covenants are capable of enforcement against the new purchaser.

8 See ch 11, p 131, below.

Whatever variation one uses on this theme, it is extremely unreliable and is given to speedy breakdowns. Developers should accordingly make sure to avoid it.

(d) *Other ways*

Various writers float other ways in which to deal with this problem. Amongst these are conditional easements, enlargements of long leases under the terms of the Law of Property Act 1925, s 153 and so on; but they all have very major drawbacks.

B. SUMMARY: THE PRESENT AND THE FUTURE

There is no doubt that the use of freeholds in flat conveyancing is at present severely restricted. We have looked at the various methods available to a developer who wishes his purchasers to take something 'better' than a leasehold estate and we have seen that none of them work in a practical way; at least not so as to permit the developer to indulge in large scale transactions without fear of repercussions in the same way that leasehold flat conveyancing does.

Nevertheless, there has been over the last few years much disquiet about the use of leaseholds, not least on the part of the building society movement because of the diminishing security they find offered to them, as the term still outstanding gets shorter and shorter. This problem also affects both lessor and lessee. It seems clear that something is going to be done about this in the fairly immediate future, but in parliamentary terms 'fairly immediate future' might be two or three years away.

However, the Law Commission have carried out a great deal of work already, to the extent of there being in existence a draft bill, supported by a great deal of research and work. What changes might be supposed to be grafted into the draft bill as it passed through Parliament is an open question, but the supposition must be that the present form of the bill would resemble the finished article to a reasonable extent.

The Building Societies Association have gone even further down the line from the Law Commission. They, too, have been looking at the present law and what changes are called for, and their propositions are somewhat more radical than those of the Law Commission, in that they are advocating changing the present system to something more resembling the Australian strata system.

Which system will be eventually introduced is at the present time an unanswerable question. To a certain extent, any discussion on the subject in this book is a waste of time, because this is a book about the present system. And yet since these changes will almost certainly take place during the lifetime of this book, some attention must be given to prospective changes. A more detailed description of what the future might bring, therefore, will be found in chs 28 and 29, below.[9]

9 Pp 309 and 325, below, respectively.

CHAPTER 4

The contents of a lease

It is beyond the scope of this book to make an intensive study of the theory of the contents of a typical residential lease for a long term. That sort of study is best left to the more specialist volumes. Nevertheless, when considering the general subject of the sale of flats, there is considerable relevance in looking at the particular sections into which a specialist lease of this sort is divided, and carrying this study to even more specialised portions of the document where this is warranted, eg to the individual tenants' covenants.

The following sections, therefore, will deal with individual components of a typical residential lease in the hope that the reader will derive from them a greater understanding of the 'raison d'etre' of the modern lease. However, this is not intended to be an exhaustive survey of the subject; rather it is a précis, and the reader is asked to treat it as such.

The chapter does not deal with those parts of a lease which will normally deal exclusively with the maintenance charge; its build up, method of computation and eventual collection. These are dealt with in chs 8–19, pp 95–228, below.

A. BASIC FEATURES OF A LEASE

The following sections are only intended as an 'aide memoire'. For a more detailed exposition, one of the learned textbooks should be consulted. Nevertheless, for a full understanding of how to use the lease format in the various situations described in this book, an elementary understanding of the different parts of the lease as an 'art form' must be achieved, otherwise the practitioner will be handicapping himself. This applies whether the information has never been known in the first place, or (which one supposes will be the case for all of us save the student element) we are merely 'reminding' ourselves!

Points which readers may find useful are as follows:

1 Any lease granted for a term which exceeds three years must be under seal.[1] Otherwise the document will be treated as an agreement for a lease.

2 Whilst it is usual to date a lease on its face, nevertheless the strict rule is that the lease will only take effect from delivery. Normally, though, the date on the document itself will be prima facie the true date.

3 Naturally, the full names and descriptions of the parties will be included, but so long as the quoted description identifies a particular party as being

1 It is assumed that in this book we shall not be touching on leases for terms shorter than three years. It is also assumed that we are only concerned with corporeal hereditaments.

distinguished from any other, that will be sufficient, if hardly good conveyancing practice.

4 The consideration for the lease of the property concerned will be:

(a) the rent; and
(b) the covenants on the part of the lessee.

It is normal for the words expressing the consideration to come before the operative words. If the financial consideration is rent alone, then this statement is sufficient but if there is also to be a premium (which inevitably there will be on the sale of property on long leases) reference to that premium at this point is essential.

Thus the wording will be something like:

'In consideration of £20,000 paid by the lessee to the lessor (receipt etc) and of the rents and covenants hereinafter reserved ... the lessor HEREBY DEMISES unto the lessee ALL THAT .'

The actual specification of the rent, that is its amount, frequency of payment, etc comes later in the 'reddendum' (see below).

5 The demise, or the 'operative' words, as sometimes described, is the central core of the lease. Of the two words most commonly used 'demise' is perhaps the more archaic, 'lease' the more modern. Either is perfectly acceptable, as indeed would any other words which sufficiently explained what the parties were trying to do, which is that the lesser is divesting himself of possession, that the lessee is taking on possession, and that the contemplated possession will be for a specific period of time, so that there is a point in time—however far into the future— when the period will come to an end, and possession will revert to the lessor or his successor in title.

6 The property which forms the subject of the lease must be described accurately. For property which is probably just one of several units in a larger block of property which is divided both vertically *and* horizontally, almost always along the line of floors and walls, there is a requirement for accurate description. Further reference should be made to the Precedent section, below.

7 The next logical section of the lease to consider is that dealing with rights granted to the lessee with the demise, such rights being over other adjoining property of the lessor, including other flats in the same block, and exceptions and reservations[2] reserved out of the property demised for the benefit of that adjoining property.

As these matters are usually dealt with by schedules, they are referred to below in the same sequence as one would expect to see them in a standard lease.

8 The habendum comes next. This is the part of the lease which contains the words 'To hold the same unto the lessee ...', and it will define:

(a) the date of commencement of the term. This need not be the same as the date of the lease, indeed it seldom is, and may be a past or future

2 It is appreciated that there is a technical distinction between an exception and a reservation: nevertheless the phrase 'exception and reservation' is used here in its 'colloquial' sense used by most practitioners.

date. If it is a past date, the interest of the lessee nevertheless vests only from the date of the lease itself. However, if the parties wish to express a past date in the habendum, the lessee will then prima facie be responsible for rent from the *commencement date*, not the date of execution of the lease, and he may also be liable for other contractual provisions in the lease, so that this point should be watched carefully by the lessee's solicitors;

(b) the length of the term. For the purposes of this book, we will only here contemplate terms expressed in precise terms, eg after the words 'to hold the same, etc ...' as set out above, there might follow: 'from the First day of January 1984 for the term of Ninety nine years.'

One point to note is that strictly speaking, if the term is expressed to start from a particular day, then that day is not included in the term, so that the last anniversary day *is* included. In the example given above, the term would start at midnight on 1/2 January 1984, and would subsist the whole of the day on 1 January 2083, finishing at midnight. Equally strictly speaking, if the expression 'on the 1st day of January' etc is used, then that day is included, and the term would finish at midnight on 31 December 2082/1 January 2083. As the word 'from' is widely used in modern drafting in preference to 'on', the position seems to be somewhat unsure. It was held in *Ladyman v Wirral Estates Ltd*[3] by Fisher J at Liverpool Assizes that whilst the word 'from' was used, the true intention of the parties was that the date of commencement was included in the term. Nevertheless he reiterated the general principle as stated above. This is obviously a point which should be watched by practitioners, as it is clear that a substantial amount subscribe to the alternative quoted as the correct one by Fisher J in the *Ladyman* case, but expressed by him therein as the exception.

9 Next in line is the reddendum. Whilst the consideration, including rents, should be mentioned previously[4] it is the reddendum which qualifies the amount of rent and all its other aspects, that is the payee (which will usually be the lessor—in which case the identity of the payee is left silent) the time and mode of payment. The time honoured phrase which will be found in most reddendums is 'Yielding and Paying therefor', but the strict wording is unnecessary and anything which indicates the method of payment is acceptable.

The matter of rent is discussed more thoroughly when we come to study the lessee's covenant to pay rent,[5] but one aspect of the subject which is best discussed here concerns not the reservation of rent itself, but that which reserves other payments as additional rent. These payments may include such matters as insurance premiums and service charges or maintenance payments.

It is normal to find insurance dealt with as part of the rent reservation. There is a school of thought, however, which prefers service charges not to be treated in this way, but instead to be dealt with as a direct covenant

3 [1968] 2 All ER 197.
4 See point no 4, above.
5 See p 26, below.

between lessor and lessee. In this latter case, of course, the reddendum would have no mention of these charges.

I have always preferred to see these payments covered by the reddendum, simply because if the worst comes to the worst and action is required, a s 146 notice is not required if the service charge is reserved as additional rent.[6] As a somewhat dubious bonus, the remedy of distress would also be available, which it would not be otherwise. How valuable this remedy is in the case of a residential tenancy is doubtful. On the other hand, those who favour the use of the direct covenant feel that it is best to separate the service charges from rental payments. Such hooking of service charges into the reddendum can actually backfire so that it is preferable to be able to opt for a simple action on the unpaid amounts without disturbing the lessor–lessee relationship. The value of this is questionable.

10 Reviews are treated separately, see 'D. Rent reviews' p 56, below.

11 Every lease will contain a lessor's covenant for quiet enjoyment, whether express or implied. The wording is standard[7] and no more need be said on the subject, except to refer readers who wish to learn more of the nature of the covenant to an appropriate textbook.[8]

12 It will be a rare lease which does not contain a lessor's right of re-entry clause. The wording is again standard[9] but one point should be noted, and that is that in former times it was only considered usual to have the right of re-entry confined to non-payment of rent, but as late as 1981 Foster J had no doubt that a right of re-entry for breach of covenant generally, as well as for non-payment of rent, was usual in a modern lease.[10]

13 Where the subject of the lease is registered, the opportunity is often taken to enter a restriction on the property register which will usually inhibit the manner in which the unit, the subject of the lease, is disposed of, except by adherence to certain laid-down guidelines. In other words, the restriction will usually make sure that the unit is not transferred without the full knowledge, and sometimes approval, of the lessor. This subject is discussed in more detail elsewhere in this book.[11]

14 We saw earlier that certain rights will normally be expected to be granted with the property as an adjunct to the demise. Typical rights will be as follows:

(a) In common with the lessor and other owners of units in the same block to rights of access over all the common parts of the block of flats, both internal and external, and (where the block of flats forms part of a development estate upon which the roads are still private and presumably under a Highways Act 1980, s 38 agreement) similar rights of way, both vehicular and pedestrian where appropriate, over the estate roads and footways leading to the nearest adopted road.
(b) Similarly rights of passage of services through the relevant pipes, cables,

6 And see further ch 27, p 297, below.
7 See eg Precedent No. 3, cl 6, p 363, below.
8 Eg *Hill & Redman's Law of Landlord and Tenant* (17th edn, Butterworths) ch 3, pp 196–206.
9 See eg Precedent No. 3, cl 7, p 363, below.
10 *Chester v Buckingham Travel Ltd* [1981] 1 All ER 386, [1981] 1 WLR 96.
11 See ch 7, p 86, below.

etc present both in the block of flats itself, and (as above where appropriate) the adjoining estate development.

NB. Obviously in both of these cases there will come a point in time when the estate roads, footpaths and service ducts—assuming the block is being built within an estate development—will become publicly owned, and to a very great extent that part of the rights granted will become irrelevant. Nevertheless on a new development they are crucial, and there are circumstances which may arise in the case of the service ducts, particularly if they do not always run under estate roads but meander instead through, eg people's back gardens, where it is important to preserve the rights.

Some practitioners would prefer the (temporary until adoption) rights over the estate roads and footways to be dealt with by a separate clause.

(c) The rights over the common parts of the block and set out in (a) above may only refer to access and egress. Access to these common parts may be required for other purposes—eg maintenance, etc. Access should certainly be available to other *units* in the block for maintenance, etc relating to the unit in question. This right should be carefully checked for its presence in any lease. All these matters discussed in this paragraph may be contained in the one clause, and should be identified as those necessary for the proper performance of the lessees' obligation under the lease.

(d) It will be necessary to include rights of support and protection referring to the unit's relationship with the other units in the same block.

(e) The demise should also carry the benefit of covenants entered into by the lessor with lessees of other units in the block.

15 Some conveyancers deal with rights to which the demise is subject as expressing them to be the mirror image of the rights granted. Most of us, though, will prefer to see the individual matters specified on a clause by clause basis:

(a) Rights of access to the demised premises by the lessor and lessees of other units in the block. This is the mirror of 14(c), above.

(b) Rights to passage of services through any service ducts within the demised premises, and the right of entry upon the demised premises in order to maintain, renew, etc such service ducts.

It will be noted that the latter right was not mentioned in paragraph 14, above as being one specifically granted as a right. The cautious conveyancer may wish to add such a clause to the rights, but there seems little doubt that it would be covered anyway by eg paragraph 14(c).

(c) Where the common parts, both internal and external, are included in part in the demise, as on the studio flat scheme[12] then it will be necessary to reserve rights over these common parts for the benefit of those other unit owners in the building and all others entitled to such rights.

(d) As a mirror of paragraph 14(d), above there will be reserved to the other units in the block rights of support and protection.

(e) The demise should be subject to the burden of covenants entered into by the lessor with lessees of other units in the same building.

12 See ch 9, p 110, below, for a description of this scheme.

16 Lessees' covenants may be divided into several different categories. The following lists are intended only to be illustrative and not definitive:

(a) Lessees' covenants to observe restrictions will be direct covenants entered into by the lessee with the lessor, and pertaining to the manner in which the lessee behaves in the premises: thus, as examples:
Not to use the premises as anything other than a private dwelling house.
Not to use the premises for any purpose from which a nuisance can arise.
Not to do anything to render void the insurance policy.
Not to cause a noise, etc, by playing musical instruments.
Not to exhibit any signs outside the demised premises.
(b) Lessees' covenants with the lessor differ from category (a), above in that they will relate to the manner in which the lessee maintains his tenancy, rather than being restrictive in a behavioural sense.
As examples:
To pay rent, and rates.
Not to make any structural alteration.
To pay s 146 notice costs.
To deliver copies of notices to lessor.
Not to sub-let or assign (in accordance with the particular covenant).
To give notice of change of ownership, etc.
To re-decorate interior of demised premises.
(c) Lessees' covenants expressed to be for the benefit of the lessor, *and* the other lessees in the same block. As examples of this type of covenant:
To maintain the demised premises in good repair and yield up in good condition.
To permit the lessor with agents to enter the demised premises to view state and condition.
To redecorate etc, exterior of demised premises (and where applicable—eg on studio flat schemes—to re-decorate appropriate parts of the common parts demised with the unit).[13]

The difference between this category of covenants and those described in categories (a) and (b) is easily discernible. Those in the former categories only affect the unit itself, or the direct relationship between the lessor and lessee. Those in this category also affect the other lessees in the block, and these covenants are to be interpreted as being entered into for the benefit of those lessees. For instance, every lessee in the block is interested in seeing that the other lessees maintain their properties in a proper manner, otherwise the appearance of the block as a whole may become affected, with a detrimental effect on the value and re-saleability of the units in it. Further deterioration within one unit may well lead to physical damage which could affect the other flats.[14]

17 Lessors' covenants will usually be fewer than lessees, but they are important for all that:

To insure.

13 See ch 9, pp 110 et seq, below.
14 Eg the cutting out of roof timbers described on p 31, below.

To lay out insurance monies on reinstatement in event of block becoming damaged.

To require other lessees to enter into similar covenants, etc.[15]

If the title of the lessor is leasehold then it will be normal to find here a covenant on its part to pay any rent reserved by the head lease, and to perform and observe any covenant into which it has therein entered.

Further, in a 'new build' situation, especially where the block is part of a larger estate development, it would be normal to find at this point the usual covenant on the part of the lessor (assuming it was also the developer) to make up the estate roads and footways, etc, and to cause them to be eventually adopted as highways maintainable at the public expense by the local highway authority.

Each separate covenant in the four preceding categories, that is, lessees' covenants of restriction, lessees' direct covenants with lessor alone, lessees' covenants for benefit of both lessor and other lessees, and lessor's covenants, requires further comment in order to offer readers a better understanding of the structure of the lease. The following sections do just that on an individual basis. Nevertheless, they are intended only as introductions, and for further information one of the standard textbooks on landlord and tenant should be consulted. It should be noted that the covenants described in the following pages are not necessarily categorised in the manner which we have just described. Rather they are taken in the order in which they might normally be expected to appear in a typical lease.

B. INTERPRETATION CLAUSES

Interpretation or definition clauses in leases seem to have been something of a growth industry in recent years. When I was in articles, not so many years ago, I can only recall heavy institutional leases carrying interpretation clauses—and I saw precious few of those in a shires county town.

Nowadays, a lease which does not have an interpretation clause seems to be the exception rather than the rule. No doubt because of this proliferation, practitioners sometimes seem bamboozled by them.

It is only because of this occasional puzzlement that space has been found for a few brief words on the subject, which can be dealt with simply by drawing attention to the following suggested basic ground rules:

(a) Only use an interpretation clause if it is really necessary. If the document is short, or by whatever manner the meaning of words in their context is clear, there should be no necessity for such a clause.
(b) Make sure that the meanings of the words in the clause itself are expressed clearly, and not so imprecisely that the meanings themselves are likely to need interpretation!

Incidentally, one point which does cause occasional concern is where the interpretation clause should go. There are those who maintain that it should

15 This is a crucial covenant. In both leases of flats, but particularly maisonettes, it is vital. For a further discussion, see eg ch 5, p 68, below.

be included as a recital; others feel it should form part of the body of the document. The answer is that it does not seem to matter, just so long as it is somewhere in the document.

C. THE TENANTS' COVENANTS

1 To pay rent

The concept of a rental on a long leasehold property is something of an anachronism which can be misunderstood and even resented by tenants. Elsewhere in this book the possibility is considered, both in the present and the future, of using a freehold basis of selling flats,[1] but if the leasehold formula is used, then there will almost always be a rent reserved. Having said that, it should be noted that the rent can be anything from nothing upwards.

There does seem to be some confusion in practitioners' minds as to the exact nature of ground rent in the case of a long residential lease, and also to the option open to the ground lessor to levy a non-monetary rent[2] or, indeed, none at all. According to *Hill & Redman's Law of Landlord and Tenant*, rent is 'the recompense paid by the lessee to the lessor for the exclusive possession of corporal hereditaments' and 'it need not consist of the payment of money'.[3] As rent is thus the product of a bargain struck freely between the two parties (or at least so the theory goes) it can be anything—money, money's worth or nothing. Again, according to *Hill & Redman*[4] it has become custom to reserve something like a peppercorn where no actual money is required, but this is not necessary and a lease may be completely rent free.

The question of what, if anything, to reserve in the way of ground rent, as it is more properly described, is necessarily tied in closely with the setting up of the management scheme. There is no point in charging a substantial ground rent as well as a service charge of some significance if what you are dealing with is a very small unit which is going to be marketed to those on tight budgets. When we discuss maintenance generally[5] we shall see that the smaller the unit, the less advisable it is to levy any sort of ground rent, *unless* the service charges are being kept to an absolute minimum (eg in a unit sold on a 'self-maintained' principle)[6] when the ground rental income is possibly the only way in which maintenance monitoring costs on the part of the landlord are going to be covered. The whole question of how much ground rent to charge is thus more logically dealt with in the section on maintenance; all that we need to consider here is that practitioners being the cautious creatures they are, the lessor's adviser will wish to see a rent (even only a peppercorn) reserved, and so probably will the lessee's adviser; so that a rent

1 See ch 3, p 13, above and ch 28, p 309, below.
2 And see ch 8, pp 98–102, below, for a discussion on the options open to the developer as to rental levels.
3 *Hill & Redman's Law of Landlord and Tenant* (17th edn) Vol 1, p. 315.
4 Ibid, p 316.
5 See ch 8, p 95, below.
6 See ch 9, p 110, below.

will be reserved, and the lessor's remedies against the lessee for non-payment of ground rent are exactly the same as in any other case.

2 To pay rates, etc

This is a perfectly standard covenant. It seems unlikely that any outgoings would be attributable to any part of the block of flats other than on the individual units themselves, but where there is the possibility of this happening (eg central recreational facilities in a large, expensive block) the outgoings on these parts would form part of the service charge.

The covenant does have slightly more to it than the bland content of the first sentence; a more detailed discussion will be found in *Hill & Redman* Vol 1, pp 306–314.[7]

3 To maintain and repair

It will be a rare lease which does not contain a clause of this type as a lessee's covenant. This covenant will usually be expressed to be with the lessor for his benefit, and the benefit of the lessees of other flats in the same block. Obviously it will be of great concern to every lessee in the same block to have re-assurance of the imposition on other lessees as to maintenance, otherwise, the block itself could be affected in the same way as a house of cards.

The wording of the covenant is usually standard, and to the point, thus:

'The Lessee will maintain and repair in good and tenantable condition the demised premises during the term and will yield up the same at the expiration of the term in like condition.'

This covenant has been long accepted as one of the 'usual' covenants to be found in a typical lease[8] save that it is not considered usual to insert on the lessee's behalf the saving words 'damage by fire or tempest only excepted.'[9]

The state of the premises which is anticipated at the end of the term should be noted. 'Good and tenantable condition' is obviously not the same condition that the demised premises would have been in at the start of the building's life, or the commencement of the term, if that came later. The phrase is to be understood as meaning a reasonable state of repair which would be acceptable to any other incoming lessee, having regard to the age, etc, of the building.

4 To re-decorate

Traditionally in a lease of a flat the lessee will only be required to perform an internal redecorating covenant. However, in the modern context a lessee may be required to covenant to redecorate other parts as well, and so discussion of this particular covenant is classified into three main sections, thus:

7 *Hill & Redman's Law of Landlord and Tenant*, (17th edn, Butterworths) Vol 1.
8 See *Hill & Redman's Law of Landlord and Tenant* (17th edn, Butterworths) Vol 1, pp 149–150.
9 According to *Hill & Redman* (at p 151) the authority for this is the old case of *Sharp v Milligan* (No 2) (1857) 23 Beau 419 at 422.

(a) redecoration of the interior of the exclusively demised premises (ie the flat);
(b) redecoration of those parts of the interior common parts which are attributable to the exclusively demised premises; and
(c) redecoration of the exterior parts of the exclusively demised premises, and, possibly, also the exterior parts of the common areas attributable to the exclusively demised premises.

Before examining these categories more closely, we should first look at the basic nature of the covenant itself—ie redecoration—and why it should be treated as a matter which is separate from general repair.

The reason is perfectly simple and straightforward. Redecoration is easily the most visible part of repair, and lack of attention to it will very quickly show, whereas defalcation in effecting general repairs will take much longer to become apparent. A window frame in need of repainting will show its condition readily, and what is more, will be in a strategic position in the building. The same applies to any type of decoration which is easily visible, for example, not only window frames but also things like rendered surfaces which have to be treated (with some such material as Snowcem).

Of course, the strategic position is only really present in a situation where the state of decoration is visible to someone other than the lessee; thus there is a strong argument that it matters not that a lessee fails to perform his internal decorating covenant, because if he does not do so only he will suffer initially in that he will live in a flat in need of decorative attention, and ultimately in that he will possibly have trouble in selling a flat in poor condition.

It should be of no consequence to a lessor that his lessee chooses to live in a flat in need of decorative attention. After all, it may be said that it is only a coincidence of circumstances that the lessee's home is one of several in an all-embracing block, and that this is the reason for the lessor/lessee relationship which may give rise to paternalism on the part of the lessor, in that he has a right to inspect, and demand improvement to the condition of, the lessee's home.

Normally, then, a lessor might not care two hoots about how the lessee is keeping his flat. On the other hand, it is undoubtedly in the interest of the lessor, or whoever is responsible for the block of flats (eg a manager) to make sure that each flat in the block is reasonably looked after, otherwise a situation might arise whereby flats up for sale were proving difficult to sell because of their poor state of repair, especially decorative repair. This situation, in its turn, could have a damaging effect to the management of the block itself. Nevertheless, the internal re-decorating covenant need not be couched in over-restrictive terms.

The particular categories set out above are now considered separately:

(a) *Internal re-decorating: individual unit*

We have already considered the basic factors affecting this aspect of decorating; what it boils down to is, on the one hand, a fight between paternalism and self-interest on the part of the lessor so that the block of flats does not get a reputation for being dilapidated and unsaleable, and on the other hand the principle of allowing each flat owner to deal with his own property in precisely the way he desires, even if that means that he does nothing. From a practical point of view, it would seem sensible, even perhaps important, that a lessor should be able to make sure that each flat in the building is being well looked-after. The only way he is going to make sure is to take a covenant from the lessee.

How should that covenant be drawn, and should it refer to frequency of decoration? The drafting should be as deliberately loose as possible, whilst still keeping within the framework of the obligation. There are still practitioners around who will incorporate all sorts of minutiae in the wording, but a fairly relaxed wording, as used in the precedent of a studio flat lease[10] is perfectly sufficient, thus:

'Once every   years to re-decorate with good quality materials the interior of the flat.'

This wording removes the rather old-fashioned references to 'oil paints' etc which one still sees used.

What about frequency? It is extremely unlikely that a lessor will knock on his lessee's front door once every three years, or whatever the frequency is, to inspect the interior of the flat. If the lessor gets to the point of requiring entry to a flat for the purposes of inspection, then it will be for a reason very much more serious than that he thinks it is about time that the lessee re-decorated his living room. Therefore some sort of reasonably vague wording as to frequency might be desirable, thus:

'As often as may be necessary ....'

But who is to interpret how often necessary is? This introduces an element of uncertainty, and so we get back to a strict timetable; probably for internal redecoration of the flat itself something between three and five years is reasonable as the cycle. The real consideration is that the covenant is a fail-safe one; it is only in the lease to be effected on a last-resort basis, so that as long as it is not overpoweringly officious, neither lessor or lessee ought to take objection to it.

(b) *Interior redecoration: common parts*

Why include a reference to interior common parts redecoration as applied to lessee's covenants? The simple fact is that owing to economic pressures, methods are having to be devised to relieve flat owners of the burden of service charges as much as possible. This subject is studied in depth in another part of this book,[11] but there are two basic ways of relieving the burden of these service charges. The first is to use materials which require little or no maintenance,[12] and the second is to divide common parts, particularly internal ones, amongst the flats, and so shift the burden of mainten-

10 See Precedent No 3, p 360, below.
11 See ch 9, p 110, below.
12 See ch 16, p 172, below, where physical aspects of materials used in the construction of blocks of flats are discussed.

ance from the lessor to the lessee. This concept is, of course, fairly revolutionary, and the principle is discussed elsewhere,[11] so that for the purposes of this part of the book we have to assume that the principle is acceptable and that it can, and is, put into practice.

The burden is shifted to the lessee by actually dividing the internal common parts into separate areas (all of which together will naturally equal the whole) and demising those areas with the flats themselves on a one-for-one basis. Each demise of a portion of the common parts will be subject to the usual rights and reservations, so that everyone has the right to use all the internal common parts, but each flat-owner will have the burden of redecorating (and of course maintaining) his section of the common parts. This is where it becomes very important to have some central thread of co-ordination running through the provisions relating to each individual section. It would be hopeless to impose a duty on each lessee to redecorate, and then leave them to it, one might end up with an internal corridor in a block of flats being redecorated in several different and violently clashing colours! The appropriate covenant must therefore incorporate a provision for supervision by the lessor on colours, thus:

'At the expiration of each (say three) years of the term hereby granted and in the final year thereof to redecorate with good quality materials of a colour designated by the lessor such parts of the interior of the common parts of the building as are included in the demised premises.'[13]

This time, (unlike in the previous section on strictly internal redecoration) it is *very* important for the lessor to be able to enforce the covenant, and on a regular basis.

(c) *Exterior redecoration: common parts*

On a flats scheme where the burden of service charges is sought to be reduced as far as possible, the principle of splitting-up the common parts maintained may extend beyond internal areas into external areas. Exactly which are external common areas and how they are divided between individual flats is dealt with specifically by each individual scheme, but in the full-blown studio flat scheme[14] the appropriate section of the external common parts demised with the flat will be the outside, load bearing wall (inter alia) so that there will fall upon the lessee the responsibility of redecorating the window-frames and/or doors which happen to be present in his portion of the external wall, and, if the wall itself were to be finished in rendering that also would be his responsibility.

Again, it is important to make sure that the covenant is enforceable on a regular basis; as an example the wording of the covenant used in the studio flat scheme lease is—[15]

13 See Precedent No 3, cl 3, Sch 5, p 366 below.
14 See ch 9, p 110 below.
15 See Precedent No 3, cl 4, Sch 5, p 366 below.

'At the expiration of (say five) years of the term hereby granted and in the final year thereof to paint with two coats of good quality paint of a colour to be designated by the lessor the exterior parts of the common parts which form part of the demised premises.'[16]

5 Not to make structural alterations

Every practitioner who deals with leasehold work is familiar with this covenant, and knows that it must appear in a lease, for the benefit and protection of co-lessees as well as for the reversioner. But how many have actually had demonstrated to them just how important the covenant is?

The following cautionary (and true) tale will serve to illustrate the covenant's importance.

The block of flats concerned was a small one of eight studio flats. The upper floor flats happened to be sold so as to include in the demise common areas contiguous to the flats.[17] Thus the roof and roof void above the flat in question was included in the demise, and so was covered by the clause under discussion. There happened to be a trap door leading out of the flat into the roof-void itself, and the lessee in question decided that he would make himself an additional room out of the roof void. As there were a number of annoying roof trusses encroaching on the space which he wanted to create, he resorted to the simple expedient of cutting out all the offending timbers, so that he had the space in which to form his extra room.

It was only by mere chance that the lessors found out about this. When they did, they moved a good deal quicker than they had for some time! Temporary repairs were effected immediately (an on-the-spot survey showed that the whole roof was in imminent danger of collapse—not only on the offending party but also, of course, on his co-lessees) and eventually the roof had to be removed and a new one built.[18]

Like many standard clauses in leases, this clause is one to which scant regard is paid on a specific basis. Nevertheless, its role is crucial.

6 User clauses

Clauses restrictive of user are more commonly expected in a commercial lease, but they are just as important in a lease of residential property.

The first proposition which has to be considered is that unless there is a specific restriction as to user in the lease, a lessee may use his property for anything he likes, subject to the one proviso that it must be a user which is not unlawful. Thus, civil remedies apart, it is perfectly lawful to make an

16 It is probably more important in the case of the exterior to be specific as to materials, quality thereof, and number of coats, as well as colours.

17 For further reference see ch 9, p 110, below.

18 The next question is, of course, what happened then? Did the lessor take action against the errant lessee, and claim as damages the money which had been spent on the repairs? Unfortunately, nothing was done other than to tick off the lessee, who was a 'man of straw', with no assets, mortgaged to the hilt—so that pursuing an action against him would have achieved nothing at all, except probably the loss of good money after bad. This is one of the factors which must be taken into account when this type of development—ie small flats—is contemplated.

excessive amount of noise, unless there happens to be some local ordinance against it. What is more, in this context the time of day when the noise is being made is probably irrelevant.

On the other hand, no one but a foolish lessor (and presumably his equally foolish adviser) will set up the leases for a block of flats, however large or small, without some restriction as to how the flats are to be used appearing in the lessees' covenants, nor should any prospective lessee (or his or her adviser) proceed with the taking of a lease without such restriction, which of course will be imposed on all the co-lessees as well as the lessee in question.

It is therefore well established that there ought to be a user covenant in a long residential lease; consideration of the type and effect of the restriction falls into two parts:

(a) *Behavioural restrictions*

The usual wording of the covenant will be something like:

'not to use . . . etc for any purpose from which a nuisance or annoyance can arise to the other occupiers of the block or the neighbourhood or for any illegal or immoral purpose.'[19]

The drafting of this covenant is fairly wide, covering not only nuisance, which might otherwise be interpreted as merely a nuisance in the strict legal technical sense, but also annoyance, which would be interpreted in more of an everyday sense. The potentially aggrieved parties are also defined widely enough so as not just to cover the co-lessees.

The breaking[20] by a lessee of this covenant is discussed in detail elsewhere in this book, but we should just remind ourselves here that this restriction is put in the lease for a purpose, and that it would be dangerous to omit it. With the growth of the market for smaller flats, especially studios, and with the ability of the larger builders to market their units aggressively, possibly to the point where sometimes unsuitable people will be sold this type of unit, problems will certainly arise. To take just one example, there was the gentleman who insisted on keeping a dog in his flat. That by itself was no particularly bad thing, but the lessor having given permission, then withdrew it, and ultimately had to start an action against the lessee because he was allowing the dog to defecate in the corridors of the block. A case may not happen often but the lessor must have something to hang his hat on, so that he can take appropriate action.

(b) *Restrictions as to type and number of occupancy*

This is a relatively new refinement of the restriction. Formerly, if there were to be a restriction as to this type of user, the wording would have been something like 'not to use other than as a single private dwelling unit', or there might well have been no such restriction at all.

However, what does the lessor do when the unit he is selling is a small

19 And see, eg Precedent No 3, cl 1, Sch 3, p 364, below.

20 For remedies open to the lessor on breach of covenant, see ch 27, p 297, below.

one? It is fine to sell a medium- to large-size flat without any occupancy restriction, or if there is one, a generalised restriction. But when one is dealing with a very small studio unit of, say, between 250 and 300 square feet (which is very small) can the lessor not restrict the occupancy?

For instance, studio flats of the sort described are not designed for children. Indeed some of them are not even designed for couples. The first studio flats marketed on a nationwide basis by the giants of the industry were intended for single person occupancy, were furnished accordingly,[1] and yet it is inconceivable to imagine that there would be no occasion when the purchaser of such a unit would not move someone in to co-habit with him or her.

What also of the situation where children arrive on the scene? This applies not only to units intended for single occupancy only, but also to those intended for double occupancy *but no more*.

The answer for the lessor is probably that he is quite entitled to impose a restriction that the user of the unit will be as a private dwelling unit, which would cope with situations where someone was causing a nuisance, etc to the co-lessees in the block by carrying on, either on a full or part time basis, a business in the unit; but then this sort of action on the part of the lessee could probably be dealt with just as efficiently under the 'nuisance or annoyance' restrictions previously discussed in section (a), although if the draftsman wants to see the 'private dwelling unit' restriction in, it will do no harm. But there is a very large question mark hanging over the right of the lessor to restrict down any further.

The drafting of such a restriction is easy enough—some wording such as 'not to use the demised premises for any purpose whatsoever other than a private dwelling unit in single occupancy only' is perfectly adequate (although I have personally received 'suggested' instructions (the phrase is used advisedly!) that the restriction extend to prohibiting occupancy by any person under the age of 18 years, ie to prohibit children).

The question mark referred to is probably one which has more to do with practicality than with legality. Although there is a suggestion that such restrictions may be contrary to public policy, they are technically at least the product of a bargain between lessor and lessee, and as they are not on the face of it unlawful, then there seems no legal objection to their appearing in the lease.

The objection has to be on practical grounds, for the following reasons:

(i) The lessor has to appreciate that human nature being what it is, in a unit designed for single occupancy, someone somewhere is going to move his/her girlfriend/boyfriend in even if only on a temporary basis, and in a unit designed for double occupancy, there is also bound to be a technical breach of the restriction sooner or later.

(ii) As everyone in the block will (or should) have the same lease, the lessor will be faced with potential complaints from co-lessees, who may, per-

1 Initially the furniture was supplied, and sold, with the flat as a 'package' and there was reference to that package in the lease, as the developers wished to tie the furniture to the bricks and mortar. But this did not work, for various reasons, so that now the furniture pack, whilst part of the overall price build-up, is sold *outright* to the first purchaser.

haps naturally, take a more serious view of the alleged breaches, and they will want the lessor to take action.

(iii) There is a very real chance that co-lessees will press the point frivolously and without real cause for complaint, yet the lessor will have to do something because of the technical breach.

(iv) The lessor will be seen as a 'Big Brother' figure in interfering with lessees' personal lives (although all he may be trying to achieve is good estate management).

(v) The lessor may find himself in a situation where the co-lessees are seeking to have him enforce a restriction (as they might well be entitled to)[2] which if it were to be enforced would create an undesirable situation (eg in a flat restricted to double occupancy only where a baby arrived the opprobrium on a lessor seeking to enforce in such circumstances would be absolute).

(vi) Because of the above, the lessor runs the risk of courting some very bad publicity.

(vii) Finally, and in any event, no lessor wants to regulate other people's private lives in such a manner.

The answer to all this is that the only words of occupancy restriction that are really feasible in a user clause are 'for the occupation of one family only' or some such similar; although these words probably have little or no effect and are mainly cosmetic. If there are problems with people who 'double up' or have children in flats which are basically too small, then if the problem is a really serious one so that the co-lessees are entitled to have the lessor take action, then the matter is probably capable of being dealt with under the usual 'nuisance or annoyance' part of the user covenant.

7 Not to make noise

Again, this lessee's covenant is more of a regulation than anything else, but nevertheless it is one which can channel a fair amount of trouble to the lessor.

The problem with flats is that they are flats, and not detached properties. We have all probably experienced the annoyance of being in a hotel, next door to a fellow resident who thinks of no-one but himself, and keeps his radio or television at uncomfortably high sound levels, or who decides to have a drinking session with friends into the small hours.

The principle is the same in flats; whether the building itself is old or new, it is only in the most expensive type of development that the sound proofing is going to be effective. In any other sort of development, there is just not enough money to support effective sound proofing.

Accordingly, whilst there is every necessity for this sort of restriction to appear in the lessees covenants, the approach of the lessor and the lessees must be reasonable. No lessee can expect to hear nothing at all from his co-lessees, and must be prepared to accept some minor background noise from

2 Ie asking the lessor to perform his covenant to enforce other lessees covenants (see eg, Sch 6, Precedent No 3 cl 3(c), p 367, below.

time to time. On the other hand, the wording of the clause should be absolute rather than qualified; apart from any other consideration, if the clause says something like (inter alia):[3] 'so as to be unreasonably audible outside the demised premises ....' the lessor may well be plunged into arguments on the interpretation of 'unreasonable'. The only real problem the lessor may experience as a result of unqualified wording in this clause is where he is called upon by other lessees to enforce performance of this particular covenant against a recalcitrant lessee. This problem is discussed elsewhere.[4]

8 Not to render the insurance void

The actual covenant to insure is dealt with elsewhere,[5] but this present covenant under discussion will depend to some extent on there being a *lessor's* covenant to insure the block as a whole.

The assumption, as always through this text, is that we are considering a block of flats with common areas,[6] whether those common areas are totally demised away (subject to rights and cross-rights), as in the studio flat system,[7] or retained as lessor's common areas subject to a service charge.

In such a block, it will be almost inevitable that the lessor will wish to take out block insurance cover. To allow the lessees to take out their own insurance would present the lessor with severe monitoring difficulties, as he would be bound to see that every flat-owner took out insurance. Having taken out block insurance, he will be concerned that no-one does anything in or to their own flat, or the common areas, that will vitiate the terms of the block policy, otherwise the action of one might well affect the cover of all, and that triggering effect on the validity of the policy might well occur without the conscious knowledge of the lessor or the co-lessees.

At the same time, the covenant is very much in the way of 'shutting the stable door after the horse has bolted'. If the lessee in question does behave in such a manner as to cause the insurance policy to become void, the covenant only protects the lessor and the co-lessees in the sense that although the act of vitiation is unavoidable they will then have a cause of action against the guilty lessee.

The uncertainty attaching to the whole question is to a large extent disposed of by having good management of the block, by whatever means. It should be part of the job of management to check that all appears to be in order in the block. Any action or inaction on the part of an individual lessee which was going to give rise to the voiding of an insurance policy would certainly make itself apparent to either the co-lessees or the manager, and as there should be ample exchange of information between the two, there should in practice be no difficulty in catching a particular problem early enough.

In cases where the lessees themselves will insure separately, eg some

3 See Precedent No 3, cl 4, Sch 3, p 365, below.
4 See ch 27, p 297, below, on enforcement of covenants.
5 See pp 43–56, below, for a commentary on the covenant to insure.
6 As opposed to eg maisonettes, where the insurance can be—and often is—dealt with by the individual unit owners, and there is no common, or 'block of flats' insurance. For further commentary, see p 43, below.
7 See ch 9, p 110, below.

maisonette schemes, there will be a covenant on the part of the lessee to insure subject to the joint names of the interest of the lessor, etc being noted.[8] Readers will have noted that we mentioned at the beginning of this section that the presence of this covenant depended *to some extent* on there being a lessor's covenant to insure. Where the lessees are bound to insure separately, it does seem that the covenant is *not always* used by practitioners, but it ought to be. It should refer to the policies of insurance of the upper/lower maisonette (as the case may be: ie the other unit to the one in question). For purposes of brevity, it is often incorporated, in these cases, with the user covenant.

9 Covenants limiting sub-letting and assignment

Residential leases will vary in their treatment of the subjects of sub-letting and assignment.

In some instances lessors seem to have developed these covenants into vehicles by means of which they appear to have the right to pick and choose to whom the lessee may transmit the whole or part of the demised premises. In some cases the covenant has become much too restrictive, thus a review of the position is called for to demonstrate what is acceptable and what is not. Of course, the point always has to be made that the incoming lessee, whether original lessee or assignee, is presented with a 'take it or leave it' situation, where often the lessor, or assignor, is in a position where either he cannot, or will not, allow any amendments; but those acting for purchasers of leasehold property should always remember that in a commercial world the lease must be a reasonably acceptable document, and if it is too restrictive in nature pressure from purchasers, and particularly their mortgagees, will very often have the effect of inducing desirable amendments, where possible.

In order not to introduce unnecessary confusion into the picture, assignments and sub-lettings are considered separately as follows:

(a) *Assignments*

In the first place, any covenant against assignment, in whatever terms, is only effective in respect of voluntary operation. Thus, if a lease is taken in execution or passes into the hands of a trustee in bankruptcy the covenant against assignment is not prima facie broken. However, there may be express words in the covenant dealing with such operation of law, and in that event the express words will prevail.[9]

There are three stages of the covenant against assignment. First, the absolute covenant against assignment; next, the covenant against assignment without the consent of the lessor; and finally, the absence of any covenant inhibiting assignment, although in this latter case there would surely be a covenant to *register* assignments, otherwise the lessor would have no way of knowing who was his lessee at any given moment in time.[10]

8 See Precedent No 1, cl 5 (16), p 339, below.
9 And see further *Hill & Redman's Law of Landlord and Tenant* (17th edn, Butterworths) pp 548 et seq.
10 And see further ch 7, p 86, below.

(i) *Absolute prohibition on assignment* The textbooks seem to be completely unclear as to whether either the legislature or the courts will permit this. There seems to be no guidance on the matter save an obiter dicta of Danckwerts LJ in the case of *Property & Bloodstock Ltd v Emerton*[11] where it was queried whether an absolute prohibition would not be construed as falling within the same category as B set out below, that is that the assignment would be permitted but with the lessor's consent, nevertheless not to be unreasonably withheld.

The general consensus of opinion, however, seems to be that such would not be the case, and an absolute prohibition on assignment would be strictly construed, presumably on the basis that the parties were contracting at arms length on fair terms, and the lessee knew what he or she was doing!

However, the likelihood of this sort of prohibition turning up in a residential lease seems remote, at least the sort of lease with which the overwhelming majority of readers will be working. Quite obviously the client would receive a strong warning from his adviser as to the restrictive nature of the document he was signing. This comment only refers to an absolute prohibition on assigning *the whole* of the premises; an absolute prohibition on assigning *part only* of the demised premises is quite normal. This is on the fairly obvious ground that the lessor, let alone the other lessees in the same block, does not want to see the custom built units therein further split up.

(ii) *Conditional prohibition on assignment.* This is much the more common type of prohibition, which will prevent any assignment taking place without the consent of the lessor. While this reposes in the lessor who has some measure of control as to whom the unit is sold, etc, it is largely illusory, because of the provisions of the Landlord and Tenant Act 1927, s 19(1), Part 11:

'**19 Provisions as to covenants not to assign, etc, without licence or consent.** (1) In all leases whether made before or after the commencement of this Act containing a covenant condition or agreement against assigning, underletting, charging or parting with the possession of demised premises or any part thereof without licence or consent, such covenant condition or agreement shall, notwithstanding any express provision to the contrary, be deemed to be subject—

(a) to a proviso to the effect that such licence or consent is not to be unreasonably withheld, but this proviso does not preclude the right of the landlord to require payment of a reasonable sum in respect of any legal or other expenses incurred in connection with such licence or consent; ...'

The rest of the clause is not relevant to our subject here, but it will be seen that whether or not the original covenant in the lease refers to the consent not having to be unreasonably withheld, these words will be deemed to be included anyway.

While this phrase 'not to be unreasonably withheld' opens up the restrictiveness of the covenant considerably from the point of view of the lessee, he or she will nevertheless wish to know just what 'unreasonably' means. It will be no good to a lessee if the lessor withholds his consent for what he maintains to be a perfectly reasonable reason, while the lessee believes it to be unreasonable, unless he, the lessee, can prove so. According to the learned text-

11 [1968] Ch 194.

books, the primary reason will be the financial status of the proposed incoming assignee. There seem to be no other real reasons which would support the contention of the lessor that he was not being unreasonable in withholding consent.[12]

The nature of the discussion in this section points unerringly to the drafting of this type of restriction being mainly for use in a commercial lease, where, eg the rent would be a full rack-rent as opposed to a ground rent. In a residential lease the emphasis is on the capital payment, and it would be no part of a lessor's duty to investigate the ability of the proposed assignee to pay the existing lessee for the property. For an investigation to be set up into the ability of the proposed assignee to pay the ground rent would be unheard of; for it to be put forward as a reason for refusing consent to an assignment, even more outlandish.

(iii) *Free choice of assignment.* This is the ideal position on a residential lease, both from the point of view of the lessee and, perhaps less so, of the lessor. The lessor has no valid reason to concern himself with influence over those who are proposing to take an assignment of the demised premises other than to make sure he knows who and where they are. He should sufficiently rely on the various lessees' covenants in the lease to regulate the incoming lessee and his behaviour in the premises. If he wishes to exercise more control over his knowledge of identities of the lessee at any given time over and above the normal 28-day notice of assignment, he should see that in the granting of the original lease an appropriate restriction is put on the register, assuming the property is being built on registered land.[13] He needs no more security than that. As for the lessee, he does not want any restriction on his rights of alienation of the premises, even if the statute says that any required consent will not be unreasonably withheld. The mere fact of having to ask for the consent is a restriction on that right.

(b) *Sub-lettings*

Sub-lettings are a quite different matter to assignments, and thus require to be discussed separately.

Again there are three stages, as follows:

(i) *Absolute prohibition on sub-letting.* As with the absolute prohibition on assignments, that on sub-lettings seems to be a matter to be agreed between the original lessor and lessee, and (subject to the comments of Danckwerts LJ in *Property & Bloodstock Ltd v Emerton*[14] which were, in any case, only obiter dicta) a covenant containing an absolute prohibition on sub-letting will be upheld as being perfectly valid. The prohibition may extend to the whole, or part only, of the premises, although it is unlikely that any normal residential lease would fail to have included in it a covenant against sub-letting part only, for the same reasons as when we were considering an assignment of part only. In any event, many modern flats are far too small to contemplate a sub-letting of part.

12 But see later in this section, on the subject of sub-letting.
13 See ch 7, pp 86 et seq, below.
14 [1968] Ch 94 at 119–20.

(ii) *Conditional prohibition on sub-letting.* Readers are referred to the Landlord and Tenant Act 1927, s 19(1) above, which refers not only to assignments, but also to 'underlettings'. Accordingly, any covenant which demands the consent of the lessor will carry the assumption under s 19(1) that the consent will not be unreasonably withheld.

As a drafting consideration, no lessor who is aware of the problems management can bring is likely to permit a sub-letting of part only of the premises. This is over and above any problems relating to Rent Act, etc statutory rights which may thereby arise. If the lease does permit sub-letting, it is more than likely that it will specifically exclude a sub-letting of part only from this permission.

(iii) *Free choice of sub-letting.* In view of the problems, indicated above, which can arise from the lease being silent on the point, one would not normally leave out totally references to sub-letting.

One point which should be borne in mind is that if the wording of any covenants dealing with sub-letting and assignments is at all vague, a situation might arise where, on the one hand, words in the covenant referring primarily to assignment will not be construed as including underletting, but on the other hand words which carry the implication of underletting may be extended to include assignment. This actually works in the right way for those dealing with residential leasehold property, because underletting provisions must be looked at more closely than those relating to assignments. However, if the clause is referring to underlettings only, it is right to include assignment as well.

The foregoing is only meant to give a rough and ready guide to the effect of covenants dealing with assignment and sub-letting. The learned textbooks have pages and pages of cases on all sorts of minute aspects of the subject, illustrating what a complex one it is.

10 Lessee to give notice of assignment, etc

This is a most important lessee's covenant, and is deserving of some study.

The principle of the covenant is simple enough: while there is a lessor/lessee relationship subsisting between parties, it is vital for a lessor to be aware of any change in identity of his lessee, otherwise the very relationship itself is destroyed, and the lessor's rights vis-à-vis the lessee, eg collection of rent, are threatened.

Like so many of the subjects considered in this book, there is both a theoretical and practical side to this matter. Although, as with major parts of this text, we are here more concerned with the practical implications than the underlying theory, in this case it is important to consider the basic rules.

According to *Hill and Redman's Law of Landlord and Tenant:*[15]

'1 In the absence of a stipulation to the contrary a tenant may assign or sub-let the demised premises.

15 *Hill and Redman's Law of Landlord and Tenant* (17th edn, Butterworths) Vol 1, ch 7, p 545 'Assignment and Devolution of Leases'.

2 There may be a covenant against assignment or sub-letting, which may be absolute or dependent on the lessor's consent.
3 Such a covenant is strictly construed against the lessor.'

Therefore, without express covenants being incorporated into the lease, the lessee may assign or sub-let as he pleases. The textbooks seem to be unclear as to whether or not there is any obligation on an outgoing lessee to advise the lessor of a sale, or on an incoming assignee notifying the lessor of his purchase.

In practice, of course, it is extremely unlikely that any lease would be drafted without some fail-safe clause which was intended to put the lessor on notice of a change of ownership of the property, the subject of the lease. These precautionary measures relating to the giving and receiving of notice can be drafted in an increasingly restrictive manner.[16]

If we analyse the lessor's motives in the incorporation of such a notice clause the obvious conclusion is that basically all that the lessor wants to do is to make sure he knows about any change of ownership of the lease. So that the most innoffensive regulatory clause will be one which does not control the assignment *before* it happens, but ensures that the lessor is given notice of the change within a reasonable time of completion of the assignment. Thus:

'The lessee shall within[17]   days of the date of every assignment sublease grant of probate or administration assent transfer mortgage charge discharge order of court or other event or document relating to the term give notice thereof in writing to the lessor.'

(There would in most cases follow a provision for payment of a registration fee.)[18]

A clause of this sort will thus make sure of the following:

(a) that the lessor is given details of the change of ownership;
(b) that he is given these details within a reasonable time of the event;
(c) that the notice not only covers a simple assignment giving effect to a sale, but also every other conceivable *document* evidencing some sort of change of ownership—or indeed change in status of the existing owner and further every other conceivable *event* similarly creating such a change—even though that event may not be recorded in a document;
(d) (usually) that the lessor is paid a registration fee for dealing with the notice.[19]

The basic problem with this type of covenant is that it is an 'after the event' covenant, and relies upon the lessee for the time being to make it work. What, for instance, happens if the assignee's solicitor (which it will be) forgets to give the notice, or even if the notice is lost in the post on the way to the lessor? The consequences for the lessee are probably not serious—no-

16 And refer to ch 7, p 86 for a further discussion on this subject.
17 It is usually left to the draftsman to decide on the appropriate period, but 28 days seems to be generally accepted.
18 Failure to provide for such a fee would seem to be a serious mistake on the part of the draftsman.
19 The registration fees may even form a part of the lessors' income, see. eg ch 9, p 123, below.

one would consider that the lease could be forfeited on account of such a breach—but for the lessor may well be more of a serious nature. The lessor is highly dependent on knowing just who his lessees are at any given time, and he cannot afford to be continually chasing around finding out the identity of persons to whom the properties in which he has a reversionary interest have been assigned. Because of this very simple potential problem, there is accordingly a very large question mark hanging over the use in the lease of a mere notice covenant, and to protect the lessor adequately, some further protection is needed.[20]

11 Not to dispose of rubbish in flat, etc

This lessee's covenant is very much in the way of a management rule, as opposed to a strictly legal covenant.

It may seem obvious to anyone with half an ounce of sense that a lessee should not try to flush unflushable objects down his WC, or wash something extremely 'gungy' down his sink, so as to gum up the works further down-stream for his co-lessees. Unfortunately people will do the strangest things, and it does happen.

Most blocks of flats will have some sort of centralised rubbish collection and control system, even if it is only a row of individual dustbin receptacles in one of the common areas. The covenant regulating rubbish disposal ought to mention adherence to the laid-down procedure on centralised collection.

As this covenant is more of a management rule, there is a case for omitting specific reference to rubbish collection from the lease itself and moving it into a set of management rules. This option[1] is discussed elsewhere.

12 No animals to be kept, etc

This clause can be very vexatious, for there is nothing more calculated to cause friction between co-lessees than the question of pets.

The draftsman has three choices when dealing with this clause; thus he can:

(a) prohibit pets altogether; or
(b) prohibit the keeping of pets without the express, specific, approval of the lessor (or the management company); or
(c) permit any sort of pet to be kept without permission: in which case he can either say nothing at all, or draft a clause which says that any pet may be kept.[2]

As well as these choices, the draftsman also has the option of including covenants such as this in the lease itself, or reducing such matters into a set of rules which may be varied by the management.[3]

20 For a more thorough discussion of the same subject, see ch 7, p 86, below.
1 And see ch 17, p 194, below, for a discussion on the desirability, or otherwise, of the lessor formulating a set of management rules.
2 Probably from the lessor's point of view, silence is to be preferred.
3 And refer to p 194, below for a discussion on the question of management rules.

Probably of all the 'rules' type of lessees' covenants, this one is the most important.

Basically there can be nothing wrong in keeping an ordinary domestic pet in a flat. The probability is that most of the pets concerned will behave as well as, if not better, than their owners. There is also nothing wrong in keeping, say, a large dog in a flat of reasonable proportions.

The real snags will only arise in two basic situations:

(a) noisy pets: and
(b) pets which are allowed to misbehave.

Small 'yappy' dogs come into the first category and the second category includes cases like a rather sad one the author came across recently. An irresponsible flat-owner left his Alsatian dog shut up alone in the flat for long periods of time. The poor dog was therefore directly responsible for noise *and* smell which greatly distressed the co-lessees, but the true fault was the owner's for not caring properly for his pet.

Probably the best position the lessor can take in a clause of this sort is to choose option (b) outlined above, in that this does not prohibit the keeping of pets per se (and it must always be borne in mind when acting for a developer that restrictions of this sort could easily lose him customers) but it does allow the lessor to 'vet' (the pun is regretted) individual cases, and—what is more—to withdraw permission if this should become justified.

13 No sign, etc to be displayed outside the premises

To an incoming lessee, this clause may seem unnecessarily restrictive. To the lessor, but more particularly the body of co-lessees as a whole, it is a protection against the building appearing like a bill-board.

This is undoubtedly one of the disadvantages of a flat from the owner's point of view, because why should a house-owner generally be able to put up political and other posters either in his windows or on posts in his garden, and the poor flat-owner not? The answer is that it is good management to have the exterior of the building looking neat, tidy, and free of superfluous matter. As evidence of good management will supposedly encourage people to buy flats in that particular building, and evidence of bad management will equally dissuade prospective buyers, it is very much in the interests of the lessees as a whole for the exterior of the building to be free of extraneous material, including advertising.

When drafting a clause of this sort, the exception relating to 'for sale' notices must not be forgotten. It would be quite inequitable to prevent the placing in an appropriate position of a notice advertising a flat for sale.

14 Lessee to pay s 146 costs
Lessee to deliver copies of notices to lessor

Both of these lessee's covenants are absolutely standard, are expected to be contained in the body of the lessee's covenants, and accordingly will not cause the practitioner any problems.

Any further discussion on their significance is beyond the scope of this book. If the practitioner finds himself or herself in need of commentary on the underlying principles in either covenant, reference should be made to more learned textbooks.

15 To permit lessor to enter and view state of repair

This is another lessee's covenant which, according to *Hill and Redman*[4] is a 'usual' covenant, in other words one which the practitioner would expect to see in a typical list of lessee's covenants.

In practical terms, the logic is fairly straightforward. The lessor will usually be responsible for the upkeep of the main structure of the block of flats, and within each separate demise of a flat unit there may well be apparatus, parts of the building, etc which are vital to the well-being of the building as a whole. The lessor must therefore reserve to himself the right to enter into each flat to view the state of repair of that unit, and so ascertain if the rest of the building is thereby being adversely affected.

The lessor also has the right to view the state of repair of the flat itself, on a more cosmetic plane, so that he can if necessary ask the lessee to bring it up to the appropriate standard. Very few lessors will actually go around inspecting their lessee's individual flats; first this would smack too much of 'Big Brother' and second very few lessors have the time to do this anyway, but for all that the right must be reserved to the lessor.

16 Covenant to insure

In leases of the sort under discussion in this book, ie long residential leases, there will nearly always be a covenant to insure. One ought to be able to say that there will *always* be such a covenant, but many are the vagaries of draftsmen, and it has been known for a lease to be silent on insurance!

There is no rule which says that either the lessor or the lessee should normally be responsible for insurance, and it is left to the parties to negotiate as to who is to be responsible. In practice, this means that the lessor will decide, and by the time the lessee sees the draft lease, it will probably be too late anyway. Nevertheless, there would theoretically be nothing to stop the responsibilities being altered, following negotiation.

Insurance covenants in long leases are usually in fairly settled and acceptable forms, and there are not likely to be too many arguments about them. However, for all that, the covenants are most important, and one should be quite clear about their application. The following points are intended to deal with all the salient features of the subject.

(a) *Insure or not?*

This, of course, is a stupid question, posed merely to illustrate that any item of property involving bricks and mortar should be insured. Accordingly, the

4 *Hill and Redman's Law of Landlord and Tenant* (17th edn, Butterworths) Vol 1, pp 148–9.

first point for a lessor is that he must have an insurance covenant in the lease he prepares, and equally the lessee must see that the lease he is preparing to take on contains an *adequate* insurance covenant.

(b) *Who is to insure?*

As we have already seen, there is no rule which says either one of the two parties to the lease must actually take out the insurance policy on the premises, but it is clear in the case of a flat that the lessor should insure. The reasoning behind this is essentially simple: that were the burden of insurance to be placed on the various lessees, a situation would ensue where each flat in the block might well be insured with a different insurance company; even if some of the companies were duplicated, it would still mean separate policies. Then there would be the common areas— the corridors, staircases, hall, the main structural shell of the building, even—these would have to be insured separately, by the lessor. All this would create administrative chaos, because each flat-owner would need to make sure that the block of flats as a whole was properly insured, and each of the insurance companies involved would be concerned to make sure of the same thing. Therefore, in a block of flats, small or large, the insuring covenant should be one *by* the lessor. He should take out the insurance on the block[5] and he will have responsibility for the administration of the policy. This may be one of the few tasks which the lessor is burdened with, in a self-maintenance situation,[6] but it is an unavoidable one.

Insurance on a block of flats is to be contrasted with, for example, leasehold houses, where it would be normal for the insurance covenant to provide that the lessee insured separately, subject usually to a proviso that the insurance company was an acceptable one. In this situation the properties concerned would not be interdependent in the same way as flats in the same block. The position with maisonettes[7] is somewhere between flats and houses. It is quite possible for the units to insure themselves, and there are many maisonettes where this happens. Nevertheless, the units are still under the *same roof*, and the lessor may feel happier about seeing to insurance himself.

(c) *Who pays for the insurance?*

When one buys a property, of whatever sort, one expects to have to insure it, so that whether directly or indirectly the lessee will always pay for the insurance.

(d) *How is the insurance paid?*

Payment may be made either in a direct manner, that is to say there will be specific sum attributable to the insurance premium, or the appropriate proportion thereof, demanded by the lessor, or there will be a general service

5 And see later, p 47 as to the 'Block of Flats' policy.
6 See ch 9 p 110, below.
7 As to what a maisonette is, see ch 1, p 1, above:

charge which will contain as just one of many elements the proportion of the insurance premium. This distinction can be equated generally with a further distinction between making the insurance payment a reservation as an additional rent, and including it in a global service charge or other payment which is merely the subject of a covenant between the two parties.[8] It must not be thought, however, that just because the insurance is treated on its own in the lease, it is being reserved by way of additional rent, or conversely that a global sum covering various services cannot be reserved as additional rent. In any case, even if a payment is reserved as additional rent, it may not be strictly rent—eg it may be recoverable by action on the agreement, but not by distress, unless an express power to distrain is given, or it is expressly made recoverable *as rent.*[9]

(e) *Method of insuring*

The covenant should specify how the insurance is to be effected. It is sometimes usual for the covenant to nominate a particular company, but generally as many options as to choice of insurer should be left open, and a covenant to insure in, eg 'Sun Alliance and London Insurance Ltd' or some other insurance office of repute' is about as specific as a lessor should want to get.

(f) *How much to insure for?*

According to *Hill and Redman,*[10] where a lessor takes the advice of the insurance company as to the amount of cover he needs, he fulfils the obligation to insure adequately even although that amount is insufficient for adequate reinstatement. Nevertheless, it hardly seems likely that any sensible lessor (and here we are assuming that it will always be the lessor's duty to insure, an assumption which it is generally safe to make) would insure for any sum less than the gross sales revenue of the block of flats in question. Indeed, the author has been involved with a great number of flat developments, on which (with the total agreement of the insurers) there has been an uplift of 10% on the initial selling price, so that the total initial cover on the block of flats would be calculated thus:

Say 8 units in the block.
2 were sold at £20,000 each
they would be:
£20,000 + 10% = £22,000 × 2 = £44,000
2 more at £21,000 each
ie £21,000 + 10% = £22,100 × 2 = £44,200
remaining 4 at £22,00 each
ie £22,000 + 10% = £24,200 × 4 = £96,800
Total initial insurance value of block = £185,000

8 And for further discussion on the subject, see p 21, above.

9 For a more erudite discussion, see *Hill and Redman's Law of Landlord and Tenant* (17th edn, Butterworths) pp 263 and 317.

10 *Hill and Redman* (17th edn) quotes *Mumford Hotels Ltd v Wheler* [1964] Ch 117, [1963] 3 All ER 250.

It is assumed that the insurance cover is subject to index linking thereafter by the Insurer.

This build-up assumes that the units are sold quickly, without too long a gap between the first and last, otherwise the earlier ones could have been subjected to index linking before the last ones were sold. The apportioned insurance value of the individual units thereafter will have to be a straight fraction, which would produce on the above figures a sum of £23,125.00 each. This calculation ought to demonstrate that, if the 10% uplift was not applied initially, the later units would in fact be covered for less than their selling prices. Undoubtedly there is a more scientific way of coping with the variations in prices as the development is sold, but this admittedly rough and ready manner does achieve more than adequate cover in all circumstances.

(g) *When is cover effective?*

The lessor will be, or ought to be, careful that he does not over-insure, but at the same time the lessee will be careful to make sure that his unit is always on cover.

These comments apply, of course, only to new flats and what follows can be forgotten if the units concerned are second-hand ones. Nevertheless, this is an important point for both lessor and lessees to consider.

It will be almost inevitable that the lessor, if he is the contractor, ie actually carrying out the building works himself, whether on a direct or sub-contract basis, will carry Contractors All Risks (CAR) insurance. If the lessor is not the contractor there may or may not be analogous insurance; it will be a question of fact, and is an essential subject of a preliminary enquiry if the information has not been volunteered by the lessor.

What sort of cover the CAR policy will provide is again a question of fact, but very often the CAR policy will dovetail with the block of flats policy which will be taken out by the lessor. This raises the question as to precisely when the block of flats cover becomes effective, which is what this section is all about, and is the central theme to which we shall return in a moment.

First of all, though, we should look at the wording of a typical CAR policy insofar as it relates to this subject. This wording is as follows, and it is stressed that the example given below is an extract from an *actual* policy:

The wording will form part of the endorsement to the policy, thus:

ENDORSEMENT
It is hereby agreed and declared that:
(inter alia)
The insurance by this policy extends to apply:
(a) to private dwelling houses or flats erected by the Insured until sold and insurance coverage effected by mortgagees and/or purchasers.
(b) Notwithstanding anything contained to the contrary in exclusion 3(a) to blocks of flats being erected or renovated by the Insured until the last flat in each block is completed and insurance coverage effected by purchaser and/or lessees.'

The exclusion referred to in (b) above will be one in respect of loss or damage due to the use or occupancy of any portion of the permanent works by any owner tenant or occupier.

There has been some discussion in conveyancing circles as to the effect of the cover on flats effected by the CAR policy, and in particular sub-clause (b) above. The wording (which is out of an existing policy) is ambiguous, and it is possible to surmise that the CAR policy extends until the *last* flat in the block is sold to a purchaser: thus the flats which had been sold previously would be covered under the CAR policy until that moment. The possibility is swept away, though, when the endorsement is considered with the exclusion, which makes it quite clear that occupancy of any flat by its owner will exclude that flat from cover.

The wording of the CAR policy insofar as it relates to, eg the common areas, and to the interrelationship of the flats covered by it to those not so covered, is either inadequate or non-existent. Unfortunately no more space can be devoted here to this aspect of the matter, and we must look instead at the effect of the CAR policy where flats are being sold. This is that when selling starts, and at whatever stage of construction the works have reached, the CAR policy covers everything. As individual flats are sold, they are taken out of the CAR policy, and it is then that the Block of Flats policy takes over. Thus there is a prolonged dovetail effect between the CAR policy at the start, and the Block of Flats policy at the end.

And so we come to the Block of Flats policy, which is the permanent insurance, and which will be the subject of the insuring covenant in the lease; although interestingly enough, as the covenant says 'The lessor shall insure and keep insured the block in the joint names of all persons having any interest therein against loss or damage by the Insured Risks in (Bloggs) Insurance Limited,'[11] the burden on the lessor is to insure the block from the moment that the first lessee completes—and as we have seen, because of the dovetail effect, the Block of Flats insurance may not at this stage be all embracing on the property. The problem is solved by the next words in the clause, 'or some other insurance office of repute ...' the interpretation necessarily being in this context that there is a dual insurance situation contemplated at the initial stages even though this is not the primary intention of the option.

As the insurers under the Flats policy will expect to cover the whole of the block from the inception of the policy, this means that there may be two lots of insurances on the same flats; that is, a flat will have cover from the CAR policy until it is legally completed, and also from the Flats policy from the time that policy is effected, which would be logically at the beginning of the development.

This two-fold cover is a nonsense, both from the point that it is unwelcome administratively especially from the standpoint of the insurers if there is a claim, and, far more elementary, simply because it is stupid for the developer to be paying out two premiums for the same cover.

The problem is that the developer cannot wait until, say, all the flats have been sold before he takes out the flats policy because then he will have left flats uncovered by either insurance as they are legally completed. So that the only real answer is to arrive at an arrangement with the Insurer if this is possible that he takes out the Flats policy at the very beginning of the

11 And see Precedent No 3, cl 1, Sch 6, p 366, below.

development, but only pays for individual flats as and when he notifies the insurer of their legal completion. Assuming he can do this, he still has the administrative burden of remembering to notify the insurer as the flats are sold. Nevertheless, the alternative is paying out double insurance premiums on unsold flats quite unnecessarily; obviously this is to be avoided.

(h) *What is the usual cover?*

Flats policies vary in detail, but a description of a typical one is perfectly sufficient for our purposes, because the differences in detail are not of any real significance.

The typical policy[12] will effect cover on:

(i) *The Buildings*. These are defined as the block of flats and its garages (where applicable), any domestic outbuildings, lessor's fixtures and fittings (including, eg fitted carpets, etc in the common parts), patios, terraces, footpaths, swimming pools, tennis courts, drives, walls, fences and gates. These subjects of the cover will be insured against loss or damage by certain causes, in other words, the insured risks. Most of these heads of cover will have exclusions spelt out by the policy; we will consider the cover and the exclusions head by head.

INSURED RISKS	EXCLUSIONS
1 Fire, lightning, explosion, earthquake.	1 Mostly there will be none in this section.
2 Storm or flood.	2 Loss or damage by frost or to fences and gates.
3 Freezing of water tanks, apparatus or pipes, or water escaping from tanks, apparatus or pipes or oil escaping from a fixed heating installation.	3 Loss or damage to any flat while the flat has been left unfurnished for more than 30 days. Loss or damage occurring while the block of flats has been left unfurnished for more than 30 days.
4 Riot, civil commotion, strike or labour disturbance.	4 Mostly none.
5 Malicious persons or vandals.	5 Loss or damage caused by the policyholder, any member of the policyholder's family, any director of the policyholder or any employee. Loss or damage caused by any resident to the flat in which he resides. Loss or damage to any residential property while the residential property has been left unfurnished for more than 30 days.

12 The author is indebted to Sun Alliance & London Insurance Group for their assistance in the preparation of this part of the text.

INSURED RISKS	EXCLUSIONS
6 Theft or attempted theft.	6 Loss or damage caused by the policyholder, any director of the policyholder or any employee. Loss or damage caused by any resident to the residential property in which he resides. Loss or damage to any residential property while the residential property has been left unfurnished for more than 30 days.
7 Subsidence and/or heave of the site on which the block of flats, its garages (if appropriate) and domestic outbuildings stand or of land belonging to them, or landslip.	7 The first (usually something in the order of £500) of each claim. Loss or damage to patios, terraces, footpaths, swimming pools, tennis courts, drives, walls, fences and gates unless the block of flats, its garages or domestic outbuildings are damaged by the same cause and at the same time. Loss or damage to solid floor slabs or loss or damage resulting from the movement of solid floor slabs unless the foundations beneath the external walls of the block of flats are damaged by the same cause and at the same time. Loss or damage resulting from coastal or river erosion, demolition of or structural alteration of structural repair to the block of flats, its garages or domestic outbuildings, faulty workmanship or the use of defective materials.
8 Falling trees or branches.	8 Loss or damage to fences or gates.
9 Falling television or radio aerials, aerial fittings or masts.	9 None.
10 Collision involving aircraft or aerial devices or anything dropped from them, vehicles or animals.	10 Loss or damage caused by domestic pets.
11 If the block of flats or any flat is damaged and made uninhabitable by any cause insured by paras 1–10 the company will pay the rent the policyholder would have received but has lost (including ground rent) during the period necessary to restore the block of flats or the flat to habitable condition. and if the flats are insured by the policyholder as manager on behalf of individual owners or lessees[13] and any such flat is	11 Any amount exceeding 20% of the sum insured on the buildings.

13 As is probable. There is thus a strong argument for the insurance to be dealt with by the manager.

INSURED RISKS	EXCLUSIONS
damaged and made uninhabitable by any cause insured by paras 1–10 the company will pay the amount of reasonable additional costs of comparable accommodation incurred by such owner or lessee during the period necessary to restore the flat to habitable condition. The Buildings Section[14] will also provide insurance for:	
12 Accidental damage for which the policyholder or the owner, lessee or tenant of any flat is legally responsible to cables or underground services supplying the buildings	12 None.
13 Accidental breakage of glass in doors or windows, washbasins, splashbacks, pedestals, baths, sinks, bidets, lavatory cisterns or lavatory pans, shower trays or shower screens all fixed to and forming part of the buildings.	13 Damage occurring in any flat while the flat has been left unfurnished for more than 30 days. Damage occurring while the block of flats has been left unfurnished for more than 30 days.

As well as the specific exclusions already noted above, there will be general exclusions, along the following lines.
1 RADIOACTIVE CONTAMINATION. Any expense, consequential loss or any loss or damage to property directly or indirectly caused by or contributed to by:
(a) ionising radiators or contamination by radioactivity from any nuclear fuel or from any nuclear waste from the combustion of nuclear fuel;
(b) the radioactive, toxic, explosive or other hazardous properties of any explosive nuclear assembly or nuclear component thereof.
2 WAR RISKS. Any consequence of war, invasion, act of foreign enemy, hostilities (whether war be declared or not) civil war, rebellion, revolution, insurrection or military or usurped power.
3 SONIC BANGS. Loss or damage by pressure waves caused by aircraft or other aerial devices travelling at sonic or supersonic speeds.

(ii) *Claims settlement*. Most insurers append to their policies and summaries of cover[15] a note explaining the claims settlement procedures. Typical wording is as follows:

'The company will pay the cost of work carried out in repairing or replacing the damaged parts of the building including fees and associated costs but not the cost of complying with building regulations, local authority or other statutory requirements if notice of the need to comply was served upon the policyholder before the damage occurred or if the regulations or requirements relate to undamaged parts of the buildings.

14 Sometimes called 'Material Damage Section'.
15 See below, p 54.

If the buildings have not been maintained in good repair or if at the time of any loss or damage the sum insured is less than the full rebuilding cost the company will pay the cost of repair or replacement less a deduction for wear and tear. If the repair or replacement is not carried out the company will pay the reduction in market value resulting from the damage not exceeding what it would have cost to repair the damage to the buildings if the repair work had been carried out without delay.

The maximum amount payable in aggregate under paragraphs 1–10, 12 and 13 is the sum insured less any excess.'

The policy will also have subsidiary sections dealing with such matters as purchaser's benefits, reinstatement of sums insured following claims and inflation protection as follows.

'SALE OF RESIDENTIAL PROPERTY. If the policyholder or the owner or lessee of any flat enters into a contract to sell his interest in any part of the buildings or in any such flat and, between exchange of contracts and completion of the sale, such part or flat is damaged by any cause insured by paragraphs 1–10, 12 and 13 the purchaser shall be entitled to benefit from this insurance, in respect of such loss or damage when the sale is completed provided such part or flat is not otherwise insured by or on behalf of the purchaser.'

'AUTOMATIC REINSTATEMENT OF THE SUM INSURED. The sum insured on buildings will not be reduced following a claim provided the policyholder carries out any recommendations the company makes to prevent further damage and the damage is made good without delay.'

'INFLATION PROTECTION. The Company will adjust the sum insured on buildings monthly in line with the House Rebuilding Cost Index prepared by the Royal Institution of Chartered Surveyors or an alternative index. Index linking of the sum insured will continue during repair or replacement following loss or damage provided the sum insured at the time of loss or damage represents the full rebuilding cost and the policyholder ensures that the work is carried out without delay.'

(iii) *Liability to the public.* It will be essential for the lessor to take out public liability cover. This is usually referred to in a subsidiary part of the covenant to insure. Typical wording is:

'... and shall also take out and keep on foot a policy of insurance in an insurance office of repute covering liability for injury to persons in the block.'

This wording is fairly pithy, but it will usually be found that the cover afforded by the average policy is rather wider drawn. The wording of a typical policy is as follows:[16]

1 The Insured is indemnified against liability at law; for damages and/or claimants costs awarded by any court of law within the geographical limits in respect of accidental bodily injury (including death disease or illness) or accidental damage to material property occurring during any period of insurance

(a) (i) in or about the residential property

1 Exclusions.

Damage to property belonging to or held in trust by or in custody or control of the Insured or any member of the Insured's family or (except for employees effects) any employee injury or damage arising out of any profession or business other than the business described in the schedule.

Liability of any resident incurred solely

16 Again the author is indebted to Sun Alliance & London Insurance Group for their cooperation.

(ii) elsewhere in the world in respect of commercial visits by the policyholder any director of the policyholder or any non-manual employee normally resident within the geographical limits in connection with the business

(b) incurred by virtue of either s 3 of the Defective Premises Act 1972 in connection with any residential property formerly owned or leased by the policyholder or lessee of any residential property described in the Schedule

provided that

—at the time of the incident giving rise to liability the Policyholder or such lessee has disposed of all legal title to and interest in the formerly owned or leased residential property—in the event of this section ceasing to apply to the lessee of any residential property described in the Schedule as a result of the sale of such residential property, the indemnity under this paragraph in respect of such residential property shall apply to such accidental bodily injury or accidental damage to material property occurring during a period of seven years from the date of such cessation, but will not apply if the liability is covered under a more recently effected or current policy.

as occupier (not as owner) of his residential property

Injury or damage arising out of ownership; possession or use by or on behalf of the Insured of mechanically propelled vehicles, caravans, aircraft, hovercraft or boats

Injury to any employee of the insured arising out of and in the course of such employment.

Liability of any director of the policyholder or any employee for which the policyholder would not have been entitled to indemnity if the claim had been made against the policyholder.

Liability assumed by agreement unless the liability would have existed without the agreement

Any liability under paragraph 1(b)

—in respect of which the Policyholder or lessee is entitled to indemnity from any other source

—which arises from ownership of any property not occupied solely for residential purposes.

2 The directors of the policyholder and employees are indemnified against liability at law, for costs awarded in connection with any prosecution brought under ss 36 or 37 of the Health and Safety at Work etc, Act 1974 arising from any offence as defined in s 33 of such Act and relating to the health, safety and welfare of any person other than an employee and happening during the period of insurance in connection with the business whether or not bodily injury has occurred.

2 Exclusions.

Prosecution consequent upon any allegedly deliberate or intentional criminal act. Fines or penalties of any kind.

The company will also pay defence costs and other expenses incurred with its written consent.

In the interpretation of this part of a typical block of flats policy, the term 'insured' means the policy-holder, and (provided they are not entitled to indemnity from any other source[17] and are subject to the terms of the policy as far as they can apply) the lessees of the flats, and the directors and/or employees of the policy-holder —always assuming that the policy-holder is a company.

(iv) *Liability to employees.* Under the terms of the Employers' Liability (Compulsory Insurance) Act 1969 there is a statutory liability for damages and claimants costs for bodily injury or disease to employees arising out of and in the course of their employment. A typical Block of Flats policy may be extended to afford cover under this head, in which case the indemnity will usually be unlimited in amount, and the cover will include approved defence costs and other expenses. Again, usually this section may be further extended to cover costs and expenses incurred in defending a prosecution under the Health and Safety at Work Act etc 1974.

Liability to the public and liability to employees are areas of cover which are usually offered by the insurers as optional extras. A lessee ought not to be concerned with liability to employees which really only concerns the relationship between the lessor/manager and his employees, but on the other hand should be concerned to see that the policy includes liability to the public because, as we have just seen above, the insured under this section specifically includes the lessees of the individual flats. We shall briefly return to this when we look shortly at what insurance points a lessee should check.

At the risk of skimping on this section, the above narrative incorporating as it does extracts from typical policies, will have to suffice, since there is simply no room to expound further on the subject. Nevertheless the section is an important one, and must be thoroughly understood.

(i) *Who is the insured?*

Not only must we be precise about the extent of the cover, but we must also understand who the insured is.

The person or corporation who actually takes out the insurance will be the original lessor, or possibly alternatively the management company. This will not always be constant, but those effecting the insurance must have some interest in the property. Nevertheless, this interest need not necessarily be one in the legal estate, thus a management company joining in the lease purely to manage might effect insurance.

Whereas we have just seen that where a Block of Flats policy incorporates a public liability section, the term 'insured' will specifically include the lessees of the individual flats, the same term will only primarily cover the actual policyholder, ie the person effecting the insurance, in the material damage section, which for the average flat lessee is probably the most important part of the policy. How then is the interest of the lessees noted on the policy?

There will usually be a section in the policy entitled 'other interests in the Insurance'. The wording may differ from company to company, but normally it will be something like:

'The interest of the lessee or owner of each flat and the mortgagees of any of them is

17 Which they might well be under, eg personal insurances.

automatically included in the Buildings section[18] without the need for it to be specially recorded.'

Despite this clearly worded part of the policy, it is by no means unusual for purchaser's and mortgagee's solicitors to insist upon a specific endorsement being placed on the policy, recording the interest of their client in respect of the particular flat. Given the wording as above—and most Block of Flats policies issued by the major insurance companies have similar wording—a specific endorsement is not necessary, and should be resisted. Specific endorsements are very largely creatures of history, at least so far as the sale of flats is concerned. Nevertheless people will no doubt still persist in asking the question.

(j) *Conclusion*

Insurance is a subject on which much more could be written. However, as a means of summing up, and also as an aide-memoire to both lessors and lessees, the following tables may be of some interest. From the lessor's point of view, the table refers more to the initial setting-up of the exercise, than to continuing responsibilities, although these come into the table as well; on the other hand, the lessee will be the owner of the flat at any given time, and insurance will accordingly be a matter of continuing interest.

(i) *Lessor's points*

(a) For preference, insure with a well-known name: avoid generally unknown insurers (remember that cost of insurance will be recovered from lessees anyway, and there will usually be a commission to be earned).

(b) Make the administration as simple as possible, thus:

 (i) if more than one block of flats is being developed there is no need for separate policies for each block, eg the property covered by the single policy could be:

 'any flat, apartment or block of flats within England and Wales in respect of which the policyholder is lessor or is the maintenance trustee or is totally responsible for management thereof' (or as the case may be—this wording is but an example);

 (ii) arrange with the insurer for them to supply enough single-sheet 'summaries of cover' for distribution to each lessee and/or his solicitors and mortgagees; and

 (iii) following each renewal date, arrange to receive a letter, or other evidence from the insurer to prove that the insurance is still in force. (The period of insurance quoted in the policy itself will only have been for one year, which may well have expired. The summary of cover will probably quote the period of insurance as 'from ... to ... annually' but this is not direct proof that the insurance is paid

18 We have already seen (p 53, above) that the lessees of flats are stated to be included in the expression 'insured' in the public liability section.

up and current, and lessee's solicitors will be justified in looking for this proof.)

(c) Make sure that the initial cover on the flats is adequate.

(d) Ensure that the cover on the flats starts at the right time and that there is no gap in cover.

(e) Make sure that interests of individual lessees and/or mortgagees, etc are sufficiently protected.

(f) Arrange for adequate inflationary cover to be built into the cover on the flats.

(ii) *Lessee's points*

(a) On initial purchase ensure:
- (i) that the flat is covered right from the moment of legal completion;
- (ii) that the cover is adequate;
- (iii) that there is inflationary indexing of the initial cover by whatever means; and
- (iv) that the interests of individual lessees and/or mortgagees, etc, is adequately noted on the policy. But remember that a general note on the policy to this effect is perfectly sufficient, and no specific noting is necessary.

(b) On subsequent purchases satisfy oneself on points (ii), (iii) and (iv) above.

(c) On all purchases:
- (i) ask to see a copy of the summary of cover. Though there is some difference of opinion amongst conveyancers, this will be perfectly sufficient, because if the summary of cover is issued by a reputable company it should be a true précis of the policy itself, which makes production of the policy unnecessary;
- (ii) ask for evidence, eg premium receipt, letter from insurers, that the policy is still in force and paid up;
- (iii) if the insurer is one whose name is completely unfamiliar, be put on notice and investigate further. Insurance, however well the policy is drawn and however shipshape the accompanying documents, will be useless if the insurer is questionable. Admittedly cases of this sort will be very rare, but the conveyancer should be able to hear the warning bells; and
- (iv) (this one is so self-evident that it might just be missed!) check through the cover afforded, together with all other salient features of the policy, and ensure that everything which should be there is there, and if it is not, investigate why not.

It is interesting that of all the sections in this chapter, devoted as it is to working our way slowly through the individual features of a typical lease, this description of insurance and its relationship to the subject has turned out to be the longest by some way. This is especially interesting because, as we have remarked before, the treatment of the subject has certainly not been one of overkill, indeed, a great deal more could have been written on it.

Nevertheless, it does illustrate the overriding importance of the subject of insurance when applied to blocks of flats. It is far more important that a block of flats should be adequately covered than a single, private dwelling house should. If the house burns down, or is blown down by a tornado, no-one but the owner of the house is going to suffer. If a flat catches fire, then the likelihood is that at least some of the other flats in the same block will be affected to a greater or lesser extent. Thus it is crucial for each individual lessee to ensure that his lease provides adequately for insurance to be effected, and that such insurance has indeed been arranged, for the one is no good without the other.

Equally it is crucial that the lessor/manager (whoever is responsible for insurance) ensures that all arrangements concerning insurance are adequately made, since of all management functions insuring is the basic one, and if whoever is running a block of flats is incapable of dealing efficiently with the insurance, he will be even more incapable of attending to the other management chores which attach to him.

Finally, it should be noted that the specimen wording of the policies of insurance as set out above is not intended to imply any commitment thereto either by Sun Alliance and London Insurance Group, who were—as always—most helpful in the preparation of this section, or by any other insurer.

D. RENT REVIEWS

In any consideration of the type of rent review clause to insert in a residential lease of a flat or maisonette, the benchmark will always be how that clause is affected, if at all, by the provisions of the Rent Act provisions as to allowable premiums on subsequent assignments.

This is a crucial factor in the drafting of the rent review clause, because the inhibiting factor which an incorrectly drawn clause can have on subsequent sales of the unit is powerful. Accordingly it is very important that the clause is drafted properly to start with.

In view of the importance of the legislation, it is set out in full.

The primary source is the Rent Act 1977, s 127, and Sch 18, as amended by the Housing Act 1980, s 78.

Section 127 states as follows:[19]

'127 Allowable premiums in relation to certain long tenancies (1) where a tenancy is both a long tenancy within the meaning of Part 1 of the Landlord and Tenant Act 1954 and a protected tenancy, then—

(a) If the conditions specified in subsection (2) below are satisfied with respect to it, nothing in this part of this Act or in Part VII of the Rent Act 1968 (provisions superseded by this Part) or the enactments replaced by the said Part VII shall apply or be deemed ever to have applied to the tenancy;

(b) if any of those conditions are not satisfied with respect to it, Part 11 of Schedule 18 to this Act shall apply and, if the tenancy was granted before the passing of this Act, be deemed always to have applied to it.

(2) The conditions mentioned in subsection (1)(a) above are—

(a) that the tenancy is not, and cannot become, terminable within 20 years of the date when it was granted by notice given to the tenant; and

(b) that, unless the tenancy was granted before 25 July 1969 or was granted in pursuance of Part 1 of the Leasehold Reform Act 1967, the sums payable by the

19 Section 78 of the 1980 Act does not *replace* s 127 of the 1977 Act. Rather it *expands* it. The only sub-clause of s 127 which is deleted by the effect of s 78 is set in italics, and those parts of s 127 which have been substituted by s 78 are indicated by asterisks.

tenant otherwise than in respect of rates, services, repairs, maintenance or insurance are not, under the terms of the tenancy, varied or liable to be varied within 20 years of the date when it was granted nor, thereafter, more than once in any 21 years; and

(c) *that assignment or underletting of the whole of the premises comprised in the tenancy is not precluded by the terms of the tenancy and, if it is subject to any consent, there is neither a term excluding section 144 of the Law of Property Act 1925 (no payment in nature of fine) nor a term requiring in connection with a request for consent the making of an offer to surrender the tenancy.*

(3) Where the condition specified in subsection (2)(b) above would be satisfied with respect to a sub-tenancy but for a term providing for one variation, within 20 years of the date when the sub-tenancy was granted, of the sums payable by the sub-tenant, that condition shall be deemed to be satisfied notwithstanding that term, if it is satisfied with respect to a superior tenancy of the premises comprised in the sub-tenancy (or of those and other premises).*

(4) Nothing in this section shall affect the recovery, in pursuance of any judgement given or order or agreement made before 20 May 1969, of any amount which it was not lawful to receive under the law in force at the time it was received.

(5) In this section 'grant' includes continuance and renewal.'*

Certain parts of s 127 were replaced and amended by the Housing Act 1980, s 78 which is reproduced below.

'78 Allowable premiums in relation to certain long tenancies. (1) Section 127 of the 1977 Act shall have effect and be deemed always to have had effect as if for paragraph (c) of sub-section (2) there were substituted the paragraph set out in subsection (2) below and at the end of subsection (5) there were added the words set out in subsection (3) below.

(2) The substituted paragraph is—

'(c) that the terms of the tenancy do not inhibit both the assignment and the underletting of the whole of the premises comprised in the tenancy.'

(3) The added words are 'and for the purposes of subsections (2)(c) and (3B)(d) above the terms of a tenancy inhibit an assignment or underletting if they—

(a) preclude it; or

(b) permit it subject to a consent but exclude section 144 of the Law of Property Act 1925 (no payment in nature of a fine); or

(c) permit it subject to a consent but require in connection with a request for consent the making of an offer to surrender the tenancy.'

(4) After subsection (3) of section 127 there are inserted the following subsections—

'(3A) If the conditions in subsection (3B) below are satisfied in respect of a tenancy, this part of this Act shall not apply to that tenancy and, together with Part VII of the Rent Act 1968 and the enactments replaced by Part VII, shall be deemed never to have applied to it.

(3B) The conditions are that—

(a) the tenancy was granted before 16 July 1980;

(b) a premium was lawfully required and paid on the grant of the tenancy;

(c) the tenancy was at the time when it was granted, a tenancy at a low rent; and

(d) the terms of the tenancy do not inhibit both the assignment and the underletting of the whole of the premises comprised in the tenancy.

(3C) If the conditions in subsection (3D) below are satisfied in respect of a tenancy, this section shall have effect, in relation to that tenancy, as if for the words '20 years' and '21 years' in subsections (2)(b) and (3) above there were substituted, respectively, the words '6 years' and '7 years'.

(3D) The conditions are that—
(a) the tenancy is granted after 15th July 1980;
(b) at the time when it is granted it is a tenancy at a low rent; and
(c) the terms of the tenancy ensure that any variation of the sums payable by the tenant otherwise than in respect of rates, services, repairs or maintenance, cannot lead to those sums exceeding an annual rate of two-thirds of the rateable value of the dwelling house at the date when the variation is made.'

For the purposes of this subsection the rateable value of a dwelling house shall be ascertained in accordance with section 25 of this Act (disregarding subsection (4)) by reference to the value shown in the valuation list at the date when the variation is made'.[20]

If the conditions specified in s 127, as amended, are not satisfied, then the provisions of Sch 18, Part 11 of the 1977 Act come into force. This reads as follows:

'PART 11. PREMIUM ALLOWED UNDER SECTIONS 121 AND 127[1]

6 (1) Where this Part of this Schedule applies to any tenancy and a premium was lawfully required and paid on the grant or an assignment of a tenancy, nothing in section 120[2] of this Act shall prevent any person from requiring or receiving, on an assignment of the tenancy, the fraction of the premium specified below (without prejudice, however, to his requiring or receiving a greater sum in a case where he may lawfully do so under Part 1 of this Schedule).
(2) If there was more than one premium, sub-paragraph (1) above shall apply to the last of them.

7 (1) The fraction is $\frac{X}{Y}$ where—

X is the residue of the term of the tenancy at the date of the assignment, and Y is the term for which the tenancy was granted. (2) Sub-paragraph (1) above shall apply where a tenancy has been assigned as it applies where a tenancy has been granted and then Y in the fraction shall be the residue, at the date of that assignment, of the term for which the tenancy was granted.

8 Where the tenancy was granted on the surrender of a previous tenancy, and a premium has been lawfully required and paid on the grant or an assignment of the previous tenancy, the surrender value of the previous tenancy shall be treated, for the purposes of this Part of this Schedule, as a premium or, as the case may be, as part of the premium, paid on the grant of the tenancy.

9 For the purposes of paragraph 8 above, the surrender value of the previous tenancy shall be taken to be the amount which, had the previous tenancy been assigned instead of being surrendered, and had this Part of this Schedule applied to it, would have been the amount that could have been required and received on the assignment in pursuance of this Part of this Schedule.

10 In determining for the purposes of this Part of this Schedule the amount which may or could have been required and received on the assignment of a tenancy terminable, before the end of the term for which it was granted, by notice to the tenant, that term shall be taken to be a term expiring at the earliest date on which

20 For the Rent Act 1977, s 25, see p 60, below.
1 Section 121 relates to tenancies which became regulated by virtue of the Counter-Inflation Act 1973, and accordingly have no relevance to this discussion.
2 Section 120 refers to prohibition of premiums and loans on assignment of *protected* tenancies (and see p 59, below on protected tenancies).

such a notice given after the date of the assignment would have been capable of taking effect.
11 In this part of this Schedule 'grant' includes continuance and renewal.'

The statutes themselves have been set out deliberately, because they are most important, and readers are advised to read them thoroughly.

As noted earlier, the subject is confusing, so much so that a good number of practitioners have been caught by it. The first part of our commentary on the legislation, therefore, should be taken on a step-by-step basis as follows:

This section is concerned with the general subject of rent reviews, but we will also consider how the effect of the rent reserved and how it is reviewed interacts with the status of the tenancy insofar as whether or not it is protected, which is also an important point for the lessor to bear in mind.

1 Any tenancy in the nature of the ownership of leasehold property which is likely to be the subject of this book is a protected tenancy. This is laid down by section 1 of the Rent Act 1977, which states:

'**1 Protected tenants and tenancies.** Subject to this Part of this Act, a tenancy under which a dwelling-house (which may be a house or part of a house) is let as a separate dwelling is a protected tenancy for the purposes of this Act.

Any reference in this Act to a protected tenancy shall be construed accordingly'.

2 However, if the rent payable is less than two-thirds of the rateable value, the tenancy reverts to being one which is not a protected one. First of all, the Rent Act 1977, s 5 states:

'**5 Tenancies at low rents.** (1) A tenancy is not a protected tenancy if under the tenancy either no rent is payable, or subject to section 17 (2)[3] of this Act, the rent payable is less than two-thirds of the rateable value which is or was the rateable value of the dwelling house on the appropriate day.
(2) Where—
(a) the appropriate day in relation to a dwelling house fell before 22 March 1973, and
(b) the dwelling house had on the appropriate day a rateable value exceeding, if it is in Greater London, £400 or, if it is elsewhere £200,
subsection (1) above shall apply in relation to the dwelling house as if the reference to the appropriate day were a reference to 22 March 1973.
(3) In this Act a tenancy falling within sub-section (1) above, is referred to as a 'tenancy at a low rent'.
(4) In determining whether a long tenancy is a tenancy at a low rent, there shall be disregarded such part (if any) of the sums payable by the tenant as is expressed (in whatever terms) to be payable in respect of rates, services, repairs, maintenance, or insurance, unless it could not have been regarded by the parties as a part so payable.
(5) In subsection (4) above 'long tenancy' means a tenancy granted for a term certain exceeding 21 years, other than a tenancy which is, or may become, terminable before the end of that term by notice given to the tenant.'

Section 5 of the 1977 Act, as set out above, refers to 'the appropriate day', and before moving on to the next stage, we must first of all study the precise

3 Section 17(2) of the 1977 Act refers to controlled tenancies on elderly properties, and is irrelevant to this discussion.

meaning of this phrase, which is defined by sub-ss (3) and (4) of s 25 of the 1977 Act:

'25 Rateable value and meaning of 'appropriate day'. (1) [Not relevant]
(2) [Not relevant]
(3) In this Act 'the appropriate day'—
(a) in relation to any dwelling house which, on 23 March 1965, was or formed part of a hereditament for which a rateable value was shown in the valuation list then in force, or consisted or formed part of more than one such hereditament, means that date, and
(b) in relation to any other dwelling house, means the date on which such a value is or was first shown in the valuation list.
(4) Where, after the date which is the appropriate day in relation to any dwelling house, the valuation list is altered so as to vary the rateable value of the hereditament of which the dwelling house consists or forms part and the alteration has effect from a date not later than the appropriate day, the rateable value of the dwelling house on the appropriate day shall be ascertained as if the value shown in the valuation list on the appropriate day had been the value shown in the list as altered.
(5) [Not relevant]'.

3 Accordingly, most tenancies created by long leasehold sales will first of all be protected under the terms of the Rent Act 1977, s 1 but immediately taken out of this status because in virtually every long leasehold property the ground rent reserved will be nowhere near two-thirds of the rateable value of the property.

For properties which were built prior to 1965, then the 'appropriate day' for determining what the rateable value is for the purpose of this calculation, will be 23 March 1965. For any other property—and most of those with which readers are concerned will come into this latter category—the 'appropriate day' is the date when the property first appeared in the valuation list, that is for all practical purposes, some time after it was completed.

The question is, what is the rateable value in respect of any particular unit? Whilst this information will need to be obtained in cases of a borderline nature, for the great majority of flats on the market it will be self-evident. This will be because it is generally unlikely that the ground rent will be more than two-thirds of the rateable value. It is clear that ground rent will virtually always be considerably less than two-thirds of the relevant figure, at least if the developer wants his properties to be readily saleable.

Accordingly, the tenancy when created will almost certainly not be protected. If this is the case, then, whilst it remains in that state, Sch 18 to the 1977 Act will not come into force anyway. This is an important point to note, and should be borne in mind constantly when considering the following discussion; as long as the tenancy is *not* protected, then the inhibiting provisions of Part 11 of Sch 18 will not apply. What does have to be considered is that because of the rent review mechanics in any particular lease, the tenancy might *change* into a protected one. It is then that the frequency of the reviews becomes important.

4 Passing on to the next stage, we now have to consider the effect which rent reviews built into the lease will have on the basic status of the tenancy.

The first point to make is that if there is no rent review at all, then, because there is such little likelihood that the rent will be more than two-thirds of the rateable value, there will be no danger of the property being, or ever becoming, a protected tenancy, and this the more so because there will be no subsequent adjustment of the rental levels.

Ground rents can generally be divided into two categories; first those which are negligible because they are something without monetary value, eg a peppercorn, or do perhaps have a monetary value but are entirely nominal, and may very well not have any review procedure, eg there are a good number of long residential leases with a 'forever' rent of something in the order of £20 per annum. Second, and it is this category with which we shall be concerned in this chapter, there are those ground rents which represent a valuable consideration, either as income in the hands of the owner or as a saleable asset.[4] In these cases the level of the ground rent will be less modest to start off with, say, for anything except a very small studio flat, £50 per annum and upwards, and with (upwards only) reviews taking place at regular intervals. As we shall see, the spacing of these intervals is relevant to this whole question.

The reviews just mentioned may either be quantified, ie there may be predetermined rental levels throughout the terms, or they may be tied into something like 'market' rental levels, so that at the review dates there may have to be an assessment made, usually by a surveyor, of what those market rental levels are.

The crucial point which must be looked at both by those advising developers and builders setting up leasehold schemes which are required to provide a reasonably commercial income, and by those who act for subsequent purchasers of the units in those schemes, is that the lease is not drafted in such a way as to result in the tenancy thus created becoming, at any subsequent time through increases in the ground rent, one which is no longer at a 'low rent' and thus excluded from the Rent Acts, and possibly open to the effects of Sch 18 because of the review time-pattern.

Unfortunately, there are a number of leases in existence which are defective, because lessors have been, and undoubtedly still are, anxious to obtain increases in their ground rental income which will at least secure them from the ravages of inflation, and continue to provide them with a significant income.

The result may be that because of the desire to obtain reviews at commercially acceptable pauses, the provisions for increasing rent, as contained in the rent review clauses in question, will not comply with the Rent Act provisions which we have already seen, and thus the vendors of properties with such defects will not, or should not, be able to obtain the full market price.

Those in such positions are then like the boxer with one hand tied behind his back, because solicitors acting for prospective purchasers and/or mortgagees may have spotted the defect, and the only real remedy that the poor lessee has is to go back to his lessor and renegotiate with him. According to an article on the subject in the *Law Society's Gazette* by H.C. Adamson,[5] in some cases lessors have been capitalising on the predicament of their lessees,

4 See ch 8, p 102, below for a discussion on ground rental values.
5 [1980] L S Gaz 1069 (29 October).

and have been making more financial gain out of them than they perhaps should in all conscience.

1 The solution

However, the provisions of the Housing Act 1980, s 78 reviewed previously,[6] came into force on 20 October 1981, and provided a solution to the problem in two different areas, depending on the date of grant of the lease, which gives rise to the problem. We will now look at these two solutions.

(a) *Leases granted before 16 July 1980*

This is, of course, in the statutes, which have already been set out. Nonetheless, the statutes are complicated and it may help the readers to have a reasonably simple resumé. As this is a difficult subject, though, and one which many practitioners find confusing, once the resumé has been grasped, readers are highly recommended to go back to the statutes set out earlier in this chapter and make sure they understand the whole picture. This is one of those cases where poor advice and/or subsequent draftsmanship may well result in the lessee not being able to recover anywhere near the full value of his investment. A mistake in this field bites clearly and hard, and is very easily attributable. So be careful!

To get back to the resumé, for leases granted prior to 16 July 1980, a premium on an assignment of the lease may be validly sought, charged, and received whatever the terms of the rent review therein, provided that:

(a) when the lease was *originally* granted, a premium was lawfully paid. This should not be too difficult to prove;
(b) when originally granted the rent[7] was a 'low' rent within the meaning of the Rent Act 1977, s 5—as we have seen[8] the very great majority of leasehold flats will fall into this category; and
(c) the lease permits assignments or sub-lettings of *the whole*.

What these provisions amount to, of course, is a virtual 'amnesty' for just about all leases granted prior to 1980.

(b) *Leases granted after 15 July 1980*

This is probably much the more important category, and naturally as time passes, it will become even more important. Both the 1977 Act, s 127 and the 1980 Act, s 78 apply, and together provide two alternatives.

(a) For Sch 18, Part 11 of the 1977 Act *not* to apply (ie the imposition of a limitation, by stated formulae, on the premium chargeable on an assignment):

6 Above, p 57.
7 It is important to note that this *whole* discussion refers only to ground rent, and not to any other payments, eg insurance, service charge, etc due under the lease, even if reserved by way of additional rent.
8 Above, p 59.

1 the tenancy must not, and must never become, terminable within 20 years of the date of its grant, by notice given to the lessee;
2 the ground rent *cannot* be reviewed initially within 20 years of the date of grant of the lease, and thereafter more frequently than once every 21 years; and
3 there must be no inhibition on the ability of the lessee to either assign or sublet the *whole* of the premises.

(b) The 1980 Act introduced the following alternative, ie if
1 the tenancy is at a low rent *at the time that it is granted,*[9] and
2 no review may lead to the rent exceeding a sum which is in excess of two-thirds of the rateable value of the property *at the time when the review operates.*

Then the initial period of 20 years and the subsequent ones of 21 years come down to 6 years and 7 years respectively.

2 What should the conveyancer look for?

Precisely what is looked at may vary slightly depending on whether the interest is in the drafting of the initial lease itself, or in an assignment, on whatever side, vendor or purchaser. Nevertheless, the overview will be the same, and in the following discussion, the distinction is not made.

The following points will summarise the position:

1 There must be no inhibition on assignment or underletting the whole.[10]
2 The review periods must be a minimum of:
(a) initially, 20 years;
(b) subsequently 21 years.
3 Providing these terms are present, then there will be no fetter at all on the assignment of the premises.

Alternatively, the shorter review periods of six years initially and seven years subsequently may be used provided (as well as the other condition mentioned in 1, above) that not only was the initial ground rent less than two-thirds of the rateable value at the *appropriate day* but that on review it never exceeds a sum which represents two-thirds of the rateable value at the time of the review. In other words, the rent as it is reviewed throughout the term stays below the two-thirds level.

The difference between the 20/21 year variety of review and the 6/7 year one is that with the former, the rent initially or upon review, need not keep to the two-thirds limit, *provided* that the 20/21 year cycles are strictly adhered to. Once those are broken, then the provisions of the 1977 Act, Sch 18, Part 11 come into force.

Alternatively, by using the 6/7 year cycle, the reviews may take place more often, *but* the drawback here is that the two-thirds rateable value rule must be absolutely adhered to throughout both on initial grant and subsequent reviews.

Thus the original lessor has the choice of swings and roundabouts. He can

9 Ie after 15 July 1980.
10 See the Rent Act 1977, s 127(5) as amended by the Housing Act 1980, s 78.

perhaps get a bigger ground rent, but will have to wait much longer for his reviews, or he can have more frequent reviews, but with a circumscribed level of rental income.

In practice, the problem may not be as great as it would otherwise seem, because the level of ground rents will be largely set by market levels, and it seems unlikely that the run-of-the-mill flat would start off with a ground rent which exceeded the two-thirds rule. The exceptions will tend to be in the upper-bracket market which the average practitioner will not come across (but then one has to consider that with those sort of properties, if there is a mistake and the premium obtainable on an assignment is inhibited, the problem is all the more serious!)

3 How are the rules catered for in the documentation?

It will be the lease itself which will tell the practitioner if there is a possible defect. What follows is intended both for those involved in drafting the leases originally, and for those involved in selling and buying flats.

(a) *20/21-year cycles*

As long as the initial review (and for the purposes of this discussion we assume that there are reviews, which there will not always be) is to take place *at least* 20 years from the grant of the lease, and subsequent review cycles will be for a minimum of 21 years, and the other conditions mentioned earlier are observed, then the position is safe.

This appears fairly straightforward, so that prima facie if the 20/21-year pattern appears in order, then the conveyancer ought to be able to assume that everything is 'OK'; *but* this is not always the case:

Consider a block of flats which is being sold with leases which adhere to the above conditions. Let us say the block is put on to the market on 1 January 1985, and the first unit is completed on 1 April 1985.

What date will be used as the commencement date of the lease term? Most conveyancers will choose 1 April 1985. They cannot choose a date after that, because the lessee's solicitors will probably not let them, for obvious reasons. (It is perfectly possible for the term to commence on a future date, but the lessee would then have no estate until that date arrived—and this is not the idea at all!) They ought not to choose a past date, because there is no point anyway, and again the lessee's solicitor would not be too happy about his client losing some of his term before he had started, unless there was a compelling reason[11] and in any event the initial 20-year period might begin to become threatened.

So the likelihood is that lease no 1 in the block is dated 1 April 1985, and will have its term commence from that date. What happens to the subsequent leases?

There is the alternative in all the succeeding leases, of either

(a) making the commencement term the same as the dates of the leases; or
(b) making the commencement term 1 April 1985 in all cases.

11 Eg if the term was a very long one—say 999 years.

Option (a) will completely get round the problems of the 20/21-year cycle being breached. However, it will bring its own problems, mainly administrative. All the leases will have started at different times, perhaps spread over many months, even years. When the time comes to operate the review clauses, whoever is dealing with the administration will have his task spread out in a completely unnecessary manner. It will be bad enough if the reviews are quantified, but if they have to be calculated by a surveyor to some laid-down formula, whatever it is, the whole thing will be an administrative mess.

Option (b) would therefore seem to be the more acceptable, but it is at this point that the conveyancer has to be very careful, as we now see.

A. He *must* make sure that every lease in the block is completed with a commencement date of 1 April 1985. *Gibson's Conveyancing* quotes the case of *Bird v Baker*[12] to support the proposition that when the date quoted as the commencement is a past date, the term runs from that date, *not* the date of the lease.

Thus, if a 21-year initial review period were used for all the units in the block in the example, all the leases would have to be sold *and* completed by 31 March 1986. This would give a 'safe' buffer period of 12 months over the statutory initial 20-year period. What if they were not?— and as the 12 months progressed, the lessor's solicitor would have to keep a careful eye on the calendar.

The answer is plain. If, say, the last lease was completed and dated on 1 June 1986, it would be in great danger of falling foul of the Rent Act provisions, because the rent would then be varied *within* 20 years of 1 June 1986, ie 1 April 2006. One could always back-date, but there is a limit to what one can do in that direction.

In these circumstances, the answer seems to be to grant the leases of any units which seem to be in danger of falling foul of the rules to a nominee who will then sell to the eventual purchaser. Nominee sales are discussed at the end of this chapter.

The above comments depend on the expression 'grant of the tenancy' meaning the date of the lease, as opposed to the date of commencement of the term. This seems to be a matter over which there seems to hang some indecision, but it would be wise to assume that such is probably the case.

B. There is still the danger that whoever is responsible for the conveyancing might arrive at a date which bites well into the 20-year initial period and suddenly realises that a clanger had been dropped. This ought not to happen, but it can, especially in situations where the person having overall control of the legal work does not have day-to-day contact with the person responsible for the actual work.

If this happens, then again, one is in trouble. The cautious draftsman can provide for this eventuality, where compliance with the 20/21-year rules have become unattainable and thus the 6/7-year rules apply, by including in the review provisions in the lease a limiting clause similar to that described in section (b) below. Further, this will only work where the initial ground rent satisfies the 'less than two-thirds of rateable value' rule (which of course for the 20/21-year cycle is unnecessary).

12 [1858] 1 E & E 12.

This is why the limiting clause appears in some leases[13] where there is a standard 21-year review cycle.

(b) *6/7 year cycles*

The emphasis is slightly different here, but the following points should be noted:

A. The time limits on the review cycles still have to be observed, so what was discussed in section (a) is still valid. There is probably a strong case for increasing the initial review period to eight, nine or even ten years to avoid the possibility of any slip-up.

B. The initial ground rent *must* be below the two-thirds rateable value limit.

C. The subsequent reviewed rents *must* also be below the same limit, although remember that the rateable value criteria are those holding good when the review is effected. The trouble here is that no-one can really predict with any great accuracy what these are going to be, so that although it is fairly likely that, providing the initial rent satisfies the rule, the limit would not be breached at any point throughout the term, some provision should be made in the lease whereby the two-thirds rule will never be broken. This applies equally to both a quantified or a formula rent review pattern.

A typical clause making this sort of provision is as follows:[14]

'But so that such reviewed rent shall never equal such a sum as would in the appropriate circumstances create an inhibition on the premium capable of being charged on an assignment of the demised premises in the same manner as set out in the Rent Act 1977, s 127 and Sch 18, Part II as amended by the Housing Act 1980, s 78 or any amending or similar legislation provided that where the said sections would otherwise operate to create such an inhibition the reviewed rent shall be set at a sum which shall be £1 per annum below the sum which would so create the said inhibition.'

(c) *Nominee leases*

We mentioned earlier the possibility of using nominees to circumvent potential problems. The following points may usefully serve as an 'aide-memoire' for this procedure.

(a) The nominees should be a trusted employee, partner, director (if the lessor is a limited company) or perhaps professional adviser of the lessor.
(b) Letters should be written between lessor and nominee, in the form as set out in Precedent Nos 8 and 9[15], below.
(c) for tax purposes, the interposition of the individual nominees may be disregarded. There will be no tax disadvantages for the nominee personally.

    Eg for the purposes of capital gains tax this is made clear by the Capital Gains Tax Act 1979, s 46(1) which provides that acts of the

13 Eg Precedent No 3 cl 1(e)(i), p 362, below.
14 This is included in Precedent No 3 p 360, below.
15 P 374, below.

nominee are to be regarded as acts of the person for whom he is a nominee.

There is no specific provision to the like effect relating to income tax but the same principle appears to apply.

(d) It is recommended that the lease is granted for basic ground rent only, with no premium. This would minimise stamp duty liability provided, of course, that the consideration could not be certified. When the nominee assigned eventually to the true purchaser, the latter would save a small amount of stamp duty, as the assignment would be stamped as a conveyance or transfer on sale.[16]

E SUMMARY

As can be seen, the whole issue is most complex. As observed before, it is even questionable that some of those leases which actually are defective have been spotted, and it is possible that there are a good number of time-bombs ticking away all over the country, only to explode when a clever conveyancer acting for an intending purchaser, spots them. (If he is acting for the vendor he will hardly point out the fault to the other side.) Thus it is incumbent on those preparing leases to bear these potential problems in mind at all times.

16 Both transactions would attract 'Produced' stamps.

CHAPTER 5

Flats and maisonettes: different conveyancing techniques

In some textbooks dealing with flats, no essential difference is drawn between the flat and the maisonette. One commentator describes the archetypal maisonette in the same way that we have in ch 1, above,[1] and then proceeds to imply that it is only to be found to any great extent in a very limited geographical area.

Another learned author offers a basic definition of the maisonette which is at one with that offered in this book. He then goes on to discuss the sale of maisonettes using freehold conveyancing techniques, as well as leasehold, and from there goes fairly deeply into the technicalities, but in so doing loses sight of the definitive difference between the two forms of housing.

In this book, we shall not pursue the theoretical course to distraction. There is insufficient space to launch into a discourse on the theory of maisonette conveyancing. What we shall do instead is highlight the appropriate features of maisonettes, which need to be considered by the conveyancer and highlight the conveyancing techniques which are appropriate.

This part of the book should perhaps have been considered for consolidation with the section on the physical differences between a flat and a maisonette, but its more correct place is with the section on conveyancing. Nevertheless, the reader should have read ch 1, above, before he comes to this present one. In drawing out the differences between flats and maisonettes from a conveyancing, as opposed to a physical, point of view, and discussing the particular techniques to be used for the maisonette, we will also be able to highlight conveyancing methods which apply to flats, specifically in the area of enforcement of covenants.

A. FREEHOLD OR LEASEHOLD?

It is probably true to say that the freehold maisonette is more common than the freehold flat. Reference to ch 3, above[2] will remind us of the basic defect of freehold conveyancing as opposed to flats, ie the difficulty in the burden of positive covenants running.

One commentator suggests that positive covenants in maisonettes are capable of being restricted to a minimum, ie in the case of an upper and lower maisonette, respectively a covenant to maintain the roof, and one to support. With all due respect, this is a simplistic approach because there is, for ex-

1 P 1, above.
2 P 13, above.

ample, just as much a burden on the upper unit to shelter, which must be interpreted much more widely than as a mere roof maintenance covenant, as on the lower to support, and both must be satisfied that the other *maintains* correctly. And this is before we come on to consider questions of insurance, because in relation to maisonettes as opposed to flats it will usually be the purchaser who takes the burden of insurance. There is just as much difficulty in creating a freehold maisonette as a freehold flat. The building societies appear to like the former no more than the latter, nor are they likely to change their opinions until the basic tenor of the law of covenants is changed.[3]

None of this prevents various schemes being put forward for the incorporation of at least some freehold element being brought into maisonette conveyancing, eg:

(a) giving the lessee of the upper unit the freehold reversion of the lower one, and vice versa, so that each is the other's landlord;[4]
(b) granting a lease on only the upper unit, and selling the lower unit on a freehold basis; and
(c) selling both units on a freehold basis, and so on.

There is, in fact, no need for any such devious schemes. The building society movement actually prefers leasehold maisonettes, and so does the market—both on the developer's side and that of the purchaser, that archetypal man, who sees nothing wrong in a leasehold unit. Whilst the law of real property remains in its present state, at least so far as the enforcement of covenants is concerned, there seems no point in the floating of technically complicated schemes just to introduce a freehold element. The application of leasehold conveyancing will serve the same function in an essentially simpler and more effective way.

B. THE PARTICULAR SNAGS

It is not an abstruse discussion on whether or not freeholds can be used in maisonettes conveyancing which should be exercising the mind of the conveyancer, but rather the particular problems which maisonettes bring with them, and how those problems are solved.

There are two principal areas which should come under consideration:

(a) The physical aspect, and
(b) the relationship between the lessor and lessee.[5]

3 See generally, ch 29, p 325, below.
4 This is all very well: the theory, ie as each is the other's landlord, there ought to be no breakdown in the chain of covenants, is unimpeachable, but in practice the system is cumbersome. Shortly after writing this chapter, the author came across one of these units where the freehold part of the transaction had 'got lost'. This is by no means unusual.
5 We shall assume from this point on that we are talking about leasehold conveyancing.

1 The physical aspect

When looking at the differences between flats and maisonettes, we come back time and time again to the physical differences.

1 Unlike flats, which by definition[6] must have common parts, maisonettes are completely separate. They share no part of the same building from the point of view of need to have access, but—

2 Nevertheless the two units, upper and lower (and for the purposes of this discussion we must assume we are dealing with maisonettes on two levels only, although it is possible—just—to have three levels) depend on each other totally.

As an illustration of this, consider a row of terraced houses. The individual units depend on each other for support and protection, at least of a kind, and they have party walls, but if a gale came along and blew one of them down—even one in the middle of the row—the others would not automatically cease to be viable, although in this illustration a little shoring up and tidying up work might be necessary. Then move on to consider a pair of maisonettes, upper and lower. If a great wind came along and blew off the upper one, the roof would go with it, and the lower unit would be completely unviable. Equally the even more outlandish example of the lower unit suffering some desperate fate: eg sinking into the ground, being blown up, etc, would leave the upper unit literally in mid air—an impossible situation.

The result of all this is that the maisonette, in whatever position, depends just as much on its compatriots as does the flat. This aspect is all the more crucial because of:

2 The lessor/lessee relationship

This is still inextricably tied in with the physical aspect. With a block of flats, the only reason that there is a 'landlord', is because there are common parts. Maisonettes do not, or should not, have common parts, and so, irrespective that the units may have been sold leasehold, so producing a technical lessor/lessee relationship, there is no need for the 'landlord' function, overseeing management. With maisonettes, there is no reason for the developer to remain on the scene in any way.

All this means that the documentation should be so drawn that each maisonette may so far as possible rely on its own remedies, because there will be no lessor with a continuing presence. If a developer builds maisonettes, he wants to walk away from them once he has sold them, and he certainly does not want to be brought into the various problems the unit owners may have, one against the other. There are naturally, other reasons why a developer will choose to build maisonettes as opposed to flats, but this one is a powerful one.

6 See ch 1, p 1, above.

C. THE EFFECT OF THE SNAGS

The principal effect of the snags which we have just described is a direct result of their attractive features. This is the conundrum in maisonette conveyancing; one creates horizontally divided units where (assuming he is selling on a leasehold[7] basis) the developer (presumably—if he understands the differences between flats and maisonettes) wants to have nothing, or as little as possible, to do with the development after he has banked his proceeds of sale. The development has been carried out in such a *physical* manner that this can be done, but may this principle be extended to the inter-relationship of the lessor to the lessees, and, perhaps more importantly, of the lessees amongst themselves?

D. THE AIM OF THE DEVELOPMENT OF THE MAISONETTE

Maisonette conveyancing has suffered a lot of tangential developments, but the true aim of maisonette development should be that the developer/lessor ends up with nothing but his profit, and any ground rental income there may be. If he chooses to develop on a freehold basis, he should end up with no responsibilities at all, but the freehold maisonette is most definitely unpopular, especially with those who fund its sales, so we will henceforward leave that subject alone, although as we observed,[8] the freehold rules closely follow the leasehold ones.

The aim of the documentation, then, should be to produce a situation where the lessor and lessee no longer have any real, practical relationship in terms of obligations, the one to the other.

1 The conveyancing problem

In considering the problem, we come back once again to the differences between positive and restrictive covenants, and in a maisonette lease, there are going to be two very important classes of positive covenants, ie:

(a) to maintain (including covenants for support and shelter, depending on the position of the unit); and
(b) to insure (usually: obliging the lessor to insure would seem to go some way to defeating the object of the maisonette).

There will also be restrictive covenants; how many depending on the zeal of the original draftsman. These will encompass use, behavioural aspects, and so on.

The two different sorts of covenants create two different results *as soon as one passes beyond the lessor/lessee relationship*.

First, though, let us remind ourselves of the position on the lessor/lessee relationship.

7 The discussion on letting schemes which follows applies also to building schemes, ie the freehold equivalent, so that in this respect the choice of leaseholds is not much different.
8 Ibid.

There are two categories to consider:

(a) covenants between the original covenantor and covenantee, their respective personal representatives, and, in respect only of the *benefit*[9] of a covenant, an assignment to a third party,[10] produce 'privity of contract' and are generally enforceable; and
(b) covenants which between lessor and lessee are entered into expressly or impliedly[11] on behalf of the *covenantors* successors in title as well as his own and have reference to the subject matter of the lease[12] are also enforceable as between the lessor for the time being and the lessee for the time being; these covenants produce 'privity of estate'.[13]

Thus, in a lessor/lessee relationship, there is no problem at all, because covenants may be enforced between the two parties, whoever they may be at the time, and whether the covenants are positive or restrictive does not matter.

But (and it is a big 'but') this presupposes that the lessor is there, willing (or under covenant)[14] to enforce covenants, because not only do we have to consider the relationship between the lessor and lessee, we have to look at that between the lessees themselves; and this is where the significance of the maisonette comes in, because in a properly set up maisonette development (and perhaps we had better add, in a perfect world) the lessees should be able to enforce covenants, the one against the other/s, without recourse to the lessor, and without distinguishment between positive and restrictive.

This idealistic situation can be brought about, but apparently only to an unsatisfactory degree.

Leasehold conveyancing has developed the doctrine of the 'letting scheme', which is analogous to the 'building scheme'. The two schemes are really the same thing, first set out by Parker J in *Elliston v Reacher*[15]. The conditions which must be present for a letting scheme to apply are:

(a) title to the units should have derived from a common lessor;
(b) the units should have been sold subject to a standard set of *restrictions* which are consistent with a scheme of development;
(c) the common lessor intended the restrictions to be for the benefit of all units; and
(d) the units must have been acquired from the common lessor, either directly or via a title chain.

9 Which obviously is no use for the purposes of this discussion; it is the *burden* of the covenant which has to have a continuing enforceability against the owner for the time being of a maisonette.
10 See also the Law of Property Act 1925, s 56 (1) where those benefitting from a covenant may include others who 'may not be named as a party to the conveyance or other interest'. The true effect of the section is not absolutely clear, though, and so cannot be relied upon.
11 Law of Property Act 1925, s 79.
12 Ibid, s 141 and 142.
13 See also ch 28, p 309, on the Law Commissions proposals.
14 See later, p 74, below.
15 [1908] 2 Ch 665.

These conditions seem to have been consolidated over the years, so that the leading textbook on restrictive covenants, *Preston and Newson*,[16] suggests that only two requirements are *essential*, ie the area of the scheme is defined (which in a block of flats/maisonettes is easy enough) and that all purchasers accept that everybody who buys a unit shall be bound by the scheme.

2 Does a letting scheme help?

In a word, no; because of the inclusion in condition 2 above of the word 'restrictions'. Thus, all the restrictions, conditions, stipulations, in a lease of a maisonette, which are of a restrictive, negative nature, will be capable of enforcement, as between the owners for the time being of the units, as long as the requirements of a letting scheme apply, which they are almost certain to do, *but* those covenants which are really important, eg maintenance and insurance, are positive, and thus cannot be the subject of a letting scheme.

Accordingly, in a lessor/lessee relationship, and here it matters little that the unit is a flat or a maisonette, the unit owners cannot enforce these crucial covenants against each other. The only person who can enforce them is the lessor, and if in a maisonette development he wishes to turn his back on it (which in any event is one of the objects of the exercise) the unit owners will be left adrift.

3 The possible solutions

(a) *Flat developments*

The incidence of positive covenants will be quite different in a flat development, as opposed to one of maisonettes. For instance, the covenant to maintain the structure of the block, the covenant to insure, and other positive aspects of the lease, will be lessor's, not lessee's covenants, so that the lessees do not need to contemplate enforcement as between themselves. Nevertheless, it is still considered important that lessee's covenants should be enforceable throughout the particular block, and whilst (having taken away the great majority of the positive obligations by making them lessor's covenants) most of the covenants are restrictive, the inter-enforceability is still necessary. This is usually achieved by inclusion of a standard clause[17] imposing on a lessor a duty to enforce covenants by the other unit owners, to the extent that they affect the particular lessee (which they probably would).

Given the fact that in a *flat* lease, the primary positive covenants of maintenance and insurance are the lessors, not the lessees, there is a strong case in support of the argument that the unit owners could rely on there being a letting scheme anyway. Whilst this is probably correct, the enforcement of covenants in that way would undoubtedly be much more difficult than merely calling upon the lessor to enforce the similar covenants of other leases.

16 *Restrictive Covenants affecting Freehold Land* (1982, Sweet & Maxwell, 7th revised edition).
17 See later, and also Precedent No 3 cl 1 3(i) and (ii), Sixth Schedule, p 367, below.

This is why leading commentators suggest that the lack of such a clause in a lease makes it defective.[18]

(b) *Maisonette developments*

The position on maisonettes is much more crucial, and can be summed up as follows:

(a) Maisonettes are different from flats in that they should not have common parts.
(b) Therefore the lessor of maisonettes should not have to maintain a continuing presence in the block, whether directly or via a manager.
(c) Nevertheless, because they are still horizontally divided, maisonettes depend totally on each other.
(d) An inescapable by-product of the lack of retained common parts so far as the lessor is concerned, and the acceptance (usually) by the lessees of positive obligations on maintenance and insurance, is a desire by the lessor to wash his hands of the whole development as soon as it is completed.
(e) At the same time, just because of the acceptance by lessees of those positive covenants, they need to be able to enforce the positive covenants on the part of the other unit owners in the block.
(f) Ideally, then, they need to be able to enforce those covenants between themselves, and not by, eg going through the lessor.
(g) The use of a letting scheme (which there probably would be on the development so far as *restrictive* covenants were concerned) is unavailable, because of the positive nature of the covenants.
(h) Therefore, if there is a bare lease between the lessor and all the lessees, they may encounter serious problems.

4 The solution

Continuing to assume that leaseholds are being used—and the following, primary, solution is not available in a freehold scenario at least without obviously complicated and artificial conveyancing devices which might have a restrictive effect on marketing—the only really effective solution is to impose on the lessor an obligation that on demand, and possibly (this is a drafting point) upon the lessee giving him proper security for his costs he will enforce the covenants (which will encompass restrictive as well as positive) on the part of the other unit owners so far as they (adversely) affect the particular lessee. The problem with this is, of course, that it is precisely what the lessor is trying to avoid. The only consolation for the lessor is that, in practice, the incidence of his being called upon to perform this obligation is remote.

The lack of such a covenant in a lease of a maisonette should most definitely be regarded as a defect, and, the conveyancer should insist on its inclusion. The problem is that if it is not in one lease, it is not likely to be in

18 On balance I would agree with this view.

the others, and there must be uniformity throughout the leases, although one supposes that if such a covenant were to be in one lease only, the lack of reciprocity would not harm it. (Any lessor who accepted such a situation would have to be mad, though!)

Any practitioner faced with such a situation in a maisonette lease, where (as we have seen) the point is much more crucial, must explain carefully to his client that if he proceeds, he may not be able to enforce important obligations on the part of his co-lessees, except with the extra-contractual co-operation of the lessor, which may very well not be available.

The position is generally unsatisfactory: the solution is only likely to come with a radical change in the law of covenants, which now seems reasonably imminent.

5 A secondary solution

The deed of covenant system may be used as a solution to this problem, as follows:

In the initial leases of the units, there are incorporated the following covenants:

(a) a covenant by the lessee that if required he will enter into a deed of covenant with the lessee for the time being (ie the incoming lessee) of the other (ie upper or lower) maisonette. We are here only talking about a double, upper/lower unit situation, but this principle could be extended, if so desired. However, the further it is extended, the more difficult it becomes to keep going;

(b) a covenant by the lessee that he will not assign, etc, his unit without inviting the owner of the other unit to enter into a similar deed of covenant with his assignee, etc;

(c) a covenant by the lessor that when he disposes of the other unit (this obviously only applies, except in unusual circumstances, to the initial grant of the lease), he will impose on the lessee an obligation to enter into the deed of covenant in the same manner as set out in the lease under discussion.

The deed of covenant contains clauses by both parties, each with the other, to maintain and insure, and provides for remedies if this does not happen.

Thus there is always a contractual relationship between the lessees for the time being of the units, meaning that they are able to enforce the positive covenants against each other. Or at least that is the theory.

The inherent snags in an exercise of this sort are legion, and make it a doubtful answer to the problem. It is true that after the initial imposition of the covenants, the lessor may in theory withdraw from the whole affair, and whenever there is a change of ownership of a unit, the respective lessees must deal directly with each other. Unfortunately it does not work like this in practice, because it depends on:

(a) each party knowing the other's identity, and how to get in touch with the other (it is not always a case of knocking on doors, and that would be translating legal matters into the everyday world, which is not really the object of the exercise); and

(b) the other party being amenable to what is being requested (he or she is under covenant to do what is required, but it is a fairly common thing for people to be most awkward in this respect).

What happens in case of difficulty? Many readers will have seen the inevitable outcome: the aggrieved party gets on to the lessor, and asks him to make a recalcitrant party do what he is supposed to do!

In other words, we are back where we started. And this is in double, ie upper and lower, cases only. The potential pitfalls which can be encountered where this type of system is tried with multiple units, as it sometimes has been, can be imagined!

Which all leads back to another reason for changing the law of, particularly, positive covenants.

CHAPTER 6

Flats conveyancing generally

A chapter, however short, on the conveyancing of flats is generally a pointless exercise, because to a very great extent the business of buying, selling and mortgaging, etc of flats and/or maisonettes is the same as it is for any other type of property, principally, of course, the archetypal freehold house.

Nevertheless, there are some matters which apply only to flats, and which the practitioner should not miss. This chapter then will quickly review the procedures which apply particularly to this branch of conveyancing. Perhaps the most effective way in which to begin is to take the standardised pre-contract enquiries which all those acting on the purchase of a flat should make, whether on law stationers forms, ready printed, or on specially devised forms drafted by the practitioner. We can pick out the main headings of such lists of queries, and then pass briefly on to matters of title. The points which will arise are not only to be taken especial note of by those acting for purchasers, but also by those looking after the interests of vendors, because they will have to provide the answers, and should be aware of the sort of information they will need to have ready.

Accordingly the main points to bear in mind are as follows:

Boundaries

Care should be taken that the lease (which by the time the pre-contract enquiries are made should be in front of the purchaser's solicitor,[1] on the assumption that he will make his pre-contract enquiries as soon as the contract arrives) accurately defines where the boundaries of the flat itself are, in relation to the other parts of the block on all sides of, and below and above the flat.

If the descriptive words in the lease are defective for any reason, the vendor should be pressed to say which parts of the construction of the flat are, in his opinion, the boundaries, although in practice he is most unlikely to be able to do this, and although annoying and indicative of bad draftsmanship, a defect of this sort is not likely to prove an insurmountable barrier to the purchase proceedings.

If the lease is unavailable at this point (and this does happen) the question should still be put in specific terms, although it is unlikely to receive a satisfactory answer.

1 But it *may* not be: eg the lease itself is not part of the register entries in the case of a registered flat, but it is still very important because it remains the central document, containing as it does the various lessor's and lessee's covenants, which will not be set out in extenso in the registers. This comment, like the majority of this chapter, relates only to 'second-hand' flats conveyancing, when the lease is already in existence.

Disputes

It is quite apparent from the nature of a block of flats that people are living in closer proximity to each other than if they were house-dwellers; therefore, it is more likely that one or more of the people in the block is or are annoying the others by their behaviour, so that disputes are more likely. There is probably a case for putting a question in more specific terms than those included in the printed forms, eg an intending purchaser might usefully ask his vendor if any of the other flats in the block had given rise to annoyance, nuisance, or inconvenience by reason of:

noise, of whatever sort, human, mechanical or electronic; smells—generated by cooking or otherwise;
behaviour which would otherwise be acceptable but is not, because it takes place at unusual hours.[2]
animals . . ., and so on.

Notices

Again, in the case of flats, the matter of any notices which may have been received, eg from the lessor, is more important than with houses. There is the further point to consider that in almost all leases there will be a lessee's covenant to bring to the attention of the lessor any notices received. The lessee should be asked to confirm that if this has happened, that he has complied with the covenant, and to explain the circumstances.

Guarantees

The questions within this category on law stationers printed forms refer to matters such as contingency insurance, policies, warranties, etc relating to the fabric of the property, and documents like Public Health Act 1936, s 18 and Highways Act 1980, s 38 agreements. These are matters which would just as easily crop up with other types of conveyancing, and so they do not require further discussion here. For most practitioners, though, the main thrust of the question relates to the NHBC documentation, and although this will also relate to other types of conveyancing, it does have a special application to flats. For a more detailed description of what is involved, see ch 25, p 289, below. The only other category which might be of interest to a flat purchaser would be guarantees relating to the treatment of infestation, etc in older blocks of flats.

Services

This subject differs little in relation to flats from the more traditional house. It is only because services which will serve the individual flats penetrate further than those serving units on a typical housing estate that the question demands any sort of particular attention. Accordingly, those acting for pur-

2 Eg outside the time period usually quoted in the lease—see as an example Precedent No 3, cl 4, Third Schedule, p 365, below.

chasers of flats should make sure that the lease contains the appropriate rights and reservations of all services.[3]

Exclusive facilities

Again, this question relates to flats more by extension rather than by exclusivity. The conveyancer should be particularly careful that the various subheadings usually found in this question are answered correctly, ie in the negative.

Shared facilities

The wording of this question will relate specifically to blocks of flats, in that there will undoubtedly be facilities used in common with the owners of other property (ie in the same block) and almost always (unless the flat has no service charge, which would be unusual) there will have been contributions made towards the cost of works on the common areas.

Adverse rights

This question does not appear to call for any specific comment, as it has the same relationship to flats as to any other type of property.

Restrictions

The wording of this question is usually strict, but one wonders how often it is asked without thought, and then answered in a 'blanket' way, eg 'Yes, to the knowledge of the vendor'. There is perhaps a case for an additional question asking for confirmation that the vendor, as the existing lessee, has adhered to the terms, restrictions, covenants and other matters contained in the lease of the premises.

Planning

Again, in this case there is no difference in the application of the question to a block of flats than to any other sort of property.

Fixtures, outgoings, completion, and new properties

None of these questions call for any specific comment.

A. LEASEHOLD ENQUIRIES

These, of course, are those specifically designed for leasehold conveyancing, and must *always* be asked. Sometimes they are not!

3 Eg those in Precedent No 2, pp 350–351, below.

Superior title

This is not the place to discuss the relative merits of the superior title being freehold, or a head lease, or an underlease; but for all that the conveyancer *must* satisfy himself on the position before he proceeds further.

Identity of lessors, etc

It is at this point that difficulties can be encountered. For instance, the lease will set out the name and address of the original lessor, but in the interim period the reversionary interest may have been sold by the lessor, or he or she, may have moved, changed names, or done something else to prevent the lessee, whoever that might be for the time being, putting himself into contact with the lessor.

Now this may seem a strange proposition, because if one owns the right to collect rent, why should one forego it? And yet it does happen. What happens then?

The reasons for inability to put oneself in touch with the lessor may be various. The problem can be notorious in the case of tenants' management companies, where the administration is actually undertaken by individual tenants themselves, and those persons do not understand the absolute necessity of quick response to those involved in transfers of the flats in the block. In cases like these, and in other sectors of this category, the purchaser and/or his adviser would no doubt be absolutely correct to suggest that without proof that the rent, etc had been paid correctly (evidenced by receipts) or that the vendor was in touch with his lessor, he should refuse to carry on. While that may be the correct attitude, it is not always the most practical one when one is acting for a purchaser who wants the flat and cannot understand the obstacles (as he thinks them to be) which his adviser is putting in his way.

Thus the purchaser should ensure, and the vendor should make every attempt to provide, that

(a) Any rent in respect of which proof of payment cannot be provided, should be deducted from the consideration. If a review has taken place, or should have taken place, the appropriate adjustment is made. If the review is not a quantifiable one, and has not taken place, then a best estimate of the likely sum involved will have to be made.
(b) The same applies to service charges, although except in unusual circumstances these will not be quantifiable. In these admittedly unusual cases, where a service charge has failed to be levied, the best that can be done is to take the last payment made and inflate it, allowing for rises in the Retail Price Index plus a bit more for safety. One assumes that the only time when the position would be that a service charge had *never* been levied, and the manager was unable to provide any sensible information as to how much it was likely to be, would be in the case of a fairly new property. The author has come across flats in fairly new blocks where the manager was so utterly disorganised that not only had he never managed to sort himself out to the extent of collecting a service charge, but when asked he could give little idea of how much it might be when

it was collected. In such cases the original lease might quote an *anticipated* service charge: this would be helpful, but over-reliance on such figures is not heartily recommended and such figures should be well topped up! If no figure was originally quoted, then someone, presumably the purchaser's solicitor, will have to think of a figure.[4]

Licences granted by lessor

This is not likely to be particularly relevant in the case of residential properties other than the very up-market ones which the average practitioner is not likely ever to come across.

Lessor's consent to assignment

The same remarks apply to this query, although it is just possible that the lease will have used a 'consent licence' procedure as described in ch 7, pp 88 et seq and illustrated in Precedent No 3, cl 8, p 363, below. Thus the lease must have been studied before this question is asked. The trouble is, very often it has not been received by the time the pre-contract enquiries are sent out (or even received!). The matter should accordingly be checked again, after the lease has been received.

B. COVENANTS

We saw how the previous question relating to restrictions would relate specifically to flats conveyancing, and we floated the possibility of a specific additional query. In most cases this will satisfy that requirement. Those acting for the vendor would do well to answer these questions carefully and, of course, those acting for purchasers should make sure that they do not get 'fobbing-off' answers. This comment naturally applies to all the leasehold enquiries.

C. SERVICE CHARGE

One of the standard questions on the printed forms refers to the possibility of the vendor having exercised his statutory right to obtain information (ie about the various components of the service charge and their cost). Very probably, few flat owners will realise that they have this right, so that although the question needs to be asked, there is little likelihood of it being answered positively. The possibility of the vendor not having the appropriate information available on the matter of the service charge in the same way as that described earlier in relation to rent, is remote, although it could happen so that reference should be made again to our earlier comments.

The purchaser should remember that just because a sale is in progress it does not mean that the lessor is obliged to provide either the vendor or the

4 In which case perhaps chs 8–19, pp 95–228, below, might form the start of some help!

purchaser with fresh information about service costs, individual quotes, etc just so long as he has complied with the requirements of the Housing Act 1980, Sch 19.[5] This may leave the intending purchaser in a position where he may not have quite enough information to give himself a full and detailed picture of the service charge liability especially if, first, the lessor or his agents have not been particularly businesslike in their dealings with flat-owners, or the vendor has, perhaps, mislaid or destroyed his own records.

Apportionment of ground rent (including other miscellaneous items reserved as rent) as well as service charges must never be forgotten.

D. INSURANCE

Where a block of flats is concerned, the likelihood is that the lessor/manager will maintain the insurance[6]. Indeed, if the conveyancer comes across any flat where insurance is the responsibility of the flat owner, he should adopt a wary attitude simply because in such cases there is the possibility that certain parts of the building will then be uninsured. Admittedly, this may be an extremely rare occurrence but in this world of ours almost anything is possible. What is important is for those representing the purchaser to find out, and for those representing the vendor, if the sale is one of a 'second-hand' flat, to provide, full information on:

insurer's identity and address (including if possible the branch dealing with the policy);
policy number;
name of the insured;
arrangements for noting interests on the policy (these are very often dealt with automatically by a proviso on the policy that the interests of all owners and mortgagees of the flats are noted, whatever they may be);
risks covered;
amount of cover;
premium renewal date;
amount of premium; and
proof that premium has been paid.

This information may be provided specifically, or perhaps a copy of the policy document itself might be available. A further possibility is that the insurer will have produced a 'Summary of Cover' which is a sheet summarising the main points of the policy. This should be equally acceptable as the policy itself.

E. OTHER MATTERS FOR CONSIDERATION

1 NHBC

A flat or maisonette in the course of sale may either:

5 And see generally ch 14, p 159, below.
6 See further ch 4, p 43, above.

(i) carry the benefit of the NHBC's standard 'Ten Year' scheme described in ch 25, p 289, below; or
(ii) carry no NHBC cover at all because either:
  (a) it is too old to have qualified for the Ten-Year scheme anyway; or
  (b) it is a 'new' flat in a conversion or renewal scheme and for one reason or another is not in the 'Six Year' scheme; or
(iii) carry the Six Year protection[7] under the NHBC's Conversions and Renewals scheme.

For a description of the Ten-Year and the Six Year schemes, the reader is referred to pp 289 and 235 respectively.

Assuming the flat *is* in one of these schemes (and the purchaser's representative must be careful that any conditions in respect of NHBC matters must be complied with) the question then arises as to how the matter is dealt with on behalf of the purchaser.

We will not review the NHBC documentation which should be available (it is assumed that this is basic knowledge) but we ought to touch upon the question of assignments of NHBC interests.

It was the practice, under the previous NHBC scheme, to take assignments of the HB5 Agreement. Prior to 1 April 1979, when the documentation used by the NHBC changed, there was an Agreement followed by the Ten Year Protection Certificate. Following 1 April 1979 there was introduced the present system of Agreement and Notices of Insurance Cover—one for the unit itself and the other for the common parts of the block of flats.

In view of the fact that the Ten Year Protection Certificate was only ever (despite its name and impressive appearance) a document by means of which the terms of the preceeding agreement were effected on a permanent basis, the document, the benefit of which a subsequent owner of the flat had to be sure was his, was the agreement.

There is still some doubt in commentator's minds as to whether strict assignment of the benefit of the agreement is necessary. There was a time when the HB12, which is the pre-printed form of assignment, was one of the most widely used documents in a conveyancers office, but the case of *Marchant v Caswell & Redgrave Ltd*[8] suggested that assignment was not necessary. However, not all practitioners have total confidence in this decision, and there are still those who will ask for an express assignment, and furthermore give notice thereof to both the NHBC and the builder. If there has been a previous break in the assignment chain (which is more than likely) this action is probably useless.

In practice, the NHBC will accept the position without there being in existence express assignments, although in such cases an owner taking some sort of step under the terms of the scheme might be involved in additional correspondence.

The present system should not give the same sort of problem, as the NHBC agreement now provides that it is made 'by the First Purchaser for himself and his successors in title and his and their mortgagees in possession. The

7 Strictly speaking, the protection is five years—see ch 20, p 235, below.
8 [1976] 240 EG 127.

vendor[9] undertakes that he shall not seek to deny liability under this agreement on the ground that it has not been assigned'.[10]

Nevertheless, there is still a reluctance amongst the more theoretically-minded practitioners to accept this, because (as they say) the house owner's rights under the agreement are a chose in action, and the contractual terms set out above are in conflict with the general rules about assignment of choses in action. Still, those who do insist on an express assignment are very much in the minority, and the important factor, which presumably is recognised by the majority of practically-minded practitioners, is that the attitude of the NHBC themselves is the over-riding aspect of the matter: that is to say, the NHBC will not allow a builder (or, presumably, themselves) to plead absence of assignment as a defence.

2 Tenants' management companies

Whether or not the reversionary interest is owned by such a company, where there is one, there may be a share certificate to transfer. There are generally two varieties of tenants' management companies, and these are dealt with on a sale as follows:

(a) *Those limited by shares*

In these cases, the share must be transferred, this being dealt with at the same time as the completion of the transfer of the flat.

(b) *Those limited by guarantee*

In ch 11, below[11] we discuss the difference between the two varieties of tenants' companies, and arrive at the conclusion that, apart from any other consideration, a company limited by guarantee is that much more efficient from everyone's point of view simply because there is that much less paperwork ie no share certificate for the vendor to find (sometimes they are *not* with the deeds) and to hand over to the purchaser and no share transfer form.

At the same time, even with a company limited by guarantee, there may be paperwork to be completed in connection with the transfer of membership, which must be contrasted with transfer of shares. Whatever the variety of management company involved, if it is a tenants' management company, the owner for the time being of the flat will have to become a member of the company, just as the outgoing vendor will have to cease to be a member. This process may very well be automatic under the terms of the unit lease and/or the articles of association of the company, but the conveyancer, particularly when acting for the purchaser, must look at the specific documentation for the flat and carry out the right actions in the right sequence. It is all rather subjective, and thus cannot warrant any further discussion here.

9 Ie the builder/developer.
10 HB5 Agreement, cl 10.
11 P 131, below.

3 Other management companies, etc

Where the management is effected by means other than a tenants' controlled company, the purchaser's adviser should seek to satisfy himself on the bona fides of the operation. Again, this is very subjective, and does not necessarily mean that, for example, a full company search should be made against every management company one comes across (although there would certainly be nothing wrong with that) but that care should be taken in finding out as much as possible about the management operation, particularly establishing that there does not seem to be anything wrong with it. Once again, a rather vague statement, but it cannot really be made any more positive.

4 The document(s) of transmission

To a very great extent conveying a flat, following the initial grant of the lease, is no different to freehold conveyancing of houses. It is all fairly standard. And yet as in freehold conveyancing, we have this strange differential between registered and unregistered.

So that if a flat is registered, it will be transferred by a transfer, which will be a very short and simple document. The Land Registration Rules 1925 prescribe various forms of transfer for use in conveyancing, but the different forms relate to matters other than the state of the title, ie leasehold or freehold (eg transfer of part, transfer of whole, transfer by company, transfer to joint proprietors, and so on) so that the familiar form 19 is in general use for transfers of flats.

The brevity of such a transfer is achieved by the fact that the usual covenants to pay rent and observe generally the provisions of the lease, including all the other tenants' covenants, are implied under the Land Registration Act 1925, s 24(1)(a) and (b). Furthermore s 24(2) of the same Act limits that covenant under s 24(1) to payment of the apportioned rent, and to the performance and observance of the lessees covenants only so far as they affect the property the subject of the transfer.

On the other hand, a transfer of an unregistered lease, which is perversely called an assignment (or is the perversity the other way around?) still has to take many words to achieve what the transfer achieves in the minimum of words.[12] For that reason, a typical (unregistered) assignment is included in the precedent Section[13] but there seems no reason to include a (registered) transfer. The reader will forgive the author if the wording of the assignment is perhaps a little archaic, but then the assignment itself is surely one of the more archaic forms of legal document still with us?

F. SUMMARY

This is not a book about conveyancing techniques. In attempting to cover the various and numerous aspects of the sale and management of flats, obviously one of them will be the conveyancing of flats, but restrictions on space demand our study to be concise. We have highlighted the main points which the conveyancer should bear in mind when acting, mainly for the purchaser but also for the vendor.

12 But see n 5 to Precedent No 20, p 418, below.
13 Precedent No 18, p 415, below.

CHAPTER 7

Keeping track of the lessee

In any management scheme, it is important that the person (whether an individual, a firm or a corporation) responsible for the management knows at all times who is the owner of any unit in the block which is under management.

We have already seen in looking at the nature and content of the tenants' covenants,[1] that one of those covenants is to give notice of assignment, etc. Obviously this is done so that the lessor is aware at all times of whom his lessees are. Because of the quasi-paternalistic nature of the landlord/tenant relationship, each side needs to know the identity of the other side. It is easy enough for a lessee to be aware of the identity of his lessor, although one supposes that there could be circumstances where this knowledge was lacking, for example, if the lessor had traded on his reversionary interest, and possibly the new lessor had failed to advise the lessees of the change of ownership. If, in these curcumstances, the lessees wished to make contact with the person holding the right to collect the rent, they might have difficulty in doing so. Readers will no doubt be able to easily envisage such circumstances and for those who remain sceptical, the author can attest to having come across this sort of situation on more than one occasion. Why anyone should own the right to collect money—a right without too many (if any) onerous duties—and fail to capitalise on it, escapes one for the moment, but it does happen.

The above circumstances relate to a situation where ground rent is the only financial tie between the two parties. Where there are other ties, and the obvious one is a service charge, then the position ought to be very different. Whether it is the lessor or some third party who is responsible for management, it is extremely unlikely that there will not be a regular contact between, on the one hand, those who have to collect, and on the other, those who have to pay.

The position just described, that is the lessees' knowledge of the identity of the lessor/manager, is capable of being sustained without the need for any special covenants in the lease. The obverse position, the lessor's manager's knowledge of the identity of the lessees, is quite different, and is very important to be sustained for a number of reasons as follows:

1 There will be multiple lessees, and the lessor must have some mechanism built into the legal documentation which enables him to keep track of lessees.

1 See generally, ch 4, p 26, above.

2 Even if there were no other reason, it is good business practice for the lessor to know who are, for the time being, the lessees.
3 As the lessees represent a source of income, which should not be disparaged however modest the ground rent, the lessor must know from whom to demand the rent, otherwise he will have his ground rent demand notes flung back in his face, with indications from the lessee that Mr Jones is *not* the owner of this flat any more!
4 The ability to identify lessees becomes even more important when we come to consider a service charge, where unlike a ground rent which is usually (or ought to be) money for jam, the income is for the main part replacing money already spent or committed by the lessor/manager.

And so it is important for the lessor/manager to be in a position at all times to know who are the lessees for the time being of the flats in the block in question. Consequently, it is important for the lessor/manager to be able to have the means of making himself aware when changes in ownership take place, and that is what this chapter is all about.

Note that we speak only of the means of making himself aware of changes; we do not need the right of controlling changes, although this is present in some leases and we shall discuss it shortly.

As we have seen, there is a need for some mechanism in the lease for notice of change being given to the lessor. The most innocuous method is the familiar notice[2] provision which is found in virtually all leases, possibly along the following lines:

'The lessee shall within (usually something of the order of 28) days of the date of every assignment sub-lease grant of probate or administration assent transfer or other event or document relating to the term give notice thereof in writing to the lessor.'

There is usually added to this covenant a provision that the notice will be accompanied by a fee payable to those registering the notice.[3] This can be a fee which is either quantified, or calculated according to a formula, eg a percentage of the value of the property the subject of the registration.[4] This provision should not be ignored, because the fees seem to be pitched at good commercial levels these days—a quantified sum of anything between £10 and £25 per notice is not in the least unusual, and on the nationwide studio flat system set up by the author,[5] a notice fee of 0·1% of the 'Notice Value', that is to say the consideration for the assignment, was levied. As studio flats were changing hands in the early 1980s, at anything between £15,000 and £30,000, depending on location, a notice fee of 0·1% was a handy amount to collect, and as far as the author is aware, no adverse comment was ever made about the level of the fee.

A covenant on the part of the lessee to give notice in this way does have disadvantages as far as the lessor is concerned. The first one is that the notice may not arrive until a month after the change of ownership, and if the date for sending out ground rent/service charge demands falls awkwardly, the

2 Discussed earlier in ch 4, p 39, above included in lessees' covenants generally.
3 This could be the lessor, the manager, or solicitors, or even agents, acting for them.
4 Eg Precedent No 3 cl 7, fourth Schedule, p 366, below.
5 See ch 9, p 110, below.

name of the lessee may be different from that quoted on the demand note, and confusion and delay in collection of monies may well ensue. The second, and much the more important one, is that the notice is the responsibility of the lessee (or more likely his professional advisers).

This means that if the lessee's side forgets to give the notice, the lessor is unaware of the change of ownership. If the lessor is running his own block of flats, and it is reasonably small, then the confusion is not going to be all-embracing and the situation can be remedied by some investigative work being done. But for anything larger than the smallest operation, the ensuing confusion can be critical, and anyway why should the lessor have to chase after his lessees to find out something which it is their duty to tell him?

Accordingly, it is suggested that for a well regulated scheme, something much tighter than the 'after the event' notice of assignment, etc (which may be forgotten anyway) is needed. But what can be done to achieve this?

There are three basic ways by means of which the lessor/manager may keep control of the movement of ownership. These are:

(a) restrictions on the register, assuming that the property concerned is registered;
(b) licence procedures; and
(c) deeds of covenant.

These are considered in turn, as follows.

A. RESTRICTIONS ON THE REGISTER

First of all, these have a most unfortunate drawback, which is, if the property is not registered, there is no register to put a restriction on! However, most urban, and a good number of rural, areas are now subject to compulsory registration, so that it is to be hoped that there will be relatively few flat schemes which are unregistered. If the lessor or manager wishes to impose some sort of a restriction on the right of alienation in an unregistered case, he must look at the deed of covenant procedure, or possibly the use of licences.[6]

Before we discuss the actual contents of the restrictions which are placed on the registers, we should consider the mechanics first of creating the restriction when the lease of the unit is being granted, and second of keeping it on the register on subsequent assignments.

In order to have a restriction placed on the register, it is necessary for both parties (it is only the lessor and the lessee who need to apply jointly—any third or subsequent party to the lease, eg a management company, does not actually need to join in the application, although of course it or they will then participate in the property both together with the benefit, of and subject to, the restriction) to apply jointly to the Chief Land Registrar for the restriction to be placed on the register.

This is done by there being included in the lease[7] a clause in the following terms, which are not absolutely definitive but are those normally used:

6 See later in ch 22, below.
7 Or whatever document is being dealt with.

'The Lessor and the Lessee hereby apply to the Registrar for the entry on the Register of the following restriction on the title to the property:'

There will then follow the precise wording of the restriction which is to be used.

As soon as both[8] parties make the application, and the inclusion of this type of clause is prima facie evidence of this, the Registry will not normally take issue with the requirement, and will automatically enter the restriction, unless the wording is such that they can foresee difficulties in its enforcement.[9]

The restriction will be entered on the Proprietorship Register, as it refers to registration of subsequent transfers into the name/s of new, intended proprietors. The advantage of this which, of course, is absolutely logical, is that when the Registry is processing a subsequent dealing, it will automatically look at the Proprietorship Register in order to delete the name of the previous proprietor and substitute that of the transferee. The disadvantage is that it is all too easy for the Registry clerk concerned to delete the restriction along with the previous proprietor.

The readers' reaction may well be—how can this happen? If the restriction itself is worded sensibly[10] it ought to be perfectly clear that it is not to be deleted on the first transfer following initial registration, but must be kept on the register for ever and a day, or at least until the appropriate parties re-apply jointly to have it deleted, which is not likely to happen.

Unfortunately, incorrect deletion of restrictions can, and does happen. The author set up a studio flat scheme some few years ago; the scheme is described elsewhere in this book[11] so that all that is necessary in this context is to say that there was a production level of some 1,500 units every year, scattered throughout the length and breadth of England and Wales, with all leases virtually identical and an absolute requirement that movements in ownership were capable of being monitored constantly. It was decided that the 'warning' type of wording described below[12] would be used for the restriction, and so the joint application to the Registrar appeared in every lease completed and put up for registration.

It did not take too long for it to be discovered—how is immaterial to this discussion—that occasionally, district land registries were inadvertently striking out the restriction on the registration of subsequent transfers. Naturally this was taken up with the Registry at Lincolns Inn Fields, as well as with the district registries themselves and, as usual, we received the fullest cooperation in the remedying of the situation. Nevertheless, what remained a worrying feature of this whole business was that we could only draw to the Registry's notice those cases where we had been fortunate enough to become involved with a studio flat *after* the registration of the dealing concerned. This was usually through acting for our client on the re-purchase of the property, usually by way of part exchange against a better property. Thus

8 Or all those who have, or will have, a legal interest in the property.
9 See p 90, below.
10 See later for the actual wording of the suggested restriction.
11 Ch 9, p 110, below.
12 See p 90, below.

had it not been for the Part Exchange Scheme, we would probably not have known about these individual cases. And as there is no way of knowing otherwise whether or not the restrictions were being kept on the registers when the properties were transferred and subsequently registered (with an annual output of 1,500 units, the cumulative effect is horrendous) we could only consider, with some trepidation, that what we had seen was only the tip of the iceberg. The effect this would have on the management programme of these studio flats is horrible to contemplate, but there is no doubt that in a proportion of these flats in the management programme, the protection of the restriction has been lost, and we are back to the basic and unsatisfactory protection of the 'after the event' notice of transfer as previously described.

This, then, is a somewhat unexpected disadvantage of the restriction procedure. But if we work on the assumption that the restriction will be retained on the register, despite any subsequent dealing, the procedure is useful and on balance is probably worth using.

We next have to decide what form the restriction should take. Here the choice is between a totally restrictive wording, introducing a consent procedure before the transfer, etc may be registered, or a wording which does not set up any necessity for consents, but merely makes sure that no transfer is going to be registered until the lessor, or manager, has been notified of the dealing.

The first alternative would probably be represented by the wording of the restriction being in the following form:[13]

> 'Except under an order of the Registrar no Transfer or Assent of the demised premises is to be registered unless a certificate is given by [as required] that it has consented to such transfer or assent.'

This wording is quite unequivocal. Before the dealing can be registered, a consent has to be issued by the lessor, etc. From the point of view of the lessor, this is marvellous, because he has to receive a request for consent from the existing owner, or the incoming purchaser, before the dealing is registered. Thus he ensures that he is told about all the assignments. But from everyone else's point of view, a restriction of this sort is not at all acceptable. For the owner of the unit, it will be a totally unnecessary fetter on his ability to deal with his property exactly as he pleases. For a mortgagee of the unit, it will be an intrusion on his security, in that a third party has power over the property. And even for the Registry, it will be unacceptable because the tendency would be for them to become involved in correspondence, etc and the ensuing extra administration which they can well do without.

Even if that time-honoured phrase 'such consent not to be unreasonably withheld' is added to the restriction, there is little difference, because the principal purpose of the restriction would still be prima facie to alienate the right of the owner of the unit to deal with it as he pleased, and in any event it would presumably be up to the lessee to prove that consent was indeed being unreasonably withheld.

There is one further aspect of such a 'consent' clause to be considered, and that is whether it may fall within the terms of the Rent Act 1979, s 127 as

13 It is up to the individual draftsman to set out the precise requirements of the restriction.

amended by the Housing Act 1980, s 78.[14] Basically, the 1977 Act s 127 deals with allowable premiums in relation to certain long tenancies. For the purposes of this discussion, we must assume that the tenancies we are dealing with are long tenancies within the meaning of this section. The section then lays down certain conditions, which, if not satisfied, bring into operation the 1977 Act, Sch 18, Part II which may restrict the premium, or price, obtainable by a flat owner on a sale of his property.

One of the conditions is as follows:

'that the terms of the tenancy do not inhibit both the assignment and the underletting of the whole of the premises comprised in the tenancy.'[15]

The 1980 Act s 78 goes on to say:[16]

'and for the purposes of subsections (2) (C) ... above the terms of a tenancy inhibit an assignment or underletting if they—
(a) preclude it, or
(b) permit it subject to a consent but exclude section 144 of the Law of Property Act 1925 (no payment in nature of a fine); or
(c) permit it subject to a consent but require in connection with a request for consent the making of an offer to surrender the tenancy.'

It seems fairly certain that no residential lease would include provisions in the nature of sub-ss (a) and (c) above but the effect of sub-s (b) should be considered carefully. If it is desired to have a consent restriction in the lease, assuming the objections of purchaser's solicitors and mortgagees, let alone the Registry, can be overcome, the wording should be carefully considered.

Accordingly, because of the inherent difficulties in framing a consent restriction, one turns to the second alternative described above; that is, the 'notice' restriction.

Consider the difference between the form of restriction quoted on p 90, above, with the following wording:

'Except under an order of the Registrar no Transfer or Assent (etc) of the demised premises is to be registered unless a certificate is given by [lessor or manager] that notice of such Transfer or Assent (etc) has been given to the said [lessor or manager].'

The emphasis this time is totally different. The person transferring the unit[17] still has to communicate with the lessor *before* completion of the transfer, but he does not rely upon the lessor having any choice about his reply. As soon as the notice of pending assignment (as the author calls it) is given to the lessor, the terms of the restriction are satisfied. But how do we prove that the notice has been given? The restriction itself does not afford any assistance here, and it is probably better that it does not. The necessary accompanying requirement on the lessor to respond to the notice is contained elsewhere, and may be drafted something like:[18]

14 For full text of the sections, see ch 4, pp 56–59, above.
15 The Housing Act 1980, s 78(2)(c), replacing the Rent Act 1977, s 127 (2) (c).
16 The words were added to the Rent Act 1977, s 127 (5) by the Housing Act 1980 s 78 (4).
17 This will probably be the intending purchaser, as it will be his job to attend to subsequent registration.
18 Refer to studio flat lease, Precedent No 3, cl 6(iii), Fourth Schedule, pp 365–6, below.

'The Lessee shall not assign the whole of the demised premises without giving prior written notice of his intention so to do to the Lessor and on receipt of such notice the Lessor shall acknowledge in writing receipt of such notice and such acknowledgement shall be in sufficient terms so as to comply with the provisions of clause ...[19] hereof.'

This clause actually repeats en clair the imposition on the unit-owner implied in the wording of the restriction; this is not strictly necessary but it does no harm. More importantly, it spells out that the lessor must himself respond in writing to the notice of pending assignment, and it is this counter notice which will provide the unit-owner with proof that the terms of the restriction have been met.[20]

Thus the procedure from start to finish is as follows:

A. The unit owner enters into a contract for sale with his purchaser.
B. He then submits a 'notice of pending assignment'[1] to the lessor, giving all relevant details.
C. The lessor is bound to return the notice receipted, and it is this receipt which proves the notice.
D. The sale is completed, and then when the purchaser applies for registration of the dealing, he encloses with the application to the DLR the receipted notice.
E. The normal 28-day notice of assignment accompanied by the usual fee, is sent to the lessor as well.

By this time readers may be asking—why go to these lengths? In order to illustrate why, it might be helpful to look at the advantages, and disadvantages, to both sides, in adopting this procedure.

1 Disadvantages

(a) *For the lessor*

The only possible disadvantage is that the receipt and return of the notice of pending assignment is an extra administrative burden.

(b) *For the unit-owner*

Again, the requirement to submit the notice of pending assignment is an added burden as might be the finding out that it has to be given, but then that is what he employs a conveyancer for. The procedure is undoubtedly an extra administrative burden for him or his conveyancer, as well as the lessor, but the advantages of the system ought to outweigh this.

2 Advantages

(a) *For the lessor*

Even if we are only talking about collection of ground rents, it is very much in the reversioner's favour if he knows the way in which the lease is drafted

19 Ie the clause containing the restriction.
20 It can be in any form, but a useful precedent is in No 6 p 372, below.
1 As a suggested format, Precedent No 6, p 372, below, may be useful.

will ensure that he is able to keep track of the lessees for the time being of the units in the particular block. But when we come to consider the collection of service charges, where for the most part the income is to be set off against money either already paid out, or if not paid probably committed, this security is even more important.

(b) *For the unit owner*

The facile view is that there is no advantage; but before the matter is dismissed so easily, the reader should consider that it is very much in his interests that monies due from all the other unit owners in a building are readily collectable. If the lessor/manager is having difficulty in collecting the ground rent and/or the service charge from any individual owners—and one of the most likely reasons will be that there is difficulty in identifying those responsible for making the payments—the management of the building will not be as smooth as it might otherwise be.

The final comment on the use of restrictions is that before one is introduced into a lease, it would be wise to seek the views of the Registry, by submitting a draft of the proposed restriction to either the appropriate district land registry, or to Lincolns Inn Fields Registry. After all, it is the registry which will have to operate the restriction, and it is only fair to show them what sort of wording is intended.

B. LICENCE PROCEDURES

It is not normal to include provision for the granting of licences in a residential lease, and only a short discussion is required here.

Nevertheless, the licence procedure is undoubtedly another way in which to secure to the lessor the knowledge that he will be aware of who his lessees are, but its inclusion in (usually) commercial leases is intended to allow the lessor to have some control over who are to be his lessees at any given time. Unlike the sort of lease we are studying in this book, which carries only a (usually) nominal ground rent, a commercial lease will be at a full rack-rent and it is important, and accepted by the market, that the lessor should be able to control to whom assignments will be made, by, eg taking up references. Until he approves the proposed assignee, he will not issue his licence, and the assignee will not (or should not!) complete the assignment.

The standard wording of a licence provision in a commercial lease is:

'Not at any time to assign etc. without the previous written consent of the Lessor first being obtained such consent not to be unreasonably withheld ...'

As can be seen, this is just a basic consent procedure, and we can compare it to the 'consent' restriction described above.[2] There is no doubt that provision for the lessor granting a licence *could* be incorporated in a residential lease, but it would be greeted with the same shouts of horror that we talked about in connection with consent restrictions, and if anything the shouts

2 See p 91, above.

would be even louder against a licence provision, simply because it is virtually never used in a residential lease.

C. DEED OF COVENANT

The use of the deed of covenant procedure is normally confined to freehold properties which share common areas (by definition external ones) and it is described in detail in another part of this book[3]. The financial implications involved would normally be service maintenance ones, so that although the procedure could just as easily be applied to leasehold property, in so far as it related to the management programme, it really would be taking a sledgehammer to crack a nut if it were also to be applied to mere ground rent.

There is no point at all in repeating in this chapter what is already contained elsewhere, but the author can assure readers that to include reference to deeds of covenant in this discussion is not especially outlandish, because he has seen at least one lease in use where the deed of covenant procedure is used to enable the lessor to keep track of his lessees. Nevertheless, for all practical purposes, we can discount the procedure.

D. SUMMARY

Before we move on to the next chapter, we would do well to briefly review the reason for our discussing these various procedures.

A great number of residential leases contain no more than the normal requirement on the lessee to give his lessor notice of an assignment etc., having occurred. This puts the burden of notice completely on the lessee, and allows the lessor no procedure which will give him knowledge of what is happening with reference to movement of ownership of flats in his building either *before* or *during* those movements, as opposed to *after*.

The author has been accused of having a bee in his bonnet about this, but surely it is not good management to set up a flat scheme where there is the possibility that movements of ownership can take place without the lessor ever necessarily knowing about them? Surely a good management scheme should give the lessor the facility of keeping track of the movements as they happen, so that no-one can move into a flat without his knowing the identity of that person?

This is precisely what the 'notice' restriction described in this chapter achieves. The various steps in the process have been described. They are simple enough, and the requirement on the lessee to give not only a notice of actual assignment, with fee, in the usual manner, but also a notice of pending assignment, which does not involve any question at all of a consent procedure is surely small enough penalty to pay for knowing that the management of his flat is professional.

3 See ch 19, p 222, below.

CHAPTER 8

Management: introduction to the options

Management is a subject which is approached with horror by too many people. Lessees particularly either do not understand what a good management programme can do for them, or they fear it, for that very reason; and lessors are sometimes even bigger offenders in not appreciating the potential of good management.

The subject matter of this book is horizontally-divided units, although brief mention is made[1] of vertically divided units (ie houses) having service charges attached to them, even when sold on a freehold basis.

Horizontally-divided units can be subdivided into flats and maisonettes, and elsewhere in this book we have already discussed the differences between these two species[2]. The main feature of a maisonette is that it should be capable of being treated as a completely separate unit, not being subject to any common areas especially internal ones and thus service charges, although in some cases there will be a service charge relating to shared *external* features. But with flats, there will be many things which will be shared: the main structure of the building, and internal and external common areas. The problem about these kinds of common areas is that responsibility for their upkeep will not be able to be parcelled out totally amongst all the flat-owners.[3] This means that some sort of central maintenance programme is going to be necessary. Depending on how the developer approaches the particular development, that programme is going to be anything between minimal and total. It should be noted that we mention as the crucial factor the attitude of the developer rather than what the particular situation calls for. This is undoubtedly the wrong way to approach the subject, but it is all too often what those advising a developer will have to cope with.

In other parts of this book, we discuss the various types of developments within the general descriptive terms of flat development, and we look at the variations on the management theme which are required to be applied. From study of these variations we can see that, although in nearly all cases of flat development some sort of centralised system of management is required, the intensity of management varies greatly between the different types of schemes under consideration, and from this we are able to progress to studying what sort of administrative organisation is necessary in order to cope with the particular management.

For instance, a sheltered housing scheme,[4] where there will certainly be a

1 See ch 19, p 222, below for a description of service charges on freehold properties.
2 See ch 1, p 1, above, for a discussion on the difference between a flat and a maisonette.
3 But see ch 9, p 110, below, on the specialist 'studio flat' scheme.
4 See ch 22, p 250, below.

warden to look after all the old dears, clearly calls for some sort of professional management. Usually, of course, a sheltered housing scheme will be administered by a housing association, but there is nothing that says that this is an absolute necessity, and it is quite possible for one to be run by any organisation, including the developer himself,[5] other than a housing association. Nevertheless, a sheltered housing scheme is probably one of the highest forms of the art of management, so that anybody attempting to take it on would need to be properly geared up for the constant administration which would be required. Also, the developer would presumably wish to carry on building other sheltered housing developments, some time, somewhere, and he would not be likely to get many customers for subsequent developments if he were unable to prove that he could provide adequate management for his existing sites.

Thus it would have to be an extremely organised developer who took on management of something at the sheltered housing end of the management spectrum. On the other hand, if all he were building were a few blocks of small studio flats, interspersed with freehold plots, he might well retain management of those, because first the actual management would be minimal, perhaps little more than cutting grass and paying electricity bills for the common areas, and second the actual administration would be minimal.[6] He might not make any sort of profit from running such management, but he would at least totally or almost cover costs, and even if there were a shortfall it might well be worthwhile to carry this, when viewed against the profits to be derived from selling the units in the first place.[7] But why accept a shortfall anyway? This would only occur if the developer sold such studio flats with an extremely low ground rental, with equally low maintenance charges, containing no 'padding' to enable his own administration costs to be covered.

The foregoing is illustrative of the wide spectrum which constitutes management options open to the developer. But it is not only in management that he has an option; he also has one relating to his reversionary interest. Unless his development is so structured that his income on ground rents is covering his actual management costs, eg on the studio flat scheme described on pp 110–127, below, there ought to be a ground rental income which is quite separate from any maintenance income. The difference between these two categories will be that ground rental income will be free income, and only the costs of collection are to be debited against it; maintenance income will, in the main, be *recovery* of expenditure already incurred, and will include only a modest amount as a 'turn' for the manager.[8]

The options thus open to the developer may accordingly be summed up as follows:

1 Full retention of reversion *and* management.
2 Full retention of reversion, but contracting out the management in some way, ie either:

5 But intending purchasers would do well to make absolutely sure that the developer could cope adequately with the management level required.
6 See ch 9, p 110, below.
7 Provided there *are* any profits! This end of the market has been very cut-throat, with the major builders paring down prices as far as possible.
8 See ch 17, p 186, below, for a discussion on the profitability permissible.

(a) by sub-contracting it out, eg to an agent, who will take it over in consideration of being able to make a reasonable profit out of it, or
(b) by incorporating in the leases of the units the joining in of a management company, so that right from the start the developer is relieved of the responsibility. The management company itself could be
   (i) a tenants' management company, or
   (ii) a management company completely outside the control of the developer, or
   (iii) one within his control—ie an associated company.

3 Dispersal of reversion, and management. By dispersal is meant sale on, not the contracting out of collection of rents, presumably in consideration of an agency charge.

These are not the only options open to the developer. We have already discussed the *degree* of management to be incorporated into any particular development, but these options will be reviewed and decided upon by the developer (and presumably his professional advisers) before the development starts, whereas only the management options described above will have to be decided upon before the start of the development and the preparation of the documentation; those relating to the reversion can be decided upon after the selling programme has got under way.

It is exceptionally difficult to discuss such options in a book of this sort; to a certain extent it is useless attempting to do so. Far better that all the surrounding circumstances are weighed up, and the developer and his solicitor decide on what sort of treatment is required. Thus, the problem is a subjective one. Also, a good number of those advising developers will know all about these problems anyway, but there will be those who do *not* have any first-hand knowledge of what line to take. It is the author's view that there will be an increase in the proportion of new leasehold units, ie principally flats being produced, rather than a decrease, simply because any given area of land is going to produce more units of this nature than, eg freehold houses. Land is becoming very much scarcer—indeed at the time of writing, the scarcity of land in some parts of the country is giving very great cause for concern to a good number of builders. Even if the Land Commissions 'Land Obligations' proposals[9] become law, this will only dispense with the reversionary, ground rent, aspect of the matter, and we will still be left with maintenance; thus the problem will really be very little different.

No single chapter can hope to achieve the answer to everyone's problems when deciding which maintenance road to take. This one is only intended to be an introduction—to let the reader get the 'feel of the water', or—if he has some experience of the subject—to remind him of the salient features, but we *can* attempt to collate the most important points to take note of, as follows. The various aspects referred to are all treated in much greater depth elsewhere in the book; this table should be treated as an exercise in orientation, so that the correct course may be selected. The table highlights the salient points, and adds commentary on each one.

9 See ch 28, p 309, below.

PRINCIPAL POINT	COMMENTARY
1 Isolate the income potential.	1 There are two principal heads of post-completion income for the developer and/or his successor in title in a development of flats. These are: (a) ground rent, and (b) profit element on maintenance payments.
2 Ground rent. Impose or not?	2 There is nothing which says the lessor *must* impose a ground rental at all. The rental which may be reserved can be anything in between: (a) nothing; and (b) the highest imaginable figure.
3 What if no ground rent is imposed?	3 This, as we have seen, is perfectly possible. But it is probably unwise from both lessor's and lessee's points of view, because: (a) as far as the lessor is concerned, by not levying any ground rent at all, he is thereby depriving himself of what is virtually free money (see point no 5). This is especially the case because most lessees will expect it anyway—there does not seem to be any sales resistance. (b) as far as the lessee is concerned, he will probably expect to pay anyway, but he may even feel uneasy about a lease which contains *absolutely* no provision to pay rent. He probably will feel happier with any payment, even a peppercorn.
4 What would be the main reason for not levying a ground-rent?	Sometimes, it is unwise to levy a ground rent because the development will simply not stand for it. In former years, flat developments tended to be sold to purchasers who were, shall we say, rather more wordly-wise about their liabilities than some of today's purchasers. Whilst we are looking at the more traditional type of block of flats, sold to people with a reasonably business-like outlook on life, then we can continue with properly built-up service charges, and separate ground rents, and expect not to run into trouble. But a great deal of these small leasehold units are being sold to first-time buyers, who probably have little or no knowledge of

PRINCIPAL POINT	COMMENTARY

such matters, and the less they are likely to be confused, the better. If this means dropping the ground rent, then so be it. Further, and this tends to be much the more overpowering factor than the former, in all probability the unit is being sold to somebody—perhaps a young couple starting out on their home-buying career—who is up to, and perhaps beyond, the limit on the mortgage, who will only just be able to afford a modest service charge,[10] and for whom a demand for a ground rent payment may be the last straw, and which may be ignored. True, the lessor has the right to start proceedings in respect of any unpaid amounts due to him,[11] but the last thing he will want is to have to get involved with proceedings.

Therefore the developer must keep an eye on:

(a) the sort of price the properties are going to be sold at, and the archetypal purchaser (this would extend to subsequent purchasers) with his or her income band;

(b) the recurring costs to which an owner of the unit will be subject; and

(c) how (b) will have an effect on (a). If he arrives at a conclusion which points to a very tight budget, he might be well advised to drop the idea of a separate ground rent, *unless* his ground rent was supporting in part or in whole the services provided to the units.[12]

5 Assuming a ground rent is charged: how much, etc?

5 If a separate ground rent is charged and not in the 'studio flat' category as above,[13] the developer will have to decide how much he should charge. As we saw above, anything may be charged. However, we are here in this book concerned only with flats sold on a long lease, with a premium being taken, so that it is extremely unlikely, for instance,

10 See, eg ch 20, p 228, below which discusses urban renewal properties, which are sold to a market of this sort.

11 See ch 27, p 297, below.

12 Eg the studio flat scheme described in ch 9, p 110, below.

13 Ibid.

PRINCIPAL POINT	COMMENTARY
	that any ground rental would get up to the level where it would make the tenancy a protected one, ie where the rent was more than two-thirds of the rateable value as at the appropriate[14] day. The actual amount of ground rent charged in practice varies, but the lowest seems to be about £20 per annum,—this being the figure which was set by a number of the major housebuilders for their studio flats programme, admittedly in 1981, so that inflation ought to have brought the figure up to £25/£30, thus representing about the lowest annual ground rental which may be economically charged. (Incidentally, although the example quoted is the studio flat scheme, where the ground rental provides a substantial cover for administrative costs,[15] this is irrelevant in the present discussion: the figures quoted have been used extensively on pure ground rental cases as well.) A median figure appears to be about £50–£60, with the top figure for all but the most luxurious types of development around the £100 per annum mark. At this level, the owner of the flat is being asked to pay £2 per week in ground rent, before he even starts on the maintenance payments. It would have to be a fairly up-market development which called for a ground rent of this proportion, or higher.
6 Should the ground rent be subject to review?	6 There is a school of thought amongst some practitioners which propounds the theory that a ground rent, once set, should not be subject to review. The author can see no reason why this should be considered an acceptable theory. If there is going to be a ground rent in the first place, then there is no reason why it should not keep up with inflation. That, after all, is basically what a review of a *residential* ground rent is attempting to do in these inflationary times. In any event, if the reversionary interest is going to be of any interest as an investment, there really has to be a review mechanism.

14 The Rent Act 1977, s 5.
15 See ch 9, p 122, below.

PRINCIPAL POINT	COMMENTARY
7 If there is a review mechanism, what should it be?	7 This is where we get into some difficulty. It is suggested that the reviews should aim to keep up with, and possibly stay slightly ahead, of inflation. The trouble is that no-one has any real idea of what inflation is going to be. The review mechanism has to cope with: (a) frequency of reviews; and (b) how the reviews are calculated. This category is further subdivided into: (i) reviews which are quantified in the mechanism, eg 'YIELDING AND PAYING THEREFOR from the date hereof until the 24th day of June 2018 the yearly rent of £50 from the 24th day of June 2018 until the 24th day of June 2051 the yearly rent of £75 and for the remainder of the term hereby granted the yearly rent of £100'; (ii) reviews which are only decided as to amount by operation of a formula set out in the lease; probably a formula relating to market value but possibly one attempting to bring the relationship of the ground rent to the value of the flat or the block in which it is situate back to the status quo as at the commencement of the term.[16] On both frequency of reviews, and the potential amount of the reviewed rent, the most important aspect to bear in mind is the possible operation on any particular review mechanism of the provisions of the Rent Act 1977 and the Housing Act 1980. These are discussed at length elsewhere in this book[17] and the practitioner *must* consider them before he settles on his review mechanism. Incidentally, the reader is warned not to lean too far to the side of caution. The author was once involved in setting up a holiday village scheme where brick-built chalets for holiday occupation only were being built for sale at a premium on a

16 Eg the mechanism used in the studio flat scheme—see Precedent No 3, cl 1 (e) (i), p 362, below.

17 And see generally, ch 4, pp 19–67, above.

PRINCIPAL POINT	COMMENTARY
	63-year term, with reviews every seven years. The reviews were pre-set at 12½% every seven years. At the time of the inception of this scheme—it was in the very late 1960s—inflation was not the dreaded animal it has since become, indeed it is doubtful if in those distant days the man in the street would have recognised the term 'inflation'. It was appreciated by those setting up the review mechanism, though, that some sort of protection should be built into the leases. The author well remembers how intense the deliberations were, and when the 12½% lift every seven years was finally settled on, we really did think that this would make the ground rental income inflation proof! What the consolidated rate of inflation between 1969 and 1983 was, heaven only knows, but it must have been many, many times the actual lift in rental income of just a little over 25%!! In those circumstances, and with hindsight, it would have been so much better to have used the 'getting the rent back to the status-quo' mechanism already discussed.[18]
8 Ground-rent income: keep it or sell it? (a) Keeping it.	8 (a) Unless the ground rental income is being used to service, in whole or in part, an embryonic management programme[19] it should be available as an investment. The rental income itself should be free of any expenditure, except that required to collect it. Thus, in itself it is an, admittedly modest, asset, and if the lessor is so minded, he may be happy to receive it for ever and a day. Even in these circumstances, the lessor has options, thus: (a) he may collect it himself; (b) he may appoint agents to collect it. In this case he would presumably be charged an agency fee by those doing the actual collecting. This might vary between, usually, 5% and 12½%;

18 See above.
19 See ch 9, p 123, below.

PRINCIPAL POINT	COMMENTARY
	(c) he may leave collection to the management company, if one is involved, and they may act as an agent in the manner described above. This is the more sensible option, rather than having ground rent and maintenance collected by two different collectors. It can only be confusing to the owner of a flat to have two different people collecting what to him looks like the same thing. If it is absolutely necessary, then it has to be done this way (eg if the lessor has sold on his reversion) but those responsible should aim to cause as little confusion as possible to those from whom they are collecting.
(b) Selling it.	(b) There are plenty of people interested in purchasing ground rents, as an investment. There will be adverts in the professional press, and there will also be mail shots directed at solicitors from time to time. There should thus be no problem in finding someone to buy out the right to collect the ground rents, ie purchase the reversionary interest, but the problem will be when terms are discussed. For the uninitiated—and the author apologises to those who regard this as elementary—ground rents are valued at a formula of 'years purchase'. Thus, if one had a ground rent of £50 per annum, and sold it on a 10 years purchase basis, the selling price would be £500.
	The number of years purchase depends very much on circumstances, including the state of the country's economy at any given time. However, as a very rough guide only, the usual range one is going to encounter will be between four and a half years and nine. If we take a median figure of six years purchase as a likely selling price, and if there were ten flats in a block, with each having a ground rent of £50 per annum, the total annual income would be:
	$$£50 \times 10 = £500$$
	and the anticipated selling price of the ground rents would be:
	$$£500 \times 6 = £3000$$
	Little enough, really, in today's terms: so little that the option of retaining them

PRINCIPAL POINT	COMMENTARY
	and the developer collecting them for himself becomes more attractive. Nevertheless, it is usually a matter for the owner of the reversion to decide.
9 Maintenance: minimal or normal? (a) Minimal	9 (a) We have already briefly touched upon the 'studio' scheme of minimal maintenance[20] which is designed to keep as much communal maintenance as possible away from the lessor, and load it on to the unit owners themselves. This might in theory work with anything up to the larger and more expensive flat type of developments but in practice really only works for the really small units built in equally small blocks. For a full description the reader is referred to pp 110–127, below but very briefly, the idea is to demise appropriate portions of the common parts—roof, foundations, corridors and staircases, external areas to the unit-owners themselves, leaving either no communal parts or minimal amounts in the direct ownership of the lessor. The unit owners have to deal with their own maintenance, and the lessor is left with those items of maintenance or management which just cannot be left to the unit-owner, like grass-cutting and electricity supply to the common parts.
(b) Maximum	(b) For 'maximum' we really ought to substitute 'ordinary' because the ordinary idea of management is that the flats are sold, leaving the common parts of the block and external areas in the ownership of the lessor. Thus the roof, the foundations, the external walls, all the internal corridors, staircases, halls, lifts and lift shafts if there are any, etc, will be centrally owned and maintained. Quite who will be responsible for that maintenance depends on how the development is structured (see below) but whoever it is will be under a duty to carry out, directly or indirectly, the maintenance and then they will re-charge it to the individual flat-owners in the proportions, which will (we hope) be laid down in the documentation.

20 See above.

PRINCIPAL POINT	COMMENTARY

The two types of management scheme, minimum and maximum, can easily be contrasted.

(a) For a very small number of units, in small blocks, minimum is perfectly workable, and has the very great advantage that the lessor or whoever owns the reversion is left with very little more than a supervisory role. It can be an answer for a developer who wants to sell properties with as few residual hang-ups as possible. However, that developer must make quite sure that the way he sets up his scheme is good enough not to (a) give him any problems on disposal, and (b) give any subsequent vendors of the flats similar problems.[1]

(b) For anything other than a small block of uncomplicated flats, there is a danger in using the 'self-help' principle, and the developer would be best advised to use some form of full management scheme. What anyone interested in a flat must always bear in mind is that, unlike a house, whether detached, semi-detached or terraced, where the owner of it has total control, and may have it looking just as neat and tidy or otherwise as he wishes, without having to rely upon anyone else, a flat-dweller owns a property which itself is part of a whole, and he *must* satisfy himself before he buys, that adequate provision has been made for the upkeep of the common parts.

The difference between these two illustrations is crucial, and is referred to throughout this book. The developer must structure his maintenance plan according to all sorts of external influences. Unless he comes up with a reasonably workable scheme, he may find that the flats will not sell at all well.

As readers will have gathered by now, this is nothing whatsoever to do with the legal niceties of flat conveyancing, but is about a pragmatic, commercial

1 See ch 9, p 110, below.

PRINCIPAL POINT	COMMENTARY

approach. The conveyancer must be equipped, first to understand the approach, and second, if necessary (which it sometimes will be) to guide the developer client to a scheme which in all the circumstances is appropriate. It is also important for those advising purchasers of such units to be able to identify if the management schemes fit the physical features of the flats.

As always, it is best to quote examples.

A. First, consider a small block—perhaps no more than ten in number—of flats which themselves are small, probably studios/one-bedroom properties. The block they are built in is simple, it has no complicated aspects, eg the external common areas are probably either grassed or tarmac/concrete footpaths and parking spaces, the internal common areas are probably finished in minimum maintenance features—facing brick walls in corridors, hardwood window frames/doors, stairs and so on. Now the units are small, so they are being sold at prices fairly low down in the price band for flats. This means that they are being sold to people whose status will probably only just support a mortgage, or the other category of purchaser for this type of unit, which is someone who is likely to be away from it a great deal. Thus the conclusion of both developer and his adviser would or should be, that the maintenance programme should be as basic as possible—this meaning low service charges—even using a form of the 'self-help' scheme,[2] because:

(i) the flat-owners who are on a tight budget just cannot afford anything other than a modest service charge;

(ii) even those in the other category discussed above will have no expectation of paying anything more than modest service charges, because of the nature of the development—ie simple features, easily maintainable finishes, etc; and

2 Yet again, refer to ch 9, p 110, below, describing the 'studio flat' system of maintenance.

PRINCIPAL POINT	COMMENTARY

(iii) if the block is built in this manner anyway, there is just no need for a large and/or complex maintenance scheme.

So that to attempt to saddle such a block with an all-out management scheme is folly, and what should be sought is the lowest possible scheme, utilising as much 'self-help' as possible.

B. The other example at the opposite end of the spectrum is the larger type of flat—usually anything from two bedrooms up, although there is nothing to say that a studio or one-bedroom unit cannot be included in this type of block, especially if it happens to be in a metropolitan area—in a complex block, complete with lift, lift shaft, sophisticated security apparatus, wall-papered internal corridors, with carpeting on floors and staircases, external grounds with complex finishes, both on the soft and hard areas, perhaps even a porter with his own flat or lodge. The people buying units in a block of this sort will be paying fairly high prices for their properties, and not only will they anticipate having fairly expensive service charges, they will expect those services to be provided for, both within the framework of the documentation, and also on a practical level. It would therefore be quite ludicrous to have anything other than a proper and full management scheme, however the management was to be dealt with, and any developer who attempted to do otherwise would probably pay for it with unsold properties. Certainly those acting for intending purchasers would be advising clients that the unit did not have the support of an adequate management scheme.

Now, the author can hear the choruses of the sceptics already—asking 'why are we being asked to read a considerable chunk of text which only tells us what is logical anyway, and which every conveyancer worth his salt ought to know in the first place?' The answer is that the author doubts very much if *every* conveyancer in the land knows anything of the sort, and

PRINCIPAL POINT	COMMENTARY

there are a good many developers and those working for them, who are in a similar position; or, they may possibly have the knowledge but desire to sell flats with the wrong sort of management scheme hooked on to them, for various reasons, some warranting accusations of culpability, others not.

This unfortunately is the way the job works, despite what those with high expectations of themselves and others, may think. The author recently had experience of an example of this sort of thing, and which illustrates that very often it will be up to the professional adviser to put his developer clients right—and also that it will be up to those advising purchasers of units that those units have got (or not got—as the case may be) a sensible management scheme attached.

The development concerned was one of about 40 units on a piece of land which had been reclaimed from a disused railway track by the simple expedient of removing the whole of the soil of the embankment which had previously been there and upon which the railway had run; thus leaving a reasonably wide site. Unfortunately, there was a bridge at one end of the site, which had to remain, and the soil was graded down from the top of the bridge to the new ground-level of the site. In order to prevent the likelihood of children clambering up this slope to the bridge, from which they could then easily have fallen, the planners quite rightly insisted that the slope be properly graded, grassed, and protected at the bottom by banks, ornamental beds, etc. The development itself was also more complex than usual. It was all flats, grouped together in admittedly small blocks, but those blocks themselves had rather more detailed treatment to, particularly, the internal common areas. The external common areas on the site were a little bit more than the usual grassed areas and ordinary tarmac footpaths. In other words, the site required management, and yet the developer client was desperately trying to keep his prices down as

PRINCIPAL POINT	COMMENTARY
	far as possible, and this included the incidental costs to the purchasers like service charges. We started off with the client demanding that the development could be treated in the same way as the 'self-help' maintenance scheme used on studio flats. Although one supposes this would have been just technically possible, that is, one could have created the documentation to give effect to it, the building societies involved would not, or should not, have accepted it, nor should solicitors acting for purchasers have acquiesced in it, nor indeed should the developer have contemplated it, had he been thinking of the long term effect on his reputation. In the end we arrived at a moderate management scheme, with as much shaved off as was possible without seriously affecting the future of the site.

SUMMARY

As can be seen from the preceding narrative there are a fair number of options open to the developer, and it is important that he appreciates what they offer him and how and when he can use them. Obviously his legal adviser should be able to offer guidance as and when necessary. The difference between a development of freehold houses and one of flats, or including flats, is significant. With the former there is really little choice. With the latter, there is a choice, but the trick is knowing which option to choose.

CHAPTER 9

The 'studio flat' scheme

Throughout this book there will be found references to 'studio flat' schemes. Different references relate to different aspects of the scheme, but, especially given the present economic circumstances, the importance and relevance of these schemes is undeniable, and thus a short chapter wholly devoted to them is required.

The term 'studio flat schemes' itself is something of a misnomer; it was so named because it was originally applied to studio flats, but it very quickly became clear that other types of flats could just as easily be dealt with in that particular manner.

Before we launch into a description of this particular variation of selling flats, it might be helpful to consider the background events leading up to the introduction of the concept on a large scale in 1981.

A. THE BACKGROUND

In times past, the average small housing unit sold on a speculative basis was the semi-detached house. Certainly in the immediately pre-war years, and then the fifties and the sixties, the average estate development consisted of row upon row of semi-detached houses. This was in the days of relatively cheap land, which was in any event not too difficult to find, and of which there was a fairly plentiful supply. Labour and materials were also relatively cheap, thus making the semi-detached house the unit which the average buyer, very often the first-time buyer, looking for a moderately priced property would choose.

Then, as we moved into the seventies, inflation began to bite, causing the price of labour and materials to escalate, and land became at the same time scarcer, and more expensive. The net result was that the semi-detached house became relatively speaking very much more expensive than it had been.

This caused housebuilders to start moving the emphasis down the scale to the terraced, or town house, and throughout the seventies this was the typical small unit, especially for the first-time buyer. But by the end of the decade, as the housebuilding industry stood on the threshold of the eighties, even the terraced house was becoming expensive to produce, and there was pressure on the industry to devise some sort of unit (in the end, it proved not to be designed for families—see later) which was smaller, more compact, and thus cheaper both to build, and to buy. If this unit happened to be more sparing in its use of land, then so much the better.

B. THE SOLUTION

The first, intermediate, step was the 'back-to-back' house: that is to say, the pair of semi-detached houses further divided *vertically* so that what one arrived at was a squarish unit comprising four individual dwellings, one at each corner, each having a downstairs and an upstairs just like any other house, but generally smaller—the archetypal unit of this sort having a living area with kitchenette downstairs, and one bedroom and a bathroom upstairs, with possibly a spiral staircase (to save space, but nevertheless providing at the same time a pleasant feature).

The back-to-back house caused problems, not only with the planners, but also with the interpretation of the building regulations. These were overcome, but the planning problems (which also were solved) arose anew with the next step downwards which the industry took; the small block of small flats.

It is important to acknowledge that it was not only maximum utilisation of space, both in terms of floor area and land, which spawned this type of unit, but also the increasing sophistication of the housing industry itself. For so long, builders had taken a guess at what the 'punter' wanted, and built row upon row of what they hoped were the right types. Not for nothing was the term 'speculative housebuilder' coined.

Now, however, modern market research techniques were applied to the job, and it was found that there was an untapped market. That market was one of well over 100,000 people who wanted to own a housing unit but did not already do so, who had the necessary status for mortgages, and who were looking for a small, self-contained unit designed for 'singles' which carried as little responsibility as possible from the point of view of day-to-day maintenance. The people who were interested in this type of unit were single or divorced, in occupations like nursing, teaching, and the like.[1]

This type of market had not previously been considered by housebuilders, *at least as a market in its own right*. The combination of the realisation of the presence of this unsatisfied sector of the buying public, and the continued pressure on builders due to spiralling land prices, and the cost of labour and materials, led to the launch of the 'Studio Solo' by Barratt Developments at the Ideal Home Exhibition of 1981. The unit in question was approximately 250 square feet in area, and was built in blocks of six or eight in two-storey form, and usually twelve in three-storey form—which latter variety was fairly rare, only being found in heavily urban locations. The resulting very small blocks of flats were not generally built on special sites of their own, as had previously been the norm with flats, nor on some secluded enclave within a normal residential housing site, but were interspersed with housing of all sizes and varieties. So that a block of studio flats might be found nextdoor to a row of terraced housing, or a detached four-bedroomed house, or as the case might be. The flats were so designed that their elevations made them most difficult to distinguish from those of an ordinary house and the blocks

1 Apparently the average profile of the initial studio flat purchaser at that time was; female, 30-ish, single, in an occupation like teaching, nursing, etc.

being very small in the first place, they were difficult to distinguish from any of the other types of housing on the site.

Whilst the author does not put forward the proposition that a small block of flats had never been built on a housing site before, he does suggest that never before had flats been intermixed with other housing to this degree, and with so little visual effect on the eye of the casual beholder.

On the introduction of these studio flats, certain difficulties were experienced with planning authorities, but in time these were overcome. On the other hand, no resistance of any sort was encountered from the buying public, and it soon became clear that the market research identifying a potential market of over 100,000 purchasers had not been over optimistic. Very soon all the major housebuilders were producing their own version of the unit, but the archetypal unit was, and still is to a very great extent, the 'Studio Solo' produced by Barratts: a unit which was followed by 'Studio Two' with just a touch more floor area, and a slightly different configuration, and designed for two *permanent* residents as opposed to one.

Since the days of introduction of the Studio Solo, the method of management devised has been extended, either wholly or in part, to other, larger types of flat. Indeed, the Studio Solo concept of management is now applied to a broad spectrum of units.

C. THE BASIC FEATURES

Initially the author was given a brief to produce a set of documentation for this type of development, including outlines of management. The main points of this brief were that:

(a) the furnishings were to be included in the initial sale of the flat, and if possible were to be tied to the lease by the legal documentation;
(b) no attempt was to be made to sell the flat on a freehold basis;
(c) a scheme of management was to be devised which
  (i) divested the company selling the flats of any residual responsibility,
  (ii) gave the purchasers of the flats as little control over their management as possible,[2]
  (iii) cost the purchasers as little as possible in the way of service charges.

Taking these points one by one:

1 Furnishings

There has been a desire in the housebuilding industry for some time that one should be able to produce a housing unit into which a purchaser might walk without having to provide anything other than linen, crockery, cutlery and personal knick-knacks. Obviously this would only be possible with the first-time buyer market, although that has not prevented some builders from supplying certain items, eg white goods and carpeting to sectors of the market beyond the first-time buyer.

2 Within the confines of the Housing Act 1980, Sch 19: see ch 14, p 159, below.

The studio flat schemes provided the opportunity of testing out the idea, so that the typical studio flat was, and still is, sold with:

carpeting;
curtains;
furniture—reasonably comprehensive range—something a little better than a very basic selection;
white goods;

so that a purchaser of such a unit really would only have to find linen, crockery, etc.

Initially, the leases of these flats included reference to a schedule of furnishings, and thus the furniture in the flat was 'leased' itself, with the idea that it would be an integral part of the flat itself, both from a legal and a practical point of view. However, this proposal did not get very far, not because it proved impossible to lease the furniture—after all, plenty of office equipment, etc is leased, and there is nothing which says that furniture in the situation we are describing cannot be the subject of a lease; but rather that in the first place the building societies, as the principal mortgagees, were discounting the cost of the furniture completely anyway, because under the Building Societies Acts they were unable to advance money on the security of a lease of furniture,[3] and in any event it was very soon realised that attempting to tie in the furniture pack with the lease itself would produce problems simply because the furniture would wear out much quicker than the flat itself would, so that after a few years part of the subject matter of the lease would have wasted away.

Thus this concept very quickly went by the board, but it did not stop the furniture pack being included in the price; now it is sold *outright* to the first purchaser, and it is up to him and subsequent owners whether or not the furniture is passed on to purchasers.

2 Freehold or leasehold?

The prohibition against a sale on a freehold basis was fairly normal; indeed selling on a freehold basis would have been virtually impossible, at least given the present state of the law.[4]

3 Management

By far the most important aspect of the whole scheme was what the management structure would be. Several different possibilities were canvassed, these being:

3 Eg see the Building Societies Act 1962, s 1 (1).

4 And see ch 28, p 309, below, on the Law Commission's proposals on freehold flat conveyancing, and ch 3, p 13, above, on the possibility of conveying flats on a freehold basis given the present state of the law.

(a) *Tenants' management companies*

To appreciate the full difficulties involved in such organisations, the reader should refer to ch 13, above,[5] but for these very small units in blocks which themselves were small the use of this management vehicle was out of the question because:

A. If a company was set up for each block, there would have been a tremendous administrative burden. Remember that we were talking about a builder with about 500 active sites, each of which would have an average of two or three of these blocks. Getting one tenants' management company away is bad enough: 1,000 plus would have been a nightmare, and in any case the cost of administration would have been unacceptably disproportionate—and someone would have had to pay for it. To expect the tenants to do so would have been going beyond the bounds of what was fair, and for the developer to accept it would have been crippling.

B. If having one tenant's management company for each block was going to be unworkable, would it have been any better to group together all the blocks on any given site? Probably not, because:

(i) it would still have produced far too many individual management companies;
(ii) it would not have worked properly because the different blocks on the same site were being sold at different times; and

C. Next, (and this was one of the main points for consideration in the management question as a whole) the ownership of the studio units would be more transitory than the normal flat or house, and it was also likely that there would be a higher proportion of absentee owners.[6] Thus there would never have been sufficient interest on the part of the unit-owners in running their own management company.

D. Finally—and even if there had been no other objections this one would have killed the whole idea—tenants' management companies can produce so much aggravation, for both sides, that a substantial proportion of the developer's staff dealing with their transfer to the owners would have ended up as potential candidates for the funny farm—and that is not an altogether facetious remark.

(b) *Mutually enforceable covenants*

These are discussed elsewhere in this book[7] where the reader will have seen that the principle is a poor solution for the particular problem. As opposed to the previous option, the size of the studio blocks would have helped rather than hindered, had this route been chosen, but again the administration on the part of the developer would have been too burdensome.

5 P 131, below.
6 These views have been borne out by practical experience.
7 P 17, above.

(c) *Contracting management out*

This might have worked especially for a smaller builder with only a relatively small number of blocks on a few sites, but the documentation would have had to have been very carefully settled, and because of the overriding necessity of keeping service charges as low as possible, it is questionable whether a commercial management organisation would have seen much to attract it in the scheme.

And so, going back to the requirement for a system of management which was as cheap and simple as possible, after a good deal of thought the system as described below was arrived at. No-one says that any part of the scheme is revolutionary, no doubt every aspect of it has been used from time to time in some particular circumstances, but what was new about this scheme was that the various facets had never before been used all at the same time, and on such a scale. Not that scale is vital for the operation of such a scheme—the scheme works with low, and medium volumes as well as high numbers. The scheme which was eventually evolved took the following form:

(d) *The developer wishes to retain as little residual liability as possible*

On a normal flat development, the unit-owners will take a demise of their flat, and they will normally only take rights over the common areas, both inside and out. These common areas will include the 'shell' of the building—roof, foundations, main structural walls, etc. The common areas will remain vested in the lessor, or the manager, and in return for looking after them he will charge the unit-owners a service charge.

This was not acceptable in this scheme, because first it would create large chunks of residual property in the shape of common areas still in the ownership of the developer. Second, there would thus have to be a service charge for looking after it.

And so instead of setting up the conveyancing exercise like the normal flat scheme, what happened was the block as a whole was demised away to the unit-owners, each of whom received an appropriate share of the common parts, so that at the end of the conveyancing exercise on each block, there was quite literally nothing left for the lessor except its reversionary interest.

The author has always used the analogy of 'building blocks' to illustrate this. The 'blocks' are made up as follows:

(a) first, there are the eight blocks each of which comprises one flat unit itself. Except for the usual rights of emergency access, and for service rights, if any are necessary, there is an exclusive demise of these areas. All the other parts of the demise are of common areas and are subject to general rights in favour of all other unit owners and any others entitled;
(b) next come the blocks which make up the common areas. These are the blocks of roof and roof space above the upper flats, the blocks of roof and roof space above the internal common areas, ie corridors, the blocks of foundations beneath the internal common areas and the blocks comprising the appropriate portions of those internal common areas;
(c) finally, there are the blocks comprising the appropriate parts of the structural, ie external walls;

(d) all these blocks together comprise the whole of the block itself.

The important point to note is that all these blocks are part of the eight individual leases; these are split up into an 'exclusive' demise of flat and a 'non-exclusive' demise of common areas, but nonetheless the *whole* of the block is taken out of the lessor's ownership, save for his reversionary interest.

The external areas are split up between the flats, leaving nothing to the lessor[8]. Thus what happens is this:

1 The developer builds the block of flats, and puts them on the market.
2 He executes a lease in favour of each unit-owner, but every individual lease comprises not only the flat itself, but also portions of the common areas of the block.
3 When he has executed the lease of the last unit in the block, he has effectively demised away all his direct interest in the block and its surrounding area.
4 All that the developer has left is his reversionary interest, and assuming that he wishes to take no further part in what goes on in, on or about the block of flats, he can then execute a concurrent lease of his reversionary interest in favour of whoever is going to 'manage' the block.[9] If he wants to be responsible for this himself, then naturally he needs to execute no such document.

The theory of this scheme is that with the lessees taking the whole of the block, there is nothing left in the way of common areas for the lessor/manager to manage. That means that there are no service charges, which in turn means that the units (which themselves are modestly priced, given that they are studio units) are all the more saleable, not being burdened by heavy management charges.

The only snag about this concept is that it just does not quite work. The lessor still runs up against the basic fact of life as applied to flats that is, where individual flats share common areas. Somebody has to take the responsibility for those areas, whether or not they are included in the unit lease, or retained in the ownership of the lessor. But the studio flat scheme we are describing here does go a long way along the road towards the lowering of costs.

To take the matter further, we must first consider the matters which have to come under some sort of central control. These are as follows:

(e) *Insurance*

Whilst maisonettes are generally able to accept the responsibility of insuring themselves, there is no way in which a block of flats, however small either in the number of units involved or their overall floor area, can adopt anything other than block insurance.[10] Therefore someone has to effect block of flats

8 See as an example, the description of the demise in Precedent No 4, p 369, below.
9 He could also sell the freehold, but the value would be negligible, because of the way in which the scheme was set up, and by retaining a reversionary interest, he maintains his potential investment, however, illusory. It does him no harm to do so.
10 And see ch 4, p 43, above, on insurance generally.

insurance, pay the premiums, and recover the proportionate part from the unit-owners.

(f) *Common electricity*

When the first major studio flats scheme was launched in the early 1980s, some thought was given to hooking in each light on landings and in corridors to the circuit of a flat, so that there would be no common electricity costs. Alternatively, consideration was given to linking the common area lighting circuit into the meter of one flat only—to be chosen at random, and charging less for that flat initially in consideration of the fact that it would have to bear the costs of the corridor lighting. Neither of these ideas was adopted in the event; the first because there were technical objections to it, the second because it was, let us face it, a senseless idea in the first place! The only really sensible solution to the problem was to have a landlord's supply separately to the common areas. Accordingly, the only way to deal with the matter is by having the lessor pay the common electricity charges, and then re-charging the appropriate proportion to the individual flat owners.

D. OTHER MAINTENANCE MATTERS

Included in this category are items such as:

(a) *TV and radio cable rental*

If there is cable radio, or TV piped into the block of flats (and the planners might specify this, as well as the lessor favouring it) then if the developer has to enter into a contract with the cable company which encompasses a rental payment, the appropriate proportion of this has to be passed on. However, it may just be that the supplier recoups its rental by charging the consumer direct. It all depends on the particular circumstances.

(b) *Entry-phone systems*

In view of the fact, as already discussed, that this type of development seeks to cut costs as much as possible, it is not likely that there will be an entry-phone system. Sometimes, though, circumstances demand one, and again the rental would have to be paid centrally and recharged proportionately.[11]

(c) *Grass cutting*

Planning authorities may very well insist that there is some sort of garden ground adjacent to the block of studio, etc. flats. The developer has therefore to choose the most easily maintainable surface, and also the cheapest to install. There is virtually no choice, in that grass is by far the cheapest to install, and also to maintain, or it should be. There is only one problem with

11 And see ch 16, p 182, below, for further discussion on entry-phone systems.

grass, and that is that it grows! In winter it is the perfect material, in that no maintenance of any sort is needed, but from April to October it has the distressing habit of growing!

When Barratts first launched their Studio Solo scheme, it was decided that the soft external common areas, ie in the main grass, should be parcelled out in the same way as the corridors, ie a portion to each individual flat (obviously with appropriate rights and reservations built in to it). Each flat-owner was to have the obligation of mowing his or her own portion of grass, just as they were to shoulder the burden of maintenance of all the other parts of the common areas, both internal and external, demised with the flat.

If those of us who were responsible for setting up the exercise had possessed any commonsense at all, and the author must take a lot of the blame here, we would have known that such a scheme would never have worked, for the following reasons:

First of all it is too much to expect that all the flat-owners in the block will be public spirited enough to mow their little piece of grass every week or fortnight throughout the summer. Second, those who do not mow their portions might not be in default deliberately, (eg they might be absentee tenants—a category which is fairly common with this sort of flat). Third, those who do attend to their obligations will become incensed at those who do not, and then at the lessor for letting this state of affairs come to pass. Fourthly, if some flat owners cut their portions of grass and others do not, the resulting checkerboard effect will look totally ridiculous, much more so than if the grass had not been cut at all. Fifthly, if those who are cutting the grass take it upon themselves to cut the other parts which are being ignored by recalcitrant flat owners, feelings of resentment will again spring up. In fact this is what generally happened in the scheme being described, and it did nothing for the relationship between the flat-owners and the developer. Finally, the first design of the blocks provided no storage areas in the common parts, so that there was nowhere to keep a lawnmower, and anyway who amongst the flat-owners would want to buy, or even contribute to the purchase of a lawn mower?

So this particular aspect of the scheme just did not work: but at the same time it is a good illustration of how important such a seemingly trivial matter can be. The developers first interpretation of how the scheme was to work in relation to grass cutting only served to mar the outward appearance of the completed blocks of flats, and for good measure it tended to strain relations with the flat-owners.

It also serves to illustrate that one cannot properly devise any scheme for a block of flats (as opposed to, eg blocks of maisonettes)[12] which obviates the necessity for maintenance, however minor. This means that there is only one way to treat grassed areas, even in low-cost blocks of flats, and that is to include it in a management programme. Admittedly, apart from insurance and common electricity charges, it might be the only item in that programme, but it is a necessary evil which apparently cannot be circumvented. As to how much this increases the annual cost to the flat-owner if professional grass cutting firms (of which there are plenty in every area of the country)

12 For a discussion on the difference between flats and maisonettes, see ch 1, p 1, above.

are given the contract is questionable, but the cost will not be absolutely minimal.

However, there are ways to cut down on cost, eg by cutting every two weeks instead of one when the growing season is at its height, and every three, or even four, weeks when the grass is not growing so strongly. And there is always the possibility, which the lessor should investigate, of providing the block (ie those with the necessary storage facilities!) with a reasonably cheap mower and persuading one of the flat-owners to be responsible for the cutting, making the appropriate financial adjustments between that person and the other owners. The trick is to get as cheap grass cutting as possible.

(d) *Miscellaneous items*

Depending on the nature of the flats, and their particular situation, there might or might not be other items of maintenance which should be dealt with in a maintenance programme. However, the whole concept of this scheme is that the recurring costs to the flat-owners are cut down to an absolute minimum so that as little as possible should be done centrally, and as much as possible should be given to the flat-owners to deal with.

E. HOW IS THE MAINTENANCE MONITORED?

If a developer is selling flats in such a block he needs to know that they are going to be looked after reasonably properly. It will do him no good for the block to fall into a state which dissuades potential customers from taking an interest in his future developments. They might look at an advert for Bloggs Ltd's new flats, and say to themselves 'We don't want anything to do with Blogg's flats—look how much of a mess his block at such and such a place is in—if we buy one of these new ones, the same may happen to us.'

Therefore, the developer, whether he retains the reversionary interest in the block, or he transfers that interest to some third party, has got to make sure that the maintenance situation is monitored.

How does he do this?

There are several ways, as follows:

1 Full-scale management

Either the lessor/manager might have a management function within his own set-up, or he can depute the task to an independent management company. But this is not really feasible, because the cost of monitoring will have to bear what will be substantial overheads. And there will have to be added into the maintenance charge a completely out-of-proportion management fee. This would be unacceptable to the parties on a practical level and there is the possibility that it would be questionable under the provisions of the Housing Act 1980.[13]

13 See ch 14, p 159, below, for commentary on the effect of the Housing Act 1980.

2 Use of agents

Wherever the block is, it is bound to be within an area where there will be an estate agency which will practise estate management. This is a stronger possibility than 1, above, but it is still unrealistic because of the potentially high costs. Agents normally charge on a percentage of the service charge, but no agent would accept that payment structure in this case because he would be on a percentage of almost nothing. Thus the management fee would again be out of proportion.

3 Self-help and ground rent

In case the above heading looks peculiar—which it undoubtedly does, we should explain that the ground rental income on a block of studio flats should be used for management purposes. The idea that the income from this source is an investment, or a potential asset, should be abandoned right from the start. No such block is large enough or important enough for the rental income to be hived off from the service element, and it makes extremely good psychology on the part of the developer to set the thing up in this way.

Before we examine this aspect of the matter, though, we shall look at the practical application.

'Self-help' means that the person who is charged with the organisation of monitoring the maintenance—whether he be the original developer or, eg a concurrent lessee[14] actually does it himself.

This can be done in two ways.

First, if the blocks of flats are within reasonably easy driving distance of the office of the lessor/manager, he can visit them himself and monitor the way in which the flat-owners are looking after them.

Second, if the blocks are too far away to be visited easily, he can appoint someone local on a part-time basis to carry out the visits. This is what was done on the national scheme in which the author was involved: the blocks which were coming under management were going to be scattered around England and Wales, so the country was divided into 12 different areas, and in each of those areas advertisements were placed in the local press for part-time 'inspectors'. The response was fairly substantial and it was interesting to see how many suitable people were keen to do this type of job. Very few of them were attracted by the money (see below)—indeed the great majority of them were people like retired police superintendents, estate agents, company directors, etc (one of them even turned up for the interview in his Rolls Royce). All of them were interested in a *very* part time job to combat partially the boredom of retirement. They were all high calibre people, so that the job of inspection was in good hands.

What actually happens on the inspection is that, say, four times every year, the inspector visits the block, armed with a check list and he checks off items such as whether or not the corridors are being kept clean, etc, etc. The check lists are sent back to the central office, and if anything looks suspicious,

14 Refer to ch 10, p 128, below on concurrent leases.

then it is followed up, either by writing to the tenant concerned, or sending the inspector back for a supplementary visit.

The cost of using 'inspectors' in this way is fairly modest. An average rate is something in the order of £6·00 per block per visit (1983 prices) plus luncheon allowance and mileage. We will refer to this cost later in this section, but of course if the lessor/manager does the inspections on an in-house basis, there will be no actual fees to pay out. Although a proportion of overheads, probably costed out on a similar basis, will have to be allocated to the cost of management.

F. THE COST OF 'MONITORING' MAINTENANCE

We now have to look at the cost of this type of maintenance from both sides.

1 The flat-owner

Based on the above narrative, the owner of the flat will be faced with some regular payments which, if he opted for a house instead of a flat, he would not be burdened with. These payments will be as follows:

(a) *Ground rent*

Whilst this would not have to be paid in the case of a house, ownership of a flat almost inevitably brings with it a ground rent, so that in imposing rental on these small flats the developer is doing no more than is expected of him, and the purchaser will not find it strange that he is expected to pay rental. That being the case, how much should the rent be? A fair figure would appear to be around £25 per annum. At £12·50 per half-yearly payment, this is surely a figure any flat owner can cope with. The figure will be subject to review, but probably only at lengthy intervals.[15]

(b) *Insurance*

This is naturally a payment which any property-owner would have to make. The only difference in this situation is that there is a block policy, and the lessor recoups the appropriate proportion from the individual flat-owner. Possibly by negotiating a good block policy rate, the lessor is getting a better deal for the flat-owner than he, the latter, would have been able to negotiate for himself. If we take a flat with a price of £25,000, insurance at 10p% (for a block policy, not an unattainable figure) will be £25 per annum, which is a very modest sum. Depending on the type and complexity of cover which the policy sets out the rate could well be higher, but the rate quoted is perfectly feasible.

15 And see ch 4, p 56, above. for a discussion on rent reviews.

(c) *Common electricity charges*

This of course is like asking how long is a piece of string. They will tend to vary but an average cost per quarter per block of eight small units will be £10–15, including standing charges, if charged, so the cost per unit per annum will be say an average of £8.

(d) *Grass cutting*

Again, this depends, totally, on local circumstances, but experience shows that an average cost per block *per year* is in the region of £200. The lessor has the choice of charging out once during the summer, or spreading the cost over the two half-yearly demands. This seems much the more sensible, so that the cost per flat per half year would be £12·50 and the annual cost £25·00.

(e) *Miscellaneous*

It should be possible to get the majority of blocks without any miscellaneous charges, so for the purpose of this exercise we shall ignore this section.

Therefore, to sum up, the typical annual cost to the owner of a unit in a block of this sort is:

Ground rent	£25·00
Insurance	£25·00
Common electricity (say)	£ 8·00
Grass cutting	£25·00
	£83·00

which seems entirely reasonable, when compared with full maintenance programmes on flats very little larger.

2 The developer/manager

Unlike the last heading, we are here concerned with both expenditure *and* income:

(a) *Income*

(i) Ground rent. Assuming the block to be an eight-unit one, the ground rental income will be £200 per annum, based on a rent of £25 per unit.

(ii) Insurance. Again, assuming the average price to be £25,000 per unit, giving at 10p% a payment of £25 per unit, a commission rate of 20% should be able to be negotiated with the insurers. Thus there ought to be commission of £40 per annum in each block. The author has known management companies which juggled with the rate of insurance, for example, charging the tenants, say 10p% whilst having negotiated a rate of 8p% with the insurers, thus giving themselves another 2p% on the whole block. This can be a significant amount—thus on total cover per block of eight × £25,000 ie

£200,000; 2p% is £40. However, this is not only questionable on moral grounds, it is probably contrary to the provisions of the Housing Act 1980, Sch 19.[16]

(iii) Assignments. In the example scheme (and refer also to Precedent No 3, cl 7, Fourth Schedule p 366, below) the fee levied on an assignment was 0·1% of the 'notice value', which basically meant the consideration given for the unit, or if it was a non-monetary transmission (eg on a death) the consideration last given for the unit. Taking the average price of a unit of this sort as, yet again, £25,000, 0·1% of this is £25, which seems high, but the author can assure readers that almost without exception it has been accepted both by incoming purchasers and their advisers. The rate itself may be adjusted if those setting it feel it to be a little too weighty, but the point about calculating the assignment fee in this manner is that it keeps up with inflationary trends in housing values. How many of us have had to deal with notices of assignments attracting such paltry fees, sometimes as little as £2, that it costs money to deal with them rather than them providing an income?

The question then remains: how many assignments can one expect to receive in each year? Probably no more than an average of one per block, but perhaps more, because these small flats tend to change hands more often than larger units. Even at one per block per year, we produce extra income of £25. (Incidentally theoretically an accompanying mortgage falls to be dealt with in a similar fashion on an assignment, but this would produce a massive registration fee, quite out of proportion to the exercise in hand, and it would seem proper to remit any accompanying fee, indeed possibly phrase the notice clause accordingly.)

(b) *Expenditure*

(i) Site costs. These will consist of the inspectors' visits, or visits by whoever is managing the property locally. Let us say that in the scheme under review, we have opted for the inspector system, and we are paying each inspector a little more than the £6 per visit we specified earlier. Say the fee is £7·50 and a similar sum is devoted to luncheon and mileage. This gives £15 per block per visit.

We have already seen that a visit every quarter is desirable. Greater frequency than this is probably pointless: lesser frequency may be dangerous, perhaps three times a year is just about reasonable, but no less. Sometimes there are problems, and the inspectors may have to be asked to go back. Experience shows that over the whole spectrum, one extra visit per year will be called for. Extra visits may be more expensive.

(ii) Overhead costs. All this activity on the part of the lessor will cost money, in the effort that he puts into controlling the programme. But rather than attempt to calculate this now, let us see what the management equation looks like.

16 And refer to ch 14, p 166, below, for commentary on Sch 19.

Example:
A block of eight units with an average value of £25,000. Insurance at 10p%, one assignment per year, and four regular, one special, inspector visits per year.

Income will be:

Ground rent = 8 × £25	200.00	
Insurance commission	40.00	
Assignment fee	25.00	£265.00
Expenditure will be:		
4 regular inspections	60.00	
1 special inspection, say	25.00	85.00
		£180.00

The operating profit per block is £180 but before everyone rushes out to set up this sort of scheme, remember it is an *operating* profit, not a net profit, and it is out of this £180 that the overheads of running the scheme have to come. Furthermore, the above equation depends on:

(a) £25 per annum being a reasonable ground rent (which it undoubted is);
(b) the lessor being able to negotiate a favourable commission rate with the insurer. This should not be too much of a problem;
(c) there being one assignment per year. Experience shows that there are likely to be more, rather than less, but nothing can be guaranteed;
(d) the lessor being able to find the right people to carry out the inspections. Do not forget that it will cost money to find, and train these people (in however rudimentary a manner). Also, if the lessor does not have many blocks it will be that much more difficult and indeed probably considerably more expensive, to find such persons, who will be looking for some sort of reasonable volume. Nevertheless, if the lessor does not have many blocks, this will probably mean that those that there are will be near his home base, so he might be able to carry out the inspections himself (and probably thus get an even cheaper service!);
(e) there being no really awkward flat-owners, What happens if:
  (i) dogs are kept locked up in flats for unreasonable periods of time, and bark themselves (and the other flat-owners) silly?
  (ii) dogs are allowed to foul corridors?
  (iii) motorbikes/car engines and other large odds and ends of mechanical gubbins are kept in corridors?
  (iv) flat-owners have noisy parties all night long?
  (v) flat-owners get up to naughty activities in their flats, and in so doing make so much noise their neighbours are disgusted and annoyed?
  (vi) flat-owners threaten to jump out of their windows in order to do themselves some (perhaps fatal) mischief on account of the behaviour of their neighbours?

All these examples actually happened—only the names have been suppressed to protect the innocent! It is when this sort of thing happens and further inspections have to be made and a lot of time devoted by the lessor to sorting out the problems that the buffer profit quoted at £180 per block begins to look less attractive. Do not lose sight of the fact that out of this £180 the following matters have to be coped with:

1 Arranging for the grass to be cut on a regular basis, and paying the contractor's costs.
2 Paying the common area electricity bills.
3 Paying the insurance.
4 Dealing with any other common matters for payment or organisation.
5 Collating all the above, apportioning it to each flat, adding the ground rent and sending out and collecting against demand notes twice a year.
6 Liaising with the inspectors, instructing them, paying them, and going through their check lists which they will send in on each block, four times a year.
7 Dealing with the assignments.
8 Attending to any correspondence, etc arising out of the general management scheme, and out of particular problems.
9 Carrying financial costs, eg unless some arrangement for spreading payments has been made with the insurer (which is quite possible) and if the scheme grows beyond the very small stage, the lessor may find himself being called upon to pay the insurance premium and have to wait at the very least several weeks before he has collected all the tenants' payments in. This sort of situation can creep up on the lessor quite insidiously.
10 Carrying specific costs relating to unpaid accounts of recalcitrant tenants, and laying out further money on pursuing them.
11 Dealing with and paying for the administration of the scheme: eg if there are a considerable number of blocks involved it might be wise to computerise the records—but this costs money.

Thus, if any particular block has a bad record, there is the possibility of loss, but on an average basis, there should be a modest profit per block.

G. ENFORCING THE MAINTENANCE

The very large drawback of this system as compared with the more traditional methods of management, where the lessor actually carries out the maintenance and then re-charges it, is that the lessor has to 'monitor' the property to see whether or not the work is being done. This is a very real problem, because it is always much easier for a lessor/manager to enforce a financial commitment than one which involves some sort of action being taken by the flat-owner.

Nevertheless, some way has to be found to ameliorate high service charges. The Government is sufficiently concerned, at the time of writing (1984) about service charges on flats escalating to the point where they become an impossible burden for tenants to have set up a committee to study the problem.

The unfortunate aspect of maintenance schemes is that even on a small, uncomplicated block, a full management programme will be expensive, probably completely out of proportion to the type of property involved. As considerations of land availability mean that builders are likely to build more blocks of flats than less, some sort of compromise has to be found, and this scheme as just described is an attempt at an answer. The writer has seen just such a scheme in operation for about four years, and it does work, perhaps to the surprise of some cynics.

The problem comes when maintenance is not performed by the flat-owners. Basically, there are two options open to the lessor as follows:

(a) regular monitoring should take place—perhaps under the inspection system described above, and recalcitrant tenants should be put under pressure at an early stage, with action resorted to in the case of non-cooperation;[17] and

(b) Undoubtedly it might be considered wise to add to the lease a proviso charging as additional rent the cost of any work which the lessor has to carry out as a result of the tenant failing to comply with his or her obligations. A right for the lessor to do this work must also be incorporated.[18] If this happens the lessor would have to be careful to co-ordinate work properly, eg redecoration of internal common areas, where each flat has responsibility for a particular portion. What if some tenants are willing to carry out their part of the work, but others are not, and the lessor has to step in to do it? It would be possible to coordinate different sections, but it would be much easier for the lessor to suggest that he did *all* the work, and recharged appropriate proportions. Indeed, the lessor might pre-empt such a decision by making that proposition in the first place. But then surely we are back to traditional management? The answer is not completely, because everyday jobs like cleaning etc, are still being performed by the tenants, and it is those jobs which really run the costs up on a full management scheme.

H. CAN THE SCHEME BE USED ON LARGER UNITS?

The scheme as described was devised for very small studio flats built in small blocks, with a very simple design. The scheme works well enough with that type of subject, although the purists tend to frown on it, but it does keep the service charges down to a manageable level, which is what it is all about. Would it work on larger units?

The answer is, as so often, 'it depends'. And what it basically depends on is size and complexity of the development. For instance, something with a lift in would not be a suitable subject for anything other than a full management scheme. But provided the block is reasonably small—say no more than at the outside 12/15 flats in the block—and uncomplicated, the fact that the units themselves are one-, two-, or even three-bedroom units need not necessarily make any difference.

17 Refer to ch 27, p 297, below for a discussion on enforcement action.
18 See Precedent No 3 cll 1(f) (v), p 363, and 6, Sixth Schedule, p 367, below.

Probably the decision as to how far to take the scheme will depend on marketing variables more than anything else, because there are still a good number of locations where nothing but a full management scheme will be acceptable if the properties are to sell.

I. MORTGAGES

Any mortgagee will be concerned to know that the property being taken as security for his loan is managed properly. When the Barratt Studio Flat scheme was introduced in 1981, the author spent a great deal of time explaining the management system to the building societies.

The very great majority of societies approached were quite happy once they saw that, although centralised management was being dispensed with to a great extent, total ultimate control was nevertheless to remain in the hands of the developer and there was a viable management function remaining.

In the author's view, this system has in many ways more to commend it to a mortgagee than, eg a flat in a block controlled by a tenants' management company.

Nevertheless, the developer intending to introduce one of these 'studio flat' schemes, whether small, medium or large, should consider consultations with a number of building societies, on however informal a basis. The fact remains, though, that there are now in existence thousands of such flats, the great majority funded by the building society movement.

CHAPTER 10

The concurrent lease

The principle of the concurrent lease in a leasehold development situation was not new when it was adapted for at least one major builder's 'small flats' scheme a few years ago, but it had not previously been used to the extent of that scheme which involved exposure to very nearly every conveyancer in the country. As a result, the principle has been questioned in some areas, so that it demands some detailed explanation here.

The specific situation in which the concurrent lease principle has been used most over the last few years has been in the sale and subsequent management of small units, where there is a high level of 'self-maintenance' by lessees and a low level of maintenance of common areas by the lessor, but nevertheless with a requirement on the lessor of *monitoring* the 'self-maintenance'.[1] Those companies actually building and selling the flats were not interested in carrying out this monitoring service themselves, and indeed very few builders or developers would be, so that a system for shifting the administrative burden had to be found.

The exact way in which the schemes for self-maintained flats are set up and organised has just been described, but the principle of the concurrent lease is dealt with here. It should not, of course, be supposed that the concurrent lease principle is synonymous with the selling of small, 'self-maintained' flats, or vice-versa; it can be used in any situation.

The whole system has been known to 'fox' people, so that it is probably best explained on a 'step-by-step' basis.

1 As the grant of a concurrent lease necessarily involves the lessor divesting himself of his basic interest in the property, there must be a settled intention on the part of the lessor *not* to have anything to do with direct management of the units. Otherwise, if the lessor were to be so involved, there would quite simply be no point in executing a concurrent lease at all.

2 There are two types of lease to be considered: First, the unit leases relating to the individual flats in the block, and second the concurrent lease. Let us assume that we are dealing with a block of flats in a block, which comprises not only the building containing the flats, but also common garden ground and other amenity areas (including parking spaces or perhaps garages and accessways and footpaths).

3 The first leases to be granted will be *all* the unit leases. Until this happens, the concurrent lease should not be granted. This is because the concurrent lease is a lease of the lessor's *reversionary interest* in the block—if he has not let all the flats, he will have more than a reversionary interest in part of the block. If he does grant the concurrent lease before he grants all the

1 Refer to previous chapter for a full description of the 'studio flat' scheme of management.

leases of the flats, then it would be the concurrent *lessee* who would be in a position to let the unsold flats. This might be acceptable if the concurrent lessee is associated in some way with the lessor, as sometimes happens, but most certainly not if he has no business connections with him. As usual, there is an answer to the problem, and this is that if the lessor wishes to deal with the concurrent lease before he has sold all his flats, he grants leases of those flats to nominees.[2]

4 When all the flat leases have been granted, the concurrent lease is granted. As we have seen, the concurrent lessee may or may not be associated with the lessor; the largest flat management programme in the country at the present time uses the concurrent lease principle, but the various lessor companies and the concurrent lessee are all part of the same group, although it is true they are all completely separate business personalities. Nevertheless, the relationship may be nothing more than a formal business one.

5 The objects of the exercise as far as the lessor is concerned, are:

(a) he will divest himself of his interest in the block, and so effectively he can forget about it, apart from any income it is producing for him. There is one slight flaw in this statement, as readers who are better technical conveyancers than the author will already have spotted, and that is that he will theoretically remain responsible in contractual terms for any breaches of covenant to his original lessees. Frankly, the author has always regarded the possibility of any untoward consequences of this slight problem as being almost totally in the realms of theory. In practice it is unlikely to cause any problems; and
(b) whilst divesting the lessor of his interest in the block, insofar as any *direct* involvement is concerned, the use of the concurrent lease retains a financial interest for the lessor, that is by way of ground rent.

6 This aspect of the ground rent available to the lessor is usually the only reason for using the scheme, but there is a subsidiary one.

First of all, the principal aim of the exercise is to provide the lessor with a regular income from the block, as well as the development income he has received from the initial sale of the flats (we are assuming that the owner of the reversion and the developer are one and the same persons). Therefore the amount of the rents on the individual flats will be tied closely to the rent which will be paid under the concurrent lease. This may be smaller than, or greater than, or the same as, the sum of the individual rents; unless the concurrent rent is a great deal less than the sum of the individual unit rents, the income is going to be at the very worst, moderately worthwhile for the concurrent lessor, and at best a tidy sum.

In order to illustrate this, let us take a block of flats comprising 15 units; which is not a terribly large figure. Say the ground rent on each of the units is £50 per annum; this again is not an outrageous sum. The rental income on the block will be £750 per annum. The concurrent lessee would collect this for himself, and he in turn would have to pay a rent to his concurrent lessor. It is probably unlikely that he would want to pay more than £750

2 And see ch 4, p 56, above on rent review patterns generally, and the effect thereon of the Rent Act 1977 and the Housing Act 1980.

per annum, although there is nothing to say that he could not, because then there would be little or no turn in the deal for him. He could well be paying £750 per annum himself, and taking his profit on the deal by way of a management fee, but it is most likely that he will be paying a concurrent rent of something less than £750 per annum, so that he will then be able to take an income from the difference between the rent collected and the rent paid, *plus* the management fee. The trick on the part of the developer, or reversioner, if they are separate, is to offer terms which will make it an attractive management proposition. Assuming the concurrent lessee is happy, then so ought the lessor to be; because he will then have the option of sitting back and collecting his ground rental without, in practice, having anything else to worry about, or selling his reversionary interest, for however many years' purchase he can get on the market. This is a luxury of choice the concurrent lessor would not have had if he had not executed the concurrent lease. (Remember that the likelihood of one, probably commercial concurrent lessee *not* paying the rent is infinitesimally low as compared with the chances of, as in the example, 15 unit owners defaulting in some way.)

Second, rather than *trading-on* his interest in the property, the concurrent lessor will, if he does not sell his reversionary interest, eventually find the terms of the flat leases, and that of the concurrent lease expiring[3] so that the whole block vests back into his immediate ownership. Admittedly, this event might well be very far into the future; one cannot see an average modern flat being sold on anything less than a 99-year term, so that the reversionary interest would only fall in well after the developer had passed on to better things, and in any event none of us can predict what restrictions the legislation of 99 years hence will have on such prospective happenings, but it is a small thought to be taken into consideration.

7 As well as juggling with the respective ground rentals of the unit leases and concurrent lease, the respective terms can be variously set. Thus, the term of the concurrent lease could be shorter or longer (or even the same—although that would be unlikely) than the terms of the units. If it is shorter, then the concurrent lease will end before the flat leases do, and thus when they do end the reversion will fall in direct to the concurrent lessor. This seems to be much more convenient than the other way around, indeed there does not seem to be much logic in setting up the scheme in that way, nor does there seem to be any logical thought in having the terms of the flat leases end more than a very few days after the concurrent term.

Incidentally, the major flat management scheme which we referred to above,[4] and which uses the concurrent lease principle, uses it for slightly different reasons; these are discussed elsewhere.[5] Readers are also referred to Precedent Nos 3 and 4 pp 360 et seq.

3 Subject to the respective terms having been judged correctly; see below, item 7.
4 Refer to item 4 above, p 129.
5 In ch 9, above.

CHAPTER 11

Tenants' management companies

The basic idea behind a tenants' management company is that, once the developer has completed the sale of all the flats, the management of the block is handed over to the owners of the flats. Whether or not the tenants' management company also takes over the developer's reversionary interest in the block, which interest may carry with it a ground rental income which will be virtually a net figure, is an open question, the answer to which should be decided by the developer at the start of the exercise.

Probably, if there is going to be a tenants' management company, it is better to transfer the reversionary interest along with the management, rather than separate them, if only to prevent the tenants from feeling that they have been burdened with management but not blessed with the reversionary interest with which they can act as their own lessors!

This may seem a rather facile statement to make, but the author has been involved with both varieties of tenants' management companies, and although in practice both can be desperately difficult to hand over to the tenants, the version without the reversionary interest is probably always the more difficult, just because the tenants feel they have been missing out! It is difficult enough to get the company away, without making artifical difficulties, and the only advantage the developer will probably get from the separation of the reversionary interest and the management is a capitalised sum for the ground rent.[1] That is, assuming that there are any ground rents. If the developer is looking to trade on his reversionary interest, then one supposes that he will create ground rents, although as we have seen in different parts of this book, there is no rule which says that one *must* have ground rents, indeed, where the management company is going to be handed over lock, stock and barrel to the tenants, including the reversionary interest, there is a very good argument for *not* reserving ground rents, because the tenants will almost inevitably treat the ground rental income as part of the general income of the company anyway. It would be very unusual for the tenants themselves to sell the capitalised ground rents, but this could be a way for them to raise some capital to cover any unforseen expenditure.[2]

Before we come to a discussion of whether the developer should or should not include the ground rents in the package he is going to pass on to the unit-owners, we will look at, first, a brief outline of the nature of the use of companies in situations of this sort, and then consider the advantages and disadvantages of the resulting method of management.

1 Refer to ch 8, p 103, above, where the value of ground rents is discussed.
2 But only if the memorandum and articles of association of the company permit this.

A. THE USE OF COMPANIES

For both cases which we will be discussing, that is where the company will hold the reversionary interest and where that interest will have been hived off by the developer before the company is operative, the nature of the company to be incorporated is the same.

The classification of companies may be structured, first, into

1 public companies, and
2 private companies

and second, into

1 companies limited by shares,
2 companies limited by guarantee, and
3 unlimited companies.

Public or private?

(a) *Public companies*

In order to become public, a company has to satisfy the following requirements

(i) the memorandum of association must state that it is a public company;[3]
(ii) the company's name must end with the words 'public limited company', or the letters 'plc' which apparently are acceptable in place of the words,
(iii) the allotted share capital must not be below the authorised minimum which at the present time is £50,000.[4] The authorised minimum is likely to be changed by statutory instrument; and
(iv) the allotted shares must have one-quarter of their nominal value paid.

It is hardly likely that any management company incorporated for the purposes at present under discussion would be a public company; there would be no advantage to be thereby gained. This is to be contrasted with, eg the corporate method of selling time-sharing discussed, ch 23, below.

(b) *Private companies*

Basically, the definition of a private company given in the Companies Act 1985, s 1(3) is as simple as it could be; a private company is 'any company which is not a public company'. No shares can be offered to the public, and there will usually be one or more articles in the articles of association of the company which restrict the transfer of shares. In the case of a tenants' management company, there will almost certainly be an article which states that only the owner of a flat in the particular development may be registered as a shareholder/member.[5] There will also usually be a provision in the lease

3 Companies Act 1985, s 1(3).
4 Ibid, ss 11, 45(2)(a).
5 There may not actually be any shares (see below).

that whoever is the lessee at any given moment in time will be a shareholder/member of the company, so that the whole thing is tied up pretty tightly.

It will thus be seen that the company is virtually certain to be a private company, indeed there would be no sense in any other course. As we noted above, there are three subsidiary categories, which we now come on to study.

(i) *Unlimited companies.* By the Companies Act 1985, s 1(2)(c) an unlimited company is defined as 'a company not having any limit on the liability of its members'. Thus, the members of such a company have the burden of unlimited liability. Incidentally, the difference between this sort of company and a partnership, where there is also unlimited liability, is that whereas the partnership itself has no separate corporate existence, an unlimited company does.

The only possible advantage that an unlimited company could have would be that by the Companies Act 1985, s 241(4) there is no statutory obligation upon it to deliver copies of its accounts to the registrar. This would seem to be no advantage at all for a tenants' management company so that we can dismiss this category completely.

(ii) *Companies limited by shares* A private company having a share capital is probably the most popular vehicle for tenants' management companies. Nevertheless, it is suggested that it should be discarded in favour of the next category for one very simple reason, that it if there are shareholdings there are going to be share certificates, and every time a flat in the development is sold, that shareholding will also have to be sold. Mention of this share transfer will probably have to be made in the contract which precedes the transfer/assignment of the flat lease, and there will be an extra piece of paper (ie the share certificate) floating around with the deeds. If any or all (which latter will be the case) of this can be avoided, so much the better.

(iii) *Companies limited by guarantee.* This is the vehicle which will avoid all the mumbo-jumbo associated with shares, as described above. Unfortunately, for some unaccountable reason, many practitioners seem to have little or no knowledge of companies limited by guarantee; lack of knowledge breeds fear, and so people shy away from the whole idea, which seems a pity.

The Companies Act 1985, s 1 (2) (b) gives the definition of a company limited by guarantee as 'a company having the liability of its members limited by the memorandum [of association] to such amount as the members may respectively thereby undertake to contribute to the assets of the company in the event of its being wound up'.[6] It is up to those incorporating the company to decide on the amount of liability quoted in the memorandum, but it will usually be a nominal sum, say £1: thus bringing the company into line with the situation which would have held had the company been one with a shareholding.

The features of a company limited by guarantee are probably best illustrated by a numerical treatment, as below:

6 See cl 5 in Memorandum, Precedent No 12, p 378, below.

(i) prior to 23 December 1980 (the relevant date under the Companies Act 1980) it was possible for a company limited by guarantee to be a public company. The 1980 Act stopped this: if a company is limited by guarantee, it *must* be a private company;
(ii) again prior to the passing of the 1980 Act, it was possible to have a company limited by guarantee *and* having a share capital. This has also been stopped—one can have either a company limited by guarantee, or one with a share capital, but not one with both features.
(iii) a company limited by guarantee is just as much a separate legal person as any other company.

The choice of vehicle for a tenants' management company therefore seems to fall between a private company limited by shares and a company limited by guarantee, which as we have seen will always be a private company. It is a matter of pure choice—presumably for the developer, but he will be guided by his legal advisers. Because of the unnecessary documentation associated with the company limited by shares, the author has always favoured the company limited by guarantee, and has never seen any reason to change his mind. Some practitioners and developers feel that that documentation is in itself an advantage, principally because the presence of a share certificate will tend to bring home more to the average flat-owner who is a member of a tenants' management company that he is indeed a member of a company, with the appropriate obligations as well as rights. This argument, it is suggested, is fairly specious.

B. THE ADVANTAGES AND DISADVANTAGES OF THE TENANTS' MANAGEMENT COMPANY

It is important for the developer to fully consider each option which is open to him insofar as management of his flat development is concerned. The tenants' management company has some very compelling attractions for the developer, but it has some equally, if not more, powerful drawbacks.

1 The advantages for the developer

(a) He is able to market his properties with the ability to tell the purchasers that he is granting them the right to control their own destiny so far as management of their block of flats is concerned. This is usually a very attractive selling point for *most* purchasers, if an illusory one.
(b) He will be able to look forward to the time, not very long after he has finished the building and selling of the block, when he can hand over the management to the flat-owners, and walk away from the development completely. This also is mostly illusory, as we shall see.

2 The disadvantages for the developer

(a) If he is divesting himself of the management of the block so early, he will probably not think it worth while to employ outside agents or a management company to look after the day-to-day management of the block from the point in time when the first flat is sold and the purchaser moves in to when the management company takes over. If the developer is collecting service charges from the flat-owners during this period, as one assumes he will, it is very easy for him to forget that he is still just as much subject to the provisions of the Housing Act 1980, particularly Sch 19, in relation to his accountability to the flat-owners as if he were managing the block on a permanent basis.[7]

(b) Far worse than the preceding drawback, though, is the difficulty he might experience in actually transferring the company to the tenants, despite what the documentation might say.

3 The advantages for the flat-owner

(a) The overpowering attraction for the flat-owner has to be that he will be totally in control of his own affairs. Here again the supposed advantage is illusory (see below under 'disadvantages'). Nevertheless, this advantage, which is about the only one there is for the flat-owner, is often puffed up to such a degree that one could easily believe that it was so important that everything else paled into insignificance.

4 The disadvantages for the flat-owner

(a) First of all, many a flat-owner who has been very much in favour of the idea of tenants' management company when he bought, has ended up despising it. Somebody will have to run the company, oversee the management, and be answerable. Those who take on these burdens are taking on something which is very much more than a sinecure.

(b) The whole concept pre-supposes that there will be some one or more persons among the flat-owners who are prepared to volunteer to run the company. If there are no such people, the whole body of the flat-owners may well be left high and dry.

(c) Very often, when there are owners willing to take on the various tasks associated with such a company, they will turn out to be a dominant minority who will tend to bully the others along, inducing in the silent majority a feeling that they are being ignored.

(d) One of the most serious disabilities of this system of flat management is that those who are buying the flats fail to check out what their expenditure on maintenance is likely to be. This happens because the developer will quote some figure to the prospective purchasers, which will persuade them that they will not necessarily be overburdened. The purchasers will have to rely on these quotes—they hardly have the expertise to carry out a detailed check on their veracity, nor, probably, have their legal advisers. No developer is going to quote to prospective purchasers maintenance figures which will put them off. Thus incoming purchasers should look very carefully at the figures they are quoted, because there is a

7 For further reference, see particularly ch 14, p 159, below.

strong chance that they may be incorrect—and it is not always a *genuine* mistake on the part of the developer which is responsible.

C. SETTING UP THE EXERCISE

When the developer looks at the pros and cons of using this system of dealing with management, the more *theoretical* advantages described above may very well outshine the more *practical* disadvantages, also described, and by the time the disadvantages have manifested themselves it will be too late. Nevertheless, the tenants' management company as a vehicle of management is still very popular, and we should next look at how it is done. This part of the chapter should be read in conjunction with Precedents Nos 10, 11 and 12[8] but readers should as always bear in mind that these precedents are but *examples* and there being as many ways of drafting a document as killing a cat are not necessarily intended to be followed slavishly. Nevertheless, they may serve as a useful starting point for readers.

1 The management company

Let us say we have decided that the tenants' management company will be a company limited by guarantee, which seems fairly logical if we are going to make the exercise as easy as possible.[9] The first step as far as the management is concerned, will be the incorporation of the company. This ought to take place at about the time that the site itself is being bought or as soon as possible afterwards, rather than leave incorporation until just before the hand-over to the flat-owners.

The main features will be as follows:

(a) *Memorandum of association*

As this document is the whole basis for the company's operations, it is important that it is drafted correctly, so that the proper conduct of its business is not impeded at a later date. The location of the registered office, and the name of the company, will precede the 'objects clause', which will set out precisely what the company is able to do.

The following is a précis of a typical objects clause for a tenants' management company:[10]

'The objects for which the Company is established are at [location of site].

(a) To acquire the (freehold or as the case may be) property together with the building erected thereon known as ... and to hold the same as an investment for the benefit of the lessees of the flats comprised in the said building.[11]

8 Pp 374, 376 and 377, below.
9 See ante on the subject of companies limited by guarantee.
10 For full text, see Precedent No 12, p 377, below.
11 Only if the reversionary interest is going to the company: see Precedent No 14, p 388, below for alternative wording when it is not.

(b) To collect the rents[11] and income of the property and to apply the same in the convenient and proper arrangement thereof. . . .
(c) To keep in repair renew rebuild decorate maintain and procure the repair . . . of the buildings erected on the property (and so on, referring to details of the management).'

There will follow other appropriate clauses relating to the required objects of the company, and finally, after the clause dealing with the liability of the members, there should appear a clause restricting admission to membership of the company. Thus:

'No persons shall be admitted to membership of the company other than the subscribers[12] hereto and the persons in whom from time to time are vested leases for terms granted originally for not less than . . . years of flats in the block of flats erected on the premises'.

(b) *Articles of association*

As the memorandum of association is the proof to the outside world of the company's right to existence, so the articles of association govern how it is actually run. To avoid possible problems over minorities of vociferous flat-owners ending up as the guiding force on the board of management, the articles should be drafted in as definite a manner as is possible, and no vagueness should be allowed to creep in.

Readers are referred to Precedent No 12, p 377, below for the full text, but the following points are worthy of note:

(i) Some mechanism is necessary for ensuring that ownership of a flat brings with it membership of the company, without the necessity of reliance being placed on the flat-owner to apply for membership. This can be achieved in a number of ways: the method adopted in our precedents is that the articles provide that initially the subscribers, and then all owners who apply in writing for membership, shall be members. If the matter were left here, then we would not achieve the automatic process referred to above, but the articles at this point are only half the equation: the other half is in the provisions of the individual flat leases themselves, which we will study very shortly.
(ii) It is important that the flat-owners do not have the opportunity of taking over the management until the developer is ready for them to do so. This will probably be when all the flats are sold. Were it to be otherwise, the developer would not have management control over the block of flats he is trying to sell, and would very possibly find himself in conflict with the flat-owners at the most inconvenient time. Thus, in our example, the articles provide that:

  1 until the subscribers cease to be members, the members (ie flat-owners) are not entitled to attend or vote at meetings; and

12 And see later, p 138.

2 the subscribers will only cease to be members when *all* the flat-owners have been registered as members.

So that there is no possibility of the flat-owners being allowed to take on the company until the end of the development. Equally they will *have* to take on the company then, because their leases oblige them to apply for registration as members.[13]

(iii) There is also provision that when a flat-owner transfers his lease, he ceases to be a member of the company.

(iv) The articles set up a representative governing body of the management company. For some odd reason, it appears unfashionable to refer to this as a board of directors, and it is usually called something like a 'council of management'.

(v) There are all the usual standard provisions relating to the internal regulation of the company.

(c) *Subscribers*

In order to incorporate a company, there need to be subscribers to the memorandum of association. These, in the context of a tenants' management company are the people who will be the first members of the company and who will be responsible for it until it is handed over to the true members.

The minimum number of subscribers for a private company, as the company will virtually be certain to be, is two, but it might be considered less unwieldy if a greater number are appointed. It might be thought wise to appoint a slightly greater number—say six, all of whom would fairly obviously be officers of the developer, or employed by, say, the developer's solicitors. The object of having more than the minimum required is that there is a sporting chance that at any given time, one or more of the subscribers will be ill, be away, have left the firm, or have found some other reason to be unavailable. In practice the presence, or signatures, of the subscribers will not be needed too often, but it is sensible to make sure that the two who might be required, eg to attest the seal, can be permed from a greater number.

2 The lease

As we saw above, the other half of the equation relating to the relationship between the company, the subscribers and the unit-owners is the unit lease itself.

This will be a fairly standard full management type of lease[14] adapted to the tenants' management company situation. Thus, there will most usually be present recitals setting out precisely what is happening:

'["The Management Company"] has been incorporated for the purposes of managing and maintaining the building and land and upon having granted the leases of all the

13 And see commentary on the lease, below, p 139.
14 Refer to Precedent No 14, p 388, below.

flats comprised in the building the Lessor intends to convey the freehold of the building and land to [the Management Company].'.
'The Lessee is or will become a member of the management company.'.

Later, in the body of the lease, there will be a covenant on the part of the lessee to regulate his membership of the management company.

In this context, first of all, there will be a covenant which will ensure that anyone to whom he transfers the flat will be a member as well:

'(a) Not to assign or transfer the demised premises except to a person who has committed himself to apply to become registered as a member of the management company.'

One supposes that at some time during the transfer process, perhaps by special condition in the contract, the incoming purchaser would be bound to make such application. In practice this will probably not happen, and (as we shall shortly see) subsequent convenants make this unnecessary.

Next comes a covenant which regulates the relationship between subsequent lessees of the unit and their purchasers, as opposed to that between the original lessor and original lessee. It is questionable that this covenant is strictly necessary, but its presence does no harm.

'That any transfer assent or disposition of this lease shall contain a covenant by the transferee devisee or disponee in terms of the preceding sub-clause (a) and if the land is registered an application for an appropriate restriction on the register shall be made.'[15]

There will then be a covenant binding the lessee for the time being to membership of the management company:

'that so long as the lessee retains any estate or interest in the demised premises he will not resign from or dispose of the rights and duties attaching to his membership of the management company to any person other than a mortgagee of the demised premises.'

This will ensure that the membership of the management company is not open to anyone other than those who have a direct interest in the unit. The reference to mortgagees is intended to put mortgagees in possession in the same capacity vis-à-vis the management company as the original owner of the unit.

Finally, the present lessee's relationship with the management company is dealt with:

'That if the lessee is not a member of the management company:
(i) the lessee will carry out the obligations attaching to members of the management company under that company's articles of association;
(ii) upon being requested by the lessor or the management company the lessee will apply to become registered as a member of the management company in any manner authorised by that company's articles of association.'

---

15 This contemplates a situation where the unit is initially unregistered, but might at a later date become registered. If it is registered in the first place, the application for the restriction would be there in the lease from the word go. See Precedent No 3, cl 8, p 363, below, and for further commentary, ch 7, p 86, above.

The sequence of events in the setting-up of membership of the unit owners in the management company is accordingly like this:

1 The first members of the company will be the subscribers, who will 'belong' to the developer, who thus retains his control over the company.
2 As each unit is sold, an application form for membership of the management company is obtained from each person who buys. This is not always done, some developers and their solicitors relying on either the recital which says that the unit-owner is or will become a member, or the simple assumption that the unit-owner will automatically be a member anyway. This is probably a dangerous assumption to make, given that there can be problems in getting the company away.[16]
3 Nevertheless, if such an application form is not obtained, reliance may be placed on the covenant in the lease that, upon being requested so to do by the lessor, the lessee will apply to become a member.
4 The subscribers choose when to resign, and under the articles, until they do so the unit-owners are virtually powerless.
5 When the subscribers resign, they date all the applications for membership and register the unit-owners as members. That means that under the articles they, the subscribers, automatically terminate their connections with the company.
6 From that point on, the unit-owners have total control over their own affairs.
7 On any subsequent transfer of any of the units, it is a requirement of the lease that the incoming purchaser commits himself/herself to become a member.

3 The reversionary interest

We discussed very briefly at the beginning of this chapter the question of whether or not the reversionary interest should be transferred with the management, or separated from it.

It is suggested that there is little point in separating the reversionary interest. There is no doubt at all that the flat-owners will think they are getting a much better deal if they do get the reversion, and its value to the developer on the open market will probably be negligible—certainly low enough that loss of a capitalised sum will make very little difference to him. In any case, the author has always felt that where a tenants management company is set up, it is wrong in principle to subject the flat-owners to a ground rent liability to an outside party.

Nevertheless, if the developer chooses to milk the development of every last drop of potential profit, the reversionary interest can be sold separately, and the documentation[17] is quite easily adapted.

On the other hand, if the reversionary interest goes to the management company, this is an equally easy procedure, and is best highlighted in the following points:

16 See later, p 141.
17 That is the lease (Precedent No 14, p 388, below) and the memorandum and articles of association (Precedent No 12, p 377, below).

(a) first, if the management company takes over the reversion, is there any sense in reserving a ground rent in the first place? Probably there is, if only to give the company a modest cushion of finance to play with. For example, a ground rent of £40 per year would not be at all out of the way on an average flat. Let us say that the management company, as soon as it is running the building, finds that it is costing more to manage than expected. It would always be possible to allocate the ground rent of £40 to management and so decrease the potential service charge by that amount, as long as the flat-owners agreed with this—and in the circumstances one would suppose that this would be certain to be the case. This will probably happen anyway;

(b) just as the developer could choose to sell on the freehold reversion for a capitalised sum, so can the management company although, given that the documentation will at that time contemplate that the tenants' management company will take over the reversion as well as the management, there will be some adjustments to make to the memorandum of association. In fact, although this is a theoretically possible option for the company, it is not one which is likely to be taken. It is all very well using a ground rental income to cushion a higher than expected service charge (see preceding paragraph) but to sell a reversionary interest for a once and for all sum in an attempt, as it almost certainly would be, to alleviate some at least of one year's service charges, would be an unwise move;

(c) the company may not realise they are getting the freehold reversion. Some care should be taken in explaining the exact position.[18]

D. ACHIEVING THE TRANSFER OF THE TENANTS' MANAGEMENT COMPANY

As with all parts of this chapter, what follows is just as important to the lessee as the lessor/developer. The practical approach to the transfer of the tenants' management company is of necessity viewed from a different vantage point than the study of the theory. There are many difficulties which can arise only too easily on the transfer, and the developer may find himself battered on all sides by angry flat-owners before he eventually manages to get the company away. Therefore, the following points may assist those acting for either side. They are taken in logical, chronological order insofar as the process is started.

1 The developer must not assume that his purchasers are going to understand the laid-down procedures of the transfer without some assistance. The documentation may be drawn in a lucid and rational way to a lawyer, but the average purchaser may have some difficulty in understanding it. This is very important because lack of understanding at this point will lead to problems later on.

How is the explanation to be given to the purchasers? There are several ways:

18 See below.

(i) *Through his legal advisers.* One would normally expect the purchaser's adviser to explain the transfer processes to his client. He certainly *ought to*, but sometimes this does not happen. This may be because, for example, he is working at such low rates that he cannot afford the necessary time to give the explanation. Or, he may be too blasé about the matter himself. There was once a client whose solicitor, when asking him to sign the contract, picked up all the supporting documentation (or 'bumph', as he called it) and threw it into the wastepaper basket, explaining to the client that it was all verbal diarrhoea anyway, and he (the client) didn't want to be bothered with it! (This, incidentally, is a true story but the solicitor retrieved the papers from his wastepaper basket as soon as the client left). There again, some legal advisers have some difficulty in understanding the process themselves.

(ii) *Via the sales outlet.* Whether the developer sells directly or via agents, whoever is responsible at the point of sale should at the very least give the purchaser a thumb-nail sketch of what the procedure of management is going to be.

(iii) *Via documentation.* Included in the documentation which the purchaser's legal adviser gets, at some stage in the transaction, there should be a hand-out explaining what is going to happen, why, and its effects.

2 Although not strictly necessary, it would be helpful if, immediately after completion, the purchaser was sent another reminder of the anticipated process of transfer of the company.

3 We saw earlier the sequence of events in the setting up of membership of the unit owners in the tenants' management company. In the author's experience, the following step is very seldom necessary, but as one never knows where problems are going to arise it is wise for the developer to obtain from the purchaser at some stage between exchange of contracts and completion, a completed written application form for membership of the management company. If there is any trouble at a later stage, the purchasers are absolutely committed to membership. From the purchaser's point of view, it is important that they have committed themselves to membership and that accordingly no-one, including the developer, can contradict that right.

4 The purchasers, once they start moving into their flats, would be well advised to set themselves up into an ad hoc residents' association. The developer would do well to encourage this. The reasons for doing this are fairly obvious:

(a) when the time of transfer of the company arrives, there will already be in existence at the very least a skeletal corporate structure which will effect the transfer the more easily, as opposed to starting from scratch;
(b) the flat-owners will have the benefit of an early, corporate voice; and
(c) from the point of view of the developer, he has a definite contact, rather than a lot of individuals. It will be equally important, once such an informal residents' association is set up, for it to open a line to the developer and make sure that he is managing the property in a correct manner, and that all necessary information is being given to the residents. From the developer's point of view, if the transition period be-

tween selling the first flat and handing over the company is so long that the end of an accounting period falls within it, he should make sure that proper accounts are shown to the residents.[19]

5 The developer should not decide on a date for the formal transfer of the company until he is satisfied that the building is in a completely satisfactory state to hand over. The residents should resist the developer as much as possible if he attempts to do otherwise.[20]

6 Having decided on a date for the formal hand-over for the company, it is wise for the developer to write to all flat-owners and remind them of the procedure on the hand-over, and he should call an informal meeting of residents. If there is an informal residents' association in being, then the arrangements about hand-over and pre-hand-over meetings will be made with the association; if not, the developer will have to take all the initiative, merely advising the individual residents what is happening.

It should be made clear to the flat-owners that the meeting is an informal one, and is certainly not a statutory meeting of the company. The sort of agenda for such a meeting would be:

(a) projected date of hand-over;
(b) method of hand-over;
(c) accounts up to date;
(d) appointment of officers;
(e) appointment of professional advisers (if considered appropriate); and
(f) any other business.

The developer should have present at such a meeting, his own professional advisers—that is to say, lawyers, accountants, or accounts staff, and someone who can talk about the technical side of things, if that is not the developer himself.

The object of such a meeting is to get as many of the flat-owners as possible together in the same room, explain to them once again the sequence of events in the hand-over, and find out from them if there is anyone who has any complaints—either about their individual flats[1] or about the block as a whole. It should be made clear to those attending that they are at the last stage, or one of the last stages, of the hand-over, and they either bring to the attention of the developer outstanding matters then, or it may well be too late.

7 The question of accounts is often a vexed one. Usually it will be found that service charges will have been underestimated by the developer, which means that there will be a running deficit. If this has happened—and it is more usual than ending up with a surplus because developers who want to dispose of their units as smoothly as possible are more likely to underestimate rather than over-load estimated service charges—it will be difficult for the developer to re-coup the deficit from the new management company. If he

19 And see ch 14, p 159, below, on the provisions of the Housing Act 1980 on conduct of lessor/ manager, and lessees' rights, in connection with service charges.
20 And see para 13, p 145, below, for more detailed comment on this aspect of the matter.
1 The meeting itself is not really the forum to examine complaints about individual flats, but the developer will want to spike as many guns as possible at this meeting.

has anticipated this situation (assuming that the development has been in being long enough up to that point) he might have taken the opportunity of raising the service charges, but if this has not happened, he can only recover his deficit by seeking an immediate payment from the company. Now as the company will have no credit balance of any sort with which to start its life, this will mean that it has to ask for a 'sub' from each of its members. Hardly a business-like way for a company to start its existence, and what is more to the point, hardly a very good exercise for the developer from the point of view of his reputation—and it is to be supposed that he will rely to at least a certain extent on his reputation to sell his next development. Some of the larger developers follow the practice of carrying any deficit on service charges themselves, whilst handing over to the company any credit balance.

8 Though this chapter is about the process of the transfer of a tenants' management company to the unit owners, and we deal elsewhere with the ability of a purchaser's legal adviser to investigate the bona fides of service charges on a flat,[2] nevertheless we ought to consider the advisability of those acting for the purchaser of a new flat looking at the estimated service charges quoted by the developer. Experience on the part of the purchaser's legal adviser will soon tell him if the estimate of the developer is too high, about right, or absurdly low, and especially if it is in the latter category he ought to warn his client, and carry out some further investigations.[3]

9 One aspect of these handovers which should not be forgotten is to make sure that the flat-owners, or those deputed to act for them within or outside the general body of tenants, are given before the hand-over, full details of all contractors who are working on the block of flats for the developer. By 'contractors' we mean people like:

grass-cutting contractors;
gardeners;
window cleaners;
cleaners responsible for internal areas, etc;
lift engineers; and so on.

Matters such as insurance should not be forgotten either. The company should be given the opportunity of awarding new contracts to the contractors, or instructing new ones or, come to that, deciding whether they wish to carry out the work themselves. All these details should be available for the unit-owners or their appointed representatives by no later than the meeting referred to in stage 6, above.

10 On the assumption that the informal meeting between the developer and the residents is successful, then the anticipated hand-over date will presumably become the actual one. The residents may or may not be represented by their own solicitors; if they are, they may wish them to act for them on the purchase of the reversion. But this is not necessarily a prerequisite, and, assuming that there is harmony between the parties, the developer's solicitors may quite easily deal with the transfer of the reversion, because:

2 See ch 6, p 77, above, on conveyancing techniques.
3 See for more detailed discussion, ch 18, p 204, below on the subject of service charge build-up.

(a) at the point immediately before, and presumably when, the transfer is sealed and delivered, the developer will still control the company;
(b) accordingly, the subscribers to the company will still be in control, and may seal the transfer, always assuming that it does need to be sealed by the purchaser.[4] At this point, of course, the subscribers themselves will be under the control of the developer;
(c) at the moment of technical delivery of the transfer, the developer procures the retirement of the subscribers, and enters on the membership register of the company the names of the owners of the flats (remember that he should have previously obtained from them completed applications for membership which he will have been holding in escrow); and
(d) at this same moment, therefore, the unit-owners become the members of the company which henceforth will be under their total control, will own the reversion in the block, and will owe no allegiance of any sort to the developer.

It is not unusual for the developer's solicitors to attend to stamping and registration (if appropriate) of the conveyance/transfer of the reversion, naturally by agreement with the residents, so that eventually there will be handed over to them a complete and correct title.

11 If the company is not to take the reversionary interest, which perhaps is being sold off separately by the developer, the steps involved are very similar, including the holding of the preliminary meeting. The steps involving the transfer of the reversion are easily enough separated out, leaving those which need to be taken to transfer the management function from the developer to the flat-owners.

12 The point arises whether the company itself has a role to play *before* the formal hand-over to the flat-owners. The consensus amongst those who practice the art of selling flats via tenants' management companies is that it is the *developer* who will be maintaining the property up to the moment of hand-over, so that the company as such will not have traded until that moment. Nevertheless, this does not relieve the developer of the burden of complying with the requirements, including accounting ones, of the Housing Act 1980 during the time he is maintaining the property.[5]

13 All this supposes a smooth ride for both flat owners and developer, but sometimes this does not happen for various reasons. There are two 'what if?' situations we must consider before we leave the subject:

(a) what if none of the tenants wishes to be involved in running the tenants' management company?

This might happen if most of the flat-owners were elderly, or were absentee, or a combination of other reasons. And it does happen—this is not mere hypothesis.

The answer here is that the flat-owners at large will still have to be persuaded to come to a meeting, at which the developer must secure the

4 It might do no harm anyway for it to be sealed by the company—purely as a public relations exercise.
5 And for further reading see ch 14, p 159, below.

attendance of, say, a local estate agent/surveyor or solicitor who is prepared to take on the management, obviously at an agreed fee-rate. There are plenty of such people, and so far as the flat-owners are concerned, there will usually be at least one who will be prepared to act as a figurehead 'chairman' and be the liaison officer between the managing agents and the flat-owners.

(b) What if the flat-owners, whilst agreeing in principle to the idea of the company being activated and taking over the management, are so incensed at the performance or attitude of the developer that they announce that they will refuse to take over the company?

Well, we have already seen that this they cannot do. The developer will have the option of transferring management and/or reversionary interest against the wishes of the flat-owners, if he so decides. Ultimately if management only is involved, he can cause the subscribers to resign, and so bring into membership the flat-owners. Presumably the developer would cancel all his contracts on the property, whilst advising the flat-owners, ie each individual, of the names and addresses of the contractors, so that fresh contracts could be entered into. If transfer of the reversion is also involved, the developer is able to effect this without recourse to the flat-owners.[6]

Nevertheless, this is a move which should only be contemplated as a last resort, and it will probably not be a last resort anyway because it will incense the flat-owners, with the possibility that they will seek advice as to the developers right to do this. Whether or not the right exists, which it does prima facie, no developer should allow matters to reach this low level. Unilateral action in the exercise of setting up flat management by means of a tenants' management company, which is supposed to be one where the flat-owners are invited run their own show, is hardly going to be beneficial for the developer.

E. SUMMARY

Hopefully, we have covered the salient features of the tenants' management company as a vehicle for carrying the developer's obligations to set up proper maintenance. As an option it does seem to be very much less popular than it used to be. One of the reasons for this is that the sort of people who will be buying flats is quite different now than formerly. There seems to have been some sort of polarisation into, on the one hand, those who are at the bottom end of the market and are probably not capable of running their own management company, and those who are just the opposite, probably making them just a little bit too 'fly' for the developer to be able to get the tenants' management company away easily. A final point for consideration is that the management of flats is something which should perhaps not be left to amateurs, and for the developer who is going to maintain a presence

6 See p 144, above.

in the area, it is important to have his developments always looking spick and span, so that his reputation is never in danger of tarnishment. He will find more difficulty in selling flats if his previous blocks are poorly managed and show it.

CHAPTER 12

Maintenance trust management

The maintenance trusteeship method of management was first used in a substantial way in 1958 by the Holding and Management Group of companies. It differs in several respects from the standard management scheme.

In basic form, maintenance trust management works as follows: Initially, following discussions between the developer/lessor (the scheme may be applied equally successfully to a new development or a 'break-up' situation) and the maintenance trustee, a trust deed is entered into between the two parties. This regulates the manner in which the maintenance is organised, and the continuing relationship between the reversioner and the maintenance trustee.

As leases of the individual units are granted, there will be three parties involved; the developer/lessor, the maintenance trustee, and the lessee. The lease will impose on the trustee the duty to collect lessees' maintenance contributions and to deal with them as trust funds, which will be used for providing repairs and service, including the creation of a separate reserve fund for future major repairs and renewals. The contents of both the trust deed and the standard maintenance trustee lease are summarised later in this section, but very briefly, the lease will set out in detail what the trustee's duties are and the purposes for which the trust funds can be used.

Whilst there are now a number of companies in this field, the innovators have undoubtedly been the Holding and Management Group, which has over the years built up a large portfolio of many thousands of flats and other units in its schemes, with a corresponding increase in expertise.

If a developer is going to involve a professional management company of this sort in any of his schemes, he must take the decision to do so before he starts selling. Nearly every practitioner must have come across the developer who has started marketing his units without considering the manner in which he is going to deal with management. The legal adviser is expected to wave a magic wand and produce legal documentation, and very often advise on and arrange management, in the twinkling of an eye. This sort of attitude is of course misguided, and especially if the maintenance trustee system is to be used it is essential to have all aspects of the scheme worked out well before selling commences.

A. HOW DOES THE TRUSTEE SCHEME WORK?

Once the decision to develop the site is taken then probably whilst the site is in the process of being purchased, or even before, the maintenance trustee must be brought in so that he may obtain all relevant information. The trustee will probably have given the developer a quotation of management costs, based on information supplied by the developer. An agreement will have been entered into between the trustee and the developer, and only then should marketing commence. Certainly the appointment of the trustee must be finalised before the completion of the first unit lease, because the trustee must be a party to that document.

The trustee will appoint a professionally qualified surveyor with effect from completion of the first sale. It is one of the advantages of the maintenance trustee scheme, when practised normally, that the developer should *never* have anything to do with the actual management of the units right from the day they are legally completed. Of course, there will be a dovetailing of certain works between the trustee and the developer during the construction period, this being dealt with in the management agreement between the trustee and the developer, but pure maintenance will be the total responsibility of the trustee right from the first day.

As the development proceeds, and more and more flats are sold, the trustee will become more involved until finally in complete charge. Full responsibility for the administration of the management[1] will be with the trustee, including such matters as liaison with any residents' association, dealing with any disputes which may arise, investment of the reserve funds, insurance, overseeing the surveyor, and so on. The object of the exercise is for the trustee to take on board executive responsibility for management, but in consultation with both lessor and lessees.

B. THE RESERVE FUND

We have discussed elsewhere in this book the concept of a reserve fund, or sinking fund as it is sometimes called. The reserve fund is an important aspect of the duties of the maintenance trustee, all the more so because it is likely that the units under management will be the more complicated ones, with more aspects of management than the average unit.

It might nevertheless be helpful if we quickly remind ourselves of the reason why a reserve fund is needed. For example, where there are common parts under management, as there inevitably will be in a maintenance trustee scheme, these will need to be redecorated, perhaps every six or seven years; the exterior will need redecoration at appreciably more frequent intervals, boilers and lift motors will require replacement, and so on. In other words, the 'big jobs' which it would be unfair to lay on the lessees in any given single year.

The reserve fund will protect the lessees from having to meet the full cost of such items in the year they arise—it will act as a fund to spread the costs equitably over the years, although, as we discuss in ch 17, below, we observe that reserve funds might not be the correct repository for such contributors, which may actually defeat the 'contingency' aims of the reserve fund. Decor-

1 More often than not, the Trustee will appoint a managing agent, usually the surveyor already referred to, to undertake the *actual* work.

ations etc, are foreseeable *actual* costs, and should perhaps more properly be included in the management programme proper.

The actual running costs—lighting and cleaning of common parts, repairs, gardening, and so on—are to be regarded separately from the major costs provided for in the reserve fund.

The reserve fund can have advantages beyond spreading the burden of major costs; for example, in the case of a resident defaulting on his service charges, the fund can be used as a 'buffer' to meet any temporary deficiency so that other residents need not be troubled whilst the maintenance trustee takes the necessary action to recover the monies due. Equally, if, let us say, the current service charges were not enough to cover the actual expenditure, which could perhaps happen if there were a sudden inflationary spiral (not unknown) the fund could be used as a buffer until the next round of service charges were due.

Except as we have just discussed, there is no practical difference between the reserve fund maintained under this maintenance trustee scheme and those which are present in the more usual maintenance schemes and described elsewhere[2] but for all that, it is still a very important feature of the scheme.

C. ADVANTAGES OF THE MAINTENANCE TRUSTEE SCHEME

1 For the lessor

The lessor undertakes no liability for repairs and services, which are undertaken by the trustee. Thus the lessor should have a trouble free ground rent investment, assuming a ground rent has been reserved. The professional maintenance trustee is *not* a managing agent. He will be an experienced professional property administrator who accepts the role of principal, not agent. Whilst an outside surveyor will generally be appointed by the trustee to look after day-to-day management, the trustee will constantly monitor his performance. The trustee will deal with the lessees, and the lessor ought to have no contact with them at all.

Where the lessor holds the property on a head lease, his obligations will be dealt with by the trustee scheme and this state of affairs will continue if he assigns his reversionary interest in the building. Thus the lessor is protected from the liability which would otherwise fall back on him were his (or any subsequent) assignee to default.

2 For the lessees

Perhaps the main advantage for the average lessee is that management of the units are undertaken by a professional management company, so that the lessees will rest secure in the knowledge that everything which ought to be done is done, and nothing is done which ought not to be. There will be no worries about absentee lessors who may fail to honour their obligations. Equally there will be no worries about changes of ownership of the building

2 See ch 17, p 191, below.

in which the flat is, because the maintenance trustee will be there continuously even though the lessor, and other residents may come and go. Usually, a professional management company will operate on a volume basis, which will mean that it will be able to negotiate better terms for goods, services, insurance cover and so on, and the benefit of these better terms will be passed on to the lessees.

The residents' funds in the nature of service charges, including the reserve fund, have the advantages of continuity and security, in that they are held in trust and are therefore completely separate from any other monies, eg the lessor's, or that belonging to the actual business of the management company itself. The trust funds are secure and will be directed only for the upkeep of the building. It follows that the income of the reserve fund bears tax only at the standard rate, without any penal rates.

At the same time as exhibiting all these advantages, it will usually be found that maintenance trustees undertaking the kind of management described in this chapter will be only too keen to work closely, liaise with, and consult with the residents of the blocks which they control.[3]

The above represents a brief description of the maintenance trustee scheme. The reader may well ask what the difference is between this type of scheme and a normal management scheme, as for instance set up in Precedent No 2, p 346, below. The main difference, of course, lies in the creation of a trust which will regulate the service charges collected from individual lessees, and particularly the reserve fund, so that (as we have just seen) these monies are theoretically totally protected from being used for any purpose other than those specified to be the objects of the trust (for which see later).

Quite to what extent service charge payments and reserve funds in what for want of a better expression, we should refer to as a 'normal' management situation are to be regarded as being held on a quasi-trustee basis, is a point which we do not have time to consider further here. The specific references to trusts and trust deeds may accordingly be somewhat illusory, but there is absolutely no doubt that the maintenance trusteeship scheme of management has been a successful one. We have already noted that it offers to the lessees continuity and security insofar as the treatment of their service charges are concerned, and this is indeed a most important point. Perhaps the scheme is best applied to the more expensive type of property, and there is no doubt that the documents involved—the trust deed and the lease itself—are lengthy and complicated and might not be best suited to an 'everyday' type of flat development.

Nevertheless, the scheme has a place in the order of 'flats' management, and the innovators in the field, the Holding and Management Group, are to be congratulated on their professionalism, which no doubt helps them remain the leaders in that particular field.

Readers will note by casting their eyes down the index of precedents that there is included in this book no precedent of either the maintenance trustee trust deed or the unit lease for use in connection therewith. This is because we are concerned in this chapter only with an introduction to the scheme,

3 And in any event the Housing Act 1980, Sch 19 provides for this to a certain extent; see ch 14, p 159, below.

and a description of its main features. The scheme itself, and the documentation, is complicated, and such complex documents are not reproduced in the precedents section to this book because that would be tantamount to an invitation to those who act for lessors, or those interested in management, to adapt the precedents for use by their clients. That would never do, since if difficulties were encountered the author might well be guilty of inducing the use of those precedents. Nor would there be any sense in reproducing them merely for prospective lessees' advisers to have the opportunity of seeing what they looked like.

We shall accordingly satisfy ourselves with a brief description of the main elements of the two documents concerned, so that readers may see how the scheme works in outline.

For those interested in taking the matter further, presumably on behalf of a developer, contact should be made with a company involved in maintenance trusteeship.

D. THE TWO DOCUMENTS: THE STANDARD TRUST DEED AND THE LEASE

The essential feature of the scheme will be that the maintenance trustee (which for sake of brevity we will hereafter call 'the trustee') will undertake, in the specific role of trustee, the obligation of:

(1) collecting the service charge from the lessees and using the same to provide repairs and services; and
(2) providing through the appointment of a chartered surveyor, for the day-to-day management of the building (of course such surveyor could be a full-time employee of the trustee, but certainly in the schemes the author has come across he will generally be an external professional carefully selected by the trustee).

All this ensures continuity of administration over the long term of the leases (notwithstanding any changes from time to time in the lessor and/or the lessees) and also provides for effective control of management.

The two documents concerned are the trust deed, the parties to which are the lessor and the trustee, and the lease, the parties to which are the lessor, the trustee, and lessee.

1 Standard trust deed

This sets out the purposes for which the service charges collected from the lessees are to be applied by the trustee

A brief summary of these purposes is as follows:

(a) employment of the surveyor for the day-to-day management of the building;
(b) decorating the exterior of the building, repairing the structure, upkeep of the gardens and grounds, and the repair and decoration of the common parts;

(c) furnishing and lighting the common parts;
(d) paying any joint assessment to rates, and rates on the common parts (and on, for example, any staff premises);
(e) providing hot water and central heating to the flats, where these are common services and the flats are not individually served;
(f) employing any necessary staff;
(g) keeping any lifts in the building in good repair and working order;
(h) repairing and decorating any flat occupied by resident staff and paying the outgoings on it;
(i) generally, paying all costs and expenses incurred in running and managing the building and collecting the rents and service charges, and also in making applications and representations in respect of statutory requirements;
(j) paying audit fees (obviously relating to the audits of the management funds which will be carried out each year);
(k) paying for any common television aerial, door porter system, and other similar matters;
(l) enforcing covenants entered into by other lessees;
(m) keeping the building insured comprehensively with the lessees included as interested parties;
(n) effecting third-party insurance;
(o) paying any taxes assessed on the maintenance fund;
(p) paying any costs in connection with the appointment of a new trustee and any retirement fee;
(q) paying pensions, annuities, etc to any staff;
(r) re-imbursing due proportions of any expenditure jointly benefiting the building and any adjoining property; and
(s) carrying out other necessary repair works improvements, etc.

There will also be incorporated in the trust deed power for the trustee to discontinue any service if it is no longer needed, or has become excessively expensive after considering the views and wishes of the majority of the flat-owners. This sort of power could almost certainly be exercised in any reasonably well set up management operation, but its being set out in specific terms is a helpful bonus, particularly for the lessees if they are faced with increasingly expensive service payments.

The trust deed also sets out:

(a) the arrangements for the appointment and retirement of the trustee;
(b) the percentages in which the service charges are payable by the lessees and the manner in which the percentages may be varied if that becomes necessary;
(c) covenants by the lessor:
    (i) to provide where appropriate, a staff flat and to keep the common parts of the building available for the provision of services;
    (ii) not to use any part of the building otherwise than for the purpose of the letting scheme and not to create any new or additional flats;
    (iii) to carry out repairs to any unsold flats;
    (iv) in the case of a new building—and, for example, in the case of a refurbished building in appropriate circumstances—to enforce its

rights against builders, architects, contractors, etc in respect of any defects in the building;

(v) not to let any flats without reserving a rent adequate to cover the ground rent and maintenance contributions;

(vi) to appoint a new trustee when required; and

(vii) to pay the service charge in respect of any unsold flat;

(d) provisions for the calculation and collection of the service charges. These will normally be collected half-yearly in advance with provision for an adjustment after the end of each year. The trustee is required to set up out of the service charges a reserve fund for long-term repairs and replacements; and

(e) the trustee's investment powers in relation to the reserve and other funds.

2 The unit lease

The lease is obviously much more of a standard document. Much of the following is fairly standard, and the average practitioner will be very familiar with the headings which are set out, but for the sake of completeness the headings are set out in full.

There will be covenants by the lessees as follows (not necessarily an exhaustive list);

1 to pay rent;
2 to pay the service charges;
3 to pay interest on rent and service charges not paid on the due date;[4]
4 to pay rates and taxes;
5 to keep the flat in good repair;
6 to redecorate the flat once every (say seven) years of the term;
7 to comply with statutes and regulations;
8 to obtain consents for any works carried out to the flat;
9 not to alter the flat;
10 not to assign or underlet part, and not to assign or underlet the whole without the consent of the trustee which is not to be unreasonably withheld;[5]
11 not to sublet except on terms that the rent covers the ground rent and the service charges;
12 to obtain certain covenants in underleases and assignments;
13 to register assignments and underlettings with the lessor;
14 to permit the lessor or the trustee to enter to inspect the state of the flat;
15 to permit the trustee or the lessor or the lessees of adjoining flats to enter for the purpose of carrying out repairs improvements or alterations;
16 to occupy the flat as a private residence only and not to carry on any business; and
17 to observe any regulations which may be made. This covenant, and

4 This is not necessarily a 'usual' covenant (for instance it is not included in the lessees' covenants reviewed in ch 4, above). Nevertheless, in maintenance trustee leases, rental, etc interest covenants are often included.

5 It is questionable how acceptable this is; the author's view is that any consent procedure is to be resisted.

certain others, are imposed as a 'letting scheme', so that each flat-owner may enforce the observance of these covenants by the other flat owners. We have seen this type of covenant in other leases studied in this book.

The standard unit lease will also contain other clauses of the type which one would expect to find in a lease of this sort.

The above narrative is merely a resumé of the scheme and the documents, and it will not be overstating the matter if we again observe that no-one should try to draft his or her own trust deed and unit lease based on the contents of this chapter.

What has hopefully been demonstrated is that the maintenance trustee scheme provides a virtually foolproof method of management for the lessor/developer who does not wish to become involved himself. The use of the trust principle for the holding of the service charge income—particularly in relation to the reserve fund—means that the lessees are virtually fireproof against any accidental or intentional diminution or disappearance of these monies. The lessor/developer is relieved of all worries and liabilities—the trustee will even collect and remit to him the ground rental income, assuming that there is one.

Perhaps the scheme is not so much an innovation as an extension of the traditional full management scheme, as laid down, for instance, in Precedent No 2, p 346, below, but it is a useful tool in the armoury of the developer, especially where complicated, as opposed to simple, blocks of flats are involved. It is likely that its use will increase, especially having regard to the professionalism which its major exponents are devoting to it.

CHAPTER 13

The management programme: factors for consideration

As with almost everything else in life, more will be derived from a maintenance programme if careful thought is put into it from its inception—indeed most of the thought should precede the actual physical inception. Careful planning will bring its own dividends.

All too often management programmes are thrown together hastily, and indeed the programme itself may be represented by no more than the clauses in the lease dealing with the management aspect, and even these may have come into the lease as part of a 'job lot', so to speak, being part of a standard precedent.

In the introduction to the Precedent section of this book, great stress is laid on the point that a precedent is merely an indication of the way in which the conveyancer should direct himself, and should never be regarded as sacrosanct to the point where it is felt that the precise wording must be left as it is. There are few precedents which can be regarded as any more than skeletons on to which are hung an individual's choice of specific variables. Nowhere does this situation arise more than the conception, and subsequent drafting, of the management programme.

In order to produce a sensible programme of management, the developer should take into account several factors, and only when he has satisfied himself on them should he proceed to implementation.

FACTORS FOR DEVELOPER'S CONSIDERATION

(a) Has the developer any experience in management?

(b) If he has experience, is it in the same area of management as that presently under consideration? E g there are all sorts of grades of management, right from the 'studio flat' type of minimal, mainly monitoring role[1] up to the full-blown scheme complete with porter/s, lifts, complex landscaped areas, etc. Experience in one will not necessarily mean that other varieties may be tackled with equanimity, although obviously if the experience is at the complex end, the other end is presumably going to be relatively easy to cope with, *but not vice versa.*

(c) If the developer is satisfied that he has the *experience*, does he have the *resources?*

(d) In cases where the developer does not have the experience, or perhaps he has the experience but not the resources, or perhaps he has both but

1 See generally, ch 9, p 110, above.

has no desire to become involved in management, does he know some person, firm or company who is willing to become involved in management?

(e) If not, then the developer's advisers should make sure that they know of a willing manager.

(f) Having arrived at the stage of identifying the manager, he should then be brought into the discussions. Unfortunately, all too often everything is cut and dried before the identity of the manager is settled; this is generally detrimental to the developer, because a good manager should be able to contribute a great deal to discussions at this early stage.

(g) If we assume that the parties concerned are taking all steps in the right order, the next job is to review the planned development and to identify what sort of materials should be used in it. This is quite clearly something which ought to be done before the architect begins to draw his plans. Whether this is likely to happen is again questionable, but what we are here concerned with is not what *usually* happens, but what *should* happen.

Ideally all the physical aspects of the development should be reviewed, and considered from two stand-points, i e.

(i) capital cost, and
(ii) maintenance cost.

All this is covered in some detail shortly,[2] but the following will serve as an illustration, even of a minor variation—a softwood window frame receiving the usual speculative builder's treatment, i e one undercoat and one topcoat, probably applied by a painter on piece work rushing to get the job done as quickly as possible, will need repainting *much* sooner than one which gets one or more additional coats, more carefully applied. The developer must weigh all these matters carefully.

If by the time this aspect of management is considered, the architect's drawings are completed, or even perhaps being put into force by the start of building operations, it may be too late to make decisions based on these sort of considerations, although the example quoted above could (just) still be implemented.

(h) After this stage, the developer and his advisers should move on to identify the aspects of maintenance which should be included in the lease, e g there is no earthly point in going for overkill in the lease provisions by talking about maintenance of lifts and lift shafts, employment of porters and maintenance and provisions of porters' lodges, and so on, unless the development is going to be large enough or complex enough to support such items. Overcomplication of the maintenance provisions in the lease will only be confusing for everyone. Further consideration of this aspect is dealt with in ch 17, below.

(i) Once the stage has been reached where
(i) identity of manager,
(ii) physical treatment, and
(iii) maintenance references in the lease,

are identified, the scale of maintenance may be settled on. This will probably have formulated itself already by this stage, because considera-

2 See ch 16, p 172, below.

tion of all the preceding points will have virtually settled the scale of maintenance, which is then dealt with by the appropriate drafting in the lease.

(j) Moving on again, the next task (which is maintenance-related) will be computation of the maintenance charge expected. This stage is very much a chicken and egg situation. The decisions on physical features, level of maintenance, etc will produce a series of figures for service charges which may be horrifying, so that the developer then selects a range of acceptable service charges and works his way back, fitting levels of maintenance, physical features, etc into scales where the calculations result in the desired range of service charges. Some practitioners might favour starting the whole sequence with the required service charges, and then working their way backwards, rather than adopting the method we have just described, but it does seem sensible to do it in the more proper, logical way, if only to see what the service charges would be (even if they are unacceptable to the developer from a marketing point of view) were the undoubtedly proper levels of maintenance to be achieved. As can be seen, this stage may owe a lot to a pragmatic approach.

(k) Finally, and as a subsidiary to the immediately preceding section, there are more ways than one of skinning a cat, and in the same manner there are several variations on the calculation of the service charge, ranging from the 'rough and ready' to that using sinking fund calculations, etc. These are discussed with illustration, in ch 18, below. It should only be at this stage that the conveyancer settles his draft lease, the manager sets up his management programme, and the developer puts his flats on to the market. Unfortunately, we do not live in an ideal world, so that the chances are this sequence as described above will rarely be adhered to. Nevertheless, that is the way it should be done, and those responsible for advising the developer should, as far as possible, try to maintain the pattern.

Having reviewed the main points for consideration, we now move on to look at the main sections one by one.

CHAPTER 14

Service charges: the current legislation

The Housing Act 1980 represents the latest consolidated effort of the legislature to codify the regulatory aspects of maintenance. Until this Act passed on to the statute book, the position between the lessor and lessee in a development of units sold on a long term of years was regulated partly by the contractual position set up between them and latterly by some previous attempts by parliament to regulate their relationship.[1]

The Act, which received the Royal Assent on 8 August 1980, relates to a large extent to the public and quasi-public sector. Those parts of it which regulate the relationship between private lessor and private lessee of a long term of years are only a very small part of the Act but, nevertheless, from our point of view, are most important, because there is imposed on lessors, or those who manage flats, duties and obligations which are comprehensive and which must be considered carefully before a development is started.

From the point of view of service charges, which for the purposes of this chapter is the only relevant part of the 1980 Act with which we are concerned, the only section to which we have to give our attention is s 136 which states as follows:

'**136 Service charges** (1) Schedule 19 to this Act shall have effect, in place of sections 90 to 91A of the 1972 Act,[2] in relation to periods ending after the commencement of this section, but subject to subsection (2) below.

(2) In relation to works begun earlier than six months after the commencement of this section—

(a) paragraphs 2 to 6 of Schedule 19 shall not apply; and

(b) sections 90 to 91A shall continue to apply.'

This section was brought into operation on 3 October 1980.[3] Accordingly, for the purposes of this book, the section, and Sch 19 to which it refers, are completely operative.

Schedule 19 is so important to the management situation that it is reproduced in full below. A commentary follows.

A. HOUSING ACT 1980, SCH 19

'SCHEDULE 19. PROVISIONS REPLACING SECTIONS 90 TO 91A OF HOUSING FINANCE ACT 1972

1 Previously the regulatory code was embodied in the Housing Finance Act 1972, ss 90–91A, as amended by Housing Act 1974, s 124 and Sch 12. The code is now laid down in the Housing Act 1980, s 136 and Sch 19.

2 I e the Housing Finance Act 1972.

3 Housing Act 1980 (Commencement No 1) Order 1980, SI 1980/1406.

Service charge and relevant costs

1 (1) For the purposes of this Schedule, a service charge is an amount payable by the tenant of a flat as part of or in addition to the rent—
(a) which is payable, directly or indirectly, for services, repairs, maintenance or insurance or the landlord's costs of management; and
(b) the whole or part of which varies or may vary according to the relevant costs;
and the relevant costs are the costs or estimated costs (including over-heads) incurred or to be incurred in any period (whether the period for which the service charge is payable or an earlier or later period) by or on behalf of the landlord or a superior landlord in connection with the matters for which the service charge is payable.
(2) Other expressions used in this Schedule are to be construed in accordance with paragraphs 16 to 20 below.

Limitation of service charge

2 The extent to which relevant costs are taken into account in determining the amount of a service charge payable for any period shall be limited in accordance with the following paragraphs, and the amount payable shall be limited accordingly; and where the service charge is payable before the relevant costs are incurred—
(a) no greater amount shall be so payable than is reasonable; and
(b) after the relevant costs have been incurred any necessary adjustments shall be made by repayment, reduction of subsequent charges or otherwise.
3 Costs are to be taken into account only to the extent that they are reasonably incurred, and costs incurred on the provision of services or the carrying out of works only if the services or works are of a reasonable standard.
4 (1) where costs incurred on the carrying out of works on a building exceed the amount prescribed by or under this paragraph the excess is not to be taken into account unless the requirements of paragraph 5 below have been complied with or are dispensed with under paragraph 6 below.
(2) The prescribed amount is £25 multiplied by the number of flats in the building or £500, whichever is the greater, but the Secretary of State may by order substitute a different amount for £25 or £500 or both.
5 (1) The requirements are as follows:
(2) At least two estimates for the works shall be obtained, one of them from a person wholly unconnected with the landlord.
(3) A notice accompanied by a copy of the estimates shall be given to each of the tenants concerned or shall be displayed in the building so as to be likely to come to the notice of all those tenants and, if there is a recognised tenants' association for the building, the notice and copy of the estimates shall also be given to the secretary of the association.
(4) The notice shall describe the works to be carried out and invite observations on them and on the estimates and shall state the name and address in the United Kingdom of the person to whom the observations may be sent and the date by which they are to be received.
(5) The date stated in the notice shall not be earlier than one month after the date on which it is given or displayed as required by sub-paragraph (3) above.
(6) The landlord shall have regard to any observations received in pursuance of the notice and, unless the works are urgently required, they shall not be begun earlier than the date specified in the notice.
(7) For the purposes of this paragraph the tenants concerned are all the landlords' tenants of flats in the building by whom a service charge is payable to which the costs of the proposed works are relevant.
6 In any proceedings relating to a service charge the court, if satisfied that the landlord acted reasonably, may dispense with all or any of the requirements.

Information as to relevant costs

7 (1) If a tenant requests the landlord in writing to supply him with a written summary of the costs incurred in the relevant period defined in sub-paragraph (5) below which are relevant to the service charges payable or demanded as payable by the tenant in that or any other period, the landlord shall do so within six months of the end of the period or within one month of the request, whichever is the later.
(2) If there is a recognised tenants' association for the building and the tenant consents, a request under sub-paragraph (1) above may be made by the secretary of the association instead of by the tenant and may then be for the supply of the summary to the secretary.
(3) The summary shall set out those costs in a way showing how they are or will be reflected in demands for service charges and, if there are more than four flats in the building or the relevant costs relate also to another building, it must be certified by a qualified accountant as in his opinion a fair summary complying with this requirement and as being sufficiently supported by accounts, receipts or other documents which have been produced to him.
(4) Where a tenant or the secretary has obtained such a summary as is referred to in sub-paragraph (1) above (whether in pursuance of this paragraph or otherwise) the tenant, or the secretary with the consent of the tenant may, within six months of obtaining it, require the landlord in writing to afford him reasonable facilities for inspecting the accounts, receipts and other documents supporting the summary and for taking copies or extracts from them, and the landlord shall then make such facilities available to the tenant or secretary for a period of two months beginning not later than one month after the request is made.
(5) The relevant period mentioned in sub-paragraph (1) above is—
(a) if the relevant accounts are made up for periods of 12 months, the last such period ending not later than the date of the request; and
(b) if none are made up for such a period, the period of 12 months ending with the request.

Information held by superior landlord

8 (1) If a request under paragraph 7 (1) above relates in whole or in part to relevant costs incurred by or on behalf of a superior landlord, and the landlord to whom the request is made is not in possession of the relevant information—
(a) he shall in turn make a written request for the relevant information to the person who is his landlord (and so on if that person is not himself the superior landlord) and the superior landlord shall then comply with the request within a reasonable time; and
(b) it shall be the duty of the immediate landlord to comply with the tenant's or secretary's request, or that part of it which relates to the relevant costs incurred by or on behalf of the superior landlord, within the time allowed by paragraph 8 or within such further time, if any, as is reasonable in the circumstances.
(2) If a request made under paragraph 7 (4) above relates to a summary of costs incurred by or on behalf of a superior landlord, the landlord to whom the request is made shall forthwith inform the tenant or secretary of that fact and of the name and address of the superior landlord, and sub-paragraph (4) shall then apply as if the superior landlord were the immediate landlord.

Service of requests under paragraph 7

9 A request under paragraph 7 above shall be deemed to be duly served on a landlord if it is served on any agent of the landlord named as such in the rent book or similar document, or on the person who receives the rent on behalf of the landlord;

and a person on whom a request is so served shall forward it as soon as may be to the landlord.

Effect of assignment

10 The assignment of a tenancy shall not affect the validity of a request made under paragraph 7 or 8 above before the assignment, but a person shall not be obliged to provide a summary or make facilities available more than once for the same flat and for the same period.

Determination of reasonableness

11 Any agreement made by a tenant of a flat, other than an arbitration agreement within the meaning of section 32 of the Arbitration Act 1950, shall be void in so far as it purports to provide for a determination in a particular manner or on particular evidence of any question whether any amount payable before costs for services, repair, maintenance, insurance or management are incurred is reasonable, whether such costs were reasonably incurred or whether services or works for which costs were incurred are of a reasonable standard.
12 A county court may make a declaration that any such amount is or is not reasonable, that any such costs were or were not reasonably incurred or that any services or works are or are not of a reasonable standard, notwithstanding that no other relief is sought in the proceedings.

Offences

13 (1) If any person without reasonable excuse fails to perform any duty imposed on him by this Schedule he shall be guilty of an offence and liable on summary conviction to a fine not exceeding £500.
(2) Where an offence under this Schedule which has been committed by a body corporate is proved to have been committed with the consent or connivance of, or to be attributable to any neglect on the part of, a director, manager, secretary or other similar officer of the body corporate, or any person who was purporting to act in such capacity, he, as well as the body corporate, shall be guilty of an offence and be liable to be proceeded against and punished accordingly.
(3) Where the affairs of a body corporate are managed by its members, sub-paragraph (2) above shall apply in relation to the acts and defaults of a member in connection with his functions of management as if he were a director of the body corporate.

Exceptions

14 (1) This Schedule does not apply to service charges payable by a tenant of any of the following bodies, that is to say—
(a) a local authority or development corporation (as defined in section 50 (1) of this Act);
(b) the council of a county,
(c) the Commission for the New Towns,
(d) the Development Board for Rural Wales.
Unless the tenancy is a long tenancy for the purposes of paragraph 1 of Schedule 3 to this Act.
(2) Where this Schedule applies to a service charge payable by the tenant of a body mentioned in sub-paragraph (1) above—
(a) paragraph 13 does not apply, and
(b) the persons who are qualified accountants include a member of the Chartered Institute of Public Finance and Accountancy and paragraph 17 (2) (b) below does not apply.

15 This Schedule does not apply to service charges payable by the tenant of a flat the rent of which is registered under Part IV of the 1977 Act, unless the amount registered is, in pursuance of section 71 (4) of that Act, entered as a variable amount.

Definition of 'flat', 'qualified accountant,' 'landlord', 'tenant' and 'recognised tenants' association'

16 A flat is a separate set of premises, whether or not on the same floor, which—
(a) forms part of a building; and
(b) is divided horizontally from some other part of that building; and
(c) is constructed or adapted for use for the purposes of a dwelling and is occupied wholly or mainly as a private dwelling.

17 (1) A qualified accountant is a person qualified for the purposes of paragraph 3 of Schedule 16, but subject to sub-paragraph (2) below.
(2) None of the following is a qualified accountant—
(a) a body corporate, except a Scottish firm;
(b) an officer or employee of the landlord or, where the landlord is a company, of a company which is the landlord's holding company or subsidiary (within the meaning of section 154 of the Companies Act 1948) or a subsidiary of the landlord's holding company; and
(c) a person who is a partner or employee of any such officer or employee.

18 'Landlord' includes any person who has a right to enforce payment of a service charge and, in relation to a flat occupied by a tenant under a right conferred by an enactment, also includes the person who, apart from that right, would be entitled to possession of the flat.

19 'Tenant' includes a person occupying a flat under a right conferred by an enactment, and, where the whole or any part of the flat is sub-let, includes also the sub-tenant.

20 A recognised tenants' association is an association of tenants of flats in a building which is recognised for the purposes of this Schedule either—
(a) by a notice in writing given by the landlord to the secretary of the association: or
(b) by a certificate of one of the persons appointed by the Lord Chancellor under the 1977 Act to the panel of persons to act as members of a rent assessment committee for the registration area in which the building is situated.

21 (1) A notice given under paragraph 20 (a) above may be withdrawn by the landlord by notice in writing given to the secretary of the association not less than six months before the date on which it is to be withdrawn; and a certificate given under paragraph 20 (b) above may be cancelled by one of the persons there mentioned.
(2) The Secretary of State may by regulations specify the matters to which regard is to be had in giving or cancelling a certificate under paragraph 20 (b) above.'

The Housing Act 1980, s 136 and Sch 19 are, as we have already seen, the primary regulatory factors in the relationship between the lessor and lessee, so far as service charges are concerned. But the statutory provisions do not set up the service charges themselves, how much they are to be, what elements of maintenance they are to include, how they are to be paid, or indeed any other aspect of maintenance, such as whether a service charge is paid to a lessor or to a management company. All that they do is to provide safeguards for the lessee, so that he may call into question the validity of individual components of the charges, and be entitled to receive full information relating both to accounts and other aspects of the management function.

It might be as well at this point, before we go back to the section and schedule in order to highlight their main provisions, to remind ourselves of the contents of the Housing Finance Act 1972, s 90, which was previously the principal statutory provision, and which was eventually replaced by s 136 and Sch 19. It was s 90 which contained the relevant information, and it is interesting to consider the text of the section itself as compared with the present legislation. The reader should, however, always bear in mind that this section is repealed and replaced by the provisions of Sch 19 to the 1980 Act.[4]

'**90 Information about service charges** (1) Where the service charges which are payable by the tenant of a flat in any calendar year, or which are demanded from the tenant as being so payable, exceed the amount specified in subsection (2) of this section, the tenant shall, in accordance with this section, be entitled to obtain a summary in writing of the relevant costs in the accounting year ending in or with that year, certified by a qualified accountant as being in his opinion—
(a) a fair summary of those costs, set out in a way which shows how they are or will be reflected in demands for service charges, and
(b) sufficiently supported by accounts, receipts and other documents which have been produced to the accountant.
and the certificate shall identify the accounting year to which the summary relates.
(2) The said amount is £80, but the Secretary of State may from time to time vary that amount by order. An order under this subsection may contain such transitional or other supplemental or incidental provisions as appear to the Secretary of State to be necessary or expedient, and shall be contained in a statutory instrument of which a draft has been approved by a resolution of each House of Parliament.
(3) The rights conferred by subsection (1) of this section shall not be exercisable—
(a) if the tenant has contractual rights exercisable in return for a reasonable payment, or without payment, enabling him to obtain from time to time statements of the relevant costs, certified by a qualified accountant, which afford all the information which could be obtained under this section or,
(b) if there are accounts, certified by a qualified accountant, which afford all the information which could be obtained under this section, and the tenant is given reasonable facilities for inspecting them, and taking copies of or extracts from them, or
(c) where there are not more than five flats in the building, and the relevant costs relate only to that building, if the tenant is afforded reasonable facilities for inspecting the receipts and other records supporting the service charges, and for taking copies of or extracts from them.
(4) The tenant shall exercise the rights conferred by this section by serving on the landlord a request in writing which states the calendar year to which the request relates, and which is so served not later than twelve months after the end of that year.
(5) It shall be the duty of the landlord to comply with the request not later than one month after the service of the request, or six months after the end of the accounting year with which the summary is to deal, whichever is the later.
(6) If the request relates in whole or in part to relevant costs incurred by or on behalf of a superior landlord, and the landlord on whom the request is served is not in possession of the relevant information about the costs so incurred—
(a) he shall in turn serve a request for the relevant information on the person who

4 And of course, as we have already seen, was expanded and amended by the Housing Act 1974, s 124 and Sch 12.

is his landlord, and it shall be the duty of that person to comply with the request within a reasonable time, and

(b) it shall be the duty of the landlord (that is to say the immediate landlord) to comply with the tenant's request, or the part of the request relating to the relevant costs incurred by or on behalf of the superior landlord, within the time allowed by subsection (5) above or within such further time, if any, as is reasonable in the circumstances.

(7) If no accounts have been made up, or if for any other reason it is impracticable to deal with an accounting year, the summary specified in sub-section (1) of this section shall be a summary of the relevant costs in the calendar year, and—

(a) the accountants' certificate shall indicate that the summary deals with relevant costs in the calendar year, and

(b) subsection (5) above shall apply with the substitution for the reference to the accounting year of a reference to the calendar year.

(8) A request under this section shall be deemed to be duly served on a landlord if it is served on any agent of the landlord named as such in a rent book or other similar document, or on the person who receives the rent on behalf of the landlord; and it shall be the duty of a person on whom the request is so served to forward it as soon as may be to the landlord.

(9) The assignment of a tenancy shall not affect the validity of a request served under this section before the assignment, but a landlord shall not be obliged to provide the summary specified in subsection (1) of this section more than once for the same flat for the same period.

(10) If any person without reasonable excuse fails to perform any duty imposed upon him by this section he shall be guilty of an offence and liable on summary conviction to a fine not exceeding £200.

(11) Proceedings for an offence under this section may be instituted by any local authority.

(12) In this section—

"accounting year" means a period of twelve months for which the accounts relating to the building in question are made up.

"Flat" means a separate set of premises, whether or not on the same floor, constructed or adapted for use for the purposes of a dwelling and forming part of a building from some other part of which it is divided horizontally, being a set of premises occupied wholly or mainly as a private dwelling. "Landlord" in relation to a flat occupied by a tenant under a right conferred by an enactment, includes the person who, apart from that right, would be entitled to possession of the flat.

"qualified accountant" means a member of—

(a) The Institute of Chartered Accountants in England and Wales,

(b) The Institute of Chartered Accountants of Scotland,

(c) The Association of Certified Accountants,

(d) The Institute of Chartered Accountants in Ireland, or

(e) any other body of Accountants established in the United Kingdom and for the time being recognised for the purposes of Section 161 (1)(a) of the Companies Act 1948 by the Secretary of State,

or a person who is for the time being authorised by the Secretary of State under section 161 (1)(b) of that Act; but excludes, except in the case of a Scottish firm every partner of which is so qualified, any body corporate.

"relevant costs" means any costs (including charges for overheads) incurred or defrayed in the period in question by or on behalf of the landlord, or any superior landlord, which affect, or may affect, the amount of the service charges for the flat for that period or for any other period, earlier or later.

"service charge" means any charge for services, repairs, maintenance or insurance,

being a charge which is payable as part of, or in addition to, the rent, and which varies or may vary according to any costs (including charges for overheads) incurred from time to time by or on behalf of the landlord or any superior landlord.
"tenant" includes a tenant under a right conferred by an enactment, and, where the whole or any part of the flat is sub-let, includes both the tenant and the sub-tenant.
13 (Commencement dates).'

Readers are encouraged to read the 1972 legislation as well as the 1980 version, in order to see to what extent the legislature has progressed, if at all, except in detail. Perhaps there has not been too much advance in the concept; the problem still remains that a determined errant lessor/manager will more than likely continue to drive a coach and horses through the legislature's provisions.

B. THE COMMENTARY

The text of the 1980 Act, Sch 19 has been reproduced in full, and it is suggested that the reader look through it very carefully because it is important for the developer and subsequent manager, if that task is to be performed by some third party. Quite obviously, it is also important for the lessee and even more important for those who advise all parties who are likely to be involved in the sale and management of any flat. The text of the 1972 Act is reproduced because readers might like to cast their eyes over it to remind themselves that the 1980 Act was by no means innovatory in attempting to regulate the whole aspect of service charges.

And yet, one wonders, how many lessors/managers still habitually transgress the provisions of Sch 19, either innocently (probably the majority) or knowingly, and how many lessees are unaware of their rights under the Act?

Probably there are a great number of transgressions of the Act by those whose job it is to administer management and collect service charges, and equally there are very few lessees who either know or care to find out what their rights are. Naturally the stance of this book is neutral and it is hoped that it will be of equal interest to lessors/managers on the one hand, and lessees on the other. But one is bound to remark that if lessors and managers scrupulously observed the provisions of the Schedule, they might well be faced with additional costs which would inevitably be passed on to the lessees, who would thus suffer rather than benefit by the Act. The selling and buying of a flat is a commercial undertaking on both sides; here is a free market, and why else does either side have professional advisers, if not to investigate matters such as this?[5]

Nevertheless, there are abuses of the system, attempted or achieved, from time to time, so that to that extent Sch 19 is important, and the reader is directed to the following points which may help as a guide, and commentary.

1 There is no substitute for sitting down and reading the Schedule thoroughly.

2 'Service charge' is defined in the Schedule[6] in a wide sense so as to bring any recharge of maintenance etc work within its scope.

5 And refer to ch 6, p 77, above, for a brief commentary on conveyancing techniques.
6 Para 1 (2).

3 In the case of service charges made in advance, 'no greater amount shall be so payable than is reasonable, and after the actual costs are incurred, there shall be made the necessary adjustments'. The interesting point to note, however, is that the Act does not demand *repayment* of any amounts overpaid on an advance service charge collection: it contemplates that an adjustment can be made on a subsequent collection.[7] The Schedule goes on to say that costs are only to be taken into account 'to the extent that they are reasonably incurred', and the works in respect of which monies are paid out are to be of a *reasonable standard.*[8] Under the provisions of paras 4, 5 and 6 of the Schedule, the lessor/manager is tied down more specifically than he was previously in the 1972 Act. These provisions are as follows:

(a) any works on the building costing more than £25 times the number of flats in a building, or £500, whichever is the greater, require *two* estimates to be obtained by the lessor, and one of those estimates has to be from someone completely unconnected with the lessor. A copy of the estimates has to be given to the recognised tenants' association (see later), and either posted on a notice board which all the tenants are likely to see, or sent to each tenant individually;

(b) the notice accompanying the estimates must give full details of the intended works, and invite observations. Those observations are to be invited within a set time period, which must not be less than one month from the date the notice is given; and

(c) if the matter comes before the court, it may dispense with any of these requirements.

In practice, this section of the Schedule is not quite as bad as it sounds. The base amount of the quote, before the provisions of the Schedule concerning quotes, notice, etc have to be complied with, is £500. Thus, in one of the small studio flat blocks we have referred to throughout this book,[9] we would have, say, eight flats. Eight times £25 is £200, so that £500 would be 'the greater'. For £500, the lessor/manager will be able to get many of the jobs done, if not all, so that he would not have to go to the lessees on every occasion that he was arranging maintenance. The sort of matters he would have to refer to the individual lessees and/or the tenants' association would be repainting of the outside woodwork, and reasonably major repair or renewal works—perhaps repainting on older buildings.[10] Something else which might come within the scope of this part of the Schedule could easily be cleaning the common parts of the block. £500 divided by £25 is 20, so that for the limiting amount to arise a block of more than 20 flats would have to be involved—a fairly large block—meaning higher cleaning costs. £500, the minimum figure, is £10 per week, and one cannot buy much in the way of cleaning services for that amount. So that the effect of the provision, although not disastrous, is insidious and the manager has to watch carefully his individual items of costs. But again, when computing cleaning

7 Para 2 (a) and (b).
8 Para 3.
9 See particularly ch 9, p 110, above.
10 See in this connection ch 16, p 172, below, which gives a commentary on materials and finishes, and relative costs.

costs, is one to look at them on an annual basis, or on a weekly basis, which is what they are usually quoted on? There seems to be no guidance in the Schedule, although it would be surprising if, in the average block, every average lessor/manager went to the trouble of obtaining annual quotes for this type of work to present to the flat-owners.

5 There is not only a burden on a lessor/manager to voluntarily supply information as to costs, in the manner described in the last section, but under the provisions of paras 7, 8 and 9, the flat-owner is entitled to ask the lessor in writing for a written summary of costs either for the last accounting period of the management of the block, or, if there is no such period (and quite often there will not be), for the 12 months immediately preceding the date of the request. Any recognised tenants' association may also make a similar request, and when the summary does turn up, it should be 'certified by a qualified accountant' and be supported by appropriate receipts, records, etc. It is only when there are less than four flats in the block in question that such certification may be dispensed with.

In the event of the immediate landlord not having this information readily available, e g if some of the costs are attributable to a superior landlord, the immediate landlord must make an identical request to his own superior landlord.

6 By para 11 of the Schedule, it is forbidden for any tenant to agree for a determination, by whatever means except a valid arbitration, as to whether any component of the service charge is reasonable.

7 The Schedule does not apply to service charges in certain circumstances, but none of them are likely to be of very much importance within the context of this book, e g the references are to tenancies with local authorities, development corporations, county councils, etc. Further, it does not apply to service charges payable by tenants of flats where the rent is registered under Part IV of the Rent Act 1977, unless the amount registered is entered as a variable amount (para 15).

8 The Schedule then goes on to define certain terms used throughout it, e g 'flat', 'qualified accountant', 'landlord', 'tenant', and 'recognised tenants' association'. For these definitions, the reader should refer back to paras 16 to 20 inclusive, p 163, above.

The Schedule as a whole, therefore, whilst comprising 21 paragraphs, is tolerably simple, and can be summed up as dealing with the following aspects:

definition of service charge;
limitation of extent of service charge, particularly by reference to financial limits, before landlord must notify tenants and have proper regard to their observations;
provision for tenants to receive upon request information about service charge costs;
determination of reasonableness;
exceptions; and
definitions.

C. THE PRACTICAL EFFECT

Schedule 19 is all very well, but does it work?

In the first place, it is drafted in fairly straightforward language, so that both the lessor/manager and the lessees should be able to comprehend just what their rights are. But there are still many blocks where service charges are paid by the lessees, and they receive in return either insufficient information or none at all. This is not to say that there are blocks where proper accounts are available for tenants—there are, but the incidence rate of reasonable approximation to the requirements of the Act is not as high as it ought to be. There are all sorts of areas where defalcation, innocent or otherwise, can occur. For example, para 7 (3) provides for the 'summary of costs' (for some reason the expression "accounts" is avoided) for any block of more than four flats to be 'certified by a qualified accountant'. Paragraph 17 (2) states that an officer or employee of the landlord, or where the landlord is a company, of a company which is the landlord's holding company or subsidiary is *not* a qualified accountant. How many sets of accounts then are actually delivered which are certified by, in this context, unqualified accountants? And what does 'certify the summary of costs' mean? Is 'certify' the same as 'audit' or does it imply some less intense investigation?

At this point, the author will commit what many may regard as heresy, and observe that far from being too restrictive, Sch 19 is not nearly restrictive enough. It is too vague to be of very much use. It is a half-hearted attempt to regulate a situation which is beyond redemption except by radical measures.

The whole problem lies in the mish-mash of management we have in this country. There are far too many half-baked tenants' management company schemes[11] still being set up by people who ought to know better: and to expect a typical tenants' management company to adhere to even the reasonably mild provisions of Sch 19 is usually asking too much.

Until changes in the law, like the introduction of development obligations, or the strata title system[12] bring in their wake more professional management, as they surely must do, Sch 19 will no doubt continue to have relatively little effect on those who choose to ignore it in whole or in part. It is to be hoped that those acting for lessees will draw their clients' attention to their basic rights under Sch 19, and thus have some effect on management generally, because better management does not mean higher service charges; rather the opposite.

11 And see ch 11, p 131, above, on tenants' management companies.
12 See ch 29, p 325, below.

CHAPTER 15

The service components

Before we study the build-up of the service charge, we first have to study its breakdown: that is to say, the individual physical components of the whole. This is because in order to understand the overall concept of the service charge, it is helpful to break it down into as many individual sectors as possible.

The example of service charge we shall mostly use in this part of the exercise is one which would relate to a scheme which was intended to be used on a reasonably complicated multi-unit block with a wide range of facilities. Nevertheless, whilst we might include in the service computation items such as porter's lodge, and payment of salary to porter/s and gardening/maintenance staff, we would not normally include items like upkeep of swimming pools, squash courts, and other similar central recreation areas. These would only be found on a very specialised up-market, extremely expensive development, but for all that they are only basically items of expenditure. Therefore, whilst every attempt has been made to make this review as comprehensive as is reasonably possible, if any items are missed out, then the treatment of those that are included may be extended to those that are excluded.

So far as the author is aware, there is no current legal textbook which has attempted to go into the subject of practical management as deeply as we try to in this book. There have been books dealing briefly with management, but only as a by-product of setting up the document on a development of flats, and even then never dealing with actual 'on-the-ground' management.

There seems no reason why the legal profession should not be able to offer its clients a comprehensive service, not only in relation to the conveyancing of a flat development, but also to advice as to what sort of scheme to adopt, and how to run it when the selling of the units has been completed. Why should estate agents have the market cornered? Why should not conveyancers go on from setting up the scheme, and acting for the client on the sales, to dealing first-hand with the management? The answer is, no reason at all; it is high time that as a profession we started getting back some lost ground.

In order to be able to do this, though, we have to understand the complexities of modern building, what sort of items will last longest, or cost less, or both; the suitability of modern materials to various situations, and then what type of scheme is appropriate; eg how much maintenance, how often, what can one afford to attend to less frequently, or not at all, and so on. Then there has to be considered how the future is catered for: thus, by way of simple inflation in the service charge components, calculation of initial service charge on a sinking fund basis, or use of a reserve fund?

The first task for the adviser is to encourage the developer to consider his management proposals from an over-view. The developer, or the manager/management company, will be the ones to take the direct role in management. It matters little that it is the one or the other: whichever option the developer takes, there must be coordination between the developer and (if there is one) any independent manager to whom he wishes to pass his burden of management.

If there is, say, a tenants' management company to be set up, the developer will have to act 'in loco parentis' to it at this stage, because even if the developer has already incorporated the company, he will not have any prospective members with whom he can consult. Thus his role in relation to setting up of the management function will in such cases be the same as if he was taking the management on board himself.

The first job the developer must undertake then, is consideration of his various physical options, and it is to those we now direct our attention.

CHAPTER 16

The physical aspects of the management programme

The whole purpose behind this book is to provide practical information, which for the main part is grafted on to the legal base as it applies to any particular aspect which is being discussed. That is why the book is subtitled 'Practice and Precedents'. The aim is to show readers what the practical problems are likely to be; how to solve them in both the legal and the practical sense, and where necessary what documentation to use in those solutions.

Nevertheless, readers may not expect to see included in the book a treatment on the building technicalities involved in the construction, etc, of flats. But if we are going to study the methods of building up management programmes, and how they are applied to particular sites, we must surely understand what components are going into those build-ups.

In any event, it is hoped that the book may not be confined to conveyancers, and that it might be found to be of some use to others involved in the field, eg property managers, agents, even builders. If that is to be the case, then it is important that it should be a straightforward practical aid.

And so we will now turn to a consideration of the types of materials and finishes which may be used in a typical flat development, before we start looking at the build up of the management programme. The assumption on which we have worked is that we are referring to new construction, but what follows will hold just as good for refurbished premises—in fact in certain areas it will be more, rather than less, pertinent.

The way in which the chapter is set out is a separate consideration of the treatment of the interior and exterior of the block of flats, and within each of those two categories, the several sub-categories are considered. Within these sub-categories we will look at both capital and maintenance costs, and in both of those sectors we review the different treatments which are available, and list them in order of cost, first from a capital (initial construction) cost, and second from a maintenance cost. Where appropriate, relevant remarks are included.

In this way, readers will be able to comprehend the matters which the developer will have under consideration when he is choosing the treatments for the various aspects of the development, and this, of course, will be useful not only to those involved with the development side, but also those involved with buying flats, because the relative cost of the different treatments will have a marked effect on the maintenance, or service, charges.[1]

1 The author is indebted to his old friend Ken Long of Colchester for the assistance given him in preparing this chapter.

A. TREATMENT OF THE INTERIOR

Insofar as the interior is concerned, we are only considering the costs as related to the *common* areas. This is because the treatment of the interiors of the flats will have no effect at all on the maintenance of common parts, and is accordingly something which is completely separate.

1. Wall finishing in corridors

In ascending order of cost, as are all the lists in this chapter, the following treatments are available:

(a) *Capital costs*

1 Blockwork whitewashed.
2 Common brickwork whitewashed.
3 Plaster and emulsion.
4 Sandlime blocks.
5 Facing bricks.

There is also the possibility of using facing blockwork, which would be between categories 4 and 5 in cost. Consideration also has to be given to the fact that with the use of categories 4 and 5, and facing blockwork, skirtings could be omitted, and so the undoubted extra cost of those materials would be offset somewhat. Categories 1 and 2 might not be generally acceptable to the house-buying public, but they still have to be considered on account of their cheapness.

(b) *Maintenance costs*

1 Facing bricks or blocks.
2 Sandlime bricks.
3 Blockwork/brickwork whitewashed.
4 Plaster and emulsion.

Obviously with self-finish materials which have a rough surface there is less likelihood of the walls getting dirty as hands are not normally placed on them quite simply because they are uncomfortable to the touch. This would be the case with facing bricks and blocks. Sandlime bricks are self-finish, but smooth; nevertheless if they do get dirty (and they will take longer to get dirty than, eg plaster and emulsion) they are easily decorated. Whitewash or emulsion decoration will last no more than four years, and sometimes with heavy usage no more than two years.

Perhaps plaster and emulsion finishes are the most common even in these enlightened times: it can be seen that they are the most expensive to maintain and yet certainly not the cheapest to build. On the other hand, while, for example facing bricks are the most expensive to build with, they are the cheapest to maintain.

2 Ceiling finishes in corridors

This will depend on the base material present (ie the underlying material on which the ceiling is laid or hung).

(a) *Capital costs where timber used as base material*

1 Plasterboard with ivory face, and decorated.
2 Baseboard and artex.
3 Baseboard skim and decoration.
4 Mineral fibre tiles.
5 Softwood boarding stained.
6 Hardwood boarding varnished or stained.

(b) *Maintenance costs where timber used as base material*

1 Baseboard and artex (merely washing down required).
2 Plasterboard with ivory face decorated and baseboard skim and decoration (re-decorating).
3 Softwood boarding stained and hardwood boarding varnished or stained (re-stain or re-varnish).
4 Mineral fibre tiles (replace, or perhaps try to re-decorate).

Interestingly enough, the boarding, particularly hardwood, which is very often associated in people's minds with facing brick walls as being an attractive finish for internal corridors in a block of flats, is, unlike the brick facing, both expensive to install and maintain, although the relevant factor will be how often the re-staining and re-varnishing is carried out. Indeed, if it is carried out only at lengthy intervals, whilst this might tend to give the boarding a slightly worn and antique look (which might not be unattractive) then it might retreat considerably in the league table of maintenance costs.

(c) *Capital costs where concrete used as base material*

1 Direct decoration.

This needs some qualification. Direct decoration can be acceptable but it depends on where it is used. It is a strange fact that cheap finishes are often used successfully in 'one-off' houses, when used with, eg expensive furniture and carpeting. In blocks of flats, though, the concrete finishing may need filling or smoothing, or even possibly a special shuttering, using very smooth or sand blasted timber to expose the grain and give a negative effect on the exposed concrete. If special shuttering is used the cost rises to between that of categories 3 and 4.

2 Artex on concrete.
3 Plaster and emulsion decoration.
4 Mineral tiles on battens.
5 Stained softwood boarding on battens.
6 Hardwood boarding on battens.

(d) *Maintenance costs where concrete used as base material*

1 Artex on concrete (wash down).
2 Direct decoration and plaster and emulsion decoration (re-decorate).
3 Stained softwood boarding and hardwood boarding (re-stain or re-varnish).
4 Mineral tiles (replace or try decoration—but decoration is not always successful).

Whilst the treatments on concrete bases vary slightly from those on timber bases, boarding holds the same position for both capital and maintenance costs.

3 Floor finishes in corridors

Again, there will be a difference between the type of base material which is present.

(a) *Capital costs where base is concrete*

1 Marley tiles of housing quality.
2 Other types of tiles, usually of a vinyl or thermoplastic mixture.
3 Grano. (A prize will be awarded to the first reader to explain what grano is!)
4 Cheap carpeting, perhaps something like Flotex or Needlecord.
5 Pure vinyl sheeting or tiles.
6 Quarry tiles. These can be very attractive, giving a 'natural' appearance. They do tend to give out a 'cold' feel, though. If there is underfloor heating (which in itself would probably be an expensive item) this takes away the coldness.
7 Terrazzo tiles.
8 Terrazzo in situ.
9 Marble.

Cheap carpeting comes fourth in the ascending order of cost: before we leave this section we ought to mention that expensive carpeting, perhaps contract grade Wilton, will come somewhere between categories 5 and 6, which is perhaps not as expensive as might at first be thought.

(b) *Maintenance costs where base is concrete*

1 Marble, the two types of terrazzo finish, quarry tiles and grano are about the same to maintain, ie very modest.
2 Pure vinyl, vinyl/thermoplastic, and Marley tiles are roughly on a par for maintenance costs.
3 Cheap carpet—by far the most expensive to maintain. If this is present in the block of flats under consideration, it is going to present fairly constant problems because it will very quickly become tatty and difficult to keep presentable. What is more, it will need replacement quite often.

Clearly some sort of tiling finish is the best from the point of view of both capital and maintenance costs, but this finish can look very cold and stark.

The ground floor of virtually any new, and a great number of existing, blocks of flats will be solid concrete. It will have to be a very old block to have a joisted floor on the ground level, so that the above lists will hold good for at least part of virtually all blocks. On the other hand, the upper floors may be concrete based, or joisted. Much depends on the particular design, although the more storeys there are in the building, the more likely the floors are to be concrete. However, for a two- or even three-storey block, that is, the type of block which is fairly popular at the present time, joisted floors may be present. If they are, then the two lists will be as follows:

(c) *Capital costs for joisted floors*

1 Chipboard with polyurethene finish.
2 Tongued and grooved boards. (This finish used to be much more prevalent than it now is—it was common for upper floors in houses, as well as blocks of flats; but now category 1 has almost taken over completely, no doubt on account of cost, and anyway, if one is covering the floor straightaway with carpet, what does it matter what there is underneath?)
3 Plywood.
4 Marley tiles of housing quality on chipboard.
5 Carpet on chipboard.
6 Marley tiles of housing quality on tongued and grooved boards and hardboard.
7 Carpet on tongued and grooved boards and hardboard.

(d) *Maintenance costs for joisted floors*

This can be worked out by applying the table used for concrete bases. In general, comparisons of carpeting with tiling are very difficult unless one knows at what level the cost limits are. For instance, cheap carpet is less effective than cheap tiles, but expensive carpet is better than expensive tiles, *so long as it is maintained properly*—and that is the crux of the whole matter, of course.

The trend at present seems to be towards carpeting. With labour costs at so expensive a level, and the cost of laying carpeting so cheap in comparison, most of the major builders are turning more to carpeting.

4 Staircase treatment

Again, the treatment differs according, this time, to usage. The author's technical mentor who provided all the information for this part of the book used the distinction of private staircases as opposed to public. By this he meant staircases *within* flats as opposed to those in common areas. A flat with a staircase in it is still a flat, if technically a duplex, and we are not really concerned here with the interior of flats, merely the parts of the block, whether inside or out, which are *outside* the individual flats.

So that the private/public distinction is a false one, but it can easily be translated into a distinction between staircases which are going to be used to a modest degree and those which are going to experience heavy traffic. Perhaps in the first category one might place the block of 'studio' flats—with no more than eight individual units and which is described more fully in ch 9.[2]

(a) *Capital cost for low-usage staircases*

1 Softwood staircase painted; this would normally incorporate plywood risers.
2 Selected softwood (eg parana pine), varnished.
3 Hardwood, varnished.

(b) *Maintenance costs for low-usage staircases*

There is very little difference between these three categories. However, if the staircase is going to have considerable usage then the following should apply:

(c) *Capital costs for high-usage staircases*

1 Steel, with hardwood and finally carpet.
2 Concrete, with screed and finally thermoplastic tiles.
3 Concrete screed and then quarry tiles.
4 Concrete screed and then terrazzo tiles.

(d) *Maintenance costs for high usage staircases*

Reference should be made to section 3, above.

5 Internal woodwork

This is the final section dealing exclusively with the internal common parts. We have looked at floors, walls, ceilings and staircases, but not yet at internal woodwork, window frames and doors. There is not included in this section any reference to the entrance doors to the flats, because, like front and/or back doors in a house, these belong to the individual flat and fall to be treated (literally) by the flat-owner. But there will often be windows in the common parts and there will be at least one door. To a very great extent, section 1 below on external window frames/doors, will automatically apply to this section and should be consulted so far as the window frames and doors are concerned (as the treatment of the frames will obviously be the same on the inside as on the outside) but there will very often be skirting and architraves around the door openings. What about these items?

(a) *Capital costs*

1 Softwood, painted (usually white).
2 Selected softwood, parana pine, varnished.

2 P 110, above.

3 Hardwood varnished.

(b) *Maintenance costs*

Repainting would have to be carried out, say, at maximum every two years, and at minimum every four years. Any longer than that and it would start to look fairly 'tatty'. Although there are plenty of flats where one suspects, the repainting cycle on common internal areas is longer than every four years. Ideally, the varnished surfaces should be renewed on a similar basis to the painted ones, although again the suspicion is that most managers would extend the cycle to some extent, and probably in these cases with more safety.

B. TREATMENT OF THE EXTERIOR

In some instances, the exterior treatment will comprise the main element of a maintenance programme, for instance in the small flats scheme of maintenance described in ch 9.[3]

In any scheme, the exterior matters will take a significant part of the maintenance costs, if only because anything which is on the outside of the block will have to withstand not only the ravages of human traffic, as does the interior, but also the ravages of the weather. For this reason, extra care should be taken when considering what materials should be used on the exterior.

1 Window frames

Again, the lists set out below represent an ascending cost, ie those at the top of the list are cheaper than those at the bottom.

(a) *Capital costs*

1 Softwood stained.
2 Softwood painted.
3 High performance timber stained.
4 High performance timber painted.
5 Hardwood varnished.
6 Aluminium mill finish.
7 Aluminium mill finish in timber frame.
8 Anodised aluminium.
9 Plastic (surprisingly enough).

(b) *Maintenance costs*

This is one of the easiest lists to remember—all one does is reverse the capital costs list. This is interesting, because one can see that painted softwood

3 P 110, above.

frames are the cheapest but one to instal, but the next to most expensive to maintain, partly because they will have to be painted quite often, a cycle of two to five years is about right, but they will also be prone to deterioration, eg wood rot.

2 External surfaces

By external surfaces is meant those other than window frames and door openings. In other words, bricks, etc.

This section is a little more difficult to put into the form of two separate lists of capital and maintenance costs, so we shall treat the subject in two principal sections; use of bricks, and alternative materials.

(a) *Brickwork*

Brickwork as a capital cost factor is neither the most expensive nor the cheapest. However, as a statement of fact this is open to query, because there are very many different types of facing bricks. Common bricks are those which are used where they are not going to be visible, facing bricks have one 'face' and the two side 'faces' which have the particular external finish which is going to be on show. Different brickworks, in different areas, have varying colours, shades and treatment of faces. Some bricks are of modest cost, but others can be very expensive.

Any ordinary facing brickwork will not be in need of maintenance for a very long time—probably a minimum period of 30 years, but after that time some repointing will be required. For those not 'au fait' with technical terms, it is not the bricks which start to deteriorate—brickwork should last for a very long time indeed, but the mortar in the joints will start to crumble, and if it is not treated, it will start to fail, and the whole construction might eventually be in some danger if no repointing was done; repointing is making good the mortar in the joints.

The only problem about repointing is that doing it 'bit by bit' can lead to a patchy finish to the brickwork. If possible, it would be wise to wait until the whole wall needs repointing. Nevertheless, if fairly small areas of brickwork can be selected, which when repointed will not contrast too badly with the unpointed areas, then a long term programme of repointing is both feasible and reasonably economic.

The only caveat to this is that on buildings of more than perhaps two, and certainly three storeys, scaffolding will be necessary for repairs of this type, and scaffolding costs are high. We shall return to this subject below.

(b) *Alternative external surfaces*

These are generally more expensive than all but the most expensive facing bricks. The only really feasible alternative on blocks of flats is external rendering.

The most important consideration when looking at both capital and maintenance costs on external rendering is what the base construction is, ie is it blockwork or brickwork?

Unlike brickwork, where the maintenance costs are long in coming, and when they do are reasonably modest, rendering requires constant maintenance—not only in replacing or renewing any worn areas of the rendering but in repainting. Thus if emulsion is used, a cycle of as low as two years has to be considered, whilst if masonry paint (which not surprisingly is more expensive than emulsion) is the material used, the cycle becomes five years. There are, however, new materials coming onto the market which have more acceptably long lives. If the buildings are more than two to three storeys in height, then there will be a constant need for scaffolding. Every time the rendering is painted, scaffolding will be required which is expensive, so there will be a constant drain on the maintenance costs. As the cost of repainting a block of flats itself is not inconsiderable, developers would be well advised to steer clear of rendered surfaces, which to be fair they generally do, and those acting for intending purchasers should ask their clients to confirm that the flat they are buying, whether new or old, is not rendered, and if it is they should explain that it will undoubtedly be more expensive to maintain.

3 Roofing

A few years ago, we might have been considering flat roofs to be the industry standard where blocks of flats were concerned. However, present day trends are away from high rise building and the average block of flats, except in some few areas in built-up situations, will not be more than four to six storeys high, and will probably have a pitched, as opposed to flat, roof.

For such properties, one would be thinking of interlocking concrete roof tiles. Experience shows that the cost of maintenance even on roofs which are five, six or even seven storeys high is minimal. The minimum maintenance free period is similar to brickwork, ie 30 years. Nevertheless, the building works must be carried out carefully. Especial care should be taken, particularly on high roofs, to ascertain the exposure conditions, and to ensure that the correct fixings are used in construction.

4 Hard external surfaces

This term refers to the surfaces outside the block of flats itself, in other words the car parking surfaces, accessways and footpaths.

The type of surface to be used depends on usage, eg for pedestrians, domestic vehicles, or heavy commercial vehicles. The following list is based on domestic usage.

(a) *Capital costs*

1 Concrete on hardcore.
2 Tarmac on stone.
3 Paving slabs on hardcore.
4 Concrete paviors on sand.
5 Brick paviors on sand or concrete.
6 Granite paviors on sand or concrete.

Items 4, 5 and 6 are fairly high specification materials, indeed they may be more than is needed, but at the same time they are the cheapest to maintain, and from the manager's and the flat-owners' point of view, if not the developer's, are the most preferable. Readers may have noticed that recently more and more public areas, including places like the central reservation areas on mini-roundabouts, are being constructed with paviors, obviously with an eye to maintenance costs.

5 Soft external surfaces

While it may be fairly obvious that hard external surfaces will require fairly minimal maintenance, soft external areas will need a great deal of looking after. Our treatment of these is slightly different because of this:

(a) *Capital costs*

When considering soft areas, we are probably looking at an ascending order of cost as follows.

1 Areas laid completely to grass, almost certainly turfed.
2 Areas laid to garden ground, with shrubs, trees, and other plants.
3 Areas perhaps one or other of the above categories or a mixture of both but with an element of ornamental areas, eg ponds/waterfalls/rockeries, etc.

(b) *Maintenance costs*

It is almost impossible to reduce the maintenance costs on soft external areas to a list. Therefore we set out the three categories from section (a) and add appropriate comments.

(i) Grassed areas. These might be thought to be by far the cheapest to maintain, but there are some surprises. For instance, whilst in winter months no work at all will be required on them, during the growing season, which is April to October inclusive, the grass will have to be cut and trimmed. The frequency of cut might well be different for the various seasons—eg in May and June once a fortnight might well be insufficient, although for an economic management programme one cannot really get any more frequent, whilst for the rest of the season it is perhaps possible to get away with a frequency of once every three weeks.

The trouble with grass is that it grows and there is nothing more unsightly than long, unkempt grass, so that if any of the soft external areas are grassed they represent a considerable demand on maintenance, the only saving grace being that this is only for just over half the year so that the costs of grass cutting can be spread over the whole year.

(ii) Garden areas. Again there will only be a commitment on maintenance during the growing season, but this time it will include any necessary replacements. Probably jobs like weeding will not be necessary on the same frequency level as grass-cutting.

(iii) Ornamental areas. If these include things like ponds, waterfalls, and the like, they are likely to cost a fair amount to maintain, especially if there is any machinery involved. Accordingly one would expect to find such areas only in an up-market scheme.

C. ADDITIONAL MATTERS FOR CONSIDERATION

The above matters represent the 'bare bones' of the make-up of a traditional block of flats, but there are one or two other areas which might stand a brief inspection, representing as they do the sort of things one might expect to find in a lot of developments. These matters are as follows:

1 Radio cables

When installed, as they usually are, these will be a direct cost to the developer. The maintenance on them is virtually zero.

2 Television cables

Their treatment is slightly different to radio cables. The principal features are as follows:

(i) the initial cost is usually shared between the developer and the cable company, although some cable companies will bear the cost totally;
(ii) if there are problems, eg planning ones, associated with having forests of aerials on the roofs of blocks of flats, or if the developer himself is against this sort of thing; or with multi-storey blocks; or where there is poor reception, then cable TV can be an excellent idea;
(iii) maintenance costs again will be virtually zero;
(iv) no information is presently available about cable TV as a service into flats. The 'cable' referred to in this section is that which brings the *normal* ie BBC and IBA programmes into the block.

3 Entry-phone systems

Entry-phone systems are generally of two different types:

(i) those which are purely an audio system and
(ii) those which incorporate some sort of video system as well—eg a video camera above the main, security door, and a small screen within the flat so that the flat-dweller is able to see who is calling.

The purely audio systems can be bought outright on installation, but the video systems are more likely to be rented (and thus form a charge on the service charge). In these cases the equipment is usually installed free of charge and rented on a quarterly basis, although there are various permutations on the cost of installation and rental. In this sort of case, where the supplier either remits any capital cost or keeps it down to an absolute minimum, the cost to the developer is purely a modest amount of building work involving chases for cables and subsequent making good.

It is difficult to quantify the cost of the installation—it is really like saying 'how long is a piece of string'—but in one case in which the author was recently involved, which dealt with fairly high class flats in the North London area, the cost of rental was about £10 per annum per flat, which for the added protection seems perfectly reasonable. Of course, it is primarily a matter of consideration of market forces as to whether or not any such system should be intalled in the first place,[4] but most definitely an entry-phone system is a feature to which many intending purchasers would not take objection, given the modest extra cost, and in the higher class type of development it would be expected to be present, and if not, the developer might suffer.

4 Metered fuel systems

Readers may already have come across blocks of flats which employ a metered system for supply of fuel from a centralised source, in other words (and this is very nearly always connected with a central heating system, although the principle can just as easily be applied to other types of supply) there will be a single boilerhouse supplying all the flats.

There are two different methods of setting up this sort of system, and we shall discuss these briefly before we turn to an examination of whether or not the idea is acceptable to those who are buying the flats. The differences in setting-up relate solely to the method of measurement and not to the basic installation, which is pretty constant.

(a) *Flow metering*

This is to be contrasted with the other type of measurement method, electronic metering, and it has largely been overtaken by the development of the sophisticated heat sensors which are now generally found in the latter type of systems. Nevertheless, flow metering systems are still sometimes found and apparently are still sometimes installed.

The principle of the flow meter is that it measures the volume of water passing through a dwelling.[5] This is usually done with a single jet vane (ie an impeller) type mechanical meter with magnetic transmission, designed to operate at hot water temperatures. The actual counter itself is in a sealed dry housing and accumulates volume of water passing through in cubic centimetres.

Heat charges within the service charge are simply accounted by totalling

4 Eg see ch 18, p 204, below where the individual service components are built up into the service charge. The developer has to consider what effect any such additional cost will have on the overall service charge he is quoting customers. This illustrates why the whole procedure described in this section of the book should be carried out as early as possible, because an item like entry-phone rental could just be the straw which broke the camel's back.

5 Remember that this is central heating from a *central* (ie in the common parts) boiler, which is heating water and pumping it round and into the individual flats, presumably through radiators.

the registrations on meters in all the flats in the block, then dividing that figure into the (known) fuel cost so as to arrive at a cost per cubic metre. Then each dwelling has its own costs calculated by multiplying by the appropriate registration particular to that flat.

This system has been used on the continent with some success but not in this country, where possibly people are more cynical and more ready to take issue with any charges levied on them of which they do not have absolute first-hand knowledge.

The basic problem is that the fundamental principle of flow metering is wrong. This assumes that volume equates to heat. For this to be true, water must arrive at each dwelling *wall* at the same temperature. Also, each dwelling must take the same amount of heat per cubic metre from the water passing through it. This is unfortunately not technically possible for 24 hours a day, 365 days a year, and the whole system is subject to uneven slippage and loss.

The mechanical flow meters themselves are easy enough to install, but even this statement assumes that the developer is careful and intelligent. For this system to work, the individual flat should have its own separate supply and return from the distribution main. It is also advisable to fit strainers upstream from meters.

(b) *Electronic metering*

Electronic heat meters represent a major advance in thermal energy measurement, and virtually completely answer the justified complaints about metering systems based on the use of flow meters.

The meter itself is an electronic integrating heat meter specifically designed for recording energy consumption in both domestic and small commercial premises connected to central boiler schemes, thus perfectly fitted for the system under discussion.

Water flow is measured by an electromagnetic flow meter, and the flow signal is combined with a temperature difference signal from two platinum resistance thermometers. The resulting thermal power signal is continuously integrated so as to give a displayed reading of energy used in kilowatt hours.

This type of meter's sophisticated electronic circuiting ensures that its accuracy may be compared with that of a domestic electricity meter, even at low flow rates and with small temperature differences.

(c) *Consumer acceptability*

With a metered system of heating, of either variety, not only the individual flats but also the internal common areas may be heated in this way. Naturally, the flat-owners will pay only a stated proportion of the costs of common area heating, but if there is an argument about the efficiency of even one meter, all parts of the building, private and common, are affected.

If there are pressure groups amongst the flat-owners, especially from the start of the development, an underlying concern about the method's inherent lack of 'equitability' as a heat charging method may result in it being discredited. If the flow system used is mechanical, this may then become extremely difficult to refute. On the other hand, the electronic method is much more foolproof, and ought to be acceptable. The trouble is, that once someone gets a bee in their bonnet about meters being unreliable, the damage has already been done.

Accordingly the points to watch are:

(d) *For lessors/developers*

(a) If you have to instal a central heat distribution system, make sure it is an electronically metered one. The extra cost is worth it.
(b) Make sure the flat-owners know right from the start about their system.
(c) Service the apparatus regularly.
(d) Resist the protests of any pressure groups who happen not to like such a system. (This is always assuming that there is any such pressure group—and also, of course, that there is nothing wrong with the system!)

(e) *For flat-owners and their advisers*

(a) Make sure you investigate thoroughly before you commit yourself to the purchase of the flat, what sort of central heating system is installed, and if it is a central flow metered system.
(b) Find out if it is mechanical or electronic.
(c) In either case, but especially the former, ask other flat-owners in the block if there have been any problems. If there have, then, as the Scots say, you should 'ca canny'.
(d) If the block is new, you cannot go around checking. In this case think carefully before you commit yourself.

The above points, relating to both inside and outside the block of flats, and including matters such as type of heating installation where there is centralisation, are important ones to bear in mind when buying a flat, either new or second hand. Naturally, they are also points for consideration by the developer/lessor of the same block of flats.

D. SUMMARY

Service charges are more and more a political hot potato, and on the one hand the lessor/manager must be seen to be giving reasonable value for money, and on the other hand the flat-owner must be sure that he is not being put upon by his lessor or manager. In order to satisfy both ends of this equation, it is important to understand about the relative capital and maintenance costs of what goes into the building of a block of flats. Some materials will be cheap to instal, but will give rise to high maintenance costs in future years. Other materials may be more expensive to instal, but will be much cheaper to maintain. Both sides will wish to see a reasonably fair balance struck. It is to be hoped that the contents of this chapter, augmented by succeeding chapters on how the maintenance charge is put together, will assist in achieving that object.

CHAPTER 17

The management programme: provisions in the lease

After discussions between the developer and his various advisers as to the type of materials and finishes which will be employed on any scheme, the next job will be for the manager principally, but in conjunction with the developer (if they are separate persons) and the legal adviser, to consider what maintenance items should be quoted in the lease.

Virtually every lease will be reasonably specific in identifying which items of maintenance the lessor/manager is to be responsible for, and thus included in the computation of the service charge. It would be most foolish to try to draft a lease which merely said of maintenance something like: 'the lessor will maintain the property in a good and workmanlike condition'. This, of course, is a nonsensical proposition, because (at least so one hopes) no intending lessee properly advised would dream of carrying on with negotiations to take a lease which was so generalised and imprecise. So, as we all acknowledge, the lease has to contain in fairly specific detail just what items of maintenance are included in the programme.

The precedents contained in this book have been selected not so much for their wording, but more as good examples of the kind of document which should be used in any given situation. Thus Precedent No 2 on p 346, below is a fairly standard, full maintenance lease, but the author would be the last to suggest that the part of the lease which sets out just what types of maintenance will be included in the programme is definitive; it is not. It is a skeletal form which the individual draftsman may adapt to his own requirements by additions, subtractions, expansion, and so on.

The task to which the developer now has to address himself is to isolate into headings what he will have to deal with under his maintenance programme. The best way to illustrate this is by example, setting out the various maintenance jobs, and ancillary matters which will need to be included in the programme.

The reader should note that, although the following list is not, and because of local variation cannot ever be, exhaustive, it does represent a reasonably typical full programme of maintenance and so must be contrasted with eg the 'small unit quasi-self-help' scheme described on pp 110–127, above. The *level* of maintenance is discussed later on in this section.

We will look at these separate provisions in two sections; first those where the manager has to make actual payments for services, of whatever variety, rendered, together with reserve fund contributions, and second, the more amorphous provisions for recouping the manager's *own* costs of managing, etc.

A. MONETARY RECOVERY

1 Direct expenditure

(a) *Re-decoration*

This will apply to:

(a) internal; and
(b) external

common areas. Those areas will be defined in the lease, either by implication, or much more probably in a well-drawn lease, by specific wording, usually also by reference to a plan. Readers should refer to Precedent Nos 2 and 3 below for suggested typical wording for a description of the individual units on the one hand, and the common areas on the other.

The heading will also refer to:

(a) quality of materials to be used; and
(b) frequency of treatment.

The quality may be expressed in the vaguest terms possible, or may not be expressed at all, although there would still be an implied reference as the lessees would be entitled to expect the lessor to use materials of a reasonable quality; or, quality may be laid down absolutely precisely, eg 'in a good and workmanlike manner to wash and paint with two coats of suitably good quality materials and to grain stain and varnish all parts etc, usually so treated and to wash distemper and whiten all ceilings and strip and repaper and renew or otherwise decorate in an appropriate manner all walls and other parts with a decorative finish'.

The choice of emphasis lays with the draftsman entirely, but he would be wise to know what materials, finishes, and where, are involved in the specific block under consideration before he finalises his wording, which is adaptable. There is no point in having a re-decoration clause which appears to be at odds with what is actually there on the ground.

The frequency may be also expressed specifically, or vaguely. Thus, the lease may say:

'as often as may in the opinion of (lessor/surveyor to lessor/manager, as the case may be) be necessary'

or he may specify precise cycles, eg:

'at least once in every ... years and in the last year of the term (terminate when it may)'.

Once again the choice is with the draftsman, although on balance, but only provided the lessor is confident he has the organisation to implement it and the lessee is confident the lessor does have that organisation, the former is preferable.

(b) *Repair*

Again, this will apply to all parts of the common areas, inside and out. In some leases, the common areas are defined differently to the main structure of the block, so that the common parts might be treated thus:

'to keep the entrance halls (including doors and doorways) staircases landings and passageways ... in good repair and condition.'

The structure would have its own clause:

'to keep the walls both interior and exterior floors ceilings the roof foundations service pipes, etc ... in good repair and condition.'

Of necessity, because while it is safe to assume that, for example, paintwork will deteriorate to an ascertainable cycle, there is no such pre-determination on general repairs, so that the appropriate clause as illustrated above will be prefaced by words such as

'At all times during the said term.'

Alternatively, a more straightforward clause, especially where the parts of the property the subject of the maintenance programme have been defined in the lease, by an expression such as 'the Maintained Property', will look like:

'Repairing rebuilding repointing improving or otherwise treating as necessary and keeping the Maintained Property and every part thereof in good and substantial repair order and condition and renewing and replacing all worn or damaged parts thereof.'

(c) *Repair and maintenance of external areas (soft)*

It is wise to treat external areas in a separate clause. Theoretically, if those areas are included in the definition of the common parts, as they usually will be, there is no need for such an extra clause, although the typical wording quoted above in section (a) and (b) would need expansion, because the type of work necessary on external areas is so different. Far better to separate external areas into a separate clause, eg:

'Keeping the gardens and grounds of the Maintained Property in a neat and tidy condition [and if greater emphasis is required—carry on with]: and tending and renewing all lawns flower beds shrubs and trees and maintaining repairing and where necessary reinstating any boundary wall hedge or fence (if any) and any benches seats garden ornaments (including water features)'.

(d) *Repair and cleaning of external areas (hard)*

There may well be private roads, parking areas, footpaths, etc which form part of the common parts. In that case another separate clause is recommended. As cycles of repair on this type of area are indeterminate, the clause itself should follow suit, eg:

'Keeping the private road/s [etc as the case requires] in good repair and in a clean and tidy condition'.

(e) *Cleaning windows and internal common areas*

There should be a clause relating to the cleaning of windows (inside and out) of the common areas, and the entrance halls, staircases, landings etc.

again on the basis of 'as necessary'. This section of the maintenance will be, interestingly enough, one of the most expensive parts of the service charge build-up, especially if a professional cleaning firm are contracted to do the job. In the author's experience, internal cleaning costs are very often the highest factor in a management programme build-up. Those in charge of management must be sure that:

(a) in the first instance they secure a contract with whoever will be responsible for cleaning in the best possible terms. This is an area where probably the requirements of the Housing Act 1980, Sch 19, relating to the taking of a minimum of two quotes[1] will be relevant, and the manager will do well to get as many quotes as he can; and
(b) the level of cleaning services is neither pitched too high, so that the service charge is bumped up unnecessarily, nor pitched too low, so that lessees become dissatisfied with the service.

As can be seen, it is all very difficult for the manager.

(f) *Operating electrical, etc, apparatus*

In even the smallest block of flats, eg the small studio blocks described in ch 9, above we have seen that there will need to be a landlord's service for the internal common areas. In more complex blocks, there may also be:

(a) Outside lighting, both
    (i) associated with the buildings, and
    (ii) eg street lighting on any private roads there may be;
(b) entry phone/video systems, radio and TV cable systems;
(c) other electrical and mechanical equipment associated with either the buildings or the external areas, eg machinery to drive the fountains in the ornamental gardens.

All this equipment should be the subject of a separate clause, eg:

'Operating maintaining and (where necessary) renewing the ... apparatus from time to time installed in the Maintained Property including the external areas thereof.'

(g) *Dustbins, etc*

It is usually wise to have a separate provision for dustbins which will encompass the provision of special areas, and dealing with the bins on a day-to-day basis, thus:

'providing and arranging for the emptying of receptacles for rubbish for the use of the lessees of the flats.'

(h) *Lifts and lift shafts*

Developers try to avoid lifts where possible. This is partly why blocks of flats now tend to be low-rise, ie not usually more than three storeys high, where one can get away with having no lift.

1 Refer also to ch 14, p 159 above, on the provisions of the Housing Act 1980, Sch 19.

The provision of lifts is expensive enough for the developer as part of his initial costs, so that it is bound to be reflected in the selling costs of the flat, but what the prospective lessee, both on the initial sale and subsequent assignments, must be careful about is the cost of maintenance. Lift maintenance is obviously a matter which simply cannot be skimped; the consequences of poor or non-maintenance are too horrific to contemplate. The incoming purchaser is therefore entitled to know that a proper maintenance contract has been arranged with qualified lift engineers. There is only one problem about such contracts, and that is that they are very expensive. Nevertheless, if one assumes that the purchaser already knows, or has been told by his adviser, that lift maintenance will have a considerable effect on the amount of the service charge he will have to pay, the main point is that the lease must adequately provide for the lessor/manager to keep the lift/s and any ancillary equipment in good working order and repair and to remedy any failures as soon as possible.

(i) *Staff premises*

This section may apply only to a very few developments although it is surprising at what an early point employment of, say, a caretaker (male) and cleaner (wife) on a development becomes more cost effective than employing outside contractors. The average conveyancer in the provinces may, however, never come across a development where there are staff premises (although quite a number of leases may well carry the provision). Nevertheless, where permanent staff are employed on the development, staff premises *may* be provided, and in those cases a clause will be necessary providing for repair, maintenance, decoration, etc of such premises and the payment of any outgoings thereon, otherwise such costs could be disallowed.

(j) *Staff*

While there will rarely be staff premises there will very often be staff, or there will be some employment function to be performed by the lessor/manager. The appropriate heads to be considered are:

(a) Staff employed to carry out maintenance. This would not apply to sub-contractors, because there the manager is paying for the performance of the contract, as opposed to paying for staff. But there may be permanent or temporary staff, employed by the manager to perform tasks related to the maintenance of the scheme. Obviously in these cases employment costs would encompass not only salary but NHI, pension, etc payments.

(b) employment of persons, firms or companies presumably on a part-time basis to carry out tasks such as (for a surveyor) overseeing the management programme as a whole or, eg (for an accountant) auditing the accounts.

This second category might conveniently be incorporated with this staff clause, or separated into a clause of its own dealing with employment of professionals and quasi-professionals.

(k) *Payment of rates, etc*

A separate clause should deal with the payment of any 'rates, taxes duties charges assessments and outgoings whatsoever (whether parliamentary parochial local or otherwise)'—a tried and tested phrase and no doubt because of that one which keeps cropping up! The covenant on the part of the manager must obviously be limited to those parts of the scheme for which he is responsible; ie the individual flats themselves are excepted from this provision.

Audit costs could fairly easily be included in this clause, although they are sometimes given a separate clause of their own, or even impliedly included in the costs of management, for which see below.

(l) *Insurance*[2]

The manager will be responsible for arranging insurance, and will pay the block premium, recouping the cost from the individual flat-owners as part of the overall service charge. This head will cover both the normal fire, etc insurance and third-party insurance.

(m) *Other provisions*

The draftsman and manager together should decide what will be specified in the lease, and what may be safely left unspecified, eg by inclusion in a 'sweeper' clause. Some of the individual items which might appear are:

(i) maintenance of fire fighting equipment;
(ii) provision and maintenance of gardening equipment;
(iii) joint expenditure with any adjoining owners, and so on.

2 Reserve fund provision

By way of introduction to this part of the subject, we reproduce clauses 23.1 and 23.2 of the Sixth Schedule to Precedent No 2 p 353, below:

'Such sum (to be fixed annually) as shall be estimated by the Management Company (whose decision shall be final)[3] to provide a reserve fund for items of expenditure referred to in this Schedule to be or expected to be incurred at any time during the period of [three] years commencing with the date on which the estimate is made.'
'The said reserve fund shall be kept in separate accounts and any interest on or income of the said fund shall be held by the Management Company in trust for the lessees of the flats and shall only be applied in accordance with the terms of this Schedule.'

All good management programmes should have reserve funds, or sinking funds, as they are sometimes called. There is nothing complex about their basic concept, which is that of a contingency fund.

There are still in existence some management programmes which provide

2 See further on insurance, ch 4, p 43, above.
3 The words in brackets are probably useless: the court has an overriding power to decide on reasonableness.

for payment of expenditure on an 'as it arises' basis. Thus the regular costs, eg cleaning of common areas, etc are paid in the normal way, ie through the (probably) half-yearly service charge, but when major items like, eg re-decoration of the outside, have to be undertaken, those lessees who happen to be in the block when the cost of that re-decoration arises, have to pay the whole cost between themselves *in that one year*.

This is clearly inequitable. What of those lessees (including those who are current) who have enjoyed the amenities of the block in previous years, and those who will also do so in years to come? They will not have been asked to share in this type of expense. The result will be that in some years some lessees may suffer very heavy service charges, and in other years other lessees may pay very little. This is unfair, which is why in the management programme build-up described in pp 204–221 below, the five-year, and perhaps also ten-year cycles of maintenance are reduced to anticipated annual charges and included in the overall service charge.

In some management programmes, the long cycles would be dealt with by way of reserve fund contributions, but this has two side effects; first, because the work involved in those cycles is expensive, this produces a very substantial reserve fund contribution each year, and second (a direct consequence of the first point) the high contribution leaves no room for additional contributions to the true contingencies. In other words, everyone *knows* that the redecorations will have to be done in five years, and new tarmac laid in ten years. This can, and should be, catered for within the cycles of the programme itself.

What the reserve fund should be for is the generally unexpected, eg if for some reason roof repairs become necessary, and are not reclaimable from some third party, including an insurer. There are many such matters which could crop up; and the manager needs a contingency fund which he can use, rather than dipping into his main fund, an action which would lead to additional levies on the lessees anyway.

There are those who would say that the contributions to the regular cycles would not be treated by the manager in the same way as reserve fund payments if the following pattern were to be followed: thus they would not be kept in 'separate accounts', 'in trust for the lessees', and interest earned on them. This is fair comment, but on balance, and based on experience, the author still prefers to see the reserve fund treated as a genuine contingency fund which can be used for unexpected expenditure, and the build-up of monies, part of the service charge payments, which will occur in respect of the longer maintenance cycles, ought to be treated by the manager in the same way as true reserve fund payments. Whether or not it is, of course, is quite another matter, but to do otherwise would surely produce a completely unbalanced reserve fund contribution, and make the whole programme more, as opposed to less, unwieldy.

Period of fund

In the example clauses quoted, the fund was to last for only three years. As this period is less than, eg the re-decoration cycles, this is yet another indication that these should remain, along with the other long cycles, in the main programme.

The point about limiting the fund for three years is that it is difficult to look further than that into the future. However, the fund will be a rolling programme; it will not stop at the end of three years. What will happen is that the fund will be set up at the beginning of the development and when it has reached a three-year level, it is maintained at that level; in other words, the year furthest away is released as the new year is added on. If the Reserve Fund monies are not being used for any purpose within the management programme, then the released years monies would be directed into the main fund. Reserve fund monies are specifically held in trust for the lessees, so once they are released, do the trust provisions lapse? Probably not, as there is in effect just as much of a quasi-trust relationship in the main fund.

What if the reserve fund monies are not so released? If we go back to the specimen clauses set out at the beginning of this sector, we see that the stated aims of the trust appear only to last for three years anyway, so that there is doubt about the status of any monies dating back beyond three years in any case. There is also the point to be made that in the specimen clauses, the amount of the reserve fund contribution in any year is in the decision of the manager/lessor, so that perhaps if there were no expenditure in any one year on contingency matters, it would be open to the manager not to levy a contribution in the following year.

What all this amounts to is that the operation of a reserve fund is a rather imprecise science. This is the answer to those who ask 'how much should a reserve fund contribution be: 5%, 10%, or what?' If a reserve fund is operated too rigidly, then the manager will soon be knee-deep in surpluses or shortfalls. If he can 'fine tune' the operation of the fund on a yearly basis, he will be able to maintain a more even balance. That is why the specimen clauses are drafted in the way they are: thus 'Such sum ... to be fixed annually ... to be estimated by the manager ...'

B. COSTS OF MANAGEMENT

All the above heads of expenditure relate to money which is repaid to some third party for work done or services rendered in connection with the scheme. If the manager has to work with a lease which stops at this point, he will have to set up administration to find, appoint, monitor, and pay all those third parties. That will cost him money, but in none of the above sections is there any return for the manager, save in the case of insurance where one supposes that he has negotiated a reasonable commission rate with the insurer. The headings which must be considered are as follows:

1 General duties which are indefinable in a precise manner

(a) *Compliance with directions, etc*

The cautious lessor/manager (and should there be any other sort?) will want to see in his list of duties/powers in respect of which he may be reimbursed a provision that he should comply with 'the requirements and directions of any competent authority and with the provisions of all statutes and all regulations orders and byelaws made thereunder relating to [the development]'.

(b) *Abatement of nuisance*

Perhaps rather similar to the above heading but sometimes expressed separately in the lease, is a provision for the lessor/manager to:

'abate any nuisance and execute such works as may be necessary for complying with any notice served by a local authority in connection with [the development] or any part thereof insofar as the same is not the liability of or attributable to the fault of any individual lessee of any flat.'

(c) *Enforcement of covenants*

A prudent lessee should see that the lease he is taking on provides that the lessor will be bound to enforce against any other lessees in the same block the same covenants as are contained in his own lease, and also (usually) that as long as any flat is unlet, at the beginning of the development, to observe those same covenants as if those flats were indeed let. Some leases contain a provision enabling a manager/lessor to recharge for any work expended in this direction.

(d) *Regulations*

A great number of flats schemes refer to regulations which are to be made by the lessor/manager, and this task may be recharged. Thus, the precise wording may be something like:

'preparing and supplying to the lessees of the flats copies of any regulations made by the management company governing the use of the flats and/or [the development].'

Now regulations are all very well, but they do seem to have rather more disadvantages than advantages. As this part of our subject is very often a largely ignored one which is nevertheless potentially troublesome, we ought to take some time to look at the pros and cons.

(i) Advantages for the lessor/manager. Regulations should not refer to the principles of the management scheme. Rather, they should deal with everyday matters which are designed to add to the general quality of life for the flat owners, eg a regulation might be made that ball games are not permitted in the external areas or even the prohibition of the playing of hi-fi's, TVs, etc outside a stated period during each day, rather than have it in the lease, as it so often is.

Thus the manager may deal with the way in which the development is regulated on almost a day-to-day basis, and what is more he can 'fine tune' the regulations from time to time. This gives him the opportunity of flexible management without having to rely upon the provisions of the lease, which will have been settled long before the flats are actually occupied and the manager can see precisely what volume of local fine tuning is required.

(ii) Advantages for the lessee. The lessee might see a system of regulations subsidiary to the lease provisions as giving him adequate protection, perhaps against his fellow lessees. At the same time, though, he might see it precisely the other way (see below).

(iii) Disadvantages for the lessor/manager. There is no doubt that responsibility for regulations adds yet another burden to the lessor. If the lease talks about regulations then the lessees will expect to receive a set of regulations. Compilation of regulations, whether on a once-and-for-all basis (although even these would call for amendment from time to time) or on an ad hoc basis, soaks up management time. For instance if, as he should do, the manager is liaising properly with a residents' association[4] the residents have every right to be heard on what regulations there should, and should not, be. All this will take up management time.

(iv) Disadvantages for the lessee. To be burdened with regulations which are additional to those provisions contained in the lease, and which relate to the 'behavioural' aspects of the relationship, may be unacceptable. Many people, including the Law Commission, the building society movement, and leading practitioners amongst others, favour a move away from the 'paternalistic' lessor/lessee relationship. The imposition of a set of regulations would appear to be moving in the opposite direction. Probably at the end of the day, it might be wise to include in the lease itself a provision allowing the formulating of regulations, but if this is done, lessees should be told as soon as they complete their leases, if not sooner, what the manager's intentions are in this direction.

(e) *Sweeper clause*

The cautious or unsure draftsman (the two adjectives are meant to refer to separate categories) may favour a clause which states that the lessor/manager may 'carry out such other repairs or improvements' and also 'defray such other costs' in relation to the development which he considers to be 'necessary to maintain [the development].' Whether such a clause is ever necessary seems to be open to question; sufficient provision ought to have been made in preceding clauses.

2 Costs of administration

(a) *Overhead recovery*

We now come to an aspect of management costs build-up which can and does sometimes cause considerable confusion. The author has been questioned on a number of occasions as to the permissibility of the manager

4 And see also the provisions of the Housing Act 1980, Sch 19, ch 14, p 159, above.

charging his overhead costs to the service charge. There is a feeling abroad that this may be prohibited by the legislature. It is not. If the reader has studied the Housing Act, Sch 19,[5] as we hope he has, there is nothing which prohibits the manager recouping his overheads, *as well as taking a management fee as profit.*[6] Before we discuss the implications of this statement, let us have a brief look at the way in which this may be expressed in the lease.

Remember that what we are discussing are the *manager's* costs of management, not costs attributable to third parties. We have already dealt with payments to third parties, which will represent the 'sub-total' global management costs in any given period. But the manager must expend money in order to arrive at that stage. Thus, he must:

1 Identify suitable subcontractors for the works, obtain quotes, where necessary take those quotes to the residents' association, and obtain approvals.

2 Following on from appointment of subcontractors, he must then monitor their performance. This (and possibly the work involved in section 1, above) may be done for him by others, eg managing agents, but whichever way the job is tackled, he will have to pay, either his own overheads or managing agent's costs, and if he chooses the latter alternative, he will still have some residual sort of overhead commitment.

Mention of managing agents leads us on at this convenient point to illustrate the sort of clause which will deal with this part of the management costs, eg:

'Generally managing and administering the Development and protecting the amenities of the Development and for that purpose if [the Management Company] think fit employing a firm of managing agents.'

3 We now pass on to overheads proper. The scale of overheads will vary tremendously. Thus, if the manager is involved only in, say, a very few blocks of flats, which are perhaps not over-complicated, and he is employing managing agents, he may have very few, or even possibly no, overheads of his own, because his managing agents will be doing all the work for him. (But remember their costs will have to be recouped as part of the service charge, which is why they are specifically mentioned in the specimen clause just quoted.)

On the other hand, if the manager is a specialist company, dealing direct with maintenance, with a reasonably large portfolio of flats, and it has its own premises, then it will have substantial overheads.

To illustrate the point, the following heads are typical of those in respect of which the manager will incur expenditure.

salaries of staff, including NHI and pension contributions;
rent, rates, of manager's office accommodation;
heating and lighting ditto;
stationery and printing;
postage;
phone bills;
motor travelling;

5 Ch 14, p 159, above.
6 See later, p 199.

vehicle leasing or purchase;
computer/other mechanical/electrical/electronic equipment;
leasing costs;
audit fees;
service charges on its own premises (ironic though this may be!);
bad debts;
repairs and renewals;
depreciation;
sundries; and
bank interest.

All these items will very soon add up to a not inconsiderable amount. If the service charge recovers only profit, in the shape of a management fee (for which see later) then these overheads will soak up those fees, and there is a very real danger that the management function may be run at a loss. This is why a great number of management programmes contemplate a recovery of overheads. The author has quite often encountered incredulity over this proposition, but viewed in a strictly commercial way, there is absolutely nothing untoward. It is true that everyone, including the government, is sufficiently concerned about the inexorable increase in service charges to have made the subject something of a hot potato, and it is also true that in all probability management costs would be challengable by individual lessees or residents associations under the terms of the Housing Act 1980, Sch 19,[7] but at the same time, management is not a charitable function and the manager must be able to make a reasonable return out of it. Any commercial organisation will include its overhead costs into its costs build-up when trying to arrive at a price it can sell its products for; it will not merely take its direct costs (ie the base cost of the product), add on its profit ratio, and hope that it can recover its overheads out of the resulting figure. That would be hopelessly uncommercial.

Therefore, the manager must include a proportion of his overhead costs into his computation of service charge. As most sensible management programmes will provide for payments of service charges in advance, perhaps on a half-yearly basis, with adjustments as related to actual costs taking place at a later date, the overhead cost content will have to be based on previous year's costs, with a mark up for inflation, if thought advisable (which it almost certainly would be).

How are the overheads recovered? This next question can be an awkward one. Given that it is proper for the manager's *own costs* in running the management to be capable of recovery, the actual allocation of proportions is not quite as easy.

If the manager has 1,000 units in his portfolio, and his management overheads are £50,000, is it right that each flat should have included in its service charge build-up £50? Probably not, because the size of the flats is bound to be different. Thus, he may have in his portfolio flats as small as studios of 250 square feet, and as large as three-bedroom units of 1,500

7 See ch 14, p 159, above.

square feet, or even more. It would clearly be inequitable for them both to suffer the same amount of overheads recharge.

How then can an equitable position be achieved? One way would be to take it purely on a square footage basis. Thus, in our example above, the studio flat would suffer only one-sixth of the overheads allocation that the large flat would. This does not mean, of course, that the large flat would have £300 (ie £50 × 6) allocated to it, nor that the small flat would have £8.33 (ie £50 ÷ 6) to it. What would happen would be that the number of flats in the portfolio would be indentifiable, and they would each be given proportions, either as a representation, say, of the floor area of the flat concerned related to the total floor areas of the flats in the programme, or based on units (see below).

What happens, though, to flats which come into the programme mid-way through an accounting year? It would be inequitable both to disregard them altogether, or include them completely.

Perhaps the best way is to look at a build-up based on units, which would represent, say, each 100 square feet of floor area of flat, so that the small flat in our illustration would be worth 2.50 units, the large one 15 units. If the large one had come into the programme, say, in the eighth month of the accounting year, the large unit could be divided into *time* sectors. We could take months, so that in its first year the large unit would only have a value of:

$$15 \times \frac{5}{12} = 6.25 \text{ units}$$

If monthly pauses are too frequent, we could use quarterly ones, in which case the result would be:

$$15 \times \frac{2}{4} = 7.50 \text{ units}$$

which would mean that the lessee lost out slightly.

The manager would have to wait until the end of the accounting year until he knew his total number of units under the programme, but he would have already collected an advance payment, or payments, depending on the time of year that the unit completed. The advance payment would have been based on the (known) unit value, both in floor area and time terms as against the total units in the programme at the beginning of the accounting period, divided into the overhead costs for the preceding year, or perhaps if the manager were in a start-up position, a projection of what current year overheads would be.

Mention of payments in advance leads us to remind ourselves that if service charge payments are made in arrears, this means that the manager will have to make all *his* payments before he recovers the relevant contributions from the lessees. This inevitably leads to further costs, in that the manager will be suffering carrying costs of monies expended; this in the author's view would be a justifiable management expense, and so far as the lessees were concerned, they would probably not be in any better position by delaying payment of their service charges on an arrears basis, as contrasted with an advance one. In any event, a good and efficient management programme is unlikely to fail to include provision for advance payments.

(b) *Profit recovery*

In moving on to this next heading, we are not leaving the last behind entirely. In order to consider this subject though, we should have looked at the last heading, and we should bring forward in our minds the gist of what we have previously discussed on overhead recovery.

It was mentioned earlier that there was sometimes considerable confusion over the ability or otherwise of the manager to recover overhead costs. There is even more confusion about profit recovery, and in the author's submission, there are some misleading pointers in what little has been written on the subject.

The problem is basically one of paucity of both statute and case law. In other parts of this book, the comment has been made that, far from being too precise in its coverage, the Housing Act 1980, Sch 19, which is the only concentrated statute law we have in this country on the regulation of management programmes, in the author's view falls a long way short of achieving what it sets out to do. That, presumably, is to regulate just what a lessee can be charged for, and in what way.

(i) Case law. The case law on this subject is very sparse. Generally, the following three cases are quoted as having some relevance to the subject: *Birmingham Corpn v Barnes (HM Inspector of Taxes)*,[8] *Oram (Inspector of Taxes) v Johnson*,[9] and *Finchbourne Ltd v Rodriguez*.[10]

The principle these cases are supposed to lay down, according to those commentators who quote them, is that the word 'costs' connotes a limitation in what can be recovered, and that specifically a lessor's costs of management must exclude a profit. If there is a management fee included in the service charge build-up, the lessor is entitled only to that part of it which actually represents costs.

In the author's view, none of these cases, nor the 1980 Act, prevent the lessor from recovering proper overhead charges, *and* a management fee in the shape of a 'profit'.

Looking at the cases first, two are tax cases; and the *Birmingham Corpn* case dates back to 1935, although the point around which the case turned—the laying of a tramway track by Birmingham Corporation for the benefit of the Dunlop Rubber Co, dated back to the immediately post-Great War period. Neither the *Birmingham Corpn* case nor the *Johnson* case have anything to do with the lessor/lessee relationship and the management function which goes with it, either on a direct or an indirect basis. The application of aspects of tax decisions to the present subject appears to the author to be highly tenuous, to say the least. Basically the *Birmingham Corpn* case turned on a payment made by Dunlop to the Corporation to get the Corporation to lay a

8 [1935] AC 292, [1935] All ER Rep 533.
9 [1980] 2 All ER 1, [1980] 1 WLR 558.
10 [1976] 3 All ER 581, 238 Estates Gazette 717.

tramway track to, and provide a tram service for, their factory, and to what extent that payment was to be taken into account into ascertaining the 'actual cost' to the Corporation of the tracks when considering allowances for wear and tear of the tracks. The *Johnson* case related to a taxpayer who tried to obtain an allowance for his own time spent in refurbishing an old cottage, and failed, because it was held that expenditure had to be in money or money's worth, which the 'labour and skill' of the taxpayer was not.

On the other hand, the *Finchbourne* case *was* about a lessor/lessee relationship, but the amount of the service contribution was to be certified by the lessor's managing agents every year and the lease included a provision that there should be included 'reasonable and proper fees payable by the lessors to its Managing Agents'. There was difficulty in establishing an actual difference of identity between the lessor and its managing agents, who appeared to be for all practical purposes, one and the same person. In addition, the lease in question was drawn in a rather vague manner, insofar as overhead and profit recovery were concerned. Thus, in the *Finchbourne* case, the wording of the lease on this point was

'(1) Keep the Reserved Property in good order repair and condition and will in particular and in a good and workmanlike manner (a) as to the external parts and (b) as to the internal parts (and there are particulars of painting and so on)
(2) (a) keep the property insured ... etc.
(3) To pay the charges incurred in meeting all outgoings paid and payable by the lessors in respect of the Property including in particular (then there are set out water rates, electricity and gas charges, the cost of renting a public telephone'

and sub-para (iv) said

'The reasonable and proper fees payable by the Lessors to its Managing Agents for the time being for the carrying out the general management and administration of the Property ...'

The clause goes on for some lines more, but we are not excluding anything which is germane to the point under discussion, which is that the above wording is much too vague, and it is hardly surprising that it did not find favour with the Court. In any event, as we have already noted, there was an indistinguishable relationship between the lessors and its 'Managing Agents'.

The *Finchbourne* case seems therefore to relate to interpretation of what was basically draftsmanship which fell some way short of the standard required, compounded by the subjective facts of the case itself. It is suggested that it was not decided in such a manner as to provide a safe precedent for those who say that overheads may be recovered, but profits may not. It was in this very area that the *Finchbourne* lease was so vague; 'reasonable and proper fees for carrying out the general management' defies construction. Are they fees which should only cover actual monies expended, or do they include a 'profit turn'? It is unclear, and would not seem to help us here.

(ii) *Statute law.* This area is just as difficult. If we look at the Housing Act 1980, Sch 19, 'service charge' is defined so as to include (cl 1(1)(a)) 'the landlord's costs of managements'.

The phraseology used here seems to suggest a failure on the part of the parliamentary draftsman to keep up with the times. True, the clause in question goes on to talk about the relevant costs of management, and quote them as being incurred by *or on behalf* of the landlord, but in a very great number of leasehold properties, the manager is brought in as a third party right from the inception of the management programme, indeed the manager is very often a party to the lease, and the management covenants may not wholly concern the lessor at all.

In the second part of Sch 19, there are set out the limitations on the service charge which may be levied. We saw in ch 14, above, that where costs are incurred *on the carrying out of works on a building* then in certain circumstances the lessor/manager must have at least two estimates to enable him to proceed.

It is clear that neither overhead recovery nor profit element fall within the heading of 'carrying out of works on a building'. Accordingly, the only reference to overheads specifically in the Schedule is in cl 1, where 'relevant costs' (ie the costs attributable to the service charge) are defined as 'the costs or estimated costs (including overheads) incurred or to be incurred in any period . . . by or on behalf of the landlord or a superior landlord in connection with the matters for which the service charge is payable'.

The first inescapable conclusion to be drawn from this then, is that overhead recovery is permitted. In what way it is permitted is not stated. The Schedule lends no assistance to those who are seeking to recover overheads, nor to those who are expected to pay it. The legislation seems to contemplate only that management will be undertaken in the main by either a tenants' management company (where although overhead recovery is important, profit recovery should not be), or the lessor himself, through a managing agent or on a direct basis.

Management nowadays though is increasingly undertaken by professional management companies who are brought into the lessor/lessee relationship, either as a third party to the lease itself, or indirectly at a later stage. For those who are trying to run such a company, the present state of statute law is less than helpful. The legislature needs to contemplate regulation of the up-to-date position, acknowledging that there are two sides to the equation, and that the equation itself is a very much more complex one than the simplistic approach of Sch 19.

So what do we find in the Schedule to help us?

1 First of all, there is nothing in statute law, and particularly in Sch 19, which appears to prevent recovery of profit element. It is true that the Schedule specifically refers to overheads but not to profits; in the author's view that is not to be interpreted as a statement that profit recovery is prohibited.

2 If profit recovery were to be prohibited, this would mean that those companies, firms, or persons engaged in management would be expected to carry on their business merely on a 'break-even' basis, and *never make a profit.* That is nonsensical, because a large part of whatever trouble there has been in the field of management is that it has been delegated in far too many cases to amateurish, half-hearted organisations. The world of flats needs good, professional management which can, and should, produce more efficient, and so most probably cheaper, management services; but if those who are interested

in providing this service cannot make a profit out of it, there is hardly any incentive for them.

3 It seems clear, from the author's experience which for a number of years has been intense, that it is generally accepted that an efficient manager should be allowed to make a profit.

4 Not that this is a legally valid argument were profit recovery to be specifically prohibited by the statutes (which it is not) but if such were to be the case there are a very considerable number of existing management leases which would be operating outside the terms of what is permitted, and many more such leases are being created every year.

5 If we look at the somewhat dated concept around which the wording of Sch 19 is built, we have to ask if profit recovery is included in 'costs to be incurred by or on behalf of the landlord'? If the lessor has so arranged the lease that management is to be undertaken by a third party, might not the whole of the costs incurred as a result of making that arrangement be allowed, and so the profit element of the manager be included as an allowable item? The answer surely cannot be anything other than 'yes' because the very strong probability would be that the lessor would be unable to find a manager to take on those responsibilities otherwise. This would also produce a nonsensical situation.

6 If we go forward on the basis of profit element, as well as overhead recovery, being allowable, we must then look at any constraints which are imposed by Sch 19. There are some constraints, as follows:

(i) in Part II of the Schedule, 'Limitation of Service Charge', cl 2 says that, *where the service charge is payable before the relevant costs are incurred* then 'no greater amount shall be so payable than is reasonable'. But if the whole clause is read together, it begins to look as though the actual meaning of these words is perhaps a little different to what we might have otherwise supposed. Is the thrust of the wording not directed against *advance* service charges as such, to make sure lessees are not asked for too much rather than a blanket caution that *any* costs—which would include overheads and profit—should be reasonable?

(ii) the situation is corrected to some degree by the following clause, 3, which states that 'Costs are to be taken into account only to the extent that they are reasonably incurred ...'. This leads us back to what is, without doubt, the underlying proposition of this whole discussion which is that it is open to the court to give relief against any harsh management provisions in a lease; and

(iii) following on from our last comment, cl 11 and 12 of the Schedule set out, respectively, that other than an agreement to arbitration (which may or may not be incorporated in the lease) no agreement by a lessee to provide for a determination as to the reasonableness of management costs is valid. In other words, whatever may be in the lease about any such questions being decided by the lessor or, eg his management agent, is irrelevant; and the county court may decide upon the reasonableness of the whole management programme and its various parts.

7 Finally, none of those constraints are such as to prevent the implementa-

tion of a genuine management programme which provides for the recovery of the manager's overheads and profits.

What must be watched carefully, though, are the provisions in the lease as to recovery of those very items.

OVERHEADS. The wording of suitable clauses may naturally differ, but that in Precedent No 2, Sixth Schedule, cl 20, p 353, below, is more than probably sufficient: eg

'Administering the Management Company itself and arranging for all necessary meetings to be held and complying with all relevant statutes and regulations and orders thereunder and (if it thinks fit) employing a suitable person or firm to deal with these matters'.

Whatever the clause says, either succinctly, as in the above example, or at length, it must be made clear that the expenses of running the management company, ie the overheads, are to be included in the build-up.

PROFITS. As we have seen earlier, overhead recovery is merely getting back (an appropriate proportion depending on the number of units involved as related to the overall work-load) what has been expended in running the management company so as to put it into a position where it can discharge its functions properly. For that reason, the recovery can never be quantified.

On the other hand, the profit element may be, and should be, quantified, but *not* as a figure, because the cost of the overall programme is not quantifiable beforehand, but as a percentage of the overall costs of management, thus as in Precedent No 2, Sixth Schedule, cl 22:

'A sum representing % of the costs expenses and outgoings referred to in the preceding clauses of this Schedule which said sum shall be the Management Fee of the Management Company or its successors in title.'

As with virtually every aspect of this subject of management, this type of clause causes problems. Some see it as a fee to include overhead recovery, but the author's view has always been that a fee is a sum which should not include overhead recovery and is free income, ie a *reward* for performing the services it is contracted to do. The *Oxford English Dictionary* includes in the meanings of 'fee' the word 'gratuity', which perhaps best illustrates the concept of the word in this context.

(c) *Amount of profit*

In deciding, on the side of either the lessor or lessee, what is an acceptable profit rate, consideration should be given to what is an acceptable *net* profitability in other businesses. The generally accepted levels of profit ratio to be incorporated in the management programme range from the 5% area, which does seem to be a little bit low, through the generally accepted $7\frac{1}{2}$–10% range to $12\frac{1}{2}$% or more, which is too high, although in a number of cases where the management fee is expressed at those levels, the fee may include overhead recovery as well. The provisions of the lease as to the management build-up need to be carefully checked before the final picture can be seen.

CHAPTER 18

Putting the programme together

The final component of the management equation is the putting-together of the programme itself. Of course, once the management is under way there will be aspects, such as accounts, with which we do not deal in this book, but management accounts are merely a variation of standard accounts, and the various aspects of management we have so far discussed hold good throughout the life of the programme just as they do at its inception.

The developer who is putting together a management programme for his development has a virtually infinite choice of variations on the theme, and it would be impossible to discuss all those options in this book.

By this stage, we have looked at the various factors which the developer should have considered at the inception of his development; leading to a decision on the type of management he thinks he needs; we have reviewed the various physical aspects of a typical flat/maisonette development, and we have indicated the various factors for consideration within that area; and we have worked our way through the different parts of the management section of the lease, and seen what sort of matters are referred to in a typical lease, and by means of what wording these matters are implemented within the lessor/lessee relationship.

We now turn to the final task which faces the manager/developer when setting up his programme: the calculation of the cost of the individual components in the programme, the putting-together of those components into a whole, and the apportionment of that whole as between the individual units in the development.

Consideration of the programme, and its initial build-up, falls into two clear parts: the putting-together of the individual components, and the subsequent apportionment to the units themselves.

The problem in a book of this sort, which attempts to give an overview, whilst dealing with the individual subjects to such an extent that it is of positive use to the reader, is to compress into a chapter necessarily restricted for space sufficient useful information.

There is no such thing as a typical management programme: there is instead an infinite variety, which starts at the very simple programme for a block of a very few units of equal size with a minimal maintenance burden, right through to the large block of flats, of many different floor areas, and with a great complexity of mantenance components, including such items as porters, lifts, and so on. In view of this, and in order to illustrate as much as possible in as few pages as possible, we shall consider the build-up of the management programme for two developments: one at the very simple end, the other of a more complicated nature. During our discussion we shall illustrate various options which are open to the manager in the way in which he constructs his programme.

A. SIMPLE MAINTENANCE

Let us take as our example, the block of studio flats which we described in ch 9.[1] Here the aim was to provide as little maintenance as possible, leaving the unit-owners the responsibility for day to day maintenance, whilst giving an overriding 'monitoring' level for the lessor.

The feature about this system of maintenance is that the lessor has as few duties as possible, but experience has shown that there are some aspects of maintenance which cannot be avoided; these are such items as common areas, electricity charges, grass cutting and minor garden maintenance, and, of course, insurance (which in any event is a totally recoverable item under the terms of the lease, but which is usually considered along with the other management items).

The computation for a block of flats of this description might be built up something like this:

1 Description of block

Small block of eight studio units, all of the same floor area. Normal construction, pitched roof with concrete interlocking tiles. Common entrance hall, stairs and first-floor landing demised (as common areas) to flats in virtually equal portions,[2] maintenance obligations of:

(i) interiors of flats;
(ii) internal common parts, and
(iii) external common parts.

imposed on *lessees*.

2 Management

Management to consist of (a) direct maintenance, and (b) indirect monitoring.

(a) *Direct maintenance*

Costs to be recharged to lessees:

1 Landlord's electricity supply to common parts (mostly lighting in hall, staircase and corridor, possibly external light/s but possibly also supply to time switches for lighting (if there are any), and entry phone of other similar system).

1 P 110, above.
2 See Precedent No 4, p 369, below, for the description of a demise for such a unit.

Say, as per estimate derived from other similar blocks run by lessor, or given by Electricity Board

per quarter	£15.00
per annum	£60.00

2 Grass cutting and minor garden maintenance. How much this might cost would depend on a number of factors. If one has to cut grass, which given that grass is the cheapest form of external area to provide is more than likely, the frequency may be minimal say every three weeks through the late spring and summer, and every four-five weeks at either end of the season. If the cuts were every one or even two weeks through the spring, summer or early autumn, the resultant costs would be high, especially if the lessor did not have any more jobs for the contractors in the area. However, say on an average frequency of cut, the annual cost for the block might be:

£200.00

3 There might be other heads of maintenance, eg the entry-phone system we mentioned earlier, or rental of a cable radio/TV service, but as inclusion of these would produce something rather more than the 'minimal maintenance' block we are talking about, we shall ignore them.

4 Insurance, which is usually included in the overall service computation, as indicated earlier, but practice varies as to how it should be billed to the lessee. It may well be included in the overall charge, but it is better practice to quote it as a separate item, simply because insurance is *not* maintenance, and further is a charge which every householder has to pay, whether he owns a small studio flat, as in this example, or a large mansion standing in acres of grounds. In order not to cause confusion, then, we shall make no further reference to insurance in this chapter.

Summary We observed at the beginning of this chapter that this example was a very simple one. What we have in the service charge computation is two items, namely

Common electricity	60.00
Grass cutting, etc	200.00
Total charge per annum	£260.00

(b) *Indirect (monitoring)*

In a 'self-help' scheme such as this, the lessor can afford to leave his lessees alone for reasonably long periods. The common electricity looks after itself; the only recurring matter might be replacement of light bulbs, and this could be imposed on the lessees under the terms of the leases. To keep things simple, we shall forget about complicated matters like repairs to internal wiring; these types of maintenance items are not likely to present a problem anyway in that their degree of incidence is absolutely minimal. The grass cutting also should look after itself, assuming the lessor issues an order to the contractor at the beginning of each growing season.

Nevertheless, the lessor, or whoever is managing the scheme, must make sure that the blocks are not falling into disrepair, or disrepute, so it is necessary for the 'eye to be kept' on them. In ch 9, on p 110, above where we described the basic studio flat system of minimal maintenance, we suggested that monitoring visits could be paid to the block, say, every three months. Who is going to pay for these visits, and any work which is necessary as a result of them?

Such expenses could be passed on to the lessees, as they are lessor's *expenses* of management, and he is quite entitled to recover them from the unit-owners. However, the point about the whole studio flat scheme was to keep the lessees' outgoings in the shape of service charges down to an absolute minimum, and in any event if the lessor has incorporated in the lease machinery to recover his expenses of management, this would not only defeat the whole object of the scheme, but produce a figure which would be quite disproportionate to the actual direct service costs. Probably in such a scheme, the lessor/manager should recover his costs by taking the ground rent, which might be £20–25 or even more, per annum per unit, using fees on notices of assignment as a secondary income, and gaining commission on the insurance premiums.

3 The service computation

This leaves us with an extraordinary simple equation, which is:

Block of 8 units:	
Total annual costs:	
Grass cutting etc	200.00
Common electricity	60.00
	£260.00
Cost per unit	£32.50

The resulting figure represents something a little over 60p per week, which is an absolute minimal service charge; certainly one which could never be an inhibition to the marketing of the units. If an average ground rent of, say, £25.00 were added, the weekly outgoing rises to £1.10. If the salesman cannot get it across to the prospective lessee that he is getting maintenance for less than the price of a packet of cigarettes, then he has no business in the sales office!

Of course, there are big snags with this system. As time goes on, the lessor might have to step in anyway and do the maintenance[3]—probably the more major items like re-decorating, (eventually) re-pointing, any necessary re-placing, etc—if it is not done by the lessee, but it will only ever be in the case of a minority of lessees.

The scheme described is at the very simple end of the market, and is

3 See Precedent No 3, p 360, below, which incorporates fail-safe provisions for such eventualities.

designed to fit in with (a) the type of property concerned, and (b) the typical purchaser of such a property, who is looking, not only for a minimal capital cost, but cheap running costs.[4] It is accepted totally that such simplicity is not to be found in every situation, so that from the simple example, we now move on to

B. TRADITIONAL MAINTENANCE OF A MORE COMPLICATED TYPE

This is an altogether more complex scenario. The build-up of the programme itself, and the consideration which goes into it, is more lengthy and subject to more pitfalls.

The first task which the developer must set himself is to arrive at a reasonably accurate service charge figure, because if he does not, he might end up with a very angry bunch of lessees in the future, assuming the estimated figures he gave them were low, rather than high.

The simplest build-up is to take each head of maintenance expenditure, cost it out, arrive at an annual figure, and thence to an overall service charge for the development which can then be apportioned to the individual units.

We therefore start by identifying the elements of the overall management plan, and the appropriate cycles. In this part of the chapter we shall assume that we are dealing with a medium-sized development with a number of blocks containing different styles of housing units, the principal differences between the various styles being the floor area. The estate is, of course, leasehold, although there could just as easily be freehold units with service charges attached to them.[5] The number of units, their size, and the way in which the development is set out, are really quite irrelevant; all we are concerned with here are examples, and what those examples are is not important because it is how the costing attached to the examples is built up and then combined in the overall plan which is important.

1 The management plan

The elements forming the overall plan might be:

(a) Expenditure

(i) Weekly. Expenditure for:

(i) maintenance of landscaped areas;
(ii) cleaning of common areas. Most of this cleaning will be internal, ie halls, corridors and stairs, but there will be some external common area cleaning not otherwise dealt with under 1 (a) (i);
(iii) Clearing rubbish from community areas. (ii) and (iii) might be dealt

4 But this does not imply poor class tenants—see ch 9, above.
5 For further discussion on this area of service charges, see the following chapter p 222.

with in consolidated form, if, eg the manager appointed a professional cleaning company to the cleaning contract. However, if the development was large enough, especially with enough common areas, both internal and external, it might be cheaper to appoint a caretaker/handyman and cleaner (ie his wife) and provide them with accommodation on the site.

This is not so radical as it might seem; cleaning contractors' bills can be surprisingly high, and the point where it will be more cost effective for the manager to employ direct labour for these tasks is probably surprisingly low, in terms of the size of development.

(ii) Quarterly. Expenditures on bills (some bills might be on other frequency cycles) for eg electricity and/or heating used in common areas, rental of entry-phone systems, radio and TV cables, and so on. Electricity might also be used externally, eg lighting and working ornamental fountains, waterfalls, etc.

(iii) Annually. Expenditure on replacement of shrubs, grass and ancilliary plants in landscaped areas, general maintenance if required to internal common areas.

The cost of insurance should not be overlooked, and as it usually falls to an annual charge, this is the most convenient place to remind readers that this will almost certainly be the lessor's responsibility, although a rechargeable item. Whether the insurance payments are 'lost' within the service charge, or invoiced separately to the lessees, is a matter of choice for the lessor to make.

(iv) Every (five) years

(i) Depending on the re-decoration cycles contained in the leases, the external paintwork, and internal common area re-decoration (ie not only pointing, but things like re-staining, emulsioning, wallpapering, and so on);

(ii) replacement of carpeting to internal common areas, assuming that there was carpeting and depending on its quality;

(iii) other refurbishment tasks in accordance with the general provisions of the lease.

(v) Every (ten) years. Again, depending this time on the state of the development, a comprehensive check to hard external common areas, eg footpaths, paviors, etc in any part of the ornamental or functional areas, car parking spaces and access ways to them, etc.

If these areas have been constructed originally from durable materials, for which see ch 16, p 180, above, no work at all may be needed after ten, or even more years. On the other hand, maintenance may be required earlier, in which case regular checks will reveal the need (see below).

(b) *Monitoring*

At frequent levels to be decided by the manager, someone must visit the site to check that everything is in order. For instance, it is useless for a manager to leave a professional cleaning company to carry out its contractual duties, say, on a weekly basis, and to arrive on site only on the anniversaries set out in section 1. There must be regular monitoring visits, which will be designed to:

(a) check that all the required work is being done properly; and
(b) identify any potential problems, and thus nip them in the bud.

Depending on whether the manager's own staff perform these monitoring duties or they are contracted out, these costs will be part of overhead recovery, or a direct management expense.

(c) *Tied housing*

Provision for housing of the handyman/cleaner as a contractual 'tied house' situation.

(d) *Reserve fund provision*

This is designed to cater for expenses which might otherwise be a crippling burden on the lessees.

Consider, for instance, a block with a lift. Lifts are expensive enough when they are behaving themselves (the manager *must* arrange regular inspections by specialist lift engineers) but when they go wrong they can be very expensive. It would be quite wrong for the lessees of units at the particular time the lift went wrong to bear the whole burden in that year's service charge.[6] So that the reserve fund payment builds up over the years, and when a major item of expenditure, which is not of a regularly recurring nature, arrives—as it will on most schemes of any consequence—there will be sufficient monies in the reserve fund to pay for it without affecting the normal service charge components.

(e) *Overheads and management fee*

These were discussed fully in the previous chapter. If the provision for charging them is included in the lease, then they must form part of the service charge computation.

There is some difficulty in arriving at a satisfactory method of allocating overheads to service charges; at best it will be only a rough and ready method, based on the proportion the development forms of the managers total work load. The management fee ought to be much easier because it will usually be expressed as a percentage of the overall service charge.

2 Illustrations

What has gone before is all very well, but any benefit it has had for the reader will be destroyed if there is no simple illustration of how all this works. We therefore reproduce below a *selection only* of the computation of service

6 And see the commentary at ch 17 p 191, above.

charge components. *All* the figures are imaginary, and are not intended to be in the slightest accurate; they are there only because in order to have an illustration, we have to have figures!

(a) *Cleaning, etc*

Cleaning of internal common areas, odd jobs, etc

At £2.25 per hour	
40 hours per week	= £90.00 weekly
	52
	£4680.00 annually

or, if with resident caretaker:

Wages for caretaker and wife, responsible for site maintenance	£120.00 weekly[7]
	52
	£6240.00 annually

(b) *Inspections*

Say, quarterly inspections	£30.00
frequency	3
	£90.00 annually
Detailed inspection	£50.00
	£140.00

(c) *Annual: shrub, etc replacement*

Replacement of shrubs, etc to landscaped area.

Area scaled off=	3750m^2
Ground coverage[8] 10%	.1
	375
Replacement need, say	.15
say	56
Cost per shrub, say	£4.50
Annual cost=	£252.00

The remaining factors will need an inflation factor built into them, because as opposed to weekly, quarterly, or annually, where costs will either be the same or virtually the same as now, the cost in five or ten years will be rather more, and an inflationary indexing will need to be incorporated.

For instance;

7 Remember, if the low wages cause raised eyebrows, they may have free accommodation. In that case the lessor would perhaps wish to include a computation of the cost of that accommodation in the service chage, depending on the provisions of the lease.

8 Ie of shrubs on the ground.

(d) *Replacement of carpeting*

Five yearly

'Provisions for replacement

Floor covering of common areas

Areas of hallways	9.35m²	
Number of hallways	53	
Area:		496
Stairs per floor	12	
m per stair	5	
	6	
stairways per entrance	3	
	18	
No of stairways	19	
Area		342
		838
Cost per m²		3.5
Cost now		£2933.00
Inflation factor 5 years, assume Annual Inflation Rate of 10%[9]		1.611
		£4725.00
80% replacement factor		.8
Cost in 5 years from now		£3780.00

or, as applied to re-decorations:

(e) *General re-decorations*

Cost of re-decorations based on estimate of Joe Bloggs Ltd.

	Today's cost	4750.00	
	5-year inflation factor[9] @ 10% rate	1.611	
			£7652.00
or	Today's cost	4750.00	
	10-year inflation factor[9]	2.594	
			£12,321.00

3 The management equation

What the manager, whoever he might be (lessor, deveoper, or independent person) will have by this stage is a series of components as follows:

1 Cyclic outgoings, ie
   weekly,
   quarterly,
   annually,
   five-yearly, and
   10-yearly; or as the case may be;

2 reserve fund expressed as a percentage of the sum of the items in section

9 See later, p 215, as to further inflation calculations.

1, or whatever is the build-up of charges in accordance with the appropriate provisions of the lease; because do not forget that management programmes are subjective—there is no such thing as a standard programme—it is whatever puts into effect the provisions of the particular lease;

3 overhead recovery; and

4 management fee, both based on the same method of calculation as section 2.

Before sections 2, 3 and 4 can be calculated, however, the cyclic outgoings in section 1 must be reduced to a common factor, which will almost inevitably be the equivalent of one year's outgoings. So that the weekly cleaning costs we looked at earlier were multiplied up to an annual basis, and equally the five-yearly costs—eg re-decorations, should be divided by five.[10]

The resulting figure will be the sum of the anticipated annual costs, including a provision for major works which will not be implemented during the year in question. Once this overall figure has been arrived at, the other figures which depend on it may be calculated, then everything is added together and the result is the amount of service charge which it is necessary to collect in any one year.[11]

4 Computation of site areas and allocations

In order to distribute the service charge equitably, there is really only one method of calculation to be used, and that is using respective floor areas. For instance, take an imaginary[12] site with five different types, and thus sizes, of flat. Say there are 133 units, with the different types represented to a greater or lesser degree. The allocation fractions for the purpose of service charges are worked out on an area basis, as follows:

Type	Area m^2	No	Total Area m^2
1 2 bed flat#1	48.16	14	674.24
2 2 bed flat#2	54.00	9	486.00
3 1 bed flat	36.96	54	1995.84
4 Studio flat#1	25.20	47	1184.40
5 Studio flat#2	27.00	9	243.00
	Totals	133	4583.48

Thus, the service charge for each individual flat will be, given that £X is the total service charge for the whole development,

10 But see later as to inflation.

11 What must *always* be borne in mind is that we are discussing here a computation of what the service charge *should be*. When the time comes for the actual calculation of the true service charge, all the contributors to the management programme up to and including, but not beyond, the annual cyclic costs will be *historic*, and *actual*. The other parts of the calculation will still hold to the original basis, though. The *actual* figure will produce either a credit to, or an extra levy upon, the individual service charges.

12 Actually not at all imaginary—these figures are taken from an actual management programme.

1 2 bed flat#1	$\frac{£X \times 48.16}{4583.48}$
2 2 bed flat#2	$\frac{£X \times 54.00}{4583.48}$
3 1 bed flat	$\frac{£X \times 36.96}{4583.48}$
4 Studio flat#1	$\frac{£X \times 25.20}{4583.48}$
5 Studio flat#2	$\frac{£X \times 27.00}{4583.48}$

How is this expressed in the lease?

On a typical full management lease, the proportion of the maintenance expenses attributable to the flat concerned will be expressed as a fraction. For instance, in Precedent No 2, p 346, below, the wording is 'The Lessee's Proportion means one [   ] part of the Maintenance Expenses ....' This assumes that the service charge computation will be capable of being expressed as a simple fraction. This will not always be so. If we look at the example of a final computation set out above, the fraction of 48.16/4583.48 for a 2 bed flat#1 is not capable of being reduced to a simple fraction of one [   ] part. The nearest one can get is one ninety five decimal point one seventh part, which is ridiculous. Equally, if one rounds up or down to the nearest whole number, one ninety-fifth will give a shortfall, and one ninety-sixth will give an over recovery, admittedly not much in either case, in fact respectively £8 and £40 (not true figures anyway, as adjustments have to be made for the four remaining calculations) but when one multiplies the unit service charge by the number of flats of that type in the development, the disparity can become troublesome.

This is why one very often finds in leases complicated fractions or decimals. Probably the latter is much the better, so that in our example, each 2 bed flat#1 would bear 1.050% of the maintenance expenses.

5 Mixed developments

At this stage, it might be useful to draw the attention of readers to the following chapter where we describe how freehold properties might have a service charge hooked on to them. What is envisaged in that chapter is that a number of freehold properties might have communal external areas, perhaps in addition to, or in substitution for, private gardens. There might be various reasons why such a situation would occur, not the least of which would be planning.

If we take the example a stage further, the freehold properties, with their communal area, might be on the same development as a number of leasehold ones, which might have their own communal areas, or more likely external common areas would be shared between the freehold and leasehold properties. But the leasehold ones would also have other common services, etc giving rise to a service charge—re-decoration, internal common parts upkeep, and so on, producing the result that there would be different types of properties on the same development, participating in the maintenance, and thus to be subject to a service charge, *to a different degree.*

The example we have used of freehold and leasehold is perhaps misleading, because there is nothing to say that a range of, eg leasehold properties on the same estate will not be able to participate in different areas of maintenance.

If this happens, the lease will obviously have to make suitable provision. Suppose, for instance, we have the intermix previously described of freehold houses with (perhaps) very small private gardens, but so laid out that they participate in the external communal areas of the development, and leasehold flats also participating in those communal areas, but having their own maintenance programme as well.

The lease of the flats would have to have a charging clause which 'doubled up', eg

'To contribute and pay a [proportion of flat maintenance costs excluding external communal areas maintenance costs] part of the costs expenses and outgoings mentioned in the [Fifth] Schedule hereto and a [proportion of external communal areas maintenance costs] part of the costs expenses and outgoings incurred in complying with the provisions of Clause [ ] hereof.'

The Schedule referred to would be the normal maintenance programme for a development of flats, *but* without reference to the external communal areas, and the clause would be something like:

'That the Lessor will keep the gardens grassed areas common grounds roads footpaths and any other part or parts of the external common areas of the estate properly cultivated laid out maintained repaired renewed and where necessary suitably cleaned.'

The freehold properties, or whatever properties were benefitting *only* from the external areas, would merely bear the costs in the clause, and would have no relationship with the matters set out in the Schedule.

Naturally this formula is capable of adaptation to almost any permutation. Perhaps some simplicity can be introduced; for example in the example just given, which is based on an actual management programme, the external areas maintenance was shared equally across the board. There were 172 properties on the development, some freehold, some leasehold, but they all were thought to benefit equally from the external common areas, and so all bore a 1/172nd part of those costs. The leasehold units bore the other costs on a floor area basis, as already described.

6 Inflation accounting

All that has gone before except for the inflation factor figures in the calculations set out previously has assumed that year one costs are constant. This, of course, is not the case.

Take, for instance, the cleaning costs which we looked at earlier on p 211 and which were estimated—presumably based on a genuine estimate from a cleaning contractor, or a costing out of a caretakers duties—on a weekly basis, which was then multiplied up to an annual figure.

The resulting figure will be year 1 costs, and all concerned, the manager and the lessees, will accept that subsequent year costs will escalate. The annual costs may be treated in the same way, but the five-yearly costs, re-decoration and the like, will need to be given a slightly different treatment.

There are two ways of approaching the problem of inflation; thus, in the case of general re-decorations on p 212, above, the cost of the job, *at today's prices* and based upon a genuine estimate, was £4750.00. The manager could simply divide this figure by five, and collect one-fifth every year, as part of the general service charge. Presumably that part of the charge which related to re-decoration would end up as a surplus, which would in every year be cumulative, so that at the end of the five-year period the manager would have sufficient monies to cover the costs. But would he, because the amount he would be collecting would be based on year one costs, and although he would probably invest the surplus, the accrued interest might not take the total accumulated amount up to the true, year five costs? Incidentally most full management leases only specifically provide for reserve funds to be held on a trustee basis, with any interest accruing to be owned by the lessees for the benefit of the management programme. As we observed in the previous chapter, to put items such as re-decoration into a reserve fund would create much too large a fund, which should be intended only for contingencies, not inevitabilities like re-decoration.

The alternative

Because it is questionable that by working on year one costs, there would be enough in 'the kitty' by the appropriate time, the manager should seriously consider the option of using inflation factors when he is arriving at an estimate of costs for the initial management programme. To illustrate this, let us recap on the re-decoration calculation we made earlier. This gave an estimate, at year one costs, of £4750.00 which needs to be spent somewhere in year five. If year one costs are used in the programme, it is just possible that the manager might be astute enough to invest that surplus part of the service charge income at sufficient rates so that he actually ended up with the same as, or perhaps even more than if he had used inflation factors in the first place. But this is unlikely, so for the sake of everyone, it is wiser to look at the problem this way:

Year 1 costs, based on estimate	£4750.00
5-year inflation factor @ 10% rate[13]	1.611
	£7652.00

And so the annual amount to be taken into account in the service charge for re-decoration will be £7652.00 ÷ 5, as opposed to £4750.00 ÷ 5. If the manager inflates the £7652.00 to more than that because of a judicious investment programme, then that should be a bonus for the lessees, in that there will be some sort of a carry-forward after paying for the re-decoration, which

13 The rate selected is obviously up to the manager.

will have an undoubted beneficial effect on the subsequent re-decoration contributions. If the worst has happened, and inflation, so far at least as re-decoration costs are concerned, has been greater than anticipated, the use of inflation factors may very well have alleviated most of the adverse effects.

One other consideration which has to be borne in mind is that by using inflation factors on these five- and ten-year recurring components of the management programme, the lessees will only suffer inflation effects in the more regularly recurring cycles, ie weekly, monthly, quarterly, annually, so that they will not in all probability see the true effect of inflation in their service charges.

7 The whole hog: sinking funds

Throughout this part of the book, on management and its related subjects, the reader may have noticed that the expression 'reserve fund' has been used when referring to the 'top-up' fund which is used for contingencies cropping up within a management programme.

This is because the term 'sinking fund' which otherwise tends to be used as synonymous with 'reserve fund', is reserved especially for the method of calculation of a management programme which in theory produces an annual service charge which should not vary, and so suffer the ravages of inflation, because inflationary tendencies are built into the computation from the start.

The author is indebted to his old friend E. (Ted) Holmes of Wakefield for invaluable help in writing this part of the book dealing with management, and particularly those references to the use of sinking funds in relation to computation of service charges. A very pleasant morning was spent with Mr Holmes, one rainy day in West Yorkshire, having the mysteries of sinking funds explained. How far into the author's brain these mysteries penetrated, remains open to question, because there is no doubt that the theory is complicated, for a mere lawyer.

The sinking fund is one of the basic tools of the surveyor's trade, though, and is a concept which is quite acceptable to them. How far the concept should be allowed to penetrate into a management programme is questionable.

Before we illustrate the operation of a sinking fund, we should run quickly through the basic points related to it.

The aim is to produce an annual charge for that part of the maintenance programme which will remain constant throughout a given period of time, and yet cover the ever-increasing cost of that particular area of maintenance up to the end of the given period.

The author of any such scheme will probably refer to the service charge element being 'based to zero balance in (say ten) years' and then state that the scheme would be revised all over again in ten years' time. 'Based to zero balance' means that at the end of the selected period there is no money left in 'the kitty'.

Naturally, certain assumptions are made in putting together such a scheme, ie assumptions on sinking fund rates themselves, inflation rates, and so on. Any variations from the assumptions will create either a surplus or a shortfall. In the event of there being a shortfall a levy would have to be implemented; with a surplus, either adjustment to the service charge may be made, or a carry forward instituted. This factor is not peculiar to sinking fund calculations; it applies to any management programme, however it is calculated. We shall return to this point at the end of the chapter.

The advantage will be that the amount of the service charge payable over the selected period, which will not usually be longer than ten years, is entirely predictable, and probably constant over the period, *given that all the components in the service charge build up are treated in the same way.*

The disadvantage will be in that very constancy; it might well be too rigid, not properly allowing for flexibility and the likelihood of the assumptions not being absolutely correct may result in variances anyway.

(a) *The illustration*

For the purposes of illustrating how a sinking fund calculation works, we shall use a weekly cycle, for caretaker's wages.

First, however, we have to go back to essentials.

(b) *What is a sinking fund?*

Basically it is the annual sum required to be invested, which will amount to £1 in a given number of years. The amount to be invested will differ according to what rate is chosen.

Thus: at a rate of 3½%

£0.085. or 8½p. would need to be invested every year to produce £1 at the end of ten years. A rate of 3½% might seem a low one to select, but valuers tend to work on cast-iron certainties, not on what the best might be!

Any valuer using sinking fund rates will probably be using *Parrys Valuation Tables*, published by the *Estates Gazette.* This, apparently, is the valuer's Bible.

The theory is capable of being expressed very simply, despite the complicated calculations which follow—included merely for the purposes of illustration.

If one thinks about what it is going to cost for, eg in our example a caretaker, over a ten-year period, quite obviously because of inflationary tendencies it is going to cost more as the period goes on to its conclusion. If one wants to arrive at a sum which can remain constant throughout the period, quite obviously the annual sum must be more than is actually expended in year one, so that there is a carry-over surplus. At some point in the period, the actual costs increase to the point where there is no longer a surplus, and indeed as the period draws to its close the surpluses which have been accumulated are themselves used up in 'making up' the annual contributions, which by then are not enough to cover the actual costs.

That is the underlying theory, and it is simple enough expressed in that way; but the implementation of it through the use of sinking funds can look dreadfully complicated. The author certainly finds them so, and he happily admits that he reproduces the following computation without professing to know its ins and outs backwards. Nevertheless, he is assured by his resident expert valuer that all the equations, etc make sense!

The format

The format used for calculating the service charge element in our example will be:

(where X = the required annual contribution)
∴ X + Amount invested at sinking fund rate

$$\left[X - \left(\text{Cost year 1}\right)\right] \times \begin{matrix}\text{Sinking fund}\\ \text{factor for 10 years}\end{matrix} + \text{———}$$

$$-\left[X - \left(\text{Cost year 1} + \begin{matrix}\text{Inflation}\\ \text{1 year}\end{matrix}\right)\right] \times \begin{matrix}\text{Sinking fund}\\ \text{factor for 9 years}\end{matrix} + \text{———}$$

—(and so on through the years, until)

$$-\left[X - \left(\text{Cost year 1} + \begin{matrix}\text{Inflation}\\ \text{9 years}\end{matrix}\right)\right] \times \begin{matrix}\text{Sinking fund}\\ \text{factor for 1 year}\end{matrix} =$$

Amount required for final year's annual charge
ie cost year 1 plus inflation for 10 years

(*c*) *Application of format*

In the caretaker examples

Wages were	£120 pw
	52
Cost now pa	£6240.00
Inflation factor	
10 years @ 6%	1.791
Cost in 10 years	£11,178.00

The cost of wages is assumed to inflate at a rate of 6% pa. The 1.791 factor is taken out of the valuation tables: it is the factor by which the base figure must be multiplied to give the end figure which 6% inflation over ten years would produce.

So we know the cost in year one, ie £6240, and we know the projected cost in ten years, ie £11,178. We now need to calculate what a constant annual contribution must be which, paid over a ten-year period, will meet the inflating costs and will (theoretically) arrive at the end of the period with neither a shortfall nor a surplus, in other words, with a 'zero' balance.

The application accordingly looks like this, based on a sinking fund rate of $3\frac{1}{2}$% (at which rate £1 invested over 10 years will produce—according to the valuation tables—£1,411).

(X − 6240) 1.411 (1.035 x − 10908) = 11.178
(Tabulated)
1.411 x = 8805
1.363 x = 9015
1.317 x = 9237
1.272 x = 9453

1.229 x = 9678
1.188 x = 9918
1.148 x = 10165
1.109 x = 10407
1.071 x = 10652
1.035 x = 10908
11178

12.143 x = 109416

Therefore service charge (x) will be $\frac{109416}{12.413}$ = £9.010 pa.

That figure applied constantly throughout the ten-year period should cater for inflation without the need for any adjustment. This will come in the eleventh year, when the scheme starts all over again.

(e) *Is a sinking fund the right choice?*

Whilst employment of the sinking fund method leads to virtually constant service charges over a fairly long period, given that the assumptions made at the inception of the scheme were correct, or more or less so, there is some doubt that it is a truly equitable method of calculating service charges. Is it right that these lessees in the earlier years should be subsidising those in the latter years which, if we accept inflation as a constant fact of life, is the case?

We do not here attempt to pronounce on such questions: what we have done is reviewed all the aspects of the management programme, from start to finish, in as comprehensive manner as space allows.

8 Establishment fee

One final element of a management programme build-up needs to be mentioned before we close; that element is the establishment fee, which is not so much an integral part of the programme, as an 'add-on' at the beginning and the important point to note about it is that *it has no affect on the lessees of the flats*; it only has relevance to the developer/lessor, and the manager.

The principle of the fee is based on the manager being quite separate from the developer/lessor; thus if there is any connection between the two sides, there is no logic in asking for and paying an establishment fee, unless for some arcane accountancy reason.

Therefore proceeding on the assumption that there is present the separation of identities, the two parties, lessor/developer and manager, will have come together at some stage, presumably at the beginning of the development, and in a great many cases, the developer will have gone to the manager for advice on his development, perhaps at such an early stage (if he is a wise developer) that the manager may be permitted, indeed encouraged, to give advice on type of development, layout, use of materials, nature of management programme to be undertaken and applied to the units in the development, and so on.

Naturally the manager is going to expend money on building up such a programme for the developer. There may well be occasions when the programme offered is unsuitable, or the developer decides not to proceed with a relationship with that manager, for whatever reason. And yet it is in the manager's interest to pursue such situations, because otherwise he is not likely to fund as much new business as he otherwise would.

In order to defray expenses of both abortive and successful management programme build-ups, there has been developed the principle of the 'establishment fee', which is a fee paid to the manager by the developer, at the point when the two parties have struck a bargain, perhaps when the formal agreement is struck, or later. It all depends on the parties concerned; an establishment fee can be paid in any way and at any time, but the logical time does seem to be upon the entering into of a formal agreement between the parties.

The fee may be levied on each unit in the development, or it may be a 'global' figure. The preference, so far as management companies are concerned, appears to be a fee *per unit*.

What the fee is to be, depends on negotiation between the parties, so that, eg the more units there are in the development the less the fee per unit is likely to be. At the time of writing, in very late 1984, the norm appears to be anything between £75 and £150 per unit, which can represent a considerable boost to the manager's cash flow, and will almost certainly represent rather more than a mere covering of overheads. From the developer's point of view, it is an acceptable expense, which will have been incorporated into his viability study and recovered eventually out of his selling prices.

CHAPTER 19

'Mixed management'—freehold and leasehold

In former times, builders developed sites which were composed mainly, or indeed wholly, of one style of building. Thus, up until very recently, we would see a complete estate of semi-detached houses, row upon row of them, or if the development was one of flats, there would probably be blocks comprising identical flats.

With the growth of sophistication amongst the house-buying public, this sort of development is no longer acceptable. Nor is it liked by the planners. Instead, the needs of the buying public are paramount considerations, and the demography of the particular area will be taken as one of the principal starting points when the developer is planning his site.[1]

Since the market which the builder is aiming for is a mixed one, that will mean that his development will generally be a mixed one. Nowadays, virtually anything goes; the mixing of different types of properties—studios up to four/five-bedroomed houses, bungalows and houses, flats and houses, and freehold and leasehold units.

Mention of the mixing of freehold and leasehold is where this discussion starts. This book is principally about *flats*, but the reader may well come across some developments where he will find a mixture of flats (which would normally be expected to be sold leasehold) and houses (where it would be usual to offer a freehold).[2] If the houses are positioned on the development in such a way that they are completely independent of the flats, and do not share any amenities with them, then they may be sold on a freehold basis without difficulty at all. But what about a case where the houses, although self-contained on an individual basis, including gardens, nevertheless share facilities with the flats? These facilities may be common garden grounds and other open areas—eg ornamental pools, etc—or possibly footpaths and roadways which are to remain private and are not intended for adoption.

The answer is essentially simple, and involves transferring the houses themselves as individual freehold units, and then vesting the freehold[3] of the common parts in a management company. This can work where the freehold units form part of a larger development, the balance of which is leasehold, or where they are completely on their own, having absolutely no connection with any other properties. It can also work where the management company is to be one set up solely for the purpose of looking after the common areas

1 As will national demographic trends and fashions—eg these have combined in some recent periods to make the three-bedroomed semi-detached house a rarity, as opposed to a standard; although this particular type is now gaining popularity again.

2 Unless they happened to be in an area, eg Birmingham, where it is apparently quite acceptable to offer houses, as opposed to flats, on a leasehold basis.

3 It is assumed that the developer's title is freehold.

on that single, specific development (in which case the owners of the freehold units themselves might be the members of the management company, which, would thus become a 'do-it-yourself' operation, or where a professional management company is asked to take over responsibility for the common areas).

An interesting illustration of freehold units on their own but making use of this management facility was experienced by the author some time ago. One of his clients was proposing to develop a small site, about 15 plots, of fairly superior detached houses. The planners were insisting that, although the roads and contiguous pathways would be accepted for adoption, the areas of landscaping and general open space should be kept private, and that proof would have to be exhibited to the planning authority that there would be a management company responsible which would be able to cope with the running of the maintenance of these private areas.

As it happened, the management side of this development was taken over by a professional management company which was part of the same group of building companies as the client concerned, but it could just as easily have been steered into a resident's management company; although in that case might not the planners concerned have been more sceptical of the ability of that company to adequately manage the site through the foreseeable future—as opposed to an independent management company totally devoted to the business of managing?

THE MECHANICS OF THE OPERATION

Whether the units to which common areas in need of management are on their own, or are intermixed with, eg leasehold properties (flats and maisonettes) is unimportant in the context of this discussion. The difference in treatment, so far as documentation is concerned, is not particularly startling.[4] The basic treatment is the same; the important point is that the use of this type of scheme enables the properties concerned to be sold on a freehold basis, *if the developer so wishes*.

As we have seen, the possibility of use of the scheme will arise when there is something present in or on the development which is to be enjoyed on a common, or shared, basis. Not all 'sharing' situations, however, call for such treatment—for example, the sharing of accessways to battery garages and of private footpaths on a development of (usually) terraced properties is common enough, but it is not dealt with by the inclusion of those areas in a management scheme, usually for two reasons. In the first place the areas concerned are usually plain tarmac or concrete, or some similar treatment which will require little or no attention for years, so that maintenance is not really necessary anyway, and second (and more relevant) there is no point in including in a management scheme areas which can just as easily be dealt with by other means. Management means administration, and that which is vital is bad enough, without including non-vital areas.

4 See Precedents Nos 25 and 26 respectively, pp 442 and 443, below.

The sort of 'sharing' situations which might call for this sort of treatment are as follows:

1 roadways and/or footpaths, where
   (a) the planners insist these remain in private ownership, or
   (b) the developer wants them to remain privately owned, as he might do on the grounds of, eg exclusivity;
2 lighting, and any other such services, on the private areas. This category would presumably be relevant only in conjunction with category 1;
3 open grassed areas which are enjoyed jointly by the houses in the scheme, or by those houses in conjunction also with other properties—eg adjoining leasehold flats/maisonettes;
4 areas of garden ground, on the same basis as category 3. These can sometimes be surprisingly complicated; it is not always a case of a piece of dug-over ground with a few shrubs stuck into it;
5 other ornamental areas, which may comprise various sorts of 'hard' external surfaces as well as 'soft' areas.[5] For instance, it is not unknown to have included in such schemes ornamental pools, complete with fountains, water gardens, seating arrangements, etc. Incidentally, it is not always the more expensive developments which are burdened by such common areas; the author well recalls one development on a cleared site in a Midlands city, where residential property was to replace industrial buildings; and the city planners were insisting on a scheme which basically comprised a circular development of flats/maisonettes/houses, on the perimeter of the site, all facing inwards on a central amenity area incorporating all the features described above. So far as the planners were concerned, it was either that sort of scheme or nothing, so that the developer was obliged to set up a management scheme of, shall we say, rather more complexity than would normally be expected. As the properties were by no means in the expensive bracket, it was just as well that there were a good number of them to spread the management costs to an acceptable level, otherwise the whole thing would have been completely unworkable. It should be stressed that this example relates to a development which was wholly leasehold, so that there was only one management scheme, whereas we are talking here about situations where there is one management scheme for the freehold properties if they are on their own, and a shared scheme if they are being built in conjunction with adjacent leasehold properties. Nevertheless, the type of layout described in this paragraph could just as easily be found in the sort of scheme under discussion.

Before we go on to study the mechanics of the 'freehold maintenance' scheme, as it has been referred to, we ought to review very quickly the alternative methods of setting-up the development.

From this point on, we shall be referring to a completely separate development of, eg houses, and not one sharing common areas with, eg flats; however, readers will be well able to 'fine tune' other choices to the latter variant.

5 For a discussion on 'hard' and 'soft' external areas, see ch 16, p 172, above.

A. First of all, the developer lets the units on long leases at a modest ground rent, plus a service charge to cover the cost of looking after the common areas, which would remain in his ownership. This would only work in the rare cases where the developer was willing to accept this burden.

B. As an extension of A, the developer could appoint an agent to manage the scheme. Care would have to be taken to draft the documentation so as to provide a profit element for the manager.[6]

C. As a further extension of A, the developer could either
   (i) execute a concurrent lease of his reversionary interest, which would include the retained common areas,[7] or
   (ii) sell his interest, whether it was freehold or (less likely) leasehold, to some person, company or organisation who would be interested on a commercial basis. Again, care would have to be taken in the drafting of the maintenance provisions so as to make such a scheme commercially attractive.

D. The developer could set up a management company, owned jointly by residents and the developer, to which would be sold the freehold interest in the site, after which the management company would grant long leases of the units. Naturally, the documentation would provide for the levying of a service charge in the normal way.

E. Again, there could be a management company set up for the site, but with the difference that it was one run completely by the residents for the time being. In this case, the developer would normally grant the leases, and then sell the (freehold) reversion to the management company for a nominal sum (say £1). It would almost inevitably be a condition of each lease that the owner of the property became a member of the company.

F. Of all the choices being reviewed, this is the one which is recommended, as it is based on a *freehold* sale. Thus, the units themselves, including any private garden grounds contiguous with the plots, would be transferred on a freehold basis, and then the freehold[8] of the common parts would be vested in a management company.

This is how the mechanics of this scheme are set up:

1 The houses are transferred on a freehold basis, using a normal building estate form of transfer[9] but amended slightly, thus:
   (a) there is incorporated a joint application by transferor and tranferee to the Chief Land Registrar for the entry on to the Register of a restriction that no transfer by a proprietor of a unit is to be registered without the consent of the management company:
   (b) included in the estate restrictions in the transfer, wherever they may be (usually in a Schedule), there will be a covenant by the transferee

6 And refer generally to ch 14, p 159, above for the effect of the Housing Act 1980, particularly Sch 19 thereto, on such a scheme.
7 See ch 10, p 128, above.
8 Or whatever the reversionary title was, although we are assuming all the way through this chapter that it will be freehold.
9 See Precedent No 25, p 442, below.

not to execute a transfer of the unit without obtaining the execution between the incoming purchaser and the management company of a deed of covenant (see below);

(c) covenants on the part of the developer are included in a separate part of the transfer that the common parts of the estate will be maintained by it until the residents take over the running of the management company, and that so long as any part of the development remains vested in it, it will itself pay appropriate portions of the common costs to the management company.

2 Each time a house is sold, (including the initial sale by the developer) a deed of covenant is entered into by the incoming purchaser with the management company. This provides for the incoming purchaser:

(a) to pay an appropriate part of the common expenses;

(b) to include, when selling the unit, a condition in the contract to the effect that the intending purchaser will become a member of the management company; and

(c) to ensure that upon any sale, a deed of covenant in similar terms is entered into with the management company.

The deed of covenant also provides for the management company:

(a) to provide the common services, which are set out in detail in the schedule to the deed of covenant; and

(b) to enter into a deed of covenant with any intending transferee of any unit and to give the appropriate consent required under the terms of the restriction imposed by the transfer (see above).

3 A management company will be in existence at the start of the development, but (if the company is to be handed over to the residents)[10] will be initially controlled by subscribers who will be officers of the developer, or perhaps his solicitors. Thus, until the unit-owners become full members of the company at the end of the development the management company is effectively controlled by the developer. Thereafter, the house-owners take over.

As we saw earlier, this particular variation of the scheme is based on there being a separate enclave of freehold houses with common areas the subject of the management scheme. However, it will be readily apparent that the nature of the scheme and the documentation which puts it into effect will differ little where the freehold units are just part of a larger, more predominantly leasehold development, so that both freehold and leasehold share some common areas. There may be some advantage in the 'mixed' development, because there is less likelihood of there being a wholly-owned residents' management company. On such a larger, mixed site one is more likely to have a professional manager, rather than the 'do-it-yourself' style, although even in a scheme such as this tenants' management companies can be used—but with caution. The author recently heard of a very large site, which to the developer was an important, prestigious site, yet he had opted for a

10 This system may be used, not only for a residents' management company, as described, but also for a professional management company, which is sometimes preferable (assuming such a company can be persuaded to take on the job).

tenants' management company. Apparently he was about half-way through the development, ie half-way to handing the management company over to the residents, and he was already experiencing almost insuperable problems with complete disinterest on the part of those residents.[11]

11 And see ch 11, p 131, above on tenants' management companies.

CHAPTER 20

Urban renewal and conversion schemes

Up to a few years ago, city centre areas were generally redeveloped by the simple expedient of knocking down everything that was already standing on the area of land selected for redevelopment, and subsequently building new dwellings on the 'quasi-virgin' land thus produced. These new dwellings might have been high rise, especially those for the public sector, or more latterly, low rise. In this modern age of 'labelling', this type of development is usually referred to by some impressive title such as 'inner-city re-development'.

We mentioned the public sector above; certainly until recent years the likelihood would have been that any such development was carried out by the local authority. But in recent years local authorities have been very much constrained in their building activities, owing to shortage of funds, and it is more usual nowadays for this type of development to be carried out by a local authority by means of a joint venture with a private developer.

Having produced a cleared area of land by demolishing and bulldozing away what was there formerly, it follows that there is no difference at all between building flats, houses or any other sort of dwelling on such a site as opposed to building on a 'greenfields' site.

The sort of development we have just been considering is symptomatic of the 'throwaway' society which in recent years has been so prevalent. But in very recent years a new attitude has surfaced, and this is not only present in the public, but also the local authorities or other bodies who generally own the basic material which we shall shortly be describing, and the builders with whom they generally work in the development of such sites.

All over the country, but more especially in urban areas, particularly those near city centres, are sites of run-down housing. They may comprise low rise housing, perhaps row upon row of terraces, or semis, or possibly three-storey blocks of maisonettes or flats. Equally they may comprise large blocks of multi-storey flats. Whatever they are, they will be run-down, and they will be empty, otherwise there would be no attraction for the developer.

Nearly all the large industrial cities have areas like these, where until recently any redevelopment would automatically lead to demolition and redevelopment with brand new properties. But the run-down housing may not be so bad that it should automatically be knocked down. It is true that it may have some basic problems, but as long as they are not basic design faults or allied to defective construction, the shells of the building may well be capable of being saved and having implanted in them new living units.

Accordingly, some of the major housebuilders have broken new ground in devising this new sort of development, which also has a label—this time 'urban renewal'. What usually happens is that the local authority is saddled with an old estate which may have been vandalised to such an extent that, for this and other reasons, it is quite beyond the financial scope of the authority to refurbish them, or indeed very often to do anything at all about the situation. At this stage along comes a developer, who first of all subjects the whole site to a thorough investigation, to identify whether there are any basic problems with either the buildings or the site, and then, having done his sums, he will make an offer.

That is one part of the subject; very closely allied to it is another type of development which has been popular in recent years, and this also has a label—usually one with the word 'refurbishment' in it. This time, the building will not be a candidate for demolition, for the very simple reason that in a great number of these cases the building will be listed by the Department of the Environment as being of special architectural or historical interest. Notwithstanding that these buildings are listed, they may very well be badly in need of refurbishment, and thus an imposition on their owners. Recently, however, some developers have been active in the field of buying these sorts of building, and refurbishing them, very nearly always as flats.

Buildings such as these are classified in three grades, or perhaps more correctly in two grades, the second one being subdivided.

Grade 1 (which represents only about 1% of the total listed buildings) are buildings of exceptional interest. It would be unusual to find a candidate for refurbishment in this grade.
Grade II are buildings of special interest, which warrant every effort being made to preserve them. Grade II* (spoken as 'Grade II starred') are particularly important buildings within that grade.[1]

Quite obviously renewal properties are completely different to refurbished ones, and are intended for a different market, as follows:

A. RENEWAL DEVELOPMENTS

While not the first case of urban renewal, the classic example was Barratt Development's operation at Minister Court, Liverpool. This hit the headlines for a number of reasons, not least because the site was right next door to the scene of the Toxteth riots. However, the flats on the site had been vacant before that notorious occurrence, and comprised four main apartment blocks, five-storeys high, with deck entrances on the sides of the blocks facing inwards from the street (the blocks were arranged in a square shape, bounded on all sides by streets).

The author viewed these apartment blocks before any work was ever done on them. They were dilapidated, generally run-down, and vandalised. Their aspect was daunting; but not to those far-sighted people—both with the local authority and the developer—who could visualise what could be done with them, rather than knocking them down—the fate they would almost certainly have suffered in less enlightened times.

A second visit when the refurbishment programme was well under way

1 DOE Circular 23/77, Appendix 1.

was truly an eye-opener, for the transformation was magical. The main fabric of the buildings had been retained, but re-furbished substantially, and on the inner faces of the blocks stairwells had been added, enclosed by conservatory-type glass structures. Part of the site had been cleared, and a mixture of new two and three storey blocks of flats were in the course of construction. The grounds were to be properly landscaped, and the whole was enclosed by a high security wall with a single entrance, with round the clock security.

And yet the market which was being aimed at was very much the lower end—the prices of the units were (1983 levels) from £13,500 for a very small one-bedroom unit to £17.500 for a reasonably sized two-bedroom unit. How could this be achieved, in a city centre site?

The factors which led to such a development were:

(a) Liverpool City Council owning a site with derelict flats. This is an (unfortunately) all too common state of affairs in our larger cities, some of which have very run down areas very near the city centre.
(b) The City Council having the foresight to enter into a deal with the developer. In recent times Liverpool as an authority has been much maligned, but in this instance (and others) they showed considerable flair and common sense (far more than another authority in a similar situation which chose to knock down its derelict buildings, without having the funds to redevelop the site).
(c) The developer having the originality and impetus to set up the deal, which basically consisted of paying a reasonably nominal sum for each flat, and then having the courage to embark upon the development.

So that when the developer took possession of the site, he had the basic shells of the apartment blocks for a (to him) nominal sum, and so was able to develop the site to a high standard, yet keep the selling prices down to affordable levels for the sort of purchaser who wanted to live in that sort of property in that location.

Circumstances differ from one development to the next, but usually the hallmark of an urban renewal development will be the provision of reasonably low cost housing in locations which are easily accessible to centres of population, services, and shopping. That is not to say that there are no urban renewal developments pitched at the better-off; there are, but they are not the archetypal schemes such as the one just described.

B. REFURBISHMENT DEVELOPMENTS

The type of property chosen for refurbishment is likely to be such that the units sold out of it will be more, rather than less, expensive. Again, there are refurbishments at the lower end of the market, but perhaps a more typical example would be that involving a country house, or older buildings in the more fashionable towns, e g Bath, where there have been a tremendous number of such schemes completed, and Bristol, particularly the Clifton area of the city, where there are approaching 4,000 listed buildings (of which, interestingly, nearly three-quarters are terraced properties).

Since refurbishment of such buildings calls for very careful treatment, matching materials and workmanship to the originals, the cost of completing the development is inevitably expensive, and, of course, there is a strong contrast to renewal properties, in that the buildings themselves are most definitely not there to be picked up for a song. Particularly in the late seventies, when refurbishment was very much the 'in' thing for builders to be involved with, owners of listed properties—and indeed anyone who owned any property which appeared to be a likely candidate for refurbishment—were asking quite ridiculous prices for their properties. Inflated purchase prices of the base property meant that units in refurbished developments became very expensive, and there is no doubt that a not inconsiderable number of developers burnt their fingers.

At the time of publication of this book, the emphasis on refurbishment seems to have swung away from the Georgian terrace/country house type of property; the latest craze seems to be warehouses and other commercial buildings fronting to rivers, particularly in the East End of London. It remains to be seen how long this will last, and whether it will be generally successful for the developers.

C. LEGAL TREATMENT

Urban renewal and refurbishments can conveniently be grouped together when considering the legal treatment.

Neither calls for any particularly specialist treatment in the preparation of the lease; they are merely variations on a leasehold theme. To that extent, this chapter is very brief and pithy and no specialist documents to use in such developments will be found in the precedents section. But if the legal aspect is bland, the management one is not: because it is crucial that:

(i) the development has built into it a full-blown management scheme; and
(ii) management should be by a professional management company. It is highly dangerous to set up a tenants' management company, and even more dangerous to try to manage the development by means of a variation on the studio flat scheme we have discussed elsewhere in this book.[2]

D. WHY FULL MANAGEMENT?

1 Renewal schemes

First consider that one is starting with an already existing building. It is not a new building, having the benefit of every modern building technique (and for those who easily scoff at modern building as 'jerry-building', it is not the case that if a building is new it is less well built than an old property—there are many old buildings which were appallingly built). Whilst the developer will have carried out a thorough survey on it, he will not have been able to strip it down completely to inspect every part of it. There may be hidden problems which will give rise to expenditure at a later date.

2 See ch 9, p 110, above.

Next, the very nature of urban renewal, taking existing buildings and turning them from a dilapidated state to acceptable housing, means that the buildings are likely to be multi-storey, i e more than certainly two or even three storeys; they will be probably fairly large, and perhaps more complicated. That also means more units in the building, with more complexity, than a simple 'self-help' type maintenance scheme like that described on p 110, above could possibly cope with.

Finally, some renewal schemes are reasonably simple from the point of view of the management of the common areas, but there are others which are complicated. Take as an example the splendid scheme at Minster Court described in the first part of this chapter. This features (inter alia) the following:

maintenance of main structures;
maintenance of private roads within the curtilage of the site, as well as footpaths;
employment of gardeners and cleaners (and there was a considerable extent of both internal common areas, and external ones, both hard and soft);
answer-phone system throughout;
private lighting on the external common areas of the site;
24-hour janitor service;
around the clock security.

Clearly only a full management scheme could cope with a development of this complexity.

2 Refurbishment schemes

To an even greater extent with these schemes, the fabric of the main structure is of importance. In a renewal scheme, the building itself is likely to be one of reasonably modern construction, so that modern construction methods, which are well understood, can be applied to it. But with a refurbishment, one may be dealing with a very old building. Some date back to Georgian times, and delightful though these are, on occasion, for example, the roofs can be in need of considerable work. One problem the intending purchaser of a unit in such a scheme has is to know whether on an elderly building all the problems have been identified correctly by the developer. However large the developer, or however high his reputation, one cannot guarantee anything, and with an NHBC exception mentioned later in this chapter, there are no written guarantees with a refurbishment scheme unit, other than those given personally by the developer—and it is up to the purchaser to decide how much this is worth.

Amongst catastrophes which have, to the author's certain knowledge, manifested themselves on developments in various parts of the country are:

(a) hitherto undetected but nevertheless massive infestation of woodworm;
(b) defective roofing requiring considerable remedial works;
(c) sinking foundations;
and so on.

It is certainly clear that on refurbishment schemes as well as renewals, it is important that there be a proper and full management scheme built into the lease. To be fair to the various developers of this type of properties up and down the country, the author has never yet seen anything other than this, but it is a point which needs to be borne in mind.

E. WHY PROFESSIONAL MANAGEMENT?

The simple answer to this second important question is based on the same reasons as on the previous point; that is, just because of the complicated nature of the building and its surroundings, and in so many of these cases the age of the fabric itself, nothing less than professional management should be contemplated.

Accordingly, those setting up such schemes must make sure that professional help is brought in when the management scheme is being set up, and those purchasing such units must equally make sure that they are satisfied that those responsible for management are able to cope with it.

There will be three basic types of management available on developments of this sort. These will be:

(a) professional management company operating its own maintenance services, etc;
(b) ditto, but contracting maintenance out to local people, or perhaps employing a local surveyor to arrange maintenance locally;
(c) tenants' management company.

This is not to say that there will not be other choices, e g;

(i) perhaps some sort of management system based on the 'small unit' one described in ch 9, above; or
(ii) possibly the developer retaining overall control but using local estate agents who may operate a management service.

These last two choices, and others on the same level, are to be avoided both by developers and prospective purchasers. Certainly the type of development under discussion is much too complex for the 'small unit' system to be at all appropriate, and unless the local agent is tolerably large, with a sizeable and experienced management department, then that option is also to be avoided.

A tenants' management company is also a vehicle to be avoided, because on complicated developments of this sort, it is wise to have the management in completely independent hands. If the unit-owners themselves are in charge, there may be the risk of those who are running the management providing a less than satisfactory service—and with a tenants' management company there will always be some sort of a clique, large or small, which will take over the direction of the company to the displeasure of the other owners, and they may pitch management at levels which are either too weak or too strong.

We therefore find ourselves left with professional management. This really is the only answer. Those who equate professional management companies with high service charges should remember that both renewal and refurbishment developments are usually more than averagely complicated, and in the end, it will pay the unit owners to have an independent, competent manager. The disadvantage, of course, is that the service charges may as a result be a little higher, but then these schemes do unfortunately tend to be full of potential disadvantages, so much so that we might usefully end the discussion by listing them.

Snags to watch out for

What follows applies just as much to those advising developers as those looking after the interests of potential purchasers, because in this sector of the market particularly it pays to know what the opposition might be thinking.

Some of the downside points, therefore, are:

(a) *These are not new buildings*

Renewal scheme buildings might not be very old; there are some derelict blocks of council flats which might qualify for a scheme but which are only a very few years old—but one always has to ask oneself why the former use stopped.

Refurbishment scheme buildings will on average be older, and again the question which has to be asked will be—'is the building worthy of all the work being done on it?'.

Given a sensible and co-operative developer, his advisers might help the other side considerably, and at the same time do themselves some good by making available as much information as possible about the basic condition of the building, and what is being done to it. If this does not happen, then the purchaser's solicitor should consider how far he should probe into this aspect of the matter.

(b) *Is the management scheme sensible?*

This has been discussed, but it is worth repeating that a development of this sort with incompetent management spells disaster.

(c) *How expensive is the management going to be?*

Developers differ in their attitude to the dissemination of specific information on the anticipated service charges. Some will give full information on the expected levels of charge, even indicating how the quoted figures are built up,[3] others will only grudgingly quote a figure while others, it has to be said, seem to have the greatest difficulty in even understanding what service charges are!

Purchasers' advisers *must* press for as much information as they can from the other side. They must then advise their clients accordingly, but certainly bearing in mind that:

3 And consider the operation of the Housing Act 1980, Sch 19. See further, ch 14, p 159, above.

(i) initial service charges on this type of development will tend to be higher, rather than lower, than those to be expected on a new development;
(ii) again, despite the protests of those who say that older property is better built than new, the likelihood is that those older properties will give rise to more maintenance, and indeed portions of renewal all over again, than new ones;
(iii) the sort of purchaser interested in this type of property is not necessarily overflowing with cash, so that, e g
  (a) taking refurbishment schemes first, a significant proportion of purchasers are retired, and very probably on fixed incomes, and
  (b) on renewal schemes, the average purchaser probably will not be in the AB social categories. Very often units in these schemes will be surprisingly cheap, but if the scheme is anything more than simple, the service charges will be substantial. This, of course, is the great conundrum of renewal schemes. How do you equate sometimes remarkably low selling prices with a continuing burden of service charges, which may well be considerably more than nominal? There seems to be no answer yet to this particular poser. Any substantial flat development with common areas gives rise to maintenance, which in its turn gives rise to charges on the flat owner.

And so, while both urban renewal and refurbishment schemes are of the greatest interest, with (especially) the former becoming more and more prevalent, there are still some basic problems which the cautious conveyancer will need to look out for. Nevertheless, it is only in these areas already described that problems may arise; otherwise there is nothing magical or special in either type of development—merely they are a variation on a theme.

F. THE NHBC CONVERSION AND RENOVATION SCHEME

Both the 'urban renewal and refurbishment' type of scheme may qualify for cover under the National Housebuilding Council's Conversion and Renovation Scheme.

As the scheme is a specialised one for specialised properties, it is dealt with in this chapter rather than in the general chapter on the NHBC Scheme as it is applied to 'ordinary' (i e new, in a new building) flats.

1 Qualifications for the scheme to apply

(a) *Builders*

(a) Those builders and developers already on the NHBC register may apply to have their conversion and renewal schemes covered. There will be no extra registration fee involved.
(b) Builders and developers who are not already registered, but who are able to show experience of this sort of work and who meet certain technical and financial requirements, may be admitted to a *special* register. There is a 'special' registration fee involved.
(c) If the builder and developer of such a scheme are different, both then must be registered. It is not enough to have only one registered.

(b) *Properties*

The scheme has to involve a building of no more than four storeys, plus a basement, and there have to be three or more units.

2 Standards to be met

The requirements for the building work to be carried out are that it should comply with current Building Regulations and that the standard of work should not be less than that required to qualify for improvement grants. On larger schemes the NHBC also obtains an independent engineer's report before satisfying itself that the scheme may be accepted.

The NHBC state in their application form for cover[4] that the normal NHBC Technical Requirements do no apply to this sort of scheme, but nevertheless in order to be eligible the 'specification and quality of workmanship must be of a reasonable standard'.

In the handbook made available to purchasers of this type of unit, the NHBC point out that conversion or renovation may be carried out in two ways, thus:

'1 It can involve spending money on things that will be needed to do a decent job, even if these are hidden from the ultimate buyer. For example, if the original building is 40 years old or more it will almost always be desirable to install new wiring and new plumbing.
2 The other way involves spending money only where the prospective buyer can see the results. The walls will gleam with new paint and wallpaper. WHO KNOWS WHAT LIES BEHIND THEM?'[5]

The NHBC concludes this section of the booklet with the comment that it will not issue insurance cover on this second variety!

3 The cover available

Everyone remembers the 'Ten-Year Protection' certificate which used to be issued by the NHBC. It was the hallmark of the scheme, and became well known as far as the public were concerned. The ten-year period still applies to the present NHBC scheme for new properties[6] but the periods for the conversion and renovation scheme are different.

(a) *Year one*

During this period, the builder/developer will be liable for *all* defects, except that if he becomes bankrupt or goes into liquidation, the NHBC will meet any arbitration award.

4 That form, and the NHBC booklet '*NHBC Protection for Buyers of Newly Converted Flats and Houses*' (which is handed to purchasers of such units) are acknowledged as source material for this section. The author is also indebted to the NHBC themselves who have, as always, been most helpful.
5 The emphasis is the NHBC's, not the authors.
6 See generally ch 25, p 289, below.

(b) *Years two to six inclusive*

During this period the NHBC will meet the cost of remedying any major damage arising from structural defects, except those arising out of subsidence or heave. These risks must be covered by the owner of the property under his normal householders policy.

Thus the scheme provides cover only for a six-year period, and because the builder/developer takes on board total liability throughout year one, the NHBC is effectively providing cover for five years, i e years two, three, four, five and six of the scheme—in other words half the period of cover available in the case of a new property.

But this is not the way to look at this scheme. It should be viewed from the opposite direction. The purchaser should perhaps count himself lucky to find NHBC cover available at all. The point is that covering the risk of such schemes is not such a cut and dried business as when new properties are involved, and the reader should not assume that every flat in a renewal or renovation development will automatically come with this type of NHBC cover. We have seen that the NHBC acceptance of a development into the scheme depends on certain minimum standards being achieved, and on its own surveyors satisfying themselves on the nature of the project. As a result of their investigations, the NHBC may ask for additional works to be undertaken. Of course it is up to the builder/developer to acquiesce or to decline to do so, in which latter case he would go forward without the NHBC cover.

4 The limit of the cover

Not surprisingly, there is a limit to the total cover available. Each unit will have an upper limit of cover in the sum of (at present) £50,000 or its purchase price, whichever is the lesser. Thus £50,000 is the maximum cover available, which in many conversion schemes will represent something of a shortfall, because the refurbishment schemes tend to be fairly 'up-market' as a rule.

Furthermore, there will be an overall limit for the scheme as a whole. If a purchaser is not told what that limit is at the time he is in the pre-contract stage, his adviser should enquire what it is.

5 What damage will be covered?

It will be clear to everyone that there will be more risk in a scheme of this sort, as opposed to new properties, quite simply because whereas what goes into a new property in the way of both work and materials can be strictly controlled, what is there as a (very often substantial) basic shell in a conversion/renewal scheme is not always able to be quantified. This is why the NHBC must reserve to themselves the right to carry out a rigorous inspection of what they are being asked to insure. Nevertheless, there are occasions when a surveyor will miss latent defects, through no fault of his own, and so the approach of the NHBC must necessarily be cautious. They say themselves that they reject one in five of all schemes submitted for consideration because 'the extent or standard of work is just not acceptable'. In the author's view, this rate of rejections is remarkably low, given the nature of the work, and the NHBC are to be congratulated on their achievement in offering substantial cover on the majority of schemes put before them.

As to the type of damage which will be covered in schemes of this sort, Section III of the special form of House Purchaser's Insurance Policy used for this scheme, the HB7D,[7] states:

> 'The Council will pay the Purchaser the cost of remedying:
> (a) Major Damage which appears and is reported during the Structural Guarantee Period and is caused by any Defect in the structure; and
> (b) any such Defect but only where such Major Damage has appeared Provided that such cost is not covered by other insurance at the time of the Claim.'

'the Structural Guarantee Period' is defined in the HB7D as 'the period commencing upon the expiry of the Initial Guarantee Period[8] and expiring six years from the date of issue of the Common Parts Notice of Insurance Cover[9]
'Defect' means a defect in the dwelling;
'Damage' means damage to the dwelling caused by any defect;
'Major Damage' means damage to the dwelling requiring complete or partial rebuilding or extensive repair work. It includes damage classified as very severe or severe in the Building Research Establishment Digest 251, 'Assessment of Damage in Low-Rise Buildings' (July 1981).[10]

For those of us who have difficulty in interpreting the above the NHBC help us, in their brochure for buyers described earlier, by saying that what is covered are all structural defects causing major damage to the building, e g foundation failure not arising from subsidence or heave, failure of load bearing walls, major roof failure, and dry rot in structural timbers, which is an important point to be covered because in elderly buildings it will very often be infestations which will be the main cause of trouble, if trouble there is going to be.

In the same booklet, the NHBC is at pains to point out that NHBC approved conversions will *not* comply in every way with modern building standards. The standards for new properties are stringent and incorporate certain matters which could not be included in conversions without costs becoming unreasonable.

The example is given of window frames in new properties requiring to have been factory-treated for protection against wet rot. In older buildings where the frames appear to be sound, it would be unreasonable to expect a builder to remove them and replace throughout with new frames. Similarly, modern standards of thermal and/or sound insulation will not always be achieved.

7 See further, below.
8 Ie the first year; one year from issue of the Standard Notice of Insurance Cover, or (if later) the completion of the dwelling.
9 This is the definition for flats, with which we are here concerned. There is a slightly different definition for houses.
10 All these definitions are taken from the HB7D.

6 The scheme in summary

1 The participation by the builder/developer in the scheme is voluntary. Just because a property is offered without the benefit of NHBC cover it does not necessarily mean that there is something wrong with it. It would be quite wrong of a purchaser and/or his advisers to dismiss a prospective property out of hand because it was not in the NHBC scheme. The approach must obviously be different for these types of properties, as opposed to new ones, where dwellings must have either NHBC cover, or in certain selected cases, an architect's certificate. Nevertheless, for a property to have NHBC cover in a conversion/renewal scheme is an added bonus. Probably at the lower end of the market, i e the majority of renewal properties and some of the refurbishment ones, the funding will be by building societies, or banks, and particularly the former may well be looking for the NHBC cover, and may indeed specify this as a condition on the mortgage offer.

2 The general aim of the scheme is to provide a 'reconditioned' dwelling, rather than a brand new one, and so the buyer is offered a warranty which is somewhat less extensive, i e in time terms, than that offered on a new property. The analogy with cars is fairly strong.

3 If the property does come with NHBC cover, then an intending purchaser may be sure that the works which the building has undergone have received careful assessment by independent experts, and that the conversion work will have been carried out in a workmanlike manner.

4 The above comments naturally lead on to the incontrovertible proposition that the property will be that much more saleable when the time comes for the purchaser to move on. Even after the Structural Guarantee Period has expired, the mere fact that the property was considered eligible for the NHBC scheme should be a powerful selling point.

5 Finally—and this is a point which might easily be overlooked—builders and developers should not forget that if they are able to have their conversion and/or renewal scheme participate in this scheme, they ought to have the competitive edge over the non-NHBC scheme when it comes to selling.

CHAPTER 21

Shared ownership

Shared ownership as a vehicle for selling and buying property is a relatively new idea; the first reported shared ownership scheme started in Birmingham only in the early seventies. As a form of house purchase, it has perhaps not enjoyed the success that some of its supporters might have hoped for, but there is no doubt that its usage has been very much more than scattered. The main problem with the concept seems to be its inherent complexity, although that very complexity probably results more from the way that the scheme is put into effect than from the basic principle.

In order to explain the scheme, we will first of all study the outlines in a way which will be understandable to lawyers and laymen alike; we will then carry on to look very briefly at what (little) underlying legislation there is, and finally we shall direct the reader's attention to the documentation by means of which such a scheme is operated. As always throughout this book, the emphasis is more on the practical than the theoretical side. Shared ownership can be very complicated indeed when one comes to consider the niceties of the system. However, we are discussing shared ownership here as an applied method of dealing with property, not as a principle. For our purposes then, the inclusion of a chapter on shared ownership in a book on the sale of flats may be justified on two counts:

1 the shared ownership concept is dealt with by way of lease, and a lease is the most common document of transmission used in the sale of flats (at least until English land law is changed);[1] and
2 nevertheless, the above represents a coincidence more than anything else, and the main justification in discussing the subject here is that it may be used for flats, and maisonettes, in the same way as it is for houses.

A. THE BASIC APPROACH

In a subject like shared ownership, where complexity can easily overpower one, it is important to start with first principles, so as to give us a basic understanding. We accordingly approach this part of the chapter on a question and answer basis, as follows.

1 What precisely is shared ownership?

As we have seen earlier, the concept started in Birmingham some years ago. It is a system where, instead of either purchasing the property in question

1 Refer to ch 28, p 309 and ch 29, p 325, below on the proposals of the Law Commission and the Building Societies Association respectively.

outright or renting it outright, there is a 'half-way' stage initially where part of the property is owned, and the other part is rented.

2 Who operates shared ownership?

Usually only a public authority, i e a local authority, new town, or a housing association. Incidentally, there is another 'similar' system of selling property, known as 'equity sharing'. This is described more fully in the author's *Residential Estate Conveyancing: Practice and Precedents*[2] and is quite different, in that an outside party, usually the vendor (e g a housebuilder), allows part of the equity, i e the unmortgaged part of the value of the property, to remain unpaid for, with the proviso that if the value of the property moves (in true equity sharing, which is equivalent to risk-sharing, the movement should be either up *or down*) then the value of the equity-holders stake moves accordingly.

The two concepts are quite different; there is risk for the sharing partner in equity sharing, and it is more in the nature of a mortgage tied to movements in value; in shared ownership there is usually no risk at all for the partner and there will be a true sharing of ownership.

3 How does shared ownership work?

The system works by the purchaser becoming an owner occupier without paying the full purchase price. This is achieved by the vendor granting the purchaser a long lease of the property; this lease

(a) defines the terms upon which the property has been bought, and
(b) provides for the payment of an annual rent.

Included in the terms set out in the lease is the 'split' between the percentage of the property which is owned outright, and that which is rented.

Thus, initially the purchaser might buy 50% of the agreed value, in which case he would pay 50% of the rent which would normally be due on that particular property were it to be included in the vendors stock of properties available for full rental. Then, if a further 10% of the market value were purchased, so that the purchaser owned 60%, the rental proportion would be reduced to 40%. Once the purchaser owns 100% of the value, he stops paying rent. If the property concerned is a house, then at that point he will have the freehold conveyed to him, or in the case of a flat/maisonette he will be granted a conventional long lease at a nominal ground rent.

4 How is the market value worked out?

There are subtle differences between different authorities in the way that they deal with valuations, whether on the initial purchase or when the purchaser is subsequently 'topping-up' his share. Mostly properties offered for sale are valued professionally, perhaps by panels of local estate agents. The position is different if the properties concerned are new ones, when the

2 (Butterworths, 1983) pp 339 et seq.

basis of valuation will be slightly varied, but at the end of the day the basic rule will be the same as for any valuation, i e it will be what sort of property in those sort of surroundings, and taking into account the economic factors in force at the given time, may reasonably be expected to fetch on the open market with vacant possession. The purchaser's rights are different depending on whether we are considering an initial valuation, or a subsequent one, e g:

(a) *Initial valuation*

The only factor here will be market forces. If the intending purchaser does not agree with the authority's valuation, he does not have to buy. Therefore he has no appeal.

(b) *Subsequent valuation*

When this comes along, by definition the purchaser is already 'tied in' to the purchase. For there to be no recourse against a valuation would be unfair, so the purchaser aggrieved by the authority's valuation of the property at the time he wishes to buy a further share in it, may appeal to the district valuer.

Generally valuations are made on the basis described above, with the rider that if the property is a flat the valuation must assume that a long lease on 'conventional' terms, with a fixed ground rent of £10 per annum will be available. Any improvements made by a purchaser will be ignored, as also will be any failure to look after the property in a proper manner.

5 How is the rent worked out?

Again the authority will work out the amount of rent due in any particular circumstance. Generally, the figure will be based on the amount of rent which a normal council tenant would pay on the whole property, reduced by whatever percentage ownership there is at any given time, with a further reduction made on account of the fact that the purchaser (whatever his share) will be responsible for maintenance.[3] Rents paid under shared ownership leases are usually reviewed on an annual basis in the same way that 'normal' council rents are reviewed.

6 What percentages of the cost may be bought?

The lion's share of the purchase must be bought on the initial purchase; normally purchasers are encouraged to take at least 50% although an initial take-up *may* be as low as 30%. The greatest initial share is 80% because there are usually no intermediate steps between 80% and the full 100% in order to discourage people 'nibbling' at the outstanding cost on the home straight and when one gets to 80%, from all points of view especially administrative, the next logical step is to completion itself.

3 This will not necessarily be the case for flats.

As to intermediate purchases, the minimum 'take' will be 10%, the reason again being that anything less will be illogical, a waste of effort on everyone's part, and administratively inefficient.

7 At what intervals do the intermediate (and final) purchases have to be made?

There are no hard and fast rules. The purchaser can elect to take his slices at whatever times he pleases. Of course, if, having just completed the purchase of one 10% slice, he then immediately gave his vendor notice that he wanted to take another 10% slice, he might not be the most popular person around, but nevertheless he would be quite within his rights.

8 Are there any special benefits available?

Purchasers in the public sector may be entitled to discounts, which will be taken off the market value, i e the price the purchaser pays will very often be *less* than the valuation.

(a) a sitting tenant in a rented property may well be entitled to a discount on the market valuation when, or if, he decides to buy;
(b) a purchaser of a new property might also be entitled to some discount on the initial price, although this is less likely, but might subsequently be offered a discount on the 'extra shares'.

Whether or not a discount is available depends on the difference between the cost of building the property and its market value. Discounts have been known to go up to 50% where the purchaser has been a 'public authority' tenant for the required period. The snag about discounts is that if the property is sold within five years of having been purchased, they are repayable on a sliding scale.

9 Is there any restriction on selling such a property?

Once the whole 100% has been purchased, there are obviously no more restrictions on the right of disposal than on any other 'normally-bought' house except that, as we have seen above in answer to question 8, the discount may have to be repaid in whole or part.

Before the purchaser has bought the whole of the 100% share there are various options open to him if, or when, he wishes to sell; which of these operates seems to depend on the authority involved. The options are:

(a) there may be a requirement for the property to be offered back to the vendor authority, with a valuation scheme operating so as to give the purchaser the full value of any increase in market value due to improvements;
(b) this, and option (c) may only be available if the vendor authority declines to repurchase under option (a), although there are authorities who

do not insist on this being a prerequisite. This option involves the purchaser finding someone else to take over his share in the property. The incoming purchaser would then stand in the shoes of his own vendor insofar as the shared ownership aspect of the property was concerned. The snag about this would seem to be that not only would the new purchaser have to find a mortgagee who would accept him; he would also have to be approved by the authority;

(c) as an alternative to the above, the property could be sold outright even though when he formed the decision to sell the purchaser has not completed the purchase of the 100% share. This would be effected by the original purchaser buying the outstanding share from the authority, and then simultaneously selling on what would then be the whole property to the incoming purchaser.

10 What sorts of property does this scheme operate on?

The scheme operates not only with what are commonly called 'council houses', i e housing built originally for rental and which are subsequently sold off to the sitting tenants, but also brand new property. In these latter cases, a public authority will get together with a housebuilder, the former providing the land, the latter the buildings. Whole estates within these parameters may be sold on shared ownership, or only pre-set (or possibly subsequently variable) proportions may be sold this way.

11 What will the cost be?

This is one of the most fascinating features of shared ownership. There are many sceptics of the whole scheme and one problem is that there has been very little written about it. Undoubtedly many practitioners who have been involved at first hand with shared ownership purchasers have bluffed their way through to a certain extent!

The best guides by far, are those booklets produced by the authorities themselves, some of which have put in a great deal of work on the development of such schemes. Two of the foremost authorities in this category are Central Lancashire Development Corporation, and Milton Keynes Development Corporation. The latter's booklet[4] is particularly good; and one of the strong points it makes very clearly is a cost comparison with 'traditional' house purchase. Thus, the table reproduced below shows the cost of buying a house costing £25,000.

(a) in the 'conventional' way, and
(b) by shared ownership.

4 Milton Keynes: *Buying your own home in easy stages—a Guide to Shared Ownership.*

	CONVENTIONAL HOUSE PURCHASE	SHARED OWNERSHIP PURCHASE		
% age purchase	100%	80%	50%	30%
Weekly mortgage repayment	£41.00	£33.00	£20.00	£12.00
Weekly rent	Nil	£3.00	£7.00	£10.00
Total	£41.00	£36.00	£27.00	£22.00

These figures are, so to speak, 'diagrammatic'. The point is that they are correct on a 'like for like' comparison of costs between outright purchase and shared ownership. It can very clearly be seen that to start buying by shared ownership and then working one's way, in however many steps, towards complete ownership is much easier than plunging in at the deep end straightaway.

Another interesting illustrative calculation contained in the Milton Keynes booklet is how shared ownership affects the capital outlay of the purchaser, thus:

A. Purchaser P buys 40% of a £23,000 house
So: (i) 40% of £23,000 = £9,200
(ii) A mortgage of £9,200 means a mortgage repayment of £15.00 per month[5]
(iii) The rental element of 60% will be, say £8.00

B. Some time later, P decides to buy another 20% of his house
So: (i) The value of the house is now £25,000
(ii) 20% of £25,000 = £5,000
(iii) (Not that either the mortgage or rental payments are relevant for this exercise;) the mortgage goes up to £23, the rent goes down to £6.

C. Finally, again some time later, P buys in the remaining 40%
So: (i) The value of the house is now £28,000
(ii) 40% of £28,000 = £11,200
(iii) Now the mortgage is £42, and of course the rent is nil.

When the shared ownership purchase is completed, the property is worth £28,000. But because it was bought in stages, the purchaser actually paid less than that for it:

First stage purchase	£9,200
Some time later	£5,000
Finally	£11,200
	£25,400

Further, whilst the purchaser was buying the property, he had the benefit of lower monthly outgoings (see above)

5 Again the figures are 'diagrammatic'.

12 What are the advantages of shared ownership?

As we have seen already, the whole subject of shared ownership can be difficult for the average layman to understand. The following summary of its advantages will help:

(a) The purchaser's monthly outgoings are lower than if he had bought outright.
(b) By using the scheme he may have the benefit of discounts to which he would not otherwise be entitled (this applies particularly, e g to a purchase of a new joint venture public authority/housebuilder property as opposed to one bought outright from a builder direct).
(c) The purchaser chooses, without influence from any third party, when to buy more shares after the initial purchase.
(d) Any increase in market values of the property attach to whatever share of it has been bought.
(e) As discount is based on there being a gap between whatever it cost the authority to build the property, and its current market value, an increase in the market value will enhance any possible discount on subsequent purchases of shares.
(f) It is possible to arrange a mortgage for 100% of the initial share. This makes sense, because the building society will be advancing much less than 100% of their valuation. Then when (presumably) the same mortgagee finances subsequent share purchases, the value of the property will have gone up anyway so that what may have been a 100% mortgage of the initial share one year may well be significantly less than 100% of the valuation of the initial share in the following year.

    The point about all this is that the purchasers may well not need to find a deposit, so releasing their cash for furniture, buying expenses, etc.
(g) Finally, the most important advantage of all is that shared ownership allows people who would not otherwise have been able to afford such a move on to the property ownership ladder.

B. SUMMARY

This chapter has deliberately not been specific to flats and/or maisonettes, nor has it been couched in technical language. As we have observed before, shared ownership as a concept has given rise to difficulties not only with intending purchasers, but also with those attempting to advise them. Accordingly, readers are advised, following a reading of this chapter, to rely to a great extent on carefully reading the appropriate precedents, which are Nos 14, and 15, below. They may look daunting at first sight, but careful perusal does bring clarification!

C. THE LEGISLATION

Surprisingly enough, this is very scant, so that the concept is more of a drafting one than a statutory one.

1 The Housing Act 1980

This Act related to shared ownership only in a peripheral way. Thus Chapter 1, Part 1, ss 1 to 27, 'The Right to Buy' were of passing relevance in that they controlled the rights of a secure tenant to buy his property. We do not have the time here to delve into the sections themselves and must leave the reader who wishes to research the subject further to read the Act. However, it will do no more than set the peripheral scene, and will not help in relation to the subject of shared ownership itself.

The only part of the 1980 Act which specifically refers to shared ownership is s 140, which excludes shared ownership tenancies from the provisions of the Leasehold Reform Act 1967. The section specifically refers to 'houses' and as we are here concerned principally with flats, the section can be seen as having little relevance.

2 The Housing and Building Control Act 1984

If the 1980 Act did not recognise shared ownership as such, except in an indirect way, the Housing and Building Control Act 1984 devoted a complete area comprising six sections, plus one Schedule, to the specific subject of shared ownership, i e ss 12–17 and Sch 3. We shall study these in outline now, although once again the reader is recommended to read the Act thoroughly in order to further advance his understanding of the subject.

However, it is most important to note that the provisions of the 1984 Act apply only to a *secure tenant* exercising his right to buy. They do *not* apply to the sale of new properties, to e g people on a council waiting list, or to those already in council accommodation, as the term 'secure tenant' is taken to refer to a person who is exercising the right to buy the property of which he is a secure tenant. Section 28 of the 1980 Act defines secure tenancies which are tenancies under which dwelling houses are let as separate dwellings, and what the Act describes as 'landlord condition' and 'tenant condition' are satisfied: these basically point to what the layman understands as a 'council house tenancy'.

Thus an important sector of shared ownership, i e the new build sector, is not affected by the 1984 Act, although one supposes that the terms of sale laid down by the 1984 Act already apply in virtually all cases of shared ownership sales, and so has not added so very much save to grant the secure tenant an inalienable right to choose the option of shared ownership, if he exercises his right to buy.

The main points of the 1984 Act are as follows:

Section 12. Provides that where a secure tenant has exercised his right to buy[6] he has the right also to a shared ownership lease, subject to certain procedural conditions which are set out in the section. The shared ownership lease should conform with Parts I and III of Sch 2 to the 1980 Act (which refer to common provisions of rights, covenants etc, to be incorporated, and the basic terms of the lease, the most identifiable term from our point of view

6 Which will be under the terms of the 1980 Act (s 1 to 27).

being that the term of the lease must be for at least 125 years and the ground rent to be not more than £10 per annum) and also with Sch 3 to the 1984 Act (for which see later).

Section 13. This regulates the procedures for the giving by the secure tenant of a written notice claiming a shared ownership lease, the required contents of the notice; e g the initial share which the tenant proposes to acquire, and it also provides for the giving of a counter notice by the landlord, either admitting the tenants right or denying it on appropriate grounds.

Section 14. Provides that where the secure tenant has exercised his right, which has been then established (by the landlord's admission or otherwise) the landlord has to serve a notice giving details of:
(a) required initial contribution;
(b) proposed discount available; and
(c) provisions to be included in the lease.

Section 15. Refers to situations where the landlord changes identity in the middle of the negotiations, and provides that any such changes shall not affect the procedures in train.

Section 16. Regulates the right to further advances to the tenant where he exercises both the right to be granted a shared ownership lease and the right to a mortgage. Obviously, if the tenant chooses shared ownership, he has to know that he can find the purchase of any subsequent shares he wishes to take on. The mortgage he has to support his initial purchase must obviously enable him to take those subsequent steps.

Section 17. Provides for procedures relating to the completion (i e legal completion of the initial purchase, not subsequent steps) of the shared ownership lease.

Schedule 3. The Schedule sets out in considerable detail what the terms of the shared ownership lease are to be. Purely as an indication of the matters which the Schedule covers, the following are its sub-headings:

Tenant's initial share;
Tenant's initial contribution;
Additional shares;
Additional contributions;
Rent;
Repayment of discount on early disposal;
Payment for outstanding share on disposal;
No disposals of part while share outstanding; and
Supplemental

D. THE DOCUMENTATION

Just as the Housing and Building Control Act 1984, Sch 3 is lengthy, so is a typical shared ownership lease. Whilst there is unfortunately no room to reproduce Sch 3 in its entirety, in order to help the reader to recognise a well drawn shared ownership lease, as well as to recognise a poorly drawn one (which is perhaps rather more important) he or she will find in Precedent No 14[7] typical shared ownership wording. The term 'wording' is used rather than 'lease' because the Precedent consists of the appropriate extracts from the form of shared ownership lease developed by Central Lancashire Development Corporation, which has been so devised that the parts of it which relate to shared ownership are concentrated, apart from two or three necessary small exceptions, into one Schedule. By devising this system, which is by no means universal, the shared ownership aspects are built on to a relatively standard form of lease, and, being in a consolidated form, are that much easier to understand.

This Precedent, as with some others in this book, is offered to the reader not because many of them, if any, will be called up on to act for a shared ownership lessor who inevitably will always have his own in-house legal advisers. The purpose of the Precedent is to *familiarise* the reader with the archetypal shared ownership lease, so that when they are called upon to act for a purchaser in that field, they will begin to have an understanding of the subject. Of course, there will be those who are well used to this type of matter, but undoubtedly they are presently very much a minority.

Those readers who wish to take the matter further can do no better than first turn to Sch 3 to the 1984 Act, which will complement their reading of Precedent No 14, below.

Precedent No 15, which follows on from the shared ownership provisions, is a precedent of a typical deed of variation dealing with the purchase of a further share beyond the initial purchase.

7 P 388, below.

CHAPTER 22

Sheltered housing

One of the more important sectors of the housing market at the present time is that providing 'sheltered housing' (i e for the elderly). As time goes by its importance is likely to increase rather than decrease as the proportion of elderly persons in the population continues to increase inexorably. Thus while the number of elderly[1] persons in the UK represented 4.7% of the population in 1901, by the year 1981 the percentage had risen to 17.7%. The projections show a continued increase, particularly in the numbers of very elderly persons, i e those aged 75 and over, from the present 2.9 million to 3.2 million by the year 1991.

The task of looking after the elderly has become more and more of a problem. With fewer numbers, the Social Services Departments through the agencies of various types of geriatric homes and the private sector, were just about able to keep up with the problem, helped out by a number of families looking after their own. The increase in numbers of the elderly has, however, caused an intolerable strain on the existing system, so that new ways of coping have had to be devised.

One important associated statistic is that among the elderly there are now far more owner-occupiers than before. As a rough guide 60% of *all* households are in this category; and that proportion does not fall significantly when people reach the age where they qualify statistically for the description 'elderly'. The fall is only to 43%. The elderly then continue to own their houses, which gives them freedom to do as they wish; it also gives them property to leave to their family. At the same time, there are disadvantages which are clear to all—the older one gets the less able and usually less inclined, one is to look after one's own property.

These various factors in combination have given rise to the considerable niche in the housebuilding industry which owner occupied sheltered housing has carved out for itself. An interesting cause and effect situation now arises because the leading housebuilders recognising that demographic trends gave rise to the need, have fed that need with a wide range of developments which have attracted the clients; those developments themselves have attracted the clients when they might not otherwise have been interested.

The sector of the market is a very important one, and the need will take a long time to be satisfied, so that a reasonably high proportion of developers will be involved in sheltered housing, and it is incumbent on those advising them to have a good working knowledge on the background, the nature of the development, and how it is put into effect.

1 Source: House builders Federation, Advisory Note on 'Sheltered' Housing for Sale. Sources attributed to the HBF throughout this chapter are based on this document.

So far as need is concerned, the House Builders Federation quote a recent study carried out by Surrey University for the Housing Research Foundation. Apparently up to 400,000 units are required, at a possible production rate of up to 15,000 per year. When one considers that this is but one sector of the overall housing market, yet equals the output of the nation's largest builder, the scale of the market can be appreciated.

A. TYPES OF DEVELOPMENT

This heading is intended not to refer to the description of the physical aspect of the undertaking, but rather to the way in which the particular sheltered housing site will be set up.

There seem to be three main methods of tackling sheltered housing:

1 Housing associations

Many conveyancers, and indeed developers, may make the unwarranted assumption that sheltered housing can only be undertaken in cooperation with a housing association. This is *not correct* but it is also incorrect for any developer to imagine that he is well able to cope with such an undertaking. The HBF in their Advisory Note[2] stress that sheltered housing 'is not an easy type of housing to build and to sell successfully, nor is the provision of sheltered accommodation an instant recipe for profitable housebuilding. *Only if such schemes are carefully designed, located, marketed and managed, are they likely to be successful*'.

As we study the subject further, we shall see how true this is, so that all but the most experienced—and here experience may well be synonymous with size—developers should opt for a cooperative venture with a housing association, which will have the expertise in all directions, and without which expertise the inexperienced housebuilder might fail dismally.

2 Specialist builders

There are throughout the country a number of specialist firms, for example, McCarthy & Stone who, at least until recently, had more or less cornered the market in their particular area. These firms have built up a great expertise over the years, and can offer a service which is the equal of, and in some cases considerably better than, housing associations.

3 In-house schemes

There is, as we have already seen, nothing to stop a housebuilder setting up his own sheltered housing scheme, although in order to do so, he would have to be ready, willing, and most important of all, able to run what at times can be complex management. Nevertheless, it is possible, and perhaps with the help of the management section of this book, it is achievable. As a

2 See note 1, above.

'half-way house' type of scheme, the builder could bring in a property management company to run the scheme for him. The only problem with this suggestion is that there are so few capable management companies.

B. WHAT IS SHELTERED HOUSING?

We should be quite clear as to what sheltered housing is. The House Builders Federation (HBF) have with a number of builders experienced in sheltered housing, housing associations with similar experience, and the National Housing and Town Planning Council (and with the NHBC as observer) formed a working party to consider the various aspects of this sort of development. The working party has, as a starting point for the study of the subject, formulated its own definition of sheltered housing. In the first place, this differs from the Government's own definition, contained in the Housing and Building Control Act 1984, thus:

4. The dwelling house is one of a group of dwelling houses which are particularly suitable, having regard to their location, size, design, heating system, and other features, for occupation by persons of pensionable age and which it is the practice of the landlord to let for occupation by such persons, or for occupation by such persons and physically disabled persons, and special facilities are provided in order to assist those persons which consist of or include either:
(a) the services of a resident warden; or
(b) the services of a non-resident warden, a system for calling him and the use of a common room in close proximity to the group of dwelling houses.

Whilst the HBF are far too polite to say so, the working party obviously found this definition much too bland, and unnecessarily wordy. The working party themselves most valuably identified the characteristics which a sheltered housing scheme should have:

(a) it must consist of a group of self-contained dwellings;[3]
(b) it must be purpose-built or converted with design features appropriate for elderly people;
(c) it must be sold exclusively to elderly[4] people (60 or over) with a provision restricting re-sales to old people;
(d) there must be a package of estate management services provided by a responsible landlord, which services will normally include structural repairs and maintenance, the provision of a resident warden, and insurance and household services to communal areas;
(e) there must *always* be an emergency alarm system, and there will *normally* be a resident warden and certain communal facilities.

With these requirements in mind, the working party have arrived at a crisp definition of sheltered housing as follows:

3 But this would not prevent the scheme from being *part* of a *larger* estate, e g of 'normal' housing, just so long as the sheltered scheme had some identifiable boundary feature—which could be an estate roadway, footpath, etc.
4 Many schemes now define 'elderly' as not being under 55.

'Housing which is purpose-built, or converted exclusively for sale to the elderly, with a package of estate management services and which consists of grouped self-contained accommodation with an alarm system, usually with communal facilities and normally with a resident warden'.

C. THE MAJOR REQUIREMENTS FOR SHELTERED HOUSING

The working party have identified four principal areas which they say are 'critical to the successful building and marketing of retirement housing'. These are:

1 the tenure used;
2 location of site;
3 design; and
4 the estate management necessary.

1 Tenure

All concerned in the provision of sheltered housing seem to agree that it should be sold on a long leasehold basis. As a certain proportion of sheltered housing are flats, this explains on a primary level why the subject demands a chapter to itself in this book, but even if we were concerned only with houses in such developments, the management aspect[5] would warrant its inclusion: and the same could be said if use was made of freehold instead of leaseholds.

The author does not hold quite the same views on the necessity of using long leaseholds as opposed to freeholds as do those who are, presently at least, mainly involved with sheltered housing. Management may quite easily be hooked on to freehold sales, as we see elsewhere in this book.[6] In any event, if the Land Obligations Bill passes through parliament reasonably unscathed,[7] then the use of leasehold would presumably become redundant.

However, for the present perhaps, long leaseholds are a cleaner, and more direct way of selling sheltered housing, with the ability to hook in the management function with slightly less documentation. And perhaps a market aimed at the elderly is not one to subject to anything other than the most tried and tested ideas.

The Advisory Note on Sheltered Housing, which we have already referred to, makes various points about what should be included in the leases of such units. There are of course, the normal points of consideration which should be included in any full management lease[8] but over and above these are specialist matters which arise only in sheltered housing: thus

(i) the duties of the warden (where provided) must be carefully set out, even down to such niceties as the hours of duty;
(ii) the terms of the leases should not be so restrictive (as they are in some

5 See later, p 256 as to estate management.
6 Refer to ch 19, p 222, above.
7 See ch 28, p 309, below.
8 See ch 17, p 186, above.

sheltered housing schemes) as to make the properties unmortgageable. Apparently very few purchasers in this sector have mortgages—this is fairly predictable—but trends may move that way in the future;

(iii) the right of alienation must be restricted, thus the lessor/manager must be able to approve the assignees so that pot-taking grannies are excluded! It is not unknown for there to be absolute prohibitions on assignments, but, if so, then the lessor must be able to guarantee that the lessee may realise the value of the investment with the minimum of time and trouble;

(iv) careful thought should be given to inclusion in the lease of provisions as to what happens when a lessee falls ill, e g the ready availability of medical and social assistance.

One final point which should be at the forefront of the minds of those setting up the schemes is not so much one which is a specialist one, but is rather general to every managed scheme, with a crucial application to sheltered housing. This concerns service charges. Very many elderly people who will be interested in buying sheltered housing will be on a fairly constricted budget. Of course it is up to the developer and/or manager to make sure that they are not selling to those who either cannot afford it now, or will find difficulty in the future given inflationary trends. There must be absolute and frank disclosure of the anticipated service charges, with indicated allowances for inflation. Nothing must be hidden from the interested purchaser. Readers may consider this remark ingenuous, but not every developer/manager concerned with schemes having a management element lays all the cards on the table all the time. With sheltered housing, this *must* happen.

We shall come back to the contents of the leases later in the chapter when we review the conveyancing aspects of such schemes.

2 Location of site

At first sight location might not seem to warrant the conveyancer's attention, but this book's appeal is to a wider audience, and the lawyer should in any case be able to advise his client on *all* aspects of a development, and even if he is not given that opportunity, he should understand all those aspects.

Location is a crucial element in any sheltered housing scheme. Remember, those living there will be in their houses much more than those of us who go out to work. They will also be buying what most of them will consider to be their very last house. Accordingly, they will be extra-critical purchasers.

On the basis that the developer has identified a demographic need for such a scheme in that particular location (and that is something that might not occur automatically to every developer) there are certain important factors that he should consider:

(a) *Topography*

In view of the age of those who will live on the site, it should be as flat as possible. While this can be a problem in some areas which are naturally undulating (e g Cornwall and other coastal areas) but which nevertheless have potentially large markets in this sector; the point is important.

(b) *Environment*

Views from the windows of principal rooms should be pleasant and interesting, and the site layout should be as varied as possible.

(c) *Mobility*

Residents of such a site may no longer be up to whizzing about all day in their boy racers, so that bus routes, for instance, should be within, at worst, easy walking distance.

(d) *Services*

The site should also afford easy access for residents to places like shops of adequate standards, especially food shops, and doctors' surgeries, banks, etc. This might be more than a little difficult to arrange, but should be the ultimate aim. There are, incidentally, all sorts of little quirks to bear in mind when planning such a site, e g if there is an incline between the site and the shops, the *uphill* walk should be when the residents *go to* the shops, not when they come back.

(e) *Facilities*

Leading on from the previous section, parks, libraries, churches, etc should be within as easy reach as possible.

3 Design

Design is probably even less a matter with which the conveyancer should bother himself, but again sheltered housing is such a specialised sector of the market that all those concerned with it should fully appreciate that a good sheltered housing scheme will not be ordinary housing with a few adaptions here and there—it will be *specially designed.*

As examples of what is recommended, the following are but the tip of the iceberg:

Alarm/audio system in (preferably) all rooms, common areas, lifts, etc;
no steps or stairs;
everything in the home within easy reach;
easy-to-grip door, etc handles;
doors to open outwards, bathroom/wc doors with lock releases outside;
master key system for warden;
fixing of grab rails in appropriate places;
additional thermal insulation;
adequate lighting, heating, and alarm sounders in common areas;
common rooms (if provided) to have toilet and kitchen facilities;

laundry rooms, suitably equipped, available;
at least one guest bedroom provided;
all aspects of the development to be designed with mobility in mind, e g doors and passages wide enough for wheelchairs or people with walking frames, handrails in corridors, lifts (where there are any) with sprung seats, shallow stair flights, etc.

The list is more or less endless. The Advisory Note itself must be consulted by those who require further information, but even for the mere conveyancer, knowledge of the sort of matters which have to be in the forefront of the designer's mind is most important, because without a basic knowledge of them, the conveyancer will not understand the nature of a sheltered housing scheme, and if he is to give his client the best possible service, he does have to possess that understanding.

4 Estate management

This is probably the most important of the four factors, from everybody's point of view. The Advisory Note draws attention to basic factors underlying sheltered housing. These are:

(a) most people become more frail with the ageing process; and
(b) most pensioners, being for the most part on fixed incomes, will become poorer as time goes on.

This means that estate management in a sheltered scheme must provide a reasonably inexpensive yet comprehensive set of management services. This is by no means easy, and is probably a very large factor in most builders who tackle sheltered housing doing so in conjunction with, usually, a housing association. Indeed, the first question the builder must ask himself when contemplating such a scheme is:

'Have I got the capability of setting up, and then administering, a management scheme for such a development?'

The answer for most will be 'no', and it is then that the housing association, or more rarely, the specialist management company, will be called in. We will shortly study the manner in which the scheme is put into effect with the management partner[9] but for the present we will confine ourselves to a description of a typical management scheme.

The usual package will consist of:

1 repairs and maintenance of the buildings within the scheme;
2 insurance of the property;
3 services; and
4 cost of warden.

These four management sectors will result in running costs, which the individual service charges will have to cover, as we shall see later. Before we do that though, we should look at the sectors in more detail, to see the

9 Refer to p 260, below.

build-up. Of course, to a certain extent, the management build-up will be similar to that for a normally managed scheme[10] but there are significant differences, the biggest being in the provision of a warden. It is really this sector which sets apart the sheltered housing management scheme from any other.

(a) *Warden services*

The features to be considered are as follows:

(a) a scheme without a warden (whether or not resident) is hardly worthy of the description 'sheltered', in fact it would be no more than a glorified standard management scheme, and the alternatives are therefore irrelevant;
(b) we have seen[11] from the working party's recommended definition of sheltered housing that it is 'normally with a resident warden'. Thus it admits of schemes where wardens may be non-resident, perhaps where two or more schemes share a warden. Nevertheless, a resident warden may very well be a strong selling point of the scheme, and it is much to be preferred, indeed in the author's view the scheme will not be a full sheltered one without a resident warden;
(c) warden accommodation will have to be provided. Thus one of the units in the scheme will be occupied by the warden. We come back to this aspect when discussing the documentation;[12]
(d) the warden's services must be quite specifically set out so that those on the site know what to expect, and perhaps more to the point, what not to expect, e g does the warden perform nursing/shopping/cleaning, etc services? This is just as important for the wardens as for the 'inmates' if we can use such a description, otherwise the warden will be deluged with unreasonable demands;
(e) the scheme must be quite clear as to how extensive in time terms the warden's duties are, and if there is any relief warden service, because no one can be expected to have no time off, especially from elderly, demanding people;
(f) it is useless to appoint as a warden someone without any training. This, probably more than any other factor, is the reason why housing associations (other than specialist firms of developers like McCarthy & Stone) are mostly to be found as management partners, as they have developed satisfactory training schemes for prospective wardens.

(b) *Repairs and maintenance*

There is nothing particularly magical about the management of a sheltered housing scheme. The Advisory Note makes a strong point about setting out all the responsibilities for maintenance, presumably in the lease, and in the

10 See also ch 18, p 204, above.
11 P 253, above.
12 See pp 261 et seq, below.

accompanying booklet it recommends should be handed to purchasers, but this is no more than should be done in a normal management scheme.

(c) *Insurance*

Very much the same remarks apply to this category as to the previous section.

(d) *Services*

Again, as in any normal management scheme, the nature and scope of the services must be set out quite clearly. Obviously because there are features in a sheltered scheme which are peculiar to it, there will be a wider range of services which will have to be provided: thus the common rooms have to be maintained, and the scheme may not provide private gardens for each property, but offer a complete communal area of grass and garden ground, which will take more maintenance than the common soft external areas in a standard flats, etc maintenance scheme. (This garden point is one which is often misinterpreted, but it is logical; the elderly residents might *want* their own private gardens, but gardens can take a great deal of looking after, and many people in their twilight years find gardening a desperately demanding aspect of their lives). A good sheltered scheme will have a design where only the bricks and mortar are the subject of the individual leases, and the garden areas are all within the common ground, yet are so designed that each resident has as much privacy as is possible.

Taking all the above items together will naturally produce the

(e) *Service charge*

This will include all the individual items that any management scheme will produce, but there will be some differences:

(i) there will be included the salary of the warden, and this will include National Insurance payments, pension contribution of employer if appropriate, (usually) telephone bills, electricity and gas bills, general and water rates;
(ii) heat, light, power, insurance, etc of the communal areas like common room/s and laundry room;
(iii) there will be a greater burden of charges in relation to the maintenance of garden areas, because (as we have seen above) there are more common garden areas in a sheltered scheme than normal;
(iv) the sinking fund should not be forgotten. The Advisory Note suggests that the fund should be an annual charge either forming part of the service charge, or deferred until the property is sold and taken as a percentate of the resale price;

    The amount of the sinking fund is recommended at something between 1% and 2%[13] if based on the resale value calculated on the

13 Compare this with the reserve, or sinking funds in a 'normal' maintenance scheme and described in ch 17, p 191, above.

original purchase price and deducted annually. Thus the treatment of the sinking fund is significantly different in sheltered housing schemes than in normal maintenance schemes, because in the latter category there is no capital sum available to the manager from which such amounts may be deducted, as opposed to sheltered housing schemes where the generally acceptable code of practice envisages the funding of long-term repairs, renewals and improvements to the development, and bona fide arrangements to provide extra care or even reduced service charges, out of the capital costs on resale.

All this presupposes that there will be a capital sum available from a resale: and this in itself presupposes that the form of lease will provide for a surrender of the lease on death. Not all sheltered housing leases provided for this, as we shall see later.

Nevertheless, the idea of the elderly person's home being surrendered back to the lessor (or some other similar device leading to the same end result) at the end of that person's occupation, and the sinking fund, on a greater or lesser scale, being deducted from the surrender/resale proceeds, i e when the elderly person is no longer in need of his unit of housing, is an attractive one, because it means that the burden of service charge is less than it might otherwise be, and (as we have already seen) economy in running costs is all important in this sector of housing, where those costs are so often necessarily high. However, in schemes where there is no surrender provision, a 'sinking fund' contribution may still be levied on a resale, e g by an appropriate restriction in the register or some other similar provision related to the lessor's consent.

5 Equity investment

Before we pass on to consideration of the way in which the scheme is interpreted in the estate documentation, we should consider the possibility of the lessor/manager taking a stake in the equity which the resident has in his dwelling unit. The author has not come across any such schemes, but apparently there have been some where the developer has taken a share in any equity enhancement.

If a resident of one of these units becomes so infirm that he or she can no longer be adequately looked after even in the sheltered housing scheme, there will almost certainly be a wish to recover the investment to provide for subsequent expenditure on more intensive nursing, etc. There is therefore every good reason for the owner of the property to maintain his investment, and possibly enhance it through increased value. If any conveyancer comes across a scheme where the residents equity is eroded in any way, it must be explained carefully to the intending purchaser.

D. THE LEGAL TREATMENT

We now turn to the manner in which the documentation regulates the development. Sheltered housing may comprise a specialist building containing flats, or the whole of an estate of bungalows or, less likely houses; or it may be merely part of a larger development. What form it takes is fairly immaterial, although the documentation will differ slightly according to whether we are considering, e g flats/maisonettes or houses/bungalows.

One constant feature will be the use of leaseholds as opposed to freehold. Obviously as soon as the Land Obligations Bill[14] reaches the statute book, things will change, but for the present we can safely assume that a typical sheltered housing site will be leasehold.

So far as the documentation is concerned, we must accept that at least for the moment housing associations are in the forefront of sheltered housing, and the practitioner is more likely to come across this variety than the specialist company scheme which we describe briefly below.

E. HOUSING ASSOCIATION JOINT VENTURES

All that the practitioner needs to know in this context is that housing associations are empowered to undertake such schemes, and what is more important, are well versed both in the setting-up and the subsequent administration of them. This applies whether the client is the developer or the purchaser. (It is hardly likely to be the association—they will usually be represented by specialist firms.)

The conveyancer is not usually concerned with the initial negotiations between the developer (assuming that he is the developer's solicitor) and the housing association, but he will have to advise him on the contents of the documentation. So will the intending purchaser's solicitors have to advise but the documentation with which each will be concerned will be different, as represented in the following diagram:

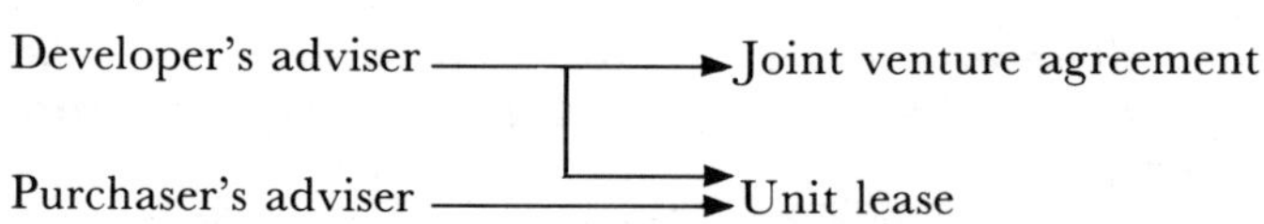

Joint venture agreement

This will provide for the following:

1 Following completion of building and granting of all leases, developer to convey reversionary interest to association, in return for an indemnity to observe all lessors covenants in leases of units.

14 See ch 28, p 309, below.

2 Developer covenants to build properties and ancillary works in a proper manner.
3 Provisions for issue of NHBC documentation.
4 (Usually) provision for payment of association's legal, etc fees.
5 Developer nominates (which really means sells to) purchasers. Association approves them and developer grants leases to them. There will usually be a provision that the association will be paid a fee out of the price the purchaser pays the developer. This varies, but a normal rate seems to be about 1.25%. This is to be compared with the 'establishment fee'[15] usually levied by a professional management company in a normal management programme. The only difference will be that the association's fee is likely to be much more than the average establishment fee. Take a perfectly normal bungalow on the south coast, selling at around £30,000. The association's fee on this would be very nearly £400, a not inconsiderable sum. The developer must be careful to include this figure in his costings, otherwise he may find his profit cut to shreds.
6 Completion of the transfer of reversionary interest usually to be a stated time after notice given by the developer that all unit leases are granted.
7 If developer does not proceed with or complete development properly, the association will usually have the right to terminate the agreement and take an indemnity from the developer in respect of lessor's obligations in the unit leases.
8 Developer has to give association notice (say 28 days) of completion of first unit lease, whereupon association has to arrange for a warden to be installed on site. The developer has to provide a unit for the warden to live in.[16] The warden occupies the warden's unit under licence.
9 During the period between completion of the first unit lease, and the transfer of the reversionary interest to the association, the Association as agent of the builder collects the service charges.
10 Finally, there will usually be an arbitration clause.

F. LEASES GENERALLY

Whether or not the scheme is being dealt with by way of a joint venture with a housing association, the document of transmission of the individual units will almost certainly be a lease.

We will briefly examine the different treatment of houses plus bungalows and flats plus maisonettes below but basically, the lease of a sheltered housing unit will be distinguished from any other lease in three principal areas, which are: rental, rights of transmission, and build-up of service charge. We examine the first two categories in more detail below; the build-up of service charge is obviously going to be more complicated for a flat than for a house and is studied in some detail in Chapters 13–18.

15 For further discussion on this concept, see ch 18, p 220, above.
16 This assumes that the warden is indeed resident (which with a housing association development he will be).

1 Ground rent

As with any other type of leasehold development, there are two basic questions: first, is any ground rent at all to be charged, and second, if there is, how much?

Taking these points backwards, if a ground rent is to be charged, then the developer is entitled to look at the market and see how much it can stand; and in fact some of the developers who have specialised in sheltered housing do charge a reasonably modest ground rent. Nevertheless, it is a common fallacy with developers that ground rent is merely to be regarded as a useful 'top-up' for the service charge. This attitude is quite wrong, for two reasons. The first is a general one which is that ground rent is most definitely *not* an adjunct to the service charge. The possibility, and in many cases the likelihood, is that it will in any event go a different way to the service charge. The ground rent should be treated as an investment either for the original developer, or for whoever he trades the ground rental income on to. The service charge is just that: a carefully constructed charge to cover all the different elements of the service charge build-up set out in the lease.

The second reason is a more specific one relating to the particular type of development in mind, i e one for the care of the elderly. We have already seen that the estate management in a sheltered scheme must provide 'a reasonably inexpensive yet comprehensive set of services'. Without becoming too accusatory, it does seem to be imposing an unnecessary extra burden on the elderly tenant, and if the manager is seeking to use the ground rental income to bolster up his management income, he is inefficient and this is a poor way of overcoming that inefficiency.

This is where we get right back to the first question we posed ourselves: whether to impose a ground rent at all? In housing association leases, and the author suggests all other sheltered schemes should follow suit, the rent of one peppercorn (if demanded) is imposed. Perhaps it might be better still not to impose any rent at all[17] and thus save the elderly purchaser any confusion about what a peppercorn is—but then we might be confusing the conveyancer, who possibly would feel uneasy about there being no ground rent at all.

A further point to note is if a ground rent is to be charged, it is assumed that some review procedure would need to be incorporated. Certainly if there was no review, then the reserved rent would be very quickly eaten away by inflation until it was hardly worth collecting the rent anyway. On the other hand, if a review procedure is incorporated, then all that this will achieve is the further burdening of the elderly owners, and indeed in the years when the rent was reviewed, the process and the resulting (presumably significantly larger) ground rent would possibly cause the elderly so much concern as to do actual damage to them. So that it does not take very much consideration to see that no rent, or a fictitious one like a peppercorn, is very much the best choice.

17 And for a further discussion on ground rent, see ch 8, pp 98–104, above.

2 Rights of transmission

These will usually differ depending on whether the scheme is run by an organisation like a housing association, or is a privately-run scheme, run by developers.

(a) *Private schemes*

It is generally found that the rights of transmission are much more relaxed in this kind of scheme than those in a housing association scheme, as we shall see later. For example, a typical private lease will have a tripartite treatment, and no more, as follows:

(i) A covenant by the lessee e g
'not to assign or underlet to or part with or share possession of the demised premises or any part thereof with any person who shall be under the age of (usually 60) years at the date of such assignment or underletting or parting with or sharing of possession'

Sometimes 'watering down' words are added, e g 'unless notwithstanding that the assignee or undertenant shall be under the age of [60] years at the date of such assignment or underletting the demised premises will be continuously occupied by a person or persons older than that age'.

(ii) A covenant by the lessor e g
'not to grant a lease of any other flat in the building to any person who shall be under the age of [60] years provided nevertheless that the lessor shall have the right to grant such lease on such conditions as it shall deem necessary to a person of under the age of [60] years for the purpose of occupation of such flat by a person or persons older than that age.'

(iii) A restriction To be included in the appropriate schedule of restrictions imposed on all flats in the same building, e g
'not to use the demised premises nor permit the same to be used for any purpose other than as a private dwelling in the occupation of one family only the members of which shall all be over [60] years of age. . . .'

As compared with the restrictions on alienation in housing association leases, which we shall examine below, those restrictions are fairly 'laid-back', in that the units may be sold not only to persons over a specific age, but also to any other person for example, the elderly person's children, just so long as the unit was to be occupied by that elderly person. Naturally, if the elderly person died, then unless there was a spouse of the minimum age left in the property, the terms of occupation would no longer be met, and the legal owners should then have to dispose of the flat, but then they would want to do so anyway.

Probably there is not a great deal of practical difference between this sort of scheme and those described below, because the tripartite restrictions set out above make sure that when the elderly person dies the unit will have to be sold to a specialised market. The likelihood is that the lessor/developer (and in this type of development the original lessor usually retains control of the management) will have set up some sort of an agency so that a qualified purchaser can be readily found.

Nevertheless, the actual legal restrictions in a lease of this sort are much less stringent, so that the purchaser might feel less hemmed in by the provisions of his lease than the typical housing association lease. For a certain type of purchaser, this may be attractive.

While we are discussing restricting categories of lessee by reference to age limits, it might be useful now, before we move on to the next section, to review the other method by which occupation is restricted. This method is, of course, by the use of planning.

Naturally the planners will be aware that they are being asked to give consent for a sheltered housing scheme. The application will inevitably describe it as such, and in any event the scheme as submitted will usually have certain physical features which will distinguish it from any other type of scheme.

Planners now take much more interest than they used to in matters concerning the management of a development, assuming there is an element of management. This interest extends to sheltered housing schemes; and most planning authorities will require to have demonstrated to them how the management is to be set up and run. They will also be interested in making sure that, having granted permission for a specialised development, its efficacy and benefit for the neighbourhood will not be eroded by the units gradually being taken over by people other than the elderly.

Obviously one can show the planning authority the documentation which will be used, and one can even undertake to use only that documentation. But this may not be enough for the planners, who will almost certainly include in the planning consent a condition that the occupation of the units shall be restricted to persons of a specified minimum age. Indeed, the planners may go even further and insist upon an agreement being entered into under the terms of the Town and County Planning Act 1971, s 52 and the Local Government (Miscellaneous Provisions) Act 1982, s 33.[18] Quite why a s 52 agreement should ever be needed in such a situation is questionable given the already significant and adequate restrictions; the only advantage of having one would seem to be that the s 52 agreement would automatically appear on the local search any intending purchaser made. But then so would the planning consent. The difference might well be that whereas the conditions of the planning consent are not usually set out in the search, and many conveyancers will not necessarily check the *original* consent, very often the main points of a s 52 agreement *will* be set out in the search, and even if they are not, a s 52 agreement appearing in a search will put most conveyancers on notice.

While on this subject, one point should be made as a reminder to readers: do not make the same mistake as the author once did, and allow a planning condition or a s 52 agreement through where there was a restriction on *anyone* under a certain minimum age living in the units, when the actual lease used in the scheme, which was a housing association scheme, only specified that

18 S 52 will deal with restrictive covenants, but for positive ones s 33 needs to be used (s 33 replaced the Housing Act 1974, s 126.)

if there was more than one occupant in any unit, then only one of them needed to have reached the minimum age. This is a point to be borne in mind when dealing with planners.

(b) *Housing association, etc schemes*

We now return to a consideration of the specific schemes, the treatment of which varies depending on whether the scheme involves on the one hand houses and bungalows or, on the other hand, flats and maisonettes. Before discussing the reason for this different treatment, however, we shall first describe the treatments.

(i) Houses and bungalows

(a) Usually there is a blanket restriction on assigning or underletting, or parting with possession of the demised premises or any part thereof.
(b) If the lessee either:
 (i) becomes incapable of managing his/her own affairs;[19] or
 (ii) has his/her affairs made subject to the jurisdiction of the Court of Protection; or
 (iii) dies;
 then there will usually be a provision entitling the lessor to determine the lease by (say three months) notice, *but* without prejudice to the right of the lessee and/or his or her personal representatives to a repayment sum (see below).
(c) Should any of the eventualities specified in (b) above come to pass, or if the lessee wishes to surrender the term voluntarily (as might happen if the lessee was moving on to some other scheme or home where there was more intensive care) then certain provisions as to recoupment of the investment come into force, as follows.
(d) The lessor takes all necessary steps, following receipt of any notice given under the above circumstances, to find a new purchaser who is willing to pay as their consideration a sum which is nearly always referred to as the 'repayment sum'.
(e) Following the determination of the term, whether by surrender or otherwise, the lessor pays to the lessee (or e g to his or her personal representatives if the operation of the clause is due to a death) on an agreed date for repayment the repayment sum.
(f) The appropriate sum to be repaid under these provisions is that sum which the property might be expected to fetch on the open market with vacant possession, and with a new term of equivalent length to the original one (e g 99 years). If that sum cannot be agreed between the parties—and in almost all cases the amount will be suggested by the lessor, not the lessee—then the matter is referred to an independent valuer to be appointed in the usual manner. The provisions of the clause will also regulate authorised deductions from the repayment sum, as follows:

19 Usually, it seems, it is up to the lessor to decide if this point has been reached.

(i) any outstanding service charge payments at the time of determination of the repayment sum;

(ii) any sums required to put the property concerned into good repair;

(iii) the costs and expenses of surrender (i e legal and incidental costs related to the surrender itself and the relevant documentation; in other words, proper costs with no penalty character);

(iv) *usually* a capital sum based on a percentage of the repayment sum. This may be equated to the lessor's costs in dealing with the surrender. Average percentages are 2% of the repayment sum, or 1% where the incoming purchaser is found by the previous lessee. 2% of the repayment sum can be fairly large—thus a transmission sum of £30–£40,000 would certainly not be unusual, especially in resort areas, where a lot of sheltered housing schemes are found. This would represent £600–£800 fees for the lessor, but then this sort of fee level is no worse, and probably much better, than the average estate agent's fee, so after all the burden on the elderly person is not really heavy at all, and of course it must be remembered that in many cases these repayment sums will be calculated following a death, where the burden will not be felt personally.

(g) The timing of the making of the repayment differs from lessor to lessor, but a fairly typical time sequence is seven days from the date when the actual sum is agreed, or determined by the valuer, if this provision operates, *or* seven days from the date when the lessor receives payment for the new lease of the premises from the incoming lessee, *whichever is the later*. In other words, the previous lessee or his or her personal representatives do not receive payment until the lessor has resold the premises. At first sight, this may seem harsh, in that some lessees or estates could be kept waiting for their cash, but on the other hand, there is no reason why the lessor should act as a banker for its lessees; this could cause it serious cash flow problems. Nevertheless, as the lessee's right of alienation is taken away completely by this sort of lease, being made to wait for their money in such circumstances is perhaps another straw on the camel's back. All these provisions are in the name of good estate management.

(h) There will almost certainly be a provision in the lease which enables the lessor to discharge any mortgages out of the repayment sum.

(ii) Flats and maisonettes

(a) For the reasons set out at the end of this chapter, there is no blanket restriction on alienation. A typical housing association lease will say that the whole of the demised premises may not be assigned except to an incoming purchaser nominated by the Association or if that does not occur, only to someone who is age-qualified, and in the latter case the person concerned must be in the opinion of the association a person in need of sheltered housing.

(b) The mechanics of assignment will be that the intending assignee must give notice of his intention to the lessor, asking if there are any suitable persons on the wating list. Those persons must be ready to pay the appropriate sum, which is the repayment sum calculated as previously. If the lessor fails to nominate a suitable person within a stated time scale (say 21 days) or if the person or persons nominated by the lessor fail to proceed (usually a period of about two months is given between receipt of a draft contract and the signing of it) then the existing lessee can assign freely subject to the incoming lessee being a suitably qualified person (see above).

(c) The fee payable to the lessor will normally in cases like this, be 1% of the repayment sum.

(d) In the case of houses or bungalows, no normal assignment is permitted, so that there is no need for a clause dealing with registration of notices. In the case under discussion, though, in certain circumstances normal assignments are permitted and accordingly the lease will contain the usual clause.

(e) As well as the provisions for assignment set out above, there will also be surrender provisions. The assignment provisions could be used if the lessee genuinely had a willing purchaser, although even here the intended sale may not be able to go ahead if the lessor has a list of suitable persons who want to buy a property on the development. The surrender provisions, on the other hand, will apply more to elderly residents either dying, or moving on to other types of accommodation, presumably better able to cope with geriatrics. If the surrender option is chosen in the case of flats and maisonettes there are one or two differences to the previously described procedure, as follows:

(i) a longer notice period is required. This may be as long as 6 months. Within that period the lessor must take steps to procure the grant of a new lease for the repayment sum; and

(ii) the fees on the disposal may be higher (2.5% seems to be the going rate) but in all other respects the surrender provisions are the same as previously described.

In both this type of lease, i e for flats and maisonettes, and that which regulates houses and bungalows, there will be the usual landlord's covenants to keep the common areas, whatever and wherever they may be, in good repair; but there will be an additional covenant on the part of the lessor that it will provide a resident warden at the property. This of course assumes that the scheme does carry a resident warden—there are some schemes which only have the services of a part-time warden, and there are even schemes where there is no warden at all, although how these can qualify for the description of sheltered schemes is open to question. Whilst the lessor will covenant to provide the services of a warden, the covenant will always carry a proviso that the lessor will not be liable for any loss damage or inconvenience arising out of the absence of a warden due to any 'accident labour dispute inability to obtain labour or to any other cause outside the control of the lessor'. A good sheltered scheme will be able to produce substitute wardens at times of holiday, illness, etc on the part of the resident warden, but these people are only human and 100% coverage is not possible.

G. THE RESTRICTIONS ON ALIENATION

We now come back to look at the reasons why there are such severe restrictions on dealing with properties comprising a sheltered housing scheme. There are two basic reasons. One is to do with management of the scheme; the other is related to the question of leasehold enfranchisement.

1 Management

We have seen that there will be a blanket restriction on alienation of houses and bungalows, with transmission only taking place through surrender of the old lease and the finding of a new lessee. With flats and maisonettes, the intending vendor of such a unit goes through a complex process before the unit can be sold on the open market, and this in itself is a misnomer, because the incoming purchaser must be approved by the lessor.

From the management point of view, these restrictions are justified, and it should be for the benefit of lessees on the development that they are maintained rigorously. If the lessor, or its immediate successor in title (e g the lessor being the housebuilder) is a housing association, it has a statutory purpose directed, inter alia, towards the provision of housing for the elderly. Even if the lessor, or the subsequent manager, is a commercial concern, it will still have set up the development as one specifically intended for the elderly, and it will have every interest in seeing that the development stays that way. If it wants to sell any more schemes, either to the builder/developer or its particular public, it must make sure that the sort of purchaser it has buying the properties on the scheme is suitable, which in most cases is neither too young, nor too frail and helpless. The elderly wish to be in a 'protected' environment with their own kind, but if there are those on the site who are too frail, they will be too demanding on the warden's time, to the detriment of the rest of the residents. Of course, it is quite possible for residents who at one time fitted into the required profile of a suitable owner to grow outside that profile. Quite what happens then depends on local circumstances; the attitude of the warden, the housing association, the other residents even. If a resident becomes too frail, then the lessor will be able to exercise its rights under the lease—e g the usual clause in a housing association lease:

> 'if the lessee shall in the judgement of the Association become incapable of managing his own affairs'

but it is to be hoped that the counselling abilities of the association would be such that this sort of clause would never need to be involved.

Nevertheless, it is not difficult to see that the powers of strict management need to be more all-enveloping on such a scheme than on any other. It is a quite unique situation, calling for unique powers.

2 Leasehold enfranchisement

There is a requirement, because of the effects of the legislation, to distinguish between the two forms of lease; i e on the one hand that for flats, etc and on the other for houses etc. The reader is generally referred to the short chapter on the effect (if any) of the Leasehold Reform Act 1967 on the subject of this book.[20] However, we will remind ourselves here that the Leasehold Reform Act 1967, s 1 states:

'1 (1) This Part of this Act shall have effect to confer on a tenant of a leasehold house ... a right to acquire on fair terms the freehold or an extended lease of the house. ...'

Section 2 of the same act defines what 'house' means:

'2 (1) For purposes of this Part of this Act, "house" includes any building designed or adapted for living in and reasonably so called ...

(a) where a building is divided horizontally, the flats or other units into which it is so divided are not separate "houses". ...'

It is quite clear that a sheltered scheme of flats or maisonettes are not within the ambit of the Act, but equally it is crystal clear, based on the wording of the sections quoted above, that the shelterd schemes of houses and/or bungalows will come within the terms of the Act. Accordingly, there must be an absolute restriction on alienation in the houses' or bungalows' leases. This is why the restrictions on alienation are less rigid in the flats leases.

Housing associations will draft their model forms of lease for houses accordingly, with the provisions of the 1967 Act in mind, and particularly, so far as the provision for determination are concerned, so as to qualify for exemption from the 1967 Act pursuant to the provisions of the Housing Act 1980, Sch 21.

On the practical side, one wonders how many elderly people would even think of enfranchisement. Even if they were able to do so, there would seem to be no practical advantage whatsoever in doing so, and as so often happens, probably the fears of the theoreticians are groundless compared with the realities of the situation.

H. SUMMARY

The subject of sheltered housing is still in its infancy and it is likely that this side of the industry will become sufficiently important in years to come that it will warrant a text book of its own. Since the subject relates only in part to flats our treatment here is necessarily restricted. Nevertheless the management aspect of sheltered housing schemes is important and it is to be hoped that our discussion will prove helpful to readers.

20 Ch 26, p 294, below.

CHAPTER 23

Time-sharing

Time-sharing is presently the great 'unknown' of English land law. It is the one area of development to have occurred in recent years where the framework of the English legal system is unable to cope with its subject in a reasonably satisfactory way. In this sense, therefore, we are disadvantaged compared with other legal systems. If we look at other common law systems, as opposed to continental codified systems, for instance those in use in the various states which comprise the USA, to a very large extent these common law systems have developed the concept of the ownership of a time-share unit on a fee simple basis. As we work our way through the subject, we shall see how much less satisfactorily our own legal system is able to cope with the concept of time-sharing.

This brings us to the first point for consideration, which is:

A. WHAT IS TIME-SHARING?

Although time-sharing has been in use in this country for little more than ten years, it has already become closely, and probably indelibly, associated with the holiday market. Nevertheless, it may be used in other applications, eg business occupations of property,[1] and it is merely coincidental that the holiday application happens to be the most appropriate one.

Time-sharing may be simply described as the right to occupy, on an exclusive basis, a particular property for a period of less than one year, generally at the same time every year, for some period of time greater than one year. Thus if one were to succeed in devising a system of selling a time-share unit on a freehold basis, there would be no limitation on the number of years over which the time-share unit could be held; it would be for ever. On the other hand, if a leasehold interest was used as the basis of selling, the term of years would be specified.

It is important to understand what a time-share unit is before we go on to look at ways of achieving its creation; accordingly, we will look once again at its main features:

(a) there will be a specified property, precisely in the same way as on the sale of property using a fee simple or term of years basis;
(b) there will be a recurring interest, and the right to occupy will only operate during the recurrence of that interest;

1 For example, a number of companies now maintain time-share units in London, their weeks coinciding with exhibition times.

(c) the interest will usually recur at precisely the same time during each cycle;
(d) the interest will be for a pre-set period, eg one week;
(e) the cycle will usually be over a period of one year, although there is nothing which says one cannot have a different period;[2]
(f) when the right to occupy operates during each cycle, it will be exclusive; and
(g) the ownership of the time-share unit should be capable of assignment, etc.

These are the main features of time-sharing. What are the advantages and disadvantages of the procedure; particularly the advantages, as it appears to have become so popular?

1 For the developer

It is unlikely that many readers will find themselves asked to act for a vendor of time-sharing units on their creation; most of the time-share developments in this country have been undertaken by the larger developers, and even those not in this category appear to have been serviced by the large City and West End firms—so that the average High Street conveyancer is not likely to be asked to set up a scheme. Nevertheless, it is important that he understand not only the mechanics of setting up a scheme, but also why it should be attractive to the developer, as well as to his prospective client.

(a) *Advantages*

The developer ought to be able to achieve very much more financially than he would by selling the unit under discussion on an outright basis. He will be able to divide the cycle of (probably) a single year into as many as 50 units of one week each, usually leaving two weeks free to allow him to have total access to the unit for repair, refurbishment, re-decoration, etc. The market price for the unit will vary according to the week of the year concerned; eg if the location is in a holiday resort, the summer weeks will be much more expensive than those in the winter, but if the development was in somewhere like Stratford-on-Avon for example, and was marketed in the USA, possibly the dip of the price during the winter months would not be so dramatic.[3]

Nevertheless, the total income of sales over the whole cycle should be considerably more than that to be derived from selling the unit on an outright basis.

2 Some of the other features can also change, eg it is theoretically possible to have different properties involved in the same time-share scheme, and the periods of occupancy could also change.

3 And consider somewhere like Aviemore, in Scotland, where there is a high season in both winter (for the skiing) and summer (for more traditional holidays); small wonder that there are a number of time-sharing schemes there.

(b) *Disadvantages*

(i) The developer will have to furnish the unit, and if he is to keep up with the prevailing UK market, he will have to spend a considerable amount of money on good, tasteful furnishings. It does appear that in this country, the generally high level of finish of units, including their furnishings, is used partly to balance out the higher possibility of inclement weather, as opposed to a unit in, eg Florida.
(ii) He will also have to spend that considerable amount of money on fitting out the unit *before* he is able to realise any sales. The general indication is that the fitting out of the unit will cost at least as much as the basic unit in the first place; probably a good deal more.
(iii) While the best weeks—probably the summer weeks in this country—will be sold fairly quickly, the poor weeks in the dead of winter may take a long time to sell. This is where clever marketing takes a hand; the trick will be to price the good weeks, not so high that they do not sell, but not so low that once they have all gone the developer has not covered his overheads.

2 For the purchaser

(a) *Advantages*

There is only one real advantage for the purchaser of a time-share unit and that is the fairly overwhelming one that he will be able to buy a holiday home (if that is what it will be) for a mere fraction of what it might otherwise have cost him.

(b) *Disadvantages*

(i) The first disadvantage is that the purchaser is still making what for him will be a fairly major investment in something which is not his totally. There will be other purchasers, possibly 49 if the sales are of single weeks, with whom he has to share his property. Not that the property itself will show any evidence of other people's occupancy; a typical time-share development will enjoy very careful and comprehensive maintenance and cleaning services. Nevertheless, this is a psychological barrier for some people.
(ii) The only other disadvantage is that of being 'locked' into the use of the property in two ways, ie
time of year, and
location
In other words, to derive the greatest benefit from his investment[4] the purchaser must visit the property *every year*, at precisely the same time of year, and obviously must go to the same place every year.
It was to allow time-share unit purchasers to escape from this strait-

4 Although, of course, the time-share unit can always be used as an investment for sub-letting (usually through the developer—the purchaser should make sure that the conditions for sub-letting are not too onerous).

jacket of usage that exchange services for time-sharing were devised. The main organisations which act as clearing houses are Interval International and Resort Condominiums International, otherwise RCI. Inevitably the owner of a time-share unit will be introduced to either or both of these organisations, or others devoted to similar aims. Through these, the owner will be able to exchange his unit of time-sharing for others, wherever they may be in the world, and thus he will be able to effect a change of timing in the cycle as well.

B. IMPLEMENTATION OF TIME-SHARING IN ENGLAND AND WALES

It will be noted that Scotland is carefully excluded from the above heading. Time-sharing is a truly international procedure. The likelihood is that a substantial proportion of people buying a time-share unit will be buying on foreign sites; but unfortunately we just do not have the space in this book for discussion of anything other than the application of English law to time-sharing. For anything with a foreign content, a specialist textbook must be consulted.

We saw earlier in this chapter that some jurisdictions, notably certain states of the USA, had developed the ability to apply a fee simple interest to a time-share unit. This has almost always been achieved by passing enabling legislation, rather than development of the common law. There has been no corresponding move towards any such enabling legislation here in England and Wales, nor is it likely. If we were blessed in these islands with glorious and dependable weather, there would undoubtedly be much more demand for time-sharing. As it is, time-sharing is directed at a fairly narrow market, and there is no sanction of popularity to help the promotion of specialist legislation.[5]

So we start with the need to use English property law in its existing state. The problem is that when that property legislation was being drafted, time-sharing was a creature of the distant future, and thus the methods by which time-sharing is sold in this country are tortuous, unsuitable, archaic and unsatisfactory, despite what the time-sharing developer's brochures will tell you.

The best way to view the present state of the art seems to be to set out the different methods which might be possible and those which are in use, and then to review them individually.

Thus the first two heads are those which cannot be used, but should be simply because the basic concepts are those most familiar to the man in the street. These are freehold and leasehold.

5 There are differences of opinion as to exactly where time-sharing started. France seems to be the likely candidate, but on the other side of the Atlantic, the concept got off the ground in a big way in Florida in the early seventies on the back of a property recession. Speculative developers were left with largely unsold blocks of apartments, in prime vacationing areas, and converted them into time-sharing, to good effect.

1 Freehold

We should just remind ourselves that by the Law of Property Act 1925:

'The only estates in land which are capable of subsisting or of being conveyed or created at law are—
(a) An estate in fee simple in possession;
(b) A term of years absolute.'[6]

By the same statute, it is provided that:[7]

'(1) An undivided share in land shall not be capable of being created except as provided by the Settled Land Act 1925, or as hereinafter mentioned.
(2) Where, after the commencement of this Act, land is expressed to be conveyed to any person in undivided shares and those persons are of full age, the conveyance shall (notwithstanding anything to the contrary in this Act) operate as if the land had been expressed to be conveyed to the grantees, or, if there are more than four grantees, to the four first names in the conveyance, as joint tenants upon the statutory trusts hereinafter mentioned and so as to give effect to the rights of the persons who would have been entitled to the shares had the conveyance operated to create these shares: ....'

The reference to the Settled Land Act 1925 in s 34 (1) of the Law of Property Act 1925, above, is to s 36 of that former Act, which basically provides that undivided shares in land are to take effect behind a trust for sale of the land. The wording of the Settled Land Act 1925, s 36 (4) closely follows that of the Law of Property Act 1925, s 34 (1), already noted: thus

'An undivided share in land shall not be capable of being created except under a trust instrument or under the Law of Property Act 1925, and shall then only take effect behind a trust for sale.'

Accordingly, the position on the attempted application of a fee simple estate to time-sharing is as follows:

(a) the fee simple estate will be in the property as a whole;
(b) the interests of the owners of the time-share units will *all* be in the same property;
(c) therefore, although the interests of the owners as related to *time periods* will be divided, their interests as related to the property itself will be undivided;
(d) thus it would be impossible to sell freehold estates to those owners;[8]
(e) if a sale of freehold shares were attempted, it would have the effect of only the first four named having the legal estates vested in them; all succeeding owners would merely have an equitable interest, and the first four would hold the property upon trust for themselves and the others. The result would be unworkable chaos. Incidentally, although consideration of Scots law is outside the scope of this book, it is interesting to note that it is perfectly possible in Scots law to create a legal estate equivalent to a fee simple into as many *independent* fractional shares as one wishes.

6 Law of Property Act 1925, s 1 (1).
7 Ibid, s 34.
8 Unless there were only four, which would be highly unlikely, it would mean each owner having 12/13 weeks each!

> The snag is that in Scotland joint owners have the right to insist on a physical division of the property, or (assuming a physical division to be difficult or impossible as it would be) to force a sale and divide the proceeds. Of course, no purchaser would initially contemplate this step but one would have to take appropriate safeguards against it, and it is highly questionable that any such safeguard would work properly.

Having thus disposed of a freehold estate as a method of disposing of a time-share unit, we turn to:

2 Leasehold

At first sight, this method would seem a likely one, but again at the end of the day, it has too many flaws.

It is said that there are at least two time-sharing developments in England where the purchasers have received a grant of a lease directly from the developer. The justification for this was based on the very old case of *Smallwood v Sheppards*.[9] The basic facts of this case involved a lease of a property for three consecutive bank holidays, ie the recurring interest we discovered earlier as a basic feature of time-sharing.[10] The Court apparently accepted this as a valid lease, but this decision may have been seriously affected by the recent case of *Cottage Holiday Associates v Customs and Excise*.[11] This was a VAT case, and so far we can only rely upon an obiter dictum of Woolfe J; but the case established that the term conferred by an instrument purporting to grant a lease of a property for one week in every year for a period of 80 years is a term of 80 weeks, not a variation on a term of 80 years. This has the unfortunate effect that, the term being less than 21 years, it is not capable of registration at HM Land Registry. The net effect of this decision is that the Registry is only prepared to make an entry in the Charges Register of the developer's title to the effect that the title is subject to such rights and interests as have been created by agreements relating to the intermittent occupation of parts thereof.

There are other implications of this decision, thus if the accrued period were to be less than eight years (which it almost certainly would) there might well be great difficulty in the developer, as landlord, being able to levy a service charge which included the cost of repairs.[12]

We have, therefore, seen that the attempted use of the term of years is generally doomed to the same sort of failure as the attempted use of the fee simple interest, although at least with leasehold, there is the glimmer of a hope. So we pass on to the schemes which actually do work.

3 Club schemes

This is probably the procedure most used in time-sharing developments in England and Wales. While it is not perfect, in that an absolutely indefeasible

9 [1895] 2 QB 627.
10 See pp 270 and 271, above.
11 [1983] QB 735, [1983] 2 WLR 861.
12 Housing Act 1961, s 32.

interest in the property itself is not passed to the purchaser, it does represent the best solution presently available.

Club schemes are divisible into two separate categories, which are:

(a) unincorporated members clubs, and
(b) incorporated members clubs,

We shall examine these in turn.

(a) *Unincorporated members clubs*

The basic difference between the unincorporated and incorporated members club is that the former does not have a separate legal personality and accordingly is unable to hold property in its own right. This problem is overcome by the use of trustees.

The procedure in the setting up of an unincorporated club is as follows; what is described below is, of course, subject to variation in several aspects of the scheme, and it is not suggested that the structure which is outlined applies to all club schemes. Nevertheless, it is typical.

(i) A name is devised for the club, and generally two founder members are appointed.

(ii) The founder members will probably be:
  (a) the developer, because he will wish to be the guiding force behind the development; and
  (b) the management company. It is assumed that there will be a management company which is incorporated as a separate entity. It would be unwise to do otherwise.

(iii) A constitution will be settled for the club; this may well require the two founder members to have the legal estate in the development transferred into the name of an independent trustee.

(iv) The independent trustee will be an organisation of unimpeachable probity. This is an important point; the time-share unit purchasers will wish to know that the organisation holding the legal interest in the development, and from which they will derive their own interests, is quite independent from the developer, and will be utterly reliable. For this reason, it has been usual for such trustees to be, eg one of the major clearing banks.

(v) The constitution will usually provide that the right to issue the ownership of the time-sharing weeks will be controlled by the developer. This right will be exercised by the selling to purchasers of 'membership certificates', each of which will refer to a given period of time, usually expressed by a week number.[13]

(vi) The founder members will also be the first 'executive' members of the club until a full committee, with representatives of the time-share unit owners, is established.

(vii) Eventually there will be a full management committee, so that to some

13 The year will be divided into separately numbered weeks, and each succeeding year will carry those numbers, so that the time-share unit owners will be able to identify precisely when their period of occupation occurs in each year.

extent there is the analogy with a tenants' management company[14] but it will generally be found that the constitution of the club will limit the powers of the owners' committee providing the management of the development is satisfactory. In any event, the owners' committee may not be so fearsome a body, because owners will probably live at a distance from the development, and will have only brief contact with it each year, so that it may meet only once every year, and even then most of the owners will probably be absent.

(viii) The club will be limited to a life of no more than 80 years, otherwise the perpetuity rules would be offended. This is one of the disadvantages of the scheme, but is unavoidable. Quite what will happen on time-share developments using this system of selling, when the eightieth year has passed, remains open to conjecture, although there is at least one major developer of time-sharing who has let it be known that when this point is reached, the exercise will be carried out again, at no capital cost to unit-owners. (One wonders!)

Documentation. In a scheme of this sort, there will typically be the following documents.

1. CLUB CONSTITUTION. This will simply set out the rules of the club, and these will deal with the relationship of individual members both with the club and as between themselves, and also with the members' rights as related to the units.

2 TRUST DEED. This will initially vest the development in the trustee, for the benefit of all the club members.[15] What the trust deed contains depends on the trustee chosen.

3 MANAGEMENT AGREEMENT. This is an agreement between the developer and the management company and controls how management is going to be organised. It should be clear to readers that management of a time-sharing development is even more important than in an everyday block of flats, because all the unit owners are absentees for the very great majority of the year, and most of them would find it logistically difficult, if not impossible, to monitor what is going on in the way of management throughout the year. From the developer's point of view as well as those of the unit owners, it is crucial to have good, efficient, management.

4 PURCHASE AGREEMENT. This will naturally be a transistory document, but it serves the same purpose as a contract in a normal land property purchase.

5 CERTIFICATE OF MEMBERSHIP. This is also variously called a membership certificate, or holiday certificate, although the latter title is misleading as not all time-sharing developments are primarily devoted to holiday occupation (as we have already seen). The certificate will confirm the membership of the individual unit-owner in the club, will bind him to observe the constitution and supporting documentation, and will set out his rights of occu-

14 Refer to ch 11, pp 131–134, above, for a description of a typical tenants' management company.

15 It is worth considering that even on a very small development of, say, 20 units, if each unit has 50 separate weeks sold there will be 1,000 members!

pancy in the unit in question. In other words, it is really his document of title.

Before we pass on to look at the advantages and disadvantages of the members club as a way of disposing of time-sharing, we should consider the incorporated members club.

(b) *Incorporated members clubs*

This will differ from the unincorporated club just described in the following ways:

(i) a company is incorporated, as opposed to a mere club;
(ii) the company is incorporated with limited liability, and will usually be limited by guarantee rather than by shares; and
(iii) accordingly the company will be able to have the legal estate in the development vested in it, and so the necessity of having an independent trustee can be dispensed with.

Incidentally, this variation should not be confused with the corporate scheme which is described below. In that scheme the right to occupancy is evidenced by a share certificate,[16] but in the variation under discussion there is still a club with a constitution, and ownership of a time-share unit is still evidenced by the issue of a membership certificate.

There is some doubt whether the use of an incorporated club is better than an unincorporated one; the use of an outside organisation such as a major clearing bank to act as the custodian trustee of the legal estate has its disadvantages, but one of the greatest advantages such a scheme can have will surely be the implicit approval that the participation of a 'famous name' financial institution brings to it. True, such implicit approval may well be largely illusory, but as a marketing ploy it may be found very useful.

What are the main 'plus' and 'minus' points in the use of the club structure, both unincorporated and incorporated?

First the 'plus' points:

(i) the scheme does not prevent investigation of title being carried out by purchasers, or (presumably) by their solicitors.[17] Those buying time-share units will be likely to belong to the property-owning classes anyway, and they will be aware that in a normal purchase situation it is usual to investigate title. If they are presented with a deal where such an investigation is denied them, they may well feel uneasy. It will probably do the developer and/or his solicitors little harm, and probably a great deal of good, to allow the underlying title to be investigated;
(ii) on the other hand, but also an advantage, is the simple document of ownership which this scheme enjoys; ie a 'membership certificate', which is easily transferable;
(iii) the purchasers may well have an opportunity of taking some active part in the management; and

16 See p 279, below.
17 See later discussion on Title Insurance, p 280.

(iv) (as we have already seen) the use of a 'big name' trustee lends authenticity to the scheme.

Now for the 'minus' points.

(i) the main one has to be the one which the scheme shares with all other methods of selling time-sharing in England and Wales; this is that the purchaser can only receive an indirect interest in the property; he cannot get a foot in the door of a direct legal estate; and
(ii) because of the inability of English law to cope with the concept of time-sharing, the documentation leading up to the issue of the membership certificate can appear tortuous to the layman.

One point which should briefly be considered here is whether a time-share interest is mortgageable. As both freehold and leasehold estates are difficult, if not impossible, vehicles to use for time-sharing, we are probably talking in the main about clubs, and corporate schemes. It has been thought that there might be some difficulty in charging a time-share interest, principally because it is merely a personal interest as opposed to real property. However, enough of the major banks and finance houses are now offering funding on time-sharing for this not to be a problem any longer. Either money is advanced as a straight personal loan, or if security is required, presumably the purchaser has a house already which has enough equity in it to have the time-share advance hooked onto that as security. This should not really be a problem.

4 Corporate schemes

These are much less popular than the club schemes, but they have been used in the past, and presumably will continue to be used, so they warrant some attention. It is not proposed here to launch into a detailed study of all the relevant points of such a scheme; rather we should satisfy ourselves with an identification of the main features, as follows:

(a) the purchaser acquires his time-sharing rights, not as a right to occupy the property, whether in the form of a lease, if this method can be used successfully, or a Membership Certificate in an unincorporated/incorporated club scheme, but in the shape of a share certificate;
(b) the share in the company represented by the share certificate entitles the purchaser to the right to occupy a specific property for a specific period in each year;
(c) thus the whole matter is regulated, not by property law as in the other schemes, but by company law. As a result, the scheme has to be put together and subsequently marketed very carefully, and this may be one of its major disadvantages;
(d) the developer will be looking to market the time-sharing to the public at large; so that he will be contemplating offering the shares of the company to the public. This means that the company involved must be a public company.[18] This in itself has drawbacks, thus:

18 Companies Act 1985, s 81.

(i) there must be a minimum allotted share capital of £50,000;[19]

(ii) each share must be paid up as to not less than one quarter of the nominal value;[20]

(e) the company to act as the vehicle for the scheme therefore, has to be incorporated as a public company in the first place, or it may be formed initially as a private company and then re-registered as a public company;

(f) The developer will obviously sell his time-sharing by means of a brochure; this will be a prospectus within the meaning of the Companies Act 1948. There is no time here to go into the consequences of this, save to remark that like the scheme in general, it imposes a rigid duty on the developer to follow the rules closely, otherwise he is in trouble;

(g) management will probably be best dealt with by having a separate management company, which will enter into a management agreement with each shareholder;

(h) the legal estate will, of course, be vested in the company, and the shareholding will be the right to occupancy of the company's property.

There are other problems associated with this type of development: one has to consider such matters as shareholders' rights, possible problems on winding-up, and so on. The scheme is undoubtedly a complex one, and the above is meant only to be an outline for purposes of familiarisation, and certainly not a guide as to how to do it.

The above methods, then, represent the main, indeed virtually the only, ways of selling time-sharing in England and Wales. The club scheme seems to be the most favoured one, and it is because of this that it is only club scheme precedents which appear in this book.[1]

Before we close the chapter, a brief word about the role of title insurance. The concept of title insurance[2] has never really taken off in this country, despite the efforts of our friends in the TI companies, which have been trying to get into the UK market for a very long time. The author well remembers being asked to deliver a presentation on 'The Relevance of Title Insurance to Time-Sharing' at an International Bar Association seminar some time ago. As a result of the research carried out on the preparation of the paper, the conclusion was reached that title insurance was not relevant to this country, even to a hybrid subject matter such as time-sharing.

Title insurance is used in countries like the USA to replace *title investigation* by lawyers acting for each individual purchaser, thus very often relieving the purchaser from appointing a lawyer at all. This is particularly the case on the west coast of the USA, but not so prevalent in states further east, where significantly enough the legal system is more heavily based on our own. Nevertheless, the use of title insurance does not mean that title investigation is not carried out—it is, but by the title insurance companies' own lawyers. It is also of more significance in legal systems where the title is not

19 Ibid, ss 45 and 117.

20 Ibid, ss 101, 112.

1 See Precedent Nos 19 to 24, pp 416–441, below.

2 Not to be confused with *defective title* insurance, ie contingency insurance.

guaranteed by governmental registers, as it is for all practical purposes with our own land registration system.

Accordingly the author arrived at the conclusion that there was really no case for using title insurance for time-sharing developments in this country, unless the TI companies were prepared to insure, not the underlying title to the legal estate, but the *method* of selling the time sharing. This, it appears, they are not interested in, so that title insurance is really as much of a non-starter in time-sharing as in any other sector of the property market in this country.[3]

3 That did not save the author from a hectic floor to podium discussion, mainly with title insurance company representatives, during the presentation previously mentioned!

CHAPTER 24

Registration

Discussion of the effect of land registration on flats and/or maisonettes is more in the nature of a technical discussion, and has no prominent place in this book.[1] Nevertheless, we ought not to talk about the sale of flats without taking a brief look at the effect of registration on what one is doing; but the following should not be used as anything other than a collection of 'pointers' and for further investigation a specialist textbook should be consulted.

A. GRANTS OF NEW LEASES

When acting for a developer who is building flats and/or maisonettes, the conveyancer will be dealing with either registered or unregistered land. It is a basic statement and is the first point which has to be considered, because if the land is not registered, then the author suggests that the developer should be advised, told, persuaded (whatever it is, depending on his relationship with his legal adviser) to apply for registration. Naturally, this only applies in areas of non-compulsory registration, because elsewhere he has no choice. In a voluntary area, as long as there is in the development a minimum of 20 units, an application for first registration will be accepted, and in view of the present Chief Land Registrar's earnest desire to see as much of the country covered by registration as possible in as short as possible a time, the application might well be acceptable anyway even if it is for less than 20 units.

One would imagine that it would be in everyone's best interests to have *any* block of flats registered, because if it is developed on an unregistered basis when the area it is situated in becomes subject to compulsory registration there is the danger of the individual units becoming registered on a piecemeal basis, and then presumably only with good leasehold title. If the developer registers his (presumably freehold) land in the first place, all the flats will be registered immediately following the creation of their terms, and they will also all have absolute leasehold title.

The Land Registry sensibly treat leasehold units on a building estate merely as a variation of a normal freehold development. Both leasehold and freehold aspects may of course be mixed together on the same site, or we

1 Ruoff and West *Concise Land Registration Practice* (3rd edn, Sweet & Maxwell) is an excellent little book if one does not want continually to refer to Ruoff and Roper *Registered Conveyancing* (4th edn, Sweet & Maxwell). As both Theodore Ruoff and Christopher West are, or were, the 'horses' mouths', one can hardly go wrong with either publication!

may be dealing with a block of flats standing on its own. The treatment is no different, and it is fully described in HM Land Registry's Practice Leaflet No 7: *Development of Registered Building Estates.* There is no intention in this book of setting out this practice leaflet in full, nor of describing in detail how to set up a building estate on registered land; however, the reader will be well advised to read the leaflet closely.[2]

The practice leaflet may be interpreted in precisely the same way on a development of flats on registered land, whether wholly or in conjunction with freehold units; all one has to do is to substitute the words 'lessor', 'lessee' and 'lease' for 'transferor', 'transferee' and 'transfer'.

The difference in treatment between leasehold and freehold units may be quickly summarised as follows:

1 (a) As registered conveyancing depends on plans, and not (usually) description, the plan of the development is of paramount importance just as much for flats;

(b) flats are housing units divided on a horizontal as well as vertical plane; therefore a plan of *each* floor lay-out must be submitted, *unless* there are floors with *absolutely* identical lay-outs. This is a point which has to be watched very closely—thus very often the ground floor will be different to intermediate floors—and so will the top floor. The ground floor will have an entrance door to the outside—a feature none of the other floors will have (we hope!). It will also have a staircase entering it only from above, whereas the intermediate floors will have staircases entering from both above *and* below, whilst the upper floor has a staircase only entering it from below. Therefore even although the layout of the flats on all of these floors is *absolutely* identical, the arrangement of the common areas may be different, however slightly, and it is probably wise to treat each such floor as separate, and lodge separate plans with the Registry, so that there would be one approved plan for the ground floor, another for the top floor, and one for the intermediate floors, no matter how many such floors there were, providing the lay-out is identical.

This point has been laboured because it is a very important one. As mere conveyancers are not trained in reading plans, subtle differences might not be spotted, and it is best to double-check the point with the developer's architect, or whoever has been responsible for the preparation of the plans.

2 Next we come to title, and in case any reader raises his eyebrows about comments on title being preceded by those on plans, let it be used as an illustration of how vital good plans are in registered conveyancing, and nowhere so vital as when dealing with the creation of flats:[3]

2 The author's companion book *Residential Estate Conveyancing: Practice and Precedents* (Butterworths 1983) has the leaflet reproduced in full, with an appropriate commentary.

3 An interesting description of flats, albeit studio flats, on different floors is in Precedent No 4, p 369, below.

(a) first of all, the assumption is that the developer has a freehold title to the land upon which the block of flats is being built, and that it is title absolute;[4]

(b) if the developer has a leasehold title, then subject to the terms of any entry to the contrary on the register (and one supposes he would not have bought the land if there were such an entry) he may grant underleases of a shorter duration than the registered term;

(c) the developer should aim to have absolute leasehold, if he has to deal with land on a leasehold basis. He will then be able to grant underleases which will themselves gain absolute title.

(d) If, however, he only has good leasehold title, this means that the ultimate title, which presumably will be freehold, will not have been examined, at least not to the satisfaction of the Registry. This has important consequences:

  (i) no-one acting for a prospective purchaser of the unit should allow him to proceed, especially if he is paying a premium, which he almost certainly will be;

  (ii) even if this escapes the net, no Lender should proceed without insisting on examining the underlying title. One must accept that these ground rules will not always be observed, admittedly sometimes because it is impossible being beyond the prospective buyer's power to insist on the underlying title being produced; nonetheless these remain strong recommendations.

3 When the lease of the particular unit is prepared, the plan used in it must naturally identify precisely where in the block it is: this includes specifying which floor the unit is on. If there is more than one intermediate floor, the plans for those floors may well be identical, as we have seen above, and if the number of the floor was not specified there would be no way of knowing exactly where the unit was. Yet again, this may seem elementary, but possibly because of that, the problem does sometimes occur.

4 The Registry will make an entry on the Charges Register of the lessor's title, of each lease as it is registered, giving brief particulars of the document. This will look something like the diagram opposite.

The schedule will be reproduced in a separate part of the Charges Register; usually on a separate page, and the schedule is entitled 'Schedule of Notices of Leases'.

The imaginary schedule reproduced does not need much commentary, because it is fairly self-explanatory. However, it should be noted that the first column will be the date the leases are noted by the Registry, and the plan reference number is the same for Plot 234 and Plot 123 with each flat described as 'part' because these are flats which are one on the top of each other, thus occupying the same *vertical* air space, and can only be separated in the legal sense by use of separate floor plans, as we have seen above.

5 If the registration of any lease of a unit is delayed for some reason or another, it is fairly obvious that it will not be listed on the schedule described

4 If it was less than absolute title, he would have to have some sort of satisfactory security, eg contingency insurance.

DATE	PLAN REF	DESCRIPTION	DATE OF LEASE	TERM		RENT	LESSEE'S
				YEARS	FROM		TITLE
19.3.1984	1 (part) 2 3	Plot 234 Bloggs Crescent (Top floor flat) Drying Area Car Parking space	31.11.1983	120	1.9.1983	£50 Subject to review	HD 12345
19.3.1984	1 (part) 4 5 6	Plot 123 Bloggs Cresent (ground floor flat) Garden Area Car Parking Space Drying Area	15.10.1983	120	1.9.1983	£50 Subject to review	HD 54321

above. It will depend on how efficient those acting for the purchasers of the units themselves are in applying for registration, as to which individual leases are noted on the register at any given time. When a conveyancer acting for a purchaser of or a lender on any particular unit sees the title supplied to him by the vendor, the lessor, there may well be some unit leases already completed but not yet registered. This should not cause any concern as long as the date stamp on the office copy entries is quoted on the search eventually made, because the search itself when returned by the Registry is a guarantee that the unit he is acting on is still in the lessor's power to sell (just so long as it does not also reveal any pending application affecting the property).

This is where we get back to the importance of plans. Even more so in a development of flats than in a normal building estate situation (where the plots are likely to be freehold) it is crucial to have clear, concise plans approved by the Registry. Otherwise 'confusion will arise'—and it is no coincidence that these are also the words the Registry itself uses in Practice Leaflet No 7 described above.

Another matter which should not be overlooked by either the lessor's solicitor, or those acting for the lessees, is that the Land Certificate belonging to the lessor must have been deposited at the Registry, in the normal way of building estate developments.

6 On the development of a freehold building estate it is a wise precaution, although not absolutely essential, to have the form of transfer 'vetted' by the Registry. In just the same way, it is sensible on the part of the lessor to submit the form of lease he is proposing to use, to the appropriate district land registry for comment. In the author's experience the registry staff are unfailingly helpful and courteous, and will often make helpful suggestions above and beyond their call of duty. The lessor's solicitor often enjoys a bonus through having so submitted his lease. As to actual form of the lease, and whether or not it has to differ in any respect from an unregistered lease, the only requirement is that as long as it refers in sufficient terms to the property demised, it is acceptable to the Registry provided, of course, that it refers to the title number of the registered land out of which it is being granted, and also that it sufficiently identifies the appropriate *part* of that title it is dealing with, eg by joint reference to unit number and plan, which should be the same as the approved layout plan (see above).

These points are the only ones to which particular notice should be given. Any conveyancer who has dealt with registered conveyancing and purchases (or indeed sales) on a freehold building estate will be able to cope perfectly well with new units on a development of flats. No mention has been made of any point which is not relevant—for instance, we have not discussed whether or not the leases of the units are *registrable* or not—they will all be for long terms if they are of units being sold for a premium, and thus it goes without saying that they *will* be registrable.

B. ASSIGNMENTS OF EXISTING LEASES

This is not meant to be a book about conveyancing techniques, although we have included a short chapter on the salient points.[5] Nevertheless, there are one or two matters to which readers' attention should be drawn, if they are acting for a vendor, or more likely, a purchaser, of an existing lease. These are as follows:

1 The office copy entries of the vendor's title should be treated as a starting point only, and are not to be relied upon as the sole document of title.

2 The other, and in many ways, more important part of the title will be the lease itself. It is just as crucial to see this.

3 The Registry will not normally supply an office copy of the registered lease, indeed it is possible for the Registry *not* to have a copy of the lease.[6]

4 The vendor should have the original lease, which should be passed from owner to owner. If for some reason the original of the document is missing, then whoever is selling ought at least to have a copy.

5 Restrictive covenants made between the original lessor and lessee will not have been entered on the Register. This is why it is so important to see the lease as well as the office copy entries.[7]

6 The office copy entries should be inspected for any restriction on the registers. We have seen elsewhere in this book[8] how important and useful these can be for the developer/manager, and their use is probably growing rather than diminishing, so the conveyancer on any dealing subsequent to the original grant of the lease must be careful to identify whether there are any such restrictions, and if there are, to secure his client (we assume here, of course, that we are dealing with the *purchaser*) in respect of them, ie he makes sure that the restrictioner either has given the consent required, or is committed to giving it.

7 Although there is supposed to be a special form to be used for transfer of leasehold properties[9] the Registry does not object in practice to the use of the more familiar Form 19.

8 Assuming that there is contained in the lease a requirement on a purchaser to register any document of transmission within a given time of its completion (which there almost certainly will be) the purchaser could be in trouble if he lodged the transfer for registration with the reversioner before he put it up for registration of the dealing at the Land Registry. If the reversioner failed to return it, the purchaser might well lose his priority with the Registry. On the other hand, he could not lodge it with the reversioner for registration *after* the Land Registry had completed registration of the

5 See ch 6, p 77, above.

6 Although one supposes that on a properly set up flat development, they should have had a copy supplied by the lessor's solicitor.

7 Eg see Land Registration Rules 1925, r 5 (1) : 'In the case of leasehold land there shall be entered in the Property Register *a reference* to the registered lease, and such particulars of the lease, and of the *exceptions and reservations* therefrom (if any) *as the applicant may desire* ....' (*author's italics*).

8 See ch 7, p 86, above.

9 Form 32.

dealing, because (a) he would almost certainly be out of time, and thus technically in breach of covenant, with the reversioner, and (b) the Registry do not return the transfer anyway! However, there is no problem, because the purchaser may submit a mere *copy* of the document to the reversioner for registration purposes.

Again, as with the previous section, these are only the basic points of difference. For those who wish to become more expert on the subject the specialist textbooks on registered conveyancing will be found to be worthwhile additional reading.

CHAPTER 25

NHBC

No discussion on the sale of flats and/or maisonettes[1] would be complete without some reference to the application of the National House-Building Council's Scheme, which is intrinsically an insurance scheme intended to compensate purchasers against faulty building.[2] Nevertheless, subject to the resumé incorporated below, we will only concern ourselves with the specialised application to flats. For those readers who wish to investigate the scheme in some depth, the following are recommended: *Guarantees for New Homes*[3] which is an excellent guide to the whole scheme; the author's own *Residential Estate Conveyancing: Practice and Precedents*,[4] for quicker reference; and finally the NHBC's own publication, *The 60 Questions Most Asked About NHBC*[5] which is a most useful little book.

First we will consider the basic NHBC documentation used in a typical estate development to see how it varies, if at all, when applied to a development of flats. There are three basic documents used by the NHBC, and they are, the HB5, (House Purchasers' Agreement) the HB7, (House Purchasers' Insurance Policy) and the HB6 (Notice of Insurance Cover). These are, briefly, as follows:

A. HOUSE PURCHASERS' AGREEMENT HB5

This is issued by the NHBC to the vendor, provided (i) the vendor is registered himself with the NHBC, and (ii) the vendor has registered the *property* with the Council (which of course includes paying the appropriate fees). It is the vendor's responsibility to distribute the HB5 and subsequent documents to the purchasers. The HB5 incorporates seven warranties given by the vendor to the purchaser:

(i) that his name is entered on the Register;
(ii) that he has undertaken to comply with the Council's rules;
(iii) that he has made an application for inspection of the building;
(iv) that the dwelling will be built in an efficient and workmanlike manner and of proper materials so as to be fit for habitation;
(v) that a standard notice of insurance cover has been or will be issued in respect of the dwelling;

1 Hereafter the expression 'flats' will be used and will include reference to maisonettes as well.
2 The author is indebted to Rhona Wyles of the NHBC for the assistance given in the preparation of this chapter.
3 Tapping and Rolfe (2nd edn, Oyez Publishing Ltd).
4 (Butterworths, 1983).
5 NHBC, Chiltern Avenue, Amersham, Bucks.

(vi) that the insurance policy will be delivered to the purchaser; and
(vii) that the notice of insurance cover will be handed over as soon as possible.

The nature of these warranties is such that everything else contained in the HB5 and the rest of the NHBC documentation flows naturally from them.

The form of HB5 issued in respect of a development of flats will be identical to that issued on a normal estate development of houses, except that, where a block of flats is being constructed by a registered builder and, instead of granting leases of the individual units to the purchasers, he grants a head lease of the building to a management company which then grants sub-leases in respect of the individual units, the standard HB5 Agreement is inappropriate. Instead, the HB5B Agreement will be used: the only difference between the two types of Agreement is that the HB5 is exchanged by the vendor, and the HB5B by the builder. Otherwise, they are identical.

The HB5B is used in other circumstances where the actual vendor is not registered, eg when a registered builder is constructing buildings (of any sort—not only flats) for sale by a public authority. Fairly obviously, prior written permission has to be obtained from the NHBC for this sort of exercise.

B. HOUSE PURCHASERS' INSURANCE POLICY HB7

As with the HB5, this is a document which will not vary as between flats and houses, although if the HB5B Agreement is used, the House Purchasers' Policy will be the HB7B. It is the document which sets out the details of the cover which is afforded to the property by the NHBC scheme. Prior to 1979, the subject matter of the present HB7 used to be contained in the First and Second Schedules of the HB5 (or HB5B).

C NOTICE OF INSURANCE COVER HB6 (or HB6B where appropriate)

Without this document the insurance cover under the Insurance Policy (the HB7) is limited to loss of deposit cover (currently £5,000, although shortly to be increased to £10,000). The HB6 is the document the issue of which is triggered off by the conclusion of the series of inspections by the NHBC inspector responsible for the site in question; it is hoped that the inspections will be satisfactory—otherwise the HB6 will not be issued. Whereas the HB7 is a closely worded document, the HB6 is a fairly pithy one, not needing to be otherwise, as it is merely required to indicate that it is bringing into operation the ten-year cover insurance with its substantial benefits as contained in the HB7.

These, then, are the basic documents of the scheme, whatever the type of property involved. Readers will have seen, however, that whilst we specifically noted, in the cases of the HB5 and HB7, that there was generally no difference between the documents used for houses and flats, there was no similar qualification in the case of the HB6, because this is where there is a difference between the treatment of flats and of houses. The difference comes not in there being variation between an HB6 issued for a flat and one issued for a house—they will be in the same basic form—but in there being an *additional* HB6 for a flat. Thus, the basic HB6 will be the same whatever the nature of the property covered; the additional cover for the flat will be the HB6D.

D. COMMON PARTS NOTICE OF INSURANCE COVER HB6D

This document was first introduced in 1979, when there was a major revision of the NHBC scheme (most practitioners will remember the revision by the disappearance of the 'Ten-Year Protection Certificate' and the introduction of the 'Notice of Insurance Cover', but the changes went much deeper than that).

The HB6D was introduced by the NHBC because there had previously been difficulty in deciding when liability for the common parts in a block of flats started to run. It is one of the basic features of a development of flats that there will be a number of individual units in the building, and there will also be those parts of the building, the common parts, which will be used jointly by all the individual units together. As these common parts are for the most part very important sectors of the building, ie the basic shell, the corridors, the staircases, lifts and lift shafts, etc it is crucial that they, as well as the flats themselves, are covered by the NHBC scheme.

It must not be thought that prior to 1979 common parts were not covered by the NHBC—they were, but each Ten-Year Protection Certificate covered a (usually indefinable) portion of the common parts, the use of which related to any particular flat, and so if there were delay in the completion of the last few flats in the building, for whatever reason, it was arguable that the cover for the common parts ran from when the last flat was sold.

This was considered to be generally unfair to the builder (although the legal position was by no means clear) because in the circumstances described above the common parts might have been completed long before certification of the last few flats. This gave rise to an actual period of cover for common parts which was, in some cases, much longer than originally intended. It was because of this anomaly that the NHBC took the opportunity of introducing in 1979, as part of its revision of the basic scheme, the new document called 'Common Parts Notice of Insurance Cover' (otherwise HB6D). There is no necessity for the builder to apply separately for this document in respect of each flat, but if the flats do have associated common parts, which are defined in the lease, it is the builder's responsibility to make the NHBC aware of the position when he completes the application for inspection form.

As soon as the common parts are physically complete, the NHBC issues a common parts notice in respect of the building. One in respect of each flat will be delivered to the builder. Thus the issue of the common parts notices does not necessarily take place at the same time as the issue of the individual notices for the flats themselves which may come before or after the common parts notice.

From the builder's point of view, the importance of the common parts notice procedure is that it does away with the uncertainty of the previous procedure, and it gives a readily identifiable starting date for the common parts cover; that starting date applying to the whole of the common parts. For example, a building comprises ten flats, the first one of which was completed on 1 January 1985, but the last one was not finished until 31 December 1988, perhaps because of difficulties in selling. The common parts could have been completed on 1 April 1985. Assuming for the sake of this example that issue of the notices coincided with physical completion,[6] the common parts notice would have been issued as soon as the common parts were completed (obviously in a development of flats the common parts will have to be in a virtual state of completion by the time the first flats are sold) and thus would have been in operation for very nearly four years by the time the last flat was completed (and presumably sold) and the builder would not have had to suffer an overrun of that period on his common parts liability. There is also no confusion (as might possibly have obtained under the pre-1979 procedure) as to when the liability for the common parts, commenced.

'Common parts' are generally defined in the lease used in the development, either directly or by implication. The NHBC's own handy definition of common parts is:[7]

> 'Those parts of a building which are:
> (a) demised jointly to all the purchasers in a block and for which all purchasers are responsible for the cost of repair or maintenance; or
> (b) owned by the freeholder and for which he is liable under the lease for the cost of repair and maintenance, but for which the individual purchaser is liable to pay a proportion of that cost under his lease.

The liability of the builder to the owner of the flat, under the terms of the HB5 Agreement and the Insurance Cover, must not be confused with the flat-owner's liabilities in respect of the common parts as set out in his lease. On the one hand, the builder is liable for what may basically be described as faults; on the other hand the flat-owner is liable (generally by way of proportionate contribution) for maintenance and upkeep, although there may be cases where the two overlap and the builder is liable to remedy defects the cost of which otherwise would have fallen on the owners.

Further, the NHBC's liability in respect of common parts is strictly controlled. It is limited to 'the extent that the Purchaser is directly or indirectly liable to share in the cost of repairing or reinstating such parts'. An indirect liability in this context is, eg where the common parts have been reserved to the lessor, to whom the flat-owner is bound to pay a proportion of the service charge. A direct liability is where the flat-owner's obligation is to a management company. Thus the liability under the NHBC Insurance Policy will be apportioned to the different flats in the building in the same ratios as the service charges attaching to these flats.

According to the NHBC Booklet previously referred to,[8] any claim in

6 There is obviously a time-lag between physical completion and the issue of notices.
7 Refer to *The 60 Questions Most Asked About NHBC* question 46, p 21.
8 *The 60 Questions Most Asked About NHBC* question 47, p 21.

respect of common parts must be made by all flat-owners jointly, or by the management company if all the owners in the building are shareholders in that company. The presence instead of a maintenance trustee or a management company limited not by shares, but by guarantee is taken to be analagous to this latter position.

Finally, it may be of some assistance to readers to have set out the wording of the standard common parts notice of insurance cover, as follows:

HB6D (1979) NATIONAL HOUSE-BUILDING COUNCIL D
COMMON PARTS NOTICE OF INSURANCE COVER

The Dwelling (*Description*)
(*Flat*)

Vendor
Address

NHBC Registration No............

Insurance Policy Number...........
Date of Issue............

First purchaser ....
Address ....
....

Purchase price............
Date of completion of first purchase.................

1 This Notice brings into operation valuable insurance benefits in respect of the Common Parts of the Building as set out in the above Insurance Policy.
2 The Council's Requirements as to design and construction have, or appear to have, been substantially complied with in relation to the Common Parts of the Building.
3 The Council employs inspectors to assist it in deciding whether to issue this Notice but they are able to make spot check inspections only. Except in accordance with the terms of the Insurance Policy, the Council, its servants or agents shall not be liable to compensate any person for any loss or damage (including consequential loss or damage) of any kind or description whatsoever, arising out of or in respect of the Common Parts of the Building or any inspection of them, and whether caused by the negligence of the Council, its servants or agents or in any other way.

(Signed, etc.)

CHAPTER 26

Leasehold enfranchisement

To some it may seem surprising to see the subject of leasehold enfranchisement receiving treatment at all in this book; but this book may well be consulted by those who are not legally qualified, including developers themselves, and among these potential readers there is almost certainly confusion about the effect of the Leasehold Reform Act 1967 on our subject.

By the Leasehold Reform Act 1967, s 1(1), there is conferred on the tenant in occupation of a leasehold house a general right to acquire the freehold or a new lease extended by 50 years, although for the purposes of this discussion, we will concentrate on the freehold aspect. Before the rights so conferred may be exercised certain requirements must be satisfied. These are as follows:

1 the house the subject of the application must be held on a long tenancy at a low rent. 'Long tenancy' means a tenancy of a term of years certain exceeding 21 years;[1] and 'low rent' means when the annual rent is less than two-thirds of the rateable value of the property on the appropriate day, or, if later, the first day of the term;[2]
2 the rateable value of the premises must have been below the relevant limit on the appropriate day applicable to the premises;[3]
3 the tenant must be occupying the premises as his residence;[4] and
4 at the relevant time (which means the time when the tenant gives notice in accordance with the Leasehold Reform Act 1967 of his desire to have the freehold or an extended lease) the tenant has been the tenant of the premises under a long tenancy at a low rent, and has occupied the premises as his residence for the previous three years, or for periods amounting to three years over the previous ten years.[5]

As can be seen, a great number of flats would come within the parameters laid down by these requirements, and so could be the subject of an application for enfranchisement or extension of lease, were it not for one overriding factor. This is, that the 1967 Act specifically refers to 'houses'.

The definition of 'house' in the context of the Leasehold Reform Act 1967 is that it

'includes any building designed or adapted for living in and reasonably so called, notwithstanding that the building is not structurally detached, or was or is not solely

1 And see the Leasehold Reform Act 1967, s 3(1).
2 Ibid, s 4(1).
3 Ibid, s 1(1)(a).
4 Ibid, s 1(1)(b).
5 The Leasehold Reform Act 1967, s 1(1)(b), as amended by the Housing Act 1980, s 141, Sch 21, para 1.

designed or adapted for living in, or is divided horizontally into flats or maisonettes; and—

(a) where a building is divided horizontally, the flats or other units into which it is so divided are not separate "houses", though the building as a whole may be; and

(b) where a building is divided vertically the building as a whole is not a "house" though any of the units into which it is divided may be.'[6]

The statute is unequivocal at this point, and makes it quite clear that a flat cannot possibly be the subject of an application for enfranchisement, although the building in which it is situated may be; so that, for instance, were the block of flats to be held on a lease according to sub-s (a), above, the block could theoretically be the subject of enfranchisement. However, for that to succeed, the conditions set out above would also have to apply, and it is difficult to see how the condition relating to the tenant having occupied the premises as his residence for the previous three years could apply. In order to arrive at the position where the main structure could be enfranchised, one would have to be dealing with something like, eg a four-floor house where the ground floor had been sub-let as (in the case reported) a betting office.[7]

It appears that there is only one case which approximates to the circumstances which this book encompasses and that is *Harris v Swick Securities Ltd*[8] where the leaseholder of a house under a tenancy complying with the requirements of the 1967 Act occupied the basement, and sub-let the other three floors. It was held that the leaseholder was entitled to acquire the freehold because, under s 1(2) of the Act, a person was entitled to say that he was occupying the premises as his residence not only when he was occupying the whole of it but also when he occupied part only and sub-let other parts.

This case illustrates how far away the normal flat is from enfranchisement. In the first place, it is clear that only in the unusual circumstances described could the premises which contained the flats itself be enfranchised; and for the average flat-owner, it matters not a jot that the title of the block itself is leasehold or freehold. Then, of course, circumstances where the majority of the flats derive title from another of the flats, as in the *Harris* case, will be unusual at least in the sort of development work with which this book is dealing. Virtually always every flat will derive title from the reversioner of the block, and *every* flat will have the same title relationship to the block. That will, of course, mean that the block will not be able to be enfranchised, because its owner is not occupying it as 'his residence'.[9] But all this is largely irrelevant, because we are concerned with the position of the individual flat-owner and we have seen by s 2(1)(a) of the 1967 Act that the individual flat is not a 'house' for the purposes of enfranchisement, and thus the conclusion is that a flat may not be enfranchised.

If it is not clear why this should be the case, one only has to consider that most flats are the subject of some sort of management programme, and the

6 The Leasehold Reform Act 1967, s 2(1).
7 *Lake v Bennett* [1970] 1 QB 663, [1970] 1 All ER 457, CA.
8 [1969] 3 All ER 1131, [1969] 1 WLR 1604, CA.
9 The Leasehold Reform Act 1967, s 1(1)(b), ante.

whole legal structure of a block of flats depends on uniformity of documentation, imposition of similar covenants, sharing of services, and provision for discharge of obligations either way. To allow enfranchisement of individual units on a piecemeal basis, converting to a legal estate which is presently less capable of dealing with the concept of the horizontally divided unit, would be unwise to say the least.

Quite what effect the introduction of a Land Obligations Act[10] would have on the likelihood of leasehold enfranchisement being extended to individual flats, one cannot say. Whereas there are arguments in favour of enfranchisement of houses, there seem to be few, whether political or practical, in favour of wholesale enfranchisement of flats. The whole concept of land obligations would have to be working well, and there would have to be a fairly basic re-working of the Leasehold Reform Act 1967, if chaos was to be avoided. It seems hardly likely to happen.

10 Refer to ch 28, p 309, for a discussion on the likely impact of the Law Commission's proposals on land obligations.

CHAPTER 27

The lessor/lessee relationship: litigation aspects[1]

Whenever there is a lessor-lessee relationship between, on the one hand, the developer or the management company (as the case may be) and on the other hand the owner of a flat, there is a danger that by reason of the owner's unwillingness or inability to discharge his financial obligations under the lease, the security of ownership of that person will be adversely affected.

This aspect of the relationship between the landlord and tenant (for such they basically are) is one which troubles a great many practitioners. It also troubles organisations like the Building Societies Association. The reasons for this disquiet are, for the most part, understandable in that there is introduced into the relationship a contingent uncertainty resulting from the parties having to opt for a system of selling, ie leasehold tenure, which they would undoubtedly not have chosen had English law been able to cope with freehold flats.[2] This disquiet also runs to cases where there is a breach of tenants' covenants, because the ultimate sanction (whether or not it is available in practical terms—the important consideration is that it is there at all) may be forfeiture both in what for ease of reference we shall refer to as 'financial' and 'non-financial' cases.

It is not the author's intention to comment on the likelihood of any actions being brought against a flat-owner for non-payment of ground rent, service charges, or for breach of tenants' covenants, and culminating in an order for forfeiture. One supposes that the courts would be ultra-reluctant to grant such an order, although if a case were bad enough then possibly the order would be made. Nor is it his intention to advise readers on the likelihood of success.

What has to be considered is that certainly a flat-owner somewhere at some time will fail to pay his or her ground rent and/or service charge to the point where the matter cannot be allowed to carry on any further, and equally another flat-owner somewhere, at some time, will be in such breach of his or her covenants that the lessor will have to take action on the matter.

Given these plain facts of life, the object of this short chapter is to outline the basic considerations, to guide the reader as to form and evidence, and to provide the appropriate precedents of the particulars of claim.[3] Any other information relating to the procedure should be sought from litigation departments.

1 The author is greatly indebted to Jonathan Winegarten of Counsel for his assistance and encouragement in the preparation of this chapter.

2 See eg ch 28, pp 309 et seq.

3 See Precedents 28 and 29, pp 446–448, below, and also the following Precedents 30, 31 and 32 which relate to the same subject.

It is convenient when discussing this subject to deal with the various aspects separately, as follows.

A FORUM

As long as the net annual value for rating of the property concerned is less than £1,500 in Greater London, or £1,000 elsewhere, the proper and indeed more convenient forum is the county court for the area in which the property is situated.

B EVIDENCE

We shall deal with those cases involving a monetary obligation (ie 'financial' cases) and those referring to any other sort of obligation ('non-financial' cases) on a separate basis.

1 Financial cases

The following documents should be made available at the hearing:

(i) the original lease of the property. This will, of course, be the counterpart, as the original will be in the possession of the lessee, or his mortgagees; it should be understood that the use of the term 'original' in this context means the *actual* document, and not a copy of it;

(ii) if there has been some sort of transmission of the lessor's interest, eg there may have been a concurrent lease of the lessor's reversionary interest[4] or a transfer, then the original documentation evidencing that transmission should be available;

(iii) if the lessee is not the original lessee, then there should also be available a certified copy of the document of transmission whereby he obtained his interest in the property. This is the ideal; one would have to rely upon the present lessee (and his predecessors in title up to the assignee from the original lessee if there had been multiple assignments) having complied with the requirements to register assignments, etc and to produce copies of the documents of transmission.[5] However, it may happen that this notice has not been given, and indeed this area of defalcation may well be associated with the failure to pay rent and/or service charges, etc. In cases where copies of these documents of assignment were not available the plaintiff lessor, etc would presumably have to prove to the court as best he could that the defendant named in the proceedings was indeed the present owner of the property;

(iv) if a rent review has taken place, the court should have available to it evidence of that rent review which would be in the form of a surveyor's determination of the new rent, provided always that the review proce-

4 Eg the studio flat scheme. See ch 9, p 110, above.)
5 It is assumed that there will have been such a provision in the lease.

dure was related to a surveyor determining a new rent. If the review procedure is different, then the evidence will have to relate to that procedure, and as there are various ways in which rent reviews are determined, we do not have the time here to consider every possible method;

(v) if any of the amount of money in arrears is in the nature of a service charge, as opposed to rent, a demand will have been made for it on at least one occasion, and therefore evidence should also be given as to those demands having been made;[6]

(vi) on the contrary, in the case of rent, no formal demand is strictly necessary, although in practice again the lessor will have been ignored. However, there are precedents in this book, notably that used on a studio flat scheme,[7] where there is included in the reentry clause a proviso that in case of default, a notice (in the precedent quoted, giving 28 days grace) must be served on the mortgagee of the property giving details of the breach complained of. (The object of this proviso is to enable the mortgagee to do something about remedying the breach. This will only work with financial cases, but in the author's experience, for every case of action having to be taken against a recalcitrant lessee on non-financial grounds, there will be hundreds of financial cases. Very often a mortgagee notified of an outstanding debt in relation to ground rent and/or service charge will settle up directly with the lessor, debit the amount to the mortgage account, and then set about the borrower/lessee without involving the lessor. The drawback of the proviso for the lessor is that he has to have the administrative ability to keep track of the current mortgagee).[8]

(vii) if any figures apart from ground rent are disputed, or likely to be disputed, the lessor should be prepared to prove them by producing in evidence the relevant accounts, etc. This would refer to service charges reserved as additional rent, so that if one was seeking to recover, inter alia, eg a proportion of grass-cutting charges, the lessor would have to produce receipted accounts from the grass-cutting contractors, quoting the properties to which it referred (so that the fraction attributable to the property in dispute could be established) and the date/s upon which the work was carried out.

Witnesses

Evidence in a financial case, as described above, should be given by an officer of the lessor, assuming it is a firm or a company. If the lessor is an individual then the likelihood is that he employs a firm of managing agents, and in that case the evidence should be given by an officer of those agents,

6 There is a case for service charge (and ground rent) demands being sent to the lessees by recorded delivery, in which case service would be marginally easier to prove; but with anything but a very small rental/service charges portfolio, using recorded delivery would amount almost to a logistical impossibility.

7 See Precedent No 3, p 360, below, and specifically cl 7, proviso.

8 And naturally there have to be the appropriate clauses in the lease, eg the proviso referred to in n 7, above.

although the relationship between him and the lessor must be established to the satisfaction of the court.

2 Non-financial cases

These, of course, are much more difficult, and in the author's view, if the matter ends up in court, then the lessor already has a failure on his hands. Everything possible should be tried before court proceedings are instituted, for example:

1 initially, the lessor should write to the unfortunate lessee and explain as simply as possible what it is that is being complained about, and requesting that he/she does something about it. There is now no typical flat-dweller, as there once used to be, and there are small, cheap flats on the market just as there are small, cheap houses. This inevitably means that a very large proportion of those living in the cheaper end of the flat market have never been property-owners before, and this sort of lessee may not totally comprehend the responsibilities of property ownership, especially where the properties concerned are in the close proximity that flats are;
2 if correspondence does no good, then before one resorts to a summons, a personal visit to the lessee by the lessor, or his officer, or of its managing agents (if any) should be tried. It is surprising how many people either fail to read their correspondence (especially official-looking examples) or fail to comprehend it properly, and 'get hold of the wrong end of the stick'! A visit to the person in default for a quiet chat *can* work wonders, although there are some risks involved because some lessees in default have been known to have an aggressive attitude. Incidentally, the lessor should be advised that a personal visit will *not* be throwing good money after bad; if he has reached the point of contemplating proceedings, it will probably cost him a considerable amount of time and money to go through with his plans, and any time and/or money spent in avoiding those proceedings is well-spent; and
3 if all the previous suggestions are followed with no positive result then (providing the identity of the mortgagee is known, and as we have touched on briefly already in (vi) on p 299, above) the lessor should consider approaching the mortgagee. He will very likely be unable to do any more good than the lessor, but there is the chance that a direct approach by him will have some effect; the average layman seems to appreciate the possible result of a displeased mortgagee more than that of a displeased lessor.

On the basis that none of the foregoing has helped the following are the documents required to prove a case of this sort:

(i) the original lease of the property
(ii) the documents evidencing transfer of (a) the lessor's and (b) the lessee's interest in the property, all as in items (i), (ii) and (iii) set out on p 298, above;
(iii) where appropriate, a copy of the s 146 notice;[9]

9 See below, pp. 303 et seq.

(iv) where appropriate, the order of the court under the Leasehold Property (Repairs) Act 1938;[10]
(v) if appropriate (which it usually will be) a copy of the letter or letters sent to the lessee asking him to desist from whatever he is doing or not doing so as to put him in breach;
(vi) the copy of the notice as referred to in item (vi), above p 299;
(vii) all relevant documentary evidence supporting the claim for damages. (This would be, eg reports by appropriate experts on damage caused as a result of the lessees' behaviour, with estimates for remedial works); and
(viii) if appropriate (this can be important—see below) all letters of complaint received about the lessee.

Witnesses

Proving the lessor's case in a non-financial matter is appreciably, and expectedly, more complicated. Briefly, the position is as follows:

(a) an officer of the lessor, or the lessor in person, or an officer of the managing agents, must produce to the court the following documents:
  (i) certified copy of transmission of the lessees interest (if appropriate);
  (ii) copy s 146 notice, if appropriate;
  (iii) copy court order under the 1938 Act,[11] items (v) to (viii) referred to above.

  This witness should be in a position to give evidence concerning the claim for damages. Where the breach of covenant does not fall within the category of case mentioned in the next sub-paragraph, this witness's evidence, eg of what he has seen on visits to the property in question,[12] will be of especial importance;
(b) in a case where the breaches complained of have given rise to complaints by other lessees of flats in the same block, or near neighbours, then as many as possible of those co-lessees and/or near neighbours should be asked to give evidence of the nature, degree and frequency of the acts. This is where the lessor may well run into difficulties, because while people are quite keen to complain about what someone is doing, or not doing, even to the point of becoming obnoxious to the lessor, it is very often quite a different matter when it comes to giving evidence in court. Unfortunately, they are likely to 'chicken out'. Yet evidence from these people will be essential in a case such as this which is based in effect on an allegation of nuisance.

A typical case, and one which is very much the most frequent in these 'non-financial' actions, is where the lessee in question has been misbehaving; let us say, for example, playing hi-fi equipment into the small hours so as to be clearly audible in the adjoining flats, having parties on a too-frequent and

10 See below, pp. 306 et seq.
11 See p 306, below.
12 It is unlikely that someone, either the lessor or someone connected with him, will not have been to the property at least once.

too-large basis, or possibly keeping a 'yappy' dog shut up on its own in the flat for hours on end.[13]

This is the sort of behaviour which only affects the co-lessees. It does not directly affect the lessor, but eventually it will do so indirectly, because first, the co-lessees will complain to him and request to him to do something about it, and later, if nothing is done, they might refuse to pay their rent and/or service charge until the lessor sorts the problem out. This is an effective sanction, because the lessor cannot reasonably take action against everyone in the block, and is thereby bound to do something about the problem.

However, the problem can be solved for the lessor in a rather interesting way. It is only the co-lessees who know and can give first-hand evidence of the nature, degree and frequency of these acts; letters of complaint are only hearsay evidence of the allegations contained in them.[14] Therefore the lessor may maintain, quite correctly, that the action will not have any chance of success without this evidence. But if these co-lessees are at the same time battering the lessor with demands that he do something, and then decline to take the trouble of appearing in court to give evidence when the lessor *does* do something, they are effectively torpedoeing the whole case, so that if they *still* continue to decline to pay rent and/or service charge—using this as an attempted sanction to produce action from the lessor, they are then hoist on their own petard, and any action by the lessor against *them* would, from their point of view, be defenceless.

Assuming co-operation from those complaining, however, it is highly desirable that, as soon as some sort of action is likely, each of them be approached and asked to prepare in diary form a note of the acts as they occur, and they will be allowed to use these, if necessary, at the hearing in order to refresh their memory.[15] Their evidence should be given of each act in chronological order.

Incidentally, although it is outside the scope of this chapter to delve into the mysteries of litigation procedure, it must be said that there is every chance that, if such an action is commenced, and the lessee does not file a defence or does not appear at the pre-trial review, the evidence of the co-lessees may be given by affidavit unless the court otherwise directs.[16] Apparently the court *will* 'otherwise direct' in any case where at trial the lessee appears and wishes to contest the action. This being the case, if the lessor is having difficulty in getting the co-lessees to agree to turn up at court to give their evidence in person, he could just risk going ahead and banking on the lessee not turning up, so that the court could be prevailed upon to accept the evidence on affidavit; but this is very much of a risk and the lessor could find himself in difficulties. In any event, if the co-lessees are not willing to put themselves out to give their own evidence in person, why should the lessor run that risk?

13 In which case the user clause, the 'no-noise' clause, and the 'pets' clause will all have been breached.

14 Although they are first-hand evidence of the fact that the lessor has received complaints.

15 But only with the court's permission!

16 See County Court Rules 1981, Ord 20, rr 6 and 7.

3 The legislation: the Law of Property Act 1925, s 146 and the Leasehold Property (Repairs) Act 1938

These two statutes were referred to in the review of evidence required by the court in 'non-financial' cases. We now turn back to them to see what relevance they have.

(a) *The Law of Property Act 1925, s 146*

This section is very glibly referred to by the majority of conveyancers; and the number who draft or approve leases containing the usual clause[17] referring to it must be legion. One wonders how many of us really know the clause and how it relates to a leasehold property? It is because of this doubt that the full text of the section is reproduced below, and readers are urged to read it carefully and thoroughly. It has a considerable degree of relevance to the subject in hand.

The section reads as follows:

'146 Restrictions on and relief against forfeiture of leases and underleases

(1) A right of re-entry or forfeiture under any proviso or stipulation in a lease for a breach of any covenant or condition inthe lease shall not be enforceable, by action or otherwise, unless and until the lessor serves on the lessee a notice—

(a) specifying the particular breach complained of; and

(b) if the breach is capable of remedy, requiring the lessee to remedy the breach; and

(c) in any case, requiring the lessee to make compensation in money for the breach; and if the lessee fails, within a reasonable time thereafter, to remedy the breach, if it is capable of remedy, and to make reasonable compensation in money, to the satisfaction of the lessor, for the breach.

(2) Where a lessor is proceeding, by action or otherwise, to enforce such a right of re-entry or forfeiture, the lessee may, in the lessor's action, if any, or in any action brought by himself, apply to the court for relief; and the court may grant or refuse relief as the court, having regard to the proceedings and conduct of the parties under the foregoing provisions of this section, and to all the other circumstances, thinks fit; and in case of relief may grant it on such terms, if any, as to costs, expenses, damages, compensation, penalty, or otherwise, including the granting of an injunction to restrain any like breach in the future, as the court, in the circumstances of each case, thinks fit.

(3) A lessor shall be entitled to recover as a debt due to him from a lessee, and in addition to damages (if any), all reasonable costs and expenses properly incurred by the lessor in the employment of a solicitor and surveyor or valuer, or otherwise, in reference to any breach giving rise to a right of re-entry or forfeiture which, at the request of the lessee, is waived by the lessor, or from which the lessee is relieved, under the provisions of this Act.

(4) Where a lessor is proceeding by action or otherwise to enforce a right of re-entry or forfeiture under any covenant, proviso, or stipulation in a lease or for non-payment of rent, the court may, on application by any person claiming as under-lessee any estate or interest in the property comprised in the lease or any part thereof, either in the lessors action (if any) or in any action brought by such person for that purpose, make an order vesting, for the whole term of the lease or any less term, the property comprised in the lease or any part thereof in any person entitled as under-lessee to

17 For typical examples see Precedent Nos 30 and 31 pp 448, et seq, below.

any estate or interest in such property upon such conditions as to execution of any deed or other document, payment of rent, costs, expenses, damages, compensation, giving security, or otherwise, as the court in the circumstances of each case may think fit, but in no case shall any such underlessee be entitled to require a lease to be granted to him for any longer term than he had under his original sub-lease.

(5) For the purposes of this section—

(a) "Lease" includes an original or derivative under-lease; also an agreement for a lease where the lessee has become entitled to have his lease granted; also a grant at a fee farm rent, or securing a rent by conditions;

(b) "Lessee" includes an original or derivative under-lessee, and the persons deriving title under a lessee; also a grantee under any such grant as aforesaid and the persons deriving title under him;

(c) "Lessor" includes an original or derivative under-lessor, and the persons deriving title under a lessor; also a person making such grant as aforesaid and the person deriving title under him;

(d) "Under-lease" includes an agreement for an underlease where the under-lessee has become entitled to have his underlease granted.

(e) "Under-lessee" includes any person deriving title under an under-lessee.

(6) This section applies although the proviso or stipulation under which the right of re-entry or forfeiture accrues is inserted in the lease in pursuance of the directions of any Act of Parliament.

(7) For the purposes of this section a lease limited to continue as long as the lessee abstains from committing a breach of covenant shall be and take effect as a lease to continue for any longer term for which it could subsist, but determinable by a proviso for re-entry on such a breach.

(8) This section does not extend—

(i) To a covenant or condition against assigning, underletting, parting with the possession, or disposing of the land leased where the breach occurred before the commencement of this Act; or

(ii) In the case of a mining lease, to a covenant or condition for allowing the lessor to have access to or inspect books, accounts, records, weighing machines or other things, or to enter or inspect the mine or the working thereof.

(9) This section does not apply to a condition for forfeiture on the bankruptcy of the lessee or on taking in execution of the lessees interest if contained in a lease of—

(a) agricultural or pastoral land;

(b) mines or minerals;

(c) a house used or intended to be used as a public-house or beer-shop;

(d) a house let as a dwelling-house, with the use of any furniture, books, works of art, or other chattels not being in the nature of fixtures;

(e) any property with respect to which the personal qualifications of the tenant are of importance for the preservation of the value or character of the property, or on the ground of neighbourhood to the lessor, or to any person holding under him.

(10) Where a condition of forfeiture on the bankruptcy of the lessee or on taking in execution of the lessee's interest is contained in any lease, other than a lease of any of the classes mentioned in the last sub-section, then—

(a) if the lessee's interest is sold within one year from the bankruptcy or taking in execution, this section applies to the forfeiture condition aforesaid;

(b) if the lessee's interest is not sold before the expiration of that year, this section only applies to the forfeiture condition aforesaid during the first year from the date of the bankruptcy or taking in execution.

(11) This section does not, save as otherwise mentioned, affect the law relating to re-entry or forfeiture or relief in case of non-payment of rent.

(12) This section has effect notwithstanding any stipulation to the contrary.'

Having set out the section in full, we are able to identify the following points:

1 The section cannot be excluded by any provision in the lease or other ancilliary document.[18]
2 It does not affect cases of non-payment of rent. Thus we saw in our review of the evidence required in both financial and non-financial cases that no notice under the section is required in the former cases, but that such a notice is required in the latter cases.
3 The notice[19] must be served on the lessee as a condition precedent to any forfeiture proceedings being taken; and it must contain all the information set out as being required in the section.[20]
4 In any event, forfeiture is not available to the lessor unless there is incorporated in the lease a forfeiture clause. Typical wording of such a clause is:
'If the rent hereby reserved or any part thereof is unpaid 21 days after becoming payable (whether formally demanded or not) or if any of the covenants on the part of the lessee herein contained are not observed and performed then and in any such case it shall be lawful for the lessor or any person or persons authorised by it in that behalf at any time thereafter to enter the demised premises or any part thereof in the name of the whole and thereupon the term hereby created shall absolutely determine ...' etc.
5 As the section is about forfeiture, as a general rule there is no need to serve a s 146 notice if forfeiture is not sought; thus a claim for damages for breach of covenant or for an injunction restraining breach of covenant would not require service of such a notice, *except* where there is a breach of a repairing covenant, when a s 146 notice must be served not only where forfeiture is the remedy sought but also when the lessor is seeking damages for the breach.[1]
The sequence is accordingly:

(i) *Financial cases*

(i) The lease must contain a forfeiture clause. (A modern lease without such a clause would be a rare animal indeed: nevertheless, anyone who is drafting a lease must consciously remember to incorporate it.);
(ii) proceedings may be taken as soon as the rent is technically outstanding. The courts will construe strictly a forfeiture clause, so that care must be exercised.

(ii) *Non-financial cases*

(i) Again, the lease must contain a forfeiture clause, which not only refers to rent, but to breaches of other covenants;
(ii) a s 146 notice must have been served in the correct form, and the lessee has not taken any remedial action. The section itself does not specify any time limits within which the lessee must respond; but uses the term 'within a reasonable time';[2]

18 Subject to the provisos in the section itself, but for our purposes, this statement is correct.
19 For Precedents, refer to Nos 30 and 31, pp 448 et seq, below.
20 Law of Property Act 1925, s 146(1)(a), (b) and (c).
1 Landlord and Tenant Act 1927, s 18(1).
2 Law of Property Act 1925, s 146(1)(c) and see the provisions of the Leasehold Property (Repairs) Act 1938, below.

(iii) proceedings may then be taken.

(b) *Leasehold Property (Repairs) Act 1938*

The purpose of this Act was to amend the law as to the enforcement by lessors of obligations to repair. Thus, it would have only restricted application to the case of a lessee in default in relation to his covenants; eg it would not apply in 'nuisance' cases and only where there was some dereliction in the manner in which the lessee was looking after the property in accordance with (or more accurately at variation with) the terms of his lease. As lessors will probably have more trouble with lessees making a nuisance of themselves, as opposed to simply not looking after their properties, the Act does not have much significance but readers should be aware of its provisions. First of all, the Act extends to every tenancy, whether a house or any other property—eg presumably a flat[3]—and irrespective of rateable value, *as long as* the following conditions are fulfilled:[4]

(a) that the tenancy was granted for a term of years certain for not less than seven years;
(b) that three years or more of the term remain unexpired at the date of the service of the s 146 notice; and
(c) that the property concerned is not an agricultural holding.

It will be seen that the Act applies to most residential tenancies, and for the purposes of this chapter, we shall assume that any tenancy under discussion is affected by it.

The operative section of the Act is s 1, which is reproduced below in full:

'**1 Restriction on enforcement of repairing covenants in long leases of small houses** (1) Where a lessor serves on a lessee under sub-section (1) of section one hundred and forty-six of the Law of Property Act 1925, a notice that relates to a breach of a covenant or agreement to keep or put in repair during the currency of the lease [all or any of the property comprised in the lease][5] and at the date of the service of the notice [three][5] years or more of the term of the lease remain unexpired, the lessee may within twenty eight days from that date serve on the lessor a counter-notice to the effect that he claims the benefit of this Act.
(2) A right to damages for a breach of such a covenant as aforesaid shall not be enforceable by action commenced at any time at which [three][5] years or more of the term of the lease remain unexpired unless the lessor has served on the lessee not less than one month before the commencement of the action such a notice as is specified in sub-section (1) of section one hundred and forty-six of the Law of Property Act 1925, and where a notice is served under this sub-section, the lessee may, within twenty-eight days from the date of the service thereof, serve on the lessor a counter-notice to the effect that he claims the benefit of this Act.
(3) Where a counter-notice is served by a lessee under this section, then, notwithstanding anything in any enactment or rule of law, no proceedings, by action or otherwise, shall be taken by the lessor for the enforcement of any right of re-entry or forfeiture under any proviso or stipulation in the lease for breach of the covenant or

3 The Act itself uses the expression 'small houses' which is misleading.
4 Landlord and Tenant Act 1954, s 51(1).
5 The words in square brackets were substituted by the Landlord and Tenant Act 1954, s 51(2), (5).

agreement in question, or for damages for breach thereof, otherwise than with the leave of the court.

(4) A notice served under sub-section (1) of section one hundred and forty-six of the Law of Property Act 1925, in the circumstances specified in sub-section (1) of this section, and a notice served under sub-section (2) of this section shall not be valid unless it contains a statement, in characters not less conspicuous than those used in any other part of the notice, to the effect that the lessee is entitled under this Act to serve on the lessor a counter-notice claiming the benefit of this Act, and a statement in the like characters specifying the time within which, and the manner in which, under this Act a counter-notice may be served and specifying the name and address for service of the lessor.

(5) Leave for the purposes of this section shall not be given unless the lessor proves—

(a) that the immediate remedying of the breach in question is requisite for preventing substantial dimunition in the value of his reversion, or that the value thereof has been substantially diminished by the breach;

(b) that the immediate remedying of the breach is required for giving effect in relation to the [premises] to the purposes of any enactment, or of any bye-law or other provision having effect under an enactment, [or for giving effect to any order of a court or requirement of any authority under any enactment or any such bye-law or other provision as aforesaid];

(c) in a case in which the lessee is not in occupation of the whole of the [premises as respects which the covenant or agreement is proposed to be enforced] that the immediate remedying of the breach is required in the interests of the occupier of [those premises] or of part thereof;

(d) that the breach can be immedately remedied at an expense that is relatively small in comparison with the much greater expense that would probably be occasioned by postponement of the necessary work; or

(e) special circumstances which in the opinion of the court, render it just and equitable that leave should be given.

(6) The court may, in granting or refusing leave for the purposes of this section, impose such terms and conditions on the lessor or on the lessee as it may think fit.'

Arising out of this section, the following points should be noted:

1 The Leasehold Property (Repairs) Act 1938 itself is a very short one, comprising only eight sections, and it is only s 1 which is directly relevant to the subject in hand. The other sections deal with interpretation, etc.
2 'The Court' as referred to in the section is the county court, other than exceptional cases.[6]
3 The section will only come into operation if the lessor has served on the lessee a Law of Property Act 1925, s 146 notice.
4 Accordingly, the section will only operate in 'non-financial' cases as described above; as by s 146(11) the law affecting re-entry or forfeiture in the case of non-payment of rent is excluded from the provisions of the 1938 Act.
5 Even within the general framework of 'non-financial' cases, the 1938 Act only applies to cases of failure to maintain. The actual wording of the section is: 'breach of a covenant or agreement to keep or put in repair'

6 Leasehold Property (Repairs) Act 1938, s 6(1).

etc. Obviously the obligation to keep in repair[7] will only apply to what has been demised to the lessee. The 1938 Act does refer to 'small houses', in which cases the obligation to repair would presumably encompass the whole of the property, ie both inside and out. On the other hand, in the case of a lease of a flat in a block where common parts were retained by the lessor or vested in a management company, all the visible parts of the block would be covered by the management scheme, and the only part for which the lessee would be responsible would be the flat itself. As, in the author's experience, lessors do not make a habit of inspecting their lessees' flats, even on an irregular basis, the significance of the 1938 Act to the subject matter of this book is slight. Possibly there might be slightly more significance in the case of a flat leased under the 'Studio' scheme described elsewhere in this book.

C. SUMMARY

It is only possible where such a broad spectrum is covered, to touch here the salient features of this subject, which is only in part a conveyancing matter. For further assistance, readers will no doubt turn to their litigation colleagues. We have reviewed the circumstances surrounding and leading up to the lessor's decision to take action against his lessee; we have set out the evidence which should be presented to the court, and the mode by which it should be delivered, and finally appropriate precedents are offered.[8] The author has already indicated that if the lessor does have to go to court, he is probably already on the way to failure. Litigation of this sort is better suited to commercial leaseholds, as opposed to residential ones, and the lessor should strive to avoid it.

7 'Put in' repair is not relevant to a normal leasehold flat situation, and in any event s 3 of the 1938 Act excludes from the operation of the Act an obligation to put premises in repair that is to be performed upon the lessee taking possession.

8 See Precedent Nos 28 to 32 pp 446–453, below.

CHAPTER 28

The future: the Law Commission's proposals

No textbook on the sale and management of flats would be complete without reference being made, in some way, to the Law Commission's proposals on possible changes to the law of positive and restrictive covenants. Indeed, should the 'Land Obligations Bill', as it is called, eventually pass on to the statute book, there may have to be a considerable change of approach to the sale of flats by conveyancers. In order to understand the reason why the Law Commission have promoted these proposed changes in the law relating to both positive and restrictive covenants, it will be necessary to consider briefly some of the background.

Although it is possible for a flat to be sold on a freehold basis,[1] traditionally flats and maisonettes have been sold on a leasehold basis. Nevertheless it is not because it is impossible to create a freehold flat that such a creature will be rare; the reason lies elsewhere, in the present state of the law of positive and restrictive covenants.

A flat, and the relationship between the lessor and lessee, will call for much more in the way of a covenantor/covenantee relationship, whichever way it lies, than will the relationship between a vendor and purchaser of a house. While it is true that in a number of transfers there will be various covenants, it would be nevertheless quite possible (if unlikely) to sell a whole estate of individual houses without the need to impose a covenant of any sort.

On the other hand, a block of flats will automatically demand a closer relationship between the vendor and various purchasers, simply because the individual flats are sharing the same basic shell, are in much closer proximity to each other than houses, and thus require some regulatory documentation, without which confusion will arise.

In view of this regulatory need, which will be interpreted as covenants in the various documents of transmission between the common vendor and the separate purchasers, the method of selling to be used must ensure that whoever is the landlord for the time being is able to enforce covenants against whoever are the tenants for the time being, and vice versa.

As there are only two basic estates in land under English law, the first proposition is quite simple—either freehold ot leasehold may be used on the creation of flats.

From this point, we pass on to the consideration as to how these two different systems of conveyancing cope with the creation and maintenance of the covenants necessary for the proper management of a block of flats. This leads us on to the second proposition, which is that a convenant will

1 See, eg ch 3, pp 13 et seq, above.

either be positive or restrictive in nature. We can now look at the way in which covenants, both positive and restrictive, are dealt with in freehold and leasehold conveyancing.

A. FREEHOLD

The position of covenants differs according to consideration of the benefit and burden thereof, at law and in equity.

(a) (i) At law, the burden of a covenant will not run with the land;
(ii) the benefit of a covenant will run with land providing the covenant has been entered into for the benefit of, or, as it is sometimes expressed, 'touching and concerning' land belonging to the person with whom the covenant is being made (ie the covenantee), and further the covenantee has to have had a legal estate in the land concerned.

(b) The position in equity is less simple. The first point to take careful note of is that the rules of equity apply only if the covenant is restrictive, not positive. The second point is that the rules have their parenthood in the case of *Tulk v Moxhay*[2] which is a case most of us will remember from our days at law school.
The doctrine of *Tulk v Moxhay* can be summarised as follows:
1 For the burden of a covenant to run;
(i) the covenant must have been for the benefit of, or 'touching and concerning' the land of the covenantee;
(ii) the covenant must have been intended to be a continuing burden on the land of the covenantor, that is the covenant will 'run with' the land in question;
(iii) a bona fide purchaser of a legal estate without notice of the covenant will not be bound by it. Therefore if the title is registered, the covenant will be of no effect if not protected by an entry on the register; if unregistered, the protection must be by means of registration under the Land Charges Act 1925;
(iv) the covenant must be restrictive, and not positive. Incidentally, it is the *substance* of the covenant, and not its wording, which will determine whether or not it is restrictive—a positive covenant can be complied with by taking some action; a restrictive one is complied with by *not* taking any action—nevertheless it is possible to have a positive covenant which begins with the words 'not to'—eg 'not to allow a wall to fall into disrepair'.
2 For the benefit of a covenant to run:
(i) the covenant must 'touch and concern' the land of the covenantee;
(ii) the owner of the land taking the benefit of the covenant must show either that;
(a) the benefit has become annexed to the land in question.

2 [1848] 2 Ph 774.

Some difficulty arises here because the wording of the covenant purporting to annex the benefit may not always be effective, or

(b) the benefit has been assigned to him. If this is to be relied upon, the requirements are that:

1 he who is seeking enforcement must own the land in question,

2 there must be a formal assignment, or at worst some agreement that the benefit of the covenant will pass, and

3 the assignment and the transfer of the land must both be part of the same transaction, or

(c) the benefit has passed under a building scheme.

This book is not the appropriate vehicle in which to launch into a detailed study of the three choices open to the owner of the land and set out above; particularly the consideration of building schemes, including the leading case of *Elliston v Reacher*[3] and for those readers wishing to look further into the background, a suitable textbook should be consulted.

It should already have been noted carefully that the *burden* of positive covenants will not run with land. Equity will only deal with restrictive covenants, and the position in law is that the burden of a covenant does not run with the land in any circumstances. This, therefore, is a serious deficiency in the way that English land law treats covenants, especially having regard to the inescapable fact that in any document regulating the position between a developer and his purchaser there will almost inevitably be a number of positive covenants, and, if the law dealt with such covenants in a more satisfactory manner, there might be many more. We speak here of *freehold*, not *leasehold*, sales: we shall be studying the treatment of covenants in leasehold situations shortly.

How, then, does English law cope with positive covenants the burden of which prima facie does not pass with the land concerned?

There are various ways. The Law Commission themselves, in their publication *Transfer of Land—the Law of Positive and Restrictive Covenants*'[4] float the ideas of using estate rent charges, rights of re-entry, enlargement of long leases, and the doctrine in the case of *Halsall v Brizell*,[5] but these, with all due respect to the Law Commission, are theoreticians' devices, and not those which would normally be considered by the average High Street conveyancer.

The method which will be best understood by the average conveyancer is the chain of indemnity covenants. This in itself is not totally satisfactory but it is the best that can be devised in the circumstances.

It is usual for the covenantor to make the covenant on his own behalf and also on behalf of succeeding owners of the land in question, and this in any event is provided for by statute.[6] The general effect on a transfer of land the subject of any such covenant will be that the vendor will remain liable even

3 [1908] 2 Ch 374 at 384.
4 HMSO Law Com No 127, 26 January 1984.
5 [1957] Ch 169.
6 Law of Property Act 1925, s 79.

although he has divested himself of the land. Yet he will be powerless to control his successors in title; accordingly, he may at a later date become unwittingly in breach of the covenant. He will normally protect himself by taking a covenant from his purchaser that he will be indemnified against any liability he may suffer as a result of any breaches, etc of the covenant.

This leads to the rather strange situation that whoever owns the land which has the benefit of the covenant will only be able to take action against the original covenantor, and assuming he has disposed of the land carrying the burden of the covenant, he will have to seek protection under his indemnity from *his* purchaser, and so on down the line. It does not take a conveyancing tyro to work out that there is every likelihood of the chain breaking down, due to the death, disappearance, or bankruptcy of someone in the chain. The chain of indemnities is accordingly a potentially weak one and is hardly a satisfactory answer.

The above represents the position as related to freehold conveyancing. Does the law treat leasehold conveyancing in any different manner?

The answer is that it does, because of the doctrine of privity of estate.

B. LEASEHOLD

Covenants in a lease will be entered into on behalf of successors in title as well as the actual covenantor. It is unimportant that this may not be specifically expressed in the document in question, because the Law of Property Act 1925, s 79 implies it anyway. Therefore, at any given time the covenantor, that is the original lessor or lessee which ever way the covenant in question is expressed, will be liable to the lessee or lessor *for the time being*, as the benefit of the covenants will have passed down the line. This is the doctrine of privity of contract in operation.

But there is the additional doctrine of *privity of estate*, which in this context means that the individual who for the time being is the lessor and the individual who for the time being is the lessee can enforce the covenants in the lease *as between each other*, and so there is no need for the chain of indemnity covenants which one sees in a freehold transfer. Although it must be said that they will still be found in assignments, presumably on the principle of playing it safe. Incidentally, the doctrine of privity of estate is not, as might generally be thought, a creature of equity; rather of statute law.[7]

The position on freehold and leasehold sales is accordingly quite different, and prima facie there would seem to be no point in altering the law of covenants as related to leaseholds. Nevertheless, the rules discussed apply only to leaseholds so long as there is privity of *estate*, and accordingly once a derivative interest, which may be a subletting or eg a mortgage, is created, the doctrine falls by the wayside, because there will be no privity of estate, and then the freehold rules set out above take over, with all their imperfections.

Having set the scene by describing in brief detail the state of the present law as applied to restrictive and positive covenants related to freehold and

7 The present legislation is the Law of Property Act 1925, ss 141 and 142.

leasehold estates, we must go on very quickly to say that the Law Commission in their Report are not concerned solely with the operation of leasehold schemes for flats as we are in this book. But that is the whole point: because in a freehold estate positive covenants do not run with the burdened land, and because in a situation where a block of flats is being sold there is a need for positive covenants, freehold conveyancing as applied to the sale of flats is virtually a dead letter.

There seems to be an accepted school of thought which is widespread amongst conveyancers that because one is dealing with a block of flats then one must use leasehold conveyancing instead of freehold, and that freehold and flats are like oil and water. *This is not the case*: flats are almost exclusively sold on a leasehold basis because that is the only safe way in which the burden of covenants can be made to run. (We shall ignore here the problem of derivative interests which we mentioned above.)

The reader is also invited to consider the commonly held belief that in order to have a freehold estate, part at least of the property concerned has physically to touch the soil. Again, this is not so. The Law Commission themselves point out the strange situation, which can occur with a block of freehold flats—that as a freehold estate is 'for ever', a situation may arise where the block of flats has ceased to exist, eg it will have been demolished, yet someone will have a freehold interest in flats on floors above the ground floor. So that the freehold estate merely exists in airspace. Nevertheless, the concept seems to be accepted by a majority of theoreticians and in fact leasehold flats are not totally free from this blight.

Accordingly, flats are not sold on a freehold basis, not because it is an impossible concept, but because there are too many technical conveyancing defects. The Law Commission's proposals encompass every conceivable situation where covenants are imposed, so that the most common area where any change in the law relating to positive and restrictive covenants would be felt would be freehold residential estate development conveyancing, but flats would also be affected, *if* conveyancers chose to switch from using leasehold to working with freehold. Whether this would actually take place is quite a different matter—conveyancers are such conservative creatures that it might well take a very long time, or indeed never, before freehold flat developments started to become the norm.

What might be the catalyst for the movement towards freehold flat conveyancing is the attitude of mortgagees, particularly the building society movement in the shape of the Building Societies Association (BSA). This body has been considering the various problems associated with leasehold flats for some considerable time, and has expressed concern over the shrinking term of years. For instance, if flats are sold on a 99-year basis they will be down to the 60 years unexpired stage very quickly, and it is at this stage that the BSA feels its member's security, if lending on such a unit, is beginning to be seriously prejudiced. One supposes the answer is that terms should be 999 years instead of 99 years, and if it is 999 years then there is no practical difference between that and freehold, except possibly a ground rental income (and it is open to the developer to adjust his prices slightly to compensate for its loss on a freehold sale).

Unfortunately, it is open to the lessor/developer to be at all times the sole arbiter of the length of term offered, and it can only be assumed that the choice of a 99-year term as opposed to one of 999 years points to the developer having an eye on the term falling in during the at least reasonably foreseeable future, rather than so far into the unforeseeable future as to be no worse than freehold.

The use of freehold conveyancing for flats would change all this, of course; and this is why the Law Commission's proposals are relevant to the subject matter of the book.

C. WHAT IS IT THEN THAT THE LAW COMMISSION IS PROPOSING?

First of all, leasehold law in its present form will stay as it is. There are no proposals to change this at all. Accordingly, those conveyancers and/or developers who wish to continue to use leasehold as a basis for their flat developments may do so. There seems little doubt that a good proportion of new flat developments will continue to be sold on a leasehold basis, and that it will take some time for the concept of the freehold flat to be accepted; that is, the freehold flat making use of the new land, or development obligations which we shall now discuss.

Before we do so, however, we should first mention that the Law Commission did consider the possibility of reforming the law of positive covenants, as an isolated case, and so as to leave the law of covenants strictly as it is at present, subject only to this change. For various reasons, the Law Commission rejected this approach.

Instead, the Commission are promoting a comprehensive reform based on the new concept of the 'land obligation', which itself comprises two classes which we shall study shortly: the 'neighbour obligation' and the 'development obligation'.

The interesting aspect of this reform is that it dispenses with the historical development and basis of the law of covenants[8] since this basis is thought to be incomplete and illogical, and replaces it with the general structure analgous to the existing law of easements, which depends upon there being both a dominant and servient tenement, or as the Commission put it, dominant and servient land. It is perhaps a pity that the rather archaic words 'dominant' and 'servient' have been chosen; more modern language might have been appropriate to the present requirement of the legal profession to display forward-looking thinking to the public at large.

The basic reasoning behind this new concept is put forward by the Commission as follows:

(a) the replacement for the covenant, whether positive or restrictive is to be called a 'land obligation'.[9] It is called thus because:
    (i) the thing in question is indeed an obligation; and
    (ii) it will only be capable of subsisting for the benefit of, and as a burden on, land;

8 Ie restrictive covenants.
9 This is the generic term, which is subdivided: see p 316, below.

(b) the land obligation will only be created expressly, and never by implication, so that the parties who are intending to create such a thing will be required to actually call it a land obligation;

(c) because it will be an obligation on *land*, and not on *individuals*, it will only be enforceable by and against the *current* owners of the land involved. Once an owner of land has disposed of it, he says goodbye to the land obligation. It is to be supposed that this will ring the death-knell of the indemnity covenant (although no doubt there will be those conveyancers who will persist in using it);

(d) it is proposed that land obligations should be registrable under the Land Charges Act 1972 and the Land Registration Act 1925. In this respect, at least, land obligations will differ from easements, on which they are to some extent modelled;

(e) where a developer is undertaking a multiple unit development, he will execute a deed wherein will be contained his 'development scheme'. The development obligation will be a special class of land obligation designed for use in property developments. The one requires the other: if a development scheme is made, there must be consequent development obligations. Equally there can be no development obligations without a development scheme preceding them;

(f) the institution of the development scheme may lead to the establishment of a manager of the development. The manager will have rights and duties vis-à-vis the unit-owners. So may the developer.

This, then, is a general introduction to the proposals of the Law Commission. We have looked briefly at the background of the present law of positive and restrictive covenants, and what is wrong with it. We have seen that the position as related to leasehold law is satisfactory, and will not change, and we have sketched out the principles of the land obligation.

The author readily admits that this present chapter is longer than was originally intended. But then the whole book is about the creation and sale of flats, and the basic method of setting up a flat development has to be the central core around which the rest of the book is built. Hitherto, leasehold law has been the accepted vehicle for conveying flats. Henceforward the prospect of the introduction of a Land Obligation Act may mean that the freehold flat becomes the accepted standard. Thus it becomes important that readers fully understand the nature and application of the concept of the land obligation.

From this point on, we will concentrate on the development obligation and its application to the setting up of a flat scheme. We must pass over the concept of the 'neighbour obligation' and all the consequential matters relating to it. Nevertheless, readers would be well advised to familiarise themselves completely with the whole subject, and they will not do better than read initially the Law Commission's own publications on the Bill.[10] The Commission write clearly and with sympathy for the reader, and are to be congratulated.

10 See note 4, p 311, above.

1 The land obligation

(a) The Bill proposes that the present law of positive and restrictive covenants is replaced by a new interest in land called a 'land obligation'.
(b) Present legislation will be amended so as to accommodate the principle of the land obligation as an interest in land, eg 'land obligations' will be inserted in the Law of Property Act 1925, s 1 (2) (a) so as to provide for a land obligation to be a legal interest provided it is 'equivalent to an estate in fee simple absolute in possession or a term of years absolute'. A land obligation which does not satisfy these requirements but is otherwise validly created will subsist as an equitable interest.
(c) Therefore a land obligation may be either a legal or an equitable interest in land.
(d) Generally, the correct analogy for the background structure of a land obligation will be that presently attaching to easements; nevertheless, the analogy is not complete and the new concept is more of a hybrid one.

2 Development obligations

(a) These will be a particular variety of land obligation, and are designed for use in multiple unit developments. They can be either of houses or of flats. Interestingly enough, the Law Commission themselves say that flats are specifically contemplated as 'land' extends upwards as well as sideways. Presumably this means that the early concept of an upper floor freehold flat, where the fabric may disappear leaving just air-space, is confirmed.
(b) In such cases of subdivision of land, either horizontally or indeed vertically, into separate units, the development obligation may be imposed on the unit which, carrying on the analogy of easement, becomes the servient land.
(c) From the point of view of the unit-owner, the development obligation does not differ substantially from the neighbour obligation. The difference comes in the other direction, ie as viewed mainly from the stance of the developer. These differences may be summarised under two heads:

(a) *The benefit*

Whereas a neighbour obligation will have the easement equivalent of servient and dominant land, with a development obligation there will be, on the one hand, the servient land (the unit itself), but the dominant land is not present and is replaced by what the Law Commission refer to as 'development land'. This title has been chosen carefully so as to point to the obvious fact that what is being dealt with is a development of *individual units*; and the development obligation is thus to be enforceable, not only by owners of other portions of servient land (ie the unit-owners) but also by a 'manager' who would be acting on behalf of all these owners. We shall explore this concept later.

(b) *The scope*

This is wider than that relating to neighbour obligations. The Law Commission give as the definitive list of development obligations the following:

(i) Restrictive

(i) An obligation imposing a restriction which benefits the whole or part of the development land on the doing of some act on the servient land, or any other part of the development land.

(ii) Positive

(i) An obligation requiring the carrying out on the servient land or any other part of the development land of works which benefit the whole of any part of the development land.

(ii) An obligation requiring the provision of services for the benefit of the whole of any part of the development land.

(iii) An obligation requiring the servient land to be used in a particular way which benefits the whole or part of the development land.

(iii) Reciprocal payment

(i) An obligation requiring the making of payments in a specified manner (whether to a person of specified description or otherwise) on account of expenditure which has been or is to be incurred by a person in complying with an obligation of type positive (i) or (ii) above.

(iv) Re-imbursement

(i) An obligation requiring the making of payments to the manager of a development scheme in respect of expenditure incurred or to be incurred in the provision of works or services provided by him in pursuance of the scheme.

(ii) An obligation requiring the making of payments to the manager of the development scheme by way of contribution towards fees, costs or expenses charged or incurred by him in discharging his functions under the scheme, which costs and expenses may include costs and expenses incurred in accordance with the scheme in connection with any application (whether made by the manager or another) to the court of the Lands Tribunal under any provision of this Act.

(v) Access

(i) An obligation requiring access to the servient land to be afforded, in such circumstances and for such purposes as may be specified, to the manager, to any servant or agent of his or to any other person authorised in writing by him.[11]

There are further supplementary provisions which are dealt with by the same Schedule (I) of the Bill which sets out the definitive list of obligations capable of subsisting as development obligations set out above. That list is contained in Part II.[12] The supplementary list is in Part III, and may be summarised as follows:

(*i*) *Information.* The right to information or to production of documents. The two examples given by the Law Commission are respectively as to the current

11 See Land Obligations Bill, Sch I, Part II.
12 Part I is the list of neighbour obligations.

ownership of the servient land and documentation dealing with transmission of ownership.

(*ii*) *Inspection.* The right of persons who may be entitled to enforce a land obligation to view the servient land to see if it has been complied with.

(*iii*) *Self-help.* The right of persons having the right to enforce a land obligation to enter servient land and carry out themselves any works the performance of which is the subject of the obligation, where those works have not been performed.

(*iv*) *Sinking fund.* Provision can be made for the setting up of such a fund, to provide for the carrying out of works or provision of services.

(*v*) *Interest.* If any payments due under the development scheme fail to be made, interest may be charged on the unpaid amounts.

(*vi*) *Charges.* There is provision for the placing on the servient land of a charge, where monies due remain unpaid.

3 The development scheme

Having reviewed the background of the Bill, and taken a brief look at land obligations and development obligations, we must now turn to a short study of the control theme, insofar as the subject matter of this book is concerned, that is, the development scheme itself.

This will apply to flats and ordinary houses equally—the Law Commission themselves say[13] that a block of flats is an area of land for the purpose of a development scheme—so that when the term 'development land', or indeed any reference to land, is used in this chapter it is in contemplation of blocks of flats being included therein.

The stated aim of the Law Commission is to introduce greater flexibility into the development world, from the point of view of the lawyer, developer, and the purchaser of units. This is important, from which it follows that no element of vagueness must creep in, and accordingly there are stated ground rules. These are as follows:

(a) *Development deed*

This title seems a little cumbersome; whether any more pithy title will be evolved remains to be seen. In order for there to be a development scheme, such a deed must be executed. This deed must:

(a) state that it creates a development scheme;
(b) identify the development land, whether by reference to a plan or otherwise, but sufficiently precisely so as to make it clear as to what land is having the development obligations imposed on it;

13 Law Commission's Report (Law Com No 127) 7; 10, p 45.

Apparently the development land may be in separate pieces *provided* that they are reasonably accessible to each other. The official wording seems to be that the different pieces of land, if there are such, must 'lie in the same locality'. This seems to mean that, eg two blocks of flats on either side of an estate road or even perhaps in different parts of the *same* estate development would be treated as capable of being dealt with under one development scheme, but two blocks, one each on different estates, even if fairly close to each other, would not be;

(c) be executed by its makers. This is where we arrive at an interesting facet of the development scheme as opposed to the traditional leasehold flat development. According to the Law Commission, *anyone* can execute a development deed. These are the words used in the Commission's Report[14] but if the relevant paragraphs are read carefully, it will be seen that in practice it will only be those who are directly involved in the development who will execute the deed, except in some special circumstances. In the Commission's words,[15] 'In practice, of course, schemes will not be made except by someone who is closely connected with the land or who intends to develop it or to control its development. But the legal arrangements for development may be complicated, involving options, contracts, associated companies and so on, and it would add great complexity to the draft bill if it sought to list all those who might, at any given moment, have a legitimate reason to make a development scheme'; and

(d) make provision for development obligations. A development scheme will be called for where land is to be divided into two or more units. The scheme itself must make adequate provision for the development obligations which are to be instituted to be imposed on that land. Whether or not the development deed itself will contain the fine detail of the development obligations seems to be a matter of some conjecture at the present time, at least on the part of the Law Commission. They give as one example a scheme which actually sets out, word for word, the development obligations which are to be imposed on all the units in the scheme, so that the subsequent[16] transfers (assuming the land to be registered) would be able to refer to the development scheme contained in the development deed, and thus be moderately concise. On the other hand, the example is also given of a scheme where the development deed is executed before the full details of the development obligations are known. Here, the obligations would be set out in full in the transfers, and the development deed itself would merely refer to the concept of the obligations. As we saw above, the development deed will be executed by its makers, who will be in virtually all cases the developer and/or the manager. The development deed will be executed in nearly all cases before any purchasers are found for the units (or that is what should happen). Therefore no unit-purchasers will be parties to the development

14 Law Commissions Report (Law Com No 127) 7; 12, p 46.

15 Ibid, 7; 14, p 46.

16 The documents transmitting the legal interest will obviously *follow* the development deed itself.

deed, and so care should be taken to note that whilst the development deed will *make provision* for the obligations, it will *not* actually *impose* them. This will be done by the transfers of the units themselves. Not all units will necessarily have the same, or indeed any, development obligations imposed on them. This will depend on the circumstances of the development.

(b) *Management*

The development scheme may, or may not, provide for a manager of the scheme.

The option is obviously necessary, because not all flat/maisonette developments call for management. Consider the case of a block of maisonettes, which under the present state of the law would almost certainly be sold on a leasehold basis, whereas assuming the Bill passes on to the Statute book, would be sold on a freehold basis. No management would be required on the present basis, so why should it under the new system? And yet the block would call for a development scheme, because of the multiplicity of units.

The scheme itself may either appoint some person, company, etc to be the manager, or it could set up the means of appointing one, leaving identification until later.

The manager will obviously have to have fairly wide powers, duties, etc: thus

(i) classes of obligations such as reimbursement obligations and access obligations[17] deal with the making of payments to the manager, and the exercise of certain rights by him;
(ii) he will have the right to enforce the obligations in general.

The enforcement of such obligations, and exercise of rights, will automatically be vested in the manager by the provisions of the Bill, despite the manager not having any legal interest whatsoever in the development, unless the development scheme excludes these provisions.

The Bill also provides for the manager to have imposed on him certain obligations. This is obviously necessary, because the owners of the units will wish to have vested in them the right to make the manager perform his functions. Otherwise the setting-up of a development scheme would be toothless so far as the unit-owners were concerned. However, the difference between the obligations imposed on the unit-owners and those imposed on the manager will be that the former will be development obligations, whereas the latter will not because a development obligation is basically a land obligation and the manager has no interest in the land.

Equally, where a manager has the automatic right to enforce development obligations, the unit-owners will not have any automatic right to enforce the 'managers obligations', unless the scheme expressly provides for this—and surely if the draftsman sets out in some detail what management functions the manager is to perform, he will provide at the same time for the enforcement of the same against the manager by the unit-owners?

17 See p 317, above.

In the same way that the manager may expressly assume obligations, the scheme makers themselves may assume them as well. Again, they will not be land obligations. Examples given by the Commission of this type of obligation are those imposing on a developer obligations to make up estate roads and lay out communal areas, and those imposing on the developer the duty of ensuring that the units actually have imposed on them the obligations which the scheme provides for. This is analogous to the covenant on the part of the developer in a lease to impose similar covenants in the leases of other units.

(c) *Enforceability of obligations*

There is to be some choice available to those setting up development schemes as to how the obligations are to be enforced. The rules may be summarised as follows:

(*i*) *Development obligations*

(a) A manager will automatically have the right to enforce these unless the scheme expressly provides to the contrary.
(b) Where the manager has the right of enforcement, no one else can enforce the obligation again unless the scheme expressly provides to the contrary; this proviso can only be used for restrictive and positive obligations and not for re-imbursement and access obligations because it would be inappropriate to have them available for enforcement by anyone other than the manager.
(c) Where the obligation is not enforceable by the manager it will be enforceable for the benefit of the land as a whole *unless* express provision is made that it is to be enforceable for the benefit of a specified part.

(*ii*) *Manager's and maker's obligations*

(a) Manager's and maker's obligations are both enforceable by the unit owners at any given time.
(b) Maker's obligations will also be enforceable by the manager if there is one.

(d) *Registration*

The Law Commission are proposing that development obligations be registered with HM Land Registry, in the case of registered land, and with HM Land Charges Registry, in the case of unregistered land.

The basic rules proposed are as follows:

(*i*) *Registered land*

(i) The burden of an obligation will be noted on the title of the servient land.
(ii) The benefit of an obligation enforceable only by a manager is incapable of registration because (as we have seen) the manager will probably

have no interest in the land and so there is no land to which the obligation is appurtenant.

(iii) For those obligations which are enforceable by some or all of the owners of other units in the development, the recommendation of the Commission is that there is no way in which the benefit of those obligations can be noted on the titles of all the other units in the same development. The Commission quote a fascinating example as an illustration as to why this would be logistically impossible. The example is of an estate of 200 units, where the first one to be sold cannot have an entry made of its benefits on the title of any other unit in the development, quite simply because at that stage none of the other 199 would have been sold. But as they are sold, theoretically the notes of No 1's benefit would be made on the titles of all subsequent 199 units. The same would apply to every single one of the remaining 199, although depending on when they were sold, there would be more or less previous titles already available for the notice to be entered, at the time of sale. The logistics of the matter are obviously impossible. Therefore the Commission recommend that there would be no obligation to register the benefit.

(*ii*) *Unregistered land* The Commission propose that a land obligation should be added to the list of registrable matters under Class C. The same rules as apply to enforceability of land charges would accordingly apply to a land obligation.

Before we close this chapter, there are two further matters which readers may wish to have drawn to their attention.

D. EXISTING FREEHOLD FLAT SCHEMES

We have briefly studied elsewhere in this book the possibility of selling a block of flats on a freehold basis. Although technically possible, the practice is rarely used, if only because the building societies are not, nor have they ever been, too keen on the concept. Nevertheless, there are some freehold flat schemes around, but because (as we have seen earlier) many of the obligations which are necessary for inclusion in a flats development are of a positive nature, and under present law the burden of positive covenants does not automatically run with freehold land, existing freehold flats can be difficult to sell.

It is the building societies and other lending institutions who have been responsible for this state of affairs (quite innocently one must add) because they have generally been uneasy about any of the devices which have been devised to get around the problem.[18] Therefore, we have, on the one hand, flat-owners who may be having difficulty in selling their property, and, on the other hand, prospective purchasers who find difficulty in financing their purchases.

The Bill as published would afford to all flat-owners in any particular freehold block the opportunity of setting up a development scheme, and then

18 Eg chains of indemnity covenants, etc.

in pursuance thereof the entering into development obligations. But this course of action presupposes a consensus of the part on *all* unit-owners, and this, for various reasons, is not always possible.

The Commission therefore propose a scheme which would be operable without the necessity of obtaining the specific approval of *everyone* concerned, whilst at the same time involving those who do not specifically approve in no risk of being placed in an unfair position.

This scheme will involve one or more of the unit-owners developing a scheme which may then be put forward to the court for approval.[19] The court must be satisfied:

(a) that the block concerned is a bona fide block of flats or maisonettes;
(b) that the principal object of the scheme is to correct some defect in the existing scheme affecting the block. There would be several examples of this type of defect, but the most obvious one would be the difficulty in selling units because of problems over enforceability of covenants, as previously discussed;
(c) that the object of the scheme is impossible without the involvement of those parties who are for one reason or another not in active agreement with those promoting the scheme;
(d) that if there are any prejudicial aspects of the scheme, insofar as those parties are concerned, they are outweighed by the benefits which will accrue to them.
(e) finally, that the scheme is a reasonable one in all the circumstances.

Use of this device, if successful before the court, will transform what may be a present-day albatross around the necks of the individual flat-owners, into a freehold block utilising the modern concept of development obligations. It remains to be seen how many such applications come before the courts, given the presumably high cost of bringing them. Perhaps if the block were reasonably old, as in all the circumstances it might well be, selling flats on a freehold basis is a practice that was used more in years past than presently—and if the majority of the unit-owners had low mortgages, they could re-mortgage to a limited extent in order to provide the capital to run such an application.[20]

E. MODEL FORMS

One of the most interesting questions which a study of the Bill prompts is, 'what about the precedents for the development deed and the transfers/ conveyances?'

The development deed will obviously be a newcomer to the ranks of conveyancing precedents, and the appropriate parts of the transfers dealing with the development obligations themselves will be new and untested. There

19 Ie the High Court, not the Lands Tribunal.

20 But the reason for their application would presumably be to convert unmortgageable properties into mortgageable ones? How could they mortgage before the application to the court was heard?

seems to be no general background of experience to call upon in order to assist in the drafting of such documents.

The Law Commission have accordingly proposed the use of model forms, to be prepared and published by the Lord Chancellor's Department. This is obviously sensible, otherwise each development could end up with a substantially different type of documentation from another, none of which would owe anything to any preceding documentation quite simply because there was none. Nevertheless, the Commission are not proposing that the use of the forms should be compulsory, so that on the basis that there will always be draftsmen who would want to produce their own version, we might eventually see the promulgated official model form only partially in use, with some developments using practitioners' own forms. There seem then to be fairly overpowering reasons why the official model forms should be the only ones in use. This course would offer uniformity throughout the country, which would surely be helpful to vendors' and purchasers' practitioners, and the courts. Further, uniformity would obviously tend to reduce costs to the public, whereas the avid draftsmen may inadvertently penalise their clients because of extra, not less, time spent on the documentation itself. There would also be obvious advantages to organisations such as HM Land Registry and also, of course, not least to the lending institutions.

The foregoing is of necessity a condensed version of the proposals incorporated in the Bill, but it is to be hoped that readers will find it useful. What has to be remembered is that the use of the freehold/development obligation method of selling flats is not necessarily going to sweep the board. The present leasehold system of selling flats will still continue, and it may well be that for some time to come it will constitute the great majority of flat development, given the innate conservatism of the English conveyancer, and his client.

However, the building societies may at the end of the day be the deciding factor, in that they have for some time past been uneasy about leaseholds generally, and will undoubtedly favour this new method if it is introduced in preference to their own choice, as described in the next chapter. It will give them the security of a freehold estate, as opposed to an inexorably diminishing term.

For those conveyancers who have constant dealings with flats developments, whether acting for lessor, lessee, or on a subsequent assignment, the future looks decidedly interesting.

CHAPTER 29

The future: the Building Societies Association's proposals

Having looked at the Law Commission's proposals on radical changes in the law relating to positive and negative covenants, thus affecting flat conveyancing, we now turn to the proposals of the Building Societies Association (BSA). These latter proposals are contained in the BSA's own publication, *Leaseholds—Time for a Change?* published in July 1984.

In specifying leaseholds generally, the BSA are referring to houses as well as flats, but the problems are, if anything, more acute on flats. Accordingly we will from this point on assume that the subject matter is flats, and no other form of housing.

After discussing the problems of enforcement of positive covenants on freehold dispositions, and identifying the subsequent use of the long leasehold as the only feasible practical method by which flats can be sold, the Report goes on to consider the special problems of leaseholds, as follows:

(a) the 'depreciating asset' problem where as time passes the term of the leasehold inexorably shortens until that very shortness has an adverse effect on the value of the property and indeed begins to represent a blight on it so far as saleability is concerned;
(b) according to the BSA, many leaseholders in blocks of flats regard themselves as no more than tenants/occupiers. This is obviously a psychological attitude which may be more prevalent in some areas than in others;
(c) even given the fact that in the landlord/tenant or, as we prefer to express it in this book, lessor/lessee relationship, positive as well as restrictive covenants are enforceable, the position and attitude of the lessor/manager is crucial, and if it is poor, then the lessees will suffer accordingly; and
(d) management is a difficulty, especially on tenants' own companies, ie tenants' management companies.

A. SHORT-TERM REFORM

The BSA considered both short-term and long-term reform. From our point of view, the latter is the more important, but we should look briefly at the short-term proposals so that we have before us the comprehensive proposals of the BSA. The basis of assessment was an examination of the various problems to see if they could be removed or improved without the basic need of replacing the present system. The following list represents suggestions that have been put forward as possible solutions.

(a) conversion of leasehold flats into freehold ones. The BSA comments that this would depend on the acceptability of any proposed new freehold system and its suitability for multiple unit developments;[1]

(b) standardisation of leases. How much this would help is questionable: after all, a proposal for standard leases was brought in as long ago as the Leases Act 1845—this hardly set the legal world on fire then and probably would have the same fate today;[2]

(c) extension of leases to something of the order of 999 years which would solve the depreciating asset problem but little else;

(d) there have been a number of Private members' Bills which attempted to deal with the problem:

(i) Lord Evan's Leasehold Reform Bill, which dealt with proposed modifications to the Leasehold Reform Act 1967, and related to houses only;

(ii) Mr John Fraser MP's Leasehold Flats Enfranchisement Bill, which proposed giving a right of extension of leases of up to 50 years. It also proposed a Commission to formulate procedures enabling lessees to acquire the reversionary interest in the block, or take over the management;

(iii) Sir Brandon Rhys Williams MP's Co-ownership of Flats Bill. This dealt with possible purchases by flat owners of their lessors interest at fair valuation.

None of these Bills progressed very far, although the understanding is that they may not have been abandoned altogether.

The BSA considered all these proposals, and offered various comments of their own. However, they concluded this part of their report with the words 'The Group puts the above suggestions forward but does so without enthusiasm and only as, in its view, a very poor second best and possibly temporary alternative to a complete revision of the present system'.[3]

B. LONG-TERM REFORM

As we have seen, the BSA considers that nothing short of basic change is desirable, and any short-term proposals are very little better than useless.

C. THE LAW COMMISSION'S PROPOSALS

These have already been set out in full in the previous section, so we do not need to reiterate them. What we should do is reproduce some of the comments of the BSA Report about the Law Commission's proposals. Whilst acknowledging the very good work done by the Commission in this field, the

1 But see also the Law Commission's proposals on freehold flats as described in the previous chapter.

2 Although there are moves in the housebuilding industry to settle standard forms of conveyance, transfer, lease etc, which would hopefully be used by as many housebuilders as possible.

3 BSA Report, p 8, para 13 (d).

BSA felt that their proposals were not radical enough. The following are extracts from the BSA's Report:

1 'The Association's conclusion ... although the concept of marketable freehold flats was a step in the right direction, the Commissions scheme leaves too much to chance and gives too much scope to developers and their advisers to concoct schemes which might in practice be unworkable, unfair, complex or otherwise against the public interest.'

2 'The only way to deal properly and fairly with developments of multiple units is for all the rights and obligations of the unit-owners, the developers and the managers to be set out in such a way that there is complete clarity and fairness and also that there are simple, straighforward procedures for resolving disputes of the type which are inevitable in these developments'.

3 'The development scheme concept is not wrong—it simply does not go far enough. In the best traditions of English law, it provides a flexible framework but, in doing so, it leaves too many doors open.'

D. THE BSA'S PROPOSALS

Given that the BSA felt that the Law Commission's proposals did not go far enough (although the Association suggested that the Commission's proposals could be used as a basis for extrapolation, but only as something of a last resort) we now arrive at the question as to whether there is an existing system of foreign conveyancing which the BSA feels would be best suited to solution of the problem.

The following systems were all examined by the BSA in some depth:

the current system in Scotland;
various condominium systems in the USA;
other condominium systems in Europe;
the sectional title system in South Africa;
the home unit systems in Australasia;
the strata title system used in Australia and New Zealand;

The Association's conclusion is that the strata title system is the one best suited for translation to the English scene; and of the different systems in use in Australasia, the New South Wales one was chosen as the most suitable. (In Australia, for example, the different states have different systems, although to be fair, all the systems have very much the same basic characteristics. Nevertheless there is much rivalry between the states as to whose system is the best. The author has a good number of Australian practitioners amongst his acquaintances, and those in Queensland appear to be most vehement about their system being the newest, and the best.)

E. THE NEW SOUTH WALES STRATA TITLE SYSTEM

The initial legislation which introduced strata title to New South Wales was the Conveyancing (Strata Titles) Act 1961. As a result of experience, this was repealed and replaced by the Strata Titles Act 1973, which remains the principal Act.

1 What does the legislation provide for?

The basis of the strata title system is:

1 Preparation and then registration of a strata plan, This will show:

(a) the whole of the land and buildings in the title; and
(b) the subdivision of each building into separate units by reference to each floor (ie the strata).

2 The appropriate local authority—one supposes this to be the equivalent of our own district councils—must approve the strata plan.

3 Once this approval has been obtained, the strata plan itself together with the certificate of approval, and any appropriate planning consents, are lodged with the Registrar-General, who is the officer responsible for all land registration in New South Wales.

4 Once registration is completed, there comes into existence, on a completely automatic basis, an organisation called 'the body corporate'. This comprises all the unit-owners. The point to note here is that no cost is involved in the birth of this body corporate, which contrasts, eg with the incorporation of a tenants' management company in this country.

5 Dealing with the conveyancing side of things first:

(a) as soon as the strata plan is registered, separate certificates of the *freehold* (note this title is freehold, not leasehold) title are issued in respect of each individual unit;
(b) at the same time a certificate of title is issued to the body corporate. This relates to the *common* property which, as in common areas in an English flat development, includes the shell of the building;
(c) the transfer of land in New South Wales is conducted under the Torrens system, of which some readers may be aware, and which thus applies equally to houses, flats, or indeed any variety of housing;
(d) each unit may be transmitted quite freely on a freehold basis. Indeed, no clauses may be used either in relation to the individual units themselves, or to the constitution of the body corporate, which inhibit this right;
(e) the boundaries of the individual units will be the *inner* surfaces of the *outer* walls, floors and ceilings;
(f) rights are *automatically* implied by the legislation, and thus need not be set out in extenso in the individual deeds, in favour of each unit for support from the remainder of the building, shelter, and the passage of services through the whole of the building including of course the units themselves.

6 Turning to the management:

(a) the phrase 'unit entitlement' is used in strata title conveyancing. This is the 'value' of each unit in relation to the value of the building as a whole;

(b) unit entitlement is related to calculation of such items as rates, voting rights in the management (as to which see later), responsibility for common parts and the work carried out in them;
(c) the common parts are, as we have seen, vested in the body corporate. This organisation becomes the agent for the unit-owners as tenants in common in shares equivalent to their unit entitlements;
(d) thus only unit-owners are members of the body corporate. The members may have different voting rights, depending on their unit entitlement. This means that where there was a block with a spread of flats, insofar as floor areas and/or prices were concerned, those people who owned the larger flats would have more votes proportionately, which seems essentially fair as those people have put more into the block;
(e) instead of the constitution of the body corporate being set out in a memorandum and articles of association, as with a management company, tenants' or otherwise, in this country and so being capable of great variation from one example to another, under the strata title system the constitution of the body corporate is set out in full in the background legislation. This factor is considered a very important one by the Building Societies Association; clearly it is a sensible and logical course to have taken, because then the flat-owner who is on the move will know what sort of management scheme he is going to—it will be virtually identical to the one he has just come from (if he was previously a flat-owner). The legislation does recognise, though, that individual blocks may need individual treatment, and there may be limited adaptations to suit individual requirements;
(f) each body corporate must hold an annual general meeting and a council of management, a term which is used in tenants' management companies in this country,[4] is elected at each such AGM. There must be a minimum of three members, and a maximum of seven. Of course, these members will be proprietors (see 6 (d), above);
(g) it is the duty of the council of management to implement the actual management of the block. Their powers, and how they implement them, are governed by the legislation and by 27 bye-laws, 11 of which are, under the terms of the legislation unalterable, and the other 16 being capable of some modification so as to meet the specific needs of the body corporate;
(h) amongst the powers of the body corporate, through its elected council, are:
    (i) to insure;
    (ii) to maintain and repair common parts;
    (iii) to comply with notices served by an authority eg the local council;
    (iv) to establish a fund for administrative expenses, eg for payment of insurance premiums, etc;
    (v) to levy service charges, which comprise maintenance and administrative expenses. These will be levied in the same proportions as the unit entitlements. There is a further power to cover any such charges which remain unpaid by action; and

4 See ch 11, p 131, above.

(vi) to appoint managing agents;

(i) managing agents are usually appointed on the larger developments, although this will be at the discretion of the body corporate itself;

(j) the legislation gives to any mortgagee who has given the appropriate notice of its interest to the body corporate the right to stand in the shoes of a defaulting owner;

(k) any disputes which are beyond the powers of the body corporate or (if there are any) the managing agents to settle may be brought before:
  (i) in the case of less serious disputes, the Strata Titles Commissioner, who is a civil servant; or
  (ii) in the case of more serious disputes or appeals from the Strata Titles Commissioner, the Strata Titles Board, which is merely the local court of first instance under another name.

2 The advantages of the strata title system

The Building Societies Association is clear in its preference for the Australian, and in particular the New South Wales, strata title system. Why should this be the case? In order to convince such an eminent body, the system must have decided advantages. And so it probably does. They are as follows:

1 the system has been invented by a country whose legal system is founded on English law. All the preparatory work has been done, on the wording of the statutes, the bye-laws, the precedents themselves, and the system has been working splendidly for a number of years. Translation to this country would thus be relatively painless;

2 by adopting this system, an immediate vehicle for conveying freehold flats would be available;

3 strata title can apply to mixed developments. Residential/commercial/industrial elements will be happily dealt with under the same scheme. It also applies equally to new-build developments, or conversion of existing schemes. Readers wishing to know more should refer to the BSA's report itself, or if that is not sufficiently detailed, there are Australian publications available for those who seek them out, but it is clear that introduction of the strata title system could deal more than satisfactorily with the problem of enfranchisement of existing leasehold flats;

4 the system is based on freehold conveyancing, and strata title unit proprietors are not burdened by a lengthy, often incomprehensible legal document as are English leaseholders. Furthermore, because of the basic concept of simplicity of ownership, and the democratic nature of the system, with (apparently) an easy and expeditious machinery available for the resolving of disputes, those who live in strata title blocks are almost without exception enthusiastic about it;

5 in New South Wales, developers are 'licensed' in very much the same way that they are in this country under the NHBC scheme. What is much more interesting is that the licensing procedures have been extended to managing agents. All such agents have to be licensed, admittedly by the Council of Auctioneers and Agents—in other words what seems to be a self-regulatory system—but they also have to contribute to a compensation

fund. There has been a movement towards a body of specialist, strata title managers, who are quite distinct from estate agencies who might devote part of their time to management. In other words, the equivalent of the professional residential property management company, of which there seem to be all too few in this country. At least 25% of developments are said to be professionally managed with this proportion increasing, and all the larger developments are in this category. It is only the small developments, say those with less than ten units, which are in the main run by the owners themselves. The author's main objection to our own brand of tenants' management companies has always been that they are unprofessional, that they develop into cliques who take over the administration, very often to the discomfiture of the silent majority, and basically are incapable of sensible management. There are, of course, exceptions, but these do seem to be in the minority. The strata title system appears to overcome those basic objections, especially given the wide use of professional management. If professional management proves too expensive, then 'self-help' management can be chosen, thus cutting down on costs. Thus the system is absolutely flexible.

F. CONCLUSIONS

The Building Societies Association has concluded, as a result of a very thorough investigation, that strata title as set up and operated in New South Wales particularly would be the best system to consider as a replacement for the present one. The points they make are as follows:

(a) that all new multiple unit developments for sale should have to be on a strata title basis;
(b) that the strata title system be optional for existing leasehold (and indeed also freehold) multiple unit developments—a 'rescue' package for enfranchisement purposes; there would be obvious advantages in forcing an unwilling landlord or any reluctant lessee in a block to convert to strata title but the question of compulsion must be a matter for government decision. (There is, however, a precedent for this compulsion principle relating to leasehold houses, in the Leasehold Reform Act 1967);
(c) that no new long leaseholds should be able to be created for houses;
(d) that there may well be room for exceptions to (a) to (c) above, for example, shared ownership leases, and assured tenancies as provided for in the Housing Act 1980, but 'these should be severely limited'.

G. FINAL THOUGHTS

So there we are—the two front runners in how we might change the present law relating to the conveyancing, and management, of blocks of flats. Is one of the sets of proposals likely to be adopted, substantially in the form that they presently take, or indeed has either got any chance at all?

The Law Commission's proposals are less radical, although strata title is not a new system, and has been proven in a common law country, so to that extent it is perhaps less of an unknown quantity than the introduction of the new concept of 'land obligations'.

The Law Society has now added its weight to the consideration of the alternatives. There appeared in the 9 January 1985 issue of the *Law Society's Gazette* (p 34) the text of a letter sent by the Society's Non-Contentious Business Department to the BSA, which gave the Law Society's considered comment on the BSA's proposals for the introduction of the strata title system. These comments bore in mind, not only the strata title proposals, but also the Law Commission's proposals.

The Law Society doubted that strata title could be introduced reasonably quickly and easily, and felt that the problem of the 'depreciating asset' in leaseholds should be tackled as separate from the proportion of reasonably radical changes in conveyancing law.

The Society therefore urged the adoption of two courses:

(a) that the draft bill annexed to the Law Commission's report be enacted at the earliest opportunity. This would bring considerable advantages affecting a wide range of properties, and would not prejudice future action on a strata title scheme;
(b) that the strata title scheme be referred to an expert body for detailed consideration of the desirability of a procedure for implementing it in this country.

The reader is left to decide which, if either, of these proposals will make any headway; but what seems clear is that there will be some substantial changes in how flats are sold and subsequently managed, and whether it is sooner or later depends on the will of the government and the amount of pressure exerted on them by organisations like the BSA. What is certain, though, is that the practitioner must know what the future is likely to bring, because when it does come, the changes are likely to be pretty substantial, and unless they are careful, some practitioners will be in danger of being left behind.

The precedents

Precedent sections of textbooks often seem to give rise to misunderstandings. This particular book is one with a very heavy practical slant; it is intended not for the theoretician, but, amongst others, for the practical conveyancer, to enable him to appreciate the position the particular job he might be doing has placed him in, how to deal with the problems which might have cropped up, and finally what sort of document he might use to enable him to deal with those problems.

Therefore, of all the practical elements in this book, the precedent section is bound to be the most practical of them all. To be of effective help, however, it must be used in a practical way.

The practitioner using any section of precedents must first of all ask himself if the individual precedents should be regarded as documents to be used slavishly in the particular context of the work in hand, or merely as indicators?

Since most situations, and the problems which flow from them, are of an endless variety, it is usually unsafe to regard a precedent as anything more than a legal skeleton upon which the flesh can be hung, according to circumstances. Indeed, the bones themselves are not sacrosanct, as they can be replaced or rearranged judiciously, as long as, at the end of the day, the fleshed-up skeleton presents a correct picture.

In case experienced practitioners feel that herein lies an invitation to those less experienced than themselves to tinker with a basic precedent to the extent that what they will end up with will be dangerous, let it be said that no precedent section is necessarily safe ground for the inexperienced. It is probably axiomatic that a certain degree of experience is necessary in the first place in order to be able to use a precedent section.

Therefore the precedents which follow are intended to be used as indicators, and are not presented as whole documents which should be followed slavishly. If any 'cutting and pasting' (to borrow an expression from word-processing) is required, then there is every reason why it should be done, and none why it should not, provided that by doing so nothing ridiculous is produced, and the practitioner who works with such precedents ought to be experienced enough to avoid this.

Some of the precedents which follow are intended as illustrations of documents of their kind, rather than precedents as such. In this category are documents such as shared ownership lease provisions (Precedent No 16) and the time-share documents (Precedents Nos 21 to 26). Most practitioners will never be called upon to draft such documents, as they will never act for clients in those fields, but many practitioners will act for clients *buying* properties subject to such schemes.

It is always difficult to choose precedents which will please everyone; indeed it is more than difficult, it is impossible. Some may complain that they will not find, for example, any precedents of contracts dealing with flat conveyancing; the reason these have been left out is because in the author's view they are not specialised enough to warrant inclusion: a contract is a contract is a contract. Others will identify what they regard as omissions. The author begs indulgence from all who find themselves in this position, and hopes that generally readers will find the Precedents useful, and welcomes any suggestions for future additions, should the book stagger to a second edition!

1 Lease of maisonette: upper or lower: provision for deed of covenant procedure

[This lease is drafted for unregistered land but is naturally easily adaptable for registered development. See for typical headings, etc Precedent No 3 p 360, below.
For a short commentary on specialist aspects of maisonettes, as opposed to flats (with particular reference to the deed of covenant procedure) see ch 5, p 68, above.]

THIS LEASE made the day of One thousand nine hundred and BETWEEN [Lessor] of/whose registered office is situate at

(hereinafter called 'the Lessor' which expression shall where the context so admits include the estate owner or estate owners for the time being of the reversion of the premises hereby demised) of the one part and [Lessee] of

(hereinafter called or collectively called 'the Lessee' which expression shall where the context so admits include the Lessee's executors administrators and assigns) of the other part

WHEREAS:

(1) The Lessor is the freeholder of an area of land situate at [general geographical location] and being part of the Lessor's [ ] Estate[1] and is in the course of developing the same by the erection thereon or on some part or parts thereof of buildings comprising maisonettes [and private garages][2]

(2) The Lessor has agreed to demise unto the Lessee the premises hereinafter described upon the terms covenants and conditions hereinafter contained

NOW in consideration of [purchase price, including receipt clause] and of the rent covenants and conditions hereinafter reserved and contained and on the part of the Lessee to be paid performed and observed

THIS DEED WITNESSETH as follows:

1 THE Lessor hereby demises unto the Lessee ALL THAT the property more particularly described in the First Part of the First Schedule hereto TOGETHER with the rights and privileges mentioned in the Second Part of the said First Schedule AND TOGETHER ALSO with the right to enforce for the benefit of the demised premises all covenants entered into by the Purchasers or Lessees of other maisonettes erected or in the course of erection at [Development][3] aforesaid for the observance and performance of similar restrictions and stipulations to those mentioned in the Second Schedule hereto BUT EXCEPT AND RESERVING unto the Lessor and subject to the rights and privileges in the Third part of the First Schedule hereto TO HOLD the same unto the Lessee (except and reserved as aforesaid) for the term of [ ] years from the [ ] day of [ ] One thousand nine hundred and [ ] YIELDING AND PAYING therefor yearly during the said term the rent of [ ] Pounds [or any other wording setting out a review situation] without any deduction by equal half yearly payments on the [ ] day of [ ] and the [ ] day of [ ] in every year the first of such payments to be made on whichever of the last mentioned dates immediately next follows the date hereof and to be a proportion from the date hereof until such date[4]

2 (1) FOR the benefit of the remainder of the Lessor's scheme of development of maisonettes at [ ] Estate aforesaid[5] and of the owners occupiers and tenants for the time being thereof and every part thereof the Lessee hereby covenants with the Lessor to the intent that the burden of this covenant may run with and bind the demised premises and every part thereof and that the benefit thereof may be annexed to and devolve with each and every part of the said [ ] Estate other than the demised premises that the Lessee will at all times hereafter duly perform and observe all and singular the restrictive and other covenants contained in the Second Schedule hereto but so that

nevertheless the Lessee shall not be personally liable for any breach of any covenant or stipulation which is only restrictive in nature occurring after he shall have parted with all interest in the demised premises in respect of which such breach shall occur and will indemnify the Lessor and its successors in title and assigns from and against all actions proceedings costs claims and liabilities in respect of any future breach non-observance or non-performance of the said covenants so far as aforesaid PROVIDED ALWAYS that the Lessor shall not be under any obligation to the Lessee to enforce any of the said stipulations in respect of any other property and shall have power from time to time by deed or deeds to vary or release any of the said stipulations in respect of any plot on the said estate

(2) IT IS HEREBY AGREED AND DECLARED that if the Lessee acquires any greater interest than the term hereby created in the demised premises the said covenant referred to in clause 2 (1) hereof shall not merge in any such greater interest but shall continue to bind the demised premises for the duration of such greater interest and the owner or owners for the time being of such greater interest shall duly perform and observe the said covenants and stipulations[6]

(3) IT IS HEREBY AGREED AND DECLARED that if at any time any dispute shall arise between the Lessee and any other owner of any interest in any part of the Lessor's development of maisonettes relating to any interest in the Lessor's development owned by them or either of them relating to the party or other walls structures roofs fences roadways passageways pathways sewers drains pipes or the combined drainage system (if any) or watercourses and other easements rights or appurtenances whatsoever relating or belonging thereto or any repairs thereto or the liability or proportion of the liability of any person for the cost thereof or any nuisance or annoyance arising therefrom then and in every such case such dispute (provided that the other party thereto shall also have agreed to become bound so as to refer the same) shall be referred to the determination and award of a surveyor appointed for the purpose by the Lessor which determination and award shall be final and binding on the Lessee[7]

[3[8] THE Lessee hereby covenants with the Lessor that he will if at any time called upon to do so by the Lessor at the joint expense of the parties thereto enter into a Deed of Covenant with the person at that time having an interest in the [upper/lower] maisonette in the same terms so far as circumstances will then permit as those contained in the model Deed of Covenant set out in the Third Schedule hereto and that the Lessee will immediately upon the execution of such Deed produce the same to the Lessor's Solicitors for registration and discharge their fee of [ ] in respect thereof]

4 IT IS HEREBY AGREED AND DECLARED between the Lessor and the Lessee that [the wall dividing the maisonette from the adjoining maisonette on the same floor shall be deemed to be a party wall and that][9] the boundary fences not shown marked with a 'T' on the said plan shall be party fences to be maintained and repaired at the joint expense of the Lessee and the tenants occupiers or owners for the time being of the adjoining property thereby separated

5 THE Lessee hereby covenants with the Lessor in manner following that is to say:

(1) To pay the rents hereby reserved at the times and in manner aforesaid without any deduction

(2) To pay and discharge (or to repay to the Lessor in the event of payment by it) all rates taxes duties assessments charges and outgoings whatsoever whether parliamentary parochial or any other description and whether of an annual or recurring nature or otherwise which now are or during the term hereby granted shall be imposed or charged on the demised premises or on the Lessor or the Lessee or occupier in respect thereof

(3) From time to time during the said term to pay all costs charges and expenses incurred by the Lessor in abating a nuisance on the demised premises and executing all such works as may be necessary for abating a nuisance in obedience to a notice served by the Local Authority

(4) Not to do or permit or suffer to be done anything whereby the policies of insurance for the time being subsisting on the demised premises against damage by fire and such other risks as are specified in sub-clause (16) hereof may become void or voidable or whereby the rate of premium thereon may be increased and forthwith on demand to pay to the Lessor all sums paid by way of increased premiums and all expenses incurred by the Lessor in or about the renewal of any policy or policies of insurance rendered necessary by a breach of this covenant all of which payments shall be made in addition to the rents hereinbefore reserved[10]

(5) In the year One thousand nine hundred and [ ][11] and thereafter once in every [ ][11] year of the said term and also during the last year thereof to paint all the outside wood iron and similar work of the demised premises and all additions thereto with a good quality gloss paint in a proper and workmanlike manner

(6) In the year One thousand nine hundred and [ ][11] and thereafter once in every [ ][11] year of the said term and also during the last year thereof to paint all the interior of the demised premises and all additions thereto usual or proper to be painted with a good quality gloss paint in a proper and workmanlike manner and also at such times as last aforesaid to grain varnish whitewash colour and paper such parts of the interior of the demised premises as are usually so treated

(7) From time to time and at all times during the said term well and substantially repair uphold support cleanse maintain drain amend and keep the premises hereby demised and all new buildings which may at any time during the said term be erected on and all additions made to the said demised premises and the fixtures therein and all sewers drains pathways passageways easements and appurtenances thereof with all necessary reparations cleansings and amendments whatsoever

(8) At all times during the said term to pay and contribute a rateable or due proportion of the expense of making repairing maintaining painting supporting rebuilding and cleansing all roofs ways passageways pathways footpaths sewers drain pipes watercourses waterpipes cisterns gutters party walls party structures and gates fences hedges and retaining walls (if any) easements appurtenances belonging to or used or capable of being used by the Lessee in common with the Lessor or the tenants or occupiers of the premises nearto or adjoining the premises hereby demised or of which the demised premises form a part such proportion in the case of difference to be settled by a surveyor appointed for that purpose by the Lessor whose decision shall be binding and to keep the Lessor indemnified against all costs claims proceedings and demands in respect thereof

(9) All the demised premises so painted repaired upheld cleansed maintained drained amended and kept as aforesaid at the expiration or sooner determination of the said term quietly to yield up unto the Lessor together with all additions and improvements made thereto in the meantime and all fixtures of every kind in or upon the demised premises or which during the said term may be affixed or fastened to or upon the same except tenant's fixtures

(10) That the Lessee will pay to the Lessor all costs charges and expenses (including legal costs and fees payable to a surveyor) which may be incurred by the Lessor in or in contemplation of any proceedings under section 146 of the Law of

Property Act 1925 notwithstanding forfeiture is avoided otherwise than by relief granted by the Court

(11) To permit the Lessor or its agents at all reasonable times during the said term with or without workmen or others to enter the demised premises and examine the state of repair and condition thereof and during the last [ ][11] years of the said term to take schedules or inventories of the fixtures and other things to be yielded up at the expiration of the said term and also to repair and make good all defects and wants of reparation which shall be discovered on any such examination and of which notice in writing shall be given by the Lessor to the Lessee within one calendar month after giving of such notice

(12) If the Lessee shall make default in any of the covenants hereinbefore contained for or relating to the repair of the demised premises it shall be lawful for the Lessor (but without prejudice to the right of re-entry under the clause hereinafter contained) to enter upon the demised premises and repair the same at the expense of the Lessee in accordance with the covenants and provisions of these presents and the expenses of such repairs shall be repaid by the Lessee to the Lessor on demand

(13) To permit the Lessor and the tenants or occupiers of the adjoining premises and their respective agents or workmen at any time or times during the said term at all reasonable hours in the daylight to enter upon the demised premises for the purpose of executing repairs or alterations of or upon such adjoining premises making good to the Lessee all damage thereby occasioned

(14) To permit the Lessor and the tenants or occupiers for the time being of the premises of which the demised premises form part or any person or persons authorised by it or them respectively in that behalf to enter upon the demised premises for the purpose of constructing laying down altering repairing cleansing emptying or maintaining any sewers watercourses cesspools gutters drains water pipes electric or telephone wires or gas pipes or a television or radio receiving aerial and connections thereto in connection with or for the accommodation of adjoining property and in particular the premises of which the demised premises form part doing as little damage as may be to the demised premises and restoring the surface of the soil and everything erected thereon without any unreasonable delay and making good any damage so caused

(15) [(a)[8] Not to assign or transfer the demised premises without first inviting the Lessor of or person having the interest in the [upper/lower] maisonette forming part of the said building (in this clause called 'the adjoining owner') to enter at the expense of the Lessee into a Deed of Covenant in the form of the model deed set out in the Third Schedule hereto with the proposed assignee or transferee (save that recitals (3) and (4) therein shall be omitted) and the adjoining owner being willing to enter into such Deed to procure on or before completion of any assignment or transfer that the Assignee or Transferee enters into the said Deed with the adjoining owner and produces the said Deed to the Lessor's Solicitors for registration and discharges their fee of [ ] in respect thereof]

[(b)][8] Within twenty one days next after any absolute transfer assignment mortgage charge or other devolution of the Lessee's interest under this present Lease in the demised premises or any part thereof to give notice in writing of such transfer assignment mortgage charge or other devolution and of the names addresses and descriptions of the parties thereto to the Lessor's solicitors and to produce to them the instrument of such transfer assignment mortgage charge or other devolution and to pay them a fee of [ ] for the registration of each document]

(16) Forthwith to insure and at all times during the said term to keep insured the

demised premises and all buildings erections and fixtures of an insurable nature which are now or may be at any time during the said term erected or placed or affixed on the demised premises against loss or damage by fire or other risks normally covered by such insurance in some insurance office to be approved in writing by the Lessor in a sum equal to the full value thereof in the joint names of the Lessor and the Lessee whether in conjunction or not in conjunction with the name or names of any persons legally or beneficially interested in the demised premises and to pay all premiums necessary for the purpose within seven days after the same shall become due and whenever required to produce to the Lessor or his agent the Policy for every insurance and the receipt for the last premium thereof and in case default shall be made in effecting or keeping on foot such insurance or producing such receipts it shall be lawful for the Lessor but without prejudice to the power of re-entry under the clause hereinafter contained to insure the said buildings against loss or damage by fire and the Lessee will forthwith repay all sums expended in effecting or keeping on foot such insurance AND in case the demised premises or any part thereof shall at any time during the said term be destroyed or damaged by fire then as often as the same shall happen with all convenient speed to lay out all moneys received in respect of such insurance on rebuilding repairing or otherwise reinstating the demised premises in a good and substantial manner to the satisfaction of the surveyor for the time being of the Lessor and in case the moneys received in respect of the said insurance shall be insufficient for the purpose to make good the deficiency out of the Lessee's own money

6 THE Lessor hereby covenants with the Lessee in manner following (that is to say):

(1) That in the event of the Lessor at any time disposing of any part of the remainder of its maisonettes at [development] aforesaid for any interest the Lessor will (subject as provided in clause 2(1) hereof) impose on the person acquiring such interest the same covenants and stipulations in so far as circumstances will then permit as are contained in clauses 2 and 5 hereof and any relevant schedule hereto

[(2)[8] That in the event of the Lessor at any time disposing of the [upper/lower] maisonette for any interest the Lessor will impose on the person acquiring such interest an obligation to enter into at the joint expense of the parties thereto a Deed of Covenant with the Lessee in the same terms so far as circumstances will then permit as those contained in the model Deed of Covenant set out in the Third Schedule hereto AND IT IS HEREBY DECLARED that in such event pending the execution by such persons of such deed the Lessor will hold the benefit of this covenant in trust for the Lessee]

(3) That the lessee paying the rent hereby reserved and performing and observing the several covenants conditions and agreements herein contained and on the Lessee's part to be performed and observed shall and may peaceably and quietly hold and enjoy the demised premises during the term hereby granted without any lawful interruption or disturbance from or by the Lessor its successors in title or any person or persons claiming under or in trust for it or them

(4)[12] That the Lessor will make up that part of any new street upon which the demised premises abut and where necessary provide and lay main drains and sewers thereunder in accordance with the requirements and to the satisfaction of and up to the minimum standard required by the proper authorities and will indemnify the Lessee and his successors in title against any proceedings costs claims and liabilities in respect thereof until such times as the said street and main drains and sewers are taken over by the proper Authorities

7 PROVIDED ALWAYS AND IT IS HEREBY AGREED AND DECLARED as follows:

(1) That if the rents hereby reserved or any part thereof shall be in arrear for

twenty one days after the same shall have become due whether the same shall have been legally demanded or not or in the event of any breach non-observance or non-performance of any of the covenants conditions and agreements on the part of the Lessee herein contained then and in any such case it shall be lawful for the Lessor or any person or persons duly authorised by it in that behalf to enter into or upon the demised premises or any part thereof in the name of the whole and peaceably hold and enjoy the same thenceforth as if these presents had not been made but without prejudice to any right of action or remedy of the Lessor in respect of any antecedent breach of any of the covenants by the Lessee thereinbefore contained

(2) That any notice hereby required or authorised to be given by the Lessor or Lessee respectively shall be in writing and may be given in any of the modes provided for by section 196 of the Law of Property Act 1925 with respect to notices to be given to Lessors or Lessees (as the case may be) under that Act[13]

(3) That words importing the masculine gender include also the feminine gender and that words importing the singular number include also the plural number and where there are two or more persons included in the term Lessee the covenants expressed to be made by the Lessee shall be deemed to be made by such persons jointly and severally and they shall be deemed to hold the demised premises as joint tenants legally and beneficially

8 Certificate of Value

IN WITNESS etc.

THE FIRST SCHEDULE before referred to

PART 1

(Lower Maisonette)

[FIRST] ALL THAT piece or parcel of land situate at [ ] and more particularly delineated and shown edged red on the plan annexed hereto TOGETHER with the maisonette erected thereon or on some part thereof and being the lower or ground floor maisonette numbered [ ] which is shown hatched yellow on the said plan and known or intended to be known as [postal address]

[AND SECONDLY ALL THAT piece or parcel of land shown coloured green on the said plan together with the garage erected thereon] ALL which said premises [FIRST AND SECONDLY] hereinbefore described form part of the Lessor's [ ] Estate and are collectively referred to in this Lease as 'the demised premises' including in this demise the upper side of the ceiling of the said maisonette but excluding from the demise the upper maisonette the floor and joists supporting the same and roof of the building erected or to be erected on the said land edged red and the entrance door and hallway of the said upper maisonette situate on the ground floor of the said building and the staircase leading thereto

(Upper Maisonette)

[FIRST] ALL THAT maisonette situate at [ ] and more particularly delineated and shown hatched yellow on the plan annexed hereto being the upper or first floor maisonette numbered [ ] and known or intended to be known as [postal address] aforesaid TOGETHER with the piece or parcel of land adjacent thereto and more particularly delineated and shown edged red on the said plan [AND SECONDLY ALL THAT piece or parcel of land shown coloured green on the said plan together with the garage erected thereon] ALL which said premises [first and secondly] hereinbefore described form part of the Lessor's [ ] Estate and are collectively referred to in this lease as 'the demised premises' including in this demise the floor and joists supporting the demised premises the roof of the building of which the demised premises form part and the entrance door and hallway of the demised premises situate on the ground floor of the said building and the staircase leading therefrom to the demised premises but excluding from the demise the lower maisonette (including the upper side of the ceiling thereof) and the foundations of the said building

PART II

Rights and privileges granted to Lessee

1[12] The right for the Lessee and all persons authorised by him in common with the Lessor and its tenants and servants and all persons authorised by them to pass and repass at all times and for all purposes connected with the use of the demised premises as a private dwelling over and along the new roads laid out or to be laid out by the Lessor on its [ ] Estate TOGETHER with the right in common as aforesaid to connect with and use the drains and sewers laid or to be laid by the Lessor under the adjoining and neighbouring premises forming part of the [ ] Estate

2 The right at all reasonable times to enter upon the property adjoining the demised premises for the purpose of executing repairs and alterations to the demised premises and cleansing and painting the same as the same shall be necessary causing as little damage as possible and making good to the tenants or occupiers of such adjoining property without any unreasonable delay all damage thereby occasioned

3 The right to support and shelter from the buildings adjoining whether at the side above or below the demised premises as the same is at present enjoyed and the free and uninterrupted right of passage and running of water and soil gas and electricity in common (where appropriate) with all others using the same from and to the demised premises through the sewers drains watercourses water pipes cisterns gas pipes electric or telephone wires and meters which are now or may hereafter during the term hereby granted be in or under the other buildings and land of the Lessor the Lessee from time to time contributing a due proportion of the expense (if any) of replacing substituting keeping and maintaining such services as are used jointly with others in a proper state of repair

4 The right to maintain one television and/or radio aerial on the roof of the building of which the demised premises forms part in such position as may be agreed with the Lessor

5[14] The right for the Lessee and all persons authorised by him in common with the Lessor and its tenants and servants and all persons authorised by it to pass and repass at all times and for all purposes connected with the use of the demised premises as a private dwelling and with or without vehicles and animals over and along the access way shown coloured yellow and unhatched on the said plan and a similar right of passage but on foot only over the pathway shown coloured yellow and hatched black on the said plan the Lessee from time to time contributing a due proportion of the expense of keeping and maintaining the said access way and pathway tidy and in good repair

PART III

Exceptions and Reservations

1 The right for the Lessor hereafter to build or rebuild on any adjoining or neighbouring land of the Lessor according to such plans (whether as to height extent or otherwise) and in such manner as the Lessor shall think fit notwithstanding any interference thereby occasioned to the access of light or air to the demised premises

2 The right for the Lessor and the tenants or occupiers of the adjoining premises including the building of which the demised premises form part or any person or persons authorised by them respectively to enter upon the demised premises or any part thereof at all reasonable times for any of the purposes mentioned and subject to the provisions contained in the covenants hereinbefore contained on the part of the Lessee to permit such entry the persons exercising such right making good without unreasonable delay all damage to the premises thereby occasioned

3 The right of support to the buildings adjoining (whether at the side above or below) the demised premises the same as is at present enjoyed from the demised premises

4 The free and uninterrupted right of passage and running of water and soil gas and electricity in common (where appropriate) with the Lessee from and to the other buildings and land of the Lessor and its tenants adjoining or near to the demised premises through the sewers drains watercourses water pipes cisterns gutters gas pipes electric wires and meters which are now or may hereafter during the term hereby granted be in or under the demised premises the persons exercising such right contributing a due proportion of the expense (if any) of keeping and maintaining such services as are used jointly with others in a proper state of repair

5[15] The right for the lessor and the owners tenants or occupiers for the time being of the upper maisonette and all persons authorised by them to pass and repass at all times and for all purposes but without vehicles over and along the footpath shown coloured blue on the said plan as a means of entrance to and exit from the upper maisonette [and garden] such owners and tenants as aforesaid paying a due proportion of the cost of maintaining the said footpath in good repair

6[16] The right for the owner tenant or occupier of the upper maisonette to store his dustbin in the dustbin recess provided and forming part of the demised premises

THE SECOND SCHEDULE before referred to
Restrictions and stipulations

1 The Lessee will at the Lessee's own expense throughout the term hereby granted properly maintain and keep the fence or fences on the side or sides of the demised premises marked 'T' within the boundary (if any are so marked) on the plan in good and substantial repair and condition

2 The Lessee will not erect any building on or over the garden or yard of the demised premises or any part thereof without the licence in writing of the Lessor

3 The Lessee will not make any alteration in or addition to the height sides front back roof walls timbers or elevations of the demised premises or the yard or garden wall or fences thereof

4 The Lessee will not use the demised premises or permit the same to be used for the purpose of any manufacture trade or business whatsoever but will use and occupy the same as and for one private dwelling in one occupation only

5 The Lessee will not do or permit to be done in or upon the demised premises any illegal or immoral act nor any act or thing which shall be or may be or grow to the annoyance nuisance damage or disturbance of the Lessor or its tenants or the owners tenants or occupiers of any adjoining or neighbouring properties

6 The Lessee will use the garden forming part of the demised premises as a garden only and will keep the same clean neat and properly tended and will not convert the same to any other use whatsoever

7 The Lessee will provide a dustbin of an adequate size and type and shall keep the same clean and disinfected and free from smell and will store it only in the dustbin recess hereinbefore mentioned and will not keep or cause or suffer to accumulate rubbish or waste matter on any part of the demised premises or the approaches thereto save in such dustbin as aforesaid

8 The Lessee will not obstruct or permit to be obstructed any of the roadways or passageways shown on the said plan

[[8]THE THIRD SCHEDULE before referred to
Specimen Deed of Covenant

THIS DEED OF COVENANT is made the day of One thousand nine hundred and
BETWEEN
of
in the County of
(hereinafter called 'the First Lessee') of the one part and

of
in the County of
(hereinafter called 'the Second Lessee') of the other part
WHEREAS:
(1) This Deed is supplemental to the two leases (short particulars whereof appear in the Schedule hereto) whereunder the First Lessee is the Lessee of the premises described therein as 'the Lower Maisonette' and the Second Lessee is the Lessee of the premises described therein as 'the Upper Maisonette'
(2) Each of the said Leases contains covenants with the Lessor by the Lessee thereunder to do certain repairs and other works in relation to the premises thereby demised respectively and to insure the said respective premises
(3) Each of the said Leases also contains a covenant with the Lessor by the Lessee thereunder that the said Lessee will if at any time called upon to do so by the Lessor enter into a Deed of Covenant with any person at that time having any interest in the Lower Maisonette or the Upper Maisonette (as the case may be) in the same terms so far as possible as those contained in the model Deed of Covenant set out in the Third Schedule to the said Leases
(4) The Lessor under the said Leases has in pursuance of the above recited covenant called upon the parties hereto respectively to enter into this deed which the parties hereto have agreed to do
NOW in pursuance of the said agreement and in consideration of the premises THIS DEED WITNESSETH as follows:
1 THE First Lessee hereby covenants with the Second Lessee that he will from time to time and at all times during the said term of the said Leases well and substantially repair uphold support cleanse maintain drain amend and keep the Lower Maisonette as defined in the said Leases and in particular any part thereof which may provide support for the Upper Maisonette as similarly defined and all new buildings which may at any time be erected on and all additions made to the Lower Maisonette and the fixtures therein and all party and other walls and fences hedges (if any) sewers drains pathways passageways easements and appurtenances thereof with all necessary reparations cleansings and amendments whatsoever
2 THE Second Lessee hereby covenants with the First Lessee that he will from time to time and at all times during the term of the said Leases well and substantially repair uphold support cleanse maintain drain amend and keep the Upper Maisonette and all new buildings which may at any time be erected on and all additions made to the Upper Maisonette and the fixtures therein and all party and other walls and fences hedges (if any) sewers drains pathways passageways easements and appurtenances thereof with all necessary reparations cleansings and amendments whatsoever and in particular keep the floors and roof of the Upper Maisonette in good weatherproof condition and free from all leakage of rain water or other elements or things which may in any way damage or affect the Lower Maisonette
3 IT IS HEREBY AGREED AND DECLARED that if either of the parties hereto shall make default in the observance or performance of any of the above covenants on his part to be observed and performed it shall be lawful for the other to enter upon the premises of the one making such default and carry out any works thereon necessary for compliance with the covenant in respect whereof default has been made and at the expense of the person making such default and the expense of such works shall be repayable on demand to the party who has carried them out
4 EACH of them the First Lessee and the Second Lessee will insure and keep insured the Lower Maisonette and the Upper Maisonette respectively in accordance with the covenants contained in the Leases thereof and will at all reasonable times produce to the other of them the receipt for the last premium and in the event of any damage to or destruction of the premises by fire or other risk insured against forthwith apply

any moneys received in respect of such insurance in reinstating the premises to which such insurance relates in accordance with the said covenants PROVIDED that in case of default in effecting and keeping on foot any such insurance it shall be lawful for the other party hereto to effect such insurance and to recover from the party in default as a liquidated debt the cost of effecting the same

5 IT IS HEREBY EXPRESSLY AGREED that in the event of either of the parties hereto assigning or transferring his interest in the premises demised to him or in the event of any devolution of his interest the other party hereto will at the expense of the party whose interest is so assigned or devolved or his personal representatives enter into a Deed of Covenant with the assignee or other person on whom such interest devolves containing the like covenants as are herein contained and the party so assigning or whose interest so devolves or his personal representatives will at his or their own expense upon such assignment being effected or the said premises being vested in any person entitled thereto procure that the assignee or such person as aforesaid shall enter into such deed with the other party and shall pay the costs of the Landlord's Solicitors in registering the same

6 PROVIDED that he shall have complied with the provisions of clause 5 hereof neither party hereto shall be under any liability to the other for any breach or non-observance of the covenants herein contained occurring after he shall have parted with all interest in the premises demised to him as aforesaid

7 IT IS HEREBY FURTHER DECLARED that if either of the parties hereto acquires any greater interest than the interest which he now has in the Lower Maisonette or the Upper Maisonette (as the case may be) the covenants herein contained and on his part to be observed and performed shall not merge in such greater interest but shall continue to be binding upon the said party

8 IN THIS DEED the expressions 'the First Lessee' and 'the Second Lessee' include their respective executors and administrators and assigns and where the context so admits the owner or owners for the time being of any interest in the Lower Maisonette or the Upper Maisonette (as the case may be)

IN WITNESS etc.

THE SCHEDULE above referred to

Date of Lease	Term	Rent	Parties	Property]

(Attestation)

Notes

1 If applicable. The maisonettes may not be on an estate; if this is the case, the words should be suitably varied.

2 Not every maisonette will have a private garage, but the wording is included on the basis that it is easier to exclude when already in, rather than not be there in the first place.

3 It seems likely that there will be more than the two, ie one up, one down, maisonettes, eg there will often be a row of lower and upper units. If there were only one double unit, the property identified at this point in the lease would be the one other than the one the subject of the lease.

4 Or if the rental payments are to be made in advance, similar wording to Precedent No 2, cl 2, p 347, below.

5 Or suitable wording to accord with the physical situation. See n 3, above.

6 Might such greater interest be a longer leasehold, or (as is probably contemplated by the document) a freehold? If the latter, then consider the effectiveness of the clause, as some of the stipulations in the Second Schedule are positive, not restrictive, in nature. See further, ch 28, pp 311 et seq on the running of positive covenants.

7 But this clause is only to be included in the lease if the lessee is willing to accept such responsibility. There may be many lessees who will not be so willing.

8 Words in square brackets only to be included if the deed of covenant principle is to be used. See heading to this precedent.
9 Words in square brackets to be omitted if there is only a single set of upper and lower maisonettes.
10 The second part of this clause refers to the proviso in sub-clause (16), following, that the lessor may insure if there is default on the part of the lessee. However, it should be noted that the primary duty to insure in this typical maisonette lease is on the lessee.
11 Or as the lessor desires.
12 If appropriate.
13 This clause may be amended to include provision for, eg recorded delivery post.
14 Inclusion of this clause will deal with rights for the upper maisonette over the approach footpaths.
15 For a lower maisonette only. This does assume that the approach footpath to the upper maisonette will be on land leased with the lower maisonette. This may not always be the case.
16 Where appropriate. The same remarks apply as n 15, above.

2 Full management lease: professional management company joining in

[The author is most indebted to his very good friend Tony Wood of the Wood Glaister Partnership, Solihull, West Midlands for permission to reproduce this precedent.]

HM LAND REGISTRY
Land Registration Acts 1925 to 1971

COUNTY AND DISTRICT:
LESSOR'S TITLE NUMBER:
PROPERTY: Flat number and Parking Space number

THIS LEASE is made on 198
BETWEEN (1) [Lessor] of/whose registered office is at

(hereinafter called 'the Lessor') (2) [Management Company] of/whose registered office is at

(hereinafter called 'the Management Company') and (3) [Lessee] of

(hereinafter called 'the Lessee')
WHEREAS:
(a) The Lessor has previously granted leases of or intends hereafter to grant leases of the Flats (other than the premises hereby demised) forming part of the Buildings as hereinafter defined each with parking space as separate and distinct properties and the Lessor has in every such lease imposed and intends in every future lease to impose the obligations set out in the Eighth Schedule hereto to the intent that the lessee for the time being of any one of the Flats may enforce the observance by the lessee of any other of the Flats of the covenants in the form set out in Part Three of the Eighth Schedule hereto
(b) The Lessor has agreed to grant to the Lessee a lease of the premises hereby demised for the consideration at the rent and on the terms and conditions hereinafter

appearing and the Management Company has agreed to join in this lease in manner hereinafter appearing

NOW THIS DEED WITNESSETH as follows:

1 In this Deed unless the context otherwise requires:

1.1 'The Lessor' includes the person for the time being entitled to the reversion immediately expectant upon the term hereby granted

1.2 'The Lessee' includes the person for the time being entitled to the term hereby granted and where the Lessee is more than one person all covenants and agreements on the part of the Lessee herein contained shall be deemed to have been made jointly and severally by all such persons constituting the Lessee

1.3 'The Development' means the land and buildings and works described in the First Schedule hereto being known for development purposes as [description of development]

[1.4 'The Adjoining Property' means the property adjoining or near to the Development now or formerly comprised in title number [ ] which comprises one block of [ ] Units with parking spaces serving the same and which property is for the purpose of better identification shown coloured blue on the plan number 1 attached hereto]

1.5 'Plan No 1' and 'Plan No 2' means the plans annexed and so numbered[1]

1.6 'The Private Road' means the road ways footpaths car parking and access areas shown hatched black and cross hatched black on Plan No 1 and any roads ways footpaths and car parking access areas substituted therefor

1.7 'The Buildings' means the buildings shown uncoloured on Plan No 1 forming part of the Development

1.8 'The Flats' means the two blocks each comprising self-contained flats shown uncoloured on Plan No 1 and lettered A and B

1.9 'The Parking Spaces' means the car-parking spaces shown uncoloured on Plan No 1 and numbered [ ] to [ ] inclusive

1.10 'The demised premises' means the property hereby demised as described in the Third Schedule hereto

1.11 'The said flat' means that part of the demised premises which is described in Part One of the Third Schedule hereto

1.12 'The said Parking Space' means that part of the demised premises which is described in Part Two of the Third Schedule hereto

1.13 'The Maintained Property' means those parts of the Development which are more particularly described in the Second Schedule hereto and the maintenance of which is the responsibility of the Management Company

1.14 'The Management Company's Lease' means a Lease dated [ ] 19 and made between (1) the Lessor and (2) the Management Company comprising the Maintained Property[2]

1.15 'The Maintenance Expenses' means the moneys actually expended or reserved for periodical expenditure by or on behalf of the management Company at all times during the term hereby granted in carrying out the obligations specified in the Sixth Schedule hereto

1.16 'The Lessee's Proportion' means the proportion of the Maintenance Expenses payable by the Lessee in accordance with the provisions of the Seventh Schedule hereto

1.17 'Service Installations' means sewers drains channels pipes watercourses gutters mains wires cables conduits aerials tanks and soakaways and any other apparatus for the supply of water electricity gas or telephone or television signals or for the disposal of foul or surface water

1.18 The masculine includes the feminine and the singular includes the plural

2 IN pursuance of the said agreement and in consideration of the premium of

[£] POUNDS now paid by the Lessee to the Lessor (the receipt whereof is hereby acknowledged) and of the rent and covenants on the part of the Lessee hereinafter reserved and contained THE LESSOR as beneficial owner [to the intent that the same covenants for title may be implied as if a demise at a rent were not excluded from the effect of Section 76 of The Law of Property Act 1925][3] HEREBY DEMISES unto the Lessee ALL AND SINGULAR the demised premises TOGETHER WITH the rights set out in the Fourth Schedule hereto TO HOLD the same unto the Lessee for the term of [ ] YEARS from the [ ] day of [ ]19 SUBJECT TO the rights set out in the Fifth Schedule hereto (which so far as not already affecting the Lessor's estate in the demised premises are hereby excepted and reserved from this demise) and to the covenants on the part of the Lessee hereinafter contained YIELDING AND PAYING therefor from the date hereof[4] until the 24th June 2015 the yearly rent of [ ] Pounds from the 24th June 2015 until the 24th June 2048 the yearly rent of [ ] Pounds and for the remainder of the term hereby granted the yearly rent of [ ] Pounds[5] being in each case free from all deductions and payable by two equal half-yearly instalments on the 24th June and the 25th December in every year[6] the first of such payments to be made on the date hereof and to be an apportioned amount for the period from the date hereof until the following half yearly instalment date

3 THE Lessee for the mutual protection of the Lessor and of the Management Company and of the lessees of the Flats and Parking Spaces HEREBY COVENANTS:

3.1 With the Lessor to observe and perform the obligations on the part of the Lessee set out in Parts One Two and Three of the Eighth Schedule hereto

3.2 With the Management Company to observe and perform the obligations on the part of the Lessee set out in Parts Two and Three of the Eighth Schedule hereto

3.3 With the lessees of the other Flats and Parking Spaces to observe and perform the obligations on the part of the Lessee set out in Part Three of the Eighth Schedule hereto

4 THE Lessor relying on the covenants on the part of the Lessee herein contained HEREBY COVENANTS with the Lessee to observe and perform the obligations on the part of the Lessor set out in the Ninth Schedule hereto

5 THE Management Company relying on the covenants on the part of the Lessee herein contained HEREBY COVENANTS with the Lessor and as a separate covenant with the Lessee to observe and perform the obligations on the part of the Management Company set out in the Tenth Schedule hereto

6 IT IS HEREBY AGREED AND DECLARED as follows:

6.1 That if any rent hereby reserved or any part thereof shall be unpaid for thirty days next after the same shall have become due (whether the same shall have been lawfully demanded or not) or if any covenant by the Lessee or condition herein contained shall not be performed or observed by the Lessee then and in any such case it shall be lawful for the Lessor or any person or persons authorised by it in that behalf at any time thereafter to re-enter the demised premises or any part thereof in the name of the whole and thereupon this demise shall absolutely determine but without prejudice to the right of action of the Lessor in respect of any antecedent breach or non-observance by the Lessee of the covenants or conditions herein contained

6.2 That all rights and obligations of the Lessor and the Lessee respectively under this Lease shall be incident to and devolve with the legal reversion immediately expectant on the term hereby granted and with the leasehold interest hereby created and shall accordingly be enjoyed and performed by the person in whom such reversion and leasehold interest respectively shall for the time being be vested

6.3 That nothing herein contained shall be construed as entitling the Lessee to require that all or any of the covenants herein contained shall be imposed upon or enforced in respect of any property adjoining or neighbouring the development[7]

6.4 Where the Lessee is more than one person it is declared that they are in equity joint tenants/tenants in common and the survivor of them can/cannot give a valid receipt for capital money arising on a disposition of this Lease. In this clause the expression 'the Lessee' means only the persons named as the third party to this Lease

6.5 Section 196 of The Law of Property Act 1925 shall apply to any notice demand or other instrument authorised to be served hereunder and any notice served by the Lessor shall be sufficiently served by any agent of the Lessor

6.6 The rights hereby granted and reserved shall only take effect in so far as they are ascertained within 21 years from the date of this lease which period shall be the perpetuity period for the purpose of this lease[8]

7 IT IS HEREBY CERTIFIED that the transaction hereby effected does not form part of a larger transaction or of a series of transactions in respect of which the amount or value or the aggregate amount or value of the consideration (other than rent) exceeds the sum of [as the case may be]

THE FIRST SCHEDULE

The Development[9]

ALL THAT PIECE OF LAND LYING OFF [Blackacre] Road Birmingham in the County of the West Midlands and having a frontage to a private road known or intended to be known as [Butterworths] Close with the flats parking spaces gardens and bin stores and drying areas erected or in course of erection thereon and the Private Road as before defined and any other buildings and any landlord's fixtures and fittings and Service Installations and any walls fences and works which may during the term hereby granted be upon or under such land which said piece of land is shown on Plan No 1 and thereon edged red and in parts hatched black cross hatched black and shaded with dots

THE SECOND SCHEDULE*

The Maintained Property

FIRST the Private Road SECONDLY the Parking Spaces THIRDLY the gardens and grounds shown for the purpose of identification only shaded with dots on Plan No 1 FOURTHLY the drying area bin and gardeners stores shown on Plan No. 1 FIFTHLY the entrance halls passages landings staircases and other parts of the Flats which are used in common by the owners or occupiers of any two or more of the Flats and the glass in the windows of such common parts SIXTHLY the structural parts of the Buildings including the roofs gutters rainwater pipes foundations floors all walls bounding individual Flats therein and all external parts of the Buildings and all Service Installations not used solely for the purpose of one Flat (but not including the glass in the windows of the individual Flats non-structural walls within the Flats the interior joinery plaster work tiling and other surfaces of floors ceilings and walls of the Flats and Service Installations which exclusively serve individual Flats or the exterior doors of the Flats except the external surfaces of them)

THE THIRD SCHEDULE

PART ONE

The Said Flat

ALL THAT [first] floor flat forming part of the Development and known for development purposes (but not for postal purposes) as Flat Number [ ] [Greenacre] Court Birmingham in the County of the West Midlands TOGETHER WITH all landlord's fixtures and fittings which are now or may from time to time during the term hereby granted be in the said flat ALL which said flat is delineated on Plan No. 2 and thereon edged red being part of the building shown uncoloured and marked 'A' on Plan No. 1 TOGETHER WITH the foundations (if any) floors ceilings roofs (if any) walls doors and windows bounding the same PROVIDED THAT in the case of any such floors ceilings or walls which also form the boundary of another Flat or building only the inner half of such floors ceilings and walls (divided in the case of floors and ceilings medially and horizontally through the main structure and in the case of walls medially and vertically through the main structure) AND TOGETHER ALSO WITH all Service Installations used solely for the purpose of the said flat whether or not within the boundaries of the said flat as hereinbefore defined but EXCEPT AND RESERVING from this demise all Service Installations not used solely for the purpose of the said flat

PART TWO

The said Parking Space

The Parking Space forming part of the Development and shown uncoloured and numbered [ ] on Plan No. 1 together with the sub-base and tarmacadamed surfacing edging kerbs and white lining and numerals

THE FOURTH SCHEDULE

Rights included in the demise

1 The benefit of the rights reserved in the Second Schedule of the Management Company's Lease[10] so far as the same relate to the demised premises

2 The right (in common with all other persons similarly entitled) to the free passage and running of water soil gas electricity telephone and other services from and to the demised premises through and from the Service installations forming part of the Development or crossing the Adjoining Property

3 The right of support and shelter for the demised premises by and from the remaining parts of the Development or (where applicable) the Adjoining Property

4.1 The right to the benefit of the covenants entered into by the lessees of the Flats and Parking Spaces (other than the demised premises) with the Lessor for the observance and performance of the covenants in the form set out in part Three of the Eighth Schedule hereto

4.2 The right to the benefit of the covenants entered into or to be entered into by the Lessor with the Lessees of Plots [to inclusive][11] on the Adjoining Property to contribute one [ ] part of the cost of maintaining the areas shown shaded with dots and hatched and cross hatched black on the Plan No. 1

5 Such rights of access to and entry upon the remaining parts of the Development or (where applicable) the Adjoining Property as are necessary for the proper performance of the Lessee's obligations hereunder or for the repair decoration maintenance or inspection of the demised premises

THE FIFTH SCHEDULE

Rights to which the demise is subject

1 The rights set out in the First Schedule to the Management Company's Lease[12] so far as the same affect the demised premises

2 The right of support and shelter for the remaining parts of the Development and (where applicable) for the Adjoining Property by and from the demised premises

3 Such rights of access to and entry upon the demised premises by the Lessor and its lessees and tenants as are necessary for the proper performance of its or their obligations hereunder or under covenants relating to other parts of the Development or (where applicable) the Adjoining Property for the repair decoration maintenance or inspection of other parts of the Development

4 The right for the Lessor at any time or times hereafter without obtaining the consent of or paying compensation to the Lessee:

4.1 To build or rebuild or alter or permit or suffer to be built or rebuilt or altered any buildings or erections upon the Development (other than the Building of which the said flat forms part) or upon the Adjoining Property according to such plans and to such height extent or otherwise and in such manner as the Lessor shall think fit notwithstanding that such buildings as so built rebuilt or altered may obstruct any lights windows or other openings in or on the demised premises

4.2 To alter the layout of the Private Road and the Adjoining Property but not so as to prejudice access to the demised premises

4.3 To make such alterations as it may think fit in the position or extent of the gardens and grounds shown shaded with dots on Plan No. 1

4.4 To tie into the walls of the Building (where appropriate) for the purpose of carrying out the remainder of its development on the Adjoining Property

5 The right (so far as necessary in common with the Lessee) for the Lessor and its lessees and tenants to the free passage and running of water soil gas electricity telephone and other services from and to those parts of the Development not included in the demised premises through and from any appropriate Service Installations within the demised premises TOGETHER WITH all easements rights and privileges necessary and proper for inspecting cleaning repairing maintaining and reinstating the same

6 The right (so far as necessary in common with the Lessee) for the Lessor and its lessees and tenants to connect to and use the communal television aerial (if any) provided by the Lessor or the Management Company and attached to the demised premises

7 The right for the Lessor and the lessees tenants or occupiers of Plots No. [to] inclusive on the Adjoining Property and its and their employees to go pass and repass at all times and for all purposes in connection with the use or occupation of such properties with or without vehicles as appropriate) over and along the areas hatched black on the Plan No. 1 such right to be conditional on such persons paying one [ ] part of the cost of repairing maintaining and when necessary reinstating the aforementioned areas

8 The right for the lessees tenants or occupiers of the plots mentioned in clause 7 hereof to use for the temporary parking of a private motor vehicle the areas shown cross hatched black on the Plan No. 1 such right to be conditional upon such persons paying one [ ] part of the cost of repairing maintaining and when necessary reinstating the aforementioned areas

THE SIXTH SCHEDULE

The Maintenance Expenses

Moneys actually expended or reserved for periodical expenditure by or on behalf of the Management Company at all times during the term hereby granted in respect of the following:

1 Repairing rebuilding repointing improving or otherwise treating as necessary and keeping the Maintained Property and every part thereof in good and substantial repair order and condition and renewing and replacing all worn or damaged parts thereof

2 Painting with two coats at least of the best quality paint so often as may (in the opinion of the Management Company) be necessary and in a proper and workmanlike manner all the wood metal stone and other work of the Maintained Property and the external surfaces of all exterior doors of the Buildings and of the Flats which usually are or ought to be painted as to the outside and inside portions thereof at least once in every four years and in the last year of the said term (terminate when

it may) and at the time of every inside painting distempering white-washing decorating and colouring all such parts of the inside of the Maintained Property as usually are or ought to be so dealt with and papering with paper of suitable quality such parts thereof as are usually papered

3 Keeping the gardens and grounds of the Maintained Property generally in a neat and tidy condition and tending and renewing all lawns flower beds shrubs and trees forming part thereof as necessary and maintaining repairing and where necessary reinstating any boundary wall hedge or fence (if any) marked with an inwards T on the Plan No. 1 and any other walls hedges or fences within the Development and any benches seats garden ornaments or drying areas

4 Keeping the Private Road in good repair and clean and tidy and edged where necessary and clearing snow from the Private Road where necessary Provided That there shall be no liability upon the Lessor or the Management Company to carry out snow clearance unless requested by not less than 85% of the persons entitled to use the Private Road

5 Paying a fair proportion (according to user) of the cost of cleaning repairing and reinstating any drains and sewers forming part of the Adjoining Property which also serve any of the Flats and Parking Spaces (such proportion to be conclusively determined by the Management Company)

6 Providing and paying such workmen as may be necessary in connection with the up-keep of the Maintained Property

7 Insuring the Buildings against loss or damage by fire storm and tempest and such other risks as the Management Company shall decide PROVIDED:

7.1 This provision is subject as mentioned in paragraph 1.2 of the Seventh Schedule

7.2 The Management Company shall obtain the approval of the Lessor (not to be unreasonably withheld) to the Company or office with which the insurance is placed and to the sum insured and to the risks covered

7.3 The insurance shall include the cost of demolition and clearing of buildings and 10% of the sum insured for architects and surveyors fees

7.4 If the money receivable under any such insurance shall be insufficient to meet the cost of the necessary works of rebuilding repair or reinstatement then the deficiency shall be treated as a further item of expense under this Schedule recoverable from the lessees of the Flats and Parking Spaces accordingly

7.5 The insurance shall be effected in the joint names of the Lessor and the Management Company and the cover shall extend to the lessees for the time being of the Flats and Parking Spaces and their mortgagees

8 Insuring any risks for which the Management Company may be liable as an employer of persons working on the Development or as the owner of the Development or any part thereof as it shall think fit

9 Cleaning as necessary the external and the internal faces of all windows in the Maintained Property and as may be necessary keeping cleaned the common entrance halls passages landings and staircases and all other common parts of the flats

10 Cleaning as necessary and if necessary re-equipping any drying areas forming part of the Maintained Property

11 Operating maintaining and (if necessary) renewing the lighting apparatus from time to time of the Maintained Property and providing such additional lighting apparatus as the Management Company may think fit

12 Providing and arranging for the emptying of receptacles for rubbish for the use of the lessees of the Flats

13 Paying all rates taxes duties charges assessments and outgoings whatsoever (whether parliamentary parochial local or of any other description) assessed charged or imposed upon or payable in respect of the Maintained Property or any part thereof except in so far as the same are the responsibility of the individual lessee of any Flat

14 Abating any nuisance and executing such works as may be necessary for complying with any notice served by a local authority in connection with the Development or any part thereof in so far as the same is not the liability of or attributable to the fault of any individual lessee of any Flat
15 Preparing and supplying to the lessees of the Flats copies of any regulations made by the Management Company governing the use of the Flats and/or the Maintained Property
16 Generally managing and administering the Development and protecting the amenities of the Development and for that purpose employing a firm of managing agents and (in so far as the Management Company think fit) enforcing or attempting to enforce the observance of the covenants on the part of any lessee of any of the Flats
17 Employing a qualified accountant for the purpose of auditing the accounts in respect of the Maintenance Expenses and certifying the total amount thereof for the period to which the account relates
18 Complying with the requirements and directions of any competent authority and with the provisions of all statutes and all regulations orders and byelaws made thereunder relating to the Development insofar as such compliance is the responsibility of the lessee of any flat
19 The purchase maintenance renewal and insurance of fire-fighting appliances for the Development and the purchase maintenance renewal and insurance of communal television aerials and such other equipment as the Management Company may from time to time consider necessary or desirable for the carrying out of the acts and things mentioned in this Schedule
20 Administering the Management Company itself and arranging for all necessary meetings thereof to be held and complying with all relevant statutes and regulations and orders thereunder and (if the Management Company thinks fit) employing a suitable person or firm to deal with these matters
21 The provision maintenance and renewal of any other equipment and the provision of any other service which in the opinion of the Management Company it is reasonable to provide and which (at the time when the equipment or service concerned is first provided) the lessees of at least two-thirds of the Flats wish the Management Company to provide
22 A sum representing [percentage sum to be fixed][13] of the costs expenses and outgoings referred to in the preceding clauses of this Schedule which said sum shall be the Management fee of the Management Company or its successors in title

23.1 Such sum (to be fixed annually) as shall be estimated by the Management Company (whose decision shall be final) to provide a reserve fund for items of expenditure referred to in this Schedule to be or expected to be incurred at any time during the period of three years commencing with the date upon which the estimate is made

23.2 The said reserve fund shall be kept in separate accounts and any interest on or income of the said fund shall be held by the Management Company in trust for the lessees of the Flats and shall only be applied in accordance with the terms of this Schedule

THE SEVENTH SCHEDULE

The Lessee's Proportion of the Maintenance Expenses

1 The Lessee's Proportion means one [ ] part of the Maintenance Expenses attributable to the matters mentioned in the Sixth Schedule hereto (but with the benefit of Clause 4.2 of the Fourth Schedule hereto) Provided Always as follows:

1.1 The certificate of the accountant for the time being of the Management Company as to the total amount of the Maintenance Expenses for the period to which the account relates shall (subject as hereinafter mentioned) be binding on the Management Company and the Lessee

1.2 If the Lessee shall at any time during the said term object to any item of the Maintenance Expenses as being unreasonable or to the insurances mentioned in the Sixth Schedule hereto being insufficient then the matter in dispute shall be determined by a person to be appointed for the purpose by the President for the time being of the Royal Institution of Chartered Surveyors whose decision shall bind both parties Provided Always that any objection by the Lessee under this sub-paragraph shall not affect the obligation of the Lessee to pay to the Management Company the Lessee's Proportion of the Maintenance Expenses in accordance with paragraph 3 of this Schedule and after the decision of any person appointed by the said President of the Royal Institution of Chartered Surveyors as aforesaid any overpayment by the Lessee shall either be credited against future payments due from the Lessee to the Management Company under this Schedule or (if the Lessee so requests) repaid by the Management Company to the Lessee

1.3 The amount of the Maintenance Expenses shall be adjusted to take into account any sums received by the Management Company as contributions towards the cost of the work mentioned in the Sixth Schedule hereto from the owners lessees or occupiers of any adjoining or neighbouring properties and the Management Company shall use its best endeavours to recover the contributions (if any) due from such persons[14]

2 An account of the Maintenance Expenses (distinguishing between actual expenditure and reserve for future expenditure) for the period ending [[15]] next following the date when construction of the Buildings shall have been completed and for each subsequent year ending on the [[15]] during the said term shall be prepared and the Management Company shall within three months of the date of each account serve on the Lessee a copy thereof and of the accountant's certificate

3 The Lessee shall pay to the Management Company the Lessee's Proportion of the Maintenance Expenses in manner following that is to say:

3.1 In advance on the [ ] day of [ ] and the [ ] day of [[16]] in every year throughout the said term one half of the Lessee's Proportion of the amount estimated by the Management Company or its managing agents as the Maintenance Expenses for the year ending on the next [[15]] the first payment to be apportioned (if necessary) from the date hereof Provided That for the first yearly period there shall be substituted the period from the date hereof to the [[17]] next following the date when construction of the Buildings shall have been completed and the payments on account shall be adjusted accordingly

3.2 Within 21 days after the service by the Management Company on the Lessee of the copy of the account and certificate referred to in paragraph 2 of this Schedule for the period in question the Lessee shall pay to the Management Company or be entitled to receive from the Management Company the balance by which the Lessee's proportion respectively exceeds or falls short of the total sums paid by the Lessee to the Management Company pursuant to paragraph 3.1 of this Schedule during the said period

THE EIGHTH SCHEDULE

Covenants by the Lessee

PART ONE

Covenants enforceable by the Lessor

1 To pay the said rent hereinbefore reserved on the days and in the manner herein provided

2 To yield up at the termination of the said term the demised premises together with any landlord's fixtures and appliances and any replacements thereof in such good and substantial repair order and condition as shall be consistent in all respects with the due performance and observance of the covenants on the part of the Lessee and the conditions herein contained

3 To pay all costs charges and expenses (including legal costs and fees payable to a Surveyor) incurred by the Lessor in or in contemplation of any proceedings or the service of any notice under Sections 146 and 147 of The Law of Property Act 1925 including the reasonable costs charges and expenses aforesaid of and incidental to the inspection of the demised premises the drawing up of schedules of dilapidations and notices and any inspection to ascertain whether any notice has been complied with and such costs charges and expenses shall be paid whether or not forfeiture for any breach shall be avoided otherwise than by relief granted by the court

4 At any time within six calendar months next before the termination of the said term to permit intending lessees and tenants authorised by order in writing of the Lessor or its agents to view the demised premises at reasonable hours in the daytime by appointment

PART TWO

Covenants enforceable by the Lessor and the Management Company

5 To pay and discharge all rates taxes assessments charges duties and other outgoings whatsoever whether parliamentary parochial or of any other kind which now are or during the said term shall be assessed on charged on or payable in respect of the demised premises or any part thereof or by the landlord tenant owner or occupier thereof in respect thereof

6 To pay to the Management Company the Lessee's Proportion of the Maintenance Expenses at the times and in the manner herein provided and also to pay any Value Added Tax chargeable in respect of the same

7 To keep the Management Company and the Lessor indemnified in respect of water rate and charges for other services payable in respect of the demised premises which the Lessor or the Management Company shall from time to time during the said term be called upon to pay such sums to be repaid to the Lessor or the Management Company on demand

8 To repair and keep the demised premises (but excluding such parts of the demised premises as are included in the Maintained Property) and every part thereof and all landlord's fixtures and fittings therein and all additions thereto in good and substantial repair order and condition at all times during the said term including the renewal and replacement forthwith of all worn or damaged parts but so that the Lessee shall not be liable for any damage which may be caused by any of the risks covered by the insurance referred to in paragraph 7 of the Sixth Schedule hereto (unless such insurance shall be wholly or partially vitiated by any act or default of the Lessee or of any member of the family employee or visitor of the Lessee or other such occupiers) or for any work for which the Management Company may be expressly liable under the covenants on the part of the Management Company hereinafter contained

9 If the Lessee shall (in the exercise of the rights conferred upon him by paragraph 5 of the Fourth Schedule hereto) require access to any other part of the Development to give at least forty eight hours notice in writing (except in cases of extreme urgency) to the Management Company's agents and to the occupiers of that part of the Development to which the Lessee requires access and the Lessee shall on giving such notice be entitled to have access to such part of the Development but shall act carefully and reasonably doing as little damage as possible to any part of the Development and making good all damage done

10 As often as may be necessary and at least once in every seventh[18] year and in the year preceding the termination of the said term to paint with two coats of the best

quality paint and in a proper and workmanlike manner all the internal wood metal stone and other work of the demised premises which usually are or ought to be painted and at the time of every inside painting to distemper whitewash decorate and colour all such parts of the inside of the demised premises as are usually or ought to be so dealt with and to paper with paper of suitable quality such parts thereof as are usually papered

11 To clean all the interior surfaces of all windows of the said flat at least once in every four weeks

12 To clean all the exterior surfaces of all windows of the said flat at least once in every four weeks

13 To permit the Lessor or the Management Company or their respective agents with or without workmen and others at any convenient hours in the daytime to enter into and upon the demised premises to take inventories of the landlord's fixtures fittings and appliances therein and to view the condition thereof and upon notice being given to the Lessee specifying any repair or works necessary to be done for which the Lessee is liable hereunder forthwith to comply with the same and if the Lessee shall not within thirty days after the service of such notice proceed diligently with the execution of such repairs or works then to permit the Lessor or the Management Company or their respective agents with or without workmen and appliances to enter upon the demised premises and cause such repairs or works to be executed and the cost thereof shall be repayable by the Lessee on demand

14 To make good any damage to any part of the Development caused by any act or omission or negligence of any occupant of or person using the demised premises and (without prejudice to the generality of the foregoing) not to damage or interfere with the aerials and services of the Development (whether or not attached to or included in the demised premises) or the fire-fighting appliances and equipment referred to in the Sixth Schedule hereto

15 Not to bring into the Flats or any part thereof any article which would impose a load of more than 1.5 kilonewtons per square metre on any part of the floor surface or any article which is or may become dangerous to the Development or the occupants thereof

16 Not to do or permit or suffer any act or omission which may render any increased or extra premium payable for the said insurance of the Development or any part thereof or which may make void or voidable any such insurance or the insurance of premises adjoining the Development and so far as the Lessee is liable hereunder to comply in all respects with the reasonable requirements of the insurer with which the Development or any part thereof may for the time being be insured

17 Forthwith to make good to the Management Company all loss or damage sustained by the Management Company consequent upon any breach of this last mentioned provision

18 Not to do or permit or suffer to be done any act matter or thing on or in respect of the demised premises which contravenes the provisions of the Town and Country Planning Act 1971 or any enactment amending or replacing it and to keep the Lessor and the Management Company indemnified against all claims demands and liabilities in respect of any such contravention

19 To comply with and make every endeavour to ensure that all persons living in or visiting the said flat or using the parking space or any part of the Maintained Property shall comply with all such regulations as the Management Company shall from time to time make for the preservation of the amenities of the Development or for the general convenience of the occupiers of the Buildings (the Management Company having the power to vary or add to such regulations from time to time as it thinks fit)

20 To deliver to the Lessor forthwith a copy of every notice or other document of

whatever description affecting or likely to affect the demised premises or any part thereof received by the Lessee from any authority or person whatsoever whether such notice or other document as aforesaid be served upon the Lessee or upon any sub-tenant of the Lessee and at the request of the Lessor to make or join with the Lessor in making such objections or representations against or in respect of any notice or other document as aforesaid as the Lessor shall deem expedient

21 To comply in all respects at the Lessee's own cost with the provisions of any statute statutory instrument order rule or regulation and of any order direction or requirement made or given by any planning authority or the appropriate minister or court (whether requiring anything to be done or omitted by landlord tenant or occupier) so far as the Lessee is liable hereunder and forthwith to give notice in writing to the Lessor of the making or giving of such order direction or requirement as aforesaid

22 Not to cut maim or injure nor to make any breach in any part of the structure of the demised premises nor without the previous consent in writing of the Lessor or its agents to make any alteration whatsoever to the plan design or elevation of the demised premises nor to make any openings therein nor to open up any floors walls or ceilings for the purpose of altering or renewing any pipes wires ducts or conduits nor to alter any of the landlord's fixtures fittings or appliances therein And not in any case to commit or allow any waste or spoil on or about the demised premises nor to display any window boxes or aerials on or from the demised premises (except aerials placed there by the Lessor or the Management Company)

23 On making application for any such consent as aforesaid to submit to the Lessor or its agents such plans block plans elevations and specifications as the Lessor or its Agents shall require and to pay the legal and surveyors fees of the Lessor in connection with any such application and to carry out any work authorised only in accordance with such plans block plans elevations and specifications as the Lessor or its agents shall approve in writing making use of good sound and substantial materials all of which shall be subject to inspection and approval by the Lessor or its agents

24 Not at any time during the said term separately to assign transfer underlet or part with the possession or occupation of any part or parts of the demised premises but only to assign transfer underlet or part with the possession thereof as a whole and not so to assign transfer underlet or part with the possession or occupation of the demised premises during the last seven years of the said term without the prior written consent of the Lessor or its agents (not to be unreasonably withheld)

25 On the occasion of every assignment or transfer of the demised premises for the term hereby granted and in every underlease or tenancy agreement (which expression shall in this sub-clause include any immediate or derivative underlease or tenancy agreement but shall not include any underlease or tenancy agreement for a term not exceeding twenty one years granted at a rack rent and without payment of a fine) of the whole of the demised premises to insert a covenant by the assignee underlessee or tenant as the case may be directly with the Management Company to observe and perform the covenants on the part of the Lessee and conditions contained in Parts Two and Three of the Eighth Schedule of this Lease

26 Within one month after the date of any and every assignment transfer mortgage charge underlease or tenancy agreement (including any immediate or derivative underlease or tenancy agreement) of the whole or part of the demised premises for any term assignment of such underlease or grant of probate or letters of administration order of court or other matter disposing of or affecting the demised premises or devolution of or transfer of title to the same to give or procure to be given to the Solicitors for the Lessor and separately to the Solicitors for the Management Company notice in writing of such disposition or devolution or transfer of title with full particulars thereof and in the case of an underlease (and if required by the Lessor or

the Management Company) a copy thereof for registration and retention by it And at the same time to produce or cause to be produced to them the document affecting or (as the case may be) evidencing such disposition or other matter And to pay or cause to be paid at the same time to the Lessor's Solicitors and to the Management Company's Solicitors such reasonable fee appropriate at the time of registration (but not being less than [[19]] Pounds in each case) in respect of any such notice perusal of documents and registration affecting the demised premises

27 Not to interfere with or obstruct in the performance of the duties from time to time imposed upon him by the Management Company any employee of the Management Company and not to carry out any work of decoration repair maintenance or otherwise upon the exterior of the Buildings

28 Not to carry out nor allow to be carried out work on any vehicle on any part of the Development or the Adjoining Property

29 Not to abandon any wheeled vehicle on any part of the Development or the Adjoining Property and in the event of any breach of this covenant it shall be lawful for the Lessor without prejudice to its rights hereunder to arrange for the removal of such abandoned vehicle and to recover from the Lessee any costs incurred by it

PART THREE

Covenants enforceable by the Lessor and the Management Company and lessees of other Flats

30 To use:

30.1 The said flat as a whole as a private residence for not more than [[20]] persons

30.2 The said parking space solely for the parking of a private motor vehicle and/or cycle used by the occupier from time to time of the said flat and not to use or suffer to be used the demised premises in any manner other than as aforesaid and in particular not to carry on or permit or suffer to be carried on in or from the demised premises any trade business or profession

31.1 Not to allow any motor vehicle wheeled vehicle or other form of transport to be parked on any part of the Development except:

31.1.1 A private vehicle and/or cycle may be parked permanently or temporarily in the said parking space

31.1.2 Any private motor vehicle used by the Lessee or his family employees or visitors may be parked temporarily and subject to availability on the car parking spaces in the bays provided forming part of the Private Road but nevertheless so as not to cause any obstruction to other users of the Private Road

32 Not to allow any trailer caravan or boat or other similar chattel to be brought on to any part of the Development or the Adjoining Property

33 Not to use or permit or suffer the demised premises to be used for any illegal immoral or improper purpose and not to do permit or suffer on the demised premises any act or thing which shall or may be or become a nuisance damage annoyance or inconvenience to the Lessor or to the lessees or occupiers of any other Flat or to the owners or occupiers of any neighbouring property and to pay all costs charges and expenses of abating a nuisance and executing all such work as may be necessary for abating a nuisance or for carying out works in obedience to a notice served by a local authority in so far as the same is the liability of or wholly or partially attributable to the default of the Lessee And not to exhibit any notice advertisement name plate or placard of any kind upon the demised premises except a notice for the sale or underletting of the demised premises which notice may be displayed only in a window of the said flat or in such other place (if any) as the Management Company may prescribe or approve by regulation or otherwise

34 That if the Management Company goes into liquidation for any reason (whether compulsory or voluntary) or fails to observe and perform its covenants under this

lease then and in any such case the Lessee will join with the other lessees of the Flats and Parking Spaces in arranging for the carying out of the matters mentioned in the Sixth Schedule hereto the Lessee contributing part of the expense of so doing

THE NINTH SCHEDULE

Covenants on the part of the Lessor

1 To ensure that the leases granted by the Lessor of all other parts of the Building comprised in the Development contain covenants on the part of the various lessees to observe the like obligations as are contained in the Eighth Schedule hereto

2 That the Lessee paying the rent hereby reserved and observing and performing the several covenants on his part and the conditions herein contained shall peaceably hold and enjoy the demised premises and the rights hereby granted during the said term without any lawful interruption from or by the Lessor or any person lawfully claiming under or in trust for it

3 That as soon as practicable after the erection of the Flats has been completed the Lessor will complete the surfacing of the Private Road and the landscaping of the grounds forming part of the Development

4 That the Lessor will make and construct at its own expense and to a reasonable standard the Private Road

THE TENTH SCHEDULE

Covenants on the part of the Management Company

1 To carry out the works and do the acts and things set out in the Sixth Schedule hereto Provided:

1.1 The Management Company shall in no way be held responsible for any damage caused by any want of repair to the Development or defects therein for which the Management Company is liable hereunder unless and until notice in writing of any such want of repair or defect has been given to the Management Company and the Management Company has failed to make good or remedy such want of repair or defect within a reasonable time of receipt of such notice

1.2 Nothing in this covenant contained shall prejudice the Management Company's right to recover from the Lessee or any other person the amount or value of any loss or damage suffered by or caused to the Management Company or the Maintained Property by the negligence or other wrongful act or default of such person

1.3 The Management Company shall not be liable for any failure to provide employees and workmen necessary in connection with the Development if it shall have used its best endeavours to obtain them

2 Forthwith unless prevented by government or other regulations strikes lockouts and other causes beyond the Management Company's control to rebuild repair or reinstate in a good and substantial manner such parts of the Development as shall from time to time be destroyed or damaged applying for the purpose the money to be received by virtue of the insurance of the Development

3 If the Management Company shall (in exercise of the rights hereinbefore reserved) require access to the demised premises to give at least forty eight hours notice in writing (except in cases of extreme urgency) to the Lessee the Management Company on giving such notice being entitled to carry out the said repairs or works to the demised premises but so that the Management Company shall act carefully and reasonably doing as little damage to the demised premises as may be and making good all damage done

4 If required by the Lessee for the reasonable protection of the demised premises to enforce or assist the Lessee in enforcing the said covenants entered into or to be entered into by a lessee of any one or more of the other Flats provided that the Lessee

shall (if required) indemnify the Management Company against all costs and expenses in respect of such enforcement and provide such security for the said costs and expenses as the Management Company may reasonably require

(Attestation)

Notes

1 Plan No. 1 is the 1/500th, (or similar, suitable scale) plan showing the layout of the relevant part of the development. Plan No. 2 will be the floor plan of the block itself (obviously on a much larger scale).

2 This assumes a lease of the common parts actually in the name of the management company.

3 Words in square brackets are optional—it is up to the conveyancer whether or not he wants them in.

4 The term can commence with the date of the lease, instead of quoting a commencement date common to all the units in the same block, because the review dates are pre-set (although care must be taken not to fall into the 'variable rent' trap—see p 61, above). However, it will mean that the terms of the flats in the same block may well end on different dates. Presumably this would be no problem.

5 The dates and sums are hypothetical.

6 Or as required.

7 This clause may not be acceptable, certainly so far as the lessees and their advisers are concerned, or even so far as the lessor is concerned. See Precedent No 3, cl 3, Sixth Schedule, p 367, below, for a clause of opposite effect.

8 Or as desired.

9 The wording is an actual description which has been amended insofar as names are concerned.

10 See Precedent No 5, p 370, below, for a precedent of the type of lease which would be used. In fact it is not necessary to execute such a lease here; this is optional.

11 Only if there are adjoining blocks which adopt a sharing role.

12 See Precedent No 5, p 370, below.

13 See ch 17, p 195, above, for a discussion on management fees.

14 This clause is only relevant where, eg the block of flats concerned is part of a greater area of new development where other properties have the use of, and are to contribute to the maintenance of, areas enjoyed in common with the block of flats.

15 The end of the financial year under the terms of the lease; eg in this case the date would be 24 June (see cl 2, p 347, above).

16 Ie the full year ending and half year ending dates—in this case 24 June and 25 December.

17 Next following half-year ending date.

18 Or as required.

19 To be decided. As in this case two notices are required—it being just as important for the management company—ie the people *actually* running the development—to know about ownership, etc movements, as for the lessor—ie the owner of the reversionary investment.

20 As required.

---

3 Typical lease for studio or other small flat. Minimal maintenance on lessor

[For background commentary, see ch 9 which is devoted to a description of the 'studio flat scheme'. This precedent should be read in conjunction with Precedent No 4, p 369 below, which is the description of the demise, and also Precedent No 5, p 370, below, which is the 'concurrent' lease which might be used to transfer the interest in the block, to eg, a manager.]

[HM LAND REGISTRY
Land Registration Acts 1925 to 1971

COUNTY AND DISTRICT:
TITLE NUMBER:
PROPERTY: FLAT][1]

THIS LEASE is made the day of One thousand nine hundred and eighty BETWEEN [Builder/Reversioner] of/ whose registered office is situate at

(hereinafter called 'the Lessor') of the one part and [lessee] of

(hereinafter called 'the Lessee') of the other part

WHEREAS:

1 In this Lease unless the context otherwise requires:

(a) 'The block' means the building together with all garden ground footpaths drying areas (if any) open spaces parking spaces and vehicular access ways as are necessary for the proper enjoyment by individual lessees in the building of their flats all as described (including by references to a plan) in the Seventh Schedule hereto

(b) 'The building' means the building in which the flats are situate but excludes all garden ground footpaths drying areas (if any) open spaces parking spaces and vehicular access ways adjacent thereto

(c) 'Flats'[2] means the flats forming part of the building and 'flat' has a corresponding meaning

(d) 'The parking space' means the parking space forming part of the block

(e) 'The common part' means that part of the block (including the building) not included either in the flat and parking space/s or portions of accessways to parking space/s but which is included in the demised premises as hereinafter defined

(f) 'The demised premises' means the property hereby demised as described in the Seventh Schedule hereto

(g) 'The reserved rent' includes as well as the rent initially reserved hereunder such additional rent as is reserved under clauses 1(e)(i), and 1(f)[3] hereof (where applicable)

(h) 'The first value of the block' means the total of the open market value selling prices achieved by the Lessor of all the flats in the block AND the certificate of the Lessor's solicitor as to the amount of such selling prices shall be accepted as conclusive unless manifestly incorrect[4]

(i) 'The review value of the block' means the total of the open market value selling prices of all the flats in the block which the Chartered Surveyor referred to in clause 1(e) hereof considers on each review would be achieved on a vacant possession sale without incumbrances AND such Chartered Surveyor is to assume that each such flat is being sold individually and that its sale is in no way inhibited by the sales of any other flat in the block

(j) 'The Insured Risks' means and includes fire lightning explosion earthquake storm or flood water damage riot civil commotion vandalism theft subsidence and/or heave and land slip together with such other risks (if any) as the Lessor may from time to time think fit

(k) 'The Notice Value' means the consideration set out in the document then being registered Save that where the consideration is nominal or the document put up for registration has no reference to consideration the expression 'The Notice Value' means the last full consideration for value relating to the flat

(l) 'The Lessor' includes the successors in title of the Lessor and any person firm or corporation to whom the Lessor may grant a concurrent lease of the block for any part of the term hereby created

(m) 'The Lessee' includes the executors administrators and assigns of the Lessee and where two or more persons are expressed to be Lessees covenants entered into by them shall be deemed to be entered into jointly and severally

2 The title of the Lessor is set out in the Seventh Schedule hereto

3 The Lessor has agreed with the Lessee to a grant to the Lessee of a lease of the demised premises for the consideration at the rent and on the terms and conditions hereinafter appearing

NOW THIS DEED WITNESSETH as follows:

1 IN pursuance of the said agreement and in consideration of the sum specified in the Seventh Schedule hereto paid by the Lessee to the Lessor (the receipt whereof the Lessor hereby acknowledges) and of the rents and covenants hereinafter reserved and contained and on the part of the Lessee to be paid and observed and performed the Lessor HEREBY DEMISES unto the Lessee ALL THOSE the demised premises

(a) Together with the rights set out in the First Schedule hereto but reserving to the Lessor the right to grant similar rights over and affecting the demised premises to other lessees of flats in the block

(b) Subject to the rights set out in the Second Schedule hereto

(c) TO HOLD the same unto the Lessee from the date specified in the Seventh Schedule hereto for the term of YEARS

(d) YIELDING AND PAYING THEREFOR during the said term the initial yearly rent of £ by equal half-yearly payments in advance on the day of and the day of in each year the first of such payments being a proportionate payment to be made on the execution hereof and to be an apportionment from the date hereof to the next day for payment of rent following the date hereof

(e) (i) Such rent to be subject to review on each anniversary of the grant hereof and shall then be increased to such sum as is the same percentage of the review value of the block as the rent reserved under the preceding sub-clause is of the first value of the block BUT so that such reviewed rent shall never equal such a sum as would in appropriate circumstances create an inhibition on the premium capable of being charged on an assignment of the demised premises in the same manner as set out in Section 127 and Schedule 18 Part 11 of the Rent Act 1977 as amended by Section 78 of the Housing Act 1980 or any amending or similar legislation[5]

(ii) The amount of the rent shall be determined by a Chartered Surveyor acting as an expert and not as an arbitrator who shall be appointed by the President for the time being of the Royal Institution of Chartered Surveyors or (if he fails to appoint one within three months of being requested to do so) by the President for the time being of the Law Society on the application by the Lessor made at any time after the expiration of the [6] year of the said term (as the case may be)

(iii) The Surveyor may be requested to determine all or any of the rents of the flats comprised in the building together

(iv) The Lessor shall pay the fees of the Surveyor appointed under this clause[7]

(f) AND ALSO paying on demand by way of further or additional rent from time to time a sum or sums of money equivalent to one[8] equal part of the amount which the Lessor may from time to time expend in

(i) effecting or maintaining the insurance of the block against loss or damage by the Insured Risks in accordance with the provisions of the Sixth Schedule hereto and

(ii) providing a supply of electricity for the purposes of lighting the common parts of the block

(iii) keeping and maintaining the door entry system (if any) in good working order and condition including the payment of the rental charge in respect thereof (if any)

(iv) maintaining (including grass cutting) the garden areas and portions of footpaths vehicular accessways and other external areas as are within the demised premises[9]

[(v) (if considered necessary: it may prove wise to have some such 'fail safe' provision for the Lessor should the Lessee prove incapable of performing his 'self maintenance' which is the feature of this lease) carrying out by default as provided for in Clause 4 hereof the duties of the Lessee set out in clauses 1, 3, 4, 5 and 6 of the said Fifth Schedule]

2 THE Lessee hereby covenants with the Lessor and with the Lessees of other flats comprised in the block that the Lessee and the persons deriving title under him will at all times hereafter observe the restrictions set forth in the Third Schedule hereto

3 THE Lessee hereby covenants with the Lessor that the Lessee will observe and perform the obligations on the part of the Lessee set out in the Fourth Schedule hereto

4 THE Lessee hereby covenants with the Lessor and with the Lessees of the other flats comprised in the block that the Lessee will observe and perform the obligations on the part of the Lessee set out in the Fifth Schedule hereto

[(if required: see optional clause 1(f)(v), ante, and Fifth Schedule) PROVIDED ALWAYS that if in the opinion of the Lessor or his Surveyor the Lessee fails to perform his obligations as set out in the said Fifth Schedule the Lessor shall have the right to serve on the Lessee a notice in writing specifying the matters outstanding thereunder and if the Lessee continues to be in breach of his said obligations following the expiry of the twenty eighth day after the date of service of the said notice the Lessor shall have the right to perform the said obligations and recharge the cost thereof to the Lessee under the provisions of clause 1(f)(v) hereof]

5 THE Lessor hereby covenants with the Lessee that it will observe and perform the obligations on its part set out in the Sixth Schedule hereto

6 THE Lessee paying the reserved rent and performing and observing the covenants on the part of the Lessee herein contained shall peaceably hold and enjoy the demised premises for the term hereby created without any interruption by the Lessor or any person lawfully claiming under or in trust for it

7 IF the rent hereby reserved or any part thereof is unpaid twenty one days after becoming payable (whether formally demanded or not) or if any of the covenants on the part of the Lessee herein contained are not observed and performed then and in any such case it shall be lawful for the Lessor or any person or persons authorised by it in that behalf at any time thereafter to re-enter the demised premises or any part thereof in the name of the whole and thereupon the term hereby created shall absolutely determine but without prejudice to any right or remedy of the Lessor in respect of any breach of the covenants on the part of the Lessee hereinbefore contained Notwithstanding the generality of the foregoing the Lessor shall not exercise the right of re-entry above referred to unless twenty eight days notice in writing of the Lessor's intention so to do is first given to any mortgagee whose interest in the demised premises (which interest shall be subsisting at the date of the Lessor's said notice) has been notified to the Lessor and the unpaid rent or other breach of covenant which shall be specified in the Lessor's said notice shall not be paid or remedied on expiry of the said notice[10]

8 THE Lessor and the Lessee hereby apply to the Registrar for the entry on the Register of the following restriction on the title to the property: 'Except under an order of the Registrar no Transfer or Assent of the demised premises is to be registered unless a certificate is given by [as required] that notice of such Transfer or Assent has been given to the said '[11]

9 Certificate of Value

THE FIRST SCHEDULE

Rights included in the demise

1 The right in common with the Lessor the owners and occupiers of all other flats in the building and all others having the like right to use for the purpose only of access to and egress from the demised premises all such parts of the other common parts in the block as afford access thereto [Continue with similar rights (which should be drafted individually for each particular development) over the Estate of which the property forms part]

2 The right of passage for running of gas (if appropriate) electricity water soil and other services necessary for the proper enjoyment of the demised premises from and to the demised premises through the sewers drains pipes wires cables ducts or conduits forming part of the block [Continue with similar rights (again to be drafted individually) over Estate]

3 All rights of support protection and other easements and all quasi easements rights and benefits of a similar nature now enjoyed or intended to be enjoyed by the demised premises

4 Such rights of access to and entry upon the other common parts in the block and the other flats therein as are necessary for the proper performance of the Lessee's obligations hereunder

5 [only where there is an outside dustbin enclosure] The right for the Lessee in common with the Lessees of other flats to place refuse from the demised premises in the receptacles in the dustbin enclosure shown on the plan annexed to the Seventh Schedule hereto together with all necessary rights of way over the other common parts in the block for this purpose

6 The benefit of any covenants entered into by the Lessor with the Lessees of the other flats (each with the other) so far as such covenants are intended to benefit the demised premises or the Lessee [any other rights which are relevant should be added here]

THE SECOND SCHEDULE

Rights to which the demise is subject

1 All rights of support and protection and other easements and quasi easements rights and benefits of a similar nature now enjoyed or intended to be enjoyed by any other part of the block over the demised premises

2 Such rights of access to and entry upon the demised premises by the Lessor and the Lessees of the other flats as are necessary for the proper performance of their obligations hereunder or under covenants relating to other flats and similar to those herein contained

3 The burden of any covenant entered into by the Lessor with the lessees of the other flats so far as such covenants are intended to bind the demised premises or the Lessee [Add any other reservations etc relevant to the particular circumstances—ie the foregoing reservations are *general* ones; those *specific* to the development or those which the practitioner usually uses must be added in]

THE THIRD SCHEDULE

Lessee's covenants to observe restrictions

1 Not to use the demised premises nor permit the same to be used for any purpose whatsoever other than as a private dwelling house in the occupation of one family only or for any purpose from which a nuisance can arise to the other occupiers of the block or the neighbourhood or for any illegal or immoral purpose

2 Not to do or permit to be done any act or thing which may render void or voidable

any policy of insurance of any flat in or being part of the block or may cause an increased premium to be payable in respect thereof

3 Not to throw dirt rubbish rags or other refuse or permit the same to be thrown into sinks basins lavatories cisterns or waste or soil pipes in the flat but to place refuse in [(only where there is an outside dustbin enclosure) the dustbins in the area more particularly referred to in the First and Seventh Schedules hereto] otherwise where, eg the dustbins are in the interior of the building, [the appropriate receptacles therefor]

4 No piano record player radio loud-speaker or other electric electronic mechanical musical or other instrument of any kind (including a computer) shall be played or used nor shall any singing be practised in the demised premises so as to cause annoyance to the other occupiers of the other flats comprised in the block or so as to be audible outside the demised premises between the hours of 11 p.m. and 9 a.m.

5 No name writing drawing signboard plate or placard of any kind shall be put on or in any window on the exterior of the demised premises or so as to be visible from outside the demised premises (except that a notice advertising the demised premises for sale or for any sub-letting permitted hereunder is allowed) and no clothes or other articles shall be hung or exposed outside the demised premises except in areas specifically reserved for the purpose (where provided)

6 No bird dog or other animal which may cause annoyance to any lessee of any other flat comprised in the block shall be kept in the demised premises and no dog cat or other animal shall be kept in the demised premises without the written consent of the Lessor which consent may be revoked at the discretion of the Lessor

THE FOURTH SCHEDULE

Covenants by Lessee with Lessor

1 The Lessee shall pay the reserved rent on the days and in the manner above mentioned

2 The Lessee shall pay all existing and future rates taxes assessments and outgoings whether Parliamentary Local or otherwise now or hereafter imposed or charged on the demised premises or any part thereof or upon the Lessor

3 The Lessee shall not make any structural alterations or structural additions to the demised premises nor erect any new buildings thereon or remove any of the Landlord's fixtures and fittings without the previous consent in writing of the Lessor

4 The Lessee will pay all costs charges and expenses (including Solicitors' costs and Surveyors' fees) incurred by the Lessor for the purpose of and incidental to the preparation and service of a notice under Section 146 of the Law of Property Act 1925 notwithstanding forfeiture may be avoided otherwise than by relief granted by the Court

5 Forthwith after service upon the Lessee of any notice affecting the demised premises served by any person body or authority (other than the Lessor) the Lessee shall deliver a true copy thereof to the Lessor and if so required by the Lessor will join the Lessor in making such representation to any such person body or authority concerning any proposals affecting the demised premises as the Lessor may consider desirable and to join with the Lessor in any such appeal against any order or direction affecting the demised premises as the Lessor may consider desirable

6 (i) The Lessee shall not sub-let the whole or any part of the demised premises save that an underletting of the whole of the demised premises (with the prior consent of the Lessor and any mortgagee of the demised premises) is permitted in the case of a term certain not exceeding three years let at a rack rent[12]

(ii) The Lessee shall not assign part only of the demised premises

(iii) The Lessee shall not assign the whole of the demised premises without giving prior written notice of his intention so to do to the Lessor and the Lessor shall acknowledge in writing receipt of such notice and such acknowledgement shall be in sufficient terms so as to comply with the provisions of clause 8 hereof[13]

7 The Lessee shall within twenty-eight days of the date of every assignment grant of Probate or Administration Assent Transfer Mortgage Charge Discharge Order of Court or other event or document relating to the term (except a mortgage effected simultaneously with the grant of this Lease)[14] give notice thereof in writing to the Lessor and pay to it a fee for registration calculated at the rate of 0.1 per cent of the Notice Value of the demised premises and in the case of a document produce a certified copy of it to the Lessor for registration with notice[15]

8 Once every three years to re-decorate with good quality materials the interior of the flat contained in the demised premises

THE FIFTH SCHEDULE

Lessees Covenants for the benefit of the Lessor and other Lessees

1 The Lessee will maintain and repair in good and tenantable condition the demised premises during the term and yield up the same at the expiration of the term in like condition

2 To permit the Lessor or its agent to enter the demised premises upon prior reasonable notice being given (except in cases of emergency) to view the state of repair and condition thereof and to leave on the demised premises notice in writing to the Lessee of all defects and wants of reparation then and there found which the Lessee is liable to make good under the covenants herein contained and if the Lessee does not proceed diligently within three months of such notice to execute such repairs the cost of so doing to be payable by the Lessee on demand and if not so paid to be recoverable as if the same were rent in arrear

3 At the expiration of each three years of the term hereby granted and in the final year thereof to redecorate with good quality materials of a colour designated by the Lessor such parts of the interior of the common parts of the building as are included in the demised premises

4 At the expiration of each five years of the term hereby granted and in the final year thereof to paint with two coats of good quality paint of a colour to be designated by the Lessor the exterior parts of the common parts which form part of the demised premises

5 To maintain in efficient working order a sufficient electric light of not less than 60 watts in the passage outside the flat included in the demised premises in a position designated by the Lessor for the benefit of persons using the block and keep the same at all times on electricity supply [and to pay the sums as demanded by the Lessor in accordance with the provisions hereinbefore specified][16]

6 To keep and maintain such parts of the common parts as are within the demised premises whether inside the building or in the grounds surrounding the same in good order and condition

7 Where the demised premises include part of the garden in the block then the Lessee shall not erect any fences thereon or other structures without the consent in writing of the Lessor and will pay to the Lessor the amount which the Lessor may from time to time expend in maintaining the same in good order and condition and properly cultivated[17]

THE SIXTH SCHEDULE

Covenants by the Lessor with the Lessee

1 The Lessor shall insure and keep insured the block in the joint names of all persons having any interest therein against loss or damage by the Insured Risks in [nominated Insurer] or some other insurance office of repute in the sum equivalent to the amount at least of the full reinstatement value from time to time of the block (including

adequate amounts in respect of professional fees) and shall also take out and keep on foot in the said names a policy of insurance in an insurance office of repute covering liability for injury to persons in the block and shall make all the payments necessary for those purposes within seven days after the same shall become payable and shall produce to the Lessee on reasonable demand the policy or policies of such insurance and the receipt for the last premium for the same PROVIDED THAT instead of effecting the said insurance in the joint names of the said persons the Lessor may ensure that the interests of the said persons are noted on the relevant policies of insurance

2 In the event of the block or part thereof being damaged or destroyed by fire or other Insured Risk the Lessor shall as soon as is reasonably practicable lay out the insurance monies received in the repair rebuilding or reinstatement of the block

3 (i) The Lessor will require every person to whom it shall hereafter grant a lease of any part of the premises comprised in the block to covenant to observe the restrictions set forth in the Third Schedule hereto and to covenant in the terms of the Fifth Schedule hereto and that whilst any of the flats comprised in the building shall not for the time being be let under a lease in the same terms as this lease (mutatis mutandis) the Lessor shall be liable to make such payments and observe and perform such obligations as the Lessee would be liable to make observe and perform if such flat were so let

(ii) That (if so required by the Lessee) it will enforce the covenants on the part of the lessee of any other flat comprised in the building on the Lessee indemnifying the Lessor against all costs and expenses in respect of such enforcement and providing such security in respect of costs and expenses as the Lessor may reasonably require

4 If the title of the Lessor is leasehold then the Lessor shall pay the rent reserved by the Head Lease and shall perform and observe the covenants on its part therein contained

5 That the Lessor shall when called upon by the appropriate Local Authority so to do at its own expense well and sufficiently form metal and kerb the said new road and footways on the Lessor's [name of development] Estate (except the access ways to the parking spaces and footpaths which are intended to be private access ways and footpaths) until taken over by the said Local Authority and will indemnify the Lessee from and against all charges costs claims or demands for sewering levelling paving metalling flagging chanelling and making good the said new roads and footways as aforesaid so far as the same are co-extensive with the demised premises to the satisfaction of the said Local Authority and until the said new roads and footpaths shall be declared repairable at the public expense

6 The Lessor will

(a) As often as may in its opinion be necessary properly cultivate and maintain in good order and condition the garden which is included in the demised premises

(b) provide a supply of electricity to the common parts of the block

[continue with any other Lessors' obligations which are thought desirable: and to match up with clause 1 (f)]

THE SEVENTH SCHEDULE

The title of the Lessor and the Lessee

1 'The Estate' is the Lessor's land at in the County of which was conveyed to the Lessor by a conveyance dated the day of 19 and made between [parties]

[or, for registered cases]

The Lessor's title is registered at HM Land Registry with Title Absolute under Title Number

2 'The Block' is the piece of land on the Estate shown edged in blue on the plan together with all buildings thereon
3 The date of commencement of the term hereby granted is the day of 19
4 The price is £
5 'The Demised Premises'[18]

Notes

1 Delete if not registered.

2 This lease is intended for small units; indeed, it is only suitable for small units in small blocks. Very often this definition has been written as 'the studio flats' or some such description, but the adjectival usage seems somewhat tortologous and can safely be discarded.

3 See later in precedent as to what is reserved.

4 For a precedent of the certificate, see Precedent No 7, p 373, below.

5 This 'status quo' method of reviewing the ground rent (which as readers will appreciate is just one of the review options available) should only be used in the lease if the lessor and/or his solicitors are confident of being able to operate the review properly in later years. See also ch 4, p 56 et seq, above, on what review periods are acceptable.

6 The end of each review period, eg on a 21-year review cycle, the figures would be 20th, 41st, 63rd, 84th, and so on.

7 It seems fair that the lessor (or, eg whoever is managing the property) should pay the costs of the review, especially as on this review formula there will be a substantial rise involved.

8 A proportion related to the flats in the block

9 Continue with other maintenance matters, as required.

10 See commentary commencing on p 297, above.

11 For full details of this restriction and the reason for its inclusion see pp 86 et seq. Refer also to Fourth Schedule, cl 6 (iii).

12 This proviso was inserted into this particular form of lease by certain building societies which did not wish to restrict the ability of their borrowers in the armed services to sub-let their properties whilst away on overseas tours. For all that, the proviso is optional.

13 This is the other part of the equation to which cl 8, the Registry restriction, forms part. It imposes on the lessor the requirement to return the notice so as to give the lessee proof of the giving of the notice. See also pp 86 et seq for a full description of the procedure.

14 Only a mortgage effected with the original lease is excepted; the lessor will require notices of mortgages on subsequent assignments of the lease so as to keep his records up to date. On the original grant, he can easily ask his purchaser for details of the mortgagee; on subsequent assignments, he must rely on the notices. However, the fee on the mortgage may be remitted.

15 A specific notice fee could, of course, be quoted but why not tie an assignment fee to value, and thus keep up with inflation?

16 The author has constantly used this clause but it is probably questionable that at the end of the day it is going to work. One would hope that lessees would be public-spirited enough to replace light bulbs. Indeed, with studio flats such as these, the aim is to cut down on service charges as much as possible, and if the lessor is going to have to replace every bulb as it goes, then this responsibility is going to bump the service charge up tremendously. So at the end of the day, it is probably necessary to keep the clause in this form, and hope the lessees observe it. The words in square brackets refer back to the reservation of additional rent—in this case cl 1 (f) (ii).

17 This refers back to cl 1 (f) (iv) which reserves amounts expended by the lessor for these items as additional rent. The principal concern of the clause is grass-cutting. Experience has taught the author that lessees of studio flats built in this manner cannot be expected to cut their own grass, so that despite how much one wants to cut out lessor performed services, in order to keep down the lessees costs, grass cutting is not one of them.

18 The description is set out separately in the next Precedent, No 4, p 369.

4 Studio or small flat lease, minimal maintenance provisions: description of demise

[See also preceding Precedent, No 3, which is the body of the lease.]

'THE DEMISED PREMISES'

(a) [For Lower Flat]

The flat is flat number   on the ground floor of the building[1] within the block[1] comprising the flat in the position shown coloured [red] on the plan[1] and includes the interior walls thereof up to the level hereinafter referred to in the definition of 'common parts', the plaster (if any) on the ceiling and on the inside of the external walls (external walls in this context being deemed to include the whole of the external walls of the flat), and the wall separating the flat from the ground floor entrance hall (but excluding the plaster (if any) on the wall on the opposite side of the flat) up to the ceiling, and the glass in the windows of the flat.

Together with the garden land shown coloured [green] on the plan [if appropriate—the part coloured [purple] on the plan of the bin area and the structure protecting the same]

(a) [For Upper Flat]

The flat is flat number   on the [first] floor of the building within the block comprising the flat in the position shown coloured [red] on the plan and includes the interior walls thereof above the level hereinafter referred to in the definition of 'common parts', the plaster (if any) on the ceiling and on the inside of the external walls (external walls in this context being deemed to include the whole of the external walls of the flat), and the wall separating the flat from the [first] floor landing (but excluding the plaster (if any) on the opposite side to the flat) above such level, and the glass in the windows of the flat

(b) Parking space: the parking space is that part of the block which is shown edged [red or, as desired]

COMMON PARTS

(c) [For Lower Flat]

The common parts are those parts of the block which comprise the lower half part in depth of the structure between the ceilings of the flat and the floors of the flat above it, and (in all cases up to the same level) (i) the nearer half part in width of the wall between the flat and the adjoining lower flat (ii) the external walls of the flat and the doors and windows (but excluding glass) therein (iii) the part [edged red—or as desired] of the entrance hall which is shown coloured [orange] on the plan including the plaster on the walls thereof (but excluding (where the same is situate in the common parts hereby demised) the staircase leading to the first floor of the building) and (iv) the whole of the wall (including the plaster (if any) on the interior thereof) separating such last mentioned part from the exterior of the building and the windows (including glass) therein and such part of the door (including glass) therein as is coextensive therewith TOGETHER with (i) the land and structure of the building below the flat and the common parts hereinbefore described including the foundations supporting the internal and external walls thereof and (ii) those parts (if any) of the paths shown coloured [yellow] on the plan as are within the [red] edging thereon

(c) [for Upper flat]

the common parts are those parts of the block which comprise the upper half part in depth of the structure between the floors of the flat and the ceilings of the flat below it and (in all cases above the same level) (i) the nearer half part in width of the wall between the flat and the adjoining upper flat (ii) the external walls of the flat and the doors and windows (but excluding glass) therein (iii) the part [edged red—or as desired] of the [first] floor landing which is shown coloured [orange] on the plan including the plaster on the walls thereof and (iv) the whole of the wall (including the plaster (if any) on the interior thereof) separating such last-mentioned part from the exterior of the building and such part of the windows (including glass) therein as is coextensive therewith TOGETHER with (i) (where applicable[2]) that part of the staircase leading from [the entrance hall on the ground floor of the building] [the floor landing][3] to the [ ] floor landing thereof which is below the area coloured [orange] and edged [red] on the plan and (ii) the roof void and structure thereof above the flat and the common parts hereinbefore described[4]

Notes

1 This description assumes the definitions set out in Precedent No 3 above. If the description is used elsewhere, the conveyancer must be careful that proper definitions are included.

2 Which would depend on where the staircase was positioned physically; it would be up to the conveyancer to interpret the individual plan.

3 This part of the wording can be varied to accommodate a block with more than two storeys.

4 Refer to ch 9, p 110, above, for a description of how this demise was evolved for a particular situation.

---

5 Concurrent lease for use in circumstances described in chapter 10 (p 128, above).

[CONCURRENT

HM LAND REGISTRY

Land Registration Acts 1925–1971

COUNTY ABND DISTRICT

TITLE NUMBER

PROPERTY FLATS AT

ESTATE][1]

THIS LEASE is made the day of One thousand nine hundred and BETWEEN [Builder/Reversioner] of/whose registered office is situate at

(hereinafter called 'the Lessor') of the one part and [Concurrent Lessee] of/whose registered office is situate at

(hereinafter called 'the Management Company') of the other part

WHEREAS:

(i) The Lessor is [registered at HM Land Registry as proprietor with Title Absolute of the [freehold][2] property comprised (inter alia) in the Title above referred to] [seised for an estate in fee simple in possession of land situate at [description]][3] which consists of [name of type of flats] known as together with parking spaces accessways thereto gardens and grounds (all of which demised premises are more particularly delineated on the plan annexed hereto and thereon edged red and are hereinafter referred to as 'the block')

(ii) The Lessor has granted Leases of the Flats parking spaces [and portions of accessways thereto] and common parts comprised in the block each for a term of [ ] years from the [ ] day of [ ] 19 (which Leases [are referred to in the Title above referred to and][1] are hereinafter called 'the Flat Leases')

NOW THIS DEED WITNESSETH AS FOLLOWS:

1 IN consideration of the rents and covenants hereinafter reserved and contained and on the part of the Management Company to be paid observed and performed the Lessor hereby demises unto the Management Company ALL THAT the Block TO HOLD the same UNTO the Management Company from the day of 19 for the term of [same term as unit leases] years less the last day thereof (hereinafter called 'the concurrent term') SUBJECT TO and with the benefit of the Flat Leases YIELDING AND PAYING THEREFOR during the concurrent term the yearly rent of [nominal sum—usually £1] to be paid on the day of in every year free of all deductions whatsoever[4]

2 THE Management Company hereby covenants with the Lessor as follows:

(i) To pay the rent hereby reserved at the times and in the manner aforesaid

(ii) To pay or otherwise effectually indemnify the Lessor against all rates taxes assessments charges impositions and outgoings which may at any time during the concurrent term be assessed charged or imposed upon the block or the owner or occupier in respect thereof (including any rent due from the Lessor under the terms of any Head Lease)

(iii) At all times during the concurrent term to perform and fulfil all the obligations of the Lessor under the Flat Leases and to indemnify and save harmless the Lessor in respect of the same

(iv) During the concurrent term to enforce the performance and also (consistently with the provisions of the Flat Leases) to perform in relation to the several flats parking spaces and portions of accessways thereto comprised in the Block the obligations of the several Lessees for the repair maintenance and decoration thereof respectively under the Flat Leases or (in the case where the Flat Leases or any of them shall have ceased to be subsisting) obligations to the like extent and effect

(v) To let the Lessor or its Agents enter upon the Block or any part thereof at any reasonable time on notice for the purpose of examining the state of repair and condition thereof and taking an inventory of the Lessors fixtures and fittings herein

(vi) Within six months after being called upon by the Lessor by notice in writing to do so to remedy any breach of any of the covenants by the Management Company hereinbefore contained concerning the repair maintenance and decoration of the block (including in particular the obligation imposed on the Management Company under paragraph (iii) of this clause)

(vii) In the event of the failure by the Management Company to perform the covenant contained in the immediately preceding paragraph to permit the Lessor with workmen and others to enter upon the Block and at the expense of the Management Company to carry out the work which the Management Company has failed to do or caused to be done and to repay the cost thereof to the Lessor on demand

(viii) Not to use or permit the use of any parking space included with the Block otherwise than for the parking or garaging (as the case may be) of private motor cars and private motor cycles

(ix) Carefully to retain and preserve at all times and on demand produce to the Lessor all notices relating to the devolution of title and grant of assignments given by the Lessees under the Flat Leases and on the expiration or sooner determination of the concurrent term to deliver the same to the Lessor

(x) Not to make any alterations or additions to the Block or any part thereof or cause or permit any damage to be done to the structure thereof

(xi) (a) Not to assign any part (as distinct from the whole) of the Block

(b) Not to assign the whole of the Block or underlet or part with possession of the whole or any part of the Block without the consent in writing of the Lessor which consent shall not be unreasonably withheld

(xii) To pay all costs charges and expenses (including Solicitors costs and Surveyors fees together with any Value Added or other tax applicable thereon) incurred by the Lessor for the purpose of or incidental to the preparation and service of a notice under Section 146 of the Law of Property Act 1925 notwithstanding forfeiture may be avoided otherwise than by relief granted by the Court

(xiii) At the expiration of or sooner determination of the concurrent term quietly to yield up the Block to the Lessor in such repair and condition as the same should be in consistently with the due performance by the Management Company of the covenants on the part of the Management Company hereinbefore contained

3 THE Lessor hereby covenants with the Management Company that the Lessor will at all times during the concurrent term allow the Management Company (so long as the Management Company shall pay the rent hereby reserved and perform the covenants on the part of the Management Company herein contained) to have quiet enjoyment of the Block (subject to the Flat Leases while subsisting) without interruption by the Lessor or any persons claiming under or in trust for it

4 IF the rent hereby reserved or any part thereof shall be in arrears twenty one days after becoming due (whether formally demanded or not) or if the Management Company shall fail to observe or perform any covenant on its part herein contained in any such event the Lessor may determine this Lease and re-enter upon the Block but without prejudice to the rights of the Lessor in respect of any antecedent breach of covenant by the Management Company

IN WITNESS etc.

Notes

1 Delete if not registered.

2 If the lessor's reversionary title is leasehold, the appropriate information should be incorporated into this recital.

3 Or appropriate suitable recital, including where lessor's reversionary title is leasehold.

4 The term and rent may depend on the lessor's reversionary title, eg he may be a leaseholder himself in which case the concurrent rental would be the rental under the lessor's lease *plus* the nominal amount. The term of the unit leases, and thus the concurrent lease, would follow that under the lessor's lease.

---

6 Notice of pending assignment: studio flats scheme[1]

MASTER COPY: DO NOT REMOVE FROM DEEDS[2]

TO BE SUBMITTED IN DUPLICATE

NOTICE OF PENDING ASSIGNMENT
AND CERTIFICATE
RE: H.M. LAND REGISTRY RESTRICTION

To: [Name and address
of lessor/manager]

Date 19

RE: FLAT: Unit/Plot No

ESTATE (if known)

POSTAL ADDRESS

H.M.L.R. TITLE NO:

Please note that there is a pending assignment in respect of this unit. The intending assignee's/s' full name/s is/are:

Kindly return the top copy of this form receipted as soon as possible.

(signed)
Full name and address of signatory (Acting for Vendor/Purchaser)

Amend or complete as necessary
From: [Name and address of lessor/manager]

Date 19

We acknowledge your Notice of Pending Assignment and request H.M. Land Registry to accept this acknowledgement as being in sufficient terms so as to comply with the Restriction on the Register of the Title of this property as set out in Clause of the lease thereof. The restriction SHOULD NOT BE REMOVED from the Register but should remain active[3]

(Authorised signatory)

Notes

1 See text, ch7, pp 86 et seq, for a full discussion

2 The idea behind this wording is that one copy of this notice should always be kept with the deeds, otherwise the lessor will receive a wide variety of forms. If one copy is with the deeds then presumably whoever gives the notice will have enough sense to know that he should use that form, and not one he has dreamed up himself. The trick, of course, is keeping the master copy with the deeds. There is almost a case for stitching a copy into the lease, with a heading such as 'This is the form of notice which should be used to satisfy the restriction.'

3 This is directed at the Registry, in an attempt to prevent the restriction from being deleted. Incidentally, the wording of this form has been agreed with the Registry.

---

7 Certificate of 'first value' of block of flats

[This is the certificate which would be required under the terms of Recital 1 (h) of Precedent No 3, p 361, above. Somebody will have to prepare this certificate as soon as the block is completely sold, and it is better prepared sooner than waiting for a later opportunity. It would seem logical for the lessor's solicitor to prepare it.]

Date 19

To whoever it may concern:

Re: [description of development by reference to unit numbers]

We hereby certify that 'the first value of the block' as defined in clause [no.] of the Unit Leases relating to the above block (being the total of the open market value selling prices achieved by the lessor of all the flats in the block) is [total figure]
Yours etc.

(Solicitors)

---

8 Letter from lessor to nominee. Nominee lease procedure, Rent Act provisions avoidance[1]

Dear Sir
We refer to the the agreement which has been reached between us whereby we will grant you a lease of [premises] at a rent of for a period of [years] from [commencement date] in the form of the draft lease enclosed.

We confirm the agreement reached between us that in accepting such grant you will be acting as our nominee and that you will deal with the lease as we may thereafter direct.

We further confirm that we will indemnify you against the rent reserved by the lease and from any other liabilities that may arise thereunder or as a result of the grant of such lease.
Yours faithfully

Notes
1 See ch 4, p 66, above.

9 Letter from nominee to lessor; nominee lease procedure, Rent Act provisions avoidance[1]

Dear Sir
I refer to your letter of relating to our agreement for the lease of [premises]

I hereby acknowledge that I will hold the lease as your nominee in trust to deal with it as you may direct. I do so on the condition that you indemnify me against the rent reserved by the lease and from any other liabilities that may arise thereunder or as a result of the grant of such lease.
Yours faithfully

Notes
1 See ch 4, p 66, above.

10 Supplemental lease

[*To be used to add property of same description to that already comprised in an existing lease.*
It sometimes happens that the parties to a lease decide, after the lease is completed, that they wish to add to the property the subject of that lease. Alternatively, they may have forgotten to include some part of the agreed subject matter in the lease! The property which is being added may be of any variety or description but inevitably it usually turns out to be something like a garage.]

[H.M. LAND REGISTRY
Land Registration Acts 1925 to 1971[1]

COUNTY AND DISTRICT:
TITLE NO:
PROPERTY:]
THIS LEASE is made the day of 19
BETWEEN [Developer] of/whose Registered Office is situate at

(hereinafter called 'the Lessor') of the one part and [Lessee] of

(hereinafter called 'the Lessee') of the other part
WHEREAS[2]
(1) This lease is supplemental to a lease (hereinafter called 'the original lease') dated the day of 19 and made between the same parties as hereto whereby [short description of the property demised by original lease—only a brief description is necessary] was demised to the Lessee for the term of years and upon the terms and conditions as set out therein [the title thereto being registered at H.M. Land Registry under Title Number]
(2) The parties hereto have agreed to enter into this supplemental lease in manner hereafter appearing
[[[NOW THIS DEED]]] WITNESSETH as follows:
1 [[[In pursuance of the said agreement and]]] [[As supplemental to a lease (hereinafter called 'the original lease') dated the day of 19 and made between the same parties as hereto whereby [short description of property demised by original lease] was demised to the Lessee for the term of years and upon the terms and conditions as set out therein [The title thereto being registered at H.M. Land Registry under Title No.] and]] in consideration of [the sum of £ paid etc (receipt etc) and of][3] the rent[4] and covenants hereinafter reserved and contained and on the part of the Lessee to be paid observed and performed the Lessor HEREBY DEMISES unto the Lessee ALL THAT [full description of what is being added] TOGETHER WITH and EXCEPT AND RESERVED[5] as set out hereafter TO HOLD the same unto the Lessee [from the [commencement date] for the term of [ ] years] or [from the same commencement date and for the same date as set out in the original lease] YIELDING AND PAYING therefor during the said term [details of rent and payment dates, in usual form; see Precedent No 2, p 348, above]
2 The rights granted exceptions and reservations made the covenants conditions restrictions stipulations and all other matters on the part of both parties contained in the original lease shall be deemed to be incorporated in this lease as though the property hereby demised had been part of the premises demised by the original lease
3 Certificate of Value

IN WITNESS, etc.

Notes

1 Where registration is appropriate, this lease must be obviously registered with the original one whereby it is supplemental. Although there will always be two separate leases, nevertheless the Registry will on application include the supplemental lease—or indeed any subsequent lease in the same category—within the original title number allocated to the first lease. The Registry will make a note on the register that the second (or any subsequent) lease is supplemental to

the original one. The only slight problem might be in relation to a registered mortgage which referred only to the original lease, although this is not a real problem and practitioners will find that the Registry will be able to cope with it.

2 It is questionable that recitals are necessary; in a registered lease they are probably superfluous. In this Precedent the body of the lease contains in double square brackets the appropriate wording to replace recitals. The wording in triple square brackets should be deleted in such cases.

3 Only where there is a consideration passing: it will not always be the case, eg there may have been a genuine omission which needs to be rectified by a supplemental lease, in which case no consideration would pass.

4 The rent may be nominal, where the supplemental lease is required because of a case of genuine omission, or monetary, where there is a genuine addition.

5 The assumption is that what is being added will be so close to, or adjoining, the subject matter of the original lease that it will not need specifically different rights and reservations. However, those dealing with the drafting of the supplemental lease should be careful to make sure that the subject matter of the supplemental lease does not need rights, reservations, and so on, specific to it, in which case these must be set out in the supplemental lease.

---

11 Deed of exchange of leasehold property[1]

[This precedent is for use where the *developer* and one of his purchasers wish to change some part of the demised property. The type of properties 'swopped' will be the same, but they will have different locations. To continue the theme from Precedent No 10, p 374–5, above, a likely sort of candidate for an exchange would be garages. It can sometimes happen that garages or perhaps parking spaces, are changed around, by mutual agreement, during the course of a development.

Again, the need for such a document might be because of some mistake, as opposed to a genuine change of requirements.

For an exchange between respective *owners* of the properties concerned (ie as opposed to one between the developer and an owner—which is what this precedent is intended for) where there is no original grant on one side, and surrender on the other, but merely a straight 'swop' of leasehold property, a different document is required. This is outside the scope of this book, but appropriate precedents are contained in the author's book *Residential Estate Conveyancing: Practice and Precedents* (Butterworths 1983) on p 441.]

[H.M. LAND REGISTRY
Land Registration Acts 1925 to 1971

COUNTY AND DISTRICT:
TITLE NOS: [respective title nos]
PROPERTIES: [brief description of both properties]
DATE]
THIS DEED OF EXCHANGE is made [the day of 19]
BETWEEN [Developer]of/whose Registered Office is situate at

(hereinafter called 'the Lessor') of the one part and [Purchaser] of

(hereinafter called 'the Lessee') of the other part
WHEREAS:[2]
(1) [as Recital (1), Precedent No 10, p 375, above]
(2) [recite Lessor's title to the development]
(3) The parties hereto have agreed that the original lease shall be amended by

[describe what is to happen: eg 'by omitting therefrom   shown edged blue on the plan annexed hereto[3] and substituting for it   shown edged red on the plan annexed hereto]

NOW THIS DEED WITNESSETH as follows:

1 The Lessee as [Beneficial owner] HEREBY SURRENDERS AND TRANSFERS unto the Lessor ALL THAT [description] comprised in the original lease [being part of [Lessees title no.]] to the intent that the term of years thereby granted in respect of such property shall merge and be absolutely extinguished in the [freehold] reversion so that the original lease may be hereby determined in all respects insofar (but not further or otherwise) as it relates to such property

2 The Lessor HEREBY DEMISES unto the Lessee ALL THAT [description] TO HOLD the same unto the Lessee [usual form of words for commencement date and term—these to be identical to those in the original lease] upon the terms of the original lease as if such property hereby demised had been part of the premises demised by the original lease

[3 The parties hereto apply to have [substituted property] amalgamated with the property comprised in [Lessee's title] and to have notice of the original lease registered against [Lessor's title] varied in accordance with the terms hereof][4]

IN WITNESS whereof

Notes

1 As to the stamp required, there is some uncertainty about this, but most authorities, including the Revenue, will accept 50p as the appropriate stamp. In the circumstances envisaged, it is unlikely that there would be any consideration. Accordingly, it would seem that no certificate of value is required. As a deed of exchange, it will not require a produced stamp, as it is not a transfer for value. For further discussion, see the author's *Residential Estate Conveyancing: Practice and Precedents* (Butterworths 1983). Land Registry Fees are assessed on the value of property exchanged, scale 3.

2 Recitals are used in this precedent, despite it being, in some cases, a registered document. One supposes that, as in Precedent No 10, p 376, note 2 above, the recitals could be dropped and the information contained therein incorporated in the body of the deed. However, most people will feel more comfortable with recitals, and they do after all serve the useful purpose—especially for non legal people reading the document—of explaining it fully before the 'nitty-gritty' part is reached.

3 The plan referred to here *could* be the plan in the original lease, but it seems more logical to have both properties shown on the same plan, ie the one attached to the deed of exchange.

4 The difference between the circumstances of an exchange, as in this precedent, and an addition, as in Precedent No 10, p 374, above, is that in the former there is merely a *substitution* within the lease which is already registered, but in the latter there is an addition, ie something new and different. Thus amalgamation is possible in the former, but not the latter.

---

12 Memorandum and articles of association of tenants management company: variations for disposal or retention of reversion

The Companies Acts 1948 to 1980

COMPANY LIMITED BY GUARANTEE AND NOT HAVING A SHARE CAPITAL

Memorandum of Association

OF

[Name of company]

1 The name of the Company is [   ] LIMITED

2 The registered office of the Company will be situate in England

3 The objects for which the Company is established are at [location of development]
Variation to be used when reversion is retained
[(A) To acquire the freehold/leasehold property together with the building/s erected thereon known as [name of development] and to hold the same as an investment for the benefit of the lessees of the flats comprised in the said building/s
(B) To collect the rents and income of the property and to apply the same in the proper and convenient arrangement thereof including [but without prejudice to the generality of the foregoing] the matters recited in paragraph (c)]
Variation to be used when reversion is disposed
[(A) to collect the service income (excluding the rents) of the freehold/leasehold property together with the building/s erected thereon known as (name of development) and to apply the same in the proper and convenient arangement thereof including (but without prejudice to the generality of the foregoing) the matters recited in paragraph (C)][1]
(C) To keep in repair renew rebuild decorate maintain and procure the repair renewal rebuilding decoration and maintenance of the buildings erected on the property including the main structure roof foundations interior exterior the common parts the common gas and water pipes drains and electric cables and wires and the grounds parking areas forecourts walls fences accessways public ways hedges and generally the whole of the property including all buildings comprising aforesaid including the cleaning and lighting of the common parts the cleaning of the windows the repair renewal replacement and maintenance of fixtures and fittings the placing and maintaining of policies of insurance in respect of the premises against loss or damage by all risks covered by a normal comprehensive policy of insurance and the placing and maintaining of policies of insurance against all third party claims normally included under Property Owners liability policies the payment of rates under rates outgoings and other charges and assessments which may become payable in respect of the premises[2]
(D) To make rules and regulations for the observance of members of the Company for the use and control of the property
(E) To borrow and raise money for the purpose of the company on such terms and on such security as may be thought fit
(F) To do all such other things as are incidental or conducive to the attainment of the above objects or are calculated to enhance the value and beneficial advantage of the property and the flats comprised in the building/s thereon
4 The liability of the members is limited
5 Every member of the Company undertakes to contribute to the assets of the Company in the event of the same being wound up while he is a member or within one year after he ceases to be a member for payment of the debts and liabilities of the Company contracted before he ceases to be a member and of the costs charges and expenses of winding up and for the adjustment of the rights of the contributories among themselves such amount as may be required not exceeding £1.00[3]
6 No person shall be admitted to Membership of the Company other than the subscribers hereto and the persons in whom from time to time are vested leases for terms granted originally for not less than [term of leases] years of flats in the block/s of flats erected on the premises. Section 23 of the Companies Act[4] shall not apply to this paragraph
WE, the several persons whose names and addresses are subscribed are desirous of being formed into a Company in pursuance of this Memorandum of Association
NAMES, ADDRESSES AND DESCRIPTIONS OF SUBSCRIBERS[5]

DATED this day of One thousand nine hundred and eighty

WITNESS to the above signatures

The Companies Acts 1948 to 1980

COMPANY LIMITED BY GUARANTEE AND NOT HAVING A SHARE CAPITAL

Articles of Association

OF

[Name of company] LIMITED

GENERAL

1 In these presents the words standing in the first column of the Table next hereinafter contained shall bear the meaning set opposite to them respectively in the second column thereof, if not inconsistent with the subject or context:

WORDS	MEANINGS
The Act	The Companies Act 1948
These presents	These Articles of Association and the regulations of the Association from time to time in force
The Association	The above-named Company
The Council	The Council of Management for the time being of the Association
The Office	The registered office of the Association
The Seal	The common seal of the Association
The United Kingdom	Great Britain and Northern Ireland
Month	Calendar month
In writing	Written, printed or lithographed, or partly one and partly another and other modes of representing or reproducing words in a visible form
Owner	A person in whom is vested a lease for a term granted originally for not less than [term of leases] years of a flat in the block of flats erected on the premises

And words importing the singular number only shall include the plural number, and vice versa

Word importing the masculine gender only shall include the feminine gender, and vice versa

Words importing persons shall include corporations

Subject as aforesaid, any words or expressions defined in the Act or any statutory modification thereof in force at the date on which these presents became binding on the Association shall, if not inconsistent with the subject or context, bear the same meanings in these presents

2 The number of members with which the Association proposes to be registered is not more than 50 but the Council may from time to time register an increase of members

3 The provisions of Section 110 of the Act shall be observed by the Association, and every member of the Association shall either sign a written consent to become a member or sign the register of members on becoming a member[6]

4 The Association is established for the purposes expressed in the Memorandum of Association

5 The Subscribers to the Memorandum of Association and all owners who apply in writing for membership shall be members of the Association. Where two or more persons are the lessees of one flat they shall together constitute one member and the person whose name first appears on the register of members shall exercise the voting and other powers vested in such member

6 (a) Until such time as all of the subscribers to the Memorandum of Association shall cease to be members of the Council of Management the members shall

not be entitled to receive notice of any General Meeting of the Association nor shall they be entitled to attend or vote at any such meeting

(b) The subscribers to the Memorandum of Association shall cease to be members as soon as owners of all of the flats erected on the premises shall have been registered as members[7]

(c) A member shall cease to be such on ceasing to be an owner and on the registration as a member of his successor in title

(d) Subject as aforesaid no member shall cease to be a member of the Association

7 The Trustee in bankruptcy of any bankrupt member or personal representative of any deceased member shall be entitled to become a member if, at the time of his application for membership, such bankrupt member or deceased member was an owner

GENERAL MEETINGS

8 The Association shall hold a General Meeting in every calendar year as its Annual General Meeting at such time and place as may be determined by the Council, and shall specify the meeting as such in the notices calling it, provided that every Annual General Meeting except the first shall be held not more than fifteen months after the holding of the last preceding Annual General Meeting, and that so long as the Association holds its first Annual General Meeting within Eighteen months after its incorporation it need not hold it in the year of its incorporation or in the following year

9 All General Meetings, other than Annual General Meetings, shall be called Extraordinary General Meetings

10 The Council may whenever they think fit convene an Extraordinary General Meeting, and Extraordinary General Meetings shall also be convened on such requisition or in default may be convened by such requisitionists, as provided by Section 132 of the Act

11 Twenty-one days' notice in writing at the least of every Annual General Meeting and of every meeting convened to pass a Special Resolution and fourteen days' notice in writing at the least of every other General Meeting (exclusive in every case both of the day on which it is served or deemed to be served and of the day for which it is given), specifying the place, the day and the hour of the meeting, and in the case of special business the general nature of that business, shall be given in manner hereinafter mentioned to such persons (including the Auditors) as are under these presents or under the Act entitled to receive such notices from the Association; but with the consent of all the members having the right to attend and vote thereat or of such proportion of them as is prescribed by the Act in the case of meetings other than Annual General Meetings, a meeting may be convened by such notice as those members may think fit

12 The accidental omission to give notice of a meeting to, or the non-receipt of such notice by, any person entitled to receive notice thereof shall not invalidate any resolution passed, or proceeding had, at any meeting

PROCEEDINGS AT GENERAL MEETINGS

13 All business shall be deemed special that is transacted at an Extraordinary General Meeting, and all that is transacted at an Annual General Meeting shall also be deemed special, with the exception of the consideration of the income and expenditure account and balance sheet, and the reports of the Council and of the Auditors, the election of members of the Council in the place of those retiring, and the appointment of, and the fixing of the remuneration of, the Auditors

14 No business shall be transacted at any General Meeting unless a quorum is present when the meeting proceeds to business Save as herein otherwise provided five mem-

bers personally present shall be a quorum/Provided always that while any of the subscribers continue to be members two members being subscribers shall constitute a quorum[8]

15 If within half an hour from the time appointed for the holding of a General Meeting a quorum is not present the meeting, if convened on the requisition of members shall be dissolved. In any other case it shall stand adjourned to the same day in the next week, at the same time and place, or at such other place as the Council may determine, and if at such adjourned meeting a quorum is not present within half an hour from time appointed for holding the meeting the members present shall be a quorum

16 The Chairman (if any) of the Council shall preside as Chairman at every General Meeting, but if there be no such Chairman, or if at any meeting he shall not be present within fifteen minutes after the time appointed for holding the same, or shall be unwilling to preside, the members present shall choose some member of the Council, or if no such member be present, or if all the members of the Council present decline to take the chair, they shall choose some member of the Association who shall be present to preside

17 The Chairman may, with the consent of any meeting at which a quorum is present (and shall if so directed by the meeting) adjourn the meeting from time to time and from place to place, but no business shall be transacted at any adjourned meeting other than the business left unfinished at the meeting from which the adjournment took place. Whenever a meeting is adjourned for thirty days or more a notice of the adjourned meeting shall be given in the same manner as of an original meeting Save as aforesaid, the members shall not be entitled to any notice of an adjournment, or of the business to be transacted at an adjourned meeting.

18 At any General Meeting a resolution put to the vote of the meeting shall be decided on a show of hands, unless a poll is, before or upon the declaration of the result of the show of hands, demanded by the Chairman or by a member or members present in person or by proxy and representing one-tenth of the total voting rights of all the members having the right to vote at the meeting, and unless a poll be so demanded a declaration by the Chairman of the meeting that a resolution had been carried, or carried unanimously or by a particular majority, or lost, or not carried by a particular majority, and an entry to that effect in the minute book of the Association, shall be conclusive evidence of the fact without proof of the number or proportion of the votes recorded in favour of or against that resolution. The demand for a poll may be withdrawn.

19 Subject to the provisions of Article 20, if a poll be demanded in manner aforesaid, it shall be taken at such time and place, and in such manner, as the Chairman of the meeting shall direct, and the result of the poll shall be deemed to be the resolution of the meeting at which the poll was demanded

20 No poll shall be demanded on the election of a Chairman of a meeting, or on any question of adjournment

21 In the case of an equality of votes, whether on a show of hands or on a poll, the Chairman of the meeting shall be entitled to a second or casting vote

22 The demand of a poll shall not prevent the continuance of a meeting for the transaction of any business other than the question on which a poll has been demanded

VOTES OF MEMBERS

23 Subject as hereinbefore provided, every member shall have one vote

24 Save as herein expressly provided no member other than a member duly registered, who shall have paid every subscription and other sum (if any) which shall be due and payable to the Association in respect of his membership or in respect of his obligations to the Association as the lessor of his flat under the lease of his flat, shall

be entitled to vote on any question either personally or by proxy or as a proxy for another member at any General Meeting

25 Votes may be given on a poll either personally or by proxy, Save as hereinafter provided on a show of hands a member present only by proxy shall have no vote, but a proxy for a corporation may vote on a show of hands. A corporation may vote by its duly authorised representative appointed as provided by Section 139 of the Act. A proxy need not be a member. A proxy who is also a mortgagee or chargee of a member's leasehold interest in a flat comprised in the property or a representative of such mortgagee or chargee shall be a Special Proxy and shall have the right to speak at meetings of the Association and to vote upon a show of hands

26 The instrument appointing a proxy shall be in writing under the hand of the appointor or his attorney duly authorised in writing, or if such appointor is a corporation under its common seal, if any, and if none, then under the hand of some officer duly authorised in that behalf

27 The instrument appointing a proxy and the power of attorney or other authority (if any) under which it is signed or a notarially certified or office copy thereof shall be deposited at the office not less than forty-eight hours before the time appointed for holding the meeting or adjourned meeting at which the person named in the instrument proposes to vote, or in the case of a poll not less than twenty-four hours before the time appointed for the taking of the poll, and in default the instrument of proxy shall not be treated as valid. No instrument appointing a proxy shall be valid after the expiration of twelve months from the date of its execution

28 A vote given in accordance with the terms of an instrument of Proxy shall be valid notwithstanding the previous death or insanity of the principal or revocation of the proxy or of the authority under which the proxy was executed, provided that no intimation in writing of the death insanity or revocation as aforesaid shall have been received at the office before the commencement of the meeting or adjourned meeting at which the proxy is used

COUNCIL OF MANAGEMENT

29 The number of the members of the Council shall be determined by the subscribers to the Memorandum of Association and after the subscribers have ceased to be members shall be determined by the members of the Council or by the Association in General Meeting[9]

30 The first members of the Council shall be the subscribers to the Memorandum of Association

31 The Council may from time to time and at any time appoint any member of the Association as a member of the Council, either to fill a casual vacancy or by way of addition to the Council provided that the prescribed maximum be not thereby exceeded. Any member so appointed shall retain his office only until the next Annual General Meeting, but he shall then be eligible for re-election

32 No person who is not a member of the Association shall in any circumstances be eligible to hold office as a member of the Council

POWERS OF THE COUNCIL

33 The business of the Association shall be managed by the Council who may pay all such expenses of, and preliminary and incidental to, the promotion, formation, establishment and registration of the Association as they think fit, and may exercise all such powers of the Association, and do on behalf of the Association all such acts as may be exercised and done by the Association, and as are not by statute or by these presents required to be exercised or done by the Association in General Meeting, subject nevertheless to any regulations of these presents to the provisions of the statutes for the time being in force and affecting the Association and to such regula-

tions, being not inconsistent with the aforesaid regulations or provisions, as may be prescribed by the Association in General Meeting, but no regulation made by the Association in General Meeting shall invalidate any prior act of the Council which would have been valid if such regulation had not been made

34 The members for the time being of the Council may act notwithstanding any vacancy in their body; provided always that in case the members of the Council shall at any time be reduced in number to less than the minimum number prescribed by or in accordance with these presents, it shall be lawful for them to act as the Council for the purpose of admitting persons to membership of the Association, filling up vacancies in their body, or of summoning a General Meeting, but not for any other purpose

SECRETARY

35 The Secretary shall be appointed by the Council for such time, at such remuneration and upon such conditions as they may think fit, and any Secretary so appointed may be removed by them. The provisions of Sections 177 and 179 of the Act shall apply and be observed. The Council may from time to time by resolution appoint an assistant or deputy Secretary, and any person so appointed may act in place of the Secretary if there be no Secretary or no Secretary capable of acting

THE SEAL

36 The seal of the Association shall not be affixed to any instrument except by the authority of a resolution of the Council, and in the presence of one member of the Council or while the subscribers remain members of the Council in the presence of one subscriber, and of the Secretary, and the said member and secretary shall sign every instrument to which the seal shall be so affixed in their presence and in favour of any purchaser or person bona fide dealing with the Association such signatures shall be conclusive evidence of the fact that the seal has been properly affixed

DISQUALIFICATION OF MEMBERS OF THE COUNCIL

37 The office of a member of the Council shall be vacated:

(a) If a receiving order is made against him or he makes any arrangement or composition with his creditors

(b) If he becomes of unsound mind

(c) If he ceases to be a member of the Association

(d) If by notice in writing to the Association he resigns his office

(e) If he ceases to hold office by reason of any order made under Section 188 of the Act

(f) If he is removed from office by a resolution duly passed pursuant to Section 184 of the Act

38 Section 185 of the Act shall not apply

ROTATION OF MEMBERS OF THE COUNCIL

39 At the first Annual General Meeting and at the Annual General Meeting to be held in every subsequent year, one-third of the members of the Council for the time being, or if their number is not a multiple of three then the number nearest to one-third shall retire from office

40 The members of the Council to retire shall be those who have been longest in office since their last election or appointment. As between members of equal seniority, the members to retire shall in the absence of agreement be selected from among them by lot. The length of time a member has been in office shall be computed from his last election or appointment. A retiring member of the Council shall be elegible for re-election

41 The Association may, at the meeting at which a member of the Council retires in manner aforesaid, fill up the vacated office by electing a person thereto, and in default the retiring member shall, if offering himself for re-election be deemed to have been re-elected, unless at such meeting it is expressly resolved not to fill such vacated office, or unless a resolution for the re-election of such member shall have been put to the meeting and lost

42 No person not being a member of the Council retiring at the meeting shall, unless recommended by the Council for election, be eligible for election to membership of the Council at any General Meeting, unless within the prescribed time before the day appointed for the meeting there shall have been given to the Secretary notice in writing, by some member duly qualified to be present and vote at the meeting for which such notice is given, of his intention to propose such person for election, and also notice in writing, signed by the person to be proposed, of his willingness to be elected. The prescribed time above mentioned shall be such that, between the date when the notice is served, or deemed to be served, and the day appointed for the meeting there shall be not less than four nor more than twenty-eight intervening days

43 Without prejudice to the provisions of Article 29 hereof the Association may from time to time in General Meeting increase or reduce the number of members of the Council, and determine in which rotation such increased or reduced number shall go out of office, and may make the appointments necessary for effecting any such increase

44 In addition and without prejudice to the provisions of Section 184 of the Act, the Association may by Extraordinary Resolution remove any member of the Council before the expiration of his period of office, and may by an Ordinary Resolution appoint another qualified member in his stead; but any person so appointed shall retain his office so long only as the member in whose place he is appointed would have held the same if he had not been removed

PROCEEDINGS OF THE COUNCIL

45 The Council may meet together for the dispatch of business adjourn and otherwise regulate their meeting as they think fit and determine the quorum necessary for the transaction of business. Unless otherwise determined two shall be a quorum[10]. Questions arising at any meeting shall be decided by a majority of votes. In case of an equality of votes the Chairman shall have a second or casting vote.

46 A member of the Council may, and on the request of a member of the Council the Secretary shall, at any time, summon a meeting of the Council by notice served upon the several members of the Council. A member of the Council who is absent from the United Kingdom shall not be entitled to notice of a meeting

47 The Chairman for the time being of the Association shall be the Chairman of the Council and shall be entitled to preside at all meetings of the Council at which he shall be present, and may determine for what period he is to hold office, but if no such Chairman be elected, or if at any meeting the Chairman be not present within five minutes after the time appointed for holding the meeting and willing to preside, the members of the Council present shall choose one of their number to be Chairman of the meeting

48 A meeting of the Council at which a quorum is present shall be competent to exercise all the authorities powers and discretions by or under the regulations of the Association for the time being invested in the Council generally

49 The Council may delegate any of their powers to committees consisting of such member or members of the Council as they think fit, and any committee so formed shall, in the exercise of the powers so delegated, conform to any regulations imposed on it by the Council. The meetings and proceedings of any such committee shall be governed by the provisions of these presents for regulating the meetings and proceed-

ings of the Council so far as applicable and so far as the same shall not be superseded by any regulations made by the Council

50 All acts bona fide done by any meeting of the Council or of any committee of the Council, or by any person acting as member of the Council, shall notwithstanding it be afterwards discovered that there was some defect in the appointment or continuance in office of any such member or person acting as aforesaid or that they or any of them were disqualified, be as valid as if every such person had been duly appointed or had duly continued in office and was qualified to be a member of the Council

51 The Council shall cause proper minutes to be made of all appointments of officers made by the Council and of the proceedings of all meetings of the Association and of the Council and of committees of the Council, and all business transacted at such meetings, and any such minutes of any meeting, if purporting to be signed by the Chairman of such meeting, or by the Chairman of the next succeeding meeting, shall be sufficient evidence without any further proof of the facts therein stated

52 A resolution in writing signed by all the members for the time being of the Council or of any committee of the Council who are entitled to receive notice of a meeting of the Council or of such committee shall be as valid and effectual as if it had been passed at the meeting of the Council or of such committee duly convened and constituted

ACCOUNTS

53 The Council shall cause proper books of accounts to be kept with respect to:

(a) all sums of money received and expended by the Association and the matters in respect of which such receipts and expenditure take place;
(b) all sales and purchases of goods by the Association and
(c) the assets and liabilities of the Association

Proper books shall not be deemed to be kept if there are not kept such books of account as are necessary to give a true and fair view of the state of affairs of the Association and to explain its transactions

54 The books of account shall be kept at the office, or, subject to Section 147 (3) of the Act, at such other place or places as the Council shall think fit, and shall always be open to the inspection of the members of the Council

55 The books of account shall be open to the inspection of any members of the Association on reasonable notice

56 At an Annual General Meeting in every year the Council shall lay before the Association a proper income and expenditure account for the period since the last preceding account (or in the case of the first account since the incorporation of the Association) made up to a date not more than four months before each meeting, together with a proper balance sheet made up as at the same date. Every such balance sheet shall be accompanied by proper reports of the Council and the Auditors, and copies of such account, balance sheet and reports (all of which shall be framed in accordance with any statutory requirements for the time being in force) and of any other documents required by law to be annexed or attached thereto or to accompany the same shall not less than twenty-one clear days before the date of the meeting subject nevertheless to the provisions of Section 158 (1) (c) of the Act, be sent to the Auditors and to all other persons entitled to receive notices of General Meetings in the manner in which notices are hereinafter directed to be served. The Auditors' report shall be open to inspection and be read before the meeting as required by Section 162 of the Act

AUDIT

57 Once at least in every year the accounts of the Association shall be examined and the correctness of the income and expenditure accounts and balance sheet ascertained by one or more properly qualified Auditor or Auditors

58 Auditors shall be appointed and their duties regulated in accordance with Sections 159 to 162 of the Act, the members of the Council being treated as directors mentioned in those sections

NOTICES

59 A notice may be served by the Association upon any member, either personally or by sending it through the post in a prepaid letter, addressed to such member at his registered address as appearing in the register of members

60 Any member described in the register of members by an address not within the United Kingdom who shall from time to time give the Association an address within the United Kingdom at which notices may be served upon him, shall be entitled to have notices served upon him at such address, but save as aforesaid and as provided by the Act, only those members who are described in the register of members by an address within the United Kingdom shall be entitled to receive notice from the Association

61 Any notice, if served by post, shall be deemed to have been served on the day following that on which the letter containing the same is put into the post, and in proving such service it shall be sufficient to prove that the letter containing the notice was properly addressed and put into the post office as a prepaid letter

PRIVATE COMPANY

62 The Association is a Private Company and accordingly:

(A) The number of members for the time being of the Association is not to exceed fifty

(B) The Association shall not offer any of its shares (if and so long as the Association shall have any share capital) or any of its debentures to the public for subscription

(C) If and so long as the Association shall at any time have any share capital, the Council may in their absolute discretion and without assigning any reason therefor decline to register any transfer of any share of the Association

NAMES, ADDRESSES AND DESCRIPTIONS OF SUBSCRIBERS

DATED this day of 19

WITNESS to the above signatures

Notes

1 See p 102, above, for discussion on relative merits of retaining or disposing of the reversionary interest.

2 To be amended as the circumstances dictate; although the wording given here is fairly general and ought to suffice in most cases.

3 This is the guarantee in relation to the incorporation of the company as one limited by guarantee.

4 Ie Companies Act 1948 (which see).

5 See p 138, above as to number of subscribers.

6 A written consent, or application, to become a member is often dispensed with, but is nevertheless desirable. See p 140, above.

7 See p 137, above. This article ensures that the company is under the control of the developer. It will be up to the developer, therefore, actually to *register* the flat owners as members.

8 The numbers may be varied to suit the circumstances, but the quorum of the subscribers should be as low as possible, ie two.

9 Experience has shown that it is unwise to specify either minimum or maximum numbers of the council of management.

10 Following on from 9, above, two must obviously be the absolute minimum number for a quorum of the council, otherwise the company could be said to be a 'one man-band'.

---

13 Agreement between developer and tenants' management company

[This should be entered into as soon as the tenants' management company has been incorporated, and (hopefully) before the development has started to sell. See, generally, text, ch 11, p 131, above.]

AN AGREEMENT made the day of One thousand nine hundred and BETWEEN [Developer] of/whose registered office is sutuate at

(hereinafter called 'the Vendor') of the one part and [Management Company] of/ whose registered office is situate at

(hereinafter called 'the Company') of the other part
WHEREBY it is agreed as follows:
1 THE Vendor shall sell and the Company shall purchase at the price of [nominal sum—usually One Pound] ALL THAT the property described in the Schedule hereto for an estate in fee simple in possession subject etc. (or, as the case may be)/AND/ SUBJECT/ALSO/TO and with the benefit of the Leases hereinafter mentioned which are to be granted by the Vendor
2 BEFORE completion the Vendor shall grant Leases of the flats comprised in the premises hereby agreed to be sold in accordance with the terms of the form of Lease annexed hereto[1] and containing all the rights easements privileges reservations and covenants set forth therein or on such other terms as may be agreed between the Vendor and the Company the Vendor shall be entitled to fix the amounts of the capital payments to be made by the Lessees on the grants of the said Leases and to retain such capital payments for its own use and benefit The amount of the rents to be reserved by each Lease shall be pounds (£) per annum
3 COMPLETION shall take place within twenty-eight days of the Vendors' solicitors serving on the Company a Notice requiring completion[2]
4 THE Vendor shall be entitled to retain for its own use and benefit the rents reserved by the said Leases for the period down to actual completion but shall pay over or allow to the Company the amount by which the aggregate of sums then received by the Vendor from the Lessees by way of service charge under the leases shall exceed the sums actually expended by the Vendor for the provision of the services covered by such service charge down to the date of completion
5 THE Vendor shall until completion of this agreement keep the Company indemnified against the reasonable expenses of the running of the Company
6 [Title clause]
7 THE property is sold SUBJECT TO:
(a) Any matter or thing registered or capable of registration in the Local Land Charges Registers and
(b) Either the entries on the Register of the Vendors' Title affecting the property or to the covenants restrictions and stipulations and all other matters (if any) contained mentioned or referred to in the Conveyance referred to in clause 6 hereof
(c) Any existing tenancies
8 THE property is sold SUBJECT TO the National Conditions of Sale (current edition) so far as the same are not varied by or inconsistent with these conditions save that

the prescribed rate of interest referred to in the said National Conditions shall be four per cent per annum above Barclays Bank PLC Base Rate

9 THE Vendor sells as Beneficial Owner

THE SCHEDULE above referred to

[description of property]

SIGNED:

A duly authorised signatory
on behalf of the Vendor

Notes

1 Model form of lease to be used should be attached to this agreement.

2 This sort of completion notice is much better for the developer, as it does not tie him down to a fixed date, even if it is a date running on from some other happening. Nevertheless, this wording is somewhat vague from the point of view of the lessees and the embryonic tenants management company. The clause could always be expanded to state that the notice should be served, say, six weeks (any less period would be administratively difficult) following completion of the last lease in the development.

---

14 Lease of flat—full management: tenants' management company to take transfer of (freehold) reversion and take on management

[See also Precedent No 12, the Memorandum and Articles of Association of the Tenants' Management Company, and ch 11, pp 131 to 147, above.]

THIS LEASE is made the day of One thousand nine hundred and

BETWEEN [Developer] of/whose registered office is situate at

(hereinafter called 'the Lessor' which expression shall where the context so admits include the estate owner or owners for the time being of the reversion of the premises hereby demised) of the one part and

[purchaser of flat] of

(hereinafter called or collectively called 'the Lessee' which expression shall where the context so admits include the Lessee's executors administrators and assigns) of the other part

WHEREAS:

(1) The Lessor is the freeholder of the land more fully described in Part 1 of the First Schedule hereto ('the land') together with the building now comprising individual flats ('the building') erected thereon or on some part thereof

(2) The Lessor has previously granted leases of or intends hereafter to grant leases of flats in the building and the Lessor has in every lease imposed and intends in every future lease to impose the restrictions set forth in the Second Schedule hereto to the intent that any lessee for the time being of any such flat shall have the benefit of the observance of the said restrictions by the owner or occupiers for the time being of the other flats in respect of which the Lessor has granted the leases

(3) The Lessor has agreed with the Lessee for the grant to the Lessee of a lease of the flat hereinafter described for the consideration at the rents and on the terms and conditions hereinafter appearing

(4) [Name of Management Company][1] ('the Management Company') has been

incorporated for the purposes of managing and maintaining the buildings and land and upon having granted the leases of all the flats comprised in the building the Lessor intends to convey the freehold of the building and land to the Management Company

(5) The Lessee is or will become a member of the Management Company

NOW THIS DEED WITNESSETH as follows:

1 In pursuance of the said agreement and in consideration of the sum of POUNDS (£) paid to the Lessor by the Lessee on or before the execution hereof (the receipt whereof the Lessor hereby acknowledges) and of the rents and covenants hereinafter reserved and contained and on the part of the Lessee to be paid observed and performed the Lessor HEREBY DEMISES unto the Lessee ALL THAT the property more particularly described in Part 11 of the First Schedule hereto ('the demised premises') TOGETHER WITH (to the exclusion of all other easements rights and privileges) the easements rights and privileges mentioned in the Third Schedule hereto subject as therein mentioned EXCEPT AND RESERVING as mentioned in the Fourth Schedule hereto TO HOLD the demised premises unto the Lessee for the term of years (years)[2] from the day of One thousand nine hundred and PAYING THEREFOR during the said term the yearly rent of [3] POUNDS (£) without any deduction by equal half yearly payments in advance on the day of and the day of [4] in every year of the term the first payment thereof being a proportionate part of the said annual sum calculated from the date hereof to the Thirtieth day of June[5] next being made on the execution hereof

2 THE Lessee hereby covenants with the Lessor and with the owners and lessees of the other flats comprised in the building and leased by the Lessor that the Lessee and the persons deriving title under him will at all times hereafter observe the restrictions set forth in the Second Schedule hereto but so that nevertheless the Lessee shall not be personally liable for any breach of any covenant or stipulation which is only restrictive in nature occurring after he shall have parted with all interest in the demised premises in respect of which such breach shall occur AND further will indemnify the Lessor and its successors in title and assigns from and against all actions proceedings costs claims and liabilities in respect of any future breach non-observance or non-performance of the said covenants and restrictions so far as aforesaid [PROVIDED ALWAYS that save as otherwise herein provided the Lessor shall not be under any obligation to the Lessee to enforce any of the said stipulations in respect of any other property and shall have power from time to time by deed or deeds to vary or release any of the said stipulations in respect of any flat in the building][6]

3 (i) THE Lessee hereby covenants with the Lessor as follows:

(a) To pay the said rent during the said term at the times and in manner aforesaid without any deduction

(b) To pay all rates taxes assessments charges impositions and outgoings which may at any time during the said term be assessed charged or imposed upon the demised premises or the owner or occupier in respect thereof and in the event of any rates taxes assessments charges impositions and outgoings being assessed charged or imposed in respect of the building of which the demised premises forms part to pay the proper proportion of such rates taxes assessments charges impositions and outgoings attributable to the demised premises

(c) Not to make any structural alterations or structural additions to the demised premises or remove any of the Lessor's fixtures without the previous consent in writing of the Lessor

(d) To pay all costs charges and expenses (including solicitors' costs and surveyors' fees) incurred by the Lessor for the purpose of or incidental to the preparation and service of a notice under Section 146 of the Law of Property Act 1925 notwithstanding forfeiture may be avoided otherwise than by relief granted by the Court

(e) Forthwith after service upon the Lessee of any notice affecting the demised premises served by any person body or authority (other than the Lessor) to deliver a true copy thereof to the Lessor and if so required by the Lessor to join with the Lessor in making such representations to any such person body or authority concerning any proposals affecting the demised premises as the Lessor may consider desirable and to join with the Lessor in any such appeal against any order or direction affecting the demised premises as the Lessor may consider desirable

(f) Within one calendar month after any such document or instrument as is hereinafter mentioned shall be executed or shall operate or take effect or purport to operate or take effect to produce to the Lessor or the Lessor's Solicitors the original or a true copy of every transfer of this lease or mortgage or legal charge of this lease of the demised premises or any part thereof and also every underlease of the demised premises or any part thereof for substantially the whole of the unexpired term and every assignment of such underlease and also every Probate Letters of Administration Order of Court or other instrument effecting or evidencing a devolution of title as regards the said term or any such Underlease as aforesaid for the purpose of registration and for such registration to pay to the said Lessor or Lessor's solicitors a fee of [to be set by Lessor] in respect of each such document or instrument so produced[7]

(g) At the expiration or sooner determination of the said term to peaceably surrender and yield up to the Lessor the demised premises together with all additions thereto and all Landlord's fixtures and fittings (if any) freshly decorated throughout and in good and tenantable repair and condition

(ii) IF the Lessor and Lessee shall fail to agree what constitutes the proper proportion of the rates taxes assessments charges impositions and outgoings under sub-paragraph (b) of sub-clause (i) of this clause the matter shall be determined by the Lessor but if the Lessee or the Lessees of any of the other flats in the building shall be unwilling to accept the determination of the Lessor he or they shall be entitled to have the matter determined by an independent surveyor nominated in default of agreement by the President of the Royal Institution of Chartered Surveyors whose fees shall be paid by the person or persons requiring such nomination to be made and such last-mentioned surveyor's determination shall be final and binding on the parties concerned

4 THE Lessee hereby further covenants with the Lessor as follows:

(a) Not to assign or transfer the demised premises except to a person who has committed himself to apply to become registered as a Member of the Management Company

(b) That any transfer assent or disposition of this Lease shall contain a covenant by the transferee devisee or disponee in terms of the preceding subclause (a) and if the land is registered an application for an appropriate restriction on the Register shall be made[8]

(c) That so long as the Lessee retains any estate or interest in the demised premises he will not resign from or dispose of the rights attaching to his membership of the Management Company to any person other than a Mortgagee of the demised premises

(d) That if the Lessee is not a member of the Management Company

(i) The Lessee will carry out the obligations attaching to members of the Management Company under that Company's Articles of Association

(ii) Upon being requested by the Lessor or the Management Company the Lessee will apply to become registered as a member of the Management

Company in any manner authorised by that Company's Articles of Association[9]

5 THE Lessee hereby covenants with the Lessor and with the owners and lessees of the other flats comprised in the building and leased by the Lessor that the Lessee will at all times hereafter:

(a) Keep the demised premises (other than the parts thereof comprised and referred to in clause 6 hereof) and all walls party walls sewers drains pipes cables wires and appurtenances thereto belonging in good and tenantable repair and condition and in particular (but without prejudice to the generality of the foregoing) so as to support shelter and protect the parts of the building other than the demised premises

(b) (i) To contribute and pay [10] of the costs expenses outgoings and matters mentioned in the Fifth Schedule hereto

(ii) The contribution under paragraph (i) of this clause for each year shall be estimated by the Lessor (whose decision shall be final) as soon as practicable after the beginning of each year of the term and the Lessee shall pay the estimated contribution in two instalments on the First day of July and the First day of January in every year of the term

The estimated contribution for the year ending the Thirtieth day of June One thousand nine hundred and eighty five[11] is £ [12] and the Lessee shall pay a proportionate part thereof calculated from the date hereof to the Thirtieth day of June next on the execution hereof

(iii) As soon as reasonably may be after the end of the year ending the Thirtieth day of June One thousand nine hundred and eighty seven and[13] each succeeding third year when the actual amount of the said costs expenses outgoings and matters for the three years ending the Thirtieth day of June One thousand nine hundred and eighty seven or each succeeding third year (as the case may be) has been ascertained the Lessee (on being supplied with a sufficient statement of account) shall forthwith pay the balance due to the Lessor or be credited in the Lessor's books with any amount overpaid

(iv) The certificate of the managing agents (if any) for the time being of the Lessor or the Lessor's Auditors as to any amount due to the Lessor under paragraph (iii) of this clause shall be final and binding on the parties

(v) Subject to paragraph (iv) of this clause in the event of any dispute between the parties arising out of this clause or the Fifth Schedule hereto the same shall be referred to an arbitrator (who shall not be a member or employee of the Lessor's managing agents) being a Chartered Surveyor appointed by the Lessor

(c) Not to do or permit to be done any act or thing which may render void or voidable any policy or policies of insurance of the building and/or the land or any policy or policies of insurance in respect of the contents of any of the flats comprised in the building or which may cause any increased premium to be payable in respect of any such policy

(d) To permit the Lessor and others authorised by it with or without workmen and others at all reasonable times on notice (except in case of emergency) to enter into and upon the demised premises or any part thereof for the following purposes namely:

(aa) to repair any part of the building or adjoining or contiguous premises and to make repair maintain rebuild cleanse and keep in order and good condition all sewers drains pipes cables watercourses gutters wires party structures or other conveniences belonging to or serving or used for the same and to lay down maintain repair and test drainage gas and water pipes and electric wires and cables and for similar purposes the Lessor or other person exercising such right (as the case may be) doing no unnecessary damage and making good all damage occasioned thereby to the demised premises

(bb) to view and examine the state and condition of the demised premises and

(cc) for the purpose of cutting off the supply of water to the demised premises or any other flat in the building in respect whereof the Lessee or the occupier of such other flat (as the case may be) shall have made default in paying his share of the Water Rate

(dd) make good all defects decays and wants of repair of which notice in writing shall be given by the Lessor to the Lessee and for which the Lessee may be liable hereunder within two months after the giving of such notice

6 THE Lessor hereby covenants with the Lessee as follows:

(a) That the Lessee paying the rents hereby reserved and performing and observing the several covenants conditions and agreements herein contained and on the Lessee's part to be performed and observed shall and may peaceably and quietly hold and enjoy the demised premises during the said term without any unlawful interruption or disturbance from or by the Lessor or any person or persons rightfully claiming under or in trust for it

(b) That the Lessor will at all times during the said term (unless such insurance shall be vitiated by any act or default of the Lessee) insure and keep insured to the full re-instatement value the building against loss or damage by fire aircraft property-owners liability and such other risks (if any) as the Lessor shall from time to time think fit in some insurance office of repute or with Lloyds' Underwriters in such sum as the Lessor shall from time to time think fit and whenever required produce to the Lessee the policy or policies of such insurance and the receipt for the last premium for the same and will in the event of the building being damaged or destroyed by fire as soon as reasonably practicable lay out the insurance monies in the repair rebuilding or re-instatement of the building[14]

(c) That the Lessor will require every person to whom it shall hereafter grant a lease of any flat comprised in the building to covenant to observe the restrictions set forth in the Second Schedule hereto

(d) That the Lessor will maintain repair decorate and renew

(i) the main structure and in particular the roof chimney stacks gutters and rainwater pipes of the building

(ii) the [gas and] water pipes drains and electric cables and wires in under and upon the building and enjoyed or used by the Lessee in common with the owners and Lessees of the other flats

(iii) the main entrance halls passages landings staircases refuse chamber (if any) and other parts of the building so enjoyed or used by the Lessee in common as aforesaid

(e) That the Lessor will so far as practicable keep clean and reasonably lighted the passage landings staircases and other parts of the building so enjoyed or used by the Lessee in common as aforesaid

(f) That (subject as aforesaid) the Lessor will so often as is reasonably required decorate the exterior including the wood and ironwork of the building in such a manner as it shall think fit[15]

(g) That the Lessor will keep the gardens and common grounds and roads and paths leading to and from the building used in connection therewith by the Lessee in common with other persons having the like right properly cultivated laid out maintained and where necessary suitably cleaned

(h) That (if the Lessor shall in its sole discretion deem it necessary or desirable) the Lessor will employ a Managing Agent to manage the building and/or a porter and/or such other staff as the Lessor shall deem reasonably necessary for the better performance of its obligations under this clause and including the provision of living accommodation (if necessary) for any person or persons so employed if the Lessor shall deem this reasonably necessary for the effective discharge of such person or persons duties

PROVIDED that the observance of the performance of the whole of the foregoing covenant on the part of the Lessor shall be conditional upon the due payment by the Lessee of all sums of money covenanted to be paid by him hereunder AND IT IS FURTHER PROVIDED AND HEREBY AGREED that in the event of the assignment by the said [developer] of the reversion immediately expectant upon the determination of the term hereby granted [developer] shall on and from the date of such assignment cease to be liable in respect of any breach or breaches of covenants on its part herein contained which may occur after the date of such assignment

PROVIDED ALWAYS AND IT IS HEREBY AGREED AND DECLARED as follows:

(1) That if the rents hereby reserved or any part thereof shall be in arrear for twenty one days after the same shall have become due whether the same shall have been legally demanded or not or in the event of any breach non-observance or non-performance of any of the covenants conditions and agreements on the part of the Lessee herein contained then and in any such case it shall be lawful for the Lessor or any person or persons duly authorised by it in that behalf to enter into and upon the demised premises or any part thereof in the name of the whole and peaceably hold and enjoy the same thenceforth as if these presents had not been made but without prejudice to any right of action or remedy of the Lessor in respect of any antecedent breach of any of the covenants by the Lessee hereinbefore contained

(2) That any notice hereby required or authorised to be given by the Lessor or Lessee respectively shall be in writing and may be given in any of the modes provided for by Section 196 of the Law of Property Act 1925 with respect to notices to be given to Lessors or Lessees (as the case may be) under that Act

(3) In this Deed where the context so admits the masculine gender shall include the feminine gender and the singular number shall include the plural number and vice versa and where there are two or more persons included in the expression 'the Lessee' covenants expressed to be made by the Lessee shall be deemed to be made by such persons jointly and severally and in this event the following clause shall apply

(4) [space for joint tenancy clause, if required]

7 [Certificate of value]

8 An acknowledgement of deeds may be given here in appropriate circumstances

IN WITNESS etc.

THE FIRST SCHEDULE before referred to

PART I

ALL THAT parcel of land situate at [location of site] in the County of shown for the purpose of identification only edged red on the plan annexed hereto

PART II

ALL THAT flat known as Flat Number [description] shown on the said plan annexed hereto and being on the floor of the building TOGETHER WITH the doors and windows thereof and the interior faces of the ceilings floors and main structural walls thereof internal walls which are not main structural and which divide the flat from adjoining flats/or the common parts of the building being party walls AND TOGETHER WITH all cisterns tanks sewers drains pipes wires ducts and conduits used solely for the purpose of the flat (EXCEPTING AND RESERVING from the demise the main structural parts of the building of which the flat forms part including the roof foundations and external parts thereof)

THE SECOND SCHEDULE before referred to

Restrictions imposed in respect of the demised premises

1 Not to use the demised premises nor permit the same to be used for any purpose whatsoever other than as a private dwelling in the occupation of one family only or for any purpose from which a nuisance can arise to the owners lessees and occupiers of the other flats comprised in the building or in the neighbourhood or for any illegal or immoral purposes

2 Not to throw dirt rubbish rags and other refuse or permit the same to be thrown into the sinks baths lavatories cisterns or waste or soil pipes in the demised premises

3 No audio equipment or musical instrument of any kind shall be played or used or any other things done or caused to be done in the demised premises so as to cause annoyance to the owners lessees or occupiers of the other flats comprised in the building or so as to be audible outside the demised premises between the hours of 11 p.m. and 8 a.m.

4 No name writing drawing signboard plate or placard of any kind shall be put on or in any window on the exterior of the demised premises (including the entrance door thereto) or so as to be visible from outside the demised premises no clothes or other articles shall be hung or exposed outside the demised premises no flower box flower pot or other like object shall be placed outside the demised premises no mat shall be shaken out of the windows of the demised premises and no bird dog or other animal which may cause annoyance to any owner lessee or occupier of the other flats comprised in the building shall be kept in the demised premises

5 No external radio or television aerial shall be erected

6 Not to obstruct in any way any of the common parts of the building or the communal roads or parking space on the land

7 No musical instruments radio sound recorders or reproducers shall be played nor shall any games or other activity be pursued or carried out in the common parts of the building or the car parking area which may prejudicially interfere with or cause damage or annoyance to the owners or occupiers of other flats in the building

THE THIRD SCHEDULE before referred to

Easements rights and privileges included in the Lease

1 Full right and liberty for the Lessee and all persons authorised by him (in common with all other persons entitled to the like right) at all times by day or by night and for all purposes to go pass and repass over and along the main entrance of the building of which the demised premises forms part and the passages landings and staircases leading to the demised premises

2 Full right and liberty for the Lessee and all persons authorised by him in common with all other persons entitled to the like right at all times by day or by night and for all purposes to go pass and repass (i) on foot only over and along the pathways laid out on the land (ii) with or without vehicles over and along the access way or ways.

3 The right to use for the purpose of recreation (but subject to all regulations from time to time made by the Lessor) those parts of the gardens and common grounds laid out on the land for that purpose

4 The right to use any refuse chamber which may be marked on the plan annexed hereto for the tidy disposal of domestic refuse only

5 The right to subjacent and lateral support and to shelter and protection from the other parts of the building and from the side and roof thereof

6 The free and uninterrupted passage and running of water and soil gas and electricity from and to the demised premises through the sewers drains and watercourses cables pipes and wires which now are or may at any time hereafter be in under or passing through the building or any part thereof

7 The right for the Lessee with servants workmen and others at all reasonable times

on notice (except in the case of emergency) to enter into and upon other parts of the building for the purpose of repairing cleansing maintaining or renewing any such sewers drains and watercourses cables pipes and wires as aforesaid and of laying down any new sewers drains and watercourses cables pipes and wires in place thereof causing as little disturbance as possible and making good any damage caused

8 The right for the Lessee with servants workmen and others at all reasonable times on notice (except in the case of emergency) to enter into and upon other parts of the building for the purpose of repairing maintaining renewing altering or rebuilding the demised premises or any part of the building giving subjacent or lateral support shelter or protection to the demised premises

9 The benefit of the restrictions contained in the Leases of the other flats comprised in the building granted or to be granted by the Lessor

10 The right to connect a television set in the flat with an aerial erected by or on behalf of the Lessors provided that nothing herein contained shall oblige the Lessor to erect any such aerial

11 All the above easements rights and privileges are subject to and conditional upon the Lessee contributing and paying as provided in clause 5 (b) (i) of this Lease

12 The exclusive right for the Lessee to use for the parking of two private motor vehicles only the car parking spaces shown coloured yellow on the said plan annexed hereto[16]

THE FOURTH SCHEDULE before referred to

Exceptions and Reservations

There are excepted and reserved out of this Lease to the Lessor and the Lessees of the other flats in the building:

1 Easement rights and privileges over along and through the demised premises equivalent to those set forth in paragraphs 5, 6, 7 and 8 of the Third Schedule to this Lease

2 Power for the Lessor and its surveyors or agents with or without workmen and others at all reasonable times on notice (except in case of emergency) to enter the demised premises for the purposes of carrying out its obligations under clause 6 of this Lease

3 The right to erect and maintain a television aerial or aerials on the roof of the building for the use of the occupiers of the building and to run wires connecting such aerial or aerials to the television sets in the flats and other parts of the building

THE FIFTH SCHEDULE before referred to

Costs expenses outgoings and matters in respect of which the Lessee is to contribute and in respect of which the Lessee's contribution is [10]

1 The expenses of and incidental to the running and administration of the Management Company whether or not the Management Company be also the Lessor

2 The expenses incurred by the Lessor in carrying out its obligations under clause 6 (b) (d) (e) (f) (g) and (h) of this Lease

3 The cost of maintaining (including any rental) communal television aerials (where there are any) for the use of the flats

4 The cost of maintaining (including any rental) any entry-phone (where there is one) (or other similar system) for the use of the flats

5 Such sum (to be fixed annually) as shall be estimated by the Lessor (whose decision shall be final) to provide a reserve fund for items of expenditure referred to in this Schedule to be or expected to be incurred at any time during the period of three years commencing with the date upon which the estimate is made

6 All rates including water rates taxes and outgoings (if any) payable in respect of any part of the building and/or the land (other than those payable solely in respect of any of the flats)

7 All other expenses (if any) incurred by the Lessor in and about the maintenance

and proper and convenient management and running of the building and the land including in particular but without prejudice to the generality of the foregoing any expenses incurred in rectifying or making good any inherent structural defect in the building any interest paid or any money borrowed by the Lessor to defray any expenses incurred by it and specified in this Schedule and any legal or other costs bona fide incurred by the Lessor in taking or defending proceedings (including any arbitration) arising out of any Lease of any part of the building or any claim by or against any lessee or tenant thereof (other than a claim for rent alone) or by any third party against the Lessor as owner or occupier of any part of the building

8 The fees and disbursements paid to any managing agent appointed by the Lessor in respect of the building and to any auditor for the purpose of this Lease

9 The Lessor or the Lessor's managing agent shall keep proper books of account (which shall be available for reasonable inspection during normal business hours by the Lessee on notice) showing the expenditure incurred under this Schedule and the contributions thereto received from the Lessees of the flats

10 The said reserve fund/s shall be kept in separate account/s Any interest on or income of the said funds shall (after deduction of any tax) be added to the funds which shall be held by the Lessor in trust for the lessees of the flats and shall only be applied in accordance with the terms of this Schedule

11 The Lessor shall be entitled to employ contractors to carry out any of its obligations under this Lease and if any repairs redecorations renewals maintenance or cleaning are carried out by the Lessor itself not being the Management Company it shall be entitled to charge as the expenses thereof its normal charge (including profit) in respect thereof

(Attestation)

Notes

1 This will be the tenants' management company incorporated at the *beginning*, not half-way through or near the end of the development.

2 The length of the term is optional, but for such a scheme, 999 years seems to be a fairly standard length. Certainly 99 years is too short.

3 See p 141, above, for the advantages of reserving a modest ground rent on a scheme such as this where it might otherwise seem to be pointless; ie if the tenants are managing the building themselves, *and* taking the reversion, ground rent might be a superfluous payment. Nevertheless, it can sometimes prove useful as a failsafe income.

4 To be chosen by developer, probably to coincide with his own.

5 This date is variable according to circumstances as mentioned in n 4 above. It will be the year ending date chosen. However as it appears in various guises throughout the document, it is used from this point on, so as to lessen confusion in the mind of the reader. But remember that the date itself is not an integral part of the lease: it could just as easily be 31 December, 31 March, and so on.

6 This proviso may not be acceptable to lessees, their mortgagees, or, indeed, the lessor. But see clause 6 (c) later which appears to answer most of the criticism. Nevertheless, this wording may be too loose for some conveyancers.

7 This is purely an 'after the event' notice of assignment procedure. In the case of a tenants' management company, where almost everybody knows almost everybody elses' business, and where the relationships will be fairly close (but not necessarily friendly) it is probably a complete waste of time using a more secure method of giving notice of movements in ownership, etc.

8 The assumption is that the property is unregistered to start with: if it is registered to start with then the original lease should contain the application for the restriction to be put on the register. The wording of the restriction will be as clause 4 (a), except that the management company's name will appear in full; the application is worded as in Precedent No 3, cl 8, p 363, above.

9 And see ch 11, pp 137 to 138, above.

10 To be decided by the developer, probably on proportionate floor areas of the individual flats.

11 We will assume that the flat is sold some time in the 12 months prior to 30 June 1985.

12 This figure should be a *sensible* estimate.

13 As nearly as possible, a date three years from the start of the development.

14 As insurance clauses go, this is fairly loosely drawn and some practitioners may choose to substitute a more rigorous one.

15 Again the wording 'so often as is reasonably required' is potentially much less strict than a cycle of years; nevertheless, it is more suitable for a block managed by a tenants' management company, where—if a quoted cycle of redecoration is quoted—a minority of awkward tenants may be insisting on performance of this covenant when it is not strictly needed, and in the face of a management company trying to save its members money.

16 Or other suitable clause.

---

15 Lease of flat. Sheltered housing development. Private (ie non-housing association type) management. Provision of warden and communal facilities

[See also ch 22, p 250, above.]

H.M. LAND REGISTRY

Land Registration Acts 1925 to 1971[1]

LEASE OF PART

COUNTY AND DISTRICT

TITLE NUMBER

PROPERTY

THIS LEASE is made the day of One thousand nine hundred and eighty BETWEEN [Lessor/Developer] of/whose Registered Office is situate at

(hereinafter called 'the Lessor' which expression shall where the context so admits include the estate owner or owners for the time being of the reversion of the premises hereby demised) of the one part and [Lessee] (hereinafter called or collectively called 'the Lessee' which expression shall where the context so admits include the Lessee's executor administrators and assigns) of the other part

WHEREAS:

(1) In this Lease unless the context otherwise requires:

(a) 'the Estate' means the property more particularly described in Part 1 of the First Schedule hereto

(b) 'the Building' means the building erected or to be erected on the Estate or on some part thereof known or intended to be known as [ ] in the County of [ ] comprising [ ] flats and a Warden's flat.

(c) 'the Management Company' means [ ] or its successors in title[2]

(d) 'the rents hereby reserved' means [not only the rent reserved in Clause 1 hereof but also] the contribution referred to in Clause 4 (b) hereof[3]

(2) The Lessor has previously granted leases of or intends hereafter to grant leases of the flats in the building other than the premises hereby demised and other than the Warden's flat and the Lessor has in every lease imposed and intends in every future lease to impose the restrictions set forth in the Second Schedule hereto to the intent that any lessee for the time being of any such flat shall have the benefit of the observance of the said restrictions by the owner or occupiers for the time being of the other flats in respect of which the Lessor has granted the leases

(3) The Lessor has agreed with the Lessee for the grant to the Lessee of a lease of the flat hereinafter described for the consideration at the rents and on the terms and conditions hereinafter appearing

(4) Upon the grant of the leases of all the flats in the building [the Lessor will enter into a concurrent underlease of the Estate for a term of one day less than the term granted in the leases of the flats with the Management Company and the Management Company will manage and maintain the Estate during its concurrent term] [the Lessor will assign its reversionary interest in the Estate to the Management Company and the Management Company will thenceforth manage and maintain the Estate][4]

NOW THIS DEED WITNESSETH as follows:

1 In pursuance of the said agreement and in consideration of the sum of [POUNDS (£)] paid to the Lessor by the Lessee on or before the execution hereof (the receipt whereof the Lessor hereby aknowledges) and of the rents and covenants hereinafter reserved and contained and on the part of the Lessee to be paid observed and performed the Lessor HEREBY DEMISES unto the Lessee ALL THAT the flat more particularly described in Part II of the First Schedule hereto ('the demised premises') TOGETHER WITH (to the exclusion of all other easements rights and privileges) the easements rights and privileges mentioned in the Third Schedule hereto subject as therein mentioned EXCEPT AND RESERVING as mentioned in the Fourth Schedule hereto TO HOLD the demised premises unto the Lessee for the term of [ ][5] years from the [ ] day of [ ] One thousand nine hundred and [ ] YIELDING AND PAYING THEREFOR during the said term [ ][6]

2 THE Lessee hereby covenants with the Lessor and with the owners and lessees of the other flats comprised in the building and leased by the Lessor that the Lessee and the persons deriving title under him will at all times hereafter observe the restrictions set forth in the Second Schedule hereto AND will indemnify the Lessor and its successors in title and assigns from and against all actions proceedings costs claims and liabilities in respect of any future breach non-observance or non-performance of the said covenants and restrictions so far as aforesaid PROVIDED ALWAYS that (save as otherwise herein provided) the Lessor shall not be under any obligation to the Lessee to enforce any of the said stipulations in respect of any other property and shall have power from time to time by deed or deeds to vary or release any of the said stipulations in respect of any flat in the building

3 (i) THE Lessee hereby covenants with the Lessor as follows:

(a) To pay the said rent during the said term at the times and in the manner aforesaid without any deduction

(b) To pay all rates taxes assessments charges impositions and outgoings which may at any time during the said term be assessed charged or imposed upon the demised premises or the owner or occupier in respect thereof and in the event of any rates taxes assessments charges impositions and outgoings being assessed charged or imposed in respect of the building and/or the Estate of which the demised premises forms part to pay the proper proportion of such rates taxes assessments charges impositions and outgoings attributable to the demised premises

(c) Not to make any structural alterations or structural additions to the demised premises or remove any of the lessor's fixtures without the previous consent in writing of the Lessor

(d) To pay all costs charges and expenses (including solicitor's costs and surveyor's fees) incurred by the Lessor for the purpose of or incidental to the preparation and service of a notice under Section 146 of the Law of Property Act 1925 or incurred in or in contemplation of proceedings under Sections 146 and 147 of that Act notwithstanding forfeiture may be avoided otherwise than by relief granted by the Court

(e) (i) Forthwith after service upon the Lessee of any notice affecting the demised premises served by any person body or authority (other than the Lessor) to deliver a true copy thereof to the Lessor and if so required by the Lessor to join with the Lessor in making such representations to any such person body or authority concerning proposals affecting the demised premises as the Lessor may consider desirable and to join with the Lessor in any such appeal against any order or direction affecting the demised premises as the Lessor may consider desirable

(ii) At all times during the said term to do and execute or cause to be done and executed all such works and to do all such things as under or by virtue of any Act or Acts of Parliament now or hereafter to be passed and Bye-Laws rules and regulations thereunder are or shall be directed or necessary to be done or executed upon or in respect of the demised premises or any part thereof or in respect of the lessees user thereof by the owner lessee tenant or occupier thereof and at all times to save harmless and to keep indemnified the Lessor against all claims demands expenses and liability in respect thereof And to pay all costs charges and expenses incurred by the Lessor in abating a nuisance and executing all such works as may be necessary for abating a nuisance or for remedying any other matter in connection with the demised premises in obedience to a Notice served by a Local Authority

(f) (1) Not at any time during the said term to divide the possession of the demised premises by an assignment or underletting or parting with possession of part only

(2) Not to assign to or underlet to or part with or share the possession of the demised premises or any part thereof with any person who shall be under the age of [sixty][7] years at the date of such assignment or underletting or parting with or sharing of possession unless notwithstanding that the assignee or under Tenant shall be under the age of [sixty][7] years at the date of such assignment or underletting the demised premises will be continuously occupied by a person or persons older than that age[8]

(3) Within one calendar month after any such document or instrument as is hereinafter mentioned shall be executed or shall operate or take effect or purport to operate or take effect to produce to the Lessor or its solicitors the original or a true copy of every transfer of this lease or mortgage or legal charge of this lease of the demised premises or any part thereof and also every underlease of the demised premises or any part thereof for substantially the whole of the unexpired term and every assignment of such underlease and also every Probate Letters of Administration Order of Court or other instrument effecting or evidencing a devolution of title as regards the said term or any such underlease as aforesaid for the purpose of registration and for such registration to pay to the Lessor or its solicitors a fee of [pounds (£)] in respect of each such document or instrument so produced[9]

(g) At the expiration or sooner determination of the said term to peaceably surrender and yield up to the Lessor the demised premises together with all additions thereto and all Landlord's fixtures and fittings (if any) freshly decorated throughout and in good and tenantable repair and condition

(ii) IF the Lessor and Lessee shall fail to agree what constitutes the proper proportion of the rates taxes assessments charges impositions and outgoings under sub-paragraph (b) of sub-clause (i) of this clause the matter shall be determined by the Lessor but if the Lessee or the Lessees of any of the other flats in the building shall be unwilling to accept the determination of the Lessor he or they shall be entitled to have the matter determined by an independent surveyor nominated in default of agreement by the President of the Royal Institution of Chartered Surveyors whose fees shall be paid by the person or persons requiring such nomination to be made and such last-mentioned surveyor's determination shall be final and binding on the parties concerned

4 THE Lessee hereby covenants with the Lessor and with the owners and lessees of the other flats comprised in the building and leased by the Lessor that the Lessee will at all times hereafter:

(a) Keep the demised premises (other than the parts thereto comprised and referred to in clause 5 hereof) and all walls party walls sewers drains pipes cables wires and appurtenances thereto belonging in good and tenantable repair and condition and in particular (but without prejudice to the generality of the foregoing) so as to support shelter and protect the parts of the building other than the demised premises

(b) (i) To contribute and pay part/s of the costs expenses outgoings and matters mentioned in the Fifth Schedule hereto[10]

(ii) The contribution under paragraph (i) of this clause for each year shall be estimated by the Lessor (whose decision shall be final) as soon as practicable after the beginning of each year of the term and the Lessee shall pay the estimated contribution in two instalments on the First day of July and the First day of January in every year of the term[11]
The estimated contribution for the year ending the Thirtieth day of June One thousand nine hundred and [ ][12] is [£] and the Lessee shall pay a proportionate part thereof calculated from the date hereof to the [ ] day of [ ][13] next on the execution hereof

(iii) As soon as reasonably may be after the end of the year ending the Thirtieth day of June one thousand nine hundred and [ ][14] and each succeeding third year when the actual amount of the said costs expenses outgoings and matters for the three years ending the Thirtieth day of June One thousand nine hundred and [ ][14] or such succeeding third year (as the case may be) has been ascertained the Lessee (on being supplied with a sufficient statement of account) shall forthwith pay the balance due to the Lessor or be credited in the Lessor's books with any amount overpaid[15]

(iv) The certificate of the managing agents (if any) for the time being of the Lessor or the Lessor's Accounts Department as to any amount due to the Lessor under paragraph (iii) of this clause shall be final and binding on the parties.

(v) Subject to paragraph (iv) of this clause in the event of any dispute between the parties arising out of this clause or the Fifth Schedule hereto the same shall be referred to an arbitrator (who shall not be a member or employee of the Lessor's managing agents) being a Chartered Surveyor appointed by the Lessor and whose decision shall be final

(c) Not to do or permit to be done any act or thing which may render void or voidable any policy or policies of insurance of the rest of the building or any policy or policies of insurance in respect of the contents of any of the flats comprised in the building or the contents of any part of the rest of the building or which may cause any increased premium to be payable in respect of any such policy

(d) To permit the Lessor and others authorised by it with or without workmen and others at all reasonable times on notice (except in case of emergency) to enter into and upon the demised premises or any part thereof for the following purposes namely:

(aa) to repair any part of the building or adjoining or contiguous premises and to make repair maintain rebuild cleanse and keep in order and good condition all sewers drains pipes cables watercourses gutters wires party structures or other conveniences belonging to or serving or used for the same and to lay down maintain repair and test drainage gas and water pipes and electric wires and cables and for similar purposes the Lessor or other person exercising such right (as the case may be) doing no unnecessary damage and making good all damage occasioned thereby to the demised premises

(bb) to view and examine the state and condition of the demised premises and

(cc) for the purpose of cutting off the supply of water to the demised premises or any flat in the building in respect whereof the Lessee or the occupier of such other flat (as the case may be) shall have made default in paying his share of the Water Rate

(dd) make good all defects decays and wants of repair of which notice in writing shall be given by the Lessor to the Lessee and for which the Lessee may be liable hereunder within two months after the giving of such notice

5 THE Lessor hereby covenants with the Lessee as follows:

(a) That the Lessee paying the rents hereby reserved and performing and observing the several covenants conditions and agreements herein contained and on the Lessee's part to be performed and observed shall and may peaceably and quietly hold and enjoy the demised premises during the said term without any unlawful interruption or disturbance from or by the lessor or any person or persons rightfully claiming under or in trust for it

(b) That the Lessor will at all times during the said term (unless such insurance shall be vitiated by any act or default of the Lessee) insure and keep insured to the full re-instatement value the building against loss or damage by fire aircraft property-owners liability and such other risks (if any) as the Lessor shall from time to time think fit in some insurance office of repute or with Lloyds' Underwriters in such sum as the Lessor shall from time to time think fit and whenever required produce to the Lessee the policy or policies of such insurance and the receipt for the last premium for the same and will in the event of the building being damaged or destroyed by fire as soon as reasonably practicable lay out the insurance monies in the repair rebuilding or re-instatement of the building AND in the event of the demised premises or any part thereof at any time during the said term being so damaged or destroyed by fire or any of the other risks insured against by the Lessor as to be unfit for habitation and use then the rents hereby reserved according to the nature and extent of the damage sustained shall be suspended until the demised premises shall again be rendered fit for habitation and use

(c) That the Lessor will require every person to whom it shall hereafter grant a lease of any flat comprised in the building to covenant to observe the restrictions set forth in the Second Schedule hereto

(d) That the Lessor will maintain repair decorate and renew

(i) the main structure and in particular the foundations the roof chimney-stacks gutters and rainwater pipes of the building

(ii) the gas and water pipes drains and electric cables and wires including the fire alarm fire extinguishment system and the audio emergency communication systems in under and upon the building and/or the Estate and enjoyed or used by the Lessee in common with the owners and Lessees of the other flats[16]

(iii) the main entrance halls passages landings staircases lift shaft refuse chamber (if any) the Wardens flat and other parts of the building and/or the Estate so enjoyed or used by the Lessee in common as aforesaid

(iv) the furniture and equipment in the community room guest-room/s and laundry room or elsewhere which are enjoyed or intended to be enjoyed by the Lessee in common with the owners and lessees of the other flats and premises comprised in the Building[17]

(e) That (subject as aforesaid) the Lessor will pay all charges assessments and outgoings for rates water electricity and gas and other services payable in respect of the common areas of the Building and Estate as aforesaid including the wardens flat

(f) That the Lessor will so far as practicable keep clean and reasonably lighted the passage landings staircases and other parts of the building and/or the Estate or used by the Lessee in common as aforesaid

(g) That (subject as aforesaid) the Lessor will so often as is reasonably required decorate the exterior including the wood and ironwork of the building in such a manner as it shall think fit

(h) That (if the Lessor shall in its sole discretion deem it necessary or desirable) the Lessor will employ a Managing Agent to manage the property for the better performance of its obligations under this clause

(i) So far as practicable to maintain the services of a Warden for the purpose of being reasonably available to the Lessees in the building to render reasonable assistance in cases of emergency and to supervise the provision of services as aforesaid in the Building and Estate and to perform such other duties as the Lessor shall in its discretion stipulate

(j) Not to grant a lease of any other flat in the Building to any person who shall be under the age of [Sixty] years provided nevertheless that the Lessor shall have the right to grant such Lease on such condition as it shall deem necessary to a person of under the age of [Sixty] years for the purpose of the occupation of such flat by a person or persons older than that age[18]

(k) That the Lessor shall insure and keep insured the furniture and equipment referred to in Clause 5 (d) (iv) hereof against such risks as the Lessor thinks fit in some Insurance Office of Repute in the full value thereof and whenever required to produce to the lessee the policy or policies of such insurance and the receipt for the last premium for the same

PROVIDED that the observance of the performance of the whole of the foregoing covenants on the part of the Lessor shall be conditional upon the due payment by the Lessee of all sums of money covenanted to be paid by him hereunder

PROVIDED ALWAYS AND IT IS HEREBY AGREED AND DECLARED as follows:

(1) That if the rents hereby reserved or any part thereof shall be in arrear for twenty one days after the same shall have become due whether the same shall have been legally demanded or not or in the event of any breach non-observance or non-performance of any of the covenants conditions and agreements on the part of the Lessee herein contained then and in any such case it shall be lawful for the Lessor or any person or persons duly authorised by it in that behalf to enter into and upon the demised premises or any part thereof in the name of the whole and peaceably hold and enjoy the same thenceforth as if these presents had not been made but without prejudice to any right of action or remedy of the Lessor in respect of any antecedent breach of any of the covenants by the Lessee hereinbefore contained

(2) That any notice hereby required or authorised to be given by the Lessor or

Lessee respectively shall be in writing and may be given in any of the modes provided for by Section 196 of the Law of Property Act 1925 with respect to notices to be given to Lessors or Lessees (as the case may be) under that Act

(3) In this Deed where the context so admits the masculine gender shall include the feminine gender and the singular number shall include the plural number and vice versa and where there are two or more persons included in the expression 'the Lessee' covenants expressed to be made by the Lessee shall be deemed to be made by such persons jointly and severally and in this event the following clause shall apply:

(4) (Joint tenancy clause if appropriate)

(5) NOTWITHSTANDING anything herein contained the Lessor shall not be liable to the lessee nor shall the lessee have any claim against the Lessor in respect of:

(i) any interruption in any of the services hereinbefore mentioned by reason of necessary repair or maintenance of any installations or apparatus or damage thereto or destruction thereof by fire water Act of God or other cause beyond the Lessor's control or by reason of mechanical or other defect or breaking down or frost or other inclement conditions or unavoidable shortage of fuel materials water or labour or

(ii) any act omission or negligence of the Warden or other servant of the Lessor in or about the performance or purported performance of any duty relating to the provision of the said services or any of them

(6) Certificate of Value

IN WITNESS etc.

THE FIRST SCHEDULE before referred to

PART I

[Description of the *whole* development (ie the Estate including the Building)]

PART II

ALL THAT flat known as Flat Number [ ] aforesaid shown on the said plan annexed hereto and being on the [ ] floor of the building TOGETHER WITH the doors and windows thereof and the interior faces of the ceilings floors and main structural walls thereof Internal walls which are not main structural walls and which divide the flat from adjoining flats or the common parts of the building being party walls AND TOGETHER WITH all cisterns tanks sewers drains pipes wires ducts and conduits used solely for the purpose of the flat (EXCEPTING AND RESERVING from the demise the main structural parts of the building of which the flat forms part including the roof the foundations and the external parts thereof)[19]

THE SECOND SCHEDULE before referred to

Restrictions imposed in respect of the demised premises

1 Not to use the demised premises nor permit the same to be used for any purpose whatsoever other than as a private dwelling in the occupation of [one family only the members of which shall all be over [Sixty] years of age] or for any purpose from which a nuisance can arise to the owners lessees and occupiers of the other flats comprised in the building or in the neighbourhood or for any illegal or immoral purposes[20]

2 Not to throw dirt rubbish rags or other refuse or permit the same to be thrown into the sinks baths lavatories cisterns or waste or soil pipes in the demised premises

3 No audio equipment or musical instrument of any kind shall be played or used or any other thing done or caused to be done in the demised premises so as to cause annoyance to the owners lessees or occupiers of the other flats comprised in the building or the owners lessees and occupiers of the rest of the building or so as to be audible outside the demised premises between the hours of [11 p.m. and 8 a.m.]

4 No name writing drawing signboard plate or placard of any kind shall be put on or in any window on the exterior of the demised premises (including the entrance door thereto) or so as to be visible from outside the demised premises no clothes or other articles shall be hung or exposed outside the demised premises no flower box flower pot or other like object shall be placed outside the demised premises no mat shall be shaken out of the windows of the demised premises and no bird dog or other animal which may cause annoyance to any owner lessee or occupier of the other flats comprised in the building or the owners lessees or occupiers of the rest of the building shall be kept in the demised premises

5 No external radio or television aerial shall be erected

6 Not to obstruct in any way any of the common parts of the building and/or the estate

7 No musical instrument radio sound recorders or reproducers shall be played nor shall any games or other activities be pursued or carried out in the common parts of the building and/or the Estate which may prejudicially interfere with or cause damage or annoyance to the owners or occupiers of other flats in the building or the owners lessees or occupiers of the rest of the building

8 (Save as hereinbefore provided for) not to park or permit or suffer to be parked any motor car or other vehicles on any part of the Estate unless with the express permission of the Lessor except that casual visitors may park in such parking areas as may be provided

THE THIRD SCHEDULE before referred to

Easements rights and privileges included in the Lease

1 Full right and liberty for the Lessee and all persons authorised by him (in common with all other persons entitled to the like right) at all times by day or by night and for all purposes to go pass and repass over and along the main entrance of the building of which the demised premises forms part and the passages landings and staircases leading to the demised premises

2 Full right and liberty for the Lessee and all persons authorised by him in common with all other persons entitled to the like right at all times by day or by night and for all purposes to go pass and repass on foot only over and along the footpaths leading from the building to the nearest public highway and to use the gardens on the Estate

3[21] The right (in common with all other persons entitled to the like right) to use the community room residents kitchen laundry room guest room and toilet in the Building (the 'facilities') TOGETHER WITH the right as aforesaid to use the Guest room/s which the Lessor proposes to construct in the building subject to the observance by the Lessee of such rules and regulations made at any time from time to time by the Lessor which the Lessor may deem necessary or expedient for the good management of those facilities

4 The right to use any refuse chamber which may be marked on the plan annexed hereto for the tidy disposal of domestic refuse only

5 The right to subjacent and lateral support and to shelter and protection from the other parts of the building and from the side and roof thereof

6 The free and uninterrupted passage and running of water and soil gas and electricity from and to the demised premises through the sewers drains and watercourses cables pipes and wires which now are or may at any time hereafter be in under or passing through the building or any part thereof

7 The right for the Lessee with servants workmen and others at all reasonable times on notice (except in the case of emergency) to enter into and upon other parts of the building for the purpose of repairing cleansing maintaining or renewing any such sewers drains and watercourses cables pipes and wires as aforesaid and of laying down any new sewers drains and watercourses cables pipes and wires in place thereof causing as little disturbance as possible and making good any damage caused

8 The right for the Lessee with servants workmen and others at all reasonable times on notice (except in the case of emergency) to enter into and upon other parts of the building for the purpose of repairing maintaining renewing altering or rebuilding the demised premises or any part of the building giving subjacent or lateral support shelter or protection to the demised premises

9 The benefit of the restrictions contained in the leases of the other flats comprised in the building granted or to be granted by the Lessor

10 The right to connect a television set in the flat with an aerial erected by or on behalf of the Lessors Provided that nothing herein contained shall oblige the Lessor to erect any such aerial

11 All the above easements rights and privileges are subject to and conditional upon the Lessee contributing and paying as provided in clause 4 (b) (i) of this Lease

THE FOURTH SCHEDULE before referred to

Exceptions and Reservations

These are excepted and reserved out of this lease to the Lessor and the Lessees of the other flats in the building and all persons rightfully claiming under it or them:

1 Easement rights and privileges over along and through the demised premises equivalent to those set forth in paragraphs 5 6 7 and 8 of the Third Schedule to this Lease

2 Power for the Lesssor and its surveyors or agents with or without workmen and others at all reasonable times on notice (except in case of emergency) to enter the demised premises for the purposes of carrying out its obligations under clause 5 of this Lease

3 The right to erect and maintain a television aerial or aerials on the roof of the building for the use of the occupiers thereof and to run wires connecting such aerial or aerials to the television sets in the flats and other parts of the building

THE FIFTH SCHEDULE before referred to

Costs expenses outgoings and matters in respect of which the Lessee is to contribute and in respect of which the Lessee's contribution is [22]

1 The expenses incurred by the Lessor in carrying out its obligations under clause 5 (b) (d) (e) (f) (g) (h) (i) and (k) of this lease

2 The cost of maintaining (including any rental) communal television aerials (where there are any) for the use of the flats

3 The cost of maintaining (including any rental) any entryphone where there is one (or other similar system) for the use of the flats

4 Such sum (to be fixed annually) as shall be estimated by the Lessor (whose decision shall be final) to provide a reserve fund for items of expenditure referred to in this Schedule to be or expected to be incurred at any time during the period of three years commencing with the date upon which the estimate is made

5 All rates including water rates taxes and outgoings (if any) payable in respect of any part of the building and/or estate (other than those payable solely in respect of any of the flats)

6 All other expenses (if any) incurred by the Lessor in and about the maintenance and proper and convenient management and running of the building and/or Estate including in particular but without prejudice to the generality of the foregoing any expenses incurred in rectifying or making good any inherent structural defect in the building any interest paid or any money borrowed by the Lessor to defray any expenses incurred by it and specified in this Schedule and any legal or other costs bona fide incurred by the Lessor in taking or defending proceedings (including any arbitration) arising out of any lease of any part of the property or any claim by or against any Lessee or tenant thereof (other than a claim for rent alone) or by any third party against the Lessor as owner or occupier of any part of the building

7 A sum representing [ ][23] of the costs expenses and outgoings referred to in the preceding clauses 1 to 6 inclusive of this Schedule which said sum shall be the Management Fee of the Management Company or its successors in title
8 The Management Company shall keep proper books of account (which shall be available for reasonable inspection during normal business hours by the Lessee on notice) showing the expenditure incurred under this Schedule and the contributions thereto received from the Lessees of the flats
9 The said reserve fund/s shall be kept in separate account/s any interest on or income of the said funds shall (after deduction of any tax) be added to the funds which shall be held by the Lessor in trust for the lessees of the flats and shall only be applied in accordance with the terms of this Schedule
10 The Lessor shall be entitled to employ contractors to carry out any of its obligations under this underlease and if any repairs redecorations renewals maintenance or cleaning are carried out by the Lessor itself it shall be entitled to charge as the expenses thereof its normal charge (including profit) in respect thereof

Notes

1 This precedent is drafted as a registered lease; for unregistered developments the alterations would be minimal and so obvious that they are not included here.

2 This lease is drafted on the basis that there will be a separate management company. In view of the complex nature of the management required in sheltering housing, this would appear to be highly desirable. The lease goes on (see recital 4) to contemplate either that a concurrent lease will be granted to the management company in the same way as in Precedents Nos 3 and 5, (pp 360 and 370 respectively) or that an assignment of the reversionary interest of the lessor to the management company will take place. Naturally, if such was required, the management company could be a party to the lease from the beginning, in the same way as Precedent No 5, p 370, above.

3 But if the rent is, eg a peppercorn (see later) the words in square brackets are irrelevant and should be omitted.

4 It is *just* possible that this lease could be used in conjunction with eg a housing association, but it is unlikely that a housing association would not have its own model form of lease.

5 99-year terms appear to be popular with housing associations. If the development were to be managed privately, a longer term might well be considered.

6 Housing associations tend to charge nominal rents, eg a peppercorn. On private sheltered housing developments market ground rents are very often reserved. The reader is referred to ch 8, pp 98 et seq for a discussion on the merits or otherwise of reserving a 'proper' ground rent. The reader is left, therefore, to provide the wording at this point—see eg Precedent No 1, p 336, above, Precedent No 2, p 346, above, and Precedent No 3 p 360, above for specimen rent reservation wording.

7 The age limit is variable, but a number of planning authorities are now imposing age limits, either by way of conditions in the planning permission, or by requiring the developer to enter into a Town and Country Planning Act 1971, s 52 agreement. Care must be taken that the sub-clause matches any such planning conditions.

8 The precise underlying requirements of the clause will vary according to the nature of the development, the attitude of the developer and/or the Planning authority, and the local market. The wording given, though, is fairly typical.

9 This precedent assumes there is no restriction on alienation at all. The same cannot be said for some Housing Association model leases. See ch 22, p 268, above for a commentary on this aspect of the matter.

10 This will depend on local circumstances, eg the respective floor areas of all the flats in the building.

11 Or such dates as the lessor requires. For purposes of illustration, the same date sequence is adhered to in the rest of the precedent.

12 The next full year ending date.

13 The next payment date.

14 The nearest anniversary to three years after the start of the development.

15 It is not contemplated that a lessee would receive a refund of overpayments provided their ownership was continuing.

16 The specialist systems referred to are important in the case of sheltered housing.

17 If there are such communal facilities (which in a block of sheltered flats there are almost bound to be). Like the other specialised parts of this lease, the wording may be adapted to local circumstances.

19 Parking rights (if there are any) should be dealt with in this part of the Schedule.

20 Age limits are variable subject to certain parameters—see earlier comments.

21 Care should be taken to ensure that the developer is providing all the amenities referred to before this clause is used.

22 See n 10, above.

23 This will be the management fee to be levied. See ch 17, pp 195–197, above, for a discussion on levels which may be expected.

---

16 Shared ownership lease of flat: extracts relating to shared ownership provisions

Like some other precedents in this book, this particular precedent is included not because many readers are expected to be instructed to draw up a shared ownership lease; they will not be unless, almost certainly, they happen to work in the local authority field, in which case they will have their own precedents and will assuredly need no help from this book. It is included because it seems sensible to include in it some definitive version of the type of document which the general practitioner will come across when he has to deal with, as he will from time to time, a property which is sold on a shared ownership basis. Thus what follows is not so much in the way of a *precedent*, it is more a *reference document*.

The clauses concerned have been supplied by Norman Allen, solicitor, Central Lancashire Development Corporation, and the author is most indebted to Mr Allen for his assistance so readily given. It is probably true to record that Central Lancs have been dealing with shared ownership for just about as long as almost any other authority, and the clauses reproduced here are the result of some considerable refinement over the period of use of shared ownership.

Nevertheless, the caveat must be entered, as so often, that the draftsman's art is a very subjective one, and no two shared ownership leases will be the same. All that these following extracts are intended to do is to indicate to readers the sort of document they are likely to come across.

The way in which this particular lease has been drafted ensures that the shared ownership provisions are concentrated into one Schedule, and thus kept apart from the rest of the document. For that reason, the body of the lease itself has not been produced, merely the shared ownership provisions as follows:

1 DEFINITIONS

Within the interpretation clause will appear the following:

'*Shared Ownership*' the definitions relating to shared ownership are contained in the [ ] Schedule hereto.

2 THE GRANT

This will read as follows:

IN consideration of the sum of [£] being the purchase price of the Initial Percentage defined in Clause 1 (c) of the [ ] Schedule hereto at page [ ] hereof now paid to the Corporation by the Lessee (the receipt whereof the Corporation hereby acknowledges) and in consideration of the rent hereinafter reserved and of the Lessee's covenants hereinafter contained the Corporation HEREBY DEMISES THE PROPERTY TOGETHER WITH (in common with the Corporation and other persons authorised by the Corporation and all other persons entitled thereto) the easements rights and privileges contained in the Second Schedule hereto but subject [usual matters] EXCEPT AND RESERVING [usual matters] TO HOLD the same unto the Lessee for a term of [ ] YEARS from the [ ] PAYING therefor unto the Corporation the yearly Revised Rent fixed by the Corporation under the provisions of the [ ] Schedule hereto in the manner therein provided the initial yearly Revised Rent therein defined being [£] payable by twelve equal instalments in advance on the 1st of every calendar month the initial monthly rent being [£] and the minimum yearly rent payable hereunder for the purposes of Section 108 (5) (d) of the Finance Act 1981 is £10 and upon the Shared Ownership provisions contained in the [ ] Schedule hereto ceasing to apply to this Lease the said yearly rent of £10 shall be payable in advance on the [ ] day of [ ] in each year AND ALSO paying by way of additional rent during the term hereby granted as and when demanded [insurance rent provisions]

3 SPECIAL CLAUSES/S

The following will appear as a separate clause in the body of the lease:

THE SHARED OWNERSHIP provisions relating to this Lease are contained in the [ ] Schedule hereto and shall apply until the Lessee purchases the Relevant Percentage therein defined and this Lease is varied in consequence thereof in the manner therein provided. Whilst applicable the provisions contained in the [ ] Schedule shall overrule any provision to the contrary that may appear in the rest of this Lease.

4 CERTIFICATE OF VALUE[1]

A composite certificate will be required in the following form:

(a) the transaction hereby effected does not form part of a transaction or of a series of transactions in respect of which the amount or value or the aggregate amount or value of the consideration other than rent exceeds £

(b) the minimum annual rent payable under this lease is £10 and the amount of £ (being the Market Value of the Property as defined in the [ ] Schedule hereto) is the premium or sum referred to in Section 108 (5) (c) of the Finance Act 1981 and the parties hereto intend Stamp Duty in respect of the Property to be charged by reference to that rent and that premium or sum and this shall constitute the statement relating thereto required by Section 108 (5) (d) of the said Act.

5 THE SCHEDULE

This contains all the provisions relating to Shared Ownership, so that these provisions are collected into one identifiable section of the document, no other part of which (except as noted in points 1–4 above) is cluttered by reference to them.

The wording of the schedule is as follows:

THE [ ] SCHEDULE before referred to

Provisions which shall apply until the Relevant Percentage hereinafter defined is purchased.

1 (a) 'market value' shall at the date hereof mean the sum of [£] (being the premium within the meaning of Section 108 (5) (c) (i) of the Finance Act 1981) and shall at any subsequent date mean the price which the Property would then fetch on a sale thereof on the open market assuming that

(i) the Corporation was granting a lease for a term of years corresponding to the then unexpired term granted by this Lease

(ii) vacant possession is available
(iii) any improvements made by the Lessee at the expense of the Lessee and any value attributed thereto were ignored
(iv) any depreciation caused by or attributable to any failure or neglect by the Lessee to comply with his obligations herein contained is disregarded
(v) neither the Lessee nor a member of his family residing with him wishes to buy the Property
(vi) the rent should not exceed £10 per annum
(vii) subject as aforesaid the grant was to be on the same terms as are contained in this Lease

(b) 'the initial payment' shall mean the sum of [£]
(c) 'the initial percentage' shall mean [ ] per centum which shall represent that portion of the market value of the Property purchased for the price specified in Clause 2 hereof[2]
(d) 'a portioned percentage' shall mean at any relevant time a portion of the then market value of the Property and the smallest percentage that the Lessee may purchase shall be 10 per centum or a multiple thereof subject to the proviso in Clause 5 (3) hereof
(e) 'the relevant percentage' shall mean at any relevant time One hundred per centum less the aggregate of the initial percentage and any portioned percentage of percentages purchased pursuant to Clause 6 hereof
(f) 'the gross rent' shall mean the yearly rent for the time being appropriate to the Property if the initial payment and any further payment or payments purchasing a portioned percentage or portioned percentages pursuant to Clause 6 hereof had not been made that is to say the yearly rent of [£] as from time to time revised in accordance with Clause 3 hereof
(g) 'the relevant discount' at any relevant date shall mean the percentage of the then market value of the Property corresponding to the percentage discount to which the Lessee is at the date entitled pursuant to a General Consent under Section 17)(1) of the New Towns Act 1981 or any other relevant consent available to the Corporation on the sale or grant of a lease of the Property to the Lessee for a term of 99 years or more
(h) 'rent day' shall mean the first day of each calendar month of the term hereby granted
(i) 'the review date' shall mean the first day of April in each year of the term hereby granted
(j) 'review notice' shall mean a notice in writing served on the Lessee pursuant to the provisions of Clause 3 (2) hereof
(k) 'the revised rent' shall be such sum as is equivalent to the relevant percentage of the gross rent of the Property which sum shall at the relevant review date be increased by a percentage equal to the average percentage increase (if any) for the rent year commencing on or about the review date made by the Corporation in the rents of comparable Corporation dwellings for letting which said rent and said increase shall be determined by the Corporation which said determinations shall be final and binding on the Corporation and the Lessee
(l) 'lending institution' shall mean a Building Society within the meaning of the Building Societies Act 1962 or the Building Societies Act (Northern Ireland) 1967 and any other lending institution as defined in paragraphs 6 to 8 inclusive of the Schedule to the Home Purchase Assistance and Housing Corporation Guarantee Act 1978.

2 The yearly revised rent payable hereunder is [£] or such rent as may from time to time be fixed by the Corporation under the provisions of Clause 3 hereof such rent to be paid by equal monthly instalments in advance on each rent day (the

first payment being a proportionate part of a months rent from the date hereof to the next rent day to be made on the date hereof) AND the Corporation hereby declares that by virtue of Section 140 of the Housing Act 1980 the tenancy hereby created is not in the opinion of the Corporation a long tenancy at a low rent for the purposes of the Leasehold Reform Act 1967 so long as the reversion immediately expectant on the determination of the term hereby created vests in any body mentioned in sub-section (2) of the said section.[3]

3 The rent payable from time to time hereunder may be revised by the Corporation as at each review date and adjusted in accordance with the following provisions.

(a) The Corporation may at any time before or after the review date ascertain in manner hereinbefore specified the revised rent of the Property at that review date.

(b) If the revised rent ascertained as hereinbefore provided exceeds the rent payable immediately prior to that review date then the Corporation may increase the latter rent up to the level of such revised rent and serve on the Lessee a review notice specifying the revised rent operative from that review date.

(c) The revised rent shall as from that review date be the rent payable hereunder and all arrears of such rent shall become due and payable to the Corporation on the rent day immediately succeeding the date of the review notice should any such review notice be served after a review date

(d) Until such revised rent shall have been ascertained the Lessee shall continue to pay the rent at the rate current immediately before the appropriate review date and such payments shall be treated as paid on account of the revised rent.

4 Until the Lessee purchases the relevant percentage the Lessee hereby covenants with the Corporation

(1) Not to mortgage or charge the Property without the previous consent in writing of the Corporation such consent not to be required in the case of a mortgage or charge in favour of a Lending Institution PROVIDED ALWAYS that the Lessee shall not mortgage or charge the property without mortgaging or charging the right to purchase the Relevant Percentage conferred by Clause 6 hereof at the same time and in favour of the same person.

(2) Not to assign or underlet the whole of the Property without the previous consent in writing of the Corporation such consent not to be unreasonably withheld in the case of a respectable and responsible assignee or underlessee or required in the case of an assignment pursuant to the provisions of clause 7 (a) hereof PROVIDED ALWAYS that

(a) For the purposes of this sub-clause (2) 'market value' shall be determined in accordance with clause 1 (a) of this Schedule but excluding (iv) thereof and where the Lessee has carried out any improvements to the Property at his own expense 'full market value' shall be determined in accordance with the said clause 1 (a) excluding (iii) thereof and 'the surrender date' shall be the later of six weeks from the Lessee's notice required by (b) below or the day of the completion of the purchase of another property by the Lessee both dates being subject to the availability of the determination by the District Valuer that may be required by the Lessee at (d) below.

(b) If the Lessee desires to assign the whole of the Property as aforesaid the Lessee shall first by notice in writing to the Corporation offer to surrender the Property with vacant possession to the Corporation by deed absolutely for consideration hereinafter mentioned on the surrender date such surrender to be prepared by the Corporation at the expense of the Lessee.

(c) The Corporation shall within fourteen days of the date of such notice notify the Lessee in writing either (i) that it does not accept such offer or (ii) that it does accept such offer such acceptance to be without prejudice to all rights and remedies of the Corporation in respect of rent or any breach of covenant on the part of the Lessee and such acceptance shall subject always to the provisions of sub-clause (4) hereof state the consideration the Corporation is prepared to pay for such surrender the said consideration being a sum equal to the aggregate of the initial percentage and any portioned percentage to which the Lessee is entitled of the market value of the Property determined by the Corporation plus the full amount of the difference between the market value and the full market value when applicable.

(d) Within fourteen days of the date of the Notice from the Corporation at (c) above the Lessee shall either:

(i) Notify the Corporation in writing accepting its determination of the market value and the full market value where applicable or

(ii) Notify the District Valuer and the Corporation simultaneously in writing that he does not accept the market value and/or full market value where applicable determined by the Corporation and requesting a determination thereof by the District Valuer stating the surrender date where known. The District Valuer shall act as expert and not as arbitrator and his decision shall be final and binding on the Corporation and the Lessee.

(e) Should the Lessee not have exchanged contracts on his sale of the Property within three months of the date of the aforesaid determination either by the Corporation or the District Valuer he may require a review thereof by the Corporation or the District Valuer as appropriate in accordance herewith.

(f) The Lessee shall not assign the whole of the Property without assigning at the same time and in favour of the same person the right to purchase the relevant percentage conferred by clause 6 hereof.

(3) Within one month of every assignment mortgage charge or other assurance of the Property to give notice thereof to the Corporation in accordance with [appropriate clause in lease].

(4) (1) To pay to the Corporation on demand the amount specified in paragraph (2) of this sub-clause if within a period of five years from the date of any subsequent purchase of a portioned percentage pursuant to the provisions of Clause 5 hereof there is a disposal falling within the meaning of paragraph (3) hereunder PROVIDED ALWAYS that if there is more than one such disposal then the provisions of this sub-clause shall apply only to the first such disposal.

(2) The amount payable by the Lessee to the Corporation pursuant to the covenant in paragraph (1) of this sub-clause is an amount equal to the sum of the relevant discounts which the Lessee has by that time received which shall be contained in the applicable deeds of variation to this Lease but reduced by one fifth of the relevant discount in respect of each subsequent purchase of a portioned percentage for each complete year which has elapsed after the date of each such purchase and before a disposal.

(3) A disposal falls within the meaning of this sub-clause if it is

(a) an assignment or surrender of the residue of the term hereby granted or

(b) the grant of any sub-lease for a term of twenty-one years or more otherwise than at a rack rent of the whole of the Property

PROVIDED ALWAYS that the creation of a mortgage term of a disposal in pursuance of an Order under Section 24 of the Matrimonial Causes Act 1973 or under Section 2 of the Inheritance (Provision for Family and Dependants) Act 1975 or a vesting in a person taking under a will or on an intestacy or by a transfer by any one joint tenant in common to the remainder is not a disposal for the purpose of this sub-clause.

(5) The Lessee hereby charges the Property with the payment of any sums which may become due under this sub-clause and such charge shall
(a) take effect as if it had been created by deed expressed to be by way of legal mortgage and
(b) have priority immediately after any legal charge securing any amount left outstanding by the Lessee or advanced to him by a lending institution for the purchase of the initial percentage or any subsequent portioned percentage or the relevant percentage or further advanced to him by that body and
(c) be protected by registration under the Land Charges Act 1975 or the Land Registration Act 1925 as the case may be.

5 With a view to purchasing a Portioned Percentage

(1) The Lessee may at any time or times during the term hereby granted on payment of a fee of [ ][4] pounds to the Corporation serve on the Corporation a notice in writing requiring the Corporation to determine the market value of the Property and the Corporation shall notify the Lessee of the amount thereof in writing within eight weeks of the service of such notice.

(2) The Lessee may within four weeks of the service of such notification by the Corporation serve on the Corporation a counter-notice requiring that the market value of the Property be determined by the District Valuer and on receipt of such counter-notice the Corporation shall forthwith refer the matter to the District Valuer who (acting as expert and not arbitrator) shall determine the same and his decision which shall be final and binding on the parties hereto shall forthwith be notified by the Corporation to the Lessee.

(3) At any time within three months of notification by the Corporation either in accordance with sub-clause (1) or sub-clause (2) hereof (whichever shall be the later) the Lessee may purchase a portioned percentage by paying to the Corporation a sum equal to that portioned percentage less the relevant discount (if any) at the date of payment and as from the first day of the month following such payment the rent payable hereunder shall be a rent equal to the then relevant percentage of the gross rent PROVIDED ALWAYS
(a) the aggregate of the initial percentage and any portioned percentage or percentages purchased under the provisions of this clause shall not exceed eighty per centum of the market value of the Property and the final twenty per centum of market value must be purchased under the provisions of clause 6 of this Schedule.
(b) that a Deed of Variation[5] in a form to be agreed recording the date and details of each such purchase shall be executed by both parties hereto who where applicable shall do all things necessary to achieve registration thereof.

6 With a view to purchasing the Relevant Percentage

(1) The Lessee may at any time or times during the term hereby granted on payment of a fee of five pounds to the Corporation serve on the Corporation notice of the desire of the Lessee to purchase the relevant percentage and on the service of such notice the relevant provisions of sub-clauses (2) to (7) hereof shall have effect.

(2) The Corporation shall within six weeks of the service of such notice notify the Lessee in writing of the market value of the Property as determined by the Corporation and the Lessee shall be deemed to refuse to purchase the relevant percentage unless the Lessee within six weeks of the service of such notice serves on the Corporation a counter-notice either agreeing to purchase at a price equal to the relevant percentage of the market value of the property less the relevant discount (if any) at the date of service of such counter-notice or requiring that the determination of the market value of the Property be referred to the District Valuer.

(3) On being served with a counter-notice requiring such determination by the District Valuer the Corporation shall forthwith refer the determination of the market value of the Property to the District Valuer who shall determine the same acting as an expert and not as an arbitrator and his decision which shall be final and binding on the Corporation and on the Lessee shall forthwith be notified by the Corporation to the Lessee in writing.

(4) The Lessee shall be deemed to refuse to purchase the relevant percentage unless the Lessee within six weeks of the notification of such decision serves on the Corporation a notice agreeing to purchase at a price equal to the relevant percentage of the market value of the property as determined by the District Valuer as aforesaid less the relevant discount (if any) at the date of service of such notice.

(5) The purchase shall be subject to the conditions hereinafter specified and shall be completed within six weeks of the service of either the counter-notice referred to in sub-clause (2) of this clause or the notice referred to in the last foregoing sub-clause as the case may be and The National Conditions of Sale Twentieth Edition or the relevant subsequent edition thereof (hereinafter called 'the General Conditions') shall apply to this sale so far as they are applicable to a sale by private treaty and are not varied by or inconsistent with any of the express terms hereof but General Condition 3 or any subsequent replacement thereof requiring a deposit shall not apply thereto.

(6) On completion of the purchase in addition to the price payable as hereinbefore provided the Lessee shall pay any arrears of rent and any other sums then due to the Corporation under the provisions of this Lease and the Corporation and the Lessee shall respectively pay their own costs and expenses in connection with such purchase.

(7) As the result of the exercise by the Lessee of his rights under this Clause this Lease shall be altered by Deed of Variation in a form to be agreed which

(a) shall provide that the yearly rent payable in respect of the Property for the residue of the term hereby granted by this Lease shall be £10 payable in advance on the First day of January in each year.

(b) shall provide that this Ninth Schedule shall cease to have effect save as is contained in (c) of this clause and that otherwise this Lease shall continue in full force and effect.

(c) shall contain a covenant and charge in like terms to Clause 4 (4) of this Schedule relating to the repayment of any relevant discount applicable when the Lessee purchases the relevant percentage and relating to any pre-existing relevant discount granted upon the purchase by the Lessee of a portioned percentage and in respect of which the Lessee's liability has not ceased by effluxion of time but so that the Lessee's liability to repay any such pre-existing relevant discount shall in no way be extended beyond the five year period applicable thereto.

7 The Corporation hereby covenants with the Lessee

(a) In the event of a mortgagee entering into possession of the property to exercise its power of sale the Corporation will (subject to and in accordance with the conditions of Clause 6 hereof save as is in this Clause hereinafter contained) sell the relevant percentage to the said mortgagee or to a purchaser nominated by the said mortgagee PROVIDED THAT at the date of completion of the sale of the relevant percentage such mortgagee or nominated purchaser is also the assignee of these presents SAVE THAT the said mortgagee and the said nominated purchaser shall not be entitled to any discount on purchasing the relevant percentage and Clause 6 (7) (c) of this Schedule shall not apply to the final deed of variation relating to such sale of the relevant percentage SAVE ALSO THAT should the said mortgagee or nominated purchaser so require the Corporation will grant a new

Lease of the Property on the terms as are contained in the said Clause 6 (7) (a) and (b) in substitution for the Deed of Variation therein mentioned.

(b) That the Lessee may at any time during the term hereby granted (but without prejudice to the provisions of Clause 4 (2) hereof) assign the benefit of his option to purchase the relevant percentage contained in Clause 6 hereof to a purchaser nominated by him in writing and in this event the Corporation will at the cost of the Purchaser sell the relevant percentage direct to the said nominated purchaser subject to and in accordance with the conditions contained in Clause 6 of this Schedule save as is in this clause hereinafter contained PROVIDED THAT at the time of the completion of the sale of the relevant percentage such nominated purchaser is also the assignee of these presents SAVE THAT the said nominated purchaser shall not be entitled to any discount on purchasing the relevant percentage and Clause 6 (7) (c) of this Schedule shall not apply to the final deed of variation relating to such sale of the relevant percentage SAVE ALSO THAT should the said nominated purchaser so require the Corporation will grant a new lease of the property upon the same terms as are contained in Clause 6 (7) (a) and (b) of this Schedule in substitution for the Deed of Variation therein mentioned.

(c) That save as herein provided the Corporation will not until the relevant percentage is purchased sell lease or dispose of its interest in the Property to any body or person or corporation who is not a Landlord to whom the security of tenure provisions of the Rent Act 1977 or any statutory modification or re-enactment thereof do not apply by virtue of Sections 13, 14 and 16 of such Act.

Notes

1 The stamp duty position on shared ownership is special: full details will always be provided by the vendor authority.

2 Ie the grant itself (see section 2, p 407, above). All other references to clauses are to clauses within the Schedule itself.

3 This provision is not in any event relevant if the clause has in mind (as is supposed) enfranchisement. See generally ch 26, p 294, above.

4 Usually, eg £5.

5 See Precedent No 17, below.

---

17 Shared ownership: deed of variation effecting purchase of further share[1] (for flats and maisonettes)

H.M. LAND REGISTRY

COUNTY DISTRICT

FREEHOLD TITLE NUMBER

LEASEHOLD TITLE NUMBER

THE CORPORATION [the Shared Ownership lessor]

THE LESSEE

THE CHARGEE

THE PROPERTY

1 THIS DEED OF VARIATION is made the day of 198 BETWEEN the Corporation of the first part the lessee of the second part and the Chargee of the third part and is supplemental to the Lease ('the Lease') of the property made between the first and second parties hereto and dated the day of 198 the Property being subject to a

Legal Charge of even date with the Lease and made between the second and third parties hereto
2 IN CONSIDERATION of the sum of [£] paid to the Corporation by the Lessee in accordance with clause 6 of the Ninth Schedule of the Lease (the receipt whereof is hereby acknowledged) being the purchase price of a Portioned Percentage of [%] of a Market Value of [£] less the relevant Discount of [£] the yearly Revised Rent shall from the date hereof be calculated and payable in accordance with the Lease as varied hereby under the terms of Clause 6 (3) of the Ninth Schedule thereof and shall be [%] (the Relevant Percentage) of the Gross Rent from time to time fixed in accordance with Clause 3 of the Ninth Schedule thereof the Lessee having previously purchased [%] of the Market Value
3 THE provisions of clause [ ] of the Lease relating to the repayment of the Relevant Discount and the charging of the Property therewith shall apply to the Relevant Discount granted hereby and in accordance therewith the Lessee hereby charges the property with the payment of any sum due thereunder
4 SAVE as varied hereby the lease shall continue in full force and effect and the definitions contained in Clause 1 thereof shall relate to this Deed of Variation the Property being described therein as the 'Demised Premises'
5 THE Lessee hereby applies to the Chief Land Registrar to make the appropriate amendment to the Lessees title and to note the Charge created hereby relating to the repayment of discount in accordance with the provisions contained in the Lease
6 THE Chargee hereby consents to the variation of the Lease in accordance herewith
7 IT is hereby declared that the Lease contained a Certificate of Value in accordance with the provisions of Section 108 (5) (c) of the Finance Act 1981 incorporating the statement relating to the payment of Stamp Duty required by Section 108 (5) (d) of that Act and the appropriate Stamp Duty amounting to [£] was paid in relation thereto

IN WITNESS etc.[2]

Notes

1 See ch 21, p 240, above, and also Precedent No 16, p 407, above (the shared ownership provisions from the lease of the property). As before, the help of Norman Allen, Solicitor, Central Lancashire Development Corporation, is gratefully acknowledged.

2 This deed is for an interim payment. We have not included a precedent for the final payment: This precedent and No 16, p 407, above, are included merely to show readers the sort of document they are likely to come across if they are involved in shared ownership, presumably from the purchasers side. Space restrictions militate against the inclusion of further documentation which in any event will be provided by the shared ownership lessor.

---

18 Covenant for assignee of leasehold premises to enter into deed of covenant with lessor

[*Note:* we have already discussed ch 7, p 86 above, the advisability of securing the lessor/lessee relationship by various devices. The ultimate device is to require any incoming assignee to enter into a direct covenant with the lessor. The recommendation was that such a device was unnecessary and in the nature of 'overkill'. Nevertheless, there are some practitioners who will opt for its use, so that we include the appropriate wording here. The covenant will appear in the usual tenants covenants section.]

'Not to assign or transfer the demised premises without the assignee or transferee entering into a Deed of Covenant directly with the lessor to pay the rent and other monies hereby reserved and made payable and to observe and perform the lessees covenants and the regulations stipulations and conditions herein contained and to which this demise is subject the form of such Deed of Covenant as aforesaid to be previously approved in writing by the lessors solicitors for the time being[1] whose reasonable fees in the matter shall be borne by the lessee

AND a duly executed duplicate of the said Deed of Covenant shall be delivered to the lessors solicitors for retention by the lessor within 14 days of the completion thereof[2] [if the covenant is intended to extend to other dealings, the following wording should be added:

AND not to grant or create any underlease or tenancy of the demised premises or any part thereof or otherwise part with possession thereof (whether furnished or unfurnished and for whatever period) without the underlease tenancy agreement or other instrument containing an express covenant by the underlessee sub-tenant or licensee with the lessee to perform and observe the covenants conditions and stipulations herein contained]

Notes

1 It is supposed that to save themselves time and trouble, the lessor and his solicitors would settle the form of deed of covenant at the start of the development, and would make sure that a specimen was placed with the title deeds on the first sale. However, loose documents such as this have been known to lose themselves; thus there is a case for stitching a blank, specimen, deed of covenant into the lease itself. As long as it had 'specimen' stamped across it prominently this would be safe enough.

2 This wording contemplates that a separate deed of covenant will be entered into. It is possible to go one further step along the road of security for the lessor, and provide that the covenant itself is to be incorporated in the actual transfer or assignment of the demised premises. If one goes to the length of requiring a direct covenant from the incoming purchaser to the lessor, then it does seem logical that it should be thus in the transfer/assignment, rather than separate. By doing this, the lessor is making absolutely certain, as far as he is able, of his security.

19 Separate deed of covenant to be entered into if covenant in Precedent No 18 (page 415) is present in lease

[*Note:* if a separate deed of covenant is not called for, but the joining of the lessor into the transfer or assignment between the lessee and his purchaser, the following wording may be adapted for inclusion in the transfer.]

THIS DEED OF COVENANT is made the day of 19

BETWEEN [Lessor] of/whose registered office is at

(hereinafter called 'the Lessor') of the one part and [incoming purchaser] of

(hereinafter called 'the Assignee') of the other part[1]

WHEREAS

(1) By a lease (hereinafter called 'the lease') dated the day of 19 and made between [appropriate parties] the Lessor demised unto [original lessee] ALL THAT flat being [full description of demised premises] All which said premises are more particularly described in the lease for the term of [ ] years from the [commencement date] at the yearly ground rent of

£[ ] SUBJECT to the lessees covenants and the conditions and stipulations therein contained.
(2) The lease contains a covenant by the lessee therein not to assign the demised premises without the Assignee entering into a covenant directly with the lessor to pay the rent and other monies reserved by the lease and to observe and perform the Lessee's covenants conditions and stipulations therein contained.
(3) The Lessee desires to assign all his estate and interest in the demised premises to the Assignees.
NOW THIS DEED WITNESSETH that the Assignees hereby [if more than one: jointly and severally] covenant with the Lessor that as from the date when the lessees estate and interest in the lease shall be assigned to them and thenceforth during the residue of the term granted by the lease the Assignees will pay the rent and other monies thereby reserved and observe and perform the covenants conditions and stipulations on the part of the Lessee herein contained.

IN WITNESS etc.

(Attestation)

Notes
1 It is permissible to have the assignors join in this deed as well, but it serves no useful purpose, other than to save them from feeling left out, as they do not actually give or receive any covenants.

---

20 Assignment of (unregistered) flat/maisonette by either original lessee or subsequent purchaser[1]

THIS ASSIGNMENT is made the day of 19 BETWEEN [Vendor] of etc, (hereinafter called 'the Vendor') of the one part and [Purchaser] of etc (hereinafter called 'the Purchaser') of the other part.
WHEREAS
[[2](1) The Vendor is possessed of the premises hereinafter described for the residue of the term of [ ] years granted by a lease (hereinafter called 'the lease') dated the day of 19 and made between [parties] subject to the annual rent [if applicable—and other payments] thereby reserved and to the covenants agreements conditions and other matters therein contained.
[(2) The lease contained (inter alia) a covenant on the part of the lessee thereof not to assign underlet or part with the possession of [any part of] the demised premises without the consent in writing of the Lessor [such consent not to be unreasonably withheld][3]
(3) The consent in writing of the Lessor to this assignment has been duly obtained][3]
(4) The Vendor has agreed with the Purchaser for the sale to him for the sum of £ [of the said premises comprised in the Lease] [of the premises hereinafter described and comprised in a lease (hereinafter called 'the lease') dated the day of 19 and made between [original lessor] of the one part and the vendor of the other part [or as the case may be, according to who the parties were]] for the residue of the term granted by the lease subject to the annual rent [and other payments] thereby reserved and to the covenants agreements conditions and other matters therein contained.

NOW THIS DEED WITNESSETH AS FOLLOWS:
1 In pursuance of the said agreement and in consideration of the sum of £ paid etc. (receipt etc.) the vendor as [Beneficial Owner[4]] HEREBY ASSIGNS into the Purchaser ALL AND SINGULAR the premises known as [description] as the same are comprised in and demised by the lease TO HOLD the same unto the Purchaser for all the residue now unexpired of the said term of [ ] years granted by the lease SUBJECT to the payment of the rent [and other payments] thereby reserved and to the covenants agreements conditions and other matters therein contained and on the part of the lessee to be observed and performed[5]
2 Certificate of Value

IN WITNESS etc.

Notes

1 See ch 6, p 77, above, for a short commentary on (registered) transfer and (unregistered) assignments contrasted.

2 Recitals (1), (4) (and where appropriate (2) and (3)) refer to a sale by a Vendor other than the original lessee. For a sale by an original lessee, recital (4) (amended as appropriate) should be used, with recitals (2) and (3) following if they are relevant.

3 An unqualified covenant will be fairly unusual in a residential lease; even a covenant qualified as to unreasonably withholding will not be so usual as to be surprising by its absence.

4 Or, as the case may be; in the case of a variation of the status of the vendor, the recitals will have to be amended.

5 If the assignment is for value, there is implied by the Law of Property Act 1925, s 77 (1) (c) a covenant by the assignee to pay the rent and to perform all the covenants agreements and conditions contained in the lease *and* to indemnify the assignor.

---

21 Time-sharing: members' club: typical club constitution

[See ch 23, pp 270–281, above. As with some other precedents in this book, those in this section relating to time-sharing, ie Nos 21 to 26, are not included because many readers are likely to be instructed to set up time-sharing documentation, but because some readers may be consulted by clients who are *buying* time-sharing, and if it happens to be in this country, the likelihood will be that it will take the form of a (probably unincorporated) members' club. The combination of these precedents and ch 23, above, may assist the reader (perhaps even *prepare him beforehand*) to comprehend what time-share is all about.

The author is very much indebted to Ian K. Ganney of McHale & Co, London EC for supplying these documents, which relate to the Broome Park, Kent, time-share site which is a perfectly beautiful development.]

THE [ ] OWNERS CLUB

CONSTITUTION

1 DEFINITIONS
In this Constitution the following expressions shall have the following meanings:

'the Advance Management Charge'	means the estimated advance payment under the Second Option in Clause 7 of the Management Agreement annexed hereto
'the club'	means The [ ] Owners Club

'the Committee'	means the body of persons appointed under Clause 11 hereof
'the Company'	[(Developer)] Limited whose registered office is at
'the Constitution'	shall mean this Constitution and any amendments hereto made in accordance with the provisions hereof
'the Deed of Trust'	means the Deed in the form annexed hereto or any similar document for the time being in operation and 'Trust Deed' shall be construed accordingly
'the Form of Surrender and Request'	means the form as annexed to the form of Holiday Certificate annexed hereto as referred to in Clause 15 hereof
'the Founder Members'	are the Company and the Management Company (as hereinafter defined)
'a Holiday Certificate'	means the certificate in the form annexed hereto more particularly referred to in Clause 8 hereof and 'Certificate' shall be construed accordingly
'the Management Agreement'	means the contract for management services more particularly referred to in Clause 11.4 hereof and any similar document for the time being in operation
'the Management Charge'	means the charge provided for under the Management Agreement
'the Management Company'	is [(Management Company)] Limited whose registered office is at [ ] as provided for in Clause 11 hereof
'Members'	means the Members from time to time of the Club including the Founder Members unless the context otherwise requires
'the ordinary members'	means all members of the Club other than the Founder Members
'the Transfer'	means the Transfer of Whole of the property known as [Time share property] registered at H.M. Land Registry under title no [ ][1] executed contemporaneously herewith by the Company in favour of [(Trustee)] Limited[2]
'Villas'[3]	means [(description of time share units)] as the same are referred to in Clause 7 hereof and 'Villa' shall be construed accordingly

Except where the context otherwise requires the words and phrases in this Constitution shall be construed in accordance with the Interpretation Act 1978 and the headings in this Constitution shall be ignored.

2 NAME

The Club shall be called 'The [ ] Owners Club'.

3 LOCATION OF CLUB

The main office of the Club shall be at [(usually Time Share location)] or at such other place as shall from time to time be determined by the committee of the Club

4 OBJECTS
The Club shall be a non-profit making Club whose object is to secure for its members:
(a) joint rights of ownership of the [Villas] at [(Time Share location)] and
(b) exclusive rights of occupation of the Villas for specified periods in each year during the period of 80 years hereinafter mentioned

5 MEMBERSHIP
The Club shall consist of not more than two Founder Members and of such number of ordinary members as shall be admitted to membership as hereinafter provided

6 FOUNDER MEMBERS
The Founder Members of the Club shall be the Company and the Management Company

7 DUTIES OF FOUNDER MEMBERS AND APPOINTMENT OF TRUSTEE
7.1 The Founder Members shall procure [the erection of [ ] villas/the conversion of [ ] into [ ] apartments on the site known as [ ] and registered at H.M. Land Registry with absolute freehold title under No [[4]] (hereinafter referred to as 'the premises'), complete with such amenities, services, fixtures, fittings, equipment, furnishings, provisions and utensils as they shall reasonably consider appropriate [and shall ensure that all members are admitted as members of the [ ] Golf & Country Club and have the right to use the facilities of the Club during each member's period of occupation under the terms of Clause 8 hereof][5]
7.2 The Founder Members shall arrange for a transfer of the villas to be vested in and for rights of access to such villas to be vested in [and for rights to use the facilities enjoyed by the [ ] Golf & Country Club] to be granted to an independent trustee (hereinafter called 'the trustee') who will hold the same upon trust for the benefit of the members of the Club from time to time upon the terms of the Deed of Trust in the form annexed hereto
7.3 The initial trustee shall be [(Trustee)] Limited, whose registered office is at [ ] and the Founder Members will arrange for the said villas and any amenity ground pertaining thereto to be transferred to and for rights of access to such villas and amenity ground to be granted to such trustee
7.4 The Deed of Trust shall at the first General Meeting of the members of the Club duly convened and held in accordance with this Constitution be ratified and confirmed

8. RIGHTS OF OCCUPATION
The exclusive rights of occupation of the Villas shall be granted in accordance with the following provisions:
8.1 for each Villa there will be issued 50 Holiday Certificates each of which will be valid for a period of 80 years from the 24th. June 19 (hereinafter called 'the initial period') and will entitle the registered holder thereof to occupy such suite to which it relates for the weekly period in each calendar year referred to therein in accordance with the provisions of this Constitution
8.2 Such weekly periods will be numbered from 2–49, 51 and 52 with the weekly period number '2' beginning for Villas numbered 12 to 24 on the second Friday in each calendar year and for Villas numbered 1 to 11 and 25 and 26 on the second Sunday in January in each calendar year. In the case of weekly periods 51 and 52 each such period shall commence at 16.00 hours and shall respectively end at 10.00 hours on the 29th December and 5th January in each calendar year. In the weekly periods numbered 2–49 (inclusive) each such period shall commence on a Friday or a Sunday (as the case may be) at 16.00 hours and shall end at 10.00 hours on the following Friday or Sunday[6]
8.3 The dates of the said weekly periods for the duration of the Club shall be as set out in the Table of Weekly Periods annexed hereto and any days unallocated

to members for weekly periods shall belong to the Company provided that the Founder Members shall ensure that there are at least 14 days per annum available for works of routine maintenance cleaning and repair for each villa

9 FIRST ISSUE OF HOLIDAY CERTIFICATES TO THE COMPANY

9.1 In consideration of the Company executing the transfer in favour of the trustee of the premises the Company will initially be entitled to (and shall be liable in respect of) all the Holiday Certificates in respect of each villa so vested in accordance with the provisions of this Constitution

10 MEMBERSHIP

10.1 Any person (not being a minor) may apply for and be admitted to membership of the Club. A person shall include an incorporated company or body and persons may purchase in joint names in which case they shall both apply for membership

10.2 No person or persons shall be registered as a holder or holders of a Holiday Certificate or be entitled to the benefit thereof unless he or they shall be a member or members of the Club

10.3 Both the Founder Members and the Committee shall have power to admit applicants to membership which each may exercise without reference to the other provided always that such power shall not be exercised so as to result in two Holiday Certificates being granted in respect of the same villa and the same weekly period

10.4 In the first instance the Company as initial holder of all Holiday Certificates (as provided in Clause 9 hereof) shall issue to members Holiday Certificates and such other evidence of membership as shall from time to time be determined by the Committee. Thereafter Holiday Certificates may be transferred from current members or the representatives of deceased members in accordance with the relevant provisions of the Constitution

10.5 Membership of the ordinary members of the Club shall cease on the occurrence of any of the following events:

(a) the transfer of a member's Holiday Certificate subject to the transferee becoming a member of the Club: or

(b) the cancellation of a member's membership in accordance with the subsequent provisions of the Constitution; or

(c) the expiry of the initial period provided always that termination of membership as aforesaid shall be without prejudice to any persons rights in respect of a member's liabilities arising prior to the said determination

10.6 Any Holiday Certificates not issued by the Company to ordinary members will belong to the Company as an ordinary member and it will be entitled to all the rights and privileges and subject to all the liabilities of being an ordinary member and Certificate Holder provided that the Company will not be subject to the obligations attached to any Holiday Certificate retained by it in respect of villas (unless otherwise provided under the provisions of Clause 18.1) used for the purpose of maintenance and repair in any year provided that no more than six Holiday Certificates in respect of each villa will be retained for such purpose. Without prejudice to the foregoing the Company will be entitled to let out the villas to which such unissued Holiday Certificates relate or otherwise to grant rights of occupation to third parties for the duration of the period of such unissued Holiday Certificates

11 APPOINTMENT OF COMMITTEE AND POWERS

11.1 The business and affairs of the Club shall (save insofar as the same may have been delegated to a management company as hereinafter provided) be managed by a Committee of not more than five persons, three of whom shall be ordinary members of the Club and two of whom shall be nominated by the Company and may be ordinary members of the Club. The Committee shall meet as often as necessary and at least once every twelve months. Any two members of the Committee may call a committee meeting by notice in writing to all members at least fourteen days prior to the date of such Committee meeting and one of the Committee members shall be appointed to act as Chairman of the Committee at the first meeting of the members of the Committee, failing which the Chairman of any meeting of the Committee will be elected by a majority of those members of the Committee present at the meeting in question. Decisions of the Committee shall be on the basis of a majority of those present and in the event of an equality of votes, the Chairman shall have the casting vote. Three members of the Committee shall form a quorum. Proper Minutes of the proceedings at Committee meetings shall be taken

11.2 The first members of the Committee will be elected at the first General Meeting of the members of the Club which will take place on or before 31st December 19 . The first Annual General Meeting of the members of the Club will be convened by the Founder Members by notice in writing sent to every member not less than twenty-eight days before the date of such meeting. At the second Annual General Meeting one member of the Committee shall retire and a new member thereof shall be elected. Retiring members may offer themselves for re-election. The order in which the first three members of the Committee retire shall be decided by drawing lots. Thereafter retirement of elected Committee members shall be by rotation each member retiring at the third Annual General Meeting to be held after their respective elections. The two Committee members nominated by the Company shall cease to be such on written notice being given to them by the Company and the Company shall then nominate a successor or successors to fill any vacancy or vacancies thereby created

11.3 Save as herein provided election or removal of members to and from the Committee shall be dealt with only at Annual General Meetings or Special General Meetings of the Club and nominations shall be made by another member of the Club in person at such meeting and shall be similarly seconded.

11.4 The Committee shall have power to do all things that may be necessary for the carrying out of the objects of the Club for its general management and shall be entitled to delegate to the Management Company hereinafter referred to such of its powers as may be appropriate to enable the Management Company to perform its functions. Until such time as the Committee shall have been constituted the management of the Club and all the powers of the Committee shall be vested in the Founder Members who will on behalf of the Club enter into an Agreement with a management company (which in the first instance is intended to be the Management Company as herein defined, namely [ ] Limited in the form annexed hereto for the management of the villas and the proper provision of the various amenities and facilities to be enjoyed by the members and any other property of the Club. The Founder Members on behalf of the Club and on behalf of the Members thereof shall have power to enter into the Deed of Trust referred to in Clause 7 hereof

11.5 Without prejudice to the generality of the foregoing the Committee shall have the following specific powers:

11.5.1 At any time to appoint a member of the Club to fill any casual vacancy amongst the elected members of the Committee occurring through any death illness resignation or otherwise. All such persons so appointed shall hold office only until the next following Annual General Meeting but shall be eligible for re-election for the un-expired portion of the period for which the Committee members whom he was so co-opted to replace would otherwise have been due to serve

11.5.2 To make By-Laws at any time for the proper regulations of the Club and such By-Laws shall be binding on all members of the Club. Such By-Laws shall not conflict with this Constitution and in the event of any apparent conflict the terms of this Constitution shall prevail

11.5.3 To appoint such sub-committees as shall be necessary for the carrying on of the management of the Club

11.5.4 At any time to cancel or suspend for a reasonable period of time the membership of any member who in the reasonable opinion of the Committee shall have committed a substantial breach of the provisions of this Constitution or any By-Laws or Regulations hereunder or whose conduct in the opinion of the Committee shall be wholly unbecoming to a member of the Club and who has not remedied the breach of conduct complained of within a reasonable time following a written request by the Committee for him to do so. Any such cancellation or suspension shall be ratified by the members of the Club at the General Meeting next following the suspension taking effect. For the avoidance of doubt any dispute or difference howsoever arising out of this subclause may be the subject of a reference of application in accordance with Clause 19 below

11.5.5 To enter into all Contracts and Agreements which the Committee may deem necessary or desirable in connection with the management of the Club and to apply the funds of the Club in payment of the expenses of management, administration and running of the Club as detailed in Clause 12 except insofar as these powers may have been delegated to the Management Company under the Management Agreement

11.5.6 To appoint a [Chartered] Accountant [being a Member of the Institute of Chartered Accountants] as auditor to audit the accounts of the Club annually and to appoint Solicitors and other professional advisers

11.5.7 To agree the remuneration of the auditors, Solicitors and any other professional advisers from time to time appointed or instructed by or on behalf of the Club and (in the event of failure to agree to remuneration of the trustee between the Company the Founder Members and the trustee) to agree the annual remuneration of the trustee

11.5.8 To bring, defend, agree to be joined, settle or compromise any proceedings or claims of any kind in relation to the affairs of the Club or the obligations of the members hereunder or under the Deed of Trust referred to in Clause 7 and in the event of any such proceedings or claims relating to some only of the members to bring, defend agree to be joined, settle or compromise the same on behalf of such members at their respective costs

11.5.9 In the event of the determination of the appointment of the initial trustee or of any trustee subsequently appointed by or on behalf of the Club in accordance with this sub-clause to appoint another body or person as trustee of the property of the Club

11.6 The Committee shall maintain or cause to be maintained a register of names and current addresses of members of the Club indicating when they became members and when, if appropriate, they ceased to be members

11.7 Without prejudice to the generality of the provisions of Clause 11.5.4 hereof in the event of the cancellation of any person's membership thereunder, the Committee shall use its best endeavours to cause to be transferred that person's Holiday Certificate(s) and is hereby irrevocably appointed as attorney for that purpose and shall immediately thereafter account for the proceeds thereof to the former member after deduction of reasonable commissions, fees or any other expenses reasonably incurred in connection with the said transfer

12 MEMBER'S LIABILITY FOR PAYMENT OF MANAGEMENT EXPENSES ETC.

12.1 The Members of the Club shall contribute in accordance with the terms of the Management Agreement to all reasonable costs incurred by the Club including and without prejudice to the generality of the foregoing the reasonable cost of the following:

12.1.1 Maintenance, repair, decoration, (where appropriate) cleansing, and where necessary repair of the Villa services and facilities provided by the Club for the benefit of the members whether exclusive or in common with others entitled thereto

12.1.2 Maintenance, repair and when necessary, replacement of furniture, equipment utensils, provisions, furnishings, fittings and fixtures in or about or pertaining to the villas

12.1.3 Insurance of the Club's property of whatsoever nature for the full reinstatement cost thereof and any other insurance which the Committee shall consider necessary or appropriate

12.1.4 All outgoings incurred in respect of the Club's property including rates and other charges or impositions whether of an annual or recurring nature or otherwise

12.1.5 All works and acts which are required to be done to comply with any statutory provisions or the directions or notices of any governmental local or public authority

12.1.6 Any reasonable management charges or any other charges whatsoever which may be incurred in the management and preservation of the value of the Club's property and the running of the Club's affairs

12.1.7 The establishment and maintenance of a sinking fund for the replacement of capital items of the Club's property

2.1.8 The establishment and maintenance of any reserve fund requested by the trustee in accordance with Clause 13 of the Deed of Trust

12.1.9 All costs, expenses, claims, demands, losses and damages paid incurred or sustained by the trustee on behalf of members pursuant to the Deed of Trust or the Transfer

12.1.10 The fees and expenses of the trustee and all other costs, expenses or payments to the trustee under the Deed of Trust and the fees and expenses of the auditor, Solicitors and other professional advisers hereinbefore referred to

12.2 Save insofar as the same may have been delegated by the Management Agreement hereinbefore referred to the Committee shall have sole discretion in deciding what monies should be spent for any of the foregoing purposes and when the same shall be expended

13 CLUB'S POWERS

The Club shall have the power:

13.1 To borrow money

13.2 To grant securities and mortgages over its property

13.3 To purchase, lease or otherwise acquire additional property and

13.4 To sell, lease, grant easements over or otherwise dispose of or deal with its property or any rights over its property

PROVIDED THAT the foregoing powers shall be exercisable only upon a decision by not less than a two thirds majority of votes cast at a General Meeting

14 FURTHER OBLIGATIONS OF MEMBERS

The Members of the Club shall automatically be bound by the terms and provisions of the Deed of Trust upon election to membership and upon execution by the Member of a Holiday Certificate such Member shall by the Acceptance of this Constitution also be deemed to have accepted the obligations imposed on the Club and the members by the provisions of the Deed of Trust

Each member of the Club shall also be subject to the following obligations (and to the intent that such obligations shall continue to bind his estate after his death and until such time as his Holiday Certificate shall be transferred to a new or other member of the Club and notwithstanding that his personal representatives may not themselves be members):

14.1 To occupy the Villa to which his Holiday Certificate relates for the appropriate period of time in each year and no longer

14.2 At all times to observe the regulations relating to the occupation of the Villas a copy whereof is annexed to this Constitution and all variations, additions and amendments thereto made by the Committee

14.3 To keep and maintain the interior of the villa and all of its contents to which his Holiday Certificate relates in a good and tenantable state and condition during the period of his occupancy and to pay or indemnify the Club against any damage deterioration, or dilapidation (over and above fair wear and tear and damage or destruction by fire or any other risk insured against which may have taken place during the period of his occupation) as to which the Committee or (during such time as the administration of the Club affairs may be delegated to it) the Management Company shall be the sole judge

14.4 In the event of any repair or maintenance work to be carried out to the Villa or its contents during the period of a Certificate holder's occupancy of the villa to allow access on reasonable notice (except in the case of emergency) to the necessary workmen and others to enable such work to be carried out provided that any such work will be carried out with all due diligence and speed and will not in so far as is reasonable interfere with members' enjoyment of their occupation of the villas

14.5 Not in any way to make alterations to the villas to which his Certificate relates or the contents thereof

14.6 To pay for all electricity consumed by him and telephone calls made in the Villa occupied by him during his occupancy

14.7 To notify the Committee and the Management Company forthwith of any change in his permanent address

14.8 To pay within one month of the same being demanded the appropriate portion of the costs referred to in Clause 12 hereof incurred by the Club in any year

14.9 Not to do anything which would make void or voidable the insurance of the Villa and its contents or any other insurance for the time being in force and relating to the Villas or which may operate to increase the premium payable in respect of any such insurance and to indemnify the Club and the trustee against any increased or additional premium which by reason of any such act or default may be required for effecting or keeping up any such insurance and in the event of the Villa or any other property as aforesaid or any part thereof being damaged or destroyed by any insured risks and the insurance money being wholly or partially irrecoverable by reason solely or in part of any act or default of such member then and in every such case to pay forthwith to the Club or the trustee or as directed by either of them the whole or as the case may require a fair proportion to be conclusively determined by a surveyor to be appointed by the Club of the cost of rebuilding and reinstatement of the same as the case may be together with the whole or such portion as aforesaid of the fees of such surveyor

14.10 During such times as the administration of the affairs of the Club shall be delegated to the said Management Company to pay the Management Company at the times provided by the Management Agreement his due proportion of the Management Charge (including where appropriate the Advance Management Charge) provided for by the Management Agreement and further to pay upon demand any charge falling due under sub-paragraphs 3, 6, 8 and/or 9 of this Clause. In the event of any of the said sums not being paid by the due date the

Committee or the Management Company as the case may be shall be entitled to refuse the member in question or any other person in his place occupation of the Villa to which his Holiday Certificate relates until all arrears have been discharged

14.11 In the event of any member letting, granting rights over or for any other reason parting with occupation of the Villa to which his Holiday Certificate relates in accordance with the terms hereof for the whole or any part of the relevant period of occupation immediately to give notice thereof to the Committee or the Management Company as the case may be together with details of the name and address of the person who has been allowed into occupation

15 TRANSFER OF HOLIDAY CERTIFICATES

15.1 Any member may subject to the provisions hereof bequeath or agree to sell or otherwise transfer the rights to which he is entitled pursuant to a Holiday Certificate in favour of a third party subject to such third party becoming a member of the Club and subject to the discharge of the member's liabilities hereunder up to the date of transfer. In the event of the death or bankruptcy of any member (or the winding up of a member being a corporation) his personal representatives, trustee in bankruptcy or liquidator as the case may be, may agree to sell such rights to a third party or to vest the same in a beneficiary subject to the third party or beneficiary becoming a member of the Club

15.2 In the event of a member agreeing to sell or otherwise dispose of the rights vested in him pursuant to his Holiday Certificate or in the case of the personal representatives, trustee in bankruptcy or liquidator as the case may be shall deliver the relevant Holiday Certificate to the Committee or the Management Company with the Form of Surrender and Request endorsed thereon duly executed by such member, personal representatives, trustee in bankruptcy or liquidator (and stamped if necessary) and by the person to whom such rights are to be transferred or vested in and, upon production of satisfactory evidence of the transfer vested or other devolution of such membership rights, and upon payment of the fee hereinafter mentioned, the Committee or the Management Company shall within 28 days of such evidence being produced issue a new Holiday Certificate in the name of the new member whose admission shall be ratified at the next following General Meeting of the Club. The register of members of the Club shall be duly completed to register such transfer

15.3 A reasonable fee may be charged for the registration of the transfer which fee may be revised by the Committee or the Management Company from time to time. A member may also let the villa to which his Certificate relates for the whole or a part of the period to which his Certificate relates subject to notification being given in terms of Clause 14.11 hereof but provided that the member will in any event during the period of such let remain the holder of the Certificate and will be primarily responsible for all the obligations encumbent on the holder of the Certificate

16 GENERAL MEETINGS OF THE CLUB

16.1 The Annual General Meeting of the Club shall be held at [ ] or such other place as the Committee shall decide on such a date in each year as shall be determined but not so as to cause a period of fifteen months to elapse between each Annual General Meeting by the Committee (subject in the case of the first such Meeting to Clause 11 hereof) and shall be convened by notice sent to all members not less than twenty-eight days before the date of the meeting together with the Agenda of the business to be conducted at such meeting

16.2 The Committee may and shall upon a request in writing from the holders of not less than ten per cent in number of the Holiday Certificates call a Special

General Meeting of the Club to be convened and held in the manner prescribed for Annual General Meetings save that fourteen days notice only shall be necessary

16.3 Notices of Special and Annual General Meetings shall contain copies of the Agenda for such meeting and the exact wording of any resolution to be voted upon at the Meeting. No business other than that specified in the Notices of Meeting and documents therewith shall be considered at the Meeting

16.4 At every General Meeting the Chairman of the Committee (and in his absence a Chairman appointed by a majority of those present at the meeting) shall preside. Each member shall be entitled to one vote for each Holiday Certificate held and voting rights shall be exercised by way of a poll and not by a show of hands. Members will be entitled to appoint a proxy to vote in their stead. A proxy need not be a member of the Club. At all meetings in the case of an equality of votes the Chairman shall have the casting vote. Any resolution to be proposed otherwise than by the Committee at any Annual or Special General Meetings of the Club shall be submitted in writing to the Committee not less than twenty-eight days before the date of the Meeting if it is an Annual General Meeting or twenty-one days if it is a Special General Meeting and shall be signed by the proposer and the seconder. Any resolution involving a change in the Constitution shall require not less than a three quarter majority of all votes cast. At all General Meetings of the Club the quorum shall be four members present in person or by Proxy. Minutes of all General Meetings will be prepared by the Committee and circulated to all members of the Club within 6 weeks of the General Meeting

16.5 The instruments appointing a Proxy shall be in writing under the hand of the appointor or his attorney duly authorised in writing or if such appointor is a corporation under its common seal, if any, and if none, then under the hand of some officer duly authorised in that behalf. The instrument appointing a Proxy and Power of Attorney or other authority if any under which it is signed or a certified or office copy thereof shall be deposited at the offices of the Club not less than forty eight hours before the time appointed for holding the meeting or adjourned meeting at which the person named in the instrument proposing to vote and in default the instrument of Proxy shall not be treated as valid. No instrument appointing a Proxy shall be valid after the expiry of twelve months from its date

16.6 Voting at all meetings of the members including Annual General Meetings and Special General Meetings shall be on the basis of the number of Holiday Certificates held whether by Founder Members or otherwise. Where a Holiday Certificate is owned jointly the vote of the first named joint owner on the Holiday Certificate only shall be counted

16.7 A resolution in writing signed by all the Members of the Club who would be entitled to receive notice of and attend and vote at a General Meeting of the Club at which such resolution was to be proposed or by their duly appointed attorney, shall be valid and effectual as if it had been passed at a General Meeting of the Club duly convened and held. Any such resolution may consist of several documents in the like form each signed by one or more of the members or their attorneys and signature in the case of a body corporate which is a member shall be sufficient if made by a director thereof or its duly appointed representative

16.8 The Deed of Trust and Management Agreement shall be adopted and ratified by the members at the first Annual General Meeting of the Club and notice of such ratification is to be given to the trustee within seven days of the said ratification

17 AUDIT

17.1 The financial year of the Club shall end on [ ] in each year or on such other date as the Committee may decide. The Committee or the Management Company as the case may be shall cause proper books of account to be kept with regard to:

17.1.1 All sums of money received and expended by the Club and the matter in respect of which such receipts and expenditure take place

17.1.2 The assets and liabilities of the Club

17.2 At the Annual General Meeting in every year the Committee shall lay before the Club an audited income and expenditure account for the period since the last preceding account (or in the case of the first account since the inception of the Club) together with an audited balance sheet made up as at the same date. Every such balance sheet shall be accompanied by proper reports of the Committee and the auditor and copies of such account balance sheets and reports shall not less than twenty-eight clear days before the meeting be sent to all members at their respective addresses

18 TERMINATION PROVISIONS

18.1 The Club shall continue in existence until the [[7]] PROVIDED THAT the Committee shall call an Extraordinary General Meeting of the members of the Club within 3 months before that date, such meeting to be held at [ ] or such other place as the Committee shall determine. The purpose of that meeting will be to consider the future of the villas and the other property of the Club and also to consider whether and if so in what manner the Club is to be continued or reconstituted for a further period. Unless otherwise resolved by a two thirds majority of those members entitled to attend such meetings, the Club shall be wound up and its assets dealt with in accordance with the provisions of this Clause

18.2 In the event of the winding up of the Club the trustee shall realise the assets of the Club with power to delay or postpone the conversion of any particular asset if so directed by the General Meeting at which the resolution to wind up the Club was passed or if so directed by any subsequent General Meeting

18.3 The sums realised pursuant to Clause 18.2 shall be distributed first in discharge of all liabilities in accordance with the provisions of any Trust Deed for the time being in force and secondly in discharge of all other debts and liabilities of the Club

18.3.1 The net assets (if any) of the Club available for distribution after the foregoing provisions of this Clause have been complied with (hereinafter called 'the net assets') shall be notionally apportioned to each of the villas in equal proportions according to the number of villas comprising the property of the Club at the time of the resolution to wind up the Club

18.3.2 The amount of the net assets apportioned to each villa as aforesaid shall be for the purpose of ascertaining the amount thereof to be distributed to each member divided into fifty equal units of value (each such unit being referred to in this Clause as a 'Unit of Value') and there shall be distributed to each member or Founder Member (as the case may be) in respect of each of the said weekly periods to which it is entitled one Unit of Value

19 MISCELLANEOUS

Any dispute or difference arising out of this Constitution shall be referred to the decision of a single arbitrator to be agreed between the parties or in default of agreement to be appointed upon the application of either party by the President for the time being of the Law Society

APPENDIX

REGULATIONS[8]
(see Clause 14.2)

Notes

1 Or as the case may be.

2 The trustee, who will usually be a large financial institution of unimpeachable character.

3 This is meant to be a definition of the time share units, so 'villas' is just one term of description.

4 Or according to the circumstances.

5 This clause is optional—there will not always be such a club.

6 This clause, like the rest of these time-share documents, is an example only, and may be varied to suit specific requirements. However, this whole set of documentation has been well tried in practice, which must be an important consideration.

7 Ie 80 years from the date specified in clause 8.1.

8 These will mainly be 'use' regulations, similar to those found in a typical lease; perhaps rather more restrictive but basically the same.

---

22 Time-sharing: members' club: typical deed of trust

[See ch 23, p 277, above.]

THE [ ] OWNERS CLUB

DEED OF TRUST

THE [ ] OWNERS CLUB

THIS DEED OF TRUST is made the day of One Thousand Nine Hundred and BETWEEN [Developer] hereinafter called 'the Company') and [Management Company] both of whose registered offices are at [ ] (hereinafter together called 'the Founder Members') of the first part and [Trustee] LIMITED whose registered office is at [ ] (hereinafter called 'the Trustee') of the second part and [Guarantor] whose registered office is at [ ] hereinafter called 'the Guarantor') of the third part

WHEREAS:

A. The Founder Members have together formed a club known as The [ ] Owners Club whose object is to secure for its members joint rights of ownership of certain [villas and apartments] at [Time Share location] and also exclusive rights of occupation of the villas and apartments for specified periods in each year during the period mentioned in the Club's Constitution (as hereinafter defined) (a copy of which is annexed hereto)

B. It is provided in the Constitution that the title to the freehold property of the club (and any other property) shall be vested in an independent trustee upon trust for the members of the Club from time to time

C. The Company is by a Transfer executed contemporaneously herewith transferring to the Trustee the freehold property more particularly described in such Transfer being registered at H.M. Land Registry with Absolute Title under No [ ] (which with all other property which may from time to time be transferred to the Trustee by the Company or otherwise to be held for the benefit of the Club upon the trusts of this Deed shall be hereinafter called 'the Property') and the Trustee has agreed to hold the same upon the trusts and terms hereinafter mentioned[1]

NOW THEREFORE THIS DEED WITNESSETH AND IT IS HEREBY AGREED as follows:

1 (A) In this Deed except where the context otherwise requires:

(a) 'Club' means the Club currently known as The [ ] Owners Club referred to in Recital (A):

(b) 'Constitution' means the Constitution of the Club from time to time

(c) 'Villas' means the [Time Share Units] constructed or in the course of construction at [Time Share location] aforesaid and 'villa' shall be construed accordingly

(d) 'Transfer' means the Transfer by which the villas and adjacent land are to be transferred, executed contemporaneously herewith between the Company and the Trustee

(e) 'Property' means the land registered at H.M. Land Registry referred to in Recital C above together with the villas and apartments situate thereon together with all other property (real or personal) which may from time to time be transferred or otherwise vested in the Trustee to be held for the benefit of the members of the Club from time to time upon the trusts of this Deed

(f) 'Members' means the members from time to time of the Club including the Founder Members

(g) 'holding company' and 'subsidiary company' shall have the meanings respectively attributed to them by Section 154 of the Companies Act 1948

(h) 'associated company' shall have the meaning attributed to it by Section 302 (1) of the Income and Corporation Taxes Act 1970

(i) 'the Committee' means the body of persons appointed under the provisions of the Constitution to manage the business and affairs of the Club in accordance with the Constitution

(B) Covenants or warranties given and obligations or liabilities otherwise assumed under the provisions of the Deed by two or more persons shall be deemed to be so given and assumed by such persons jointly and severally

(C) Where reference is made herein to directions of the Committee of the Club the Trustee shall be entitled to rely on and accept firstly decisions of the Committee which shall be stated by the Chairman of the Committee Meeting at which the relevant decision was reached to have so reached in accordance with the relevant rules of the Constitution and without prejudice to the generality of the foregoing the Trustee shall not be concerned to enquire or satisfy itself in any way as to the election of Committee members or of the Chairman of the Committee Meeting or calling of Committee Meetings or the procedure adopted or the reaching of decisions thereat and secondly resolutions in writing in respect of which it shall have been certified by the Founder Members that the provisions of Clause 16.7 of the Constitution have been fully observed

2 THE Founder Members hereby appoint the Trustee and the Trustee hereby agrees to act as trustee on behalf of the Club and the members thereof from time to time on the terms set out in this Deed and the general terms and conditions upon which the Trustee acts as a trustee last published before the date hereof which are more particularly set out in the Schedule hereto. The said general terms and conditions shall apply and be incorporated herein and if there shall be any conflict between the same and the other provisions of this Deed then such terms and conditions set out in the Schedule shall pro tanto prevail. The Title Deeds of the Property will remain throughout the period of this Deed in the custody of the Trustee

3 THE Trustee shall hold the Property as trustee upon trust for the members from time to time of the Club entitled thereto under the Constitution and shall deal with the same and every part thereof only in accordance with the written directions and

requests of the Committee of the Club or (until such Committee has been established) of the Founder Members pursuant to the Constitution and not otherwise PROVIDED ALWAYS

(i) that the Trustee shall not be bound to concur in or perform any act or acts which in the opinion of the Trustee shall be illegal or shall be inconsistent with the trusts thereby declared or shall constitute a breach of trust or shall involve the Trustee in any personal liability or in any action which may be improper or disreputable or which may in the opinion of the Trustee constitute a breach of the conditions or covenants affecting the Property

(ii) PROVIDED FURTHER that notwithstanding any direction of the Committee or of the Founder members the Trustee shall not be obliged to charge or otherwise incumber the Property or any part thereof

4 (a) THE Trustee shall have no responsibility for the rebuilding repair maintenance renewal upkeep decoration administration or management of the Property and shall not be liable for any damage or loss or depreciation which may result in any way to the Property and gives no guarantee or warranty with regard to the validity or otherwise of the title to the Property

(b) THE Trustee shall not be bound to concern itself in any way with the management of the Club or its assets or finances nor with the rights duties or obligations of members or any other matter to which members may be subject nor with the replacement or retrieval or renewal of any of the contents furniture fittings or fixtures of the villas whether the said contents furniture fittings or fixtures be broken lost stolen or damaged or otherwise mislaid or misplaced and the Trustee shall bear no liability to the members in respect of such matters

5 THE Trustee shall not be required to take any legal or other action whatever in relation to any matter whatsoever relating to the Property unless fully indemnified by the Club or the Founder members to the reasonable satisfaction of the Trustee for all costs and liabilities likely to be incurred or suffered by the Trustee

6 THE Trustee shall be entitled at the expense of the Club or the Founder Members to obtain legal advice from its Solicitors for the time being and/or the Opinion of Counsel on any matter relating to the Property or in relation to the trust hereby constituted or the exercise of the Trustee's powers or rights or the observance or performance of the Trustees liabilities or duties hereunder

7 THE Company shall initially be entitled to occupy the Property pursuant to Clause 9 of the Constitution and shall be entitled to grant the rights of occupation of parts thereof in accordance therewith

8 THE Company and the Founder Members on behalf of the Club and as a separate covenant for themselves hereby jointly and severally warrant that save as otherwise ordered by a Court of competent jurisdiction or as provided herein the Trustee shall not by entering into and acting in pursuance of the terms and conditions of this Deed owe any duty or obligation or incur any liability to any person or persons (whether corporate or individual) other than the members of the Club and that no such person or persons are entitled to require or oblige the Trustee to transfer or deal with the Property

9 THE Company and the Founder Members on behalf of the Club and as a separate covenant for themselves hereby jointly and severally warrant that the Trustee's name shall not appear on any literature or document or on any advertisement issued by or on behalf of the Company the Founder members or the Club without the prior approval in writing of the Trustee having first been obtained

10 THE Trustee shall not be responsible for any loss suffered by the Club or any member thereof arising out of or in respect of any act or omission on the part of the Trustee its officers employees or agents in respect of the Property unless the same

shall have been caused by or arisen from fraud or negligence on behalf of the Trustee or its said officers employees or agents

11 THE Founder Members shall pay to the Trustee as remuneration for the performance of its duties hereunder such fees (together with any Value Added Tax thereon) as may from time to time be separately agreed upon between the Founder members and the Trustee (or failing which between the Club and the Trustee) and all out-of-pocket expenses (together with any Value Added Tax thereon) incurred by the Trustee in the performance of its duties under this Deed and in default of such payment the Founder Members hereby jointly and severally undertake that the Club will pay to the Trustee all such sums PROVIDED THAT as between the Company and the Founder Members on behalf of the Club the Club shall be primarily liable to pay all such sums

12 (A) IN connection with the Property the Founder Members on behalf of the Club and (as a separate covenant) for themselves covenant with the Trustee:

(a) on demand to pay as the Trustee may direct all outgoings whatsoever (including rates, service charge, interest, costs, expenses and damages) covenanted or agreed to be paid (whether contingently or otherwise) in respect of the property

(b) at all times to observe and perform all the covenants terms and conditions contained in the Land Certificate referred to in Recital C hereto

(c) to indemnify and keep fully and effectually indemnified the Trustee from and against all actions claims demands losses damages costs and expenses made against or suffered or incurred by the Trustee arising from any breach non-observance or non-performance of any of the covenants contained in paragraphs (a) and (b) of this Clause

(B) The Founder members on behalf of the Club and (as a separate covenant) for themselves covenant with the Trustee henceforth to observe and perform and that there have been observed and performed up to the date hereof all conditions and restrictions attaching to or subject to which any planning permissions under The Town & Country Planning Act 1971 have been granted in respect of the Property

13 THE Company and on behalf of the Club and as a separate covenant for themselves the Founder members hereby agree jointly and severally to indemnify and hold harmless the Trustee against all claims actions proceedings charges fees costs liabilities and expenses to which it may be entitled or which may result from or be incurred in connection with the performance by the Trustee of its duties hereunder and the Trustee shall be kept fully indemnified jointly and severally by the Founder Members and the Club against all losses claims demands actions damages costs and expenses made or incurred in connection with the Property or in any other way in connection with the holding by the Trustee of the office of trustee hereunder. The Trustee shall have the right if at any time it considers it desirable so to do to require that the Founder Members of the Club shall deposit with the Trustee such sum as the Trustee shall reasonably consider to be necessary in support of the indemnities contained in the Clause provided that in connection with the fees and expenses payable to the Trustee under the provisions of Clause 15 (b) (i) and (ii) hereof but without prejudice to the generality thereof the Trustee shall not require there to be deposited at any time any greater sum than shall be equal to five times the annual remuneration payable to the Trustee under Clause 11 hereof unless it is reasonable in the circumstances for the Trustee to require such greater sum

14 THE Trustee shall be entitled to be indemnified out of the Property or the proceeds of the sale thereof for all sums expended by the Trustee in or about or in any way in connection with the trusts of this Deed and for all sums (including remuneration) payable to the Trustee hereunder and for such purposes shall have all the powers of

an absolute owner to sell, let, mortgage or otherwise dispose of the Property or any part thereof unrestricted by Clause 3 hereof or the Constitution

15 THIS Deed shall continue until [[2]] or until terminated either by the Club giving not less than six months notice in writing to the Trustee or by the Trustee giving the Company and the Club not less than six months notice in writing. Any notice given under this Clause shall expire on the last day of any calendar month and such notice shall not be given in any event before the expiry of one year from the date hereof

Upon termination of this Deed the Founder Members (of failing which the Club) shall pay to the Trustee all remuneration then owing to the Trustee together with any outstanding out-of-pocket expenses and all expenses incurred by the Trustee in conveying or assigning or otherwise disposing of the title to the Property in manner hereinafter provided. The Trustee shall in the event of this Deed being terminated convey or assign the Property or procure the same to be conveyed or transferred (at the expense of the Club or failing which at the expense of the Founder Members) to any succeeding trustee or otherwise as the Committee of the Club in writing may direct.

In the event that no such direction of the Committee is received by the Trustee by the date of determination then the Trustee is entitled thereafter

(a) to sell the property in such manner as it may choose and so that the Trustee shall not be liable to the Founder Members or either of them or to any other person or persons in respect of the consideration received for any such sale or for any loss or damage suffered in respect thereof: and

(b) to deduct from the consideration received:
   (i) all payments due to the Trustee under this Deed
   (ii) all expenses incurred in connection with any such sale or sales: and
   (iii) The Trustee's fees for acting on the termination of the Club and the subsequent distribution of the net proceeds of sale

Such fee to be in addition to any remuneration payable to the Trustee under Clause 11 hereof;

and

(c) after the deduction of all sums referred to in paragraph (b) of this Clause to distribute the net proceeds of sale to such persons as would be entitled under Clause 18 of the Constitution to such proceeds upon dissolution of the Club and pending distribution to invest the net proceeds of sale in any investment authorised by law and to employ [ ] or any subsidiary or holding company thereof as bankers without being liable to account for any profit arising therefrom

16 (1) THE Company and the Founder Members on behalf of the club and as a separate covenant for themselves jointly and severally undertake:
   (a) to give to the Trustee the names and addresses of all officers of the Club
   (b) to inform the Trustee within 21 days of any change in the holders of any office with the full name and address of each new officer
   (c) to give to the Trustee within 21 days of admission of each member to membership the name and address of each such member and details of any change of address of such member within 21 days of such change occurring
   (d) that within seven days of the relevant meeting there shall be delivered to the Trustee duly certified by the Chairman or Secretary of the Committee of the Club an excerpt from the Minutes of any meeting of the Committee or of the members of the Club minuting the resignation of any officer or other member of the Committee or the election or appointment of a new

officer or Committee member and any change in the Constitution of the Club approved by the members thereof

(e) that there shall be delivered to the Trustee

(i) a copy of each annual audited account of the Club as soon as the same is available
and

(ii) notice of any General Meetings of the Club and a copy of the agenda and of any resolution to be proposed at the meeting at least 14 days prior to such meeting and

(iii) minutes of any such meeting as soon as the same is available

(iv) a copy of any contract relating to the management of the Club

(2) The Trustee shall have the right to attend all General Meetings of the members of the Club but shall have no right to vote at any such meetings

17 NOTWITHSTANDING the provisions of this Deed neither the Trustee nor any holding subsidiary or associated company of the Trustee shall be precluded from acting as banker investment manager or adviser to either or both of the Founder Members or the Club or the Guarantor nor shall the Trustee nor any holding subsidiary or associated company thereof be precluded from making any advances to either or both the Founder Members of the Club or the Guarantor on such terms as may be agreed or making any contract or entering into any financial or other transaction in the ordinary course of business with either or both of the Founder Members or the Club or the Guarantor and shall be entitled to charge interest on overdrawn accounts and make the usual banker's charges and shall not be liable to account either to the Founder Members or either of them or the Club or the Guarantor for any profit made in connection therewith

18 ANY Notice which is required to be given in pursuance to any provision of this Deed shall be given or served by pre-paid first class post, telegram, cable or telex addressed to the Company to the Founder Members or to the Trustee as the case may be at their respective registered offices or (in the case of notice to be served on the Club to the Committee) to the Committee of the Club at [Time Share location] and any notice sent by post shall be deemed to have been given or served forty-eight hours after the despatch and any notice sent by telegram, cable or telex shall be deemed to have been given or served at the time of despatch

19 THE Guarantor hereby covenants with the Trustee that the Company and the Founder Members and (as the case may be) the Club will perform and observe all the covenants conditions and warranties contained herein and on the part of the Company the Founder Members and the Club to be performed and observed and will pay all sums herein covenanted to be paid by the Company and the Club at the time specified and that if any of the Company the Founder Members of the Club shall make any default in such performance observance or payment then and in every such case the Guarantor will pay and make good to the Trustee on demand anything whatsoever which ought to be performed observed or paid as aforesaid including all losses damages costs and expenses sustained by the Trustee through such default of the Company the Founder Members or (as the case may be) the Club PROVIDED ALWAYS that any neglect delay or forbearance of the Trustee in enforcing against the Company the Founder Members of the Club any such performance observance or payment of the giving of time by the Trustee to the Company the Founder Members or the Club in relation thereto or any variation in the terms of these presents or the release of the Guarantor from liability hereunder or any other act or omission matter or thing whatever either wholly or in part from this guarantee other than a release under seal given by the Trustee shall not release or in any way lessen or affect the liability of the Guarantor hereunder

20 THE Trustee and the Founder Members shall be entitled by deed supplemental

hereto to modify alter or add to the provisions of these present in such manner and to such extent as they may consider expedient for any purpose: PROVIDED THAT unless the Trustee shall certify in writing that in its opinion such modification alteration or addition does not prejudice the interests of the members and does not operate to release the Trustee or the Founder Members from any responsibility to the members no such modification alteration or addition shall be made without the sanction of a resolution of Extraordinary General Meeting of members duly convened and held in accordance with the Constitution of the Club or of a written resolution of the members in accordance with Rule 16.7 of the Constitution of the Club: PROVIDED ALSO THAT no such modification alteration or addition shall impose upon any member any obligation to make any further payments in respect of his membership of the Club or to accept any liability in respect thereof

21 THIS Deed shall be governed by and construed in accordance with English law

IN WITNESS whereof the parties hereto have hereunto caused their Common Seals to be affixed the day and year first above written

THE SCHEDULE

General terms and conditions upon which the Trustee accepts appointment

1 The Trustee may act by a proper officer or officers

2 The Trustee's remuneration for its services shall be free of all taxes or fiscal impositions whatsoever and a first charge upon the estate or trust fund and shall be exclusive of all legal costs and disbursements, agents charges staff travel costs postages telephone calls and other expenses properly incurred and paid

3 Subject to any express provisions to the contrary in the Will or Codocil or Trust instruments, the Trustee may in its absolute discretion determine how remuneration due to the Trustee shall be borne as between different parts of an estate or trust or as between the beneficiaries and every such determination shall be binding upon all persons concerned

4 The Trustee may without being liable to account for any profit thereby made:

(a) act as banker and transact any banking or allied business on normal banking terms
(b) retain the customary share of brokerage and other commissions
(c) perform any service on behalf of the estate or trust and make charges commensurate with the service rendered
(d) employ at the expense and on behalf of the estate or trust any parent or associated or subsidiary company as banker or to transact any allied business or for any purpose for which a Trustee is entitled to employ any agents
(e) retain any remuneration received as a result of any appointment of a nominee as a director or officer of any other company whose shares or expenses shall from time to time be held in the estate or trust

5 The Trustee shall not be required by reason only of the general rule preventing a trustee from deriving a profit from his trusteeship to account to the estate or trust for any profit made in the ordinary course of business by the Trustee or any holding or associated or subsidiary company arising from the exercise of any power or discretion conferred by the Will, Codicil or Trust instrument or by Law

6 The Trustee may at its discretion vest any property of the estate or trust in any person or corporate body as its nominee

7 In any case in which the Trustee shall act as executor administrator or trustee jointly with another or others all monies securities title deeds and documents belonging to or relating to the estate or trust shall be under the exclusive custody and control of the Trustee, any other executor administrator or trustee having all reasonable facilities for verification or inspection and the name of the trustee or the name of its nominee shall be placed first in the Register of all stock, shares, securities or property

8 Unless otherwise provided in the Will, Codicil or Trust instrument, every appointment whether under the statutory power or under any special power of a new trustee during the period of trusteeship of the Trustee shall be subject to the consent in writing of the Trustee

(Attestation)

Notes

1 The description of the title will naturally change according to specific circumstances.

2 Same date as the termination date in clause 18.1 of the Constitution: Precedent No 21, p 428, above.

---

23 Time-sharing: members' club: typical purchase agreement

[See ch 23, p 277, above.]

THE [ ] OWNERS CLUB

PURCHASE AGREEMENT

THIS AGREEMENT is made the day of 198 BETWEEN [Developer] whose registered office is at ('the Company') of the first part [Management Company] whose registered office is at ['the Manager'] of the second part (the Company and the Manager are hereinafter together called 'the Founder Members') and the Purchaser named in Paragraph 1 of the Schedule ('the Purchaser') of the third part

IT IS HEREBY AGREED as follows:

(1) The Purchaser hereby applies for membership of the [ ] Owners Club ('the Club') of which the Company and the Manager are Founder Members

(2) The Purchaser hereby agrees to be bound by the Constitution of the Club and the Trust Deed referred to therein (copies of which have been supplied to the Purchaser prior to the signing of this Agreement and which the Purchaser shall be deemed to have inspected) and without prejudice to the generality of the foregoing agrees to pay within one month of the same being demanded the management charge for which the Purchaser may be liable as holder of the Holiday Certificate hereinafter mentioned

(3) The Company will following payment by the Purchaser of the purchase monies referred to in Clause 4 hereof transfer or cause to be transferred to the Purchaser a Holiday Certificate in respect of the weekly period (as referred to in Clause 8 of the Constitution of the club) stated in paragraph 2 of the Schedule relating to the villa or apartment specified in paragraph 4 of the Schedule and which is shown more particularly on the site plan a copy of which has been made available for inspection by the Purchaser and which the Purchaser shall be deemed to have inspected

(4) In consideration of the transfer of the said Holiday Certificate by the Company to the Purchaser the Purchaser will pay to the Company the purchase price stated in paragraph 3 of the Schedule of which a deposit of ten per cent (10%) thereof shall be paid to the Company's Solicitors [ ] as Agents for the Company on the date hereof and the balance shall be payable on the completion date stated in paragraph 5 of the Schedule. In the event of the Purchaser failing to complete within seven (7) days of being given written notice to that effect by the Company or its Solicitors (of which time shall be of the essence of completion) the said deposit will be forfeited to the Company but in the event that the Company shall fail to deliver

to the Purchaser the said Holiday Certificate within two(2) weeks the said deposit shall be repaid to the Purchaser on demand

(5) It is hereby agreed between the Founder Members on behalf of the Club and the Purchaser that the management charge payable by the Purchaser as holder of the said Holiday Certificate will until the [ ] be at the rate per annum specified in paragraph 6 of the Schedule together with any Value Added Tax which is required by law to be collected from the Purchaser. The said management charge will become due and payable on the completion date specified in Clause 4 hereof and on each successive anniversary of that date

(6) Subject to the payment by the Purchaser of the management charge as aforesaid the Manager as the Management Company referred to in the Constitution of the Club hereby undertakes with the Purchaser to observe and perform the obligations imposed upon it by the Management Agreement for the time being in force during the Purchaser's period of occupancy of the apartment referred to in Clause 3 hereof

(7) Where the context so admits and requires the provisions of this Agreement shall remain in full force and effect notwithstanding completion of the issue of the said Holiday Certificate to the Purchaser.

THE SCHEDULE

1 PURCHASER:	Name Address
2 WEEKLY PERIOD(S):	until
3 PURCHASE PRICE:	POUNDS (£)
4 VILLA:	
5 COMPLETION DATE:	
6 INITIAL MANAGEMENT CHARGE:	POUNDS (£) EXCLUSIVE OF V.A.T.

(Attestation)

---

24 Time-sharing: members' club: typical management agreement

[See ch 23, p 636, above.]

THE [ ] OWNERS CLUB
MANAGEMENT AGREEMENT

THIS AGREEMENT is made the Day of One Thousand Nine Hundred and BETWEEN [Developer] having its registered office at and [Management Company] having its registered office at (hereinafter together called 'the Founder Members')) of the one part and the said [Management Company] (hereinafter called 'the Management Company') of the other part

WHEREAS:

1 The Founder Members have together formed a club known as The [ ] Owners Club (hereinafter called 'the Club') whose object is to secure for its members joint rights of ownership of [Time Share Units] at [Time Share Location] and exclusive rights of occupation of such suites for specified periods in each year during the period mentioned in the Club's Constitution

2 In pursuance of Clause 11 of the said Constitution the Founder Members have agreed to delegate to the Management Company the general management and administration of the Club

NOW THIS AGREEMENT WITNESSETH AND IT IS HEREBY AGREED as follows:
1 SUBJECT to the rights of the Committee of the Club to intervene where necessary or appropriate the Management Company will undertake on behalf of the Club and the Club hereby delegates to the Management Company the management and administration of the whole of the Club's property at [Time Share location]. Without prejudice to the generality of the foregoing the Management Company will be responsible for the provision of all items detailed in Clause 12 of the Constitution of the Club. The Management Company will ensure that the management and administration aforesaid are carried out with all due diligence and in the best interests of the members of the Club and will comply with all requirements of the Committee of the Club in the performance of its duties hereunder and will effect all maintenance repairs renewals and redecoration and the insurance of the property of the Club and the facilities available to the members of the Club when the same shall be necessary and in a good and workmanlike manner with all due speed and diligence but not so as to interfere except insofar as reasonably necessary with the members' enjoyment of their occupation of the villas and apartments as aforesaid
2 THE appointment of the Management Company will continue (subject to determination as hereinafter provided) from [[1]] until [[1]] (hereinafter called 'the Management Period')
3 SUBJECT to the right of the Committee to intervene as aforesaid the Management Company shall during the Management Period be entitled to exercise all the powers of the Committee of the Club referred to in the Club's Constitution relating to the management and administration of the Club's property and affairs including the power to collect from each member any sum or sums by him pursuant to Clause 12 of the Constitution including any management charge referred to in Clause 14.8 of the Constitution PROVIDED ALWAYS that the exercise of any power or discretion relating to the Club's property which shall require the Trustee of such property to do or concur in any act shall at all times remain vested in the Club and/or (as the Constitution may require) the Committee
4 (A) THE Committee of the Club may by not less than three (3) months written notice to the Management Company to that effect require the Management Company to cease to provide any service for the time being provided by the Management Company hereunder
(B) Following service of any such notice the Committee of the Club and the Management Company shall use their best endeavours to ascertain the amount by which the Management Charge referred to hereafter shall be reduced. Following the date of expiry of such notice and in default of agreement as to such reduction within two (2) months of the service of such notice the matter shall be referred to a Chartered Surveyor in accordance with Clause 13
(C) (i) The Committee of the Club may by not less than three (3) months written notice to the Management Company to that effect request the Management Company to provide such reasonable additional services as may be specified in such notice in addition to all services for the time being provided by the Management Company hereunder
(ii) As soon as reasonably possible after receipt of such notice the Management Company shall submit to the Committee of the Club a written statement setting out its computation of the addition to the Management Charge resulting from the additional services such computation to be based on the estimated cost to the Management Company of the provision of the additional services
(iii) Within two (2) months of the receipt of such statement the Committee of the Club shall elect by written notice to the Management Company as

to whether or not to accept such computation and if it shall so accept the Management Company shall commence the provision of the relevant services within one (1) month thereafter and the Management Charge shall thenceforth be increased by the amount of such computation

(iv) in the event of the Committee of the club electing not to accept such computation and being in a position to enter into an agreement with a third party for the provision of that service at a cost acceptable to the Committee of the Club the Committee of the Club shall not enter into any such agreement unless the Management Company shall have been given at least one (1) month's written notice of such intention and does not offer to provide the service itself on similar terms

5 THE Management Period shall be deemed to commence on [[2]] and during the first three (3) years of the period each member of the Club shall pay the Management Company by way of a management charge (hereinafter called 'the initial management charge') a fixed sum per each Holiday Certificate held (such sum to be determined by the Management Company and notified to the member in writing at the time of issue of his Holiday Certificate) and in each subsequent year after the third year he shall pay by way of management charge:

(a) the fixed sum per each Holiday Certificate held as aforesaid plus

(b) an increment of such percentage of the management charge as is equal to the percentage increase in the figure at which the Index of Retail Prices (all items) published by the Department of Employment or by any other governmental department upon which duties in connection with such index shall have devolved stands at each last anniversary of the date of commencement of the Management Period over the Index figure of such Index at the [[2]] No fall in the figure at which the said Index stands shall cause a variation to be made in the management charge or in the amount of any increment previously so determined. In the event of any change in the reference base used to compile the said Index the figure taken to be shown in the said Index after such change shall be the figure which would have been shown in the said Index if the reference base current at [[2]] has been retained PROVIDED THAT in the event of it becoming impossible by reason of any change after the date hereof in the method used to compile the said Index or for any other reason whatsoever to calculate the said additional sum payable in any year by reference to the said Index or if any dispute or any difference whatsoever shall arise between the Club and the Management Company with respect to the amount of such additional sum or with respect to the construction or effect of this Clause the determination of the additional sum or other matter in difference shall be determined by an expert appointed in pursuance of the terms of this Agreement and he shall have full power to determine on such date as he shall deem appropriate what would have been the increase in the said Index had it continued on the same basis and given the information assumed to be available for the operation of this Clause

6 NOT later than three (3) months before the end of the third year of the Management Period either the Committee (acting on the authority of the resolution of the Club in general meeting) may given written notice to the Management Company or the Management Company may give written notice to the Committee that with effect from the commencement of the fourth year of the Management Period (that is from [ ]) the provision for the ascertainment of the management charge as set out in Clause 5 above ('the First Option') is to be discounted and replaced by the alternative set out in Clause 7 below (hereinafter referred to as the 'Second Option'). In such event the First Option shall be so discontinued and shall be so replaced. If the said election to discontinue the First Option and replace it by the Second Option shall not be exercised during the period aforesaid the Club and the Management

Company shall each have a like right to elect to discontinue the First Option and replace it by the Second Option from any of the sixth, ninth, twelfth and subsequent three yearly intervals from the commencement of the Management Period upon giving at least three months written notice one party to the other. Thereafter the First Option shall not be reinstated except by the mutual agreement of both the Club and the Management Company.

7 UNDER the Second Option (as herein defined) each member of the Club shall (for each Holiday Certificate held by him) pay the Management Company by way of annual management charge a proportionate part of the total cost to the Management Company in each year of providing the services it hereby agrees to provide including all the overhead expenses outlays and outgoings properly incurred by the Management Company in the performance of its duties hereunder and the salaries of all employees of the Management Company to the extent that they are engaged in the provision of these services calculated in accordance with the following formula:

$$D = \frac{A}{B} \times C$$

Where

A = The initial management charge referred to in Clause 5 hereof

B = [£] being the total of all the initial management charge based on an availability of 50 weeks per annum for each villa or apartment

C = 115% of the cost of providing the aforesaid services

D = Annual Management Charge per each Holiday Certificate

Under the Second Option the Management Company shall as soon as reasonably practicable after the commencement of each new year of the Management Period give written notice to each member requiring him to pay an estimated advance payment (hereinafter called 'the Advance Management Charge') of his liability for that year in respect of the annual management charge of each Holiday Certificate held by him and each member shall forthwith pay the Management Company his Advance Management Charge. The amount of the Advance Management Charge shall be such amount as the Management Company shall in their discretion determine to be a fair and reasonable charge but in the event of a dispute as to the amount of the charge the matter shall be resolved as provided in Clause 13 hereof. Under the Second Option the amount of the total management charge for each year shall be ascertained and certified annually by a Certificate signed by the auditors of the Management Company as soon as reasonably practicable after the end of the year in question and as soon as reasonably practicable after the signature of the Certificate every member shall be furnished with an account of the said total management charge including the additional 15% addition and secondly the proportionate amount payable by each member in respect of each Holiday Certificate held by him and after giving each member credit for the Advance Management Charge already paid by him and showing such adjustment if any as may be necessary there shall forthwith be paid by each member to the Management Company any balance still payable by him in respect of the proportionate amount aforesaid due from him in respect of the annual management charge or (as the case may be) there shall be forthwith paid by the Management Company to the member any amount which may have been overpaid by the member by way of an Advance Management Charge

8 ON the issue of each new Holiday Certificate to a member of the Club and if the First Option is in operation such new member shall forthwith pay in advance the management charge (duly apportioned when necessary by time) due from him in respect of such Holiday Certificate for the remainder of the year in which such Holiday Certificate shall be issued to him and where the Second Option is in opera-

tion the same principle shall apply to the Advance Management Charge subject to any due apportionment by time if necessary

9 THE Management Company shall arrange for the prompt collection (and payment if necessary) of the management charge payable by each ordinary member and the Founder Members and shall properly pay and discharge out of all such monies collected by it from ordinary members and Founder Members all expenses in relation to which such amounts have been collected and shall ensure that proper records and books of account relating to the management of the Club's property and affairs are maintained at all times on behalf of the members and that such records and books of account are at all reasonable times available for inspection by any member of the Club or any person on his behalf or the trustee of the Club's property

10 DURING the Management Period the Management Company shall not be entitled to any remuneration in respect of its duties and obligations hereunder save insofar as the aggregate of the management charges collected by it from all ordinary members and the Founder Members shall in respect of each calendar year be sufficient for that purpose

11 THE Management Period shall forthwith terminate:

(a) if the Management Company being a Corporation shall pass a resolution to wind up or enter into liquidation whether compulsory or voluntary (except for the purpose of amalgamation or reconstruction) or suffer a Receiver to be appointed or being an individual or individuals shall commit an act of bankruptcy

or

(b) if the [ ] Owners Club shall be wound up or for any reason shall cease to exist

or

(c) if the Management Company shall have committed a breach of this Agreement and shall neglect or otherwise fail to remedy such breach (whether capable of remedy or not) within one (1) month of being required in writing to do so by the Committee of the Club and the Committee thereafter serves upon the Management Company a notice in writing summarily terminating the Management Period

12 THE Founder Members on behalf of the members of the Club shall indemnify and keep indemnified the Management Company from and against all claims demands proceedings damages liabilities and costs and expenses arising out of or incidental to the proper and reasonable performance by the Management Company of its duties under this Agreement

13 ANY dispute or difference arising out of this Agreement shall be referred to the decision of a single expert to be agreed between the Committee and the Management Company or in default of agreement to be appointed on the application of either party by the President for the time being of the Royal Institution of Chartered Surveyors

IN WITNESS etc.

Notes

1 The 80-year period set out in the constitution.

2 Commencement date.

25 Time-sharing: members' club: typical holiday certificate

[This is the document of title, if such it can be called. See also ch 23, p 277, above.]

THE [ ] OWNERS CLUB

HOLIDAY CERTIFICATE

[Developer] whose registered office is at and [Management Company] whose registered office is at (together hereinafter referred to as 'the Grantors') as Founder Members of The [ ]Owners Club ('the Club') and in pursuance of the Constitution of the Club HEREBY admit to membership of the Club AND GRANT to the Member whose name and address is stated in paragraph 1 of the Schedule and who has paid to [Developer] (receipt whereof is hereby acknowledged) the sum stated in Paragraph 2 of the Schedule the right to occupy and enjoy the villa described in Paragraph 3 of the Schedule and all other facilities and amenities of the Club for the Weekly Period or Periods in each calendar year stated in Paragraph 4 of the Schedule for eighty years from the date of this Deed in all respects in accordance with and subject to the observance by the member of the said Constitution and the Trust Deed referred to therein including but without prejudice to the generality of the foregoing the provisions relating to payment of management charges.

IT IS HEREBY CERTIFIED THAT the transaction hereby effected does not form part of a larger transaction or of a series of transactions in respect of which the amount or value or the aggregate amount or value of the consideration exceeds [POUNDS]

IN WITNESS whereof the Grantors and the member have executed this Deed the day and year below written in Paragraph 5 of this Schedule

The Common Seal of [Developer] was hereunto affixed in the presence of
Director
Secretary

1 Member	Name Address
2 Purchase price	(£) Pounds
3 Villa	
4 Weekly periods	from the day of 19 until the day of 20
5 Date of deed	day of 19

The Common Seal of [Management Company] was hereunto affixed in the presence of

Director
Secretary

SIGNED SEALED and DELIVERED by the MEMBER

MEMBER

26 Time-sharing: members' club: typical form of surrender and request

[See also ch 23, p 277, above.]

FORM OF SURRENDER AND REQUEST (Pursuant to Clause 15 of the Constitution of the Club)

I/We, the within written member(s)

of

being the

of the within written member(s) hereby surrender this Holiday Certificate pursuant to Clause 15 of the Constitution of The [ ] Owners Club subject to the issue of the new Holiday Certificate in accordance with the Request contained below and hereby agree to use my/our best endeavours at the cost of the person or persons named below to procure that such person or persons is/are admitted to membership of the Club in accordance with the Constitution and pending such admission declare that I/we hold my/our interest as a member(s) of the Club (to the extent that such interest may be so held) upon trust for such person or persons and I/we

[Purchaser's Name]
of

hereby request the issue of a new Holiday Certificate to me/us in respect of the suite within mentioned and undertake that with effect from the date mentioned below I/we shall observe and perform all the obligations of membership of The [ ] Owners Club pursuant to the said Constitution

DATED the day of

(Attestation)

---

27 Form of transfer for use in 'freehold' management situation

H.M. LAND REGISTRY

Land Registration Acts 1925 to 1971

TRANSFER OF PART

COUNTY AND DISTRICT:
TITLE NUMBER:
PROPERTY:
DATE: 19

1 IN CONSIDERATION OF
pounds (£) receipt whereof is hereby acknowledged
[Developer] of/whose registered office is situate at

(hereinafter called 'the Transferor') as Beneficial Owner hereby transfers to
[Purchaser] of

(hereinafter called 'the Transferee') the land shown and coloured red on the plan annexed hereto and known (or to be known) as
[postal address]

(hereinafter referred to as the Property) being part of the land comprised in the above-mentioned title (which land is hereinafter referred to as the Development) and TOGETHER WITH the easements and other rights set out in the First Schedule hereto but EXCEPTING AND RESERVING the easements and other rights set out in the Second Schedule hereto AND SUBJECT TO the covenants and conditions on the part of the Transferee and the Transferor set out in the Third and Fourth Schedules respectively hereto.

2 The Property is transferred subject also to and with the benefit of the stipulations hereinafter contained subject to and with the benefit of which the Property is to be held by virtue of its forming part of the Transferor's Development at [description] aforesaid in accordance with the scheme of development as shown and edged green[1] on the plan annexed hereto

3 The Transferee hereby covenants with the Transferor and its successors in title and the owner or owners of any other part of the land comprised in the development for the benefit of the remainder of the land comprised in the Development and each and every part thereof with intent to bind the Property into whosoever hands the same may come but not so as to render the Transferee or persons deriving title under him personally liable for any breach or omission after he or they shall have parted with his or their interest in the Property that he and the persons deriving title under him will observe and perform the stipulations to which all the land comprised in the Development is subject particulars of which are set out in the Third Schedule hereto

4 The Transferor expressly reserves the right of making from time to time any alteration in the mode of laying out the Development in the number and area of the plots in the class of building and in the special and general conditions of sale to withdraw vary release or abandon in favour of the owner or owners from time to time of any part of the development (including the Property) of any of the special conditions or any covenants restrictions stipulations and conditions entered into or to be entered into in such manner as the Transferor shall think fit.

5 IT IS HEREBY DECLARED that all stipulations imposed by or in pursuance of the Development on different Transferees from the Transferor of parts of the land comprised in the Development are intended to be mutually enforceable inter se by such Transferees and their successors in title regardless of the date or dates of their respective purchases

6 IT IS HEREBY AGREED AND DECLARED as follows:

(i) The Transferee shall not by virtue of this transfer acquire or be entitled to any easement or right of light or air which would prejudice the free use or enjoyment of any adjoining or neighbouring land of the Transferor for building or other purposes and any enjoyment of light or air had by the Transferee from or over any adjoining or neighbouring land of the Transferor shall be deemed to be had by consent of the Transferor

(ii) any wall erected or to be erected which shall separate the buildings erected or to be erected on the development shall after erection be deemed to be a party wall and shall be maintained and repaired accordingly

(iii) all eaves spouts down rainwater spouts cisterns passages drains waterpipes and electricity cables and all other matters and things now used or intended to be used and enjoyed in common by the owners and occupiers for the time being of the Property and of any other land comprised in the Development shall continue to be so used and enjoyed and shall be repaired and maintained at the fair and proportionate expenses of those persons entitled to the use and enjoyment thereof

7 The Transferor and the Transferee hereby apply to the Registrar to enter in the Register such of the easements rights exceptions reservations covenants conditions and stipulations herein contained as are capable of registration and in particular the Transferor hereby applies for and the Transferee hereby consents to the entry on the Register of the following Restriction on the Title to the Property:

> Except under an Order of the Registrar no Transfer or lease by the proprietor of the land is to be registered without the consent of [Management Company]

8 In this transfer the expression 'the Transferor' and 'the Transferee' shall where the context so admits include the successors in title of the Transferor and the Transferee respectively and the expression 'the Transferee' shall further include the masculine the feminine the plural and the singular and where two or more persons constitute the Transferee all covenants or agreements made by or with them shall be deemed to be made by or with them jointly and severally [and the following declaration shall form part of this Transfer

space for joint tenancy clause/s, if so required]

9 Certificate of Value

FIRST SCHEDULE

[Any typical estate rights schedule]

SECOND SCHEDULE

[Any typical estate exceptions and reservations schedule]

THIRD SCHEDULE

[Normal estate restrictions, plus:]
The transferee will not transfer the property without obtaining simultaneously to such Transfer the execution by the intending Transferee of a Deed of Covenant between the intending Transferee and [Management Company] in the terms of the Deed of Covenant made between the Transferee and the said Company and bearing even date herewith

FOURTH SCHEDULE

1 The Transferor at its own expense will and sufficiently form metal and kerb the new roads and footways upon the said land coloured blue and will maintain and repair the same [or, substitute and/or add such items as are appropriate to the particular Development in hand] [in the case of a Tenants Management Company: until such time as the subscribers to the Memorandum of Association of [Management Company] have under the provisions of [appropriate Article] of the Articles of Association of the said Company ceased to be members of the said Company] [or in the case of a professional management company—until the same is handed over for management to [Management Company]]

2 The Transferor will so long as any part of the land comprised in the Development remains vested in the transferor pay to [Management Company] such part of any costs and expenses incurred by the said Company in providing procuring and performing in respect of the said land coloured blue the services set out in the Schedule to a Deed of Covenant made between the said Company of the one part and the Transferee of the other part and bearing even date herewith as if the Transferor had entered into a Deed of Covenant in like terms with the said company in respect of the land remaining vested in the Transferor

(Attestation)

Notes

1 The full extent of the development. This clause and subsequent ones are additional to the 'standard' transfer, and they specifically set up a building scheme. The clause is probably optional, because it is likely that a building scheme would be set up anyway. However, in view of the management situation which is being set up, it is probably better that the initial transfers of each individual property spell out the creation of a building scheme, so to this extent this precedent is to be preferred to the 'standard' one. See also pp 303–306 of the author's *Residential Estate Conveyancing: Practice and Precedents* (Butterworths, 1983).

---

28 Deed of covenant between management company and incoming purchaser: freehold management

[See ch 19, p 222, above. It is important for the proper working of the scheme described therein that this Deed of Covenant is obtained from *all* incoming purchasers on the development, or that part of it comprising this 'freehold management'. 'All incoming purchasers' means the initial ones as well.]

THIS DEED OF COVENANT is made the day of 19
BETWEEN [Management Company] LIMITED of/whose registered office is situate at

(hereinafter called 'the Company') of the one part and [Incoming Purchaser] of

(hereinafter called 'the Transferee') of the other part

WHEREAS:

(A) The Transferee has agreed to purchase/[or in the case of a subsequent purchase: to a transfer of] the property known as [description of property] TOGETHER WITH the easements and other rights in respect of the Communal Land set out in the First Schedule to a transfer [in the case of the initial purchase: bearing even date herewith] [in the case of a subsequent purchase: dated the day of 19] and made between [Developer] of the one part and/the Transferee/[or: the initial purchaser] of the other part

(B) The Transferee has agreed to enter into this Deed in the manner hereinafter appearing/[or for a subsequent purchaser: the said transfer provides that the transferee and his successors in title will enter into a Deed of Covenant in the manner set out in the said transfer and the parties hereto have agreed to enter into these presents accordingly]

NOW THIS DEED WITNESSETH and it is hereby agreed and declared as follows:

1 In this Deed the following expressions shall unless the context requires bear the following meanings.

'The Communal Land' means the land shown coloured blue on the plan annexed to the above-mentioned transfer.

'The Transferee' includes where the context so admits the successors in title of the Transferee

'The Scheduled Services' means the services set out in the schedule hereto

2 The Transferee hereby applies to be registered and the Company hereby undertakes to register the Transferee as a member of the Company[1]

3 The Company hereby covenants with the Transferee that it will:

(a) provide procure and perform in relation to the Communal Land the Scheduled Services

(b) enter into a Deed of Covenant with any intended Transferee of the Property in the terms of this Deed and will give any consent required to H.M. Land Registry to allow registration of any proposed dealing in the property provided that the Transferee shall have observed and performed the covenants on his part herein contained and fulfilled the obligations on his part contained in the Articles of Association of the Company

4 The Transferee hereby covenants with the Company that he will:

(a) pay to the Company [fraction][2] part of the costs and expenses incurred by the Company in providing securing and performing the Scheduled Services including the costs of and incidental to the administration and conduct of the Company's affairs

(b) in any contract for the transfer of the Property include a condition that the intending Transferee shall upon completion of such contract apply to become registered as a member of the company[1]

(c) include in any contract for the transfer of the property a condition precedent that the intending transferee shall enter into a Deed of Covenant with the Company in the terms of this Deed and that the intending Transferee shall bear all costs of and incidental to the preparation and execution of such Deed including any stamp duty payable thereon

5 Where the Transferee is more than one person all covenants and agreements on the part of the Transferee hereinbefore contained shall be deemed to have been made jointly and severally by all such persons constituting the Transferee

THE SCHEDULE[3]

1 The provision and maintenance of all necessary boundary walls fences roads footpaths drives sewers and other services as are necessary passing in under upon and over the Communal Land

2 The mowing and upkeep of all grassed areas and the upkeep of all garden areas when considered expedient

3 The provision of lighting (including the cost of replacement and supply of electricity) where the same is not the responsibility of any Local Authority or other authority

4 All such other services and matters which the Company may from time to time think fit

5 The employment of all such agents managers contractors or other persons as shall in the opinion of the [Council of the] Company be necessary[4]

6 The payment of all rates insurance premiums and other charges of a like nature which may be charged upon or incurred in relation to the Communal Land

IN WITNESS, etc.

(Attestation)

Notes

1 This clause will only apply where the management company is a tenants' management company. If the management company has no connection with the residents other than a contractual one, the clause should be deleted totally.

2 The fraction depends on the number of units concerned.

3 The precise nature of the works to be set out in the Schedule are, of course, variable, but those included in this precedent are typical and will give readers an insight into the sort of matters which may be covered.

4 Delete the words in brackets if the management company is a professional one. Incidentally, the 'Council' is the same as a board of directors.

29 Consent required under terms of restriction set out in Precedent No 27, clause 7, p 445, above

CONSENT TO DEALING
H.M. LAND REGISTRY
Land Registration Acts 1925 to 1971

COUNTY AND DISTRICT:
SHORT DESCRIPTION OF PROPERTY:
TITLE NUMBER:
[Management Company] LIMITED whose registered office is situate at

hereby consents to the registration of a Transfer dated 19 BETWEEN [parties] in respect of [property the subject of the restriction] being the land comprised in the above title

Dated this day of 19
[to be sealed by Management Company]

---

30 Model form particulars of claim: 'financial cases'[1]

[The author is indebted to Mr Jonathan Winegarten of Counsel for permission to use this Precedent; also for assistance in the text, pp 297 to 308, which are complementary to this and the following precedent.]

IN THE [ ] COUNTY COURT[2] PLAINT NO [ ]

BETWEEN:

Plaintiff

—and—
[A. B.] *Defendant*

PARTICULARS OF CLAIM

1 By a Lease (hereinafter called 'the Lease') dated [ ] and made between [ ] as Lessor of the one part and [*if A.B. was the original Lessee*: the Defendant] [*if A.B. is an assignee*: XY] as Lessee of the other part [lessor] demised to [the Defendant] [XY] all that flat known as Flat No. [ ] and situate at [*address*] [if the demise contains eg parking space/common parts etc. a brief description of these should be included here] (therein and hereinafter called 'the Demised premises') for a term of [ ] years from [date of commencement of term as specified in lease] at a rent [hereinafter called 'the Basic Rent')] payable [half-yearly in advance] on the [dates of payment] in each year of [£] p.a. [subject to review on each [ ] anniversary of the grant] [and at a further additional rent (hereinafter called 'the Additional Rent') payable on demand from time to time of a sum or sums equivalent to a [*specify fraction*] equal part of the amount which the Lessor might from time to time expend in effecting or maintaining insurance] [and in providing electricity to the common parts.][3]

2 By [appropriate clause/s] of the Lease the Lessee covenanted to pay the rent on the days and in the manner in the lease mentioned.

3 [*If forfeiture as well as a money judgement is sought, add:*

[Specify appropriate Clause number] of the Lease contained a proviso for re-entry by the Lessor in the event of rent or any part thereof remaining unpaid for 21 days after becoming payable (whether formally demanded or not) and in the event of breach of covenant by the Lessee [which proviso for re-entry was subject to the following restriction, namely that the Lessor should not exercise the right of re-entry unless 28-days' notice in writing of the Lessor's intention so to do had been first given to any mortgagee whose interest in the Demised Premises (which interest was subsisting at the date of the said notice) had been notified to the Lessor and the unpaid rent or the breach of covenant had not been paid or remedied by the expiration of the said notice][4]

4 The reversion immediately expectant on the Lease is vested in the Plaintiff.

5 [*If the Defendant is an assignee, add:*]

The term of years demised by the Lease is vested in the Defendant.

6 [*If the Defendant is in arrear with the Basic rent and a rent review has taken place: add*]

By virtue of a rent review effective from [*date*] the Basic rent is now £[ ] p.a.

7 The Defendant is in arrear with his rent by reason whereof the Lease has become forfeited.

PARTICULARS OF ARREARS

(a) Arrears of Basic Rent [*give particulars*] £[X]

(b) Arrears of Additional Rent [*give particulars and add, in respect of this item, the date of demand or demands for the Additional Rent if the appropriate clause in the lease states that it is only payable on demand*][5]

£[Y]

£[Z]

[Paragraph 8 only applies to leases where there is included a proviso to the forfeiture clause (eg Precedent No 3, cl 7, p 363, above) restraining the right of forfeiture until (28 days) notice is given to any mortgagee]

8 [*If forfeiture as well as a money judgement is sought, add:*]

[*Either:*] In accordance with Clause [appropriate clause of lease in question] of the Lease [a] 28 days notice[s] in writing [has] [have] been served on [*specify*] being [a] mortgagee[s] of the Demised Premises whose interest therein had been notified to the Plaintiff but the arrears of rent were not paid by the expiration of the said notice[s] and have not been paid subsequently.

[*or:*] The Plaintiff has not been notified for the purposes of Clause [appropriate Clause] of the Lease of the interest in the Demised Premises of any mortgagee.]

8/9 [*If forfeiture is sought, add:*

The net annual value for rating of the Demised Premises is £[ ]

AND THE PLAINTIFF CLAIMS:

1 [*If forfeiture is sought:*]

Possession of the Demised Premises.

2 Payment of £[Z], arrears of rent.

3 Interest pursuant to Section 97A of the County Courts Act 1959.

4 Further or other relief.

5 Costs.

DATED etc [*Signature*]

Notes

1 Refer also to pp 297–308, above.

2 It is assumed that the action will take place in the appropriate county court; for financial limits, see p 298, above.

3 Vary wording as necessary to fit the lease in question. This wording refers to the studio flat lease set out in Precedent No 3, p 360, above; but if full maintenance is included the wording can be easily varied to suit the circumstances.

4 This wording is only relevant if the appropriate proviso is present in the lease; see Precedent No 3, cl 7, p 363, above, and see also ch 29, p 299, above.

5 See, eg cl 1 (f) of studio flat lease: Precedent No 3, p 362, above, which commences 'And also paying on demand by way of further or additional rent from time to time a sum or sums of money . . . .' etc.

---

31 Model form particulars of claim: 'non-financial' cases[1]

[The author is indebted to Mr Jonathan Winegarten of Counsel for permission to use this Precedent.]

IN THE [ ] COUNTY COURT[2] PLAINT NO [ ]

BETWEEN:

Plaintiff

—and—

[A.B.]

Defendant

PARTICULARS OF CLAIM

1 As paragraph 1, Precedent No 30, p 448, above.

2 The Lease contained, inter alia, the following covenant[s] on the part of the Lessee, namely:

[*In this paragraph or these sub-paragraphs there should be set out and by reference to the relevant Clause* (*and Paragraph in the Schedules if appropriate*) *in the Lease the covenant or covenants of which the Defendant is in breach.*

Thus, for example:

'(1) (*Clause 2 and Paragraph 1 Third Schedule*):
Not to use the Demised Premises [etc]

(2) (*Clause 2 and Paragraph 3 Third Schedule*):
Not to throw dirt, rubbish, rags, [etc]

(3) (*Clause 4 and Paragraph 1 Fifth Schedule*):
To maintain and repair [etc.]']

3 [*If* (*a*) *forfeiture on any non-financial ground is sought and/or* (*b*) *damages for breach of a* repairing *covenant is sought, add:*]

By Clause [appropriate number] of the Lease [and (also quote any other relevant part/s of the Lease)] the Lessee covenanted to pay all costs charges and expenses (including solicitors' costs and surveyors' fees) incurred by the Lessor for the purpose of and incidental to the preparation and service of a notice under Section 146 of the Law of Property Act 1925 notwithstanding that forfeiture might be avoided otherwise than by relief granted by the Court.

4 [*If forfeiture as well as a money judgement is sought, add:*]

Clause [appropriate number] of the Lease contained a proviso for re-entry by the Lessor in the event of breach of covenant by the Lessee [which proviso for re-entry was subject to the following restriction, namely that the Lessor should not exercise the right of re-entry unless 28 days notice in writing of the Lessor's intention so to do had been first given to any mortgagee whose interest in the Demised Premises (which interest was subsisting at the date of the said notice) had been notified to the Lessor and the breach of covenant had not been remedied by the expiration of the said notice.][3]

5 The reversion immediately expectant on the Lease is vested in the Plaintiff.

6 [*If the Defendant is an assignee, add*:]

The term of years demised by the Lease is vested in the Defendant.

7 Wrongfully and in breach of covenant the Defendant has

[*Set out here the breach or various breaches complained of. If more than one, set them out in numbered sub-paragraphs in the same order as the sub-paragraphs in Paragraph 2, above. Thus, for example*:

'(1) Used the Demised Premises [etc]

(2) Thrown dirt, rubbish, rags [etc]

(3) Failed to maintain and repair [etc]'

In appropriate cases particulars (*under a heading* 'PARTICULARS') *should be given*]

8 [If forfeiture and/or damages are sought, add:]

By reason of the matters hereinbefore set out [the Lease has become forfeited] [and] [the Plaintiff has suffered loss and damage]

PARTICULARS OF SPECIAL DAMAGE

[*Give itemised particulars with their appropriate figures, and then give a total* £[*A*]]

9 [*If* (*a*) *forfeiture on any non-financial ground is sought and/or* (*b*) *damages for breach of a repairing covenant is sought add*:]

On [ ] the Plaintiff served on the Defendant a notice in writing pursuant to Section 146 of the Law of Property Act 1925 [*and if* (*a*) *forfeiture on the grounds of breach of a repairing covenant is sought and/or* (*b*) *damages for breach of a repairing covenant is sought, add in addition*: containing the statement required by Section 1 of the Leasehold Property (Repairs) Act 1938] *but* [*if forfeiture on the grounds of breach of a repairing covenant is sought, add*: (notwithstanding that the fact that the said notice had been served on him was known to the Defendant and notwithstanding that a time reasonably sufficient to enable the repairs specified in the said notice to be executed has elapsed since the time when the fact of the service of the said notice came to the knowledge of the Defendant)] the Defendant has failed to comply with the terms of the said notice. The costs charges and expenses incurred by the Plaintiff for the purpose of and incidental to the preparation and service of the said notice was £[B]

10 [*If* (*a*) *forfeiture on the grounds of a breach of a repairing covenant is sought and/or* (*b*) *damages for a breach of a repairing covenant is sought add one or other of the following alternatives as appropriate*

[*Either:* By an Order of this Court dated [ ] the Plaintiff was granted leave under the Leasehold Property (Repairs) Act 1938 to commence this action]

or: The Defendant did not [validly] claim the benefit of the leasehold Property (Repairs) Act 1938]'

11 [*If forfeiture is* not *sought but an injunction is sought, add:*

By a [letter] [series of letters] dated [ ] [respectively] and served on the Defendant the Plaintiff required the Defendant to cease carrying out the acts complained of in [sub-paragraph [ ] of] Paragraph 7, above but the Defendant has wrongfully failed or refused to comply with such requirement. In the premises the Defendant will or is likely to continue to carry out the said acts unless restrained by injunction.

12 (Paragraph 12 only applies to leases where there is included a proviso to the forfeiture clause (eg Precedent No 3, cl 7, p 363, above) restraining the right of forfeiture until (28 days) notice is given to any mortgagee)

[*If forfeiture is sought, add*:]

Either In accordance with Clause [appropriate number] of the Lease [a] 28 days notice[s] in writing [has] [have] been served on [specify] being [a] mortgagee[s] the Demised Premises whose interest therein has been notified to the Plaintiff but [breach of covenant was] [breaches of covenants were] not remedied by the of the said notice[s] and [has] [have] not been remedied subsequently.]

or: The Plaintiff has not been notified for the purposes of Clause [appropriate number] of the Lease of the interest in the Demised Premises of any mortgagee.]

13 [*If either forfeiture or an injunction is sought, add:*]
The net annual value for rating of the demised premises is £[ ]

AND THE PLAINTIFF CLAIMS:
[*If forfeiture is sought*:
(1) Possession of the Demised Premises]
[*If, in the alternative* (*and 'ex hypothesi' this must be an alternative to forfeiture*), *an injunction is sought*:
(1) An order restraining the Defendant whether by himself his servants agents and licenses or howsoever from [etc]
(2) *Under Paragraph 8*, £ [A] damages
(3) *Under Paragraph 9*, £[B·
(4) Interest pursuant to Section 69 of the County Courts Act 1984
(5) Further or other relief
(6) Costs]

DATED etc [Signature]

Notes

1 Refer also to pp 297–308, above.

2 The limits for the county court are generous—see p 298, above, it is therefore assumed that the very great majority of cases will be commenced in that forum.

3 This wording is only relevant if the appropriate proviso is present in the lease:—see Precedent No 3, cl 7, p 363 and see also ch 27, p 299, above.

---

32 Law of Property Act 1925 section 146 notice to which Leasehold Property (Repairs) Act 1938 does not apply

[Opening paragraph as in Precedent No 33, p 453, below]

We [name] Solicitors and Agents for the above-mentioned [Reversioner] HEREBY GIVE YOU NOTICE as follows:

1 By the said lease [if A.B. is the original lessee: you] [if A.B. is an assignee: the lessee] covenanted [set out using the wording of the covenants, the covenant or various covenants which is or are said to have been broken. For example:
'(Clause X and paragraph Y Third Schedule: Not to use the Demised Premises [etc.].)
(Clause A and paragraph B Third Schedule: Not to throw dirt, rubbish, rags [etc.]')]

2 The said covenant[s] has [have] been broken and the particular breaches which are complained of are [set out here the particular breaches complained of].

3 [Reversioner] requires you to remedy all the said breaches [and to make compensation to [Reversioner] in money for such breaches].
4 On your failure to comply with this notice within a reasonable time [alternatively specify here a time from service of the notice which is reasonable for remedying all the breaches, thus: within [weeks] [months]] it is the intention of [Reversioner] to re-enter upon the said flat and premises and forfeit the said lease and claim damages for the said breaches of covenant[s].

DATED ETC

Signed (Solicitors)
Solicitors and Agents for the
above-mentioned Reversioner

---

33 Law of Property Act 1925 section 146 notice: to which Leasehold Property (Repairs) Act 1938 applies

[See pp 297–308, above.]

To [A.B.] of etc, the lessee of the flat and premises known as Flat No. [ ] and situate at [address] [if the demise contains, eg parking space/common parts etc, a brief description should be included here] comprised in a lease dated
and made between [lessor] as lessor of the one part and [if A.B. was the original lessee: you] [if A.B. is an assignee: X.Y.] as lessee of the other part [if A.B. is an assignee add: the term of which lease is now vested in you] [if there has been a transfer of the reversionary interest: the reversion of which lease is now vested in [ ]] and to all others whom it may concern.
We [name] Solicitors and Agents for the above-mentioned [Reversioner][1] HEREBY GIVE YOU NOTICE as follows:
1 By the said lease [if A.B. is the original lessee: you] [if A.B. is an assignee: the lessee] covenanted
[set out, using the wording of the covenants, the repairing covenants or various repairing covenants which is or are said to have been broken. For example.
'Clause X and paragraph Y Fifth Schedule: To maintain and repair [etc.]']
2 The said covenant[s] has [have] been broken and the particular breaches which are complained of are [permitting or allowing the dilapidations and want of repair mentioned in the Schedule annexed hereto.]
3 [Reversioner] requires you to remedy all the said breaches [and to make compensation to [Reversioner] in money for such breaches].
4 On your failure to comply with this notice within [ ] months [specify here a time from service of the notice which is reasonable for remedying all the breaches, being in any event a time not less than one calendar month from the date of service] it is the intention of [Reversioner] to re-enter upon the said flat and premises and forfeit the said lease and claim damages for the said breaches of covenant[s].
5 You are entitled under the Leasehold Property (Repairs) Act 1938 to serve on the lessor a counter-notice claiming the benefit of that Act. Such counter-notice must be in writing, must be to the effect that you claim the benefit of that Act and must be served within 28 days of the service upon you of this notice.
The name and address for service of such counter-notice on your lessor are:
[Give details][2]
Your counter-notice may be served by leaving it at that address, or by sending it by

post, in a registered letter or by a recorded delivery service, provided in either case that the letter is not returned through the Post Office undelivered.

DATED etc

THE SCHEDULE above referred to

[Set out here the dilapidations and want of repair complained of]

Signed (Solicitor)
Solicitors and Agents for [Reversioner]

NOTE: *The whole of the above notice should be set out in uniform type, in order to comply with Leasehold Property (Repairs) Act 1938, s 1.*

Notes

1 If the lessor has retained the lease, then this will be the lessor, otherwise whoever he has transferred his reversionary interest to.

2 This should ideally be the reversioner himself, as opposed to his solicitor or other agent.

34 Originating application under terms of Leasehold Property (Repairs) Act 1938[1]

IN THE [ ] COUNTY COURT PLAINT NO [ ]

IN THE MATTER of the Leasehold Property (Repairs) Act 1938

AND IN THE MATTER of a Lease dated and made between [lessor] (1) and [if the Respondent was the original lessee: A.B.] [otherwise put original lessee: X.Y.][2]

BETWEEN:

[Reversioner][2] *Applicant*

—and—

[A.B.] *Respondent*

[Reversioner] [of] [whose registered office is situate at] applies to the Court for an Order in the following terms, namely:

1 That [Reversioner] being the person in whom is vested the reversion expectant on the above-mentioned lease, may be granted leave under the above-mentioned Act to take proceedings in this Court against the Respondent for the enforcement of the right of [Reversioner] for [re-entry or forfeiture] [and] [damages] for breach of covenant or agreement under the terms and provisions of the said lease

2 That the costs of this application may be provided for

The ground upon which [Reversioner] claims to be entitled to such Order are as follows:

1 The said Lease was entered into on the between [original lessor][3] as Lessor of the one part and [if A.B. was the original lessee: the Respondent] [if A.B. is an assignee: X.Y.] as lessee of the other part.

2 By the said lease [original lessor] demised to [the Respondent] [X.Y.] all that flat known as Flat No. [ ] and situate at [address] [if the demise contains eg parking space/common parts etc. a brief description should be included here] (therein and hereinafter called 'the Demised Premises') for a term of [ ] years from [specify date of commencement of term].

3 The said lease contained the following covenant[s] relating to the repair of the Demised Premises:

[*Set out here the wording of the repairing covenant which is said to have been broken. For example,* '(Clause A and Paragraph X Fifth Schedule(: To maintain and repair [etc].']

[4 The reversion immediately expectant on the said Lease is now vested in the Applicant [Specify].][4]

5 [*If the Respondent is an assignee, add*:] The term of years demised by the said lease is now vested in the Respondent

6 Wrongfully and in breach of the said covenant[s] the Respondent has:

[*set out here, and if necessary in numbered sub-paragraphs, the breach or various breaches of the repairing covenant or convenants*]

7 On [Reversioner] served on the Respondent a notice in writing pursuant to Section 146 of the Law of Property Act 1925 containing the statement required by Section 1 of the Leasehold Property (Repairs) Act 1938

8 On the Respondent served on [Reversioner] a counter-notice, claiming the benefit of the Leasehold Property (Repairs) Act 1938

9 [Reversioner] applies to the Court for leave under Section 1 of the Leasehold Property (Repairs) Act 1938 on the grounds

[*set out here the particular ground contained in Section 1(5) of the 1938 Act which is relied on. The wording of the relevant sub-paragraph of Section 1(5) should be adhered to as far as possible. For example,*

'That the breach can be immediately remedied at an expense that is relatively small in comparison with the much greater expense that would probably be occasioned by postponement of the necessary work,'

The name and address of the person on whom it is intended to serve this application is A.B. of [address]

The address for service of [Reversioner] is [address]

DATED etc

TO the Registrar of the Court, and
TO The Respondent

(signature)

[Solicitors for the Applicant]

Notes

1 Only necessary when the lessee claims the benefit of the 1938 Act, see pp 306 et seq.

2 The identity of the Applicant will only be different to that of the lessor if there has been some sort of a transmission of the reversionary interest; otherwise they will be one and the same.

3 If not a different person, then this will be the applicant.

4 Only to be included if appropriate.

Index to Precedents

Index